Commentaries and Cases on the Law of Business Organization

2016-2017 Statutory Supplement

COMMENTARIES AND CASES ON THE LAW OF BUSINESS ORGANIZATION

2016-2017 Statutory Supplement

William T. Allen
Jack Nusbaum Professor of Law and Business
New York University
Of Counsel, Wachtell, Lipton, Rosen and Katz

Reinier Kraakman
Ezra Ripley Thayer Professor of Law
Harvard Law School

Wolters Kluwer

Published by Wolters Kluwer in New York.

Wolters Kluwer Legal & Regulatory US serves customers worldwide with CCH, Aspen Publishers, and Kluwer Law International products. (www.WKLegaledu.com)

To contact Customer Service, e-mail customer.service@wolterskluwer.com, call 1-800-234-1660, fax 1-800-901-9075, or mail correspondence to:

Wolters Kluwer
Attn: Order Department
PO Box 990
Frederick, MD 21705

Printed in the United States of America.

2 3 4 5 6 7 8 9 0

ISBN 978-1-4548-4054-1

About Wolters Kluwer Legal & Regulatory US

Wolters Kluwer Legal & Regulatory Solutions U.S. delivers expert content and solutions in the areas of law, corporate compliance, health compliance, reimbursement, and legal education. Its practical solutions help customers successfully navigate the demands of a changing environment to drive their daily activities, enhance decision quality and inspire confident outcomes.

Serving customers worldwide, its legal and regulatory solutions portfolio includes products under the Aspen Publishers, CCH Incorporated, Kluwer Law International, ftwilliam.com and MediRegs names. They are regarded as exceptional and trusted resources for general legal and practice-specific knowledge, compliance and risk management, dynamic workflow solutions, and expert commentary.

Contents

ACKNOWLEDGMENTS

We are grateful for permission to reprint copyrighted material from the following:

New York Stock Exchange Listed Company Manual, as available on NYSE's website at the time of publication. Copyright © 2016 NYSE Group, Inc. Used with permission of NYSE Group, Inc.

Principles of Corporate Governance: Analysis and Recommendations (1994). Copyright 1994 by The American Law Institute. All rights reserved. Reprinted with permission.

Restatement (Second) of Agency. Copyright 1958 by The American Law Institute. All rights reserved. Reprinted with permission.

Uniform Partnership Act (1914); Uniform Partnership Act (1997), ©1994, 1996, 1997, 2014 by National Conference of Commissioners on Uniform State Laws; and Uniform Limited Partnership Act (2001), © 2001 by National Conference of Commissioners on Uniform State Laws. All rights reserved. Reprinted with permission of the National Conference of Commissioners on Uniform State Laws.

Commentaries and Cases on the Law of Business Organization

2016-2017 Statutory Supplement

RESTATEMENT (2d) AGENCY (1958)

Chapter 1. Introductory Matters

§ 1. Agency; Principal; Agent

(1) Agency is the fiduciary relation which results from the manifestation of consent by one person to another that the other shall act on his behalf and subject to his control, and consent by the other so to act.

(2) The one for whom action is to be taken is the principal.

(3) The one who is to act is the agent.

§ 2. Master; Servant; Independent Contractor

(1) A master is a principal who employs an agent to perform service in his affairs and who controls or has the right to control the physical conduct of the other in the performance of the service.

(2) A servant is an agent employed by a master to perform service in his affairs whose physical conduct in the performance of the service is controlled or is subject to the right to control by the master.

(3) An independent contractor is a person who contracts with another to do something for him but who is not controlled by the other nor subject to the other's right to control with respect to his physical conduct in the performance of the undertaking. He may or may not be an agent.

Comment:

a. Servants and non-servant agents. A master is a species of principal, and a servant is a species of agent. The words "master" and "servant" are herein used to indicate the relation from which arises both the liability of an employer for the physical harm caused to third persons by the tort of an employee (see § § 219-249) and the special duties and immunities of an employer to the employee. See § § 473-528. Although for brevity the definitions in this Section refer only to the control or right to control the physical conduct of the servant, there are many factors which are considered by the courts in defining the relation. These factors which distinguish a servant from an independent contractor are stated in Section 220.

§ 3. General Agent; Special Agent

(1) A general agent is an agent authorized to conduct a series of transactions involving a continuity of service.

(2) A special agent is an agent authorized to conduct a single transaction or a series of transactions not involving continuity of service.

§ 4. Disclosed Principal; Partially Disclosed Principal; Undisclosed Principal

(1) If, at the time of a transaction conducted by an agent, the other party thereto has notice that the agent is acting for a principal and of the principal's identity, the principal is a disclosed principal.

(2) If the other party has notice that the agent is or may be acting for a principal but has no notice of the principal's identity, the principal for whom the agent is acting is a partially disclosed principal.

(3) If the other party has no notice that the agent is acting for a principal, the one for whom he acts is an undisclosed principal.

§ 6. Power

A power is an ability on the part of a person to produce a change in a given legal relation by doing or not doing a given act.

Comment:

a. The word "power" denotes not a physical or mental quality but a legal attribute, the ability to change legal relations. This ability may be rightfully exercised, as where an agent makes an authorized contract; or it may be wrongly exercised, as where an agent, having apparent authority so to do, makes an unauthorized contract.

§ 7. Authority

Authority is the power of the agent to affect the legal relations of the principal by acts done in accordance with the principal's manifestations of consent to him.

Comment:

a. Authority distinguished from other powers. "Authority" as used in the Restatement of this Subject, is the power of the agent to do an act or to conduct a transaction on account of the principal which, with respect to the principal, he is privileged to do because of the principal's manifestations to him.

§ 8. Apparent Authority

Apparent authority is the power to affect the legal relations of another person by transactions with third persons, professedly as agent for the other, arising from and in accordance with the other's manifestations to such third persons.

Comment:

a. Apparent authority results from a manifestation by a person that another is his agent, the manifestation being made to a third person and not, as when authority is created, to the agent. It is entirely distinct from authority, either express or implied.

Comment:

c. Belief by third person. Apparent authority exists only to the extent that it is reasonable for the third person dealing with the agent to believe that the agent is authorized. Further, the third person must believe the agent to be authorized. In this respect apparent authority differs from authority since an agent who is authorized can bind the principal to a transaction with a third person who does not believe the agent to be authorized.

§ 8A. Inherent Agency Power

Inherent agency power is a term used in the restatement of this subject to indicate the power of an agent which is derived not from authority, apparent authority or estoppel, but solely from the agency relation and exists for the protection of persons harmed by or dealing with a servant or other agent.

Comment:

a. Rationale. The power of an agent to bind his principal is the distinctive feature of the Anglo-American agency relation. In many situations, however, its existence and extent can be based upon other legal principles. Thus, the liability of a principal for the authorized acts and contracts of an agent is responsive to the tort rule that one is liable for what he intentionally causes, and to the rule in contracts that one who manifests assent to another is bound by the resulting transaction. Contractual liability based upon apparent authority, or its close relation, estoppel, can equally be referred to tort or to contract principles. Likewise restitutional principles may require a principal to surrender property by which he has been unjustly enriched.

However there are situations in which the principal is made liable because of an act done or a transaction entered into by an agent even though there is no tort, contract or restitutional theory upon which the liability can be rested. A principle which will explain such cases can be found if it is assumed that a power can exist purely as a product of the agency relation. Because such a power is derived solely from the agency relation and is not based upon principles of contracts or torts, the term inherent agency power is used to distinguish it from other powers of an agent which are sustained upon contract or tort theories.

The principles of agency have made it possible for persons to utilize the services of others in accomplishing far more than could be done by their unaided efforts. Although the agency relation may exist without reference to mercantile affairs, as in the case of domestic servants, its primary function in modern life is to make possible the commercial enterprises which could not exist otherwise. The common law has properly been responsive to the needs of commerce, permitting what older systems of law denied, namely a direct relation between the principal and a third person with whom the agent deals, even when the principal is undisclosed. Partnerships and corporations, through which most of the work of the world is done today, depend for their existence upon agency principles. The rules designed to promote the interests of these enterprises are necessarily accompanied by rules to police them. It is inevitable that in doing their work, either through negligence or excess of zeal, agents will harm third persons or will deal with them in unauthorized ways. It would be unfair for an enterprise to have the benefit of the work of its agents without making it responsible to some extent for their excesses and failures to act carefully.

§ 8B. Estoppel — Change of Position

(1) A person who is not otherwise liable as a party to a transaction purported to be done on his account, is nevertheless subject to liability to persons who have changed their positions because of their belief that the transaction was entered into by or for him, if

(a) he intentionally or carelessly caused such belief, or

(b) knowing of such belief and that others might change their positions because of it, he did not take reasonable steps to notify them of the facts.

(2) An owner of property who represents to third persons that another is the owner of the property or who permits the other so to represent, or who realizes that third persons believe that another is the owner of the property, and that he could easily inform the third persons of the facts, is subject to the loss of the property if the other disposes of it to third persons who, in ignorance of the facts, purchase the property or otherwise change their position with reference to it.

(3) Change of position, as the phrase is used in the restatement of this subject, indicates payment of money, expenditure of labor, suffering a loss or subjection to legal liability.

§ 13. Agent as a Fiduciary

An agent is a fiduciary with respect to matters within the scope of his agency.

Comment:

a. Existence and effect of fiduciary duties. The agreement to act on behalf of the principal causes the agent to be a fiduciary, that is, a person having a duty, created by his undertaking, to act primarily for the benefit of another in matters connected with his undertaking. Among the agent's fiduciary duties to the principal is the duty to account for profits arising out of the employment, the duty not to act as, or on account of, an adverse party without the principal's consent, the duty not to compete with the principal on his own account or for another in matters relating to the subject matter of the agency, and the duty to deal fairly with the principal in all transactions between them.

Chapter 3. Creation and Interpretation of Authority and Apparent Authority

§ 26. Creation of Authority; General Rule

Except for the execution of instruments under seal or for the performance of transactions required by statute to be authorized in a particular way, authority to do an act can be created by written or spoken words or other conduct of the principal which, reasonably interpreted, causes the agent to believe that the principal desires him so to act on the principal's account.

§ 27. Creation of Apparent Authority: General Rule

Except for the execution of instruments under seal or for the conduct of transactions required by statute to be authorized in a particular way, apparent authority to do an act is created as to a third person by written or spoken words or any other conduct of the principal which, reasonably interpreted, causes the third person to believe that the principal consents to have the act done on his behalf by the person purporting to act for him.

§ 35. When Incidental Authority Is Inferred

Unless otherwise agreed, authority to conduct a transaction includes authority to do acts which are incidental to it, usually accompany it, or are reasonably necessary to accomplish it.

§ 43. Acquiescence by Principal in Agent's Conduct

(1) Acquiescence by the principal in conduct of an agent whose previously conferred authorization reasonably might include it, indicates that the conduct was authorized; if clearly not included in the authorization, acquiescence in it indicates affirmance.

(2) Acquiescence by the principal in a series of acts by the agent indicates authorization to perform similar acts in the future.

Chapter 4. Ratification

§ 82. Ratification

Ratification is the affirmance by a person of a prior act which did not bind him but which was done or professedly done on his account, whereby the act, as to some or all persons, is given effect as if originally authorized by him.

§ 83. Affirmance

Affirmance is either

(a) a manifestation of an election by one on whose account an unauthorized act has been done to treat the act as authorized, or

(b) conduct by him justifiable only if there were such an election.

§ 94. Failure to Act as Affirmance

An affirmance of an unauthorized transaction can be inferred from a failure to repudiate it.

§ 100. Effect of Ratification; in General

Except as stated in Section 101, the liabilities resulting from ratification are the same as those resulting from authorization if, between the time when the original act was performed and when it was affirmed, there has been no change in the capacity of the principal or third person or in the legality of authorizing or performing the original act.

Chapter 5. Termination of Agency Powers

§ 118. Revocation or Renunciation

Authority terminates if the principal or the agent manifests to the other dissent to its continuance.

Comment:

a. Such termination by act of the principal is revocation; by act of the agent, it is renunciation.

b. Power to revoke or renounce. The principal has power to revoke and the agent has power to renounce, although doing so is in violation of a contract between the parties and although the authority is expressed to be irrevocable. A statement in a contract that the authority cannot be terminated by either party is effective only to create liability for its wrongful termination.

Illustrations:

1. In consideration of A's agreement to advertise and give his best energies to the sale of Blackacre, its owner, P, grants to A "a power of attorney, irrevocable for one year" to sell it. A advertises and spends time trying to sell Blackacre. At the end of three months P informs A that he revokes. A's authority is terminated.

2. In consideration of $1000 and A's promise to endeavor to sell, P grants to A for a period of one year a power of attorney to sell property, with compensation at 25 per cent. of the selling price, the power of attorney ending with this phrase: "Hereby intending and agreeing that this power shall be irrevocable during one year, and that during this period A shall have a power coupled with an interest which shall not be affected by my death or other circumstances." At the end of three months P informs A that he revokes. A's authority is terminated.

§ 124A. Effect of Termination of Authority Upon Apparent Authority and Other Powers

The termination of authority does not thereby terminate apparent authority. All other powers of the agent resulting from the relation terminate except powers necessary for the protection of his interests or of those of the principal.

§ 136. Notification Terminating Apparent Authority

(1) Unless otherwise agreed, there is a notification by the principal to the third person of revocation of an agent's authority or other fact indicating its termination:

(a) when the principal states such fact to the third person; or

(b) when a reasonable time has elapsed after a writing stating such fact has been delivered by the principal

(i) to the other personally;

(ii) to the other's place of business;

(iii) to a place designated by the other as one in which business communications are received; or

(iv) to a place which, in view of the business customs or relations between the parties is reasonably believed to be the place for the receipt of such communications by the other.

(2) Unless otherwise agreed, a notification to be effective in terminating apparent authority must be given by the means stated in Subsection (1) with respect to a third person:

(a) who has previously extended credit to or received credit from the principal through the agent in reliance upon a manifestation from the principal of continuing authority in the agent;

(b) to whom the agent has been specially accredited;

(c) with whom the agent has begun to deal, as the principal should know; or

(d) who relies upon the possession by the agent of indicia of authority entrusted to him by the principal.

(3) Except as to the persons included in Subsection (2), the principal can properly give notification of the termination of the agent's authority by:

(a) advertising the fact in a newspaper of general circulation in the place where the agency is regularly carried on; or

(b) giving publicity by some other method reasonably adapted to give the information to such third person.

Chapter 6. Liability of the Principal to Third Persons; Contracts and Conveyances

§ 140. Liability Based Upon Agency Principles

The liability of the principal to a third person upon a transaction conducted by an agent, or the transfer of his interests by an agent, may be based upon the fact that:

(a) the agent was authorized;

(b) the agent was apparently authorized; or

(c) the agent had a power arising from the agency relation and not dependent upon authority or apparent authority.

Comment:

a. As stated in Sections 144, 159, a principal is subject to liability upon a transaction conducted by his agent, whom he has authorized or apparently authorized to conduct it in the way in which it is conducted, as if he had personally entered into the transaction. In transactions in which there is neither authority nor apparent authority, the principal may be subjected to liability because, in view of the relations of the parties or the subject matter involved, policy requires that the agent should have power to bind the principal, described in Section 8A as inherent agency powers.

§ 144. General Rule

A disclosed or partially disclosed principal is subject to liability upon contracts made by an agent acting within his authority if made in proper form and with the understanding that the principal is a party.

§ 159. Apparent Authority

A disclosed or partially disclosed principal is subject to liability upon contracts made by an agent acting within his apparent authority if made in proper form and with the understanding that the apparent principal is a party. The rules as to the liability of a principal for authorized acts, are applicable to unauthorized acts which are apparently authorized.

§ 161. Unauthorized Acts of General Agent

A general agent for a disclosed or partially disclosed principal subjects his principal to liability for acts done on his account which usually accompany or are incidental to transactions which the agent is authorized to conduct if, although they are forbidden by the principal, the other party reasonably believes that the agent is authorized to do them and has no notice that he is not so authorized.

Comment:

a. Rationale. The rule in this Section, and the corresponding rule stated in Section 194 dealing with the general agents of undisclosed principals, are applicable to cases in which the agent has neither authority nor apparent authority and acts disobediently or ignorantly on account of the principal. Both rules are important illustrations of inherent powers, that is, powers held by an agent, the exercise of which are effective to subject the principal to liability in transactions in which the agent has neither authority nor apparent authority, but in which the agent derives his power wholly from his relation with the principal. They are called inherent agency powers since there is no other common designation which adequately describes them. See § 8A.

§ 186. General Rule

An undisclosed principal is bound by contracts and conveyances made on his account by an agent acting within his authority, except that the principal is not bound by a contract which is under seal or which is negotiable, or upon a contract which excludes him.

Comment:

a. Rationale. The rules with reference to undisclosed principals appear to violate one of the basic theories of contracts. The relation between the principal and a person with whom the agent has made an authorized contract is spoken of as contractual, although by definition there has been no manifestation of consent by the third person to the principal or by the principal to him. In fact, the contract, in the common law sense, is between the agent and the third person. In spite of this, the law of agency finds it expedient to create rights and liabilities between the other party to the transaction and the principal as if the latter were a contracting party. It may be said that the principal becomes a party to the contract by operation of law, without the will of the third party and, in some cases, contrary to the will of the principal.

§ 194. Acts of General Agents

A general agent for an undisclosed principal authorized to conduct transactions subjects his principal to liability for acts done on his account, if usual or necessary in such transactions, although forbidden by the principal to do them.

§ 195. Acts of Manager Appearing to Be Owner

An undisclosed principal who entrusts an agent with the management of his business is subject to liability to third persons with whom the agent enters into transactions usual in such businesses and on the principal's account, although contrary to the directions of the principal.

Comment:

a. This Section is a special application of Section 194. The fact that the agent is the apparent owner of the business does not result in liability of the principal, except to the extent of the assets of the business, or to the extent to which the principal has been benefited by things received from the third person. The liability of the principal upon the contract itself and without reference to benefits received or to the assets of the business is dependent upon the rule of agency stated in Section 194, the Comments to which are applicable

Chapter 7. Liability of the Principal to Third Persons; Torts

§ 215. Conduct Authorized but Unintended by Principal

A master or other principal who unintentionally authorizes conduct of a servant or other agent which constitutes a tort to a third person is subject to liability to such person.

§ 216. Unauthorized Tortious Conduct

A master or other principal may be liable to another whose interests have been invaded by the tortious conduct of a servant or other agent, although the principal does not personally violate a duty to such other or authorize the conduct of the agent causing the invasion.

§ 217C. Punitive Damages

Punitive damages can properly be awarded against a master or other principal because of an act by an agent if, but only if:

(a) the principal authorized the doing and the manner of the act, or

(b) the agent was unfit and the principal was reckless in employing him, or

(c) the agent was employed in a managerial capacity and was acting in the scope of employment, or

(d) the principal or a managerial agent of the principal ratified or approved the act.

§ 217D. Penalties

A principal may be subject to penalties enforced under the rules of the criminal law, for acts done by a servant or other agent.

§ 219. When Master Is Liable for Torts of His Servants

(1) A master is subject to liability for the torts of his servants committed while acting in the scope of their employment.

(2) A master is not subject to liability for the torts of his servants acting outside the scope of their employment, unless:

(a) the master intended the conduct or the consequences, or

(b) the master was negligent or reckless, or

(c) the conduct violated a non-delegable duty of the master, or

(d) the servant purported to act or to speak on behalf of the principal and there was reliance upon apparent authority, or he was aided in accomplishing the tort by the existence of the agency relation.

§ 220. Definition of Servant

factors for employee

(1) A servant is a person employed to perform services in the affairs of another and who with respect to the physical conduct in the performance of the services is subject to the other's control or right to control.

(2) In determining whether one acting for another is a servant or an independent contractor, the following matters of fact, among others, are considered:

(a) the extent of control which, by the agreement, the master may exercise over the details of the work;

(b) whether or not the one employed is engaged in a distinct occupation or business;

(c) the kind of occupation, with reference to whether, in the locality, the work is usually done under the direction of the employer or by a specialist without supervision;

(d) the skill required in the particular occupation;

(e) whether the employer or the workman supplies the instrumentalities, tools, and the place of work for the person doing the work;

(f) the length of time for which the person is employed;

(g) the method of payment, whether by the time or by the job;

(h) whether or not the work is a part of the regular business of the employer;

(i) whether or not the parties believe they are creating the relation of master and servant; and

(j) whether the principal is or is not in business.

Comment on Subsection (1):

. . . *c. Generality of definition.* The relation of master and servant is one not capable of exact definition. It is an important relation in that upon it depends the liability of the master to third persons and to his employees under the provisions of various statutes as well as under the common law; the relation may prevent liability, as in the case of the fellow servant rule. It cannot, however, be defined in general terms with substantial accuracy. The factors stated in Subsection (2) are all considered in determining the question, and it is for the triers of fact to determine whether or not there is a sufficient group of favorable factors to establish the relation. . . .

d. Control or right to control. Although control or right to control the physical conduct of the person giving service is important and in many situations is determinative, the control or right to control needed to establish the relation of master and servant may be very attenuated. In some types of cases which involve persons customarily considered as servants, there may even be an understanding that the employer shall not exercise control. . . .

e. Independent contractors. It is important to distinguish between a servant and an agent who is not a servant, since ordinarily a principal is not liable for the incidental physical acts of negligence in the performance of duties committed by an agent who is not a servant.

§ 228. General Statement

(1) Conduct of a servant is within the scope of employment if, but only if:

(a) it is of the kind he is employed to perform;

(b) it occurs substantially within the authorized time and space limits;

(c) it is actuated, at least in part, by a purpose to serve the master, and

(d) if force is intentionally used by the servant against another, the use of force is not unexpectable by the master.

(2) Conduct of a servant is not within the scope of employment if it is different in kind from that authorized, far beyond the authorized time or space limits, or too little actuated by a purpose to serve the master.

§ 230. Forbidden Acts

An act, although forbidden, or done in a forbidden manner, may be within the scope of employment.

Comment:

. . . *b. Acts specifically forbidden.* A master cannot avoid responsibility for the negligence of a servant by telling him to act carefully. He cannot limit the servant to the pound of flesh and direct him not to spill blood. But the rule stated in this Section goes much further; it includes specifically forbidden acts and forbidden means of accomplishing results. A master cannot direct a servant to accomplish a result and anticipate that he will always use the means which he directs or will refrain from acts which it is natural to expect that servants may do.

§ 231. Criminal Or Tortious Acts

An act may be within the scope of employment although consciously criminal or tortious.

§ 232. Failure to Act

The failure of a servant to act may be conduct within the scope of employment.

Chapter 13. Duties and Liabilities of Agent to Principal

§ 379. Duty of Care and Skill

(1) Unless otherwise agreed, a paid agent is subject to a duty to the principal to act with standard care and with the skill which is standard in the locality for the kind of work which he is employed to perform and, in addition, to exercise any special skill that he has.

(2) Unless otherwise agreed, a gratuitous agent is under a duty to the principal to act with the care and skill which is required of persons not agents performing similar gratuitous undertakings for others.

§ 381. Duty to Give Information

Unless otherwise agreed, an agent is subject to a duty to use reasonable efforts to give his principal information which is relevant to affairs entrusted to him and which, as the agent has notice, the principal would desire to have and which can be communicated without violating a superior duty to a third person.

§ 385. Duty to Obey

(1) Unless otherwise agreed, an agent is subject to a duty to obey all reasonable directions in regard to the manner of performing a service that he has contracted to perform.

(2) Unless he is privileged to protect his own or another's interests, an agent is subject to a duty not to act in matters entrusted to him on account of the principal contrary to the directions of the principal, even though the terms of the employment prescribe that such directions shall not be given.

Comment on Subsection (1):

a. Unless otherwise agreed, a contract of agency is interpreted as including a promise by the agent to act with reference to the subject matter of the agency in accordance with the reasonable directions of the principal.

§ 387. General Principle

Unless otherwise agreed, an agent is subject to a duty to his principal to act solely for the benefit of the principal in all matters connected with his agency.

§ 388. Duty to Account for Profits Arising Out of Employment

Unless otherwise agreed, an agent who makes a profit in connection with transactions conducted by him on behalf of the principal is under a duty to give such profit to the principal.

§ 389. Acting as Adverse Party Without Principal's Consent

Unless otherwise agreed, an agent is subject to a duty not to deal with his principal as an adverse party in a transaction connected with his agency without the principal's knowledge.

§ 390. Acting as Adverse Party with Principal's Consent

An agent who, to the knowledge of the principal, acts on his own account in a transaction in which he is employed has a duty to deal fairly with the principal and to disclose to him all facts which the agent knows or should know would reasonably affect the principal's judgment, unless the principal has manifested that he knows such facts or that he does not care to know them.

Comment:

a. Facts to be disclosed. One employed as agent violates no duty to the principal by acting for his own benefit if he makes a full disclosure of the facts to an acquiescent principal and takes no unfair advantage of him. Before dealing with the principal on his own account, however, an agent has a duty, not only to make no misstatements of fact, but also to disclose to the principal all relevant facts fully and completely. A fact is relevant if it is one which the agent should realize would be likely to affect the judgment of the principal in giving his consent to the agent to enter into the particular transaction on the specified terms. Hence, the disclosure must include not only the fact that the agent is acting on his own account (see § 389), but also all other facts which he should realize have or are likely to have a bearing upon the desirability of the transaction from the viewpoint of the principal. This includes, in the case of sales to him by the principal, not only the price which can be obtained, but also all facts affecting the desirability of sale, such as the likelihood of a higher price being obtained later, the possibilities of dealing with the property in another way, and all other matters which a disinterested and skillful agent advising the principal would think reasonably relevant.

If the principal has limited business experience, an agent cannot properly fail to give such information merely because the principal says he does not care for it; the agent's duty of fair dealing is satisfied only if he reasonably believes that the principal understands the implications of the transaction....

Comment:

c. Fairness. The agent must not take advantage of his position to persuade the principal into making a hard or improvident bargain. If the agent is one upon whom the principal naturally would rely for advice, the fact that the agent discloses that he is acting as an adverse party does not relieve him from the duty of giving the principal impartial advice based upon a carefully formed judgment as to the principal's interests. If he cannot or does not wish to do so, he has a duty to see that the principal secures the advice of a competent and disinterested third person. An agent who is in a close confidential relation to the principal, such as a family attorney, has the burden of proving that a substantial gift to him was not the result of undue influence. Even though an agent employed to sell is not in such a position, payment of less than the reasonable market value for property he buys from the principal is evidence that the bargain was unfair. If the principal is not in a dependent position, however, and the agent fully performs his duties of disclosure, a transaction of purchase and sale between them is not voidable merely because the principal receives an inadequate price or pays too great a price.

§ 391. Acting for Adverse Party Without Principal's Consent

Unless otherwise agreed, an agent is subject to a duty to his principal not to act on behalf of an adverse party in a transaction connected with his agency without the principal's knowledge.

§ 393. Competition as to Subject Matter of Agency

Unless otherwise agreed, an agent is subject to a duty not to compete with the principal concerning the subject matter of his agency.

Comment:

a. The reasons for the rule stated in this Section are the same as those which prevent an agent from dealing with the principal as an adverse party, and the rule stated in Section 390 as to the duties of disclosure and fair dealing is applicable.

There is no violation of the agent's duty if the principal understands that the agent is to compete; a course of dealing between the parties may indicate that this is understood. Likewise, an agent can properly act freely on his own account in matters not within the field of his agency and in matters in which his interests are not antagonistic to those of the principal, except that he can not properly thus use confidential information.

§ 395. Using or Disclosing Confidential Information

Unless otherwise agreed, an agent is subject to a duty to the principal not to use or to communicate information confidentially given him by the principal or acquired by him during the course of or on account of his agency or in violation of his duties as agent, in competition with or to the injury of the principal, on his own account or on behalf of another, although such information does not relate to the transaction in which he is then employed, unless the information is a matter of general knowledge.

RESTATEMENT (3d) AGENCY (2006)

CHAPTER 1. INTRODUCTORY MATTERS

§ 1.01 Agency Defined

Agency is the fiduciary relationship that arises when one person (a "principal") manifests assent to another person (an "agent") that the agent shall act on the principal's behalf and subject to the principal's control, and the agent manifests assent or otherwise consents so to act.

§ 1.02 Parties' Labeling and Popular Usage Not Controlling

An agency relationship arises only when the elements stated in § 1.01 are present. Whether a relationship is characterized as agency in an agreement between parties or in the context of industry or popular usage is not controlling.

§ 1.03 Manifestation

A person manifests assent or intention through written or spoken words or other conduct.

§ 1.04 Terminology

(1) *Coagents.* Coagents have agency relationships with the same principal. A coagent may be appointed by the principal or by another agent actually or apparently authorized by the principal to do so.

(2) *Disclosed, undisclosed, and unidentified principals.*

(a) *Disclosed principal.* A principal is disclosed if, when an agent and a third party interact, the third party has notice that the agent is acting for a principal and has notice of the principal's identity.

(b) *Undisclosed principal.* A principal is undisclosed if, when an agent and a third party interact, the third party has no notice that the agent is acting for a principal.

(c) *Unidentified principal.* A principal is unidentified if, when an agent and a third party interact, the third party has notice that the agent is acting for a principal but does not have notice of the principal's identity.

(3) *Gratuitous agent.* A gratuitous agent acts without a right to compensation.

(4) *Notice.* A person has notice of a fact if the person knows the fact, has reason to know the fact, has received an effective notification of the fact, or should know the fact to fulfill a duty owed to another person. Notice of a fact that an agent knows or has reason to know is imputed to the principal as stated in §§ 5.03 and 5.04. A notification given to or by an agent is effective as notice to or by the principal as stated in § 5.02.

(5) *Person.* A person is (a) an individual; (b) an organization or association that has legal capacity to possess rights and incur obligations; (c) a government, political subdivision, or instrumentality or entity created by government; or (d) any other entity that has legal capacity to possess rights and incur obligations.

(6) *Power given as security.* A power given as security is a power to affect the legal relations of its creator that is created in the form of a manifestation of actual authority and held for the benefit of the holder or a third person. It is given to protect a legal or equitable title or to secure the performance of a duty apart from any duties owed the holder of the power by its creator that are incident to a relationship of agency under § 1.01.

(7) *Power of attorney.* A power of attorney is an instrument that states an agent's authority.

(8) *Subagent.* A subagent is a person appointed by an agent to perform functions that the agent has consented to perform on behalf of the agent's principal and for whose conduct the appointing agent is responsible to the

principal. The relationship between an appointing agent and a subagent is one of agency, created as stated in § 1.01.

(9) *Superior and subordinate coagents*. A superior coagent has the right, conferred by the principal, to direct a subordinate coagent.

(10) *Trustee and agent-trustee*. A trustee is a holder of property who is subject to fiduciary duties to deal with the property for the benefit of charity or for one or more persons, at least one of whom is not the sole trustee. An agent-trustee is a trustee subject to the control of the settlor or of one or more beneficiaries.

CHAPTER 2. PRINCIPLES OF ATTRIBUTION

§ 2.01 Actual Authority

An agent acts with actual authority when, at the time of taking action that has legal consequences for the principal, the agent reasonably believes, in accordance with the principal's manifestations to the agent, that the principal wishes the agent so to act.

Comment:

Comment b. Terminology. As defined in this section, "actual authority" is a synonym for "true authority," a term used in some opinions. The definition in this section does not attempt to classify different types of actual authority on the basis of the degree of detail in the principal's manifestation, which may consist of written or spoken words or other conduct. See § 1.03. As commonly used, the term "express authority" often means actual authority that a principal has stated in very specific or detailed language. The term "implied authority" has more than one meaning. "Implied authority" is often used to mean actual authority either (1) to do what is necessary, usual, and proper to accomplish or perform an agent's express responsibilities or (2) to act in a manner in which an agent believes the principal wishes the agent to act based on the agent's reasonable interpretation of the principal's manifestation in light of the principal's objectives and other facts known to the agent. These meanings are not mutually exclusive. Both fall within the definition of actual authority. Section 2.02, which delineates the scope of actual authority, subsumes the practical consequences of implied authority. The term "inherent agency power," used in Restatement Second, Agency, and defined therein by § 8 A, is not used in this Restatement. Inherent agency power is defined as "a term used . . . to indicate the power of an agent which is derived not from authority, apparent authority or estoppel, but solely from the agency relation and exists for the protection of persons harmed by or dealing with a servant or other agent." Other doctrines stated in this Restatement encompass the justifications underpinning § 8 A, including the importance of interpretation by the agent in the agent's relationship with the principal, as well as the doctrines of apparent authority, estoppel, and restitution.

§ 2.02 Scope of Actual Authority

(1) An agent has actual authority to take action designated or implied in the principal's manifestations to the agent and acts necessary or incidental to achieving the principal's objectives, as the agent reasonably understands the principal's manifestations and objectives when the agent determines how to act.

(2) An agent's interpretation of the principal's manifestations is reasonable if it reflects any meaning known by the agent to be ascribed by the principal and, in the absence of any meaning known to the agent, as a reasonable person in the agent's position would interpret the manifestations in light of the context, including circumstances of which the agent has notice and the agent's fiduciary duty to the principal.

(3) An agent's understanding of the principal's objectives is reasonable if it accords with the principal's manifestations and the inferences that a reasonable person in the agent's position would draw from the circumstances creating the agency.

§ 2.03 Apparent Authority

Apparent authority is the power held by an agent or other actor to affect a principal's legal relations with third parties when a third party reasonably believes the actor has authority to act on behalf of the principal and that belief is traceable to the principal's manifestations.

§ 2.04 Respondeat Superior

An employer is subject to liability for torts committed by employees while acting within the scope of their employment.

§ 2.05 Estoppel to Deny Existence of Agency Relationship

A person who has not made a manifestation that an actor has authority as an agent and who is not otherwise liable as a party to a transaction purportedly done by the actor on that person's account is subject to liability to a third party who justifiably is induced to make a detrimental change in position because the transaction is believed to be on the person's account, if

(1) the person intentionally or carelessly caused such belief, or

(2) having notice of such belief and that it might induce others to change their positions, the person did not take reasonable steps to notify them of the facts.

§ 2.06 Liability of Undisclosed Principal

(1) An undisclosed principal is subject to liability to a third party who is justifiably induced to make a detrimental change in position by an agent acting on the principal's behalf and without actual authority if the principal, having notice of the agent's conduct and that it might induce others to change their positions, did not take reasonable steps to notify them of the facts.

(2) An undisclosed principal may not rely on instructions given an agent that qualify or reduce the agent's authority to less than the authority a third party would reasonably believe the agent to have under the same circumstances if the principal had been disclosed.

§ 2.07 Restitution of Benefit

If a principal is unjustly enriched at the expense of another person by the action of an agent or a person who appears to be an agent, the principal is subject to a claim for restitution by that person.

CHAPTER 3. CREATION AND TERMINATION OF AUTHORITY AND AGENCY RELATIONSHIPS

§ 3.01 Creation of Actual Authority

Actual authority, as defined in § 2.01, is created by a principal's manifestation to an agent that, as reasonably understood by the agent, expresses the principal's assent that the agent take action on the principal's behalf.

§ 3.02 Formal Requirements

If the law requires a writing or record signed by the principal to evidence an agent's authority to bind a principal to a contract or other transaction, the principal is not bound in the absence of such a writing or record. A principal may be estopped to assert the lack of such a writing or record when a third party has been induced to make a detrimental change in position by the reasonable belief that an agent has authority to bind the principal that is traceable to a manifestation made by the principal.

§ 3.03 Creation of Apparent Authority

Apparent authority, as defined in § 2.03, is created by a person's manifestation that another has authority to act with legal consequences for the person who makes the manifestation, when a third party reasonably believes the actor to be authorized and the belief is traceable to the manifestation.

Comment:

. . . *e. Organizational executives and corporate officers*

(1). Organizational executives — corporations. The corporate form of organization makes it necessary that a corporation act through agents as well as undertaking commitments that are expressly authorized by resolutions adopted by its board of directors. Corporate legislation contemplates that a corporation's directors and in some instances its shareholders have power to and will appoint officers as agents of the corporation. Some contemporary statutes are flexible and do not prescibe titles for holders of offices. Officer positions are often specified in bylaws but may be designated by directors acting in accord with the bylaws. The term "officer" usually means an executive has been appointed directly by the board to the position held. Persons hired by officers are typically employees of the corporation, not subagents of the officers themselves. See § 1.04(8), which defines subagent. In a corporation of any size, many managerial agents will not hold statutorily defined positions as officers. It is not always clear whether a person is an officer, and the answer to the question may vary with the context in which it is asked. For purposes of the federal securities laws, "executive officer" is a defined term encompassing officers who perform policy-making functions.

Questions of apparent authority turn on the reasonableness of a third party's belief in an executive's authority and whether these beliefs are traceable to conduct of the corporation, in particular, conduct by its board of directors. In the absence of a link to conduct of the corporation, a third party's belief in an executive's authority is not encompassed by apparent authority if it is based solely on the executive's own representations of authority.

When present, apparent authority expands an executive's effective ability to bind the corporation, typically because the third party is unaware when the executive's actual authority is limited in a manner not customary for an executive in a comparable position. Less typically, apparent authority expands an executive's authority when the corporation's directors acted in a manner that led a third party reasonably to belive that the directors acquiesced in conduct by the executive that had not been authorized by the board.

It is not reasonable for a third party to believe a corporate executive to be authorized simply on the basis of the physical grandeur of the executive's work space or other atmospherics. In contrast, apparent authority may be based on the third party's observations of how the executive customarily functions and the scope of the executive's evident responsibility in dealing with third parties and directing corporate business. It may not be reasonable to believe that an executive has authority to speak as to a matter that is within the province of others' functionally defined responsibilities.

If an executive proposes a transaction that will generate proceeds inuring solely to the executive's personal benefit, the fact that the third party is shown what purports to be a resolution from the corporation's board authorizing such a transaction does not in itself establish the reasonableness of the third party's belief in the executive's authority. It is a question of fact whether, under all relevant circumstances, a reasonable third party would inquire further into the propriety of the transaction, the genuineness of the resolution, or the confirmation of authority.

It is, of course, possible for the same individual to serve as an agent of more than one corporation or, for example, to be both an officer of a corporation and a partner in a partnership. The authority that such an agent may have in connection with one such association does not in itself create apparent authority as to the other association.

A corporation may create an appearance of authority by acquiescing in the continuing exercise of a corporate officer's function by an individual who has never been duly appointed or elected to office. Such an individual is often characterized as a "de facto" corporate officer to protect third parties who deal with the corporation through the purported officer, reasonably believing the appearance that the individual has the status of an officer. For these purposes, a shareholder is not a "third party" but is a member of the corporate principal itself. The question is whether the third party had a reasonable basis to believe that the officer with whom the interaction occurred had authority to bind the firm, a basis that might be present if the other shareholders led the third party to believe the officer had such authority.

(2). Organizational executives — partnerships and other unincorporated associations. As an organizational structure, a general partnership is flatter than a structure defined by the corporate form. A general partnership results when two or more persons associate for the purpose of carrying on as co-owners a business for profit, unless they structure their association pursuant to some other organizational form. General partnership is thus the legal structure applicable to an ongoing business that extends beyond a single project. An association limited to a single project is a joint venture. A joint venture is treated as a form of partnership, in which duties and authority are limited by the scope of the venture. Partnership legislation characterizes all general partners as agents of the partnership "for the purpose of its business . . ." Partnership thus automatically links ownership with agency, which the corporate form does not. Under the Uniform Partnership Act § 9(1), the partnership is bound by "the act of every partner . . . for apparently carrying on in the usual way the business of the partnership" unless the partner lacks authority so to act and the person with whom the partner deals "has knowledge of the fact that [the partner] has no such authority," Under the Revised Uniform Partnership Act § 301, a partner's act binds the partnership "for apparently carrying on in the ordinary course the partnership business or business of the kind carried on by the partnership" unless the partner lacks authority so to act and the person with whom the partner deals "knew or had received a notification that the partner lacked authority." Under both formulations, a partner's apparent authority is linked, not to a specific manifestation by the partnership about the particular partner, but to the scope or nature of the partnership's business and whether the partner's particular act carries it on in "the usual way" or "in the ordinary course." What is determinative is the connection between the act and the business in which the partnership is engaged, as well as the connection between the act and the type of activities typical or characteristic of the business.

The consequences of defined position within a hierarchical organizational structure do not affect appearances of authority in a general partnership to the degree they shape such appearances in a corporate context. Apparent authority in the partnership context is a question of the reasonableness of the third party's belief about authority as defined by the partnership's business and by known limits on a partner's actual authority. A third party may reasonably believe that the partnership has acquiesced or consented to a partner's expansion of the nature of "the business of the partnership" if the third party observes dealings or a pattern of conduct between the individual partner and the partnership supportive of that belief.

§ 3.06 Termination of Actual Authority — In General

An agent's actual authority may be terminated by:

(1) the agent's death, cessation of existence, or suspension of powers as stated in § 3.07(1) and (3); or

(2) the principal's death, cessation of existence, or suspension of powers as stated in § 3.07(2) and (4); or

(3) the principal's loss of capacity, as stated in § 3.08(1) and (3); or

(4) an agreement between the agent and the principal or the occurrence of circumstances on the basis of which the agent should reasonably conclude that the principal no longer would assent to the agent's taking action on the principal's behalf, as stated in § 3.09; or

(5) a manifestation of revocation by the principal to the agent, or of renunciation by the agent to the principal, as stated in § 3.10(1); or

(6) the occurrence of circumstances specified by statute.

§ 3.09 Termination by Agreement or by Occurrence of Changed Circumstances

An agent's actual authority terminates (1) as agreed by the agent and the principal, subject to the provisions of § 3.10; or (2) upon the occurrence of circumstances on the basis of which the agent should reasonably conclude that the principal no longer would assent to the agent's taking action on the principal's behalf.

§ 3.10 Manifestation Terminating Actual Authority

(1) Notwithstanding any agreement between principal and agent, an agent's actual authority terminates if the agent renounces it by a manifestation to the principal or if the principal revokes the agent's actual authority by a manifestation to the agent. A revocation or a renunciation is effective when the other party has notice of it.

(2) A principal's manifestation of revocation is, unless otherwise agreed, ineffective to terminate a power given as security or to terminate a proxy to vote securities or other membership or ownership interests that is made irrevocable in compliance with applicable legislation. See §§ 3.12-3.13.

§ 3.11 Termination of Apparent Authority

(1) The termination of actual authority does not by itself end any apparent authority held by an agent.

(2) Apparent authority ends when it is no longer reasonable for the third party with whom an agent deals to believe that the agent continues to act with actual authority.

§ 3.12 Power Given as Security; Irrevocable Proxy

(1) A power given as security is a power to affect the legal relations of its creator that is created in the form of a manifestation of actual authority and held for the benefit of the holder or a third person. This power is given to protect a legal or equitable title or to secure the performance of a duty apart from any duties owed the holder of the power by its creator that are incident to a relationship of agency under § 1.01. It is given upon the creation of the duty or title or for consideration. It is distinct from actual authority that the holder may exercise if the holder is an agent of the creator of the power.

(2) A power to exercise voting rights associated with securities or a membership interest may be conferred on a proxy through a manifestation of actual authority. The power may be given as security under (1) and may be made irrevocable in compliance with applicable legislation.

Comment:

... *b. Distinguished from agency and actual authority.* A power given as security creates neither a relationship of agency as defined in § 1.01 nor actual authority as defined in § 2.01, although the power enables its holder to affect the legal relations of the creator of the power. The power arises from a manifestation of assent by its creator that the holder of the power may properly create liability against the creator, or dispose of property or other interests of the creator, or perfect or otherwise protect a title already held by the holder of the power or the person for whose benefit the holder is to act. If the power is given as security for the performance of a duty, it must be supported by consideration, but consideration is not necessary if the power is given to facilitate transfers of title to the power holder.

The rights created by a power given as security, or by an irrevocable proxy, entitle the holder to take specfic actions. If the creator of a validly created power given as security purports to revoke the holder's authority contrary to the agreement pursuant to which the creator granted the power, specific enforcement of the holder's rights is an appropriate remedy, subject to the court's discretion in granting an equitable remedy. Likewise, specific enforcement may be warranted to protect the rights of the holder of a validly created irrevocable proxy. In both cases, it will often be difficult or impossible for the holder to prove quantifiable damages or to obtain a substitute performance. See Restatement Second, Contracts § 360, Comments *b* and *c*.

A power given as security does not create a relationship of agency as defined in § 1.01 because it is neither given for, nor exercised for, the benefit of the person who creates it. The holder is not subject to the creator's control and the holder does not owe fiduciary duties to the creator. An agent's right to act, created by actual authority, does not consititue a power given as security although the agent has an interest in earning a commission by performing services and the principal has contracted with the agent not to revoke the agent's actual authority. An agent's interest in being paid a commission is an ordinary incident of agency and its presence does not convert the agent's authority into a power held for the agent's benefit. In contrast, cases interpreting statutes applicable to irrevocable proxies hold that a proxy holder's interest in an employment agreement with the corporation suffices to support irrevocability. See Comment *d*. However, if a power holder has a distinct interest in the subject matter of an agency relationship, seprate from acting as an agent, a power given to protect that interest is a power given as security, as is a power given to protect a distinct relationship, separate from the agency relationship, between the agent and the principal. A power may be granted irrevocably for the benefit of its creator as well as the holder.

A power given as security may also be created and held for the benefit of a third party, other than the holder of the power. The creator of the power and the holder have the ability to create an enforceable right in a third party to benefit from the power, just as two parties to a contarct have the ability to create a right in a third party beneficiary. See Restatement Second, Contracts § 304, Comment *b*.

CHAPTER 4. RATIFICATION

§ 4.01 Ratification Defined

(1) Ratification is the affirmance of a prior act done by another, whereby the act is given effect as if done by an agent acting with actual authority.

(2) A person ratifies an act by

(a) manifesting assent that the act shall affect the person's legal relations, or

(b) conduct that justifies a reasonable assumption that the person so consents.

(3) Ratification does not occur unless

(a) the act is ratifiable as stated in § 4.03,

(b) the person ratifying has capacity as stated in § 4.04,

(c) the ratification is timely as stated in § 4.05, and

(d) the ratification encompasses the act in its entirety as stated in § 4.07.

§ 4.02 Effect of Ratification

(1) Subject to the exceptions stated in subsection (2), ratification retroactively creates the effects of actual authority.

(2) Ratification is not effective:

(a) in favor of a person who causes it by misrepresentation or other conduct that would make a contract voidable;

(b) in favor of an agent against a principal when the principal ratifies to avoid a loss; or

(c) to diminish the rights or other interests of persons, not parties to the transaction, that were acquired in the subject matter prior to the ratification.

§ 4.03 Acts That May Be Ratified

A person may ratify an act if the actor acted or purported to act as an agent on the person's behalf.

§ 4.04 Capacity to Ratify

(1) A person may ratify an act if

(a) the person existed at the time of the act, and

(b) the person had capacity as defined in § 3.04 at the time of ratifying the act.

(2) At a later time, a principal may avoid a ratification made earlier when the principal lacked capacity as defined in § 3.04.

§ 4.05 Timing of Ratification

A ratification of a transaction is not effective unless it precedes the occurrence of circumstances that would cause the ratification to have adverse and inequitable effects on the rights of third parties. These circumstances include:

(1) any manifestation of intention to withdraw from the transaction made by the third party;

(2) any material change in circumstances that would make it inequitable to bind the third party, unless the third party chooses to be bound; and

(3) a specific time that determines whether a third party is deprived of a right or subjected to a liability.

§ 4.06 Knowledge Requisite to Ratification

A person is not bound by a ratification made without knowledge of material facts involved in the original act when the person was unaware of such lack of knowledge.

§ 4.07 No Partial Ratification

A ratification is not effective unless it encompasses the entirety of an act, contract, or other single transaction.

§ 4.08 Estoppel to Deny Ratification

If a person makes a manifestation that the person has ratified another's act and the manifestation, as reasonably understood by a third party, induces the third party to make a detrimental change in position, the person may be estopped to deny the ratification.

CHAPTER 5. NOTIFICATIONS AND NOTICE

§ 5.01 Notifications and Notice — In General

(1) A notification is a manifestation that is made in the form required by agreement among parties or by applicable law, or in a reasonable manner in the absence of an agreement or an applicable law, with the intention of affecting the legal rights and duties of the notifier in relation to rights and duties of persons to whom the notification is given.

(2) A notification given to or by an agent is effective as notification to or by the principal as stated in § 5.02.

(3) A person has notice of a fact if the person knows the fact, has reason to know the fact, has received an effective notification of the fact, or should know the fact to fulfill a duty owed to another person.

(4) Notice of a fact that an agent knows or has reason to know is imputed to the principal as stated in §§ 5.03 and 5.04.

§ 5.02 Notification Given by or to an Agent

(1) A notification given to an agent is effective as notice to the principal if the agent has actual or apparent authority to receive the notification, unless the person who gives the notification knows or has reason to know that the agent is acting adversely to the principal as stated in § 5.04.

(2) A notification given by an agent is effective as notification given by the principal if the agent has actual or apparent authority to give the notification, unless the person who receives the notification knows or has reason to know that the agent is acting adversely to the principal as stated in § 5.04.

§ 5.03 Imputation of Notice of Fact to Principal

For purposes of determining a principal's legal relations with a third party, notice of a fact that an agent knows or has reason to know is imputed to the principal if knowledge of the fact is material to the agent's duties to the principal, unless the agent

(a) acts adversely to the principal as stated in § 5.04, or

(b) is subject to a duty to another not to disclose the fact to the principal.

§ 5.04 An Agent Who Acts Adversely to a Principal

For purposes of determining a principal's legal relations with a third party, notice of a fact that an agent knows or has reason to know is not imputed to the principal if the agent acts adversely to the principal in a transaction or matter, intending to act solely for the agent's own purposes or those of another person. Nevertheless, notice is imputed

(a) when necessary to protect the rights of a third party who dealt with the principal in good faith; or

(b) when the principal has ratified or knowingly retained a benefit from the agent's action.

A third party who deals with a principal through an agent, knowing or having reason to know that the agent acts adversely to the principal, does not deal in good faith for this purpose.

CHAPTER 6. CONTRACTS AND OTHER TRANSACTIONS WITH THIRD PARTIES

§ 6.01 Agent for Disclosed Principal

When an agent acting with actual or apparent authority makes a contract on behalf of a disclosed principal,

(1) the principal and the third party are parties to the contract; and

(2) the agent is not a party to the contract unless the agent and third party agree otherwise.

§ 6.02 Agent for Unidentified Principal

When an agent acting with actual or apparent authority makes a contract on behalf of an unidentified principal,

(1) the principal and the third party are parties to the contract; and

(2) the agent is a party to the contract unless the agent and the third party agree otherwise.

§ 6.03 Agent for Undisclosed Principal

When an agent acting with actual authority makes a contract on behalf of an undisclosed principal,

(1) unless excluded by the contract, the principal is a party to the contract;

(2) the agent and the third party are parties to the contract; and

(3) the principal, if a party to the contract, and the third party have the same rights, liabilities, and defenses against each other as if the principal made the contract personally, subject to §§ 6.05-6.09.

§ 6.04 Principal Does Not Exist or Lacks Capacity

Unless the third party agrees otherwise, a person who makes a contract with a third party purportedly as an agent on behalf of a principal becomes a party to the contract if the purported agent knows or has reason to know that the purported principal does not exist or lacks capacity to be a party to a contract.

§ 6.10 Agent's Implied Warranty of Authority

A person who purports to make a contract, representation, or conveyance to or with a third party on behalf of another person, lacking power to bind that person, gives an implied warranty of authority to the third party and is subject to liability to the third party for damages for loss caused by breach of that warranty, including loss of the benefit expected from performance by the principal, unless

(1) the principal or purported principal ratifies the act as stated in § 4.01; or

(2) the person who purports to make the contract, representation, or conveyance gives notice to the third party that no warranty of authority is given; or

(3) the third party knows that the person who purports to make the contract, representation, or conveyance acts without actual authority.

§ 6.11 Agent's Representations

(1) When an agent for a disclosed or unidentified principal makes a false representation about the agent's authority to a third party, the principal is not subject to liability unless the agent acted with actual or apparent authority in making the representation and the third party does not have notice that the agent's representation is false.

(2) A representation by an agent made incident to a contract or conveyance is attributed to a disclosed or unidentified principal as if the principal made the representation directly when the agent had actual or apparent authority to make the contract or conveyance unless the third party knew or had reason to know that the representation was untrue or that the agent acted without actual authority in making it.

(3) A representation by an agent made incident to a contract or conveyance is attributed to an undisclosed principal as if the principal made the representation directly when

(a) the agent acted with actual authority in making the representation, or

(b) the agent acted without actual authority in making the representation but had actual authority to make true representations about the same matter.

The agent's representation is not attributed to the principal when the third party knew or had reason to know it was untrue.

(4) When an agent who makes a contract or conveyance on behalf of an undisclosed principal falsely represents to the third party that the agent does not act on behalf of a principal, the third party may avoid the contract or conveyance if the principal or agent had notice that the third party would not have dealt with the principal.

CHAPTER 7. TORTS—LIABILITY OF AGENT AND PRINCIPAL

§ 7.03 Principal's Liability—In General

(1) A principal is subject to direct liability to a third party harmed by an agent's conduct when

(a) as stated in § 7.04, the agent acts with actual authority or the principal ratifies the agent's conduct and

(i) the agent's conduct is tortious, or

(ii) the agent's conduct, if that of the principal, would subject the principal to tort liability; or

(b) as stated in § 7.05, the principal is negligent in selecting, supervising, or otherwise controlling the agent; or

(c) as stated in § 7.06, the principal delegates performance of a duty to use care to protect other persons or their property to an agent who fails to perform the duty.

(2) A principal is subject to vicarious liability to a third party harmed by an agent's conduct when

(a) as stated in § 7.07, the agent is an employee who commits a tort while acting within the scope of employment; or

(b) as stated in § 7.08, the agent commits a tort when acting with apparent authority in dealing with a third party on or purportedly on behalf of the principal.

§ 7.04 Agent Acts with Actual Authority

A principal is subject to liability to a third party harmed by an agent's conduct when the agent's conduct is within the scope of the agent's actual authority or ratified by the principal; and

(1) the agent's conduct is tortious, or

(2) the agent's conduct, if that of the principal, would subject the principal to tort liability.

§ 7.05 Principal's Negligence in Conducting Activity Through Agent; Principal's Special Relationship with Another Person

(1) A principal who conducts an activity through an agent is subject to liability for harm to a third party caused by the agent's conduct if the harm

was caused by the principal's negligence in selecting, training, retaining, supervising, or otherwise controlling the agent.

(2) When a principal has a special relationship with another person, the principal owes that person a duty of reasonable care with regard to risks arising out of the relationship, including the risk that agents of the principal will harm the person with whom the principal has such a special relationship.

§ 7.06 Failure in Performance of Principal's Duty of Protection

A principal required by contract or otherwise by law to protect another cannot avoid liability by delegating performance of the duty, whether or not the delegate is an agent.

§ 7.07 Employee Acting Within Scope of Employment

(1) An employer is subject to vicarious liability for a tort committed by its employee acting within the scope of employment.

(2) An employee acts within the scope of employment when performing work assigned by the employer or engaging in a course of conduct subject to the employer's control. An employee's act is not within the scope of employment when it occurs within an independent course of conduct not intended by the employee to serve any purpose of the employer.

(3) For purposes of this section,

(a) an employee is an agent whose principal controls or has the right to control the manner and means of the agent's performance of work, and

(b) the fact that work is performed gratuitously does not relieve a principal of liability.

§ 7.08 Agent Acts with Apparent Authority

A principal is subject to vicarious liability for a tort committed by an agent in dealing or communicating with a third party on or purportedly on behalf of the principal when actions taken by the agent with apparent authority constitute the tort or enable the agent to conceal its commission.

Comment:

Comment a. Scope and cross-references. The rule stated in this section applies to (1) agents, whether or not they are employees as defined in § 7.07(3); and (2) agents who are employees as defined in § 7.07(3) whose tortious conduct is not within the scope of employment under § 7.07(2). The torts to which this section applies are those in which an agent appears to deal or communicate on behalf of a principal and the agent's appearance of authority enables the agent to commit a tort or conceal its commission. Such torts include fraudulent and negligent misrepresentations, defamation, tortious institution of legal proceedings, and conversion of property obtained by an agent purportedly at the principal's direction. Apparent authority stems from a manifestation made by the principal. See § 2.03. . . .

Comment b. Connection between apparent authority and agent's tortious conduct. An agent acts with apparent authority with regard to a third party when the third party reasonably believes that the agent or other actor has authority to act on behalf of the principal and that belief is traceable to manifestations made by the principal. See § 2.03. Manifestation is defined in § 1.03. When an agent acts with apparent authority, the agent's motivation is immaterial to the legal consequences that the agent's action carries for the principal. Likewise, the fact that an agent's conduct is not in fact beneficial to the principal does not shield the principal from legal consequences. This is because apparent authority holds a principal accountable for the results of third-party beliefs about an actor's authority to act as an agent when the belief is reasonable and is traceable to a manifestation made by the principal. See § 2.03, Comment *c*. So to charge a principal is fair because it is the principal's manifestation that clothes the agent with the appearance of authority to act on the principal's behalf and that induces the third party reasonably to believe that the agent acts with actual authority. See id. Apparent-authority doctrine thus focuses on the reasonable expectations of third parties with whom an agent deals. This focus is inapposite to many instances of tort liability. However, apparent-authority doctrine is operative in explaining a principal's vicarious liability when a third party's reasonable belief in an agent's authority to speak or deal on behalf of a principal stems from a manifestation made by the principal and it is through statements or dealings that the agent acts tortiously. A principal's liability under the rule stated in this section does not depend on whether the principal benefits from the agent's tortious conduct.

CHAPTER 8. DUTIES OF AGENT AND PRINCIPAL TO EACH OTHER

§ 8.01 General Fiduciary Principle

An agent has a fiduciary duty to act loyally for the principal's benefit in all matters connected with the agency relationship.

§ 8.02 Material Benefit Arising out of Position

An agent has a duty not to acquire a material benefit from a third party in connection with transactions conducted or other actions taken on behalf of the principal or otherwise through the agent's use of the agent's position.

§ 8.03 Acting as or on Behalf of an Adverse Party

An agent has a duty not to deal with the principal as or on behalf of an adverse party in a transaction connected with the agency relationship.

§ 8.04 Competition

Throughout the duration of an agency relationship, an agent has a duty to refrain from competing with the principal and from taking action on behalf of or otherwise assisting the principal's competitors. During that time, an agent may take action, not otherwise wrongful, to prepare for competition following termination of the agency relationship.

§ 8.05 Use of Principal's Property; Use of Confidential Information

An agent has a duty

(1) not to use property of the principal for the agent's own purposes or those of a third party; and

(2) not to use or communicate confidential information of the principal for the agent's own purposes or those of a third party.

§ 8.06 Principal's Consent

(1) Conduct by an agent that would otherwise constitute a breach of duty as stated in §§ 8.01, 8.02, 8.03, 8.04, and 8.05 does not constitute a breach of duty if the principal consents to the conduct, provided that

(a) in obtaining the principal's consent, the agent

(i) acts in good faith,

(ii) discloses all material facts that the agent knows, has reason to know, or should know would reasonably affect the principal's judgment unless the principal has manifested that such facts are already known by the principal or that the principal does not wish to know them, and

(iii) otherwise deals fairly with the principal; and

(b) the principal's consent concerns either a specific act or transaction, or acts or transactions of a specified type that could reasonably be expected to occur in the ordinary course of the agency relationship.

(2) An agent who acts for more than one principal in a transaction between or among them has a duty

(a) to deal in good faith with each principal,

(b) to disclose to each principal

(i) the fact that the agent acts for the other principal or principals, and

(ii) all other facts that the agent knows, has reason to know, or should know would reasonably affect the principal's judgment unless the principal has manifested that such facts are already known by the principal or that the principal does not wish to know them, and

(c) otherwise to deal fairly with each principal.

§ 8.07 Duty Created by Contract

An agent has a duty to act in accordance with the express and implied terms of any contract between the agent and the principal.

§ 8.08 Duties of Care, Competence, and Diligence

Subject to any agreement with the principal, an agent has a duty to the principal to act with the care, competence, and diligence normally exercised by agents in similar circumstances. Special skills or knowledge possessed by an agent are circumstances to be taken into account in determining whether the agent acted with due care and diligence. If an agent claims to possess special skills or knowledge, the agent has a duty to the principal to act with the care, competence, and diligence normally exercised by agents with such skills or knowledge.

§ 8.09 Duty to Act Only Within Scope of Actual Authority and to Comply with Principal's Lawful Instructions

(1) An agent has a duty to take action only within the scope of the agent's actual authority.

(2) An agent has a duty to comply with all lawful instructions received from the principal and persons designated by the principal concerning the agent's actions on behalf of the principal.

§ 8.10 Duty of Good Conduct

An agent has a duty, within the scope of the agency relationship, to act reasonably and to refrain from conduct that is likely to damage the principal's enterprise.

§ 8.11 Duty to Provide Information

An agent has a duty to use reasonable effort to provide the principal with facts that the agent knows, has reason to know, or should know when

(1) subject to any manifestation by the principal, the agent knows or has reason to know that the principal would wish to have the facts or the facts are material to the agent's duties to the principal; and

(2) the facts can be provided to the principal without violating a superior duty owed by the agent to another person.

§ 8.14 Duty to Indemnify

A principal has a duty to indemnify an agent

(1) in accordance with the terms of any contract between them; and

(2) unless otherwise agreed,

(a) when the agent makes a payment

(i) within the scope of the agent's actual authority, or

(ii) that is beneficial to the principal, unless the agent acts officiously in making the payment; or

(b) when the agent suffers a loss that fairly should be borne by the principal in light of their relationship.

§ 8.15 Principal's Duty to Deal Fairly and in Good Faith

A principal has a duty to deal with the agent fairly and in good faith, including a duty to provide the agent with information about risks of physical harm or pecuniary loss that the principal knows, has reason to know, or should know are present in the agent's work but unknown to the agent.

RESTATEMENT (SECOND) OF TRUSTS

§ 203. Accountability for Profits in the Absence of a Breach of Trust

The trustee is accountable for any profit made by him through or arising out of the administration of the trust, although the profit does not result from a breach of trust

any profit goes back to the trust

§ 205. Liability in Case of Breach of Trust

If the trustee commits a breach of trust, he is chargeable with

(a) any loss or depreciation in value of the trust estate resulting from the breach of trust; or

(b) any profit made by him through the breach of trust; or

(c) any profit which would have accrued to the trust estate if there had been no breach of trust.

§ 206. Liability for Breach of Loyalty

The rule stated in § 205 is applicable where the trustee in breach of trust sells trust property to himself individually, or sells his individual property to himself as trustee, or otherwise violates his duty of loyalty.

UNIFORM PARTNERSHIP ACT (1914)

§ 6. Partnership Defined

(1) A partnership is an association of two or more persons to carry on as co-owners a business for profit.

(2) But any association formed under any other statute of this state, or any statute adopted by authority, other than the authority of this state, is not a partnership under this act, unless such association would have been a partnership in this state prior to the adoption of this act; but this act shall apply to limited partnerships except in so far as the statutes relating to such partnerships are inconsistent herewith.

§ 7. Rules for Determining the Existence of a Partnership

In determining whether a partnership exists, these rules shall apply:

(1) Except as provided by section 16 persons who are not partners as to each other are not partners as to third persons.

(2) Joint tenancy, tenancy in common, tenancy by the entireties, joint property, common property, or part ownership does not of itself establish a partnership, whether such co-owners do or do not share any profits made by the use of the property.

(3) The sharing of gross returns does not of itself establish a partnership, whether or not the persons sharing them have a joint or common right or interest in any property from which the returns are derived.

(4) The receipt by a person of a share of the profits of a business is prima facie evidence that he is a partner in the business, but no such inference shall be drawn if such profits were received in payment:

(a) As a debt by installments or otherwise,

(b) As wages of an employee or rent to a landlord,

(c) As an annuity to a widow or representative of a deceased partner,

(d) As interest on a loan, though the amount of payment vary with the profits of the business,

(e) As the consideration for the sale of a good-will of a business or other property by installments or otherwise.

§ 8. Partnership Property

(1) All property originally brought into the partnership stock or subsequently acquired by purchase or otherwise, on account of the partnership, is partnership property.

(2) Unless the contrary intention appears, property acquired with partnership funds is partnership property.

(3) Any estate in real property may be acquired in the partnership name. Title so acquired can be conveyed only in the partnership name.

(4) A conveyance to a partnership in the partnership name, though without words of inheritance, passes the entire estate of the grantor unless a contrary intent appears.

§ 9. Partner Agent of Partnership as to Partnership Business

(1) Every partner is an agent of the partnership for the purpose of its business, and the act of every partner, including the execution in the partnership name of any instrument, for apparently carrying on in the usual way the business of the partnership of which he is a member binds the partnership, unless the partner so acting has in fact no authority to act for the partnership in the particular matter, and the person with whom he is dealing has knowledge of the fact that he has no such authority.

(2) An act of a partner which is not apparently for the carrying on of the business of the partnership in the usual way does not bind the partnership unless authorized by the other partners.

(3) Unless authorized by the other partners or unless they have abandoned the business, one or more but less than all the partners have no authority to:

(a) Assign the partnership property in trust for creditors or on the assignee's promise to pay the debts of the partnership,

(b) Dispose of the good-will of the business,

(c) Do any other act which would make it impossible to carry on the ordinary business of a partnership,

(d) Confess a judgment,

(e) Submit a partnership claim or liability to arbitration or reference.

(4) No act of a partner in contravention of a restriction on authority shall bind the partnership to persons having knowledge of the restriction.

§ 10. Conveyance of Real Property of the Partnership

(1) Where title to real property is in the partnership name, any partner may convey title to such property by a conveyance executed in the partnership name; but the partnership may recover such property unless the partner's act binds the partnership under the provisions of paragraph (1) of section 9, or unless such property has been conveyed by the grantee or a person claiming through such grantee to a holder for value without knowledge that the partner, in making the conveyance, has exceeded his authority.

(2) Where title to real property is in the name of the partnership, a conveyance executed by a partner, in his own name, passes the equitable interest of the partnership, provided the act is one within the authority of the partner under the provisions of paragraph (1) of section 9.

(3) Where title to real property is in the name of one or more but not all the partners, and the record does not disclose the right of the partnership, the partners in whose name the title stands may convey title to such property, but the partnership may recover such property if the partners' act does not bind the partnership under the provisions of paragraph (1) of section 9, unless the purchaser or his assignee, is a holder for value, without knowledge.

(4) Where the title to real property is in the name of one or more or all the partners, or in a third person in trust for the partnership, a conveyance executed by a partner in the partnership name, or in his own name, passes the equitable interest of the partnership, provided the act is one within the authority of the partner under the provisions of paragraph (1) of section 9.

(5) Where the title to real property is in the names of all the partners a conveyance executed by all the partners passes all their rights in such property.

§ 11. Partnership Bound by Admission of Partner

An admission or representation made by any partner concerning partnership affairs within the scope of his authority as conferred by this act is evidence against the partnership.

§ 12. Partnership Charged with Knowledge of or Notice to Partner

Notice to any partner of any matter relating to partnership affairs, and the knowledge of the partner acting in the particular matter, acquired while a partner or then present to his mind, and the knowledge of any other partner who reasonably could and should have communicated it to the acting partner, operate as notice to or knowledge of the partnership, except in the case of a fraud on the partnership committed by or with the consent of that partner.

§ 13. Partnership Bound by Partner's Wrongful Act

Where, by any wrongful act or omission of any partner acting in the ordinary course of the business of the partnership or with the authority of his co-partners, loss or injury is caused to any person, not being a partner in the partnership, or any penalty is incurred, the partnership is liable therefor to the same extent as the partner so acting or omitting to act.

§ 14. Partnership Bound by Partner's Breach of Trust

The partnership is bound to make good the loss:

(a) Where one partner acting within the scope of his apparent authority receives money or property of a third person and misapplies it; and

(b) Where the partnership in the course of its business receives money or property of a third person and the money or property so received is misapplied by any partner while it is in the custody of the partnership.

§ 15. Nature of Partner's Liability— Gen. P'ship

All partners are liable

(a) Jointly and severally for everything chargeable to the partnership under sections 13 and 14.

(b) Jointly for all other debts and obligations of the partnership; but any partner may enter into a separate obligation to perform a partnership contract.

§ 16. Partner by Estoppel

(1) When a person, by words spoken or written or by conduct, represents himself, or consents to another representing him to any one, as a partner in an existing partnership or with one or more persons not actual partners, he is liable to any such person to whom such representation has been made, who has, on the faith of such representation, given credit to the actual or apparent partnership, and if he has made such representation or consented to its being made in a public manner he is liable to such person, whether the representation has or has not been made or communicated to such person so giving credit by or with the knowledge of the apparent partner making the representation or consenting to its being made.

(a) When a partnership liability results, he is liable as though he were an actual member of the partnership.

(b) When no partnership liability results, he is liable jointly with the other persons, if any, so consenting to the contract or representation as to incur liability, otherwise separately.

(2) When a person has been thus represented to be a partner in an existing partnership, or with one or more persons not actual partners, he is an agent of the persons consenting to such representation to bind them to the same extent and in the same manner as though he were a partner in fact, with respect to persons who rely upon the representation. Where all the members of the existing partnership consent to the representation, a partnership act or obligation results; but in all other cases it is the joint act or obligation of the person acting and the persons consenting to the representation.

§ 17. Liability of Incoming Partner

A person admitted as a partner into an existing partnership is liable for all the obligations of the partnership arising before his admission as though he had been a partner when such obligations were incurred, except that this liability shall be satisfied only out of partnership property.

§ 18. Rules Determining Rights and Duties of Partners

The rights and duties of the partners in relation to the partnership shall be determined, subject to any agreement between them, by the following rules:

(a) Each partner shall be repaid his contributions, whether by way of capital or advances to the partnership property and share equally in the profits and surplus remaining after all liabilities, including those to partners, are satisfied; and must contribute towards the losses, whether of capital or otherwise, sustained by the partnership according to his share in the profits.

(b) The partnership must indemnify every partner in respect of payments made and personal liabilities reasonably incurred by him in the ordinary and proper conduct of its business, or for the preservation of its business or property.

(c) A partner, who in aid of the partnership makes any payment or advance beyond the amount of capital which he agreed to contribute, shall be paid interest from the date of the payment or advance.

(d) A partner shall receive interest on the capital contributed by him only from the date when repayment should be made.

(e) All partners have equal rights in the management and conduct of the partnership business.

(f) No partner is entitled to remuneration for acting in the partnership business, except that a surviving partner is entitled to reasonable compensation for his services in winding up the partnership affairs.

(g) No person can become a member of a partnership without the consent of all the partners.

(h) Any difference arising as to ordinary matters connected with the partnership business may be decided by a majority of the partners; but no act in contravention of any agreement between the partners may be done rightfully without the consent of all the partners.

§ 19. Partnership Books

The partnership books shall be kept, subject to any agreement between the partners, at the principal place of business of the partnership, and every partner shall at all times have access to and may inspect and copy any of them.

§ 20. Duty of Partners to Render Information

Partners shall render on demand true and full information of all things affecting the partnership to any partner or the legal representative of any deceased partner or partner under legal disability.

§ 21. Partner Accountable as a Fiduciary

(1) Every partner must account to the partnership for any benefit, and hold as trustee for it any profits derived by him without the consent of the other partners from any transaction connected with the formation, conduct, or liquidation of the partnership or from any use by him of its property.

(2) This section applies also to the representatives of a deceased partner engaged in the liquidation of the affairs of the partnership as the personal representatives of the last surviving partner.

§ 22. Right to an Account

Any partner shall have the right to a formal account as to partnership affairs:

(a) If he is wrongfully excluded from the partnership business or possession of its property by his co-partners,

(b) If the right exists under the terms of any agreement,

(c) As provided by section 21,

(d) Whenever other circumstances render it just and reasonable.

§ 23. Continuation of Partnership Beyond Fixed Term

(1) When a partnership for a fixed term or particular undertaking is continued after the termination of such term or particular undertaking without any express agreement, the rights and duties of the partners remain the same as they were at such termination, so far as is consistent with a partnership at will.

(2) A continuation of the business by the partners or such of them as habitually acted therein during the term, without any settlement or liquidation of the partnership affairs, is prima facie evidence of a continuation of the partnership.

§ 24. Extent of Property Rights of a Partner

The property rights of a partner are (1) his rights in specific partnership property, (2) his interest in the partnership, and (3) his right to participate in the management.

§ 25. Nature of a Partner's Right in Specific Partnership Property

(1) A partner is co-owner with his partners of specific partnership property holding as a tenant in partnership.

(2) The incidents of this tenancy are such that:

(a) A partner, subject to the provisions of this act and to any agreement between the partners, has an equal right with his partners to possess specific partnership property for partnership purposes; but he has no right to possess such property for any other purpose without the consent of his partners.

(b) A partner's right in specific partnership property is not assignable except in connection with the assignment of rights of all the partners in the same property.

(c) A partner's right in specific partnership property is not subject to attachment or execution, except on a claim against the partnership. When partnership property is attached for a partnership debt the partners, or any of them, or the representatives of a deceased partner, cannot claim any right under the homestead or exemption laws.

(d) On the death of a partner his right in specific partnership property vests in the surviving partner or partners, except where the deceased was the last surviving partner, when his right in such property vests in his legal representative. Such surviving partner or partners, or the legal representative of the last surviving partner, has no right to possess the partnership property for any but a partnership purpose.

(e) A partner's right in specific partnership property is not subject to dower, curtesy, or allowances to widows, heirs, or next of kin.

§ 26. Nature of Partner's Interest in the Partnership

A partner's interest in the partnership is his share of the profits and surplus, and the same is personal property.

§ 27. Assignment of Partner's Interest

(1) A conveyance by a partner of his interest in the partnership does not of itself dissolve the partnership, nor, as against the other partners in the absence of agreement, entitle the assignee, during the continuance of the partnership, to interfere in the management or administration of the partnership business or affairs, or to require any information or account of

partnership transactions, or to inspect the partnership books; but it merely entitles the assignee to receive in accordance with his contract the profits to which the assigning partner would otherwise be entitled.

(2) In case of a dissolution of the partnership, the assignee is entitled to receive his assignor's interest and may require an account from the date only of the last account agreed to by all the partners.

§ 28. Partner's Interest Subject to Charging Order

(1) On due application to a competent court by any judgment creditor of a partner, the court which entered the judgment, order, or decree, or any other court, may charge the interest of the debtor partner with payment of the unsatisfied amount of such judgment debt with interest thereon; and may then or later appoint a receiver of his share of the profits, and of any other money due or to fall due to him in respect of the partnership, and make all other orders, directions, accounts and inquiries which the debtor partner might have made, or which the circumstances of the case may require.

(2) The interest charged may be redeemed at any time before foreclosure, or in case of a sale being directed by the court may be purchased without thereby causing a dissolution:

(a) With separate property, by any one or more of the partners, or

(b) With partnership property, by any one or more of the partners with the consent of all the partners whose interests are not so charged or sold.

(3) Nothing in this act shall be held to deprive a partner of his right, if any, under the exemption laws, as regards his interest in the partnership.

§ 29. Dissolution Defined

The dissolution of a partnership is the change in the relation of the partners caused by any partner ceasing to be associated in the carrying on as distinguished from the winding up of the business.

§ 30. Partnership Not Terminated by Dissolution

On dissolution the partnership is not terminated, but continues until the winding up of partnership affairs is completed.

§ 31. Causes of Dissolution

Dissolution is caused:

(1) Without violation of the agreement between the partners,

(a) By the termination of the definite term or particular undertaking specified in the agreement,

(b) By the express will of any partner when no definite term or particular undertaking is specified,

(c) By the express will of all the partners who have not assigned their interests or suffered them to be charged for their separate debts, either before or after the termination of any specified term or particular undertaking,

(d) By the expulsion of any partner from the business bona fide in accordance with such a power conferred by the agreement between the partners;

(2) In contravention of the agreement between the partners, where the circumstances do not permit a dissolution under any other provision of this section, by the express will of any partner at any time;

(3) By any event which makes it unlawful for the business of the partnership to be carried on or for the members to carry it on in partnership;

(4) By the death of any partner;

(5) By the bankruptcy of any partner or the partnership;

(6) By decree of court under section 32.

§ 32. Dissolution by Decree of Court

(1) On application by or for a partner the court shall decree a dissolution whenever:

(a) A partner has been declared a lunatic in any judicial proceeding or is shown to be of unsound mind,

(b) A partner becomes in any other way incapable of performing his part of the partnership contract,

(c) A partner has been guilty of such conduct as tends to affect prejudicially the carrying on of the business,

(d) A partner wilfully or persistently commits a breach of the partnership agreement, or otherwise so conducts himself in matters relating to the partnership business that it is not reasonably practicable to carry on the business in partnership with him,

(e) The business of the partnership can only be carried on at a loss,

(f) Other circumstances render a dissolution equitable.

(2) On the application of the purchaser of a partner's interest under sections [27 or 28]:

(a) After the termination of the specified term or particular undertaking,

(b) At any time if the partnership was a partnership at will when the interest was assigned or when the charging order was issued.

§ 33. General Effect of Dissolution on Authority of Partner

Except so far as may be necessary to wind up partnership affairs or to complete transactions begun but not then finished, dissolution terminates all authority of any partner to act for the partnership,

(1) With respect to the partners,

(a) When the dissolution is not by the act, bankruptcy or death of a partner; or

(b) When the dissolution is by such act, bankruptcy or death of a partner, in cases where section 34 so requires.

(2) With respect to persons not partners, as declared in section 35.

§ 34. Right of Partner to Contribution from Co-partners After Dissolution

Where the dissolution is caused by the act, death or bankruptcy of a partner, each partner is liable to his co-partners for his share of any liability created by any partner acting for the partnership as if the partnership had not been dissolved unless

(a) The dissolution being by act of any partner, the partner acting for the partnership had knowledge of the dissolution, or

(b) The dissolution being by the death or bankruptcy of a partner, the partner acting for the partnership had knowledge or notice of the death or bankruptcy.

§ 35. Power of Partner to Bind Partnership to Third Persons After Dissolution

(1) After dissolution a partner can bind the partnership except as provided in Paragraph (3).

(a) By any act appropriate for winding up partnership affairs or completing transactions unfinished at dissolution;

(b) By any transaction which would bind the partnership if dissolution had not taken place, provided the other party to the transaction

(I) Had extended credit to the partnership prior to dissolution and had no knowledge or notice of the dissolution; or

(II) Though he had not so extended credit, had nevertheless known of the partnership prior to dissolution, and, having no knowledge or notice of dissolution, the fact of dissolution had not been advertised in a newspaper of general circulation in the place (or in each place if more than one) at which the partnership business was regularly carried on.

§ 36. Effect of Dissolution on Partner's Existing Liability

(1) The dissolution of the partnership does not of itself discharge the existing liability of any partner.

(2) A partner is discharged from any existing liability upon dissolution of the partnership by an agreement to that effect between himself, the partnership creditor and the person or partnership continuing the business; and such agreement may be inferred from the course of dealing between the creditor having knowledge of the dissolution and the person or partnership continuing the business.

(3) Where a person agrees to assume the existing obligations of a dissolved partnership, the partners whose obligations have been assumed shall be discharged from any liability to any creditor of the partnership who, knowing of the agreement, consents to a material alteration in the nature or time of payment of such obligations.

(4) The individual property of a deceased partner shall be liable for all obligations of the partnership incurred while he was a partner but subject to the prior payment of his separate debts.

§ 37. Right to Wind Up

Unless otherwise agreed the partners who have not wrongfully dissolved the partnership or the legal representative of the last surviving partner, not bankrupt, has the right to wind up the partnership affairs; provided, however, that any partner, his legal representative or his assignee, upon cause shown, may obtain winding up by the court.

§ 38. Rights of Partners to Application of Partnership Property

(1) When dissolution is caused in any way, except in contravention of the partnership agreement, each partner, as against his co-partners and all persons claiming through them in respect of their interests in the partnership, unless otherwise agreed, may have the partnership property applied to discharge its liabilities, and the surplus applied to pay in cash the net amount owing to the respective partners. But if dissolution is caused by expulsion of a partner, bona fide under the partnership agreement and if the expelled partner is discharged from all partnership liabilities, either by payment or agreement under section 36(2), he shall receive in cash only the net amount due him from the partnership.

(2) When dissolution is caused in contravention of the partnership agreement the rights of the partners shall be as follows:

(a) Each partner who has not caused dissolution wrongfully shall have,

I. All the rights specified in paragraph (1) of this section, and

II. The right, as against each partner who has caused the dissolution wrongfully, to damages for breach of the agreement.

(b) The partners who have not caused the dissolution wrongfully, if they all desire to continue the business in the same name, either by themselves or jointly with others, may do so, during the agreed term for the partnership and for that purpose may possess the partnership property, provided they secure the payment by bond approved by the court, or pay to any partner who has caused the dissolution wrongfully, the value of his interest in the partnership at the dissolution, less any damages recoverable under clause (2a II) of this section, and in like manner indemnify him against all present or future partnership liabilities.

(c) A partner who has caused the dissolution wrongfully shall have:

I. If the business is not continued under the provisions of paragraph (2b) all the rights of a partner under paragraph (1), subject to clause (2a II), of this section,

II. If the business is continued under paragraph (2b) of this section the right as against his co-partners and all claiming through them in respect of their interests in the partnership, to have the value of his interest in the partnership, less any damages caused to his co-partners by the dissolution, ascertained and paid to him in cash, or the payment secured by bond approved by the court, and to be released from all existing liabilities of the partnership; but in ascertaining the value of the partner's interest the value of the good-will of the business shall not be considered.

§ 39. Rights Where Partnership Is Dissolved for Fraud or Misrepresentation

Where a partnership contract is rescinded on the ground of the fraud or misrepresentation of one of the parties thereto, the party entitled to rescind is, without prejudice to any other right, entitled,

(a) To a lien on, or a right of retention of, the surplus of the partnership property after satisfying the partnership liabilities to third persons for any sum of money paid by him for the purchase of an interest in the partnership and for any capital or advances contributed by him; and

(b) To stand, after all liabilities to third persons have been satisfied, in the place of the creditors of the partnership for any payments made by him in respect of the partnership liabilities; and

(c) To be indemnified by the person guilty of the fraud or making the representation against all debts and liabilities of the partnership.

§ 40. Rules for Distribution

In settling accounts between the partners after dissolution, the following rules shall be observed, subject to any agreement to the contrary:

(a) The assets of the partnership are:

I. The partnership property,

II. The contributions of the partners necessary for the payment of all the liabilities specified in clause (b) of this paragraph.

(b) The liabilities of the partnership shall rank in order of payment, as follows:

I. Those owing to creditors other than partners,

II. Those owing to partners other than for capital and profits,

III. Those owing to partners in respect of capital,

IV. Those owing to partners in respect of profits.

(c) The assets shall be applied in order of their declaration in clause (a) of this paragraph to the satisfaction of the liabilities.

(d) The partners shall contribute, as provided by section 18 (a) the amount necessary to satisfy the liabilities; but if any, but not all, of the partners are insolvent, or, not being subject to process, refuse to contribute, the other partners shall contribute their share of the liabilities, and, in the relative proportions in which they share the profits, the additional amount necessary to pay the liabilities.

(e) An assignee for the benefit of creditors or any person appointed by the court shall have the right to enforce the contributions specified in clause (d) of this paragraph.

(f) Any partner or his legal representative shall have the right to enforce the contributions specified in clause (d) of this paragraph, to the extent of the amount which he has paid in excess of his share of the liability.

(g) The individual property of a deceased partner shall be liable for the contributions specified in clause (d) of this paragraph.

(h) When partnership property and the individual properties of the partners are in possession of a court for distribution, partnership creditors shall have priority on partnership property and separate creditors on individual property, saving the rights of lien or secured creditors as heretofore.

(i) Where a partner has become bankrupt or his estate is insolvent the claims against his separate property shall rank in the following order:

I. Those owing to separate creditors,

II. Those owing to partnership creditors,

III. Those owing to partners by way of contribution.

§ 41. Liability of Persons Continuing the Business in Certain Cases

(1) When any new partner is admitted into an existing partnership, or when any partner retires and assigns (or the representative of the deceased partner assigns) his rights in partnership property to two or more of the partners, or to one or more of the partners and one or more third persons, if the business is continued without liquidation of the partnership affairs, creditors of the first or dissolved partnership are also creditors of the partnership so continuing the business.

(2) When all but one partner retire and assign (or the representative of a deceased partner assigns) their rights in partnership property to the remaining partner, who continues the business without liquidation of partnership affairs, either alone or with others, creditors of the dissolved partnership are also creditors of the person or partnership so continuing the business.

(3) When any partner retires or dies and the business of the dissolved partnership is continued as set forth in paragraphs (1) and (2) of this section, with the consent of the retired partners or the representative of the deceased partner, but without any assignment of his right in partnership property, rights of creditors of the dissolved partnership and of the creditors of the person or partnership continuing the business shall be as if such assignment had been made.

(4) When all the partners or their representatives assign their rights in partnership property to one or more third persons who promise to pay the debts and who continue the business of the dissolved partnership, creditors of the dissolved partnership are also creditors of the person or partnership continuing the business.

(5) When any partner wrongfully causes a dissolution and the remaining partners continue the business under the provisions of section 38(2b), either alone or with others, and without liquidation of the partnership affairs, creditors of the dissolved partnership are also creditors of the person or partnership continuing the business.

(6) When a partner is expelled and the remaining partners continue the business either alone or with others, without liquidation of the partnership affairs, creditors of the dissolved partnership are also creditors of the person or partnership continuing the business.

(7) The liability of a third person becoming a partner in the partnership continuing the business, under this section, to the creditors of the dissolved partnership shall be satisfied out of partnership property only.

(8) When the business of a partnership after dissolution is continued under any conditions set forth in this section the creditors of the dissolved partnership, as against the separate creditors of the retiring or deceased partner or the representative of the deceased partner, have a prior right to any claim of the retired partner or the representative of the deceased partner against the person or partnership continuing the business, on account of the retired or deceased partner's interest in the dissolved partnership or on account of any consideration promised for such interest or for his right in partnership property.

(9) Nothing in this section shall be held to modify any right of creditors to set aside any assignment on the ground of fraud.

(10) The use by the person or partnership continuing the business of the partnership name, or the name of a deceased partner as part thereof, shall not of itself make the individual property of the deceased partner liable for any debts contracted by such person or partnership.

§ 42. Rights of Retiring or Estate of Deceased Partner When the Business Is Continued

When any partner retires or dies, and the business is continued under any of the conditions set forth in section 41 (1, 2, 3, 5, 6), or section 38(2b) without any settlement of accounts as between him or his estate and the person or partnership continuing the business, unless otherwise agreed, he or his legal representative as against such persons or partnership may have the value of his interest at the date of dissolution ascertained, and shall receive as an ordinary creditor an amount equal to the value of his interest in the dissolved partnership with interest, or, at his option or at the option of his legal representative, in lieu of interest, the profits attributable to the use of his right in the property of the dissolved partnership; provided that the creditors of the dissolved partnership as against the separate creditors, or the representative of the retired or deceased partner, shall have priority on any claim arising under this section, as provided by section 41(8) of this act.

§ 43. Accrual of Actions

The right to an account of his interest shall accrue to any partner, or his legal representative, as against the winding up partners or the surviving partners or the person or partnership continuing the business, at the date of dissolution, in the absence of any agreement to the contrary

UNIFORM PARTNERSHIP ACT (1997)

Article 1. General Provisions

§ 101. Definitions

In this [Act]:

(1) "Business" includes every trade, occupation, and profession.

(2) "Debtor in bankruptcy" means a person who is the subject of:

(i) an order for relief under Title 11 of the United States Code or a comparable order under a successor statute of general application; or

(ii) a comparable order under federal, state, or foreign law governing insolvency.

(3) "Distribution" means a transfer of money or other property from a partnership to a partner in the partner's capacity as a partner or to the partner's transferee.

(4) "Foreign limited liability partnership" means a partnership that:

(i) is formed under laws other than the laws of this State; and

(ii) has the status of a limited liability partnership under those laws.

(5) "Limited liability partnership" means a partnership that has filed a statement of qualification under Section 1001 and does not have a similar statement in effect in any other jurisdiction.

(6) "Partnership" means an association of two or more persons to carry on as co-owners a business for profit formed under Section 202, predecessor law, or comparable law of another jurisdiction.

(7) "Partnership agreement" means the agreement, whether written, oral, or implied, among the partners concerning the partnership, including amendments to the partnership agreement.

(8) "Partnership at will" means a partnership in which the partners have not agreed to remain partners until the expiration of a definite term or the completion of a particular undertaking.

(9) "Partnership interest" or "partner's interest in the partnership" means all of a partner's interests in the partnership, including the partner's transferable interest and all management and other rights.

(10) "Person" means an individual, corporation, business trust, estate, trust, partnership, association, joint venture, government, governmental subdivision, agency, or instrumentality, or any other legal or commercial entity.

(11) "Property" means all property, real, personal, or mixed, tangible or intangible, or any interest therein.

(12) "State" means a State of the United States, the District of Columbia, the Commonwealth of Puerto Rico, or any territory or insular possession subject to the jurisdiction of the United States.

(13) "Statement" means a statement of partnership authority under Section 303, a statement of denial under Section 304, a statement of dissociation under Section 704, a statement of dissolution under Section 805, a statement of merger under Section 907, a statement of qualification under Section 1001, a statement of foreign qualification under Section 1102, or an amendment or cancellation of any of the foregoing.

(14) "Transfer" includes an assignment, conveyance, lease, mortgage, deed, and encumbrance.

§ 102. Knowledge and Notice

(a) A person knows a fact if the person has actual knowledge of it.

(b) A person has notice of a fact if the person:

(1) knows of it;

(2) has received a notification of it; or

(3) has reason to know it exists from all of the facts known to the person at the time in question.

(c) A person notifies or gives a notification to another by taking steps reasonably required to inform the other person in ordinary course, whether or not the other person learns of it.

(d) A person receives a notification when the notification:

(1) comes to the person's attention; or

(2) is duly delivered at the person's place of business or at any other place held out by the person as a place for receiving communications.

(e) Except as otherwise provided in subsection (f), a person other than an individual knows, has notice, or receives a notification of a fact for purposes of a particular transaction when the individual conducting the transaction knows, has notice, or receives a notification of the fact, or in any event when the fact would have been brought to the individual's attention if the person had exercised reasonable diligence. The person exercises reasonable diligence if it maintains reasonable routines for communicating significant information to the individual conducting the transaction and there is reasonable compliance with the routines. Reasonable diligence does not require an individual acting for the person to communicate information unless the communication is part of the individual's regular duties or the individual has reason to know of the transaction and that the transaction would be materially affected by the information.

(f) A partner's knowledge, notice, or receipt of a notification of a fact relating to the partnership is effective immediately as knowledge by, notice to, or receipt of a notification by the partnership, except in the case of a fraud on the partnership committed by or with the consent of that partner.

§ 103. Effect of Partnership Agreement; Nonwaivable Provisions

(a) Except as otherwise provided in subsection (b), relations among the partners and between the partners and the partnership are governed by the partnership agreement. To the extent the partnership agreement does not otherwise provide, this [Act] governs relations among the partners and between the partners and the partnership.

(b) The partnership agreement may not:

(1) vary the rights and duties under Section 105 except to eliminate the duty to provide copies of statements to all of the partners;

(2) unreasonably restrict the right of access to books and records under Section 403(b);

(3) eliminate the duty of loyalty under Section 404(b) or 603(b)(3), but:

(i) the partnership agreement may identify specific types or categories of activities that do not violate the duty of loyalty, if not manifestly unreasonable; or

(ii) all of the partners or a number or percentage specified in the partnership agreement may authorize or ratify, after full disclosure of all material facts, a specific act or transaction that otherwise would violate the duty of loyalty;

(4) unreasonably reduce the duty of care under Section 404(c) or 603(b)(3);

(5) eliminate the obligation of good faith and fair dealing under Section 404(d), but the partnership agreement may prescribe the standards by which the performance of the obligation is to be measured, if the standards are not manifestly unreasonable;

(6) vary the power to dissociate as a partner under Section 602(a), except to require the notice under Section 601(1) to be in writing;

(7) vary the right of a court to expel a partner in the events specified in Section 601(5);

(8) vary the requirement to wind up the partnership business in cases specified in Section 801(4), (5), or (6);

(9) vary the law applicable to a limited liability partnership under Section 106(b); or

(10) restrict rights of third parties under this [Act].

§ 106. Governing Law

(a) Except as otherwise provided in subsection (b), the law of the jurisdiction in which a partnership has its chief executive office governs relations among the partners and between the partners and the partnership.

(b) The law of this State governs relations among the partners and between the partners and the partnership and the liability of partners for an obligation of a limited liability partnership.

Article 2. Nature of Partnership

§ 201. Partnership as Entity

(a) A partnership is an entity distinct from its partners.

(b) A limited liability partnership continues to be the same entity that existed before the filing of a statement of qualification under Section 1001.

§ 202. Formation of Partnership

(a) Except as otherwise provided in subsection (b), the association of two or more persons to carry on as co-owners a business for profit forms a partnership, whether or not the persons intend to form a partnership.

(b) An association formed under a statute other than this [Act], a predecessor statute, or a comparable statute of another jurisdiction is not a partnership under this [Act].

(c) In determining whether a partnership is formed, the following rules apply:

(1) Joint tenancy, tenancy in common, tenancy by the entireties, joint property, common property, or part ownership does not by itself establish a partnership, even if the co-owners share profits made by the use of the property.

(2) The sharing of gross returns does not by itself establish a partnership, even if the persons sharing them have a joint or common right or interest in property from which the returns are derived.

(3) A person who receives a share of the profits of a business is presumed to be a partner in the business, unless the profits were received in payment:

(i) of a debt by installments or otherwise;

(ii) for services as an independent contractor or of wages or other compensation to an employee;

(iii) of rent;

(iv) of an annuity or other retirement or health benefit to a beneficiary, representative, or designee of a deceased or retired partner;

(v) of interest or other charge on a loan, even if the amount of payment varies with the profits of the business, including a direct or indirect present or future ownership of the collateral, or rights to income, proceeds, or increase in value derived from the collateral; or

(vi) for the sale of the goodwill of a business or other property by installments or otherwise.

§ 203. Partnership Property

Property acquired by a partnership is property of the partnership and not of the partners individually.

§ 204. When Property Is Partnership Property

(a) Property is partnership property if acquired in the name of:

(1) the partnership; or

(2) one or more partners with an indication in the instrument transferring title to the property of the person's capacity as a partner or of the existence of a partnership but without an indication of the name of the partnership.

(b) Property is acquired in the name of the partnership by a transfer to:

(1) the partnership in its name; or

(2) one or more partners in their capacity as partners in the partnership, if the name of the partnership is indicated in the instrument transferring title to the property.

(c) Property is presumed to be partnership property if purchased with partnership assets, even if not acquired in the name of the partnership or of one or more partners with an indication in the instrument transferring title to the property of the person's capacity as a partner or of the existence of a partnership.

(d) Property acquired in the name of one or more of the partners, without an indication in the instrument transferring title to the property of the person's capacity as a partner or of the existence of a partnership and without use of partnership assets, is presumed to be separate property, even if used for partnership purposes.

Article 3. Relations of Partners to Persons Dealing with Partnership

§ 301. Partner Agent of Partnership

Subject to the effect of a statement of partnership authority under Section 303:

(1) Each partner is an agent of the partnership for the purpose of its business. An act of a partner, including the execution of an instrument in the partnership name, for apparently carrying on in the ordinary course the partnership business or business of the kind carried on by the partnership binds the partnership, unless the partner had no authority to act for the partnership in the particular matter and the person with whom the partner was dealing knew or had received a notification that the partner lacked authority.

(2) An act of a partner which is not apparently for carrying on in the ordinary course the partnership business or business of the kind carried on by the partnership binds the partnership only if the act was authorized by the other partners.

§ 303. Statement of Partnership Authority

(a) A partnership may file a statement of partnership authority, which:

(1) must include:

(i) the name of the partnership;

(ii) the street address of its chief executive office and of one office in this State, if there is one;

(iii) the names and mailing addresses of all of the partners or of an agent appointed and maintained by the partnership for the purpose of subsection (b); and

(iv) the names of the partners authorized to execute an instrument transferring real property held in the name of the partnership; and

(2) may state the authority, or limitations on the authority, of some or all of the partners to enter into other transactions on behalf of the partnership and any other matter.

(b) If a statement of partnership authority names an agent, the agent shall maintain a list of the names and mailing addresses of all of the partners and make it available to any person on request for good cause shown.

(c) If a filed statement of partnership authority is executed pursuant to Section 105(c) and states the name of the partnership but does not contain all of the other information required by subsection (a), the statement nevertheless operates with respect to a person not a partner as provided in subsections (d) and (e).

(d) Except as otherwise provided in subsection (g), a filed statement of partnership authority supplements the authority of a partner to enter into transactions on behalf of the partnership as follows:

(1) Except for transfers of real property, a grant of authority contained in a filed statement of partnership authority is conclusive in favor of a person who gives value without knowledge to the contrary, so long as and to the extent that a limitation on that authority is not then contained in another filed statement. A filed cancellation of a limitation on authority revives the previous grant of authority.

(2) A grant of authority to transfer real property held in the name of the partnership contained in a certified copy of a filed statement of partnership authority recorded in the office for recording transfers of that real property is conclusive in favor of a person who gives value without knowledge to the contrary, so long as and to the extent that a certified copy of a filed statement containing a limitation on that authority is not then of record in the office for recording transfers of that real property. The recording in the office for recording transfers of that real

property of a certified copy of a filed cancellation of a limitation on authority revives the previous grant of authority.

(e) A person not a partner is deemed to know of a limitation on the authority of a partner to transfer real property held in the name of the partnership if a certified copy of the filed statement containing the limitation on authority is of record in the office for recording transfers of that real property.

(f) Except as otherwise provided in subsections (d) and (e) and Sections 704 and 805, a person not a partner is not deemed to know of a limitation on the authority of a partner merely because the limitation is contained in a filed statement.

(g) Unless earlier canceled, a filed statement of partnership authority is canceled by operation of law five years after the date on which the statement, or the most recent amendment, was filed with the [Secretary of State].

§ 305. Partnership Liable for Partner's Actionable Conduct

(a) A partnership is liable for loss or injury caused to a person, or for a penalty incurred, as a result of a wrongful act or omission, or other actionable conduct, of a partner acting in the ordinary course of business of the partnership or with authority of the partnership.

(b) If, in the course of the partnership's business or while acting with authority of the partnership, a partner receives or causes the partnership to receive money or property of a person not a partner, and the money or property is misapplied by a partner, the partnership is liable for the loss.

§ 306. Partner's Liability

(a) Except as otherwise provided in subsections (b) and (c), all partners are liable jointly and severally for all obligations of the partnership unless otherwise agreed by the claimant or provided by law.

(b) A person admitted as a partner into an existing partnership is not personally liable for any partnership obligation incurred before the person's admission as a partner.

(c) An obligation of a partnership incurred while the partnership is a limited liability partnership, whether arising in contract, tort, or otherwise, is solely the obligation of the partnership. A partner is not personally liable, directly or indirectly, by way of contribution or otherwise, for such an obligation solely by reason of being or so acting as a partner. This subsection applies notwithstanding anything inconsistent in the partnership agreement that existed immediately before the vote required to become a limited liability partnership under Section 1001(b).

§ 307. Actions By and Against Partnership and Partners

(a) A partnership may sue and be sued in the name of the partnership.

(b) An action may be brought against the partnership and, to the extent not inconsistent with Section 306, any or all of the partners in the same action or in separate actions.

(c) A judgment against a partnership is not by itself a judgment against a partner. A judgment against a partnership may not be satisfied from a partner's assets unless there is also a judgment against the partner.

(d) A judgment creditor of a partner may not levy execution against the assets of the partner to satisfy a judgment based on a claim against the partnership unless the partner is personally liable for the claim under Section 306 and:

(1) a judgment based on the same claim has been obtained against the partnership and a writ of execution on the judgment has been returned unsatisfied in whole or in part;

(2) the partnership is a debtor in bankruptcy;

(3) the partner has agreed that the creditor need not exhaust partnership assets;

(4) a court grants permission to the judgment creditor to levy execution against the assets of a partner based on a finding that partnership assets subject to execution are clearly insufficient to satisfy the judgment, that exhaustion of partnership assets is excessively burdensome, or that the grant of permission is an appropriate exercise of the court's equitable powers; or

(5) liability is imposed on the partner by law or contract independent of the existence of the partnership.

(e) This section applies to any partnership liability or obligation resulting from a representation by a partner or purported partner under Section 308.

§ 308. Liability of Purported Partner

(a) If a person, by words or conduct, purports to be a partner, or consents to being represented by another as a partner, in a partnership or with one or more persons not partners, the purported partner is liable to a person to whom the representation is made, if that person, relying on the representation, enters into a transaction with the actual or purported partnership. If the representation, either by the purported partner or by a person with the purported partner's consent, is made in a public manner, the purported partner is liable to a person who relies upon the purported partnership even if the purported partner is not aware of being held out as a partner to the claimant. If partnership liability results, the purported partner is liable with respect to that liability as if the purported partner were a partner. If no partnership liability results, the purported partner is liable with respect to that liability jointly and severally with any other person consenting to the representation.

(b) If a person is thus represented to be a partner in an existing partnership, or with one or more persons not partners, the purported partner is an agent of persons consenting to the representation to bind them to the same extent and in the same manner as if the purported partner were a partner, with respect to persons who enter into transactions in reliance upon the representation. If all of the partners of the existing partnership consent to the representation, a partnership act or obligation results. If fewer than all of the partners of the existing partnership consent to the representation, the person acting and the partners consenting to the representation are jointly and severally liable.

(c) A person is not liable as a partner merely because the person is named by another in a statement of partnership authority.

(d) A person does not continue to be liable as a partner merely because of a failure to file a statement of dissociation or to amend a statement of partnership authority to indicate the partner's dissociation from the partnership.

(e) Except as otherwise provided in subsections (a) and (b), persons who are not partners as to each other are not liable as partners to other persons.

Article 4. Relations of Partners to Each Other and to Partnership

§ 401. Partner's Rights and Duties

(a) Each partner is deemed to have an account that is:

(1) credited with an amount equal to the money plus the value of any other property, net of the amount of any liabilities, the partner contributes to the partnership and the partner's share of the partnership profits; and

(2) charged with an amount equal to the money plus the value of any other property, net of the amount of any liabilities, distributed by the partnership to the partner and the partner's share of the partnership losses.

(b) Each partner is entitled to an equal share of the partnership profits and is chargeable with a share of the partnership losses in proportion to the partner's share of the profits.

(c) A partnership shall reimburse a partner for payments made and indemnify a partner for liabilities incurred by the partner in the ordinary course of the business of the partnership or for the preservation of its business or property.

(d) A partnership shall reimburse a partner for an advance to the partnership beyond the amount of capital the partner agreed to contribute.

(e) A payment or advance made by a partner which gives rise to a partnership obligation under subsection (c) or (d) constitutes a loan to the partnership which accrues interest from the date of the payment or advance.

(f) Each partner has equal rights in the management and conduct of the partnership business.

(g) A partner may use or possess partnership property only on behalf of the partnership.

(h) A partner is not entitled to remuneration for services performed for the partnership, except for reasonable compensation for services rendered in winding up the business of the partnership.

(i) A person may become a partner only with the consent of all of the partners.

(j) A difference arising as to a matter in the ordinary course of business of a partnership may be decided by a majority of the partners. An act outside the ordinary course of business of a partnership and an amendment to the partnership agreement may be undertaken only with the consent of all of the partners.

(k) This section does not affect the obligations of a partnership to other persons under Section 301.

§ 403. Partner's Rights and Duties with Respect to Information

(a) A partnership shall keep its books and records, if any, at its chief executive office.

(b) A partnership shall provide partners and their agents and attorneys access to its books and records. It shall provide former partners and their agents and attorneys access to books and records pertaining to the period during which they were partners. The right of access provides the opportunity to inspect and copy books and records during ordinary business hours. A partnership may impose a reasonable charge, covering the costs of labor and material, for copies of documents furnished.

(c) Each partner and the partnership shall furnish to a partner, and to the legal representative of a deceased partner or partner under legal disability:

(1) without demand, any information concerning the partnership's business and affairs reasonably required for the proper exercise of the partner's rights and duties under the partnership agreement or this [Act]; and

(2) on demand, any other information concerning the partnership's business and affairs, except to the extent the demand or the information demanded is unreasonable or otherwise improper under the circumstances.

§ 404. General Standards of Partner's Conduct

(a) The only fiduciary duties a partner owes to the partnership and the other partners are the duty of loyalty and the duty of care set forth in subsections (b) and (c).

(b) A partner's duty of loyalty to the partnership and the other partners is limited to the following:

(1) to account to the partnership and hold as trustee for it any property, profit, or benefit derived by the partner in the conduct and winding up of the partnership business or derived from a use by the partner of partnership property, including the appropriation of a partnership opportunity;

(2) to refrain from dealing with the partnership in the conduct or winding up of the partnership business as or on behalf of a party having an interest adverse to the partnership; and

(3) to refrain from competing with the partnership in the conduct of the partnership business before the dissolution of the partnership.

(c) A partner's duty of care to the partnership and the other partners in the conduct and winding up of the partnership business is limited to refraining from engaging in grossly negligent or reckless conduct, intentional misconduct, or a knowing violation of law.

(d) A partner shall discharge the duties to the partnership and the other partners under this [Act] or under the partnership agreement and exercise any rights consistently with the obligation of good faith and fair dealing.

(e) A partner does not violate a duty or obligation under this [Act] or under the partnership agreement merely because the partner's conduct furthers the partner's own interest.

(f) A partner may lend money to and transact other business with the partnership, and as to each loan or transaction the rights and obligations of the partner are the same as those of a person who is not a partner, subject to other applicable law.

(g) This section applies to a person winding up the partnership business as the personal or legal representative of the last surviving partner as if the person were a partner.

Article 5. Transferees and Creditors of Partner

§ 501. Partner Not Co-owner of Partnership Property

A partner is not a co-owner of partnership property and has no interest in partnership property which can be transferred, either voluntarily or involuntarily.

§ 502. Partner's Transferable Interest in Partnership

The only transferable interest of a partner in the partnership is the partner's share of the profits and losses of the partnership and the partner's right to receive distributions. The interest is personal property.

§ 503. Transfer of Partner's Transferable Interest

(a) A transfer, in whole or in part, of a partner's transferable interest in the partnership:

(1) is permissible;

(2) does not by itself cause the partner's dissociation or a dissolution and winding up of the partnership business; and

(3) does not, as against the other partners or the partnership, entitle the transferee, during the continuance of the partnership, to participate in the management or conduct of the partnership business, to require access to information concerning partnership transactions, or to inspect or copy the partnership books or records.

(b) A transferee of a partner's transferable interest in the partnership has a right:

(1) to receive, in accordance with the transfer, distributions to which the transferor would otherwise be entitled;

(2) to receive upon the dissolution and winding up of the partnership business, in accordance with the transfer, the net amount otherwise distributable to the transferor; and

(3) to seek under Section 801(6) a judicial determination that it is equitable to wind up the partnership business.

(c) In a dissolution and winding up, a transferee is entitled to an account of partnership transactions only from the date of the latest account agreed to by all of the partners.

(d) Upon transfer, the transferor retains the rights and duties of a partner other than the interest in distributions transferred.

(e) A partnership need not give effect to a transferee's rights under this section until it has notice of the transfer.

(f) A transfer of a partner's transferable interest in the partnership in violation of a restriction on transfer contained in the partnership agreement is ineffective as to a person having notice of the restriction at the time of transfer.

§ 504. Partner's Transferable Interest Subject to Charging Order

(a) On application by a judgment creditor of a partner or of a partner's transferee, a court having jurisdiction may charge the transferable interest of the judgment debtor to satisfy the judgment. The court may appoint a receiver of the share of the distributions due or to become due to the judgment debtor in respect of the partnership and make all other orders, directions, accounts, and inquiries the judgment debtor might have made or which the circumstances of the case may require.

(b) A charging order constitutes a lien on the judgment debtor's transferable interest in the partnership. The court may order a foreclosure of the interest subject to the charging order at any time. The purchaser at the foreclosure sale has the rights of a transferee.

(c) At any time before foreclosure, an interest charged may be redeemed:

(1) by the judgment debtor;

(2) with property other than partnership property, by one or more of the other partners; or

(3) with partnership property, by one or more of the other partners with the consent of all of the partners whose interests are not so charged.

(d) This [Act] does not deprive a partner of a right under exemption laws with respect to the partner's interest in the partnership.

(e) This section provides the exclusive remedy by which a judgment creditor of a partner or partner's transferee may satisfy a judgment out of the judgment debtor's transferable interest in the partnership.

Article 6. Partner's Dissociation

§ 601. Events Causing Partner's Dissociation

A partner is dissociated from a partnership upon the occurrence of any of the following events:

(1) the partnership's having notice of the partner's express will to withdraw as a partner or on a later date specified by the partner;

(2) an event agreed to in the partnership agreement as causing the partner's dissociation;

(3) the partner's expulsion pursuant to the partnership agreement;

(4) the partner's expulsion by the unanimous vote of the other partners if:

(i) it is unlawful to carry on the partnership business with that partner;

(ii) there has been a transfer of all or substantially all of that partner's transferable interest in the partnership, other than a transfer for security purposes, or a court order charging the partner's interest, which has not been foreclosed;

(iii) within 90 days after the partnership notifies a corporate partner that it will be expelled because it has filed a certificate of dissolution or the equivalent, its charter has been revoked, or its right to conduct business has been suspended by the jurisdiction of its incorporation, there is no revocation of the certificate of dissolution or no reinstatement of its charter or its right to conduct business; or

(iv) a partnership that is a partner has been dissolved and its business is being wound up;

(5) on application by the partnership or another partner, the partner's expulsion by judicial determination because:

(i) the partner engaged in wrongful conduct that adversely and materially affected the partnership business;

(ii) the partner willfully or persistently committed a material breach of the partnership agreement or of a duty owed to the partnership or the other partners under Section 404; or

(iii) the partner engaged in conduct relating to the partnership business which makes it not reasonably practicable to carry on the business in partnership with the partner;

(6) the partner's:

(i) becoming a debtor in bankruptcy;

(ii) executing an assignment for the benefit of creditors;

(iii) seeking, consenting to, or acquiescing in the appointment of a trustee, receiver, or liquidator of that partner or of all or substantially all of that partner's property; or

(iv) failing, within 90 days after the appointment, to have vacated or stayed the appointment of a trustee, receiver, or liquidator of the partner or of all or substantially all of the partner's property obtained without the partner's consent or acquiescence, or failing within 90 days after the expiration of a stay to have the appointment vacated;

(7) in the case of a partner who is an individual:

(i) the partner's death;

(ii) the appointment of a guardian or general conservator for the partner; or

(iii) a judicial determination that the partner has otherwise become incapable of performing the partner's duties under the partnership agreement;

(8) in the case of a partner that is a trust or is acting as a partner by virtue of being a trustee of a trust, distribution of the trust's entire transferable interest in the partnership, but not merely by reason of the substitution of a successor trustee;

(9) in the case of a partner that is an estate or is acting as a partner by virtue of being a personal representative of an estate, distribution of the estate's entire transferable interest in the partnership, but not merely by reason of the substitution of a successor personal representative; or

(10) termination of a partner who is not an individual, partnership, corporation, trust, or estate.

§ 602. Partner's Power to Dissociate; Wrongful Dissociation

(a) A partner has the power to dissociate at any time, rightfully or wrongfully, by express will pursuant to Section 601(1).

(b) A partner's dissociation is wrongful only if:

(1) it is in breach of an express provision of the partnership agreement; or

(2) in the case of a partnership for a definite term or particular undertaking, before the expiration of the term or the completion of the undertaking:

(i) the partner withdraws by express will, unless the withdrawal follows within 90 days after another partner's dissociation by death or otherwise under Section 601(6) through (10) or wrongful dissociation under this subsection;

(ii) the partner is expelled by judicial determination under Section 601(5);

(iii) the partner is dissociated by becoming a debtor in bankruptcy; or

(iv) in the case of a partner who is not an individual, trust other than a business trust, or estate, the partner is expelled or otherwise dissociated because it willfully dissolved or terminated.

(c) A partner who wrongfully dissociates is liable to the partnership and to the other partners for damages caused by the dissociation. The liability is in addition to any other obligation of the partner to the partnership or to the other partners.

§ 603. Effect of Partner's Dissociation

(a) If a partner's dissociation results in a dissolution and winding up of the partnership business, [Article] 8 applies; otherwise, [Article] 7 applies.

(b) Upon a partner's dissociation:

(1) the partner's right to participate in the management and conduct of the partnership business terminates, except as otherwise provided in Section 803;

(2) the partner's duty of loyalty under Section 404(b)(3) terminates; and

(3) the partner's duty of loyalty under Section 404(b)(1) and (2) and duty of care under Section 404(c) continue only with regard to matters arising and events occurring before the partner's dissociation, unless the partner participates in winding up the partnership's business pursuant to Section 803.

Article 7. Partner's Dissociation When Business Not Wound Up

§ 701. Purchase of Dissociated Partner's Interest

(a) If a partner is dissociated from a partnership without resulting in a dissolution and winding up of the partnership business under Section 801, the partnership shall cause the dissociated partner's interest in the partnership to be purchased for a buyout price determined pursuant to subsection (b).

(b) The buyout price of a dissociated partner's interest is the amount that would have been distributable to the dissociating partner under Section 807(b) if, on the date of dissociation, the assets of the partnership were sold at a price equal to the greater of the liquidation value or the value based on a sale of the entire business as a going concern without the dissociated partner and the partnership were wound up as of that date. Interest must be paid from the date of dissociation to the date of payment.

(c) Damages for wrongful dissociation under Section 602(b), and all other amounts owing, whether or not presently due, from the dissociated partner to the partnership, must be offset against the buyout price. Interest must be paid from the date the amount owed becomes due to the date of payment.

(d) A partnership shall indemnify a dissociated partner whose interest is being purchased against all partnership liabilities, whether incurred before or after the dissociation, except liabilities incurred by an act of the dissociated partner under Section 702.

(e) If no agreement for the purchase of a dissociated partner's interest is reached within 120 days after a written demand for payment, the partnership shall pay, or cause to be paid, in cash to the dissociated partner the amount the partnership estimates to be the buyout price and accrued interest, reduced by any offsets and accrued interest under subsection (c).

(f) If a deferred payment is authorized under subsection (h), the partnership may tender a written offer to pay the amount it estimates to be the buyout price and accrued interest, reduced by any offsets under subsection (c), stating the time of payment, the amount and type of security for payment, and the other terms and conditions of the obligation.

(g) The payment or tender required by subsection (e) or (f) must be accompanied by the following:

(1) a statement of partnership assets and liabilities as of the date of dissociation;

(2) the latest available partnership balance sheet and income statement, if any;

(3) an explanation of how the estimated amount of the payment was calculated; and

(4) written notice that the payment is in full satisfaction of the obligation to purchase unless, within 120 days after the written notice, the dissociated partner commences an action to determine the buyout price, any offsets under subsection (c), or other terms of the obligation to purchase.

(h) A partner who wrongfully dissociates before the expiration of a definite term or the completion of a particular undertaking is not entitled to payment of any portion of the buyout price until the expiration of the term or completion of the undertaking, unless the partner establishes to the satisfaction of the court that earlier payment will not cause undue hardship to the business of the partnership. A deferred payment must be adequately secured and bear interest.

(i) A dissociated partner may maintain an action against the partnership, pursuant to Section 405(b)(2)(ii), to determine the buyout price of that partner's interest, any offsets under subsection (c), or other terms of the obligation to purchase. The action must be commenced within 120 days after the partnership has tendered payment or an offer to pay or within one year after written demand for payment if no payment or offer to pay is tendered. The court shall determine the buyout price of the dissociated partner's interest, any offset due under subsection (c), and accrued interest, and enter judgment for any additional payment or refund. If deferred payment is authorized under subsection (h), the court shall also determine the security for payment and other terms of the obligation to purchase. The court may assess reasonable attorney's fees and the fees and expenses of appraisers or other experts for a party to the action, in amounts the court finds equitable, against a party that the court finds acted arbitrarily, vexatiously, or not in good faith. The finding may be based on the partnership's failure to tender payment or an offer to pay or to comply with subsection (g).

§ 702. Dissociated Partner's Power to Bind and Liability to Partnership

(a) For two years after a partner dissociates without resulting in a dissolution and winding up of the partnership business, the partnership, including a surviving partnership under [Article] 9, is bound by an act of the dissociated partner which would have bound the partnership under Section 301 before dissociation only if at the time of entering into the transaction the other party:

(1) reasonably believed that the dissociated partner was then a partner;

(2) did not have notice of the partner's dissociation; and

(3) is not deemed to have had knowledge under Section 303(e) or notice under Section 704(c).

(b) A dissociated partner is liable to the partnership for any damage caused to the partnership arising from an obligation incurred by the dissociated partner after dissociation for which the partnership is liable under subsection (a).

§ 703. Dissociated Partner's Liability to Other Persons

(a) A partner's dissociation does not of itself discharge the partner's liability for a partnership obligation incurred before dissociation.

A dissociated partner is not liable for a partnership obligation incurred after dissociation, except as otherwise provided in subsection (b).

(b) A partner who dissociates without resulting in a dissolution and winding up of the partnership business is liable as a partner to the other party in a transaction entered into by the partnership, or a surviving partnership under [Article] 9, within two years after the partner's dissociation, only if the partner is liable for the obligation under Section 306 and at the time of entering into the transaction the other party:

(1) reasonably believed that the dissociated partner was then a partner;

(2) did not have notice of the partner's dissociation; and

(3) is not deemed to have had knowledge under Section 303(e) or notice under Section 704(c).

(c) By agreement with the partnership creditor and the partners continuing the business, a dissociated partner may be released from liability for a partnership obligation.

(d) A dissociated partner is released from liability for a partnership obligation if a partnership creditor, with notice of the partner's dissociation but without the partner's consent, agrees to a material alteration in the nature or time of payment of a partnership obligation.

§ 704. Statement of Dissociation

(a) A dissociated partner or the partnership may file a statement of dissociation stating the name of the partnership and that the partner is dissociated from the partnership.

(b) A statement of dissociation is a limitation on the authority of a dissociated partner for the purposes of Section 303(d) and (e).

(c) For the purposes of Sections 702(a)(3) and 703(b)(3), a person not a partner is deemed to have notice of the dissociation 90 days after the statement of dissociation is filed.

Article 8. Winding Up Partnership Business

§ 801. Events Causing Dissolution and Winding Up of Partnership Business

A partnership is dissolved, and its business must be wound up, only upon the occurrence of any of the following events:

(1) in a partnership at will, the partnership's having notice from a partner, other than a partner who is dissociated under Section 601(2) through (10), of that partner's express will to withdraw as a partner, or on a later date specified by the partner;

(2) in a partnership for a definite term or particular undertaking:

(i) within 90 days after a partner's dissociation by death or otherwise under Section 601(6) through (10) or wrongful dissociation under Section 602(b), the express will of at least half of the remaining partners to wind up the partnership business, for which purpose a partner's rightful dissociation pursuant to Section 602(b)(2)(i) constitutes the expression of that partner's will to wind up the partnership business;

(ii) the express will of all of the partners to wind up the partnership business; or

(iii) the expiration of the term or the completion of the undertaking;

(3) an event agreed to in the partnership agreement resulting in the winding up of the partnership business;

(4) an event that makes it unlawful for all or substantially all of the business of the partnership to be continued, but a cure of illegality within 90 days after notice to the partnership of the event is effective retroactively to the date of the event for purposes of this section;

(5) on application by a partner, a judicial determination that:

(i) the economic purpose of the partnership is likely to be unreasonably frustrated;

(ii) another partner has engaged in conduct relating to the partnership business which makes it not reasonably practicable to carry on the business in partnership with that partner; or

(iii) it is not otherwise reasonably practicable to carry on the partnership business in conformity with the partnership agreement; or

(6) on application by a transferee of a partner's transferable interest, a judicial determination that it is equitable to wind up the partnership business:

(i) after the expiration of the term or completion of the undertaking, if the partnership was for a definite term or particular undertaking at the time of the transfer or entry of the charging order that gave rise to the transfer; or

(ii) at any time, if the partnership was a partnership at will at the time of the transfer or entry of the charging order that gave rise to the transfer.

§ 802. Partnership Continues After Dissolution

(a) Subject to subsection (b), a partnership continues after dissolution only for the purpose of winding up its business. The partnership is terminated when the winding up of its business is completed.

(b) At any time after the dissolution of a partnership and before the winding up of its business is completed, all of the partners, including any dissociating partner other than a wrongfully dissociating partner, may waive the right to have the partnership's business wound up and the partnership terminated. In that event:

(1) the partnership resumes carrying on its business as if dissolution had never occurred, and any liability incurred by the partnership or a

partner after the dissolution and before the waiver is determined as if dissolution had never occurred; and

(2) the rights of a third party accruing under Section 804(1) or arising out of conduct in reliance on the dissolution before the third party knew or received a notification of the waiver may not be adversely affected.

§ 803. Right to Wind Up Partnership Business

(a) After dissolution, a partner who has not wrongfully dissociated may participate in winding up the partnership's business, but on application of any partner, partner's legal representative, or transferee, the [designate the appropriate court], for good cause shown, may order judicial supervision of the winding up.

(b) The legal representative of the last surviving partner may wind up a partnership's business.

(c) A person winding up a partnership's business may preserve the partnership business or property as a going concern for a reasonable time, prosecute and defend actions and proceedings, whether civil, criminal, or administrative, settle and close the partnership's business, dispose of and transfer the partnership's property, discharge the partnership's liabilities, distribute the assets of the partnership pursuant to Section 807, settle disputes by mediation or arbitration, and perform other necessary acts.

§ 804. Partner's Power to Bind Partnership After Dissolution

Subject to Section 805, a partnership is bound by a partner's act after dissolution that:

(1) is appropriate for winding up the partnership business; or

(2) would have bound the partnership under Section 301 before dissolution, if the other party to the transaction did not have notice of the dissolution.

§ 807. Settlement of Accounts and Contributions Among Partners

(a) In winding up a partnership's business, the assets of the partnership, including the contributions of the partners required by this section, must be applied to discharge its obligations to creditors, including, to the extent permitted by law, partners who are creditors. Any surplus must be applied to pay in cash the net amount distributable to partners in accordance with their right to distributions under subsection (b).

(b) Each partner is entitled to a settlement of all partnership accounts upon winding up the partnership business. In settling accounts among the partners, profits and losses that result from the liquidation of the partnership assets must be credited and charged to the partners' accounts. The partnership shall make a distribution to a partner in an amount equal to any excess of the credits over the charges in the partner's account. A partner shall contribute to the partnership an amount equal to any excess of the charges over the credits in the partner's account but excluding from the calculation charges attributable to an obligation for which the partner is not personally liable under Section 306.

(c) If a partner fails to contribute the full amount required under subsection (b), all of the other partners shall contribute, in the proportions in which those partners share partnership losses, the additional amount necessary to satisfy the partnership obligations for which they are personally liable under Section 306. A partner or partner's legal representative may recover from the other partners any contributions the partner makes to the extent the amount contributed exceeds that partner's share of the partnership obligations for which the partner is personally liable under Section 306.

(d) After the settlement of accounts, each partner shall contribute, in the proportion in which the partner shares partnership losses, the amount necessary to satisfy partnership obligations that were not known at the time of the settlement and for which the partner is personally liable under Section 306.

(e) The estate of a deceased partner is liable for the partner's obligation to contribute to the partnership.

(f) An assignee for the benefit of creditors of a partnership or a partner, or a person appointed by a court to represent creditors of a partnership or a partner, may enforce a partner's obligation to contribute to the partnership.

Article 10. Limited Liability Partnership

§ 1001. Statement of Qualification

(a) A partnership may become a limited liability partnership pursuant to this section.

(b) The terms and conditions on which a partnership becomes a limited liability partnership must be approved by the vote necessary to amend the partnership agreement except, in the case of a partnership agreement that expressly considers obligations to contribute to the partnership, the vote necessary to amend those provisions.

(c) After the approval required by subsection (b), a partnership may become a limited liability partnership by filing a statement of qualification. The statement must contain:

(1) the name of the partnership;

(2) the street address of the partnership's chief executive office and, if different, the street address of an office in this State, if any;

(3) if the partnership does not have an office in this State, the name and street address of the partnership's agent for service of process;

(4) a statement that the partnership elects to be a limited liability partnership; and

(5) a deferred effective date, if any.

(d) The agent of a limited liability partnership for service of process must be an individual who is a resident of this State or other person authorized to do business in this State.

(e) The status of a partnership as a limited liability partnership is effective on the later of the filing of the statement or a date specified in the statement. The status remains effective, regardless of changes in the partnership, until it is canceled pursuant to Section 105(d) or revoked pursuant to Section 1003.

(f) The status of a partnership as a limited liability partnership and the liability of its partners is not affected by errors or later changes in the information required to be contained in the statement of qualification under subsection (c).

(g) The filing of a statement of qualification establishes that a partnership has satisfied all conditions precedent to the qualification of the partnership as a limited liability partnership.

(h) An amendment or cancellation of a statement of qualification is effective when it is filed or on a deferred effective date specified in the amendment or cancellation.

§ 1002. Name

The name of a limited liability partnership must end with "Registered Limited Liability Partnership", "Limited Liability Partnership", "R.L.L.P.", "L.L.P.", "RLLP", or "LLP".

§ 1003. Annual Report

(a) A limited liability partnership, and a foreign limited liability partnership authorized to transact business in this State, shall file an annual report in the office of the [Secretary of State] which contains:

(1) the name of the limited liability partnership and the State or other jurisdiction under whose laws the foreign limited liability partnership is formed;

(2) the street address of the partnership's chief executive office and, if different, the street address of an office of the partnership in this State, if any; and

(3) if the partnership does not have an office in this State, the name and street address of the partnership's current agent for service of process.

(b) An annual report must be filed between [January 1 and April 1] of each year following the calendar year in which a partnership files a statement of qualification or a foreign partnership becomes authorized to transact business in this State.

(c) The [Secretary of State] may revoke the statement of qualification of a partnership that fails to file an annual report when due or pay the required filing fee. To do so, the [Secretary of State] shall provide the partnership at least 60 days' written notice of intent to revoke the statement. The notice must be mailed to the partnership at its chief executive office set forth in the last filed statement of qualification or annual report. The notice must specify the annual report that has not been filed, the fee that has not been paid, and the effective date of the revocation. The revocation is not effective if the annual report is filed and the fee is paid before the effective date of the revocation.

(d) A revocation under subsection (c) only affects a partnership's status as a limited liability partnership and is not an event of dissolution of the partnership.

(e) A partnership whose statement of qualification has been revoked may apply to the [Secretary of State] for reinstatement within two years after the effective date of the revocation. The application must state:

(1) the name of the partnership and the effective date of the revocation; and

(2) that the ground for revocation either did not exist or has been corrected.

(f) A reinstatement under subsection (e) relates back to and takes effect as of the effective date of the revocation, and the partnership's status as a limited liability partnership continues as if the revocation had never occurred.

DELAWARE LIMITED LIABILITY COMPANY ACT

Del. Code Ann. Title 6, Chapter 18

Subchapter I. General Provisions

§ 18-101. Definitions

As used in this chapter unless the context otherwise requires:

. . .

(2) "Certificate of formation" means the certificate referred to in § 18-201 of this title, and the certificate as amended.

(3) "Contribution" means any cash, property, services rendered or a promissory note or other obligation to contribute cash or property or to perform services, which a person contributes to a limited liability company in the person's capacity as a member.

(4) "Foreign limited liability company" means a limited liability company formed under the laws of any state or under the laws of any foreign country or other foreign jurisdiction and denominated as such under the laws of such state or foreign country or other foreign jurisdiction.

(5) "Knowledge" means a person's actual knowledge of a fact, rather than the person's constructive knowledge of the fact.

(6) "Limited liability company" and "domestic limited liability company" means a limited liability company formed under the laws of the State of Delaware and having 1 or more members.

(7) "Limited liability company agreement" means any agreement (whether referred to as a limited liability company agreement, operating agreement or otherwise), written, oral or implied, of the member or members as to the affairs of a limited liability company and the conduct of its business. A member or manager of a limited liability company or an assignee of a limited liability company interest is bound by the limited liability company agreement whether or not the member or manager or assignee executes the limited liability company agreement. A limited liability company is not required to execute its limited liability company agreement. A limited liability company is bound by its limited liability company agreement whether or not the limited liability company executes the limited liability company agreement. A limited liability company agreement of a limited liability company having only 1 member shall not be unenforceable by reason of there being only 1 person who is a party to the limited liability company agreement. A limited liability company agreement is not subject to any statute of frauds (including § 2714 of this title). A limited liability company agreement may provide rights to any person, including a person who is not a party to the limited liability company agreement, to the extent set forth therein. A written limited liability company agreement or another written agreement or writing:

a. May provide that a person shall be admitted as a member of a limited liability company, or shall become an assignee of a limited liability company interest or other rights or powers of a member to the extent assigned:

1. If such person (or a representative authorized by such person orally, in writing or by other action such as payment for a limited liability company interest) executes the limited liability company agreement or any other writing evidencing the intent of such person to become a member or assignee; or

2. Without such execution, if such person (or a representative authorized by such person orally, in writing or by other action such as payment for a limited liability company interest) complies with the conditions for becoming a member or assignee as set forth in the limited liability company agreement or any other writing; and

b. Shall not be unenforceable by reason of its not having been signed by a person being admitted as a member or becoming an assignee as provided in paragraph (7)a. of this section, or by reason of its having been signed by a representative as provided in this chapter.

(8) "Limited liability company interest" means a member's share of the profits and losses of a limited liability company and a member's right to receive distributions of the limited liability company's assets.

(9) "Liquidating trustee" means a person carrying out the winding up of a limited liability company.

(10) "Manager" means a person who is named as a manager of a limited liability company in, or designated as a manager of a limited liability company pursuant to, a limited liability company agreement or similar instrument under which the limited liability company is formed.

(11) "Member" means a person who is admitted to a limited liability company as a member as provided in § 18-301 of this title or, in the case of a foreign limited liability company, in accordance with the laws of the state or foreign country or other foreign jurisdiction under which the foreign limited liability company is formed.

(12) "Person" means a natural person, partnership (whether general or limited), limited liability company, trust (including a common law trust, business trust, statutory trust, voting trust or any other form of trust), estate, association (including any group, organization, co-tenancy, plan, board, council or committee), corporation, government (including a country, state, county or any other governmental subdivision, agency or instrumentality), custodian, nominee or any other individual or entity (or series thereof) in its own or any representative capacity, in each case, whether domestic or foreign.

(13) "Personal representative" means, as to a natural person, the executor, administrator, guardian, conservator or other legal representative thereof and, as to a person other than a natural person, the legal representative or successor thereof.

(14) "State" means the District of Columbia or the Commonwealth of Puerto Rico or any state, territory, possession or other jurisdiction of the United States other than the State of Delaware.

§ 18-104. Registered Office; Registered Agent

(a) Each limited liability company shall have and maintain in the State of Delaware:

(1) A registered office, which may but need not be a place of its business in the State of Delaware; and

(2) A registered agent for service of process on the limited liability company, having a business office identical with such registered office, which agent may be any of:

a. The limited liability company itself,

b. An individual resident in the State of Delaware,

c. A domestic limited liability company (other than the limited liability company itself), a domestic corporation, a domestic partnership (whether general (including a limited liability partnership) or limited (including a limited liability limited partnership)), or a domestic statutory trust, or

d. A foreign corporation, a foreign partnership (whether general (including a limited liability partnership) or limited (including a limited liability limited partnership)), a foreign limited liability company, or a foreign statutory trust.

(b) A registered agent may change the address of the registered office of the limited liability company(ies) for which it is registered agent to another address in the State of Delaware by paying a fee as set forth in § 18-1105(a)(2) of this title and filing with the Secretary of State a certificate, executed by such registered agent, setting forth the address at which such registered agent has maintained the registered office for each of the limited liability companies for which it is a registered agent, and further certifying to the new address to which each such registered office will be changed on a given day, and at which new address such registered agent will thereafter maintain the registered office for each of the limited liability companies for which it is a registered agent. Upon the filing of such certificate, the Secretary of State shall furnish to the registered agent a certified copy of the same under the Secretary's hand and seal of office, and thereafter, or until further change of address, as authorized by law, the registered office in the State of Delaware of each of the limited liability companies for which the agent is a registered agent shall be located at the new address of the registered agent thereof as given in the certificate. In the event of a change of name of any person acting as a registered agent of a limited liability company, such registered agent shall file with the Secretary of State a certificate executed by such registered agent setting forth the new name of such registered agent, the name of such registered agent before it was changed, and the address at which such registered agent has maintained the registered office for each of the limited liability companies for which it is a registered agent, and shall pay a fee as set forth in § 18-1105(a)(2) of this title. Upon the filing of such certificate, the Secretary of State shall furnish to the registered agent a certified copy of the certificate under the Secretary of State's own hand and seal of office. A change of name of any person acting as a registered agent of a limited liability company as a result of a merger or consolidation of the registered agent with or into another person which succeeds to its assets and liabilities by operation of law shall be deemed a change of name for purposes of this section. Filing a certificate under this section shall be deemed to be an amendment of the certificate of formation of each limited liability company affected thereby, and each such limited liability company shall not be required to take any further action with respect thereto to amend its certificate of formation under § 18-202 of this title. Any registered agent filing a certificate under this section shall promptly, upon such filing, deliver a copy of any such certificate to each limited liability company affected thereby.

(c) The registered agent of 1 or more limited liability companies may resign and appoint a successor registered agent by paying a fee as set forth in § 18-1105(a)(2) of this title and filing a certificate with the Secretary of State stating that it resigns and the name and address of the successor registered agent. There shall be attached to such certificate a statement of each affected limited liability company ratifying and approving such change of registered agent. Upon such filing, the successor registered agent shall become the registered agent of such limited liability companies as have ratified and approved such substitution, and the successor registered agent's address, as stated in such certificate, shall become the address of each such limited liability company's registered office in the State of Delaware. The Secretary of State shall then issue a certificate that the successor registered agent has become the registered agent of the limited liability companies so ratifying and approving such change and setting out the names of such limited liability companies. Filing of such certificate of resignation shall be deemed to be an amendment of the certificate of formation of each limited liability company affected thereby, and each such limited liability company shall not be required to take any further action with respect thereto to amend its certificate of formation under § 18-202 of this title.

(d) The registered agent of 1 or more limited liability companies may resign without appointing a successor registered agent by paying a fee as set forth in § 18-1105(a)(2) of this title and filing a certificate of resignation with the Secretary of State, but such resignation shall not become effective until 30 days after the certificate is filed. The certificate shall contain a statement that written notice of resignation was given to each affected limited liability company at least 30 days prior to the filing of the certificate by mailing or delivering such notice to the limited liability company at its address last known to the registered agent and shall set forth the date of such notice. After receipt of the notice of the resignation of its registered agent, the limited liability company for which such registered agent was acting shall obtain and designate a new registered agent, to take the place of the registered agent so resigning. If such limited liability company fails to obtain and designate a new registered agent as aforesaid prior to the expiration of the period of 30 days after the filing by the registered agent of the certificate of resignation, the certificate of formation of such limited liability company shall be canceled. After the resignation of the registered agent shall have become effective as provided in this section and if no new registered agent shall have been obtained and designated in the time and manner aforesaid, service of legal process against each limited liability company for which the resigned registered agent had been acting shall thereafter be upon the Secretary of State in accordance with § 18-105 of this title.

(e) Every registered agent shall:

(1) If an entity, maintain a business office in the State of Delaware which is generally open, or if an individual, be generally present at a designated location in the State of Delaware, at sufficiently frequent times to accept service of process and otherwise perform the functions of a registered agent;

(2) If a foreign entity, be authorized to transact business in the State of Delaware;

(3) Accept service of process and other communications directed to the limited liability companies and foreign limited liability companies for which it serves as registered agent and forward same to the limited liability company or foreign limited liability company to which the service or communication is directed; and

(4) Forward to the limited liability companies and foreign limited liability companies for which it serves as registered agent the statement for the annual tax described in § 18-1107 of this title or an electronic notification of same in a form satisfactory to the Secretary of State.

(f) Any registered agent who at any time serves as registered agent for more than 50 entities (a "commercial registered agent"), whether domestic or foreign, shall satisfy and comply with the following qualifications:

(1) A natural person serving as a commercial registered agent shall:

a. Maintain a principal residence or a principal place of business in the State of Delaware;

b. Maintain a Delaware business license;

c. Be generally present at a designated location within the State of Delaware during normal business hours to accept service of process and otherwise perform the functions of a registered agent as specified in subsection (e) of this section; and

d. Provide the Secretary of State upon request with such information identifying and enabling communication with such commercial registered agent as the Secretary of State shall require.

(2) A domestic or foreign corporation, a domestic or foreign partnership (whether general (including a limited liability partnership) or limited (including a limited liability limited partnership)), a domestic or foreign limited liability company, or a domestic or foreign statutory trust serving as a commercial registered agent shall:

a. Have a business office within the State of Delaware which is generally open during normal business hours to accept service of process and otherwise perform the functions of a registered agent as specified in subsection (e) of this section;

b. Maintain a Delaware business license;

c. Have generally present at such office during normal business hours an officer, director or managing agent who is a natural person; and

d. Provide the Secretary of State upon request with such information identifying and enabling communication with such commercial registered agent as the Secretary of State shall require.

(3) For purposes of this subsection and paragraph (i)(2)a. of this section, a commercial registered agent shall also include any registered agent which has an officer, director or managing agent in common with any other registered agent or agents if such registered agents at any time during such common service as officer, director or managing agent collectively served as registered agents for more than 50 entities, whether domestic or foreign.

(g) Every limited liability company formed under the laws of the State of Delaware or qualified to do business in the State of Delaware shall provide to its registered agent and update from time to time as necessary the name, business address and business telephone number of a natural person who is a member, manager, officer, employee or designated agent of the limited liability company, who is then authorized to receive communications from the registered agent. Such person shall be deemed the communications contact for the limited liability company. A limited liability company, upon receipt of a request by the communications contact delivered in writing or by electronic transmission, shall provide the communications contact with the name, business address and business telephone number of a natural person who has access to the record required to be maintained pursuant to § 18-305(h) of this title. Every registered agent shall retain (in paper or electronic form) the above information concerning the current communications contact for each limited liability company and each foreign limited liability company for which that registered agent serves as registered agent. If the limited liability company fails to provide the registered agent with a current communications contact, the registered agent may resign as the registered agent for such limited liability company pursuant to this section. For purposes of this subsection, the term "electronic transmission" means any form of communication not directly involving the physical transmission of paper that creates a record that may be retained, retrieved and reviewed by a recipient thereof and that may be directly reproduced in paper form by such a recipient through an automated process.

(h) The Secretary of State is authorized to issue such rules and regulations as may be necessary or appropriate to carry out the enforcement of subsections (e), (f) and (g) of this section, and to take actions reasonable and necessary to assure registered agents' compliance with subsections (e), (f) and (g) of this section. Such actions may include refusal to file documents submitted by a registered agent.

(i) Upon application of the Secretary of State, the Court of Chancery may enjoin any person or entity from serving as a registered agent or as an officer, director or managing agent of a registered agent.

(1) Upon the filing of a complaint by the Secretary of State pursuant to this section, the court may make such orders respecting such proceeding as it deems appropriate, and may enter such orders granting interim or final relief as it deems proper under the circumstances.

(2) Any 1 or more of the following grounds shall be a sufficient basis to grant an injunction pursuant to this section:

a. With respect to any registered agent who at any time within 1 year immediately prior to the filing of the Secretary of State's complaint is a commercial registered agent, failure after notice and warning to comply with the qualifications set forth in subsection (e) of this section and/or the requirements of subsection (f) or (g) of this section above;

b. The person serving as a registered agent, or any person who is an officer, director or managing agent of an entity registered agent, has been convicted of a felony or any crime which includes an element of dishonesty or fraud or involves moral turpitude; or

c. The registered agent has engaged in conduct in connection with acting as a registered agent that is intended to or likely to deceive or defraud the public.

(3) With respect to any order the court enters pursuant to this section with respect to an entity that has acted as a registered agent, the Court may also direct such order to any person who has served as an officer, director or managing agent of such registered agent. Any person who, on or after January 1, 2007, serves as an officer, director or managing agent of an entity acting as a registered agent in the State of Delaware shall be deemed thereby to have consented to the appointment of such registered agent as agent upon whom service of process may be made in any action brought pursuant to this section, and service as an officer, director or managing agent of an entity acting as a registered agent in the State of Delaware shall be a signification of the consent of such person that any process when so served shall be of the same legal force and validity as if served upon such person within the State of Delaware, and such appointment of the registered agent shall be irrevocable.

(4) Upon the entry of an order by the Court enjoining any person or entity from acting as a registered agent, the Secretary of State shall mail or deliver notice of such order to each affected limited liability company:

a. That has specified the address of a place of business in a record of the Secretary of State, to the address specified, or

b. An address of which the Secretary of State has obtained from the limited liability company's former registered agent, to the address obtained.

If such a limited liability company is a domestic limited liability company and fails to obtain and designate a new registered agent within 30 days after such notice is given, the certificate of formation of such limited liability company shall be canceled. If such a limited liability company is a foreign limited liability company and fails to obtain and designate a new registered agent within 30 days after such notice is given, such foreign limited liability company shall not be permitted to do business in the State of Delaware and its registration shall be canceled. If any other affected limited liability company is a domestic limited liability company and fails to obtain and designate a new registered agent within 60 days after entry of an order by the Court enjoining such limited liability company's registered agent from acting as a registered agent, the certificate of formation of such limited liability company shall be canceled. If any other affected limited liability company is a foreign limited liability company and fails to obtain and designate a new registered agent within 60 days after entry of an order by court enjoining such limited liability company's registered agent from acting as a registered agent, such foreign limited liability company shall not be permitted to do business in the State of Delaware and its registration shall be canceled. If the Court enjoins a person or entity from acting as a registered agent as provided in this section and no new registered agent shall have been obtained and designated in the time and manner aforesaid, service of legal process against the limited liability company for which the registered agent had been acting shall thereafter be upon the Secretary of State in accordance with § 18-105 or § 18-911 of this title. The Court of Chancery may, upon application of the Secretary of State on notice to the former registered agent, enter such orders as it deems appropriate to give the Secretary of State access to information in the former registered agent's possession in order to facilitate communication with the limited liability companies the former registered agent served.

(j) The Secretary of State is authorized to make a list of registered agents available to the public, and to establish such qualifications and issue such rules and regulations with respect to such listing as the Secretary of State deems necessary or appropriate.

(k) As contained in any certificate of formation, application for registration as a foreign limited liability company, or other document filed in the office of the Secretary of State under this chapter, the address of a registered agent or registered office shall include the street, number, city and postal code.

§ 18-105. Service of Process on Domestic Limited Liability Companies

(a) Service of legal process upon any domestic limited liability company shall be made by delivering a copy personally to any manager of the limited liability company in the State of Delaware or the registered agent of the limited liability company in the State of Delaware, or by leaving it at the dwelling house or usual place of abode in the State of Delaware of any such manager or registered agent (if the registered agent be an individual), or at the registered office or other place of business of the limited liability company in the State of Delaware. If the registered agent be a corporation, service of process upon it as such may be made by serving, in the State of Delaware, a copy thereof on the president, vice-president, secretary, assistant secretary or any director of the corporate registered agent. Service by copy left at the dwelling house or usual place of abode of a manager or registered agent, or at the registered office or other place of business of the limited liability company in the State of Delaware, to be effective, must be delivered thereat at least 6 days before the return date of the process, and in the presence of an adult person, and the officer serving the process shall distinctly state the manner of service in the officer's return thereto. Process returnable forthwith must be delivered personally to the manager or registered agent. . . .

§ 18-106. Nature of Business Permitted; Powers

(a) A limited liability company may carry on any lawful business, purpose or activity, whether or not for profit, with the exception of the business of banking as defined in § 126 of Title 8.

(b) A limited liability company shall possess and may exercise all the powers and privileges granted by this chapter or by any other law or by its limited liability company agreement, together with any powers incidental thereto, including such powers and privileges as are necessary or convenient to the conduct, promotion or attainment of the business, purposes or activities of the limited liability company.

(c) Notwithstanding any provision of this chapter to the contrary, without limiting the general powers enumerated in subsection (b) of this section, a limited liability company shall, subject to such standards and restrictions, if any, as are set forth in its limited liability company agreement, have the power and authority to make contracts of guaranty and suretyship and enter into interest rate, basis, currency, hedge or other swap agreements or cap, floor, put, call, option, exchange or collar agreements, derivative agreements, or other agreements similar to any of the foregoing.

(d) Unless otherwise provided in a limited liability company agreement, a limited liability company has the power and authority to grant, hold or exercise a power of attorney, including an irrevocable power of attorney.

§ 18-107. Business Transactions of Member or Manager with the Limited Liability Company

Except as provided in a limited liability company agreement, a member or manager may lend money to, borrow money from, act as a surety, guarantor or endorser for, guarantee or assume 1 or more obligations of, provide collateral for, and transact other business with, a limited liability company and, subject to other applicable law, has the same rights and obligations with respect to any such matter as a person who is not a member or manager.

§ 18-108. Indemnification

Subject to such standards and restrictions, if any, as are set forth in its limited liability company agreement, a limited liability company may, and shall have the power to, indemnify and hold harmless any member or manager or other person from and against any and all claims and demands whatsoever.

§ 18-109. Service of Process on Managers and Liquidating Trustees

(a) A manager or a liquidating trustee of a limited liability company may be served with process in the manner prescribed in this section in all civil actions or proceedings brought in the State of Delaware involving or relating to the business of the limited liability company or a violation by the manager or the liquidating trustee of a duty to the limited liability company or any member of the limited liability company, whether or not the manager or the liquidating trustee is a manager or a liquidating trustee at the time suit is commenced. A manager's or a liquidating trustee's serving as such constitutes such person's consent to the appointment of the registered agent of the limited liability company (or, if there is none, the Secretary of State) as such person's agent upon whom service of process may be made as provided in this section. . . .

§ 18-110. Contested Matters Relating to Managers; Contested Votes

(a) A manager or a liquidating trustee of a limited liability company may be served with process in the manner prescribed in this section in all civil actions or proceedings brought in the State of Delaware involving or relating to the business of the limited liability company or a violation by the manager or the liquidating trustee of a duty to the limited liability company or any member of the limited liability company, whether or not the manager or the liquidating trustee is a manager or a liquidating trustee at the time suit is commenced. A manager's or a liquidating trustee's serving as such constitutes such person's consent to the appointment of the registered agent of the limited liability company (or, if there is none, the Secretary of State) as such person's agent upon whom service of process may be made as provided in this section. Such service as a manager or a liquidating trustee shall signify the consent of such manager or liquidating trustee that any process when so served shall be of the same legal force and validity as if served upon such manager or liquidating trustee within the State of Delaware and such appointment of the registered agent (or, if there is none, the Secretary of State) shall be irrevocable. As used in this subsection (a) and in subsections (b), (c) and (d) of this section, the term "manager" refers (i) to a person who is a manager as defined in § 18-101(10) of this title and (ii) to a person, whether or not a member of a limited liability company, who, although not a manager as defined in § 18-101(10) of this title, participates materially in the management of the limited liability company; provided however, that the power to elect or otherwise select or to participate in the election or selection of a person to be a manager as defined in § 18-101(10) of this title shall not, by itself, constitute participation in the management of the limited liability company.

(b) Service of process shall be effected by serving the registered agent (or, if there is none, the Secretary of State) with 1 copy of such process in the manner provided by law for service of writs of summons. In the event service is made under this subsection upon the Secretary of State, the plaintiff shall pay to the Secretary of State the sum of $50 for the use of the State of Delaware, which sum shall be taxed as part of the costs of the proceeding if the plaintiff shall prevail therein. In addition, the Prothonotary or the Register in Chancery of the court in which the civil action or proceeding is pending shall, within 7 days of such service, deposit in the United States mails, by registered mail, postage prepaid, true and attested copies of the process, together with a statement that service is being made pursuant to this section, addressed to such manager or liquidating trustee at the registered office of the limited liability company and at the manager's or liquidating trustee's address last known to the party desiring to make such service.

(c) In any action in which any such manager or liquidating trustee has been served with process as hereinabove provided, the time in which a defendant shall be required to appear and file a responsive pleading shall be computed from the date of mailing by the Prothonotary or the Register in Chancery as provided in subsection (b) of this section; however, the court in which such action has been commenced may order such continuance or continuances as may be necessary to afford such manager or liquidating trustee reasonable opportunity to defend the action.

(d) In a written limited liability company agreement or other writing, a manager or member may consent to be subject to the nonexclusive jurisdiction of the courts of, or arbitration in, a specified jurisdiction, or the exclusive jurisdiction of the courts of the State of Delaware, or the exclusivity of arbitration in a specified jurisdiction or the State of Delaware, and to be served with legal process in the manner prescribed in such limited liability company agreement or other writing. Except by agreeing to arbitrate any arbitrable matter in a specified jurisdiction or in the State of Delaware, a member who is not a manager may not waive its right to maintain a legal action or proceeding in the courts of the State of Delaware with respect to matters relating to the organization or internal affairs of a limited liability company.

(e) Nothing herein contained limits or affects the right to serve process in any other manner now or hereafter provided by law. This section is an extension of and not a limitation upon the right otherwise existing of service of legal process upon nonresidents.

(f) The Court of Chancery and the Superior Court may make all necessary rules respecting the form of process, the manner of issuance and return thereof and such other rules which may be necessary to implement this section and are not inconsistent with this section.

§ 18-111. Interpretation and Enforcement of Limited Liability Company Agreement

Any action to interpret, apply or enforce the provisions of a limited liability company agreement, or the duties, obligations or liabilities of a limited liability company to the members or managers of the limited liability company, or the duties, obligations or liabilities among members or managers and of members or managers to the limited liability company, or the rights or powers of, or restrictions on, the limited liability company, members or managers, or any provision of this chapter, or any other instrument, document, agreement or certificate contemplated by any provision of this chapter, may be brought in the Court of Chancery.

Subchapter II. Formation; Certificate of Formation

§ 18-201. Certificate of Formation

(a) In order to form a limited liability company, 1 or more authorized persons must execute a certificate of formation. The certificate of formation shall be filed in the office of the Secretary of State and set forth:

(1) The name of the limited liability company;

(2) The address of the registered office and the name and address of the registered agent for service of process required to be maintained by § 18-104 of this title; and

(3) Any other matters the members determine to include therein.

(b) A limited liability company is formed at the time of the filing of the initial certificate of formation in the office of the Secretary of State or at any later date or time specified in the certificate of formation if, in either case, there has been substantial compliance with the requirements of this section. A limited liability company formed under this chapter shall be a separate legal entity, the existence of which as a separate legal entity shall continue until cancellation of the limited liability company's certificate of formation.

(c) The filing of the certificate of formation in the office of the Secretary of State shall make it unnecessary to file any other documents under Chapter 31 of this title.

(d) A limited liability company agreement shall be entered into or otherwise existing either before, after or at the time of the filing of a certificate of formation and, whether entered into or otherwise existing before, after or at the time of such filing, may be made effective as of the effective time of such filing or at such other time or date as provided in or reflected by the limited liability company agreement.

§ 18-202. Amendment to Certificate of Formation

(a) A certificate of formation is amended by filing a certificate of amendment thereto in the office of the Secretary of State. The certificate of amendment shall set forth:

(1) The name of the limited liability company; and

(2) The amendment to the certificate of formation.

(b) A manager or, if there is no manager, then any member who becomes aware that any statement in a certificate of formation was false when made, or that any matter described has changed making the certificate of formation false in any material respect, shall promptly amend the certificate of formation.

(c) A certificate of formation may be amended at any time for any other proper purpose.

(d) Unless otherwise provided in this chapter or unless a later effective date or time (which shall be a date or time certain) is provided for in the certificate of amendment, a certificate of amendment shall be effective at the time of its filing with the Secretary of State.

§ 18-203. Cancellation of Certificate

(a) A certificate of formation shall be canceled upon the dissolution and the completion of winding up of a limited liability company, or as provided in § 18-104(d) or (i)(4) or § 18-1108 of this title, or upon the filing of a certificate of merger or consolidation or a certificate of ownership and merger if the limited liability company is not the surviving or resulting entity in a merger or consolidation or upon the future effective date or time of a certificate of merger or consolidation or a certificate of ownership and merger if the limited liability company is not the surviving or resulting entity in a merger or consolidation, or upon the filing of a certificate of transfer or upon the future effective date or time of a certificate of transfer, or upon the filing of a certificate of conversion to non-Delaware entity or upon the future effective date or time of a certificate of conversion to non-Delaware entity. A certificate of cancellation shall be filed in the office of the Secretary of State to accomplish the cancellation of a certificate of formation upon the dissolution and the completion of winding up of a limited liability company and shall set forth:

(1) The name of the limited liability company;

(2) The date of filing of its certificate of formation;

(3) The future effective date or time (which shall be a date or time certain) of cancellation if it is not to be effective upon the filing of the certificate; and

(4) Any other information the person filing the certificate of cancellation determines.

(b) A certificate of cancellation that is filed in the office of the Secretary of State prior to the dissolution or the completion of winding up of a limited liability company may be corrected as an erroneously executed certificate of cancellation by filing with the office of the Secretary of State a certificate of correction of such certificate of cancellation in accordance with § 18-211 of this title.

(c) The Secretary of State shall not issue a certificate of good standing with respect to a limited liability company if its certificate of formation is canceled.

§ 18-207. Notice

The fact that a certificate of formation is on file in the office of the Secretary of State is notice that the entity formed in connection with the filing of the certificate of formation is a limited liability company formed under the laws of the State of Delaware and is notice of all other facts set forth therein which are required to be set forth in a certificate of formation by§ 18-201(a)(1) and (2) of this title and which are permitted to be set forth in a certificate of formation by § 18-215(b) of this title . . .

§ 18-209. Merger and Consolidation

(a) As used in this section and in § 18-204 of this title, "other business entity" means a corporation, a statutory trust, a business trust, an association, a real estate investment trust, a common-law trust, or any other unincorporated business or entity, including a partnership (whether general (including a limited liability partnership) or limited (including a limited liability limited partnership)), and a foreign limited liability company, but excluding a domestic limited liability company. As used in this section and in §§ 18-210 and 18-301 of this title, "plan of merger" means a writing approved by a domestic limited liability company, in the form of resolutions or otherwise, that states the terms and conditions of a merger under subsection (i) of this section.

(b) Pursuant to an agreement of merger or consolidation, 1 or more domestic limited liability companies may merge or consolidate with or into 1 or more domestic limited liability companies or 1 or more other business entities formed or organized under the laws of the State of Delaware or any other state or the United States or any foreign country or other foreign jurisdiction, or any combination thereof, with such domestic limited liability company or other business entity as the agreement shall provide being the surviving or resulting domestic limited liability company or other business entity. Unless otherwise provided in the limited liability company agreement, an agreement of merger or consolidation or a plan of merger shall be approved by each domestic limited liability company which is to merge or consolidate by members who own more than 50 percent of the then current percentage or other interest in the profits of the domestic limited liability company owned by all of the members. In connection with a merger or consolidation hereunder, rights or securities of, or interests in, a domestic limited liability company or other business entity which is a constituent party to the merger or consolidation may be exchanged for or converted into cash, property, rights or securities of, or interests in, the surviving or resulting domestic limited liability company or other business entity or, in addition to or in lieu thereof, may be exchanged for or converted into cash, property, rights or securities of, or interests in, a domestic limited liability company or other business entity which is not the surviving or resulting limited liability company or other business entity in the merger or consolidation, may remain outstanding or may be canceled. Notwithstanding prior approval, an agreement of merger or consolidation or a plan of merger may be terminated or amended pursuant to a provision for such termination or amendment contained in the agreement of merger or consolidation or plan of merger. Unless otherwise provided in a limited liability company agreement, a limited liability company whose original certificate of formation was filed with the Secretary of State and effective on or prior to July 31, 2015, shall continue to be governed by the second sentence of this subsection as in effect on July 31, 2015.

(c) Except in the case of a merger under subsection (i) of this section, if a domestic limited liability company is merging or consolidating under this section, the domestic limited liability company or other business entity surviving or resulting in or from the merger or consolidation shall file a certificate of merger or consolidation executed by 1 or more authorized persons on behalf of the domestic limited liability company when it is the surviving or resulting entity in the office of the Secretary of State. The certificate of merger or consolidation shall state:

(1) The name, jurisdiction of formation or organization and type of entity of each of the domestic limited liability companies and other business entities which is to merge or consolidate;

(2) That an agreement of merger or consolidation has been approved and executed by each of the domestic limited liability companies and other business entities which is to merge or consolidate;

(3) The name of the surviving or resulting domestic limited liability company or other business entity;

(4) In the case of a merger in which a domestic limited liability company is the surviving entity, such amendments, if any, to the certificate of formation of the surviving domestic limited liability company to change its name, registered office or registered agent as are desired to be effected by the merger;

(5) The future effective date or time (which shall be a date or time certain) of the merger or consolidation if it is not to be effective upon the filing of the certificate of merger or consolidation;

(6) That the agreement of merger or consolidation is on file at a place of business of the surviving or resulting domestic limited liability company or other business entity, and shall state the address thereof;

(7) That a copy of the agreement of merger or consolidation will be furnished by the surviving or resulting domestic limited liability company or other business entity, on request and without cost, to any member of any domestic limited liability company or any person holding an interest in any other business entity which is to merge or consolidate; and

(8) If the surviving or resulting entity is not a domestic limited liability company, or a corporation, partnership (whether general (including a limited liability partnership) or limited (including a limited liability limited partnership)) or statutory trust organized under the laws of the State of Delaware, a statement that such surviving or resulting other business entity agrees that it may be served with process in the State of Delaware in any action, suit or proceeding for the enforcement

of any obligation of any domestic limited liability company which is to merge or consolidate, irrevocably appointing the Secretary of State as its agent to accept service of process in any such action, suit or proceeding and specifying the address to which a copy of such process shall be mailed to it by the Secretary of State. Process may be served upon the Secretary of State under this subsection by means of electronic transmission but only as prescribed by the Secretary of State. The Secretary of State is authorized to issue such rules and regulations with respect to such service as the Secretary of State deems necessary or appropriate. In the event of service hereunder upon the Secretary of State, the procedures set forth in § 18-911(c) of this title shall be applicable, except that the plaintiff in any such action, suit or proceeding shall furnish the Secretary of State with the address specified in the certificate of merger or consolidation provided for in this section and any other address which the plaintiff may elect to furnish, together with copies of such process as required by the Secretary of State, and the Secretary of State shall notify such surviving or resulting other business entity at all such addresses furnished by the plaintiff in accordance with the procedures set forth in § 18-911(c) of this title.

(d) Unless a future effective date or time is provided in a certificate of merger or consolidation, or in the case of a merger under subsection (i) of this section in a certificate of ownership and merger, in which event a merger or consolidation shall be effective at any such future effective date or time, a merger or consolidation shall be effective upon the filing in the office of the Secretary of State of a certificate of merger or consolidation or a certificate of ownership and merger.

(e) A certificate of merger or consolidation or a certificate of ownership and merger shall act as a certificate of cancellation for a domestic limited liability company which is not the surviving or resulting entity in the merger or consolidation. A certificate of merger that sets forth any amendment in accordance with paragraph (c)(4) of this section shall be deemed to be an amendment to the certificate of formation of the limited liability company, and the limited liability company shall not be required to take any further action to amend its certificate of formation under § 18-202 of this title with respect to such amendments set forth in the certificate of merger. Whenever this section requires the filing of a certificate of merger or consolidation, such requirement shall be deemed satisfied by the filing of an agreement of merger or consolidation containing the information required by this section to be set forth in the certificate of merger or consolidation.

(f) An agreement of merger or consolidation or a plan of merger approved in accordance with subsection (b) of this section may:

(1) Effect any amendment to the limited liability company agreement; or

(2) Effect the adoption of a new limited liability company agreement, for a limited liability company if it is the surviving or resulting limited liability company in the merger or consolidation.

Any amendment to a limited liability company agreement or adoption of a new limited liability company agreement made pursuant to the foregoing sentence shall be effective at the effective time or date of the merger or consolidation and shall be effective notwithstanding any provision of the limited liability company agreement relating to amendment or adoption of a new limited liability company agreement, other than a provision that by its terms applies to an amendment to the limited liability company agreement or the adoption of a new limited liability company agreement, in either case, in connection with a merger or consolidation. The provisions of this subsection shall not be construed to limit the accomplishment of a merger or of any of the matters referred to herein by any other means provided for in a limited liability company agreement or other agreement or as otherwise permitted by law, including that the limited liability company agreement of any constituent limited liability company to the merger or consolidation (including a limited liability company formed for the purpose of consummating a merger or consolidation) shall be the limited liability company agreement of the surviving or resulting limited liability company.

(g) When any merger or consolidation shall have become effective under this section, for all purposes of the laws of the State of Delaware, all of the rights, privileges and powers of each of the domestic limited liability companies and other business entities that have merged or consolidated, and all property, real, personal and mixed, and all debts due to any of said domestic limited liability companies and other business entities, as well as all other things and causes of action belonging to each of such domestic limited liability companies and other business entities, shall be vested in the surviving or resulting domestic limited liability company or other business entity, and shall thereafter be the property of the surviving or resulting domestic limited liability company or other business entity as they were of each of the domestic limited liability companies and other business entities that have merged or consolidated, and the title to any real property vested by deed or otherwise, under the laws of the State of Delaware, in any of such domestic limited liability companies and other business entities, shall not revert or be in any way impaired by reason of this chapter; but all rights of creditors and all liens upon any property of any of said domestic limited liability companies and other business entities shall be preserved unimpaired, and all debts, liabilities and duties of each of the said domestic limited liability companies and other business entities that have merged or consolidated shall thenceforth attach to the surviving or resulting domestic limited liability company or other business entity, and may be enforced against it to the same extent as if said debts, liabilities and duties had been incurred or contracted by it. Unless otherwise agreed, a merger or consolidation of a domestic limited liability company, including a domestic limited liability company which is not the surviving or resulting entity in the merger or consolidation, shall not require such domestic limited liability company to wind up its affairs under § 18-803 of this title or pay its liabilities and distribute its assets under § 18-804 of this title, and the merger or consolidation shall not constitute a dissolution of such limited liability company.

(h) A limited liability company agreement may provide that a domestic limited liability company shall not have the power to merge or consolidate as set forth in this section.

(i) In any case in which (i) at least 90% of the outstanding shares of each class of the stock of a corporation or corporations (other than a corporation which has in its certificate of incorporation the provision required by § 251(g)(7)(i) of Title 8), of which class there are outstanding shares that, absent § 267(a) of Title 8, would be entitled to vote on such merger, is owned by a domestic limited liability company, (ii) 1 or more of such corporations is a corporation of the State of Delaware, and (iii) any corporation that is not a corporation of the State of Delaware is a corporation of any other state or the District of Columbia or another jurisdiction, the laws of which do not forbid such merger, the domestic limited liability company having such stock ownership may either merge the corporation or corporations into itself and assume all of its or their obligations, or merge itself, or itself and 1 or more of such corporations, into 1 of the other corporations, pursuant to a plan of merger. If a domestic limited liability company is causing a merger under this subsection, the domestic limited liability company shall file a certificate of ownership and merger executed by 1 or more authorized persons on behalf of the domestic limited liability company in the office of the Secretary of State. The certificate of ownership and merger shall certify that such merger was authorized in accordance with the domestic limited liability company's limited liability company agreement and this chapter, and if the domestic limited liability company shall not own all the outstanding stock of all the corporations that are parties to the merger, shall state the terms and conditions of the merger, including the securities, cash, property, or rights to be issued, paid, delivered or granted by the surviving domestic limited liability company or corporation upon surrender of each share of the corporation or corporations not owned by the domestic limited liability company, or the cancellation of some or all of such shares. If a corporation surviving a merger under this subsection is not a corporation organized under the laws of the State of Delaware, then the terms and conditions of the merger shall obligate such corporation to agree that it may be served with process in the State of Delaware in any proceeding for enforcement of any obligation of the domestic limited liability company or any obligation of any constituent corporation of the State of Delaware, as well as for enforcement of any obligation of the surviving corporation, including any suit or other proceeding to enforce the right of any stockholders as determined in appraisal proceedings pursuant to § 262 of Title 8, and to irrevocably appoint the Secretary of State as its agent to accept service of process in any such suit or other proceedings, and to specify the address to which a copy of such process shall be mailed by the Secretary of State. Process may be served upon the

Secretary of State under this subsection by means of electronic transmission but only as prescribed by the Secretary of State. The Secretary of State is authorized to issue such rules and regulations with respect to such service as the Secretary of State deems necessary or appropriate. In the event of such service upon the Secretary of State in accordance with this subsection, the Secretary of State shall forthwith notify such surviving corporation thereof by letter, directed to such surviving corporation at its address so specified, unless such surviving corporation shall have designated in writing to the Secretary of State a different address for such purpose, in which case it shall be mailed to the last address so designated. Such letter shall be sent by a mail or courier service that includes a record of mailing or deposit with the courier and a record of delivery evidenced by the signature of the recipient. Such letter shall enclose a copy of the process and any other papers served on the Secretary of State pursuant to this subsection. It shall be the duty of the plaintiff in the event of such service to serve process and any other papers in duplicate, to notify the Secretary of State that service is being effected pursuant to this subsection and to pay the Secretary of State the sum of $50 for the use of the State of Delaware, which sum shall be taxed as part of the costs in the proceeding, if the plaintiff shall prevail therein. The Secretary of State shall maintain an alphabetical record of any such service setting forth the name of the plaintiff and the defendant, the title, docket number and nature of the proceeding in which process has been served, the fact that service has been effected pursuant to this subsection, the return date thereof, and the day and hour service was made. The Secretary of State shall not be required to retain such information longer than 5 years from receipt of the service of process.

§ 18-210. Contractual Appraisal Rights

A limited liability company agreement or an agreement of merger or consolidation or a plan of merger may provide that contractual appraisal rights with respect to a limited liability company interest or another interest in a limited liability company shall be available for any class or group or series of members or limited liability company interests in connection with any amendment of a limited liability company agreement, any merger or consolidation in which the limited liability company is a constituent party to the merger or consolidation, any conversion of the limited liability company to another business form, any transfer to or domestication or continuance in any jurisdiction by the limited liability company, or the sale of all or substantially all of the limited liability company's assets. The Court of Chancery shall have jurisdiction to hear and determine any matter relating to any such appraisal rights.

. . .

§ 18-214. Conversion of Certain Entities to a Limited Liability Company

(a) As used in this section and in § 18-204 of this title, the term "other entity" means a corporation, a statutory trust, a business trust, an association, a real estate investment trust, a common-law trust or any other unincorporated business or entity, including a partnership (whether general (including a limited liability partnership) or limited (including a limited liability limited partnership)) or a foreign limited liability company.

(b) Any other entity may convert to a domestic limited liability company by complying with subsection (h) of this section and filing in the office of the Secretary of State in accordance with § 18-206 of this title...

§ 18-215. Series of Members, Managers, Limited Liability Company Interests or Assets

(a) A limited liability company agreement may establish or provide for the establishment of 1 or more designated series of members, managers, limited liability company interests or assets. Any such series may have separate rights, powers or duties with respect to specified property or obligations of the limited liability company or profits and losses associated with specified property or obligations, and any such series may have a separate business purpose or investment objective.

(b) Notwithstanding anything to the contrary set forth in this chapter or under other applicable law, in the event that a limited liability company agreement establishes or provides for the establishment of 1 or more series, and if the records maintained for any such series account for the assets associated with such series separately from the other assets of the limited liability company, or any other series thereof, and if the limited liability company agreement so provides, and if notice of the limitation on liabilities of a series as referenced in this subsection is set forth in the certificate of formation of the limited liability company, then the debts, liabilities, obligations and expenses incurred, contracted for or otherwise existing with respect to a particular series shall be enforceable against the assets of such series only, and not against the assets of the limited liability company generally or any other series thereof, and, unless otherwise provided in the limited liability company agreement, none of the debts, liabilities, obligations and expenses incurred, contracted for or otherwise existing with respect to the limited liability company generally or any other series thereof shall be enforceable against the assets of such series. Assets associated with a series may be held directly or indirectly, including in the name of such series, in the name of the limited liability company, through a nominee or otherwise. Records maintained for a series that reasonably identify its assets, including by specific listing, category, type, quantity, computational or allocational formula or procedure (including a percentage or share of any asset or assets) or by any other method where the identity of such assets is objectively determinable, will be deemed to account for the assets associated with such series separately from the other assets of the limited liability company, or any other series thereof. Notice in a certificate of formation of the limitation on liabilities of a series as referenced in this subsection shall be sufficient for all purposes of this subsection whether or not the limited liability company has established any series when such notice is included in the certificate of formation, and there shall be no requirement that any specific series of the limited liability company be referenced in such notice. The fact that a certificate of formation that contains the foregoing notice of the limitation on liabilities of a series is on file in the office of the Secretary of State shall constitute notice of such limitation on liabilities of a series.

(c) A series established in accordance with subsection (b) of this section may carry on any lawful business, purpose or activity, whether or not for profit, with the exception of the business of banking as defined in § 126 of Title 8. Unless otherwise provided in a limited liability company agreement, a series established in accordance with subsection (b) of this section shall have the power and capacity to, in its own name, contract, hold title to assets (including real, personal and intangible property), grant liens and security interests, and sue and be sued.

(d) Notwithstanding § 18-303(a) of this title, under a limited liability company agreement or under another agreement, a member or manager may agree to be obligated personally for any or all of the debts, obligations and liabilities of one or more series.

(e) A limited liability company agreement may provide for classes or groups of members or managers associated with a series having such relative rights, powers and duties as the limited liability company agreement may provide, and may make provision for the future creation in the manner provided in the limited liability company agreement of additional classes or groups of members or managers associated with the series having such relative rights, powers and duties as may from time to time be established, including rights, powers and duties senior to existing classes and groups of members or managers associated with the series. A limited liability company agreement may provide for the taking of an action, including the amendment of the limited liability company agreement, without the vote or approval of any member or manager or class or group of members or managers, including an action to create under the provisions of the limited liability company agreement a class or group of the series of limited liability company interests that was not previously outstanding. A limited liability company agreement may provide that any member or class or group of members associated with a series shall have no voting rights.

(f) A limited liability company agreement may grant to all or certain identified members or managers or a specified class or group of the members or managers associated with a series the right to vote separately or with all or any class or group of the members or managers associated with the series, on any matter. Voting by members or managers associated with a series may be on a per capita, number, financial interest, class, group or any other basis.

(g) Unless otherwise provided in a limited liability company agreement, the management of a series shall be vested in the members associated with such series in proportion to the then current percentage or other interest of members in the profits of the series owned by all of the members associated with such series, the decision of members owning more than 50 percent of the said percentage or other interest in the profits controlling; provided, however, that if a limited liability company agreement provides for the management of the series, in whole or in part, by a manager, the management of the series, to the extent so provided, shall be vested in the manager who shall be chosen in the manner provided in the limited liability company agreement. The manager of the series shall also hold the offices and have the responsibilities accorded to the manager as set forth in a limited liability company agreement. A series may have more than 1 manager. Subject to § 18-602of this title, a manager shall cease to be a manager with respect to a series as provided in a limited liability company agreement. Except as otherwise provided in a limited liability company agreement, any event under this chapter or in a limited liability company agreement that causes a manager to cease to be a manager with respect to a series shall not, in itself, cause such manager to cease to be a manager of the limited liability company or with respect to any other series thereof.

(h) Notwithstanding § 18-606 of this title, but subject to subsections (i) and (l) of this section, and unless otherwise provided in a limited liability company agreement, at the time a member associated with a series that has been established in accordance with subsection (b) of this section becomes entitled to receive a distribution with respect to such series, the member has the status of, and is entitled to all remedies available to, a creditor of the series, with respect to the distribution. A limited liability company agreement may provide for the establishment of a record date with respect to allocations and distributions with respect to a series.

(i) Notwithstanding § 18-607(a) of this title, a limited liability company may make a distribution with respect to a series that has been established in accordance with subsection (b) of this section. A limited liability company shall not make a distribution with respect to a series that has been established in accordance with subsection (b) of this section to a member to the extent that at the time of the distribution, after giving effect to the distribution, all liabilities of such series, other than liabilities to members on account of their limited liability company interests with respect to such series and liabilities for which the recourse of creditors is limited to specified property of such series, exceed the fair value of the assets associated with such series, except that the fair value of property of the series that is subject to a liability for which the recourse of creditors is limited shall be included in the assets associated with such series only to the extent that the fair value of that property exceeds that liability. For purposes of the immediately preceding sentence, the term "distribution" shall not include amounts constituting reasonable compensation for present or past services or reasonable payments made in the ordinary course of business pursuant to a bona fide retirement plan or other benefits program. A member who receives a distribution in violation of this subsection, and who knew at the time of the distribution that the distribution violated this subsection, shall be liable to a series for the amount of the distribution. A member who receives a distribution in violation of this subsection, and who did not know at the time of the distribution that the distribution violated this subsection, shall not be liable for the amount of the distribution. Subject to § 18-607(c) of this title, which shall apply to any distribution made with respect to a series under this subsection, this subsection shall not affect any obligation or liability of a member under an agreement or other applicable law for the amount of a distribution.

(j) Unless otherwise provided in the limited liability company agreement, a member shall cease to be associated with a series and to have the power to exercise any rights or powers of a member with respect to such series upon the assignment of all of the member's limited liability company interest with respect to such series. Except as otherwise provided in a limited liability company agreement, any event under this chapter or a limited liability company agreement that causes a member to cease to be associated with a series shall not, in itself, cause such member to cease to be associated with any other series or terminate the continued membership of a member in the limited liability company or cause the termination of the series, regardless of whether such member was the last remaining member associated with such series.

(k) Subject to § 18-801 of this title, except to the extent otherwise provided in the limited liability company agreement, a series may be terminated and its affairs wound up without causing the dissolution of the limited liability company. The termination of a series established in accordance with subsection (b) of this section shall not affect the limitation on liabilities of such series provided by subsection (b) of this section. A series is terminated and its affairs shall be wound up upon the dissolution of the limited liability company under § 18-801 of this title or otherwise upon the first to occur of the following:

(1) At the time specified in the limited liability company agreement;

(2) Upon the happening of events specified in the limited liability company agreement;

(3) Unless otherwise provided in the limited liability company agreement, upon the affirmative vote or written consent of members associated with such series who own more than 2/3 of the then-current percentage or other interest in the profits of the series of the limited liability company owned by all of the members associated with such series; or

(4) The termination of such series under subsection (m) of this section.

Unless otherwise provided in a limited liability company agreement, a limited liability company whose original certificate of formation was filed with the Secretary of State and effective on or prior to July 31, 2015, shall continue to be governed by paragraph (3) of this subsection as in effect on July 31, 2015.

(*l*) Notwithstanding § 18-803(a) of this title, unless otherwise provided in the limited liability company agreement, a manager associated with a series who has not wrongfully terminated the series or, if none, the members associated with the series or a person approved by the members associated with the series, in either case, by members who own more than 50 percent of the then current percentage or other interest in the profits of the series owned by all of the members associated with the series, may wind up the affairs of the series; but, if the series has been established in accordance with subsection (b) of this section, the Court of Chancery, upon cause shown, may wind up the affairs of the series upon application of any member or manager associated with the series, or the member's personal representative or assignee, and in connection therewith, may appoint a liquidating trustee. The persons winding up the affairs of a series may, in the name of the limited liability company and for and on behalf of the limited liability company and such series, take all actions with respect to the series as are permitted under § 18-803(b) of this title. The persons winding up the affairs of a series shall provide for the claims and obligations of the series and distribute the assets of the series as provided in § 18-804 of this title, which section shall apply to the winding up and distribution of assets of a series. Actions taken in accordance with this subsection shall not affect the liability of members and shall not impose liability on a liquidating trustee. Unless otherwise provided in a limited liability company agreement, a limited liability company whose original certificate of formation was filed with the Secretary of State and effective on or prior to July 31, 2015, shall continue to be governed by the first sentence of this subsection as in effect on July 31, 2015.

(m) On application by or for a member or manager associated with a series established in accordance with subsection (b) of this section, the Court of Chancery may decree termination of such series whenever it is not reasonably practicable to carry on the business of the series in conformity with a limited liability company agreement.

(n) If a foreign limited liability company that is registering to do business in the State of Delaware in accordance with § 18-902 of this title is governed by a limited liability company agreement that establishes or provides for the establishment of designated series of members, managers, limited liability company interests or assets having separate rights, powers or duties with respect to specified property or obligations of the foreign limited liability company or profits and losses associated with specified property or obligations, that fact shall be so stated on the application for registration as a foreign limited liability company. In addition, the foreign limited liability company shall state on such application whether the debts, liabilities and obligations incurred, contracted for or otherwise existing with respect to a particular series, if any, shall be enforceable against the assets of such series only, and not against the assets of the foreign limited liability company generally or any other series thereof, and whether any of the debts, liabilities, obligations and expenses incurred, contracted for or otherwise existing with respect to the foreign limited liability company generally or any other series thereof shall be enforceable against the assets of such series.

§ 18-216. Approval of Conversion of a Limited Liability Company

(a) Upon compliance with this section, a domestic limited liability company may convert to a corporation, a statutory trust, a business trust, an association, a real estate investment trust, a common-law trust or any other unincorporated business or entity, including a partnership (whether general (including a limited liability partnership) or limited (including a limited liability limited partnership)) or a foreign limited liability company.

(b) If the limited liability company agreement specifies the manner of authorizing a conversion of the limited liability company, the conversion shall be authorized as specified in the limited liability company agreement. If the limited liability company agreement does not specify the manner of authorizing a conversion of the limited liability company and does not prohibit a conversion of the limited liability company, the conversion shall be authorized in the same manner as is specified in the limited liability company agreement for authorizing a merger or consolidation that involves the limited liability company as a constituent party to the merger or consolidation. If the limited liability company agreement does not specify the manner of authorizing a conversion of the limited liability company or a merger or consolidation that involves the limited liability company as a constituent party and does not prohibit a conversion of the limited liability company, the conversion shall be authorized by the approval by members who own more than 50 percent of the then current percentage or other interest in the profits of the domestic limited liability company owned by all of the members. Unless otherwise provided in a limited liability company agreement, a limited liability company whose original certificate of formation was filed with the Secretary of State and effective on or prior to July 31, 2015, shall continue to be governed by the third sentence of this subsection as in effect on July 31, 2015.

(c) Unless otherwise agreed, the conversion of a domestic limited liability company to another entity or business form pursuant to this section shall not require such limited liability company to wind up its affairs under § 18-803 of this title or pay its liabilities and distribute its assets under § 18-

804 of this title, and the conversion shall not constitute a dissolution of such limited liability company. When a limited liability company has converted to another entity or business form pursuant to this section, for all purposes of the laws of the State of Delaware, the other entity or business form shall be deemed to be the same entity as the converting limited liability company and the conversion shall constitute a continuation of the existence of the limited liability company in the form of such other entity or business form.

(d) In connection with a conversion of a domestic limited liability company to another entity or business form pursuant to this section, rights or securities of or interests in the domestic limited liability company which is to be converted may be exchanged for or converted into cash, property, rights or securities of or interests in the entity or business form into which the domestic limited liability company is being converted or, in addition to or in lieu thereof, may be exchanged for or converted into cash, property, rights or securities of or interests in another entity or business form, may remain outstanding or may be canceled.

(e) If a limited liability company shall convert in accordance with this section to another entity or business form organized, formed or created under the laws of a jurisdiction other than the State of Delaware, a certificate of conversion to non-Delaware entity executed in accordance with § 18-204 of this title, shall be filed in the office of the Secretary of State in accordance with § 18-206 of this title...

Subchapter III. Members

§ 18-301. Admission of Members

(a) In connection with the formation of a limited liability company, a person is admitted as a member of the limited liability company upon the later to occur of:

(1) The formation of the limited liability company; or

(2) The time provided in and upon compliance with the limited liability company agreement or, if the limited liability company agreement does not so provide, when the person's admission is reflected in the records of the limited liability company.

(b) After the formation of a limited liability company, a person is admitted as a member of the limited liability company:

(1) In the case of a person who is not an assignee of a limited liability company interest, including a person acquiring a limited liability company interest directly from the limited liability company and a person to be admitted as a member of the limited liability company without acquiring a limited liability company interest in the limited liability company at the time provided in and upon compliance with the limited liability company agreement or, if the limited liability company agree-

ment does not so provide, upon the consent of all members and when the person's admission is reflected in the records of the limited liability company;

(2) In the case of an assignee of a limited liability company interest, as provided in § 18-704(a) of this title and at the time provided in and upon compliance with the limited liability company agreement or, if the limited liability company agreement does not so provide, when any such person's permitted admission is reflected in the records of the limited liability company; or

(3) In the case of a person being admitted as a member of a surviving or resulting limited liability company pursuant to a merger or consolidation approved in accordance with § 18-209(b) of this title, as provided in the limited liability company agreement of the surviving or resulting limited liability company or in the agreement of merger or consolidation or plan of merger, and in the event of any inconsistency, the terms of the agreement of merger or consolidation or plan of merger shall control; and in the case of a person being admitted as a member of a limited liability company pursuant to a merger or consolidation in which such limited liability company is not the surviving or resulting limited liability company in the merger or consolidation, as provided in the limited liability company agreement of such limited liability company.

. . .

(d) A person may be admitted to a limited liability company as a member of the limited liability company and may receive a limited liability company interest in the limited liability company without making a contribution or being obligated to make a contribution to the limited liability company. Unless otherwise provided in a limited liability company agreement, a person may be admitted to a limited liability company as a member of the limited liability company without acquiring a limited liability company interest in the limited liability company. Unless otherwise provided in a limited liability company agreement, a person may be admitted as the sole member of a limited liability company without making a contribution or being obligated to make a contribution to the limited liability company or without acquiring a limited liability company interest in the limited liability company.

(e) Unless otherwise provided in a limited liability company agreement or another agreement, a member shall have no preemptive right to subscribe to any additional issue of limited liability company interests or another interest in a limited liability company.

§ 18-302. Classes and Voting

(a) A limited liability company agreement may provide for classes or groups of members having such relative rights, powers and duties as the limited liability company agreement may provide, and may make provision for the future creation in the manner provided in the limited liability company agreement of additional classes or groups of members having such relative rights, powers and duties as may from time to time be established, including rights, powers and duties senior to existing classes and groups of members. A limited liability company agreement may provide for the taking of an action, including the amendment of the limited liability company agreement, without the vote or approval of any member or class or group of members, including an action to create under the provisions of the limited liability company agreement a class or group of limited liability company interests that was not previously outstanding. A limited liability company agreement may provide that any member or class or group of members shall have no voting rights.

(b) A limited liability company agreement may grant to all or certain identified members or a specified class or group of the members the right to vote separately or with all or any class or group of the members or managers, on any matter. Voting by members may be on a per capita, number, financial interest, class, group or any other basis.

(c) A limited liability company agreement may set forth provisions relating to notice of the time, place or purpose of any meeting at which any matter is to be voted on by any members, waiver of any such notice, action by consent without a meeting, the establishment of a record date, quorum requirements, voting in person or by proxy, or any other matter with respect to the exercise of any such right to vote.

(d) Unless otherwise provided in a limited liability company agreement, meetings of members may be held by means of conference telephone or other communications equipment by means of which all persons participating in the meeting can hear each other, and participation in a meeting pursuant to this subsection shall constitute presence in person at the meeting. Unless otherwise provided in a limited liability company agreement, on any matter that is to be voted on, consented to or approved by members, the members may take such action without a meeting, without prior notice and without a vote if consented to, in writing or by electronic transmission, by members having not less than the minimum number of votes that would be necessary to authorize or take such action at a meeting at which all members entitled to vote thereon were present and voted. Unless otherwise provided in a limited liability company agreement, if a person (whether or not then a member) consenting as a member to any matter provides that such consent will be effective at a future time (including a time determined upon the happening of an event), then such person shall be deemed to have consented as a member at such future time so long as such person is then a member. Unless otherwise provided in a limited liability company agreement, on any matter that is to be voted on by members, the members may vote in person or by proxy, and such proxy may be granted in writing, by means of electronic transmission or as otherwise permitted by applicable law. Unless otherwise provided in a limited liability company agreement, a consent transmitted by electronic transmission by a member or by a person or persons authorized to act for a member shall be deemed to be written and signed for purposes of this subsection. For purposes of this subsection, the term "electronic transmission" means any form of communication not directly involving the physical transmission of paper that creates a record that may be retained, retrieved and reviewed by a recipient thereof and that may be directly reproduced in paper form by such a recipient through an automated process.

(e) If a limited liability company agreement provides for the manner in which it may be amended, including by requiring the approval of a person who is not a party to the limited liability company agreement or the satisfaction of conditions, it may be amended only in that manner or as otherwise permitted by law, including as permitted by § 18-209(f) of this title (provided that the approval of any person may be waived by such person and that any such conditions may be waived by all persons for whose benefit such conditions were intended). Unless otherwise provided in a limited liability company agreement, a supermajority amendment provision shall only apply to provisions of the limited liability company agreement that are expressly included in the limited liability company agreement. As used in this section, "supermajority amendment provision" means any amendment provision set forth in a limited liability company agreement requiring that an amendment to a provision of the limited liability company agreement be adopted by no less than the vote or consent required to take action under such latter provision.

(f) If a limited liability company agreement does not provide for the manner in which it may be amended, the limited liability company agreement may be amended with the approval of all of the members or as otherwise permitted by law, including as permitted by § 18-209(f) of this title. This subsection shall only apply to a limited liability company whose original certificate of formation was filed with the Secretary of State on or after January 1, 2012.

§ 18-303. Liability to 3rd Parties

(a) Except as otherwise provided by this chapter, the debts, obligations and liabilities of a limited liability company, whether arising in contract, tort or otherwise, shall be solely the debts, obligations and liabilities of the limited liability company, and no member or manager of a limited liability company shall be obligated personally for any such debt, obligation or liability of the limited liability company solely by reason of being a member or acting as a manager of the limited liability company.

(b) Notwithstanding the provisions of subsection (a) of this section, under a limited liability company agreement or under another agreement, a member or manager may agree to be obligated personally for any or all of the debts, obligations and liabilities of the limited liability company.

§ 18-304. Events of Bankruptcy

A person ceases to be a member of a limited liability company upon the happening of any of the following events:

(1) Unless otherwise provided in a limited liability company agreement, or with the written consent of all members, a member:

a. Makes an assignment for the benefit of creditors;

b. Files a voluntary petition in bankruptcy;

c. Is adjudged a bankrupt or insolvent, or has entered against the member an order for relief, in any bankruptcy or insolvency proceeding;

d. Files a petition or answer seeking for the member any reorganization, arrangement, composition, readjustment, liquidation, dissolution or similar relief under any statute, law or regulation;

e. Files an answer or other pleading admitting or failing to contest the material allegations of a petition filed against the member in any proceeding of this nature;

f. Seeks, consents to or acquiesces in the appointment of a trustee, receiver or liquidator of the member or of all or any substantial part of the member's properties; or

(2) Unless otherwise provided in a limited liability company agreement, or with the written consent of all members, 120 days after the commencement of any proceeding against the member seeking reorganization, arrangement, composition, readjustment, liquidation, dissolution or similar relief under any statute, law or regulation, if the proceeding has not been dismissed, or if within 90 days after the appointment without the member's consent or acquiescence of a trustee, receiver or liquidator of the member or of all or any substantial part of the member's properties, the appointment is not vacated or stayed, or within 90 days after the expiration of any such stay, the appointment is not vacated.

§ 18-305. Access to and Confidentiality of Information; Records

(a) Each member of a limited liability company, in person or by attorney or other agent, has the right, subject to such reasonable standards (including standards governing what information and documents are to be furnished at what time and location and at whose expense) as may be set forth in a limited liability company agreement or otherwise established by the manager or, if there is no manager, then by the members, to obtain from the limited liability company from time to time upon reasonable demand for any purpose reasonably related to the member's interest as a member of the limited liability company:

(1) True and full information regarding the status of the business and financial condition of the limited liability company;

(2) Promptly after becoming available, a copy of the limited liability company's federal, state and local income tax returns for each year;

(3) A current list of the name and last known business, residence or mailing address of each member and manager;

(4) A copy of any written limited liability company agreement and certificate of formation and all amendments thereto, together with executed copies of any written powers of attorney pursuant to which the limited liability company agreement and any certificate and all amendments thereto have been executed;

(5) True and full information regarding the amount of cash and a description and statement of the agreed value of any other property or services contributed by each member and which each member has agreed to contribute in the future, and the date on which each became a member; and

(6) Other information regarding the affairs of the limited liability company as is just and reasonable.

(b) Each manager shall have the right to examine all of the information described in subsection (a) of this section for a purpose reasonably related to the position of manager.

(c) The manager of a limited liability company shall have the right to keep confidential from the members, for such period of time as the manager deems reasonable, any information which the manager reasonably believes to be in the nature of trade secrets or other information the disclosure of which the manager in good faith believes is not in the best interest of the limited liability company or could damage the limited liability company or its business or which the limited liability company is required by law or by agreement with a third party to keep confidential.

(d) A limited liability company may maintain its records in other than a written form if such form is capable of conversion into written form within a reasonable time.

(e) Any demand under this section shall be in writing and shall state the purpose of such demand. In every instance where an attorney or other agent shall be the person who seeks the right to obtain the information described in subsection (a) of this section, the demand shall be accompanied by a power of attorney or such other writing which authorizes the attorney or other agent to so act on behalf of the member.

(f) Any action to enforce any right arising under this section shall be brought in the Court of Chancery. If the limited liability company refuses to permit a member, or attorney or other agent acting for the member, to obtain or a manager to examine the information described in subsection (a) of this section or does not reply to the demand that has been made within 5 business days (or such shorter or longer period of time as is provided for in a limited liability company agreement but not longer than 30 business days) after the demand has been made, the demanding member or manager may apply to the Court of Chancery for an order to compel such disclosure. The Court of Chancery is hereby vested with exclusive jurisdiction to determine whether or not the person seeking such information is entitled to the information sought. The Court of Chancery may summarily order the limited liability company to permit the demanding member to obtain or manager to examine the information described in subsection (a) of this section and to make copies or abstracts therefrom, or the Court of Chancery may summarily order the limited liability company to furnish to the demanding member or manager the information described in subsection (a) of this section on the condition that the demanding member or manager first pay to the limited liability company the reasonable cost of obtaining and furnishing such information and on such other conditions as the Court of Chancery deems appropriate. When a demanding member seeks to obtain or a manager seeks to examine the information described in subsection (a) of this section, the demanding member or manager shall first establish:

(1) That the demanding member or manager has complied with the provisions of this section respecting the form and manner of making demand for obtaining or examining of such information, and

(2) That the information the demanding member or manager seeks is reasonably related to the member's interest as a member or the manager's position as a manager, as the case may be. The Court of Chancery may, in its discretion, prescribe any limitations or conditions with reference to the obtaining or examining of information, or award such other or further relief as the Court of Chancery may deem just and proper.

The Court of Chancery may order books, documents and records, pertinent extracts therefrom, or duly authenticated copies thereof, to be brought within the State of Delaware and kept in the State of Delaware upon such terms and conditions as the order may prescribe.

(g) The rights of a member or manager to obtain information as provided in this section may be restricted in an original limited liability company agreement or in any subsequent amendment approved or adopted by all of the members or in compliance with any applicable requirements of the limited liability company agreement. The provisions of this subsection shall not be construed to limit the ability to impose restrictions on the rights of a member or manager to obtain information by any other means permitted under this chapter.

(h) A limited liability company shall maintain a current record that identifies the name and last known business, residence or mailing address of each member and manager.

§ 18-306. Remedies for Breach of Limited Liability Company Agreement by Member

A limited liability company agreement may provide that:

(1) A member who fails to perform in accordance with, or to comply with the terms and conditions of, the limited liability company

agreement shall be subject to specified penalties or specified consequences; and

(2) At the time or upon the happening of events specified in the limited liability company agreement, a member shall be subject to specified penalties or specified consequences.

Such specified penalties or specified consequences may include and take the form of any penalty or consequence set forth in § 18-502(c) of this title.

Subchapter IV. Managers

§ 18-401. Admission of Managers

A person may be named or designated as a manager of the limited liability company as provided in § 18-101(10) of this title.

§ 18-402. Management of Limited Liability Company

Unless otherwise provided in a limited liability company agreement, the management of a limited liability company shall be vested in its members in proportion to the then current percentage or other interest of members in the profits of the limited liability company owned by all of the members, the decision of members owning more than 50 percent of the said percentage or other interest in the profits controlling; provided however, that if a limited liability company agreement provides for the management, in whole or in part, of a limited liability company by a manager, the management of the limited liability company, to the extent so provided, shall be vested in the manager who shall be chosen in the manner provided in the limited liability company agreement. The manager shall also hold the offices and have the responsibilities accorded to the manager by or in the manner provided in a limited liability company agreement. Subject to § 18-602 of this title, a manager shall cease to be a manager as provided in a limited liability company agreement. A limited liability company may have more than 1 manager. Unless otherwise provided in a limited liability company agreement, each member and manager has the authority to bind the limited liability company.

§ 18-403. Contributions by a Manager

A manager of a limited liability company may make contributions to the limited liability company and share in the profits and losses of, and in distributions from, the limited liability company as a member. A person who is both a manager and a member has the rights and powers, and is subject to the restrictions and liabilities, of a manager and, except as provided in a limited liability company agreement, also has the rights and powers, and is subject to the restrictions and liabilities, of a member to the extent of the manager's participation in the limited liability company as a member.

§ 18-404. Classes and Voting

(a) A limited liability company agreement may provide for classes or groups of managers having such relative rights, powers and duties as the limited liability company agreement may provide, and may make provision for the future creation in the manner provided in the limited liability company agreement of additional classes or groups of managers having such relative rights, powers and duties as may from time to time be established, including rights, powers and duties senior to existing classes and groups of managers. A limited liability company agreement may provide for the taking of an action, including the amendment of the limited liability company agreement, without the vote or approval of any manager or class or group of managers, including an action to create under the provisions of the limited liability company agreement a class or group of limited liability company interests that was not previously outstanding.

(b) A limited liability company agreement may grant to all or certain identified managers or a specified class or group of the managers the right to vote, separately or with all or any class or group of managers or members, on any matter. Voting by managers may be on a per capita, number, financial interest, class, group or any other basis.

(c) A limited liability company agreement may set forth provisions relating to notice of the time, place or purpose of any meeting at which any matter is to be voted on by any manager or class or group of managers, waiver of any such notice, action by consent without a meeting, the establishment of a record date, quorum requirements, voting in person or by proxy, or any other matter with respect to the exercise of any such right to vote.

(d) Unless otherwise provided in a limited liability company agreement, meetings of managers may be held by means of conference telephone or other communications equipment by means of which all persons participating in the meeting can hear each other, and participation in a meeting pursuant to this subsection shall constitute presence in person at the meeting. Unless otherwise provided in a limited liability company agreement, on any matter that is to be voted on, consented to or approved by managers, the managers may take such action without a meeting, without prior notice and without a vote if consented to, in writing or by electronic transmission, by managers having not less than the minimum number of votes that would be necessary to authorize or take such action at a meeting at which all managers entitled to vote thereon were present and voted. Unless otherwise provided in a limited liability company agreement, if a person (whether or not then a manager) consenting as a manager to any matter provides that such consent will be effective at a future time (including a time determined upon the happening of an event), then such person shall be deemed to have consented as a manager at such future time so long as such person is then a manager. Unless otherwise provided in a limited liability company agreement, on any matter that is to be voted on by managers, the managers may vote in person or by proxy, and such proxy may be granted in writing, by means of electronic transmission or as otherwise permitted by applicable law. Unless otherwise provided in a limited liability company agreement, a consent transmitted by electronic transmission by a manager or by a person or persons authorized to act for a manager shall be deemed to be written and signed for purposes of this subsection. For purposes of this subsection, the term "electronic transmission" means any form of communication not directly involving the physical transmission of paper that creates a record that may be retained, retrieved and reviewed by a recipient thereof and that may be directly reproduced in paper form by such a recipient through an automated process.

§ 18-405. Remedies for Breach of Limited Liability Company Agreement by Manager

A limited liability company agreement may provide that:

(1) A manager who fails to perform in accordance with, or to comply with the terms and conditions of, the limited liability company agreement shall be subject to specified penalties or specified consequences; and

(2) At the time or upon the happening of events specified in the limited liability company agreement, a manager shall be subject to specified penalties or specified consequences.

§ 18-406. Reliance on Reports and Information by Member or Manager

A member, manager or liquidating trustee of a limited liability company shall be fully protected in relying in good faith upon the records of the limited liability company and upon information, opinions, reports or statements presented by another manager, member or liquidating trustee, an officer or employee of the limited liability company, or committees of the limited liability company, members or managers, or by any other person as to matters the member, manager or liquidating trustees reasonably believes are within such other person's professional or expert competence, including information, opinions, reports or statements as to the value and amount of the assets, liabilities, profits or losses of the limited liability company, or the value and amount of assets or reserves or contracts, agreements or other undertakings that would be sufficient to pay claims and obligations of the limited liability company or to make reasonable provision to pay such claims and obligations, or any other facts pertinent to the existence and amount of assets from which distributions to members or creditors might properly be paid.

§ 18-407. Delegation of Rights and Powers to Manage

Unless otherwise provided in the limited liability company agreement, a member or manager of a limited liability company has the power and authority to delegate to 1 or more other persons the member's or manager's, as the case may be, rights and powers to manage and control the business and affairs of the limited liability company, including to delegate to agents, officers and employees of a member or manager or the limited liability company, and to delegate by a management agreement or another agreement with, or otherwise to, other persons. Unless otherwise provided in the limited liability company agreement, such delegation by a member or manager shall be irrevocable if it states that it is irrevocable. Unless otherwise provided in the limited liability company agreement, such delegation by a member or manager of a limited liability company shall not cause the member or manager to cease to be a member or manager, as the case may be, of the limited liability company or cause the person to whom any such rights and powers have been delegated to be a member or manager, as the case may be, of the limited liability company.

Subchapter V. Finance

§ 18-501. Form of Contribution

The contribution of a member to a limited liability company may be in cash, property or services rendered, or a promissory note or other obligation to contribute cash or property or to perform services.

§ 18-502. Liability for Contribution

(a) Except as provided in a limited liability company agreement, a member is obligated to a limited liability company to perform any promise to contribute cash or property or to perform services, even if the member is unable to perform because of death, disability or any other reason. If a member does not make the required contribution of property or services, the member is obligated at the option of the limited liability company to contribute cash equal to that portion of the agreed value (as stated in the records of the limited liability company) of the contribution that has not been made. The foregoing option shall be in addition to, and not in lieu of, any other rights, including the right to specific performance, that the limited liability company may have against such member under the limited liability company agreement or applicable law.

(b) Unless otherwise provided in a limited liability company agreement, the obligation of a member to make a contribution or return money or other property paid or distributed in violation of this chapter may be compromised only by consent of all the members. Notwithstanding the compromise, a creditor of a limited liability company who extends credit, after the entering into of a limited liability company agreement or an amendment thereto which, in either case, reflects the obligation, and before the amendment thereof to reflect the compromise, may enforce the original obligation to the extent that, in extending credit, the creditor reasonably relied on the obligation of a member to make a contribution or return. A conditional obligation of a member to make a contribution or return money or other property to a limited liability company may not be enforced unless the conditions of the obligation have been satisfied or waived as to or by such member. Conditional obligations include contributions payable upon a discretionary call of a limited liability company prior to the time the call occurs.

(c) A limited liability company agreement may provide that the interest of any member who fails to make any contribution that the member is obligated to make shall be subject to specified penalties for, or specified consequences of, such failure. Such penalty or consequence may take the form of reducing or eliminating the defaulting member's proportionate interest in a limited liability company, subordinating the member's limited liability company interest to that of nondefaulting members, a forced sale of that limited liability company interest, forfeiture of the defaulting member's limited liability company interest, the lending by other members of the amount necessary to meet the defaulting member's commitment, a fixing of the value of the defaulting member's limited liability company interest by appraisal or by formula and redemption or sale of the limited liability company interest at such value, or other penalty or consequence.

§ 18-503. Allocation of Profits and Losses

The profits and losses of a limited liability company shall be allocated among the members, and among classes or groups of members, in the manner provided in a limited liability company agreement. If the limited liability company agreement does not so provide, profits and losses shall be allocated on the basis of the agreed value (as stated in the records of the limited liability company) of the contributions made by each member to the extent they have been received by the limited liability company and have not been returned.

§ 18-504. Allocation of Distributions

Distributions of cash or other assets of a limited liability company shall be allocated among the members, and among classes or groups of members, in the manner provided in a limited liability company agreement. If the limited liability company agreement does not so provide, distributions shall be made on the basis of the agreed value (as stated in the records of the limited liability company) of the contributions made by each member to the extent they have been received by the limited liability company and have not been returned.

§ 18-505. Defense of Usury Not Available

No obligation of a member or manager of a limited liability company to the limited liability company, or to a member or manager of the limited liability company, arising under the limited liability company agreement or a separate agreement or writing, and no note, instrument or other writing evidencing any such obligation of a member or manager, shall be subject to the defense of usury, and no member or manager shall interpose the defense of usury with respect to any such obligation in any action.

Subchapter VI. Distributions and Resignation

§ 18-601. Interim Distributions

Except as provided in this subchapter, to the extent and at the times or upon the happening of the events specified in a limited liability company agreement, a member is entitled to receive from a limited liability company distributions before the member's resignation from the limited liability company and before the dissolution and winding up thereof.

§ 18-602. Resignation of Manager

A manager may resign as a manager of a limited liability company at the time or upon the happening of events specified in a limited liability company agreement and in accordance with the limited liability company agreement. A limited liability company agreement may provide that a manager shall not have the right to resign as a manager of a limited liability company. Notwithstanding that a limited liability company agreement provides that a manager does not have the right to resign as a manager of a limited liability company, a manager may resign as a manager of a limited liability company at any time by giving written notice to the members and other managers. If the resignation of a manager violates a limited liability company agreement, in addition to any remedies otherwise available under applicable law, a limited liability company may recover from the resigning manager damages for breach of the limited liability company agreement and offset the damages against the amount otherwise distributable to the resigning manager.

§ 18-603. Resignation of Member

A member may resign from a limited liability company only at the time or upon the happening of events specified in a limited liability company agreement and in accordance with the limited liability company agreement. Notwithstanding anything to the contrary under applicable law, unless a limited liability company agreement provides otherwise, a member may not resign from a limited liability company prior to the dissolution and winding up of the limited liability company. Notwithstanding anything to the contrary under applicable law, a limited liability company agreement may provide that a limited liability company interest may not be assigned prior to the dissolution and winding up of the limited liability company.

Unless otherwise provided in a limited liability company agreement, a limited liability company whose original certificate of formation was filed with the Secretary of State and effective on or prior to July 31, 1996, shall continue to be governed by this section as in effect on July 31, 1996.

§ 18-604. Distribution Upon Resignation

Except as provided in this subchapter, upon resignation any resigning member is entitled to receive any distribution to which such member is entitled under a limited liability company agreement and, if not otherwise provided in a limited liability company agreement, such member is entitled to receive, within a reasonable time after resignation, the fair value of such member's limited liability company interest as of the date of resignation based upon such member's right to share in distributions from the limited liability company.

§ 18-605. Distribution in Kind

Except as provided in a limited liability company agreement, a member, regardless of the nature of the member's contribution, has no right to demand and receive any distribution from a limited liability company in any form other than cash. Except as provided in a limited liability company agreement, a member may not be compelled to accept a distribution of any asset in kind from a limited liability company to the extent that the percentage of the asset distributed exceeds a percentage of that asset which is equal to the percentage in which the member shares in distributions from the limited liability company. Except as provided in the limited liability company agreement, a member may be compelled to accept a distribution of any asset in kind from a limited liability company to the extent that the percentage of the asset distributed is equal to a percentage of that asset which is equal to the percentage in which the member shares in distributions from the limited liability company.

§ 18-606. Right to Distribution

Subject to §§ 18-607 and 18-804 of this title, and unless otherwise provided in a limited liability company agreement, at the time a member becomes entitled to receive a distribution, the member has the status of, and is entitled to all remedies available to, a creditor of a limited liability company with respect to the distribution. A limited liability company agreement may provide for the establishment of a record date with respect to allocations and distributions by a limited liability company.

§ 18-607. Limitations on Distribution

(a) A limited liability company shall not make a distribution to a member to the extent that at the time of the distribution, after giving effect to the distribution, all liabilities of the limited liability company, other than liabilities to members on account of their limited liability company interests and liabilities for which the recourse of creditors is limited to specified property of the limited liability company, exceed the fair value of the assets of the limited liability company, except that the fair value of property that is subject to a liability for which the recourse of creditors is limited shall be included in the assets of the limited liability company only to the extent that the fair value of that property exceeds that liability. For purposes of this subsection (a), the term "distribution" shall not include amounts constituting reasonable compensation for present or past services or reasonable payments made in the ordinary course of business pursuant to a bona fide retirement plan or other benefits program.

(b) A member who receives a distribution in violation of subsection (a) of this section, and who knew at the time of the distribution that the distribution violated subsection (a) of this section, shall be liable to a limited liability company for the amount of the distribution. A member who receives a distribution in violation of subsection (a) of this section, and who did not know at the time of the distribution that the distribution violated subsection (a) of this section, shall not be liable for the amount of the distribution. Subject to subsection (c) of this section, this subsection shall not affect any obligation or liability of a member under an agreement or other applicable law for the amount of a distribution.

(c) Unless otherwise agreed, a member who receives a distribution from a limited liability company shall have no liability under this chapter or other applicable law for the amount of the distribution after the expiration of 3 years from the date of the distribution unless an action to recover the distribution from such member is commenced prior to the expiration of the said 3-year period and an adjudication of liability against such member is made in the said action.

Subchapter VII. Assignment of Limited Liability Company Interests

§ 18-701. Nature of Limited Liability Company Interest

A limited liability company interest is personal property. A member has no interest in specific limited liability company property.

§ 18-702. Assignment of Limited Liability Company Interest

(a) A limited liability company interest is assignable in whole or in part except as provided in a limited liability company agreement. The assignee of a member's limited liability company interest shall have no right to participate in the management of the business and affairs of a limited liability company except as provided in a limited liability company agreement or, unless otherwise provided in the limited liability company agreement, upon the affirmative vote or written consent of all of the members of the limited liability company.

(b) Unless otherwise provided in a limited liability company agreement:

(1) An assignment of a limited liability company interest does not entitle the assignee to become or to exercise any rights or powers of a member;

(2) An assignment of a limited liability company interest entitles the assignee to share in such profits and losses, to receive such distribution or distributions, and to receive such allocation of income, gain, loss, deduction, or credit or similar item to which the assignor was entitled, to the extent assigned; and

(3) A member ceases to be a member and to have the power to exercise any rights or powers of a member upon assignment of all of

the member's limited liability company interest. Unless otherwise provided in a limited liability company agreement, the pledge of, or granting of a security interest, lien or other encumbrance in or against, any or all of the limited liability company interest of a member shall not cause the member to cease to be a member or to have the power to exercise any rights or powers of a member.

(c) Unless otherwise provided in a limited liability company agreement, a member's interest in a limited liability company may be evidenced by a certificate of limited liability company interest issued by the limited liability company. A limited liability company agreement may provide for the assignment or transfer of any limited liability company interest represented by such a certificate and make other provisions with respect to such certificates. A limited liability company shall not have the power to issue a certificate of limited liability company interest in bearer form.

(d) Unless otherwise provided in a limited liability company agreement and except to the extent assumed by agreement, until an assignee of a limited liability company interest becomes a member, the assignee shall have no liability as a member solely as a result of the assignment.

(e) Unless otherwise provided in the limited liability company agreement, a limited liability company may acquire, by purchase, redemption or otherwise, any limited liability company interest or other interest of a member or manager in the limited liability company. Unless otherwise provided in the limited liability company agreement, any such interest so acquired by the limited liability company shall be deemed canceled.

§ 18-703. Member's Limited Liability Company Interest Subject to Charging Order

(a) On application by a judgment creditor of a member or of a member's assignee, a court having jurisdiction may charge the limited liability company interest of the judgment debtor to satisfy the judgment. To the extent so charged, the judgment creditor has only the right to receive any distribution or distributions to which the judgment debtor would otherwise have been entitled in respect of such limited liability company interest.

(b) A charging order constitutes a lien on the judgment debtor's limited liability company interest.

(c) This chapter does not deprive a member or member's assignee of a right under exemption laws with respect to the judgment debtor's limited liability company interest.

(d) The entry of a charging order is the exclusive remedy by which a judgment creditor of a member or a member's assignee may satisfy a judgment out of the judgment debtor's limited liability company interest and attachment, garnishment, foreclosure or other legal or equitable remedies are not available to the judgment creditor, whether the limited liability company has 1 member or more than 1 member.

(e) No creditor of a member or of a member's assignee shall have any right to obtain possession of, or otherwise exercise legal or equitable remedies with respect to, the property of the limited liability company.

(f) The Court of Chancery shall have jurisdiction to hear and determine any matter relating to any such charging order.

. . .

§ 18-704. Right of Assignee to Become Member

(a) An assignee of a limited liability company interest may become a member:

(1) As provided in the limited liability company agreement; or

(2) Unless otherwise provided in the limited liability company agreement, upon the affirmative vote or written consent of all of the members of the limited liability company.

(b) An assignee who has become a member has, to the extent assigned, the rights and powers, and is subject to the restrictions and liabilities, of a member under a limited liability company agreement and this chapter. Notwithstanding the foregoing, unless otherwise provided in a limited liability company agreement, an assignee who becomes a member is liable for the obligations of the assignor to make contributions as provided in § 18-502 of this title, but shall not be liable for the obligations of the assignor under subchapter VI of this chapter. However, the assignee is not obligated for liabilities, including the obligations of the assignor to make contributions as provided in § 18-502 of this title, unknown to the assignee at the time the assignee became a member and which could not be ascertained from a limited liability company agreement.

(c) Whether or not an assignee of a limited liability company interest becomes a member, the assignor is not released from liability to a limited liability company under subchapters V and VI of this chapter.

§ 18-705. Powers of Estate of Deceased or Incompetent Member

If a member who is an individual dies or a court of competent jurisdiction adjudges the member to be incompetent to manage the member's person or property, the member's personal representative may exercise all of the member's rights for the purpose of settling the member's estate or administering the member's property, including any power under a limited liability company agreement of an assignee to become a member. If a member is a corporation, trust or other entity and is dissolved or terminated, the powers of that member may be exercised by its personal representative.

Subchapter VIII. Dissolution

§ 18-801. Dissolution

(a) A limited liability company is dissolved and its affairs shall be wound up upon the first to occur of the following:

(1) At the time specified in a limited liability company agreement, but if no such time is set forth in the limited liability company agreement, then the limited liability company shall have a perpetual existence;

(2) Upon the happening of events specified in a limited liability company agreement;

(3) Unless otherwise provided in a limited liability company agreement, upon the affirmative vote or written consent of members who own more than 2/3 of the then-current percentage or other interest in the profits of the limited liability company owned by all of the members;

(4) At any time there are no members; provided, that the limited liability company is not dissolved and is not required to be wound up if:

a. Unless otherwise provided in a limited liability company agreement, within 90 days or such other period as is provided for in the limited liability company agreement after the occurrence of the event that terminated the continued membership of the last remaining member, the personal representative of the last remaining member agrees in writing to continue the limited liability company and to the admission of the personal representative of such member or its nominee or designee to the limited liability company as a member, effective as of the occurrence of the event that terminated the continued membership of the last remaining member; provided, that a limited liability company agreement may provide that the personal representative of the last remaining member shall be obligated to agree in writing to continue the limited liability company and to the admission of the personal representative of such member or its nominee or designee to the limited liability company as a member, effective as of the occurrence of the event that terminated the continued membership of the last remaining member, or

b. A member is admitted to the limited liability company in the manner provided for in the limited liability company agreement, effective as of the occurrence of the event that terminated the continued membership of the last remaining member, within 90 days or such other period as is provided for in the limited liability company agreement after the occurrence of the event that terminated the continued membership of the last remaining member, pursuant to a provision of the limited liability company agreement that specifically provides for the admission of a member to the limited liability company after there is no longer a remaining member of the limited liability company.

(5) The entry of a decree of judicial dissolution under § 18-802 of this title.

Unless otherwise provided in a limited liability company agreement, a limited liability company whose original certificate of formation was filed with the Secretary of State and effective on or prior to July 31, 2015, shall continue to be governed by paragraph (a)(3) of this section as in effect on July 31, 2015.

(b) Unless otherwise provided in a limited liability company agreement, the death, retirement, resignation, expulsion, bankruptcy or dissolution of any member or the occurrence of any other event that terminates the continued membership of any member shall not cause the limited liability company to be dissolved or its affairs to be wound up, and upon the occurrence of any such event, the limited liability company shall be continued without dissolution.

§ 18-802. Judicial Dissolution

On application by or for a member or manager the Court of Chancery may decree dissolution of a limited liability company whenever it is not reasonably practicable to carry on the business in conformity with a limited liability company agreement.

§ 18-803. Winding Up

(a) Unless otherwise provided in a limited liability company agreement, a manager who has not wrongfully dissolved a limited liability company or, if none, the members or a person approved by the members, in either case, by members who own more than 50 percent of the then current percentage or other interest in the profits of the limited liability company owned by all of the members, may wind up the limited liability company's affairs; but the Court of Chancery, upon cause shown, may wind up the limited liability company's affairs upon application of any member or manager, or the member's personal representative or assignee, and in connection therewith, may appoint a liquidating trustee. Unless otherwise provided in a limited liability company agreement, a limited liability company whose original certificate of formation was filed with the Secretary of State and effective on or prior to July 31, 2015, shall continue to be governed by this subsection as in effect on July 31, 2015.

(b) Upon dissolution of a limited liability company and until the filing of a certificate of cancellation as provided in § 18-203 of this title, the persons winding up the limited liability company's affairs may, in the name of, and for and on behalf of, the limited liability company, prosecute and defend suits, whether civil, criminal or administrative, gradually settle and close the limited liability company's business, dispose of and convey the limited liability company's property, discharge or make reasonable provision for the limited liability company's liabilities, and distribute to the members any remaining assets of the limited liability company, all without affecting the liability of members and managers and without imposing liability on a liquidating trustee.

§ 18-804. Distribution of Assets

(a) Upon the winding up of a limited liability company, the assets shall be distributed as follows:

(1) To creditors, including members and managers who are creditors, to the extent otherwise permitted by law, in satisfaction of liabilities of the limited liability company (whether by payment or the making of reasonable provision for payment thereof) other than liabilities for which reasonable provision for payment has been made and liabilities for distributions to members and former members under § 18-601 or § 18-604 of this title;

(2) Unless otherwise provided in a limited liability company agreement, to members and former members in satisfaction of liabilities for distributions under § 18-601 or § 18-604 of this title; and

(3) Unless otherwise provided in a limited liability company agreement, to members first for the return of their contributions and second respecting their limited liability company interests, in the proportions in which the members share in distributions.

(b) A limited liability company which has dissolved:

(1) Shall pay or make reasonable provision to pay all claims and obligations, including all contingent, conditional or unmatured contractual claims, known to the limited liability company;

(2) Shall make such provision as will be reasonably likely to be sufficient to provide compensation for any claim against the limited liability company which is the subject of a pending action, suit or proceeding to which the limited liability company is a party; and

(3) Shall make such provision as will be reasonably likely to be sufficient to provide compensation for claims that have not been made known to the limited liability company or that have not arisen but that, based on facts known to the limited liability company, are likely to arise or to become known to the limited liability company within 10 years after the date of dissolution.

If there are sufficient assets, such claims and obligations shall be paid in full and any such provision for payment made shall be made in full. If there are insufficient assets, such claims and obligations shall be paid or provided for according to their priority and, among claims of equal priority, ratably to the extent of assets available therefor. Unless otherwise provided in the limited liability company agreement, any remaining assets shall be distributed as provided in this chapter. Any liquidating trustee winding up a limited liability company's affairs who has complied with this section shall not be personally liable to the claimants of the dissolved limited liability company by reason of such person's actions in winding up the limited liability company.

(c) A member who receives a distribution in violation of subsection (a) of this section, and who knew at the time of the distribution that the distribution violated subsection (a) of this section, shall be liable to the limited liability company for the amount of the distribution. For purposes of the immediately preceding sentence, the term "distribution" shall not include amounts constituting reasonable compensation for present or past services or reasonable payments made in the ordinary course of business pursuant to a bona fide retirement plan or other benefits program. A member who receives a distribution in violation of subsection (a) of this section, and who did not know at the time of the distribution that the distribution violated subsection (a) of this section, shall not be liable for the amount of the distribution. Subject to subsection (d) of this section, this subsection shall not affect any obligation or liability of a member under an agreement or other applicable law for the amount of a distribution.

(d) Unless otherwise agreed, a member who receives a distribution from a limited liability company to which this section applies shall have no liability under this chapter or other applicable law for the amount of the distribution after the expiration of 3 years from the date of the distribution unless an action to recover the distribution from such member is commenced prior to the expiration of the said 3-year period and an adjudication of liability against such member is made in the said action.

(e) Section 18-607 of this title shall not apply to a distribution to which this section applies.

§ 18-805. Trustees or Receivers for Limited Liability Companies; Appointment; Powers; Duties

When the certificate of formation of any limited liability company formed under this chapter shall be canceled by the filing of a certificate of cancellation pursuant to § 18-203 of this title, the Court of Chancery, on application of any creditor, member or manager of the limited liability company, or any other person who shows good cause therefor, at any time, may either appoint 1 or more of the managers of the limited liability company to be trustees, or appoint 1 or more persons to be receivers, of and for the limited liability company, to take charge of the limited liability company's property, and to collect the debts and property due and belonging to the limited liability company, with the power to prosecute and defend, in the name of the limited liability company, or otherwise, all such suits as may be necessary or proper for the purposes aforesaid, and to appoint an agent or agents under them, and to do all other acts which might be done by the limited liability company, if in being, that may be necessary for the final settlement of the unfinished business of the limited liability company. The powers of the trustees or receivers may be continued as long as the Court of Chancery shall think necessary for the purposes aforesaid.

§ 18-806. Revocation of Dissolution

If a limited liability company agreement provides the manner in which a dissolution may be revoked, it may be revoked in that manner and, unless a limited liability company agreement prohibits revocation of dissolution, then notwithstanding the occurrence of an event set forth in § 18-801(a)(1), (2), (3) or (4) of this title, the limited liability company shall not be dissolved and its affairs shall not be wound up if, prior to the filing of a certificate of cancellation in the office of the Secretary of State, the limited liability company is continued, effective as of the occurrence of such event:

(1) In the case of dissolution effected by the affirmative vote or written consent of the members or other persons, pursuant to such affirmative vote or written consent (and the approval of any members or other persons whose approval is required under the limited liability company agreement to revoke a dissolution contemplated by this paragraph);

(2) In the case of dissolution under § 18-801(a)(1) or (2) of this title (other than a dissolution effected by the affirmative vote or written consent of the members or other persons or the occurrence of an event that causes the last remaining member to cease to be a member), pursuant to such affirmative vote or written consent that, pursuant to the terms of the limited liability company agreement, is required to amend the provision of the limited liability company agreement effecting such dissolution (and the approval of any members or other persons whose approval is required under the limited liability company agreement to revoke a dissolution contemplated by this paragraph); and

(3) In the case of dissolution effected by the occurrence of an event that causes the last remaining member to cease to be a member, pursuant to the affirmative vote or written consent of the personal representative of the last remaining member of the limited liability company or the assignee of all of the limited liability company interests in the limited liability company (and the approval of any other persons whose approval is required under the limited liability company agreement to revoke a dissolution contemplated by this paragraph).

If there is no remaining member of the limited liability company and the personal representative of the last remaining member or the assignee of all of the limited liability company interests in the limited liability company votes in favor of or consents to the continuation of the limited liability company, such personal representative or such assignee, as applicable, shall be required to agree in writing to the admission of a nominee or designee as a member, effective as of the occurrence of the event that terminated the continued membership of the last remaining member. The provisions of this section shall not be construed to limit the accomplishment of a revocation of dissolution by other means permitted by law. . . .

Subchapter X. Derivative Actions

§ 18-1001. Right to Bring Action

A member or an assignee of a limited liability company interest may bring an action in the Court of Chancery in the right of a limited liability company to recover a judgment in its favor if managers or members with authority to do so have refused to bring the action or if an effort to cause those managers or members to bring the action is not likely to succeed.

§ 18-1002. Proper Plaintiff

In a derivative action, the plaintiff must be a member or an assignee of a limited liability company interest at the time of bringing the action and:

(1) At the time of the transaction of which the plaintiff complains; or

(2) The plaintiff's status as a member or an assignee of a limited liability company interest had devolved upon the plaintiff by operation of law or pursuant to the terms of a limited liability company agreement from a person who was a member or an assignee of a limited liability company interest at the time of the transaction.

§ 18-1003. Complaint

In a derivative action, the complaint shall set forth with particularity the effort, if any, of the plaintiff to secure initiation of the action by a manager or member or the reasons for not making the effort.

§ 18-1004. Expenses

If a derivative action is successful, in whole or in part, as a result of a judgment, compromise or settlement of any such action, the court may award the plaintiff reasonable expenses, including reasonable attorney's fees, from any recovery in any such action or from a limited liability company.

Subchapter XI. Miscellaneous

§ 18-1101. Construction and Application of Chapter and Limited Liability Company Agreement

(a) The rule that statutes in derogation of the common law are to be strictly construed shall have no application to this chapter.

(b) It is the policy of this chapter to give the maximum effect to the principle of freedom of contract and to the enforceability of limited liability company agreements.

(c) To the extent that, at law or in equity, a member or manager or other person has duties (including fiduciary duties) to a limited liability company or to another member or manager or to another person that is a party to or is otherwise bound by a limited liability company agreement, the member's or manager's or other person's duties may be expanded or restricted or eliminated by provisions in the limited liability company agreement; provided, that the limited liability company agreement may not eliminate the implied contractual covenant of good faith and fair dealing.

(d) Unless otherwise provided in a limited liability company agreement, a member or manager or other person shall not be liable to a limited liability company or to another member or manager or to another person that is a party to or is otherwise bound by a limited liability company agreement for breach of fiduciary duty for the member's or manager's or other person's good faith reliance on the provisions of the limited liability company agreement.

(e) A limited liability company agreement may provide for the limitation or elimination of any and all liabilities for breach of contract and breach of duties (including fiduciary duties) of a member, manager or other person to a limited liability company or to another member or manager or to another person that is a party to or is otherwise bound by a limited liability company agreement; provided, that a limited liability company agreement may not limit or eliminate liability for any act or omission that constitutes a bad faith violation of the implied contractual covenant of good faith and fair dealing.

(f) Unless the context otherwise requires, as used herein, the singular shall include the plural and the plural may refer to only the singular. The use of any gender shall be applicable to all genders. The captions contained herein are for purposes of convenience only and shall not control or affect the construction of this chapter.

(g) Sections 9-406 and 9-408 of this title do not apply to any interest in a limited liability company, including all rights, powers and interests arising under a limited liability company agreement or this chapter. This provision prevails over §§ 9-406 and 9-408 of this title.

(h) Action validly taken pursuant to 1 provision of this chapter shall not be deemed invalid solely because it is identical or similar in substance to an action that could have been taken pursuant to some other provision of this chapter but fails to satisfy 1 or more requirements prescribed by such other provision.

(i) A limited liability company agreement that provides for the application of Delaware law shall be governed by and construed under the laws of the State of Delaware in accordance with its terms.

(j) The provisions of this chapter shall apply whether a limited liability company has 1 member or more than 1 member.

§ 18-1104. Cases Not Provided for in This Chapter

In any case not provided for in this chapter, the rules of law and equity, including the law merchant, shall govern.

DELAWARE GENERAL CORPORATION LAW

Subchapter I. Formation

§ 101. Incorporators; How Corporation Formed; Purposes

(a) Any person, partnership, association or corporation, singly or jointly with others, and without regard to such person's or entity's residence, domicile or state of incorporation, may incorporate or organize a corporation under this chapter by filing with the Division of Corporations in the Department of State a certificate of incorporation which shall be executed, acknowledged and filed in accordance with § 103 of this title.

(b) A corporation may be incorporated or organized under this chapter to conduct or promote any lawful business or purposes, except as may otherwise be provided by the Constitution or other law of this State.

(c) Corporations for constructing, maintaining and operating public utilities, whether in or outside of this State, may be organized under this chapter, but corporations for constructing, maintaining and operating public utilities within this State shall be subject to, in addition to this chapter, the special provisions and requirements of Title 26 applicable to such corporations.

§ 102. Contents of Certificate of Incorporation

(a) The certificate of incorporation shall set forth:

(1) The name of the corporation, which (i) shall contain 1 of the words "association," "company," "corporation," "club," "foundation," "fund," "incorporated," "institute," "society," "union," "syndicate," or "limited," (or abbreviations thereof, with or without punctuation), or words (or abbreviations thereof, with or without punctuation) of like import of foreign countries or jurisdictions (provided they are written in roman characters or letters); provided, however, that the Division of Corporations in the Department of State may waive such requirement (unless it determines that such name is, or might otherwise appear to be, that of a natural person) if such corporation executes, acknowledges and files with the Secretary of State in accordance with § 103 of this title a certificate stating that its total assets, as defined in § 503(i) of this title, are not less than $10,000,000, or, in the sole discretion of the Division of Corporations in the Department of State, if the corporation is both a nonprofit nonstock corporation and an association of professionals, (ii) shall be such as to distinguish it upon the records in the office of the Division of Corporations in the Department of State from the names that are reserved on such

records and from the names on such records of each other corporation, partnership, limited partnership, limited liability company or statutory trust organized or registered as a domestic or foreign corporation, partnership, limited partnership, limited liability company or statutory trust under the laws of this State, except with the written consent of the person who has reserved such name or such other foreign corporation or domestic or foreign partnership, limited partnership, limited liability company or statutory trust, executed, acknowledged and filed with the Secretary of State in accordance with § 103 of this title, or except that, without prejudicing any rights of the person who has reserved such name or such other foreign corporation or domestic or foreign partnership, limited partnership, limited liability company or statutory trust, the Division of Corporations in the Department of State may waive such requirement if the corporation demonstrates to the satisfaction of the Secretary of State that the corporation or a predecessor entity previously has made substantial use of such name or a substantially similar name, that the corporation has made reasonable efforts to secure such written consent, and that such waiver is in the interest of the State, (iii) except as permitted by § 395 of this title, shall not contain the word "trust," and (iv) shall not contain the word "bank," or any variation thereof, except for the name of a bank reporting to and under the supervision of the State Bank Commissioner of this State or a subsidiary of a bank or savings association (as those terms are defined in the Federal Deposit Insurance Act, as amended, at 12 U.S.C. § 1813), or a corporation regulated under the Bank Holding Company Act of 1956, as amended, 12 U.S.C. § 1841 et seq., or the Home Owners' Loan Act, as amended, 12 U.S.C. § 1461 et seq.; provided, however, that this section shall not be construed to prevent the use of the word "bank," or any variation thereof, in a context clearly not purporting to refer to a banking business or otherwise likely to mislead the public about the nature of the business of the corporation or to lead to a pattern and practice of abuse that might cause harm to the interests of the public or the State as determined by the Division of Corporations in the Department of State;

(2) The address (which shall be stated in accordance with § 131(c) of this title) of the corporation's registered office in this State, and the name of its registered agent at such address;

(3) The nature of the business or purposes to be conducted or promoted. It shall be sufficient to state, either alone or with other businesses or purposes, that the purpose of the corporation is to engage in any lawful act or activity for which corporations may be organized under the General Corporation Law of Delaware, and by such statement all lawful acts and activities shall be within the purposes of the corporation, except for express limitations, if any;

(4) If the corporation is to be authorized to issue only 1 class of stock, the total number of shares of stock which the corporation shall have authority to issue and the par value of each of such shares, or a statement that all such shares are to be without par value. If the corporation is to be

authorized to issue more than 1 class of stock, the certificate of incorporation shall set forth the total number of shares of all classes of stock which the corporation shall have authority to issue and the number of shares of each class and shall specify each class the shares of which are to be without par value and each class the shares of which are to have par value and the par value of the shares of each such class. The certificate of incorporation shall also set forth a statement of the designations and the powers, preferences and rights, and the qualifications, limitations or restrictions thereof, which are permitted by § 151 of this title in respect of any class or classes of stock or any series of any class of stock of the corporation and the fixing of which by the certificate of incorporation is desired, and an express grant of such authority as it may then be desired to grant to the board of directors to fix by resolution or resolutions any thereof that may be desired but which shall not be fixed by the certificate of incorporation. The foregoing provisions of this paragraph shall not apply to nonstock corporations. In the case of nonstock corporations, the fact that they are not authorized to issue capital stock shall be stated in the certificate of incorporation. The conditions of membership, or other criteria for identifying members, of nonstock corporations shall likewise be stated in the certificate of incorporation or the bylaws. Nonstock corporations shall have members, but failure to have members shall not affect otherwise valid corporate acts or work a forfeiture or dissolution of the corporation. Nonstock corporations may provide for classes or groups of members having relative rights, powers and duties, and may make provision for the future creation of additional classes or groups of members having such relative rights, powers and duties as may from time to time be established, including rights, powers and duties senior to existing classes and groups of members. Except as otherwise provided in this chapter, nonstock corporations may also provide that any member or class or group of members shall have full, limited, or no voting rights or powers, including that any member or class or group of members shall have the right to vote on a specified transaction even if that member or class or group of members does not have the right to vote for the election of the members of the governing body of the corporation. Voting by members of a nonstock corporation may be on a per capita, number, financial interest, class, group, or any other basis set forth. The provisions referred to in the 3 preceding sentences may be set forth in the certificate of incorporation or the bylaws. If neither the certificate of incorporation nor the bylaws of a nonstock corporation state the conditions of membership, or other criteria for identifying members, the members of the corporation shall be deemed to be those entitled to vote for the election of the members of the governing body pursuant to the certificate of incorporation or bylaws of such corporation or otherwise until thereafter otherwise provided by the certificate of incorporation or the bylaws;

(5) The name and mailing address of the incorporator or incorporators;

(6) If the powers of the incorporator or incorporators are to terminate upon the filing of the certificate of incorporation, the names and mailing addresses of the persons who are to serve as directors until the first annual meeting of stockholders or until their successors are elected and qualify.

(b) In addition to the matters required to be set forth in the certificate of incorporation by subsection (a) of this section, the certificate of incorporation may also contain any or all of the following matters:

(1) Any provision for the management of the business and for the conduct of the affairs of the corporation, and any provision creating, defining, limiting and regulating the powers of the corporation, the directors, and the stockholders, or any class of the stockholders, or the governing body, members, or any class or group of members of a nonstock corporation; if such provisions are not contrary to the laws of this State. Any provision which is required or permitted by any section of this chapter to be stated in the bylaws may instead be stated in the certificate of incorporation;

(2) The following provisions, in haec verba, (i), for a corporation other than a nonstock corporation, viz:

Whenever a compromise or arrangement is proposed between this corporation and its creditors or any class of them and/or between this corporation and its stockholders or any class of them, any court of equitable jurisdiction within the State of Delaware may, on the application in a summary way of this corporation or of any creditor or stockholder thereof or on the application of any receiver or receivers appointed for this corporation under § 291 of Title 8 of the Delaware Code or on the application of trustees in dissolution or of any receiver or receivers appointed for this corporation under § 279 of Title 8 of the Delaware Code order a meeting of the creditors or class of creditors, and/or of the stockholders or class of stockholders of this corporation, as the case may be, to be summoned in such manner as the said court directs. If a majority in number representing three fourths in value of the creditors or class of creditors, and/or of the stockholders or class of stockholders of this corporation, as the case may be, agree to any compromise or arrangement and to any reorganization of this corporation as consequence of such compromise or arrangement, the said compromise or arrangement and the said reorganization shall, if sanctioned by the court to which the said application has been made, be binding on all the creditors or class of creditors, and/or on all the stockholders or class of stockholders, of this corporation, as the case may be, and also on this corporation"; or

(ii), for a nonstock corporation, viz:

"Whenever a compromise or arrangement is proposed between this corporation and its creditors or any class of them and/or between this corporation and its members or any class of them, any court of equitable jurisdiction within the State of Delaware may, on the application in a summary way of this corporation or of any creditor or member thereof or on the application of any receiver or receivers appointed for this corporation under § 291 of Title 8 of the Delaware Code or on the application of trustees in dissolution or of any receiver or receivers appointed for this corporation under § 279 of Title 8 of the Delaware Code order a meeting of the creditors or class of creditors, and/or of the members or class of members of this corporation, as the case may be, to be summoned in such manner as the said court directs. If a majority in number representing three fourths in value of the creditors or class of creditors, and/or of the members or class of members of this corporation, as the case may be, agree to any compromise or arrangement and to any reorganization of this corporation as consequence of such compromise or arrangement, the said compromise or arrangement and the said reorganization shall, if sanctioned by the court to which the said application has been made, be binding on all the creditors or class of creditors, and/or on all the members or class of members, of this corporation, as the case may be, and also on this corporation";

(3) Such provisions as may be desired granting to the holders of the stock of the corporation, or the holders of any class or series of a class thereof, the preemptive right to subscribe to any or all additional issues of stock of the corporation of any or all classes or series thereof, or to any securities of the corporation convertible into such stock. No stockholder shall have any preemptive right to subscribe to an additional issue of stock or to any security convertible into such stock unless, and except to the extent that, such right is expressly granted to such stockholder in the certificate of incorporation. All such rights in existence on July 3, 1967, shall remain in existence unaffected by this paragraph unless and until changed or terminated by appropriate action which expressly provides for the change or termination;

(4) Provisions requiring for any corporate action, the vote of a larger portion of the stock or of any class or series thereof, or of any other securities having voting power, or a larger number of the directors, than is required by this chapter;

(5) A provision limiting the duration of the corporation's existence to a specified date; otherwise, the corporation shall have perpetual existence;

(6) A provision imposing personal liability for the debts of the corporation on its stockholders to a specified extent and upon specified conditions; otherwise, the stockholders of a corporation shall not be personally liable for the payment of the corporation's debts except as they may be liable by reason of their own conduct or acts;

(7) A provision eliminating or limiting the personal liability of a director to the corporation or its stockholders for monetary damages for breach of fiduciary duty as a director, provided that such provision shall not eliminate or limit the liability of a director: (i) For any breach of the director's duty of loyalty to the corporation or its stockholders; (ii) for acts or omissions not in good faith or which involve intentional

misconduct or a knowing violation of law; (iii) under § 174 of this title; or (iv) for any transaction from which the director derived an improper personal benefit. No such provision shall eliminate or limit the liability of a director for any act or omission occurring prior to the date when such provision becomes effective. All references in this paragraph to a director shall also be deemed to refer to such other person or persons, if any, who, pursuant to a provision of the certificate of incorporation in accordance with § 141(a) of this title, exercise or perform any of the powers or duties otherwise conferred or imposed upon the board of directors by this title.

(c) It shall not be necessary to set forth in the certificate of incorporation any of the powers conferred on corporations by this chapter.

(d) Except for provisions included pursuant to paragraphs (a)(1), (a)(2), (a)(5), (a)(6), (b)(2), (b)(5), (b)(7) of this section, and provisions included pursuant to paragraph (a)(4) of this section specifying the classes, number of shares, and par value of shares a corporation other than a nonstock corporation is authorized to issue, any provision of the certificate of incorporation may be made dependent upon facts ascertainable outside such instrument, provided that the manner in which such facts shall operate upon the provision is clearly and explicitly set forth therein. The term "facts," as used in this subsection, includes, but is not limited to, the occurrence of any event, including a determination or action by any person or body, including the corporation.

§ 103. Execution, Acknowledgment, Filing, Recording and Effective Date of Original Certificate of Incorporation and Other Instruments; Exceptions

(a) Whenever any instrument is to be filed with the Secretary of State or in accordance with this section or chapter, such instrument shall be executed as follows:

(1) The certificate of incorporation, and any other instrument to be filed before the election of the initial board of directors if the initial directors were not named in the certificate of incorporation, shall be signed by the incorporator or incorporators (or, in the case of any such other instrument, such incorporator's or incorporators' successors and assigns). If any incorporator is not available then any such other instrument may be signed, with the same effect as if such incorporator had signed it, by any person for whom or on whose behalf such incorporator, in executing the certificate of incorporation, was acting directly or indirectly as employee or agent, provided that such other instrument shall state that such incorporator is not available and the reason therefor, that such incorporator in executing the certificate of incorporation was acting directly or indirectly as employee or agent for or on behalf of such

person, and that such person's signature on such instrument is otherwise authorized and not wrongful.

(2) All other instruments shall be signed:

a. By any authorized officer of the corporation; or

b. If it shall appear from the instrument that there are no such officers, then by a majority of the directors or by such directors as may be designated by the board; or

c. If it shall appear from the instrument that there are no such officers or directors, then by the holders of record, or such of them as may be designated by the holders of record, of a majority of all outstanding shares of stock; or

d. By the holders of record of all outstanding shares of stock.

(b) Whenever this chapter requires any instrument to be acknowledged, such requirement is satisfied by either:

(1) The formal acknowledgment by the person or 1 of the persons signing the instrument that it is such person's act and deed or the act and deed of the corporation, and that the facts stated therein are true. Such acknowledgment shall be made before a person who is authorized by the law of the place of execution to take acknowledgments of deeds. If such person has a seal of office such person shall affix it to the instrument.

(2) The signature, without more, of the person or persons signing the instrument, in which case such signature or signatures shall constitute the affirmation or acknowledgment of the signatory, under penalties of perjury, that the instrument is such person's act and deed or the act and deed of the corporation, and that the facts stated therein are true.

(c) Whenever any instrument is to be filed with the Secretary of State or in accordance with this section or chapter, such requirement means that:

(1) The signed instrument shall be delivered to the office of the Secretary of State;

(2) All taxes and fees authorized by law to be collected by the Secretary of State in connection with the filing of the instrument shall be tendered to the Secretary of State; and

(3) Upon delivery of the instrument, the Secretary of State shall record the date and time of its delivery. Upon such delivery and tender of the required taxes and fees, the Secretary of State shall certify that the instrument has been filed in the Secretary of State's office by endorsing upon the signed instrument the word "Filed", and the date and time of its filing. This endorsement is the "filing date" of the instrument, and is conclusive of the date and time of its filing in the absence of actual fraud. The Secretary of State shall file and index the endorsed instrument. Except as provided in paragraph (c)(4) of this section and in subsection (i) of this section, such filing date of an instrument shall be the date and time of delivery of the instrument.

(4) Upon request made upon or prior to delivery, the Secretary of State may, to the extent deemed practicable, establish as the filing date of an instrument a date and time after its delivery.

. . .

(d) Any instrument filed in accordance with subsection (c) of this section shall be effective upon its filing date. Any instrument may provide that it is not to become effective until a specified time subsequent to the time it is filed, but such time shall not be later than a time on the ninetieth day after the date of its filing . . .

. . .

§ 104. Certificate of Incorporation; Definition

The term "certificate of incorporation," as used in this chapter, unless the context requires otherwise, includes not only the original certificate of incorporation filed to create a corporation but also all other certificates, agreements of merger or consolidation, plans of reorganization, or other instruments, howsoever designated, which are filed pursuant to § 102, §§ 133-136, § 151, §§ 241-243, § 245, §§ 251-258, §§ 263-264, § 267, § 303, or any other section of this title, and which have the effect of amending or supplementing in some respect a corporation's original certificate of incorporation.

. . .

§ 106. Commencement of Corporate Existence

Upon the filing with the Secretary of State of the certificate of incorporation, executed and acknowledged in accordance with § 103 of this title, the incorporator or incorporators who signed the certificate, and such incorporator's or incorporators' successors and assigns, shall, from the date of such filing, be and constitute a body corporate, by the name set forth in the certificate, subject to § 103(d) of this title and subject to dissolution or other termination of its existence as provided in this chapter.

§ 107. Powers of Incorporators

If the persons who are to serve as directors until the first annual meeting of stockholders have not been named in the certificate of incorporation, the incorporator or incorporators, until the directors are elected, shall manage the affairs of the corporation and may do whatever is necessary and proper to perfect the organization of the corporation, including the adoption of the original bylaws of the corporation and the election of directors.

§ 108. Organization Meeting of Incorporators or Directors Named in Certificate of Incorporation

(a) After the filing of the certificate of incorporation an organization meeting of the incorporator or incorporators, or of the board of directors if the initial directors were named in the certificate of incorporation, shall be held, either within or without this State, at the call of a majority of the incorporators or directors, as the case may be, for the purposes of adopting bylaws, electing directors (if the meeting is of the incorporators) to serve or hold office until the first annual meeting of stockholders or until their successors are elected and qualify, electing officers if the meeting is of the directors, doing any other or further acts to perfect the organization of the corporation, and transacting such other business as may come before the meeting.

(b) The persons calling the meeting shall give to each other incorporator or director, as the case may be, at least 2 days' written notice thereof by any usual means of communication, which notice shall state the time, place and purposes of the meeting as fixed by the persons calling it. Notice of the meeting need not be given to anyone who attends the meeting or who signs a waiver of notice either before or after the meeting.

(c) Any action permitted to be taken at the organization meeting of the incorporators or directors, as the case may be, may be taken without a meeting if each incorporator or director, where there is more than 1, or the sole incorporator or director where there is only 1, signs an instrument which states the action so taken.

§ 109. Bylaws

(a) The original or other bylaws of a corporation may be adopted, amended or repealed by the incorporators, by the initial directors of a corporation other than a nonstock corporation or initial members of the governing body of a nonstock corporation if they were named in the certificate of incorporation, or, before a corporation other than a nonstock corporation has received any payment for any of its stock, by its board of directors. After a corporation other than a nonstock corporation has received any payment for any of its stock, the power to adopt, amend or repeal bylaws shall be in the stockholders entitled to vote. In the case of a nonstock corporation, the power to adopt, amend or repeal bylaws shall be in its members entitled to vote. Notwithstanding the foregoing, any corporation may, in its certificate of incorporation, confer the power to adopt, amend or repeal bylaws upon the directors or, in the case of a nonstock corporation, upon its governing body. The fact that such power has been so conferred upon the directors or governing body, as the case may be, shall not divest the stockholders or members of the power, nor limit their power to adopt, amend or repeal bylaws.

(b) The bylaws may contain any provision, not inconsistent with law or with the certificate of incorporation, relating to the business of the corporation, the conduct of its affairs, and its rights or powers or the rights or powers of its stockholders, directors, officers or employees.

§ 111. Jurisdiction to Interpret, Apply, Enforce or Determine the Validity of Corporate Instruments and Provisions of This Title

(a) Any civil action to interpret, apply, enforce or determine the validity of the provisions of:

(1) The certificate of incorporation or the bylaws of a corporation;

(2) Any instrument, document or agreement by which a corporation creates or sells, or offers to create or sell, any of its stock, or any rights or options respecting its stock;

(3) Any written restrictions on the transfer, registration of transfer or ownership of securities under § 202 of this title;

(4) Any proxy under § 212 or § 215 of this title;

(5) Any voting trust or other voting agreement under § 218 of this title;

(6) Any agreement, certificate of merger or consolidation, or certificate of ownership and merger governed by §§ 251-253, §§ 255-258, §§ 263-264, or § 267 of this title;

(7) Any certificate of conversion under § 265 or § 266 of this title;

(8) Any certificate of domestication, transfer or continuance under § 388, § 389 or § 390 of this title; or

(9) Any other instrument, document, agreement, or certificate required by any provision of this title;

may be brought in the Court of Chancery, except to the extent that a statute confers exclusive jurisdiction on a court, agency or tribunal other than the Court of Chancery.

(b) Any civil action to interpret, apply or enforce any provision of this title may be brought in the Court of Chancery.

§ 112. Access to Proxy Solicitation Materials

The bylaws may provide that if the corporation solicits proxies with respect to an election of directors, it may be required, to the extent and subject to such procedures or conditions as may be provided in the bylaws, to include in its proxy solicitation materials (including any form of proxy it distributes), in addition to individuals nominated by the board of directors, 1 or more individuals nominated by a stockholder. Such procedures or conditions may include any of the following:

(1) A provision requiring a minimum record or beneficial ownership, or duration of ownership, of shares of the corporation's capital stock, by the nominating stockholder, and defining beneficial ownership to take into account options or other rights in respect of or related to such stock;

(2) A provision requiring the nominating stockholder to submit specified information concerning the stockholder and the stockholder's nominees, including information concerning ownership by such persons of shares of the corporation's capital stock, or options or other rights in respect of or related to such stock;

(3) A provision conditioning eligibility to require inclusion in the corporation's proxy solicitation materials upon the number or proportion of directors nominated by stockholders or whether the stockholder previously sought to require such inclusion;

(4) A provision precluding nominations by any person if such person, any nominee of such person, or any affiliate or associate of such person or nominee, has acquired or publicly proposed to acquire shares constituting a specified percentage of the voting power of the corporation's outstanding voting stock within a specified period before the election of directors;

(5) A provision requiring that the nominating stockholder undertake to indemnify the corporation in respect of any loss arising as a result of any false or misleading information or statement submitted by the nominating stockholder in connection with a nomination; and

(6) Any other lawful condition.

§ 113. Proxy Expense Reimbursement

(a) The bylaws may provide for the reimbursement by the corporation of expenses incurred by a stockholder in soliciting proxies in connection with an election of directors, subject to such procedures or conditions as the bylaws may prescribe, including:

(1) Conditioning eligibility for reimbursement upon the number or proportion of persons nominated by the stockholder seeking reimbursement or whether such stockholder previously sought reimbursement for similar expenses;

(2) Limitations on the amount of reimbursement based upon the proportion of votes cast in favor of 1 or more of the persons nominated by the stockholder seeking reimbursement, or upon the amount spent by the corporation in soliciting proxies in connection with the election;

(3) Limitations concerning elections of directors by cumulative voting pursuant to § 214 of this title; or

(4) Any other lawful condition.

(b) No bylaw so adopted shall apply to elections for which any record date precedes its adoption.

Subchapter II. Powers

§ 121. General Powers

(a) In addition to the powers enumerated in § 122 of this title, every corporation, its officers, directors and stockholders shall possess and may exercise all the powers and privileges granted by this chapter or by any other law or by its certificate of incorporation, together with any powers incidental thereto, so far as such powers and privileges are necessary or convenient to the conduct, promotion or attainment of the business or purposes set forth in its certificate of incorporation.

(b) Every corporation shall be governed by the provisions and be subject to the restrictions and liabilities contained in this chapter.

§ 122. Specific Powers

Every corporation created under this chapter shall have power to:

(1) Have perpetual succession by its corporate name, unless a limited period of duration is stated in its certificate of incorporation;

(2) Sue and be sued in all courts and participate, as a party or otherwise, in any judicial, administrative, arbitrative or other proceeding, in its corporate name;

(3) Have a corporate seal, which may be altered at pleasure, and use the same by causing it or a facsimile thereof, to be impressed or affixed or in any other manner reproduced;

(4) Purchase, receive, take by grant, gift, devise, bequest or otherwise, lease, or otherwise acquire, own, hold, improve, employ, use and otherwise deal in and with real or personal property, or any interest therein, wherever situated, and to sell, convey, lease, exchange, transfer or otherwise dispose of, or mortgage or pledge, all or any of its property and assets, or any interest therein, wherever situated;

(5) Appoint such officers and agents as the business of the corporation requires and to pay or otherwise provide for them suitable compensation;

(6) Adopt, amend and repeal bylaws;

(7) Wind up and dissolve itself in the manner provided in this chapter;

(8) Conduct its business, carry on its operations and have offices and exercise its powers within or without this State;

(9) Make donations for the public welfare or for charitable, scientific or educational purposes, and in time of war or other national emergency in aid thereof;

(10) Be an incorporator, promoter or manager of other corporations of any type or kind;

(11) Participate with others in any corporation, partnership, limited partnership, joint venture or other association of any kind, or in any transaction, undertaking or arrangement which the participating corporation would have power to conduct by itself, whether or not such participation involves sharing or delegation of control with or to others;

(12) Transact any lawful business which the corporation's board of directors shall find to be in aid of governmental authority;

(13) Make contracts, including contracts of guaranty and suretyship, incur liabilities, borrow money at such rates of interest as the corporation may determine, issue its notes, bonds and other obligations, and secure any of its obligations by mortgage, pledge or other encumbrance of all or any of its property, franchises and income, and make contracts of guaranty and suretyship which are necessary or convenient to the conduct, promotion or attainment of the business of (a) a corporation all of the outstanding stock of which is owned, directly or indirectly, by the contracting corporation, or (b) a corporation which owns, directly or indirectly, all of the outstanding stock of the contracting corporation, or (c) a corporation all of the outstanding stock of which is owned, directly or indirectly, by a corporation which owns, directly or indirectly, all of the outstanding stock of the contracting corporation, which contracts of guaranty and suretyship shall be deemed to be necessary or convenient to the conduct, promotion or attainment of the business of the contracting corporation, and make other contracts of guaranty and suretyship which are necessary or convenient to the conduct, promotion or attainment of the business of the contracting corporation;

(14) Lend money for its corporate purposes, invest and reinvest its funds, and take, hold and deal with real and personal property as security for the payment of funds so loaned or invested;

(15) Pay pensions and establish and carry out pension, profit sharing, stock option, stock purchase, stock bonus, retirement, benefit, incentive and compensation plans, trusts and provisions for any or all of its directors, officers and employees, and for any or all of the directors, officers and employees of its subsidiaries;

(16) Provide insurance for its benefit on the life of any of its directors, officers or employees, or on the life of any stockholder for the purpose of acquiring at such stockholder's death shares of its stock owned by such stockholder.

(17) Renounce, in its certificate of incorporation or by action of its board of directors, any interest or expectancy of the corporation in, or in

being offered an opportunity to participate in, specified business opportunities or specified classes or categories of business opportunities that are presented to the corporation or 1 or more of its officers, directors or stockholders.

§ 123. Powers Respecting Securities of Other Corporations or Entities

Any corporation organized under the laws of this State may guarantee, purchase, take, receive, subscribe for or otherwise acquire; own, hold, use or otherwise employ; sell, lease, exchange, transfer or otherwise dispose of; mortgage, lend, pledge or otherwise deal in and with, bonds and other obligations of, or shares or other securities or interests in, or issued by, any other domestic or foreign corporation, partnership, association or individual, or by any government or agency or instrumentality thereof. A corporation while owner of any such securities may exercise all the rights, powers and privileges of ownership, including the right to vote.

§ 124. Effect of Lack of Corporate Capacity or Power; Ultra Vires

No act of a corporation and no conveyance or transfer of real or personal property to or by a corporation shall be invalid by reason of the fact that the corporation was without capacity or power to do such act or to make or receive such conveyance or transfer, but such lack of capacity or power may be asserted:

(1) In a proceeding by a stockholder against the corporation to enjoin the doing of any act or acts or the transfer of real or personal property by or to the corporation. If the unauthorized acts or transfer sought to be enjoined are being, or are to be, performed or made pursuant to any contract to which the corporation is a party, the court may, if all of the parties to the contract are parties to the proceeding and if it deems the same to be equitable, set aside and enjoin the performance of such contract, and in so doing may allow to the corporation or to the other parties to the contract, as the case may be, such compensation as may be equitable for the loss or damage sustained by any of them which may result from the action of the court in setting aside and enjoining the performance of such contract, but anticipated profits to be derived from the performance of the contract shall not be awarded by the court as a loss or damage sustained;

(2) In a proceeding by the corporation, whether acting directly or through a receiver, trustee or other legal representative, or through stockholders in a representative suit, against an incumbent or former officer or director of the corporation, for loss or damage due to such incumbent or former officer's or director's unauthorized act;

(3) In a proceeding by the Attorney General to dissolve the corporation, or to enjoin the corporation from the transaction of unauthorized business.

Subchapter III. Registered Office and Registered Agent

§ 131. Registered Office in State; Principal Office or Place of Business in State

(a) Every corporation shall have and maintain in this State a registered office which may, but need not be, the same as its place of business.

. . .

§ 132. Registered Agent in State; Resident Agent

(a) Every corporation shall have and maintain in this State a registered agent, which agent may be any of:

(1) The corporation itself;

(2) An individual resident in this State;

(3) A domestic corporation (other than the corporation itself), a domestic partnership (whether general (including a limited liability partnership) or limited (including a limited liability limited partnership)), a domestic limited liability company or a domestic statutory trust; or

(4) A foreign corporation, a foreign partnership (whether general (including a limited liability partnership) or limited (including a limited liability limited partnership)), a foreign limited liability company or a foreign statutory trust.

have to have an office and a person in DE

. . .

Subchapter IV. Directors and Officers

§ 141. Board of Directors; Powers; Number, Qualifications, Terms and Quorum; Committees; Classes of Directors; Nonstock Corporations; Reliance Upon Books; Action Without Meeting; Removal

(a) The business and affairs of every corporation organized under this chapter shall be managed by or under the direction of a board of directors, except as may be otherwise provided in this chapter or in its certificate of incorporation. If any such provision is made in the certificate of incorporation, the powers and duties conferred or imposed upon the board of directors by this chapter shall be exercised or performed to such extent and by such person or persons as shall be provided in the certificate of incorporation.

(b) The board of directors of a corporation shall consist of 1 or more members, each of whom shall be a natural person. The number of directors shall be fixed by, or in the manner provided in, the bylaws, unless the certificate of incorporation fixes the number of directors, in which case a change in the number of directors shall be made only by amendment of the certificate. Directors need not be stockholders unless so required by the certificate of incorporation or the bylaws. The certificate of incorporation or bylaws may prescribe other qualifications for directors. Each director shall hold office until such director's successor is elected and qualified or until such director's earlier resignation or removal. Any director may resign at any time upon notice given in writing or by electronic transmission to the corporation. A resignation is effective when the resignation is delivered unless the resignation specifies a later effective date or an effective date determined upon the happening of an event or events. A resignation which is conditioned upon the director failing to receive a specified vote for reelection as a director may provide that it is irrevocable. A majority of the total number of directors shall constitute a quorum for the transaction of business unless the certificate of incorporation or the bylaws require a greater number. Unless the certificate of incorporation provides otherwise, the bylaws may provide that a number less than a majority shall constitute a quorum which in no case shall be less than 1/3 of the total number of directors except that when a board of 1 director is authorized under this section, then 1 director shall constitute a quorum. The vote of the majority of the directors present at a meeting at which a quorum is present shall be the act of the board of directors unless the certificate of incorporation or the bylaws shall require a vote of a greater number.

(c)(1) All corporations incorporated prior to July 1, 1996, shall be governed by this paragraph (c)(1) of this section, provided that any such corporation may by a resolution adopted by a majority of the whole board elect to be governed by paragraph (c)(2) of this section, in which case this paragraph (c)(1) of this section shall not apply to such corporation. All corporations incorporated on or after July 1, 1996, shall be governed by paragraph (c)(2) of this section. The board of directors may, by resolution passed by a majority of the whole board, designate 1 or more committees, each committee to consist of 1 or more of the directors of the corporation. The board may designate 1 or more directors as alternate members of any committee, who may replace any absent or disqualified member at any meeting of the committee. The bylaws may provide that in the absence or disqualification of a member of a committee, the member or members present at any meeting and not disqualified from voting, whether or not the member or members present constitute a quorum, may unanimously appoint another member of the board of directors to act at the meeting in the place of any such absent or disqualified member. Any such committee, to the extent provided in the resolution of the board of directors, or in the bylaws of the corporation, shall have and may exercise all the powers and authority of the board of directors in the management of the business and affairs of the corporation, and may authorize the seal of the corporation to be affixed to all papers which may require it; but no such committee shall have the power or authority in reference to amending the certificate of incorporation (except that a committee may, to the extent authorized in the resolution or resolutions providing for the issuance of shares of stock adopted by the board of directors as provided in § 151(a) of this title, fix the designations and any of the preferences or rights of such shares relating to dividends, redemption, dissolution, any distribution of assets of the corporation or the conversion into, or the exchange of such shares for, shares of any other class or classes or any other series of the same or any other class or classes of stock of the corporation or fix the number of shares of any series of stock or authorize the increase or decrease of the shares of any series), adopting an agreement of merger or consolidation under § 251, § 252, § 254, § 255, § 256, § 257, § 258, § 263 or § 264 of this title, recommending to the stockholders the sale, lease or exchange of all or substantially all of the corporation's property and assets, recommending to the stockholders a dissolution of the corporation or a revocation of a dissolution, or amending the bylaws of the corporation; and, unless the resolution, bylaws or certificate of incorporation expressly so provides, no such committee shall have the power or authority to declare a dividend, to authorize the issuance of stock or to adopt a certificate of ownership and merger pursuant to § 253 of this title.

(2) The board of directors may designate 1 or more committees, each committee to consist of 1 or more of the directors of the corporation. The board may designate 1 or more directors as alternate members of any committee, who may replace any absent or disqualified member at any meeting of the committee. The bylaws may provide that in the absence or disqualification of a member of a committee, the member or members present at any meeting and not disqualified from voting, whether or not such member or members constitute a quorum, may unanimously appoint another member of the board of directors to act at the meeting in the place of any such absent or disqualified member. Any such committee, to the extent provided in the resolution of the board of directors, or in the bylaws of the corporation, shall have and may exercise all the powers and authority of the board of directors in the management of the business and affairs of the corporation, and may authorize the seal of the corporation to be affixed to all papers which may require it; but no such committee shall have the power or authority in reference to the following matter: (i) approving

or adopting, or recommending to the stockholders, any action or matter (other than the election or removal of directors) expressly required by this chapter to be submitted to stockholders for approval or (ii) adopting, amending or repealing any bylaw of the corporation.

(3) Unless otherwise provided in the certificate of incorporation, the bylaws or the resolution of the board of directors designating the committee, a committee may create 1 or more subcommittees, each subcommittee to consist of 1 or more members of the committee, and delegate to a subcommittee any or all of the powers and authority of the committee.

(d) The directors of any corporation organized under this chapter may, by the certificate of incorporation or by an initial bylaw, or by a bylaw adopted by a vote of the stockholders, be divided into 1, 2 or 3 classes; the term of office of those of the first class to expire at the first annual meeting held after such classification becomes effective; of the second class 1 year thereafter; of the third class 2 years thereafter; and at each annual election held after such classification becomes effective, directors shall be chosen for a full term, as the case may be, to succeed those whose terms expire. The certificate of incorporation or bylaw provision dividing the directors into classes may authorize the board of directors to assign members of the board already in office to such classes at the time such classification becomes effective. The certificate of incorporation may confer upon holders of any class or series of stock the right to elect 1 or more directors who shall serve for such term, and have such voting powers as shall be stated in the certificate of incorporation. The terms of office and voting powers of the directors elected separately by the holders of any class or series of stock may be greater than or less than those of any other director or class of directors. In addition, the certificate of incorporation may confer upon 1 or more directors, whether or not elected separately by the holders of any class or series of stock, voting powers greater than or less than those of other directors. Any such provision conferring greater or lesser voting power shall apply to voting in any committee or subcommittee, unless otherwise provided in the certificate of incorporation or bylaws. If the certificate of incorporation provides that 1 or more directors shall have more or less than 1 vote per director on any matter, every reference in this chapter to a majority or other proportion of the directors shall refer to a majority or other proportion of the votes of the directors.

(e) A member of the board of directors, or a member of any committee designated by the board of directors, shall, in the performance of such member's duties, be fully protected in relying in good faith upon the records of the corporation and upon such information, opinions, reports or statements presented to the corporation by any of the corporation's officers or employees, or committees of the board of directors, or by any other person as to matters the member reasonably believes are within such other person's professional or expert competence and who has been selected with reasonable care by or on behalf of the corporation.

(f) Unless otherwise restricted by the certificate of incorporation or bylaws, any action required or permitted to be taken at any meeting of the board of directors or of any committee thereof may be taken without a meeting if all members of the board or committee, as the case may be, consent thereto in writing, or by electronic transmission and the writing or writings or electronic transmission or transmissions are filed with the minutes of proceedings of the board, or committee. Such filing shall be in paper form if the minutes are maintained in paper form and shall be in electronic form if the minutes are maintained in electronic form. Any person (whether or not then a director) may provide, whether through instruction to an agent or otherwise, that a consent to action will be effective at a future time (including a time determined upon the happening of an event), no later than 60 days after such instruction is given or such provision is made and such consent shall be deemed to have been given for purposes of this subsection at such effective time so long as such person is then a director and did not revoke the consent prior to such time. Any such consent shall be revocable prior to its becoming effective.

(g) Unless otherwise restricted by the certificate of incorporation or bylaws, the board of directors of any corporation organized under this chapter may hold its meetings, and have an office or offices, outside of this State.

(h) Unless otherwise restricted by the certificate of incorporation or bylaws, the board of directors shall have the authority to fix the compensation of directors.

(i) Unless otherwise restricted by the certificate of incorporation or bylaws, members of the board of directors of any corporation, or any committee designated by the board, may participate in a meeting of such board, or committee by means of conference telephone or other communications equipment by means of which all persons participating in the meeting can hear each other, and participation in a meeting pursuant to this subsection shall constitute presence in person at the meeting.

(j) The certificate of incorporation of any nonstock corporation may provide that less than 1/3 of the members of the governing body may constitute a quorum thereof and may otherwise provide that the business and affairs of the corporation shall be managed in a manner different from that provided in this section. Except as may be otherwise provided by the certificate of incorporation, this section shall apply to such a corporation, and when so applied, all references to the board of directors, to members thereof, and to stockholders shall be deemed to refer to the governing body of the corporation, the members thereof and the members of the corporation, respectively; and all references to stock, capital stock, or shares thereof shall be deemed to refer to memberships of a nonprofit nonstock corporation and to membership interests of any other nonstock corporation.

(k) Any director or the entire board of directors may be removed, with or without cause, by the holders of a majority of the shares then entitled to vote at an election of directors, except as follows:

(1) Unless the certificate of incorporation otherwise provides, in the case of a corporation whose board is classified as provided in subsection (d) of this section, stockholders may effect such removal only for cause; or

(2) In the case of a corporation having cumulative voting, if less than the entire board is to be removed, no director may be removed without cause if the votes cast against such director's removal would be sufficient to elect such director if then cumulatively voted at an election of the entire board of directors, or, if there be classes of directors, at an election of the class of directors of which such director is a part.

Whenever the holders of any class or series are entitled to elect 1 or more directors by the certificate of incorporation, this subsection shall apply, in respect to the removal without cause of a director or directors so elected, to the vote of the holders of the outstanding shares of that class or series and not to the vote of the outstanding shares as a whole.

§ 142. Officers; Titles, Duties, Selection, Term; Failure to Elect; Vacancies

(a) Every corporation organized under this chapter shall have such officers with such titles and duties as shall be stated in the bylaws or in a resolution of the board of directors which is not inconsistent with the bylaws and as may be necessary to enable it to sign instruments and stock certificates which comply with §§ 103(a)(2) and 158 of this title. One of the officers shall have the duty to record the proceedings of the meetings of the stockholders and directors in a book to be kept for that purpose. Any number of offices may be held by the same person unless the certificate of incorporation or bylaws otherwise provide.

(b) Officers shall be chosen in such manner and shall hold their offices for such terms as are prescribed by the bylaws or determined by the board of directors or other governing body. Each officer shall hold office until such officer's successor is elected and qualified or until such officer's earlier resignation or removal. Any officer may resign at any time upon written notice to the corporation.

(c) The corporation may secure the fidelity of any or all of its officers or agents by bond or otherwise.

(d) A failure to elect officers shall not dissolve or otherwise affect the corporation.

(e) Any vacancy occurring in any office of the corporation by death, resignation, removal or otherwise, shall be filled as the bylaws provide. In the absence of such provision, the vacancy shall be filled by the board of directors or other governing body.

§ 143. Loans to Employees and Officers; Guaranty of Obligations of Employees and Officers

Any corporation may lend money to, or guarantee any obligation of, or otherwise assist any officer or other employee of the corporation or of its subsidiary, including any officer or employee who is a director of the corporation or its subsidiary, whenever, in the judgment of the directors, such loan, guaranty or assistance may reasonably be expected to benefit the corporation. The loan, guaranty or other assistance may be with or without interest, and may be unsecured, or secured in such manner as the board of directors shall approve, including, without limitation, a pledge of shares of stock of the corporation. Nothing in this section contained shall be deemed to deny, limit or restrict the powers of guaranty or warranty of any corporation at common law or under any statute.

§ 144. Interested Directors; Quorum

(a) No contract or transaction between a corporation and 1 or more of its directors or officers, or between a corporation and any other corporation, partnership, association, or other organization in which 1 or more of its directors or officers, are directors or officers, or have a financial interest, shall be void or voidable solely for this reason, or solely because the director or officer is present at or participates in the meeting of the board or committee which authorizes the contract or transaction, or solely because any such director's or officer's votes are counted for such purpose, if:

(1) The material facts as to the director's or officer's relationship or interest and as to the contract or transaction are disclosed or are known to the board of directors or the committee, and the board or committee in good faith authorizes the contract or transaction by the affirmative votes of a majority of the disinterested directors, even though the disinterested directors be less than a quorum; or

(2) The material facts as to the director's or officer's relationship or interest and as to the contract or transaction are disclosed or are known to the stockholders entitled to vote thereon, and the contract or transaction is specifically approved in good faith by vote of the stockholders; or

(3) The contract or transaction is fair as to the corporation as of the time it is authorized, approved or ratified, by the board of directors, a committee or the stockholders.

(b) Common or interested directors may be counted in determining the presence of a quorum at a meeting of the board of directors or of a committee which authorizes the contract or transaction.

§ 145. Indemnification of Officers, Directors, Employees and Agents; Insurance

(a) A corporation shall have power to indemnify any person who was or is a party or is threatened to be made a party to any threatened, pending or completed action, suit or proceeding, whether civil, criminal, administrative or investigative (other than an action by or in the right of the corporation) by reason of the fact that the person is or was a director, officer, employee or agent of the corporation, or is or was serving at the request of the corporation as a director, officer, employee or agent of another corporation, partnership, joint venture, trust or other enterprise, against expenses (including attorneys' fees), judgments, fines and amounts paid in settlement actually and reasonably incurred by the person in connection with such action, suit or proceeding if the person acted in good faith and in a manner the person reasonably believed to be in or not opposed to the best interests of the corporation, and, with respect to any criminal action or proceeding, had no reasonable cause to believe the person's conduct was unlawful. The termination of any action, suit or proceeding by judgment, order, settlement, conviction, or upon a plea of nolo contendere or its equivalent, shall not, of itself, create a presumption that the person did not act in good faith and in a manner which the person reasonably believed to be in or not opposed to the best interests of the corporation, and, with respect to any criminal action or proceeding, had reasonable cause to believe that the person's conduct was unlawful.

(b) A corporation shall have power to indemnify any person who was or is a party or is threatened to be made a party to any threatened, pending or completed action or suit by or in the right of the corporation to procure a judgment in its favor by reason of the fact that the person is or was a director, officer, employee or agent of the corporation, or is or was serving at the request of the corporation as a director, officer, employee or agent of another corporation, partnership, joint venture, trust or other enterprise against expenses (including attorneys' fees) actually and reasonably incurred by the person in connection with the defense or settlement of such action or suit if the person acted in good faith and in a manner the person reasonably believed to be in or not opposed to the best interests of the corporation and except that no indemnification shall be made in respect of any claim, issue or matter as to which such person shall have been adjudged to be liable to the corporation unless and only to the extent that the Court of Chancery or the court in which such action or suit was brought shall determine upon application that, despite the adjudication of liability but in view of all the circumstances of the case, such person is fairly and reasonably entitled to indemnity for such expenses which the Court of Chancery or such other court shall deem proper.

(c) To the extent that a present or former director or officer of a corporation has been successful on the merits or otherwise in defense of any action, suit or proceeding referred to in subsections (a) and (b) of this section, or in defense of any claim, issue or matter therein, such person shall be indemnified against expenses (including attorneys' fees) actually and reasonably incurred by such person in connection therewith.

(d) Any indemnification under subsections (a) and (b) of this section (unless ordered by a court) shall be made by the corporation only as authorized in the specific case upon a determination that indemnification of the present or former director, officer, employee or agent is proper in the circumstances because the person has met the applicable standard of conduct set forth in subsections (a) and (b) of this section. Such determination shall be made, with respect to a person who is a director or officer of the corporation at the time of such determination:

(1) By a majority vote of the directors who are not parties to such action, suit or proceeding, even though less than a quorum; or

(2) By a committee of such directors designated by majority vote of such directors, even though less than a quorum; or

(3) If there are no such directors, or if such directors so direct, by independent legal counsel in a written opinion; or

(4) By the stockholders.

(e) Expenses (including attorneys' fees) incurred by an officer or director of the corporation in defending any civil, criminal, administrative or investigative action, suit or proceeding may be paid by the corporation in advance of the final disposition of such action, suit or proceeding upon receipt of an undertaking by or on behalf of such director or officer to repay such amount if it shall ultimately be determined that such person is not entitled to be indemnified by the corporation as authorized in this section. Such expenses (including attorneys' fees) incurred by former directors and officers or other employees and agents of the corporation or by persons serving at the request of the corporation as directors, officers, employees or agents of another corporation, partnership, joint venture, trust or other enterprise may be so paid upon such terms and conditions, if any, as the corporation deems appropriate.

(f) The indemnification and advancement of expenses provided by, or granted pursuant to, the other subsections of this section shall not be deemed exclusive of any other rights to which those seeking indemnification or advancement of expenses may be entitled under any bylaw, agreement, vote of stockholders or disinterested directors or otherwise, both as to action in such person's official capacity and as to action in another capacity while holding such office. A right to indemnification or to advancement of expenses arising under a provision of the certificate of incorporation or a bylaw shall not be eliminated or impaired by an amendment to the certificate of incorporation or the bylaws after the occurrence of the act or omission that is the subject of the civil, criminal, administrative or investigative action, suit or proceeding for which indemnification or advancement of expenses is sought, unless the provision in effect at the time of such act or omission explicitly authorizes such elimination or impairment after such action or omission has occurred.

(g) A corporation shall have power to purchase and maintain insurance on behalf of any person who is or was a director, officer, employee or agent of the corporation, or is or was serving at the request of the corporation as a director, officer, employee or agent of another corporation, partnership, joint venture, trust or other enterprise against any liability asserted against such person and incurred by such person in any such capacity, or arising out of such person's status as such, whether or not the corporation would have the power to indemnify such person against such liability under this section.

(h) For purposes of this section, references to "the corporation" shall include, in addition to the resulting corporation, any constituent corporation (including any constituent of a constituent) absorbed in a consolidation or merger which, if its separate existence had continued, would have had power and authority to indemnify its directors, officers, and employees or agents, so that any person who is or was a director, officer, employee or agent of such constituent corporation, or is or was serving at the request of such constituent corporation as a director, officer, employee or agent of another corporation, partnership, joint venture, trust or other enterprise, shall stand in the same position under this section with respect to the resulting or surviving corporation as such person would have with respect to such constituent corporation if its separate existence had continued.

(i) For purposes of this section, references to "other enterprises" shall include employee benefit plans; references to "fines" shall include any excise taxes assessed on a person with respect to any employee benefit plan; and references to "serving at the request of the corporation" shall include any service as a director, officer, employee or agent of the corporation which imposes duties on, or involves services by, such director, officer, employee or agent with respect to an employee benefit plan, its participants or beneficiaries; and a person who acted in good faith and in a manner such person reasonably believed to be in the interest of the participants and beneficiaries of an employee benefit plan shall be deemed to have acted in a manner "not opposed to the best interests of the corporation" as referred to in this section.

(j) The indemnification and advancement of expenses provided by, or granted pursuant to, this section shall, unless otherwise provided when authorized or ratified, continue as to a person who has ceased to be a director, officer, employee or agent and shall inure to the benefit of the heirs, executors and administrators of such a person.

(k) The Court of Chancery is hereby vested with exclusive jurisdiction to hear and determine all actions for advancement of expenses or indemnification brought under this section or under any bylaw, agreement, vote of stockholders or disinterested directors, or otherwise. The Court of Chancery may summarily determine a corporation's obligation to advance expenses (including attorneys' fees).

§ 146. Submission of Matters for Stockholder Vote

A corporation may agree to submit a matter to a vote of its stockholders whether or not the board of directors determines at any time subsequent to approving such matter that such matter is no longer advisable and recommends that the stockholders reject or vote against the matter.

Subchapter V. Stock and Dividends

§ 151. Classes and Series of Stock; Redemption; Rights

(a) Every corporation may issue 1 or more classes of stock or 1 or more series of stock within any class thereof, any or all of which classes may be of stock with par value or stock without par value and which classes or series may have such voting powers, full or limited, or no voting powers, and such designations, preferences and relative, participating, optional or other special rights, and qualifications, limitations or restrictions thereof, as shall be stated and expressed in the certificate of incorporation or of any amendment thereto, or in the resolution or resolutions providing for the issue of such stock adopted by the board of directors pursuant to authority expressly vested in it by the provisions of its certificate of incorporation. Any of the voting powers, designations, preferences, rights and qualifications, limitations or restrictions of any such class or series of stock may be made dependent upon facts ascertainable outside the certificate of incorporation or of any amendment thereto, or outside the resolution or resolutions providing for the issue of such stock adopted by the board of directors pursuant to authority expressly vested in it by its certificate of incorporation, provided that the manner in which such facts shall operate upon the voting powers, designations, preferences, rights and qualifications, limitations or restrictions of such class or series of stock is clearly and expressly set forth in the certificate of incorporation or in the resolution or resolutions providing for the issue of such stock adopted by the board of directors. The term "facts," as used in this subsection, includes, but is not limited to, the occurrence of any event, including a determination or action by any person or body, including the corporation. The power to increase or decrease or otherwise adjust the capital stock as provided in this chapter shall apply to all or any such classes of stock.

(b) Any stock of any class or series may be made subject to redemption by the corporation at its option or at the option of the holders of such stock or upon the happening of a specified event; provided however, that immediately following any such redemption the corporation shall have outstanding 1 or more shares of 1 or more classes or series of stock, which share, or shares together, shall have full voting powers. Notwithstanding the limitation stated in the foregoing proviso:

(1) Any stock of a regulated investment company registered under the Investment Company Act of 1940 [15 U.S.C. § 80 a-1 et seq.], as heretofore or hereafter amended, may be made subject to redemption by the corporation at its option or at the option of the holders of such stock.

(2) Any stock of a corporation which holds (directly or indirectly) a license or franchise from a governmental agency to conduct its business or is a member of a national securities exchange, which license, franchise or membership is conditioned upon some or all of the holders of its stock possessing prescribed qualifications, may be made subject to redemption by the corporation to the extent necessary to prevent the loss of such license, franchise or membership or to reinstate it.

Any stock which may be made redeemable under this section may be redeemed for cash, property or rights, including securities of the same or another corporation, at such time or times, price or prices, or rate or rates, and with such adjustments, as shall be stated in the certificate of incorporation or in the resolution or resolutions providing for the issue of such stock adopted by the board of directors pursuant to subsection (a) of this section.

(c) The holders of preferred or special stock of any class or of any series thereof shall be entitled to receive dividends at such rates, on such conditions and at such times as shall be stated in the certificate of incorporation or in the resolution or resolutions providing for the issue of such stock adopted by the board of directors as hereinabove provided, payable in preference to, or in such relation to, the dividends payable on any other class or classes or of any other series of stock, and cumulative or noncumulative as shall be so stated and expressed. When dividends upon the preferred and special stocks, if any, to the extent of the preference to which such stocks are entitled, shall have been paid or declared and set apart for payment, a dividend on the remaining class or classes or series of stock may then be paid out of the remaining assets of the corporation available for dividends as elsewhere in this chapter provided.

(d) The holders of the preferred or special stock of any class or of any series thereof shall be entitled to such rights upon the dissolution of, or upon any distribution of the assets of, the corporation as shall be stated in the certificate of incorporation or in the resolution or resolutions providing for the issue of such stock adopted by the board of directors as hereinabove provided.

(e) Any stock of any class or of any series thereof may be made convertible into, or exchangeable for, at the option of either the holder or the corporation or upon the happening of a specified event, shares of any other class or classes or any other series of the same or any other class or classes of stock of the corporation, at such price or prices or at such rate or rates of exchange and with such adjustments as shall be stated in the certificate of incorporation or in the resolution or resolutions providing for the issue of such stock adopted by the board of directors as hereinabove provided.

(f) If any corporation shall be authorized to issue more than 1 class of stock or more than 1 series of any class, the powers, designations, preferences and relative, participating, optional, or other special rights of each class of stock or series thereof and the qualifications, limitations or restrictions of such preferences and/or rights shall be set forth in full or summarized on the face or back of the certificate which the corporation shall issue to represent such class or series of stock, provided that, except as otherwise provided in § 202 of this title, in lieu of the foregoing requirements, there may be set forth on the face or back of the certificate which the corporation shall issue to represent such class or series of stock, a statement that the corporation will furnish without charge to each stockholder who so requests the powers, designations, preferences and relative, participating, optional, or other special rights of each class of stock or series thereof and the qualifications, limitations or restrictions of such preferences and/or rights. Within a reasonable time after the issuance or transfer of uncertificated stock, the corporation shall send to the registered owner thereof a written notice containing the information required to be set forth or stated on certificates pursuant to this section or § 156, § 202(a) or § 218(a) of this title or with respect to this section a statement that the corporation will furnish without charge to each stockholder who so requests the powers, designations, preferences and relative participating, optional or other special rights of each class of stock or series thereof and the qualifications, limitations or restrictions of such preferences and/or rights. Except as otherwise expressly provided by law, the rights and obligations of the holders of uncertificated stock and the rights and obligations of the holders of certificates representing stock of the same class and series shall be identical.

(g) When any corporation desires to issue any shares of stock of any class or of any series of any class of which the powers, designations, preferences and relative, participating, optional or other rights, if any, or the qualifications, limitations or restrictions thereof, if any, shall not have been set forth in the certificate of incorporation or in any amendment thereto but shall be provided for in a resolution or resolutions adopted by the board of directors pursuant to authority expressly vested in it by the certificate of incorporation or any amendment thereto, a certificate of designations setting forth a copy of such resolution or resolutions and the number of shares of stock of such class or series as to which the resolution or resolutions apply shall be executed, acknowledged, filed and shall become effective, in accordance with § 103 of this title. Unless otherwise provided in any such resolution or resolutions, the number of shares of stock of any such series to which such resolution or resolutions apply may be increased (but not above the total number of authorized shares of the class) or decreased (but not below the number of shares thereof then outstanding) by a certificate likewise executed, acknowledged and filed setting forth a statement that a specified increase or decrease therein had been authorized and directed by a resolution or resolutions likewise adopted by the board of directors. In case the number of such shares shall be decreased the number of shares so specified in the certificate shall resume the status which they had prior to the adoption of the first resolution or resolutions. When no shares of any such class or series are outstanding, either because none were issued or because no issued shares of any such class or series remain outstanding, a certificate setting forth a resolution or resolutions adopted by the board of directors that none of the authorized shares of such class or series are outstanding, and that none will be issued subject to the certificate of designations previously filed with respect to such class or series, may be executed, acknowledged and filed in accordance with § 103 of this title and, when such certificate becomes effective, it shall have the effect of eliminating from the certificate of incorporation all matters set forth in the certificate of designations with respect to such class or series of stock. Unless otherwise provided in the certificate of incorporation, if no shares of stock have been issued of a class or series of stock established by a resolution of the board of directors, the voting powers, designations, preferences and relative, participating, optional or other rights, if any, or the qualifications, limitations or restrictions thereof, may be amended by a resolution or resolutions adopted by the board of directors. A certificate which:

(1) States that no shares of the class or series have been issued;

(2) Sets forth a copy of the resolution or resolutions; and

(3) If the designation of the class or series is being changed, indicates the original designation and the new designation,

shall be executed, acknowledged and filed and shall become effective, in accordance with § 103 of this title. When any certificate filed under this subsection becomes effective, it shall have the effect of amending the certificate of incorporation; except that neither the filing of such certificate nor the filing of a restated certificate of incorporation pursuant to § 245 of this title shall prohibit the board of directors from subsequently adopting such resolutions as authorized by this subsection.

§ 152. Issuance of Stock; Lawful Consideration; Fully Paid Stock

The consideration, as determined pursuant to § 153(a) and (b) of this title, for subscriptions to, or the purchase of, the capital stock to be issued by a corporation shall be paid in such form and in such manner as the board of directors shall determine. The board of directors may authorize capital stock to be issued for consideration consisting of cash, any tangible or intangible property or any benefit to the corporation, or any combination thereof. The resolution authorizing the issuance of capital stock may provide that any stock to be issued pursuant to such resolution may be issued in 1 or more transactions in such numbers and at such times as are set forth in or determined by or in the manner set forth in the resolution, which may include a determination or action by any person or body, including the corporation, provided the resolution fixes a maximum number of shares that may be issued pursuant to such resolution, a time period during which such shares may be issued and a minimum amount of consideration for which such shares may be issued. The board of directors may determine the amount of consideration for which shares may be issued by setting a minimum amount of consideration or approving a formula by which the amount or minimum amount of consideration is determined. The formula may include or be made dependent upon facts ascertainable outside the formula, provided the manner in which such facts shall operate upon the formula is clearly and expressly set forth in the formula or in the resolution approving the formula. In the absence of actual fraud in the transaction, the judgment of the directors as to the value of such consideration shall be conclusive. The capital stock so issued shall be deemed to be fully paid and nonassessable stock upon receipt by the corporation of such consideration; provided, however, nothing contained herein shall prevent the board of directors from issuing partly paid shares under § 156 of this title.

§ 153. Consideration for Stock

(a) Shares of stock with par value may be issued for such consideration, having a value not less than the par value thereof, as determined from time to time by the board of directors, or by the stockholders if the certificate of incorporation so provides.

(b) Shares of stock without par value may be issued for such consideration as is determined from time to time by the board of directors, or by the stockholders if the certificate of incorporation so provides.

(c) Treasury shares may be disposed of by the corporation for such consideration as may be determined from time to time by the board of directors, or by the stockholders if the certificate of incorporation so provides.

(d) If the certificate of incorporation reserves to the stockholders the right to determine the consideration for the issue of any shares, the stockholders shall, unless the certificate requires a greater vote, do so by a vote of a majority of the outstanding stock entitled to vote thereon.

§ 154. Determination of Amount of Capital; Capital, Surplus and Net Assets Defined

Any corporation may, by resolution of its board of directors, determine that only a part of the consideration which shall be received by the corporation for any of the shares of its capital stock which it shall issue from time to time shall be capital; but, in case any of the shares issued shall be shares having a par value, the amount of the part of such consideration so determined to be capital shall be in excess of the aggregate par value of the shares issued for such consideration having a par value, unless all the shares issued shall be shares having a par value, in which case the amount of the part of such consideration so determined to be capital need be only equal to the aggregate par value of such shares. In each such case the board of directors shall specify in dollars the part of such consideration which shall be capital. If the board of directors shall not have determined (1) at the time of issue of any shares of the capital stock of the corporation issued for cash or (2) within 60 days after the issue of any shares of the capital stock of the corporation issued for consideration other than cash what part of the consideration for such shares shall be capital, the capital of the corporation in respect of such shares shall be an amount equal to the aggregate par value of such shares having a par value, plus the amount of the consideration for such shares without par value. The amount of the consideration so determined to be capital in respect of any shares without par value shall be the stated capital of such shares. The capital of the corporation may be increased from time to time by resolution of the board of directors directing that a portion of the net assets of the corporation in excess of the amount so determined to be capital be transferred to the capital account. The board of directors may direct that the portion of such net assets so transferred shall be treated as capital in respect of any shares of the corporation of any designated class or classes. The excess, if any, at any given time, of the net assets of the corporation over the amount so determined to be capital shall be surplus. Net assets means the amount by which total assets exceed total liabilities. Capital and surplus are not liabilities for this purpose. Notwithstanding anything in this section to the contrary, for purposes of this section and §§ 160 and 170 of this title, the capital of any nonstock corporation shall be deemed to be zero.

§ 155. Fractions of Shares

A corporation may, but shall not be required to, issue fractions of a share. If it does not issue fractions of a share, it shall (1) arrange for the disposition of fractional interests by those entitled thereto, (2) pay in cash the fair value of fractions of a share as of the time when those entitled to receive such fractions are determined or (3) issue scrip or warrants in registered form (either represented by a certificate or uncertificated) or in bearer form (represented by a certificate) which shall entitle the holder to receive a full share upon the surrender of such scrip or warrants aggregating a full share. A certificate for a fractional share or an uncertificated fractional share shall, but scrip or warrants shall not unless otherwise provided therein, entitle the holder to exercise voting rights, to receive dividends thereon and to participate in any of the assets of the corporation in the event of liquidation. The board of directors may cause scrip or warrants to be issued subject to the conditions that they shall become void if not exchanged for certificates representing the full shares or uncertificated full shares before a specified date, or subject to the conditions that the shares for which scrip or warrants are exchangeable may be sold by the corporation and the proceeds thereof distributed to the holders of scrip or warrants, or subject to any other conditions which the board of directors may impose.

§ 156. Partly Paid Shares

Any corporation may issue the whole or any part of its shares as partly paid and subject to call for the remainder of the consideration to be paid therefor. Upon the face or back of each stock certificate issued to represent any such partly paid shares, or upon the books and records of the corporation in the case of uncertificated partly paid shares, the total amount of the consideration to be paid therefor and the amount paid thereon shall be stated. Upon the declaration of any dividend on fully paid shares, the corporation shall declare a dividend upon partly paid shares of the same class, but only upon the basis of the percentage of the consideration actually paid thereon.

§ 157. Rights and Options Respecting Stock

(a) Subject to any provisions in the certificate of incorporation, every corporation may create and issue, whether or not in connection with the issue and sale of any shares of stock or other securities of the corporation, rights or options entitling the holders thereof to acquire from the corporation any shares of its capital stock of any class or classes, such rights or options to be evidenced by or in such instrument or instruments as shall be approved by the board of directors.

(b) The terms upon which, including the time or times which may be limited or unlimited in duration, at or within which, and the consideration (including a formula by which such consideration may be determined) for which any such shares may be acquired from the corporation upon the exercise of any such right or option, shall be such as shall be stated in the certificate of incorporation, or in a resolution adopted by the board of directors providing for the creation and issue of such rights or options, and, in every case, shall be set forth or incorporated by reference in the instrument or instruments evidencing such rights or options. A formula by which such consideration may be determined may include or be made dependent upon facts ascertainable outside the formula, provided the manner in which such facts shall operate upon the formula is clearly and expressly set forth in the formula or in the resolution approving the formula. In the absence of actual fraud in the transaction, the judgment of the directors as to the consideration for the issuance of such rights or options and the sufficiency thereof shall be conclusive.

(c) The board of directors may, by a resolution adopted by the board, authorize 1 or more officers of the corporation to do 1 or both of the following: (i) designate officers and employees of the corporation or of any of its subsidiaries to be recipients of such rights or options created by the corporation, and (ii) determine the number of such rights or options to be received by such officers and employees; provided, however, that the resolution so authorizing such officer or officers shall specify the total number of rights or options such officer or officers may so award. The board of directors may not authorize an officer to designate himself or herself as a recipient of any such rights or options.

(d) In case the shares of stock of the corporation to be issued upon the exercise of such rights or options shall be shares having a par value, the consideration so to be received therefor shall have a value not less than the par value thereof. In case the shares of stock so to be issued shall be shares of stock without par value, the consideration therefor shall be determined in the manner provided in § 153 of this title.

§ 158. Stock Certificates; Uncertificated Shares

The shares of a corporation shall be represented by certificates, provided that the board of directors of the corporation may provide by resolution or resolutions that some or all of any or all classes or series of its stock shall be uncertificated shares. Any such resolution shall not apply to shares represented by a certificate until such certificate is surrendered to the corporation. Every holder of stock represented by certificates shall be entitled to have a certificate signed by, or in the name of the corporation by the chairperson or vice-chairperson of the board of directors, or the president or vice-president, and by the treasurer or an assistant treasurer, or the secretary or an assistant secretary of such corporation representing the number of shares registered in certificate form. Any or all the signatures on the certificate may be a facsimile. In case any officer, transfer agent or registrar who has signed or whose facsimile signature has been placed upon a certificate shall have ceased to be such officer, transfer agent or registrar before such certificate is issued, it may be issued by the corporation with the same effect as if such person were such officer, transfer agent or registrar at the date of issue. A corporation shall not have power to issue a certificate in bearer form.

§ 159. Shares of Stock; Personal Property, Transfer and Taxation

The shares of stock in every corporation shall be deemed personal property and transferable as provided in Article 8 of subtitle I of Title 6.

No stock or bonds issued by any corporation organized under this chapter shall be taxed by this State when the same shall be owned by nonresidents of this State, or by foreign corporations. Whenever any transfer of shares shall be made for collateral security, and not absolutely, it shall be so expressed in the entry of transfer if, when the certificates are presented to the corporation for transfer or uncertificated shares are requested to be transferred, both the transferor and transferee request the corporation to do so.

§ 160. Corporation's Powers Respecting Ownership, Voting, etc., of Its Own Stock; Rights of Stock Called for Redemption

(a) Every corporation may purchase, redeem, receive, take or otherwise acquire, own and hold, sell, lend, exchange, transfer or otherwise dispose of, pledge, use and otherwise deal in and with its own shares; provided, however, that no corporation shall:

(1) Purchase or redeem its own shares of capital stock for cash or other property when the capital of the corporation is impaired or when such purchase or redemption would cause any impairment of the capital of the corporation, except that a corporation other than a nonstock corporation may purchase or redeem out of capital any of its own shares which are entitled upon any distribution of its assets, whether by dividend or in liquidation, to a preference over another class or series of its stock, or, if no shares entitled to such a preference are outstanding, any of its own shares, if such shares will be retired upon their acquisition and the capital of the corporation reduced in accordance with §§ 243 and 244 of this title. Nothing in this subsection shall invalidate or otherwise affect a note, debenture or other obligation of a corporation given by it as consideration for its acquisition by purchase, redemption or exchange of its shares of stock if at the time such note, debenture or obligation was delivered by the corporation its capital was not then impaired or did not thereby become impaired;

(2) Purchase, for more than the price at which they may then be redeemed, any of its shares which are redeemable at the option of the corporation; or

(3)a. In the case of a corporation other than a nonstock corporation, redeem any of its shares, unless their redemption is authorized by § 151(b) of this title and then only in accordance with such section and the certificate of incorporation, or

b. In the case of a nonstock corporation, redeem any of its membership interests, unless their redemption is authorized by the certificate of incorporation and then only in accordance with the certificate of incorporation.

(b) Nothing in this section limits or affects a corporation's right to resell any of its shares theretofore purchased or redeemed out of surplus and which have not been retired, for such consideration as shall be fixed by the board of directors.

(c) Shares of its own capital stock belonging to the corporation or to another corporation, if a majority of the shares entitled to vote in the election of directors of such other corporation is held, directly or indirectly, by the corporation, shall neither be entitled to vote nor be counted for quorum purposes. Nothing in this section shall be construed as limiting the right of any corporation to vote stock, including but not limited to its own stock, held by it in a fiduciary capacity.

(d) Shares which have been called for redemption shall not be deemed to be outstanding shares for the purpose of voting or determining the total number of shares entitled to vote on any matter on and after the date on which written notice of redemption has been sent to holders thereof and a sum sufficient to redeem such shares has been irrevocably deposited or set aside to pay the redemption price to the holders of the shares upon surrender of certificates therefor.

§ 161. Issuance of Additional Stock; When and by Whom

The directors may, at any time and from time to time, if all of the shares of capital stock which the corporation is authorized by its certificate of incorporation to issue have not been issued, subscribed for, or otherwise committed to be issued, issue or take subscriptions for additional shares of its capital stock up to the amount authorized in its certificate of incorporation.

§ 162. Liability of Stockholder or Subscriber for Stock Not Paid in Full

(a) When the whole of the consideration payable for shares of a corporation has not been paid in, and the assets shall be insufficient to satisfy the claims of its creditors, each holder of or subscriber for such shares shall be bound to pay on each share held or subscribed for by such holder or subscriber the sum necessary to complete the amount of the unpaid balance of the consideration for which such shares were issued or are to be issued by the corporation.

(b) The amounts which shall be payable as provided in subsection (a) of this section may be recovered as provided in § 325 of this title, after a writ of execution against the corporation has been returned unsatisfied as provided in said § 325.

(c) Any person becoming an assignee or transferee of shares or of a subscription for shares in good faith and without knowledge or notice that the full consideration therefor has not been paid shall not be personally liable for any unpaid portion of such consideration, but the transferor shall remain liable therefor.

(d) No person holding shares in any corporation as collateral security shall be personally liable as a stockholder but the person pledging such shares shall be considered the holder thereof and shall be so liable. No executor, administrator, guardian, trustee or other fiduciary shall be personally liable as a stockholder, but the estate or funds held by such executor, administrator, guardian, trustee or other fiduciary in such fiduciary capacity shall be liable.

(e) No liability under this section or under § 325 of this title shall be asserted more than 6 years after the issuance of the stock or the date of the subscription upon which the assessment is sought.

(f) In any action by a receiver or trustee of an insolvent corporation or by a judgment creditor to obtain an assessment under this section, any stockholder or subscriber for stock of the insolvent corporation may appear and contest the claim or claims of such receiver or trustee.

§ 163. Payment for Stock Not Paid in Full

The capital stock of a corporation shall be paid for in such amounts and at such times as the directors may require. The directors may, from time to time, demand payment, in respect of each share of stock not fully paid, of such sum of money as the necessities of the business may, in the judgment of the board of directors, require, not exceeding in the whole the balance remaining unpaid on said stock, and such sum so demanded shall be paid to the corporation at such times and by such installments as the directors shall direct. The directors shall give written notice of the time and place of such payments, which notice shall be mailed at least 30 days before the time for such payment, to each holder of or subscriber for stock which is not fully paid at such holder's or subscriber's last known post-office address.

§ 164. Failure to Pay for Stock; Remedies

When any stockholder fails to pay any installment or call upon such stockholder's stock which may have been properly demanded by the directors, at the time when such payment is due, the directors may collect the amount of any such installment or call or any balance thereof remaining unpaid, from the said stockholder by an action at law, or they shall sell at public sale such part of the shares of such delinquent stockholder as will pay all demands then due from such stockholder with interest and all incidental expenses, and shall transfer the shares so sold to the purchaser, who shall be entitled to a certificate therefor.

Notice of the time and place of such sale and of the sum due on each share shall be given by advertisement at least 1 week before the sale, in a newspaper of the county in this State where such corporation's registered office is located, and such notice shall be mailed by the corporation to such delinquent stockholder at such stockholder's last known post-office address, at least 20 days before such sale.

If no bidder can be had to pay the amount due on the stock, and if the amount is not collected by an action at law, which may be brought within the county where the corporation has its registered office, within 1 year from the date of the bringing of such action at law, the said stock and the amount previously paid in by the delinquent stockholder on the stock shall be forfeited to the corporation.

§ 165. Revocability of Preincorporation Subscriptions

Unless otherwise provided by the terms of the subscription, a subscription for stock of a corporation to be formed shall be irrevocable, except with the consent of all other subscribers or the corporation, for a period of 6 months from its date.

§ 166. Formalities Required of Stock Subscriptions

A subscription for stock of a corporation, whether made before or after the formation of a corporation, shall not be enforceable against a subscriber, unless in writing and signed by the subscriber or by such subscriber's agent.

§ 167. Lost, Stolen or Destroyed Stock Certificates; Issuance of New Certificate or Uncertificated Shares

A corporation may issue a new certificate of stock or uncertificated shares in place of any certificate theretofore issued by it, alleged to have been lost, stolen or destroyed, and the corporation may require the owner of the lost, stolen or destroyed certificate, or such owner's legal representative to give the corporation a bond sufficient to indemnify it against any claim that may be made against it on account of the alleged loss, theft or destruction of any such certificate or the issuance of such new certificate or uncertificated shares.

§ 168. Judicial Proceedings to Compel Issuance of New Certificate or Uncertificated Shares

(a) If a corporation refuses to issue new uncertificated shares or a new certificate of stock in place of a certificate theretofore issued by it, or by any corporation of which it is the lawful successor, alleged to have been lost, stolen or destroyed, the owner of the lost, stolen or destroyed certificate or such owner's legal representatives may apply to the Court of Chancery for an order requiring the corporation to show cause why it should not issue new uncertificated shares or a new certificate of stock in place of the certificate so lost, stolen or destroyed. Such application shall be by a complaint which shall state the name of the corporation, the number and date of the certificate, if known or ascertainable by the plaintiff, the number of shares of stock represented thereby and to whom issued, and a statement of the circumstances attending such loss, theft or destruction. Thereupon the court shall make an order requiring the corporation to show cause at a time and place therein designated, why it should not issue new uncertificated shares or a new certificate of stock in place of the one described in the complaint. A copy of the complaint and order shall be served upon the corporation at least 5 days before the time designated in the order.

(b) If, upon hearing, the court is satisfied that the plaintiff is the lawful owner of the number of shares of capital stock, or any part thereof, described in the complaint, and that the certificate therefor has been lost, stolen or destroyed, and no sufficient cause has been shown why new uncertificated shares or a new certificate should not be issued in place thereof, it shall make an order requiring the corporation to issue and deliver to the plaintiff new uncertificated shares or a new certificate for such shares. In its order the court shall direct that, prior to the issuance and delivery to the plaintiff of such new uncertificated shares or a new certificate, the plaintiff give the corporation a bond in such form and with such security as to the court appears sufficient to indemnify the corporation against any claim that may be made against it on account of the alleged loss, theft or destruction of any such certificate or the issuance of such new uncertificated shares or new certificate. No corporation which has issued uncertificated shares or a certificate pursuant to an order of the court entered hereunder shall be liable in an amount in excess of the amount specified in such bond.

§ 169. Situs of Ownership of Stock

For all purposes of title, action, attachment, garnishment and jurisdiction of all courts held in this State, but not for the purpose of taxation, the situs of the ownership of the capital stock of all corporations existing under the laws of this State, whether organized under this chapter or otherwise, shall be regarded as in this State.

§ 170. Dividends; Payment; Wasting Asset Corporations

(a) The directors of every corporation, subject to any restrictions contained in its certificate of incorporation, may declare and pay dividends upon the shares of its capital stock either:

(1) Out of its surplus, as defined in and computed in accordance with §§ 154 and 244 of this title; or

(2) In case there shall be no such surplus, out of its net profits for the fiscal year in which the dividend is declared and/or the preceding fiscal year.

If the capital of the corporation, computed in accordance with §§ 154 and 244 of this title, shall have been diminished by depreciation in the value of its property, or by losses, or otherwise, to an amount less than the aggregate amount of the capital represented by the issued and outstanding stock of all classes having a preference upon the distribution of assets, the directors of such corporation shall not declare and pay out of such net profits any dividends upon any shares of any classes of its capital stock until the deficiency in the amount of capital represented by the issued and outstanding stock of all classes having a preference upon the distribution of assets shall have been repaired. Nothing in this subsection shall invalidate or otherwise affect a note, debenture or other obligation of the corporation paid by it as a dividend on shares of its stock, or any payment made thereon, if at the time such note, debenture or obligation was delivered by the corporation, the corporation had either surplus or net profits as provided in (a)(1) or (2) of this section from which the dividend could lawfully have been paid.

(b) Subject to any restrictions contained in its certificate of incorporation, the directors of any corporation engaged in the exploitation of wasting assets (including but not limited to a corporation engaged in the exploitation of natural resources or other wasting assets, including patents, or engaged primarily in the liquidation of specific assets) may determine the net profits derived from the exploitation of such wasting assets or the net proceeds derived from such liquidation without taking into consideration the depletion of such assets resulting from lapse of time, consumption, liquidation or exploitation of such assets.

...

§ 171. Special Purpose Reserves

The directors of a corporation may set apart out of any of the funds of the corporation available for dividends a reserve or reserves for any proper purpose and may abolish any such reserve.

§ 172. Liability of Directors and Committee Members as to Dividends or Stock Redemption

A member of the board of directors, or a member of any committee designated by the board of directors, shall be fully protected in relying in good faith upon the records of the corporation and upon such information, opinions, reports or statements presented to the corporation by any of its officers or employees, or committees of the board of directors, or by any other person as to matters the director reasonably believes are within such other person's professional or expert competence and who has been selected with reasonable care by or on behalf of the corporation, as to the value and amount of the assets, liabilities and/or net profits of the corporation or any other facts pertinent to the existence and amount of surplus or other funds from which dividends might properly be declared and paid, or with which the corporation's stock might properly be purchased or redeemed.

§ 173. Declaration and Payment of Dividends

No corporation shall pay dividends except in accordance with this chapter. Dividends may be paid in cash, in property, or in shares of the corporation's capital stock. If the dividend is to be paid in shares of the corporation's theretofore unissued capital stock the board of directors shall, by resolution, direct that there be designated as capital in respect of such shares an amount which is not less than the aggregate par value of par value shares being declared as a dividend and, in the case of shares without par value being declared as a dividend, such amount as shall be determined by the board of directors. No such designation as capital shall be necessary if shares are being distributed by a corporation pursuant to a split-up or division of its stock rather than as payment of a dividend declared payable in stock of the corporation.

§ 174. Liability of Directors for Unlawful Payment of Dividend or Unlawful Stock Purchase or Redemption; Exoneration from Liability; Contribution Among Directors; Subrogation

(a) In case of any wilful or negligent violation of § 160 or § 173 of this title, the directors under whose administration the same may happen shall be jointly and severally liable, at any time within 6 years after paying such unlawful dividend or after such unlawful stock purchase or redemption, to the corporation, and to its creditors in the event of its dissolution or insolvency, to the full amount of the dividend unlawfully paid, or to the full amount unlawfully paid for the purchase or redemption of the corporation's stock, with interest from the time such liability accrued. Any director who may have been absent when the same was done, or who may have dissented from the act or resolution by which the same was done, may be exonerated from such liability by causing his or her dissent to be entered on the books containing the minutes of the proceedings of the directors at the time the same was done, or immediately after such director has notice of the same.

(b) Any director against whom a claim is successfully asserted under this section shall be entitled to contribution from the other directors who voted for or concurred in the unlawful dividend, stock purchase or stock redemption.

(c) Any director against whom a claim is successfully asserted under this section shall be entitled, to the extent of the amount paid by such director as a result of such claim, to be subrogated to the rights of the corporation against stockholders who received the dividend on, or assets for the sale or redemption of, their stock with knowledge of facts indicating that such dividend, stock purchase or redemption was unlawful under this chapter, in proportion to the amounts received by such stockholders respectively.

Subchapter VI. Stock Transfers

§ 201. Transfer of Stock, Stock Certificates and Uncertificated Stock

Except as otherwise provided in this chapter, the transfer of stock and the certificates of stock which represent the stock or uncertificated stock shall be governed by Article 8 of subtitle I of Title 6. To the extent that any provision of this chapter is inconsistent with any provision of subtitle I of Title 6, this chapter shall be controlling.

§ 202. Restrictions on Transfer and Ownership of Securities

(a) A written restriction or restrictions on the transfer or registration of transfer of a security of a corporation, or on the amount of the corporation's securities that may be owned by any person or group of persons, if permitted by this section and noted conspicuously on the certificate or certificates representing the security or securities so restricted or, in the case of uncertificated shares, contained in the notice or notices sent pursuant to § 151(f) of this title, may be enforced against the holder of the restricted security or securities or any successor or transferee of the holder including an executor, administrator, trustee, guardian or other fiduciary entrusted with like responsibility for the person or estate of the holder. Unless noted conspicuously on the certificate or certificates representing the security or securities so restricted or, in the case of uncertificated shares, contained in the notice or notices sent pursuant to § 151(f) of this title, a restriction, even though permitted by this section, is ineffective except against a person with actual knowledge of the restriction.

(b) A restriction on the transfer or registration of transfer of securities of a corporation, or on the amount of a corporation's securities that may be owned by any person or group of persons, may be imposed by the certificate of incorporation or by the bylaws or by an agreement among any number of security holders or among such holders and the corporation. No restrictions so imposed shall be binding with respect to securities issued prior to the adoption of the restriction unless the holders of the securities are parties to an agreement or voted in favor of the restriction.

(c) A restriction on the transfer or registration of transfer of securities of a corporation or on the amount of such securities that may be owned by any person or group of persons is permitted by this section if it:

(1) Obligates the holder of the restricted securities to offer to the corporation or to any other holders of securities of the corporation or to any other person or to any combination of the foregoing, a prior opportunity, to be exercised within a reasonable time, to acquire the restricted securities; or

(2) Obligates the corporation or any holder of securities of the corporation or any other person or any combination of the foregoing, to purchase the securities which are the subject of an agreement respecting the purchase and sale of the restricted securities; or

(3) Requires the corporation or the holders of any class or series of securities of the corporation to consent to any proposed transfer of the restricted securities or to approve the proposed transferee of the restricted securities, or to approve the amount of securities of the corporation that may be owned by any person or group of persons; or

(4) Obligates the holder of the restricted securities to sell or transfer an amount of restricted securities to the corporation or to any other holders of securities of the corporation or to any other person or to any combination of the foregoing, or causes or results in the automatic sale or transfer of an amount of restricted securities to the corporation or to any other holders of securities of the corporation or to any other person or to any combination of the foregoing; or

(5) Prohibits or restricts the transfer of the restricted securities to, or the ownership of restricted securities by, designated persons or classes of persons or groups of persons, and such designation is not manifestly unreasonable.

(d) Any restriction on the transfer or the registration of transfer of the securities of a corporation, or on the amount of securities of a corporation that may be owned by a person or group of persons, for any of the following purposes shall be conclusively presumed to be for a reasonable purpose:

(1) Maintaining any local, state, federal or foreign tax advantage to the corporation or its stockholders, including without limitation:

a. Maintaining the corporation's status as an electing small business corporation under subchapter S of the United States Internal Revenue Code [26 U.S.C. § 1371 et seq.], or

b. Maintaining or preserving any tax attribute (including without limitation net operating losses), or

c. Qualifying or maintaining the qualification of the corporation as a real estate investment trust pursuant to the United States Internal Revenue Code or regulations adopted pursuant to the United States Internal Revenue Code, or

(2) Maintaining any statutory or regulatory advantage or complying with any statutory or regulatory requirements under applicable local, state, federal or foreign law.

(e) Any other lawful restriction on transfer or registration of transfer of securities, or on the amount of securities that may be owned by any person or group of persons, is permitted by this section.

§ 203. Business Combinations with Interested Stockholders

(a) Notwithstanding any other provisions of this chapter, a corporation shall not engage in any business combination with any interested stockholder for a period of 3 years following the time that such stockholder became an interested stockholder, unless:

(1) Prior to such time the board of directors of the corporation approved either the business combination or the transaction which resulted in the stockholder becoming an interested stockholder;

board approval

(2) Upon consummation of the transaction which resulted in the stockholder becoming an interested stockholder, the interested stockholder owned at least 85% of the voting stock of the corporation outstanding at the time the transaction commenced, excluding for purposes of determining the voting stock outstanding (but not the outstanding voting stock owned by the interested stockholder) those shares owned (i) by persons who are directors and also officers and (ii) employee stock plans in which employee participants do not have the right to determine confidentially whether shares held subject to the plan will be tendered in a tender or exchange offer; or

(3) At or subsequent to such time the business combination is approved by the board of directors and authorized at an annual or special meeting of stockholders, and not by written consent, by the affirmative vote of at least 66 2/3% of the outstanding voting stock which is not owned by the interested stockholder.

(b) The restrictions contained in this section shall not apply if:

(1) The corporation's original certificate of incorporation contains a provision expressly electing not to be governed by this section;

can opt-out in corp. charter

(2) The corporation, by action of its board of directors, adopts an amendment to its bylaws within 90 days of February 2, 1988, expressly

electing not to be governed by this section, which amendment shall not be further amended by the board of directors;

(3) The corporation, by action of its stockholders, adopts an amendment to its certificate of incorporation or bylaws expressly electing not to be governed by this section; provided that, in addition to any other vote required by law, such amendment to the certificate of incorporation or bylaws must be approved by the affirmative vote of a majority of the shares entitled to vote. An amendment adopted pursuant to this paragraph shall be effective immediately in the case of a corporation that both (i) has never had a class of voting stock that falls within any of the 2 categories set out in paragraph (b)(4) of this section, and (ii) has not elected by a provision in its original certificate of incorporation or any amendment thereto to be governed by this section. In all other cases, an amendment adopted pursuant to this paragraph shall not be effective until 12 months after the adoption of such amendment and shall not apply to any business combination between such corporation and any person who became an interested stockholder of such corporation on or prior to such adoption. A bylaw amendment adopted pursuant to this paragraph shall not be further amended by the board of directors;

(4) The corporation does not have a class of voting stock that is: (i) Listed on a national securities exchange; or (ii) held of record by more than 2,000 stockholders, unless any of the foregoing results from action taken, directly or indirectly, by an interested stockholder or from a transaction in which a person becomes an interested stockholder;

(5) A stockholder becomes an interested stockholder inadvertently and (i) as soon as practicable divests itself of ownership of sufficient shares so that the stockholder ceases to be an interested stockholder; and (ii) would not, at any time within the 3-year period immediately prior to a business combination between the corporation and such stockholder, have been an interested stockholder but for the inadvertent acquisition of ownership;

(6) The business combination is proposed prior to the consummation or abandonment of and subsequent to the earlier of the public announcement or the notice required hereunder of a proposed transaction which (i) constitutes 1 of the transactions described in the second sentence of this paragraph; (ii) is with or by a person who either was not an interested stockholder during the previous 3 years or who became an interested stockholder with the approval of the corporation's board of directors or during the period described in paragraph (b)(7) of this section; and (iii) is approved or not opposed by a majority of the members of the board of directors then in office (but not less than 1) who were directors prior to any person becoming an interested stockholder during the previous 3 years or were recommended for election or elected to succeed such directors by a majority of such directors. The proposed transactions referred to in the preceding sentence are limited to (x) a merger or consolidation of the corporation (except for a merger in respect of which, pursuant to § 251(f)

of this title, no vote of the stockholders of the corporation is required); (y) a sale, lease, exchange, mortgage, pledge, transfer or other disposition (in 1 transaction or a series of transactions), whether as part of a dissolution or otherwise, of assets of the corporation or of any direct or indirect majority-owned subsidiary of the corporation (other than to any direct or indirect wholly-owned subsidiary or to the corporation) having an aggregate market value equal to 50% or more of either that aggregate market value of all of the assets of the corporation determined on a consolidated basis or the aggregate market value of all the outstanding stock of the corporation; or (z) a proposed tender or exchange offer for 50% or more of the outstanding voting stock of the corporation. The corporation shall give not less than 20 days' notice to all interested stockholders prior to the consummation of any of the transactions described in clause (x) or (y) of the second sentence of this paragraph; or

(7) The business combination is with an interested stockholder who became an interested stockholder at a time when the restrictions contained in this section did not apply by reason of any of paragraphs (b)(1) through (4) of this section, provided, however, that this paragraph (b)(7) shall not apply if, at the time such interested stockholder became an interested stockholder, the corporation's certificate of incorporation contained a provision authorized by the last sentence of this subsection (b).

Notwithstanding paragraphs (b)(1), (2), (3) and (4) of this section, a corporation may elect by a provision of its original certificate of incorporation or any amendment thereto to be governed by this section; provided that any such amendment to the certificate of incorporation shall not apply to restrict a business combination between the corporation and an interested stockholder of the corporation if the interested stockholder became such prior to the effective date of the amendment.

(c) As used in this section only, the term:

(1) "Affiliate" means a person that directly, or indirectly through 1 or more intermediaries, controls, or is controlled by, or is under common control with, another person.

(2) "Associate," when used to indicate a relationship with any person, means: (i) Any corporation, partnership, unincorporated association or other entity of which such person is a director, officer or partner or is, directly or indirectly, the owner of 20% or more of any class of voting stock; (ii) any trust or other estate in which such person has at least a 20% beneficial interest or as to which such person serves as trustee or in a similar fiduciary capacity; and (iii) any relative or spouse of such person, or any relative of such spouse, who has the same residence as such person.

(3) "Business combination," when used in reference to any corporation and any interested stockholder of such corporation, means:

(i) Any merger or consolidation of the corporation or any direct or indirect majority-owned subsidiary of the corporation with (A) the interested stockholder, or (B) with any other corporation, partnership, unincorporated association or other entity if the merger or consolidation is caused by the interested stockholder and as a result of such merger or consolidation subsection (a) of this section is not applicable to the surviving entity;

(ii) Any sale, lease, exchange, mortgage, pledge, transfer or other disposition (in 1 transaction or a series of transactions), except proportionately as a stockholder of such corporation, to or with the interested stockholder, whether as part of a dissolution or otherwise, of assets of the corporation or of any direct or indirect majority-owned subsidiary of the corporation which assets have an aggregate market value equal to 10% or more of either the aggregate market value of all the assets of the corporation determined on a consolidated basis or the aggregate market value of all the outstanding stock of the corporation;

(iii) Any transaction which results in the issuance or transfer by the corporation or by any direct or indirect majority-owned subsidiary of the corporation of any stock of the corporation or of such subsidiary to the interested stockholder, except: (A) Pursuant to the exercise, exchange or conversion of securities exercisable for, exchangeable for or convertible into stock of such corporation or any such subsidiary which securities were outstanding prior to the time that the interested stockholder became such; (B) pursuant to a merger under § 251(g) of this title; (C) pursuant to a dividend or distribution paid or made, or the exercise, exchange or conversion of securities exercisable for, exchangeable for or convertible into stock of such corporation or any such subsidiary which security is distributed, pro rata to all holders of a class or series of stock of such corporation subsequent to the time the interested stockholder became such; (D) pursuant to an exchange offer by the corporation to purchase stock made on the same terms to all holders of said stock; or (E) any issuance or transfer of stock by the corporation; provided however, that in no case under items (C)-(E) of this subparagraph shall there be an increase in the interested stockholder's proportionate share of the stock of any class or series of the corporation or of the voting stock of the corporation;

(iv) Any transaction involving the corporation or any direct or indirect majority-owned subsidiary of the corporation which has the effect, directly or indirectly, of increasing the proportionate share of the stock of any class or series, or securities convertible into the stock of any class or series, of the corporation or of any such subsidiary which is owned by the interested stockholder, except as a result of immaterial changes due to fractional share adjustments or as a result of any purchase or redemption of any shares of stock not caused, directly or indirectly, by the interested stockholder; or

(v) Any receipt by the interested stockholder of the benefit, directly or indirectly (except proportionately as a stockholder of such corporation), of any loans, advances, guarantees, pledges or other financial benefits (other than those expressly permitted in paragraphs (c)(3)(i)-(iv) of this section) provided by or through the corporation or any direct or indirect majority-owned subsidiary.

(4) "Control," including the terms "controlling," "controlled by" and "under common control with," means the possession, directly or indirectly, of the power to direct or cause the direction of the management and policies of a person, whether through the ownership of voting stock, by contract or otherwise. A person who is the owner of 20% or more of the outstanding voting stock of any corporation, partnership, unincorporated association or other entity shall be presumed to have control of such entity, in the absence of proof by a preponderance of the evidence to the contrary; Notwithstanding the foregoing, a presumption of control shall not apply where such person holds voting stock, in good faith and not for the purpose of circumventing this section, as an agent, bank, broker, nominee, custodian or trustee for 1 or more owners who do not individually or as a group have control of such entity.

(5) "Interested stockholder" means any person (other than the corporation and any direct or indirect majority-owned subsidiary of the corporation) that (i) is the owner of 15% or more of the outstanding voting stock of the corporation, or (ii) is an affiliate or associate of the corporation and was the owner of 15% or more of the outstanding voting stock of the corporation at any time within the 3-year period immediately prior to the date on which it is sought to be determined whether such person is an interested stockholder, and the affiliates and associates of such person; provided, however, that the term "interested stockholder" shall not include (x) any person who (A) owned shares in excess of the 15% limitation set forth herein as of, or acquired such shares pursuant to a tender offer commenced prior to, December 23, 1987, or pursuant to an exchange offer announced prior to the aforesaid date and commenced within 90 days thereafter and either (I) continued to own shares in excess of such 15% limitation or would have but for action by the corporation or (II) is an affiliate or associate of the corporation and so continued (or so would have continued but for action by the corporation) to be the owner of 15% or more of the outstanding voting stock of the corporation at any time within the 3-year period immediately prior to the date on which it is sought to be determined whether such a person is an interested stockholder or (B) acquired said shares from a person described in item (A) of this paragraph by gift, inheritance or in a transaction in which no consideration was exchanged; or (y) any person whose ownership of shares in excess of the 15% limitation set forth herein is the result of action taken solely by the corporation; provided that such person shall be an interested stockholder if thereafter such person acquires additional shares of voting stock of the corporation, except as a result of further corporate action not caused, directly or indirectly, by such person. For the purpose of determining whether a

person is an interested stockholder, the voting stock of the corporation deemed to be outstanding shall include stock deemed to be owned by the person through application of paragraph (9) of this subsection but shall not include any other unissued stock of such corporation which may be issuable pursuant to any agreement, arrangement or understanding, or upon exercise of conversion rights, warrants or options, or otherwise.

(6) "Person" means any individual, corporation, partnership, unincorporated association or other entity.

(7) "Stock" means, with respect to any corporation, capital stock and, with respect to any other entity, any equity interest.

(8) "Voting stock" means, with respect to any corporation, stock of any class or series entitled to vote generally in the election of directors and, with respect to any entity that is not a corporation, any equity interest entitled to vote generally in the election of the governing body of such entity. Every reference to a percentage of voting stock shall refer to such percentage of the votes of such voting stock.

(9) "Owner," including the terms "own" and "owned," when used with respect to any stock, means a person that individually or with or through any of its affiliates or associates:

(i) Beneficially owns such stock, directly or indirectly; or

(ii) Has (A) the right to acquire such stock (whether such right is exercisable immediately or only after the passage of time) pursuant to any agreement, arrangement or understanding, or upon the exercise of conversion rights, exchange rights, warrants or options, or otherwise; provided, however, that a person shall not be deemed the owner of stock tendered pursuant to a tender or exchange offer made by such person or any of such person's affiliates or associates until such tendered stock is accepted for purchase or exchange; or (B) the right to vote such stock pursuant to any agreement, arrangement or understanding; provided, however, that a person shall not be deemed the owner of any stock because of such person's right to vote such stock if the agreement, arrangement or understanding to vote such stock arises solely from a revocable proxy or consent given in response to a proxy or consent solicitation made to 10 or more persons; or

(iii) Has any agreement, arrangement or understanding for the purpose of acquiring, holding, voting (except voting pursuant to a revocable proxy or consent as described in item (B) of subparagraph (ii) of this paragraph), or disposing of such stock with any other person that beneficially owns, or whose affiliates or associates beneficially own, directly or indirectly, such stock.

(d) No provision of a certificate of incorporation or bylaw shall require, for any vote of stockholders required by this section, a greater vote of stockholders than that specified in this section.

(e) The Court of Chancery is hereby vested with exclusive jurisdiction to hear and determine all matters with respect to this section.

Subchapter VII. Meetings, Elections, Voting and Notice

§ 211. Meetings of Stockholders

(a)(1) Meetings of stockholders may be held at such place, either within or without this State as may be designated by or in the manner provided in the certificate of incorporation or bylaws, or if not so designated, as determined by the board of directors. If, pursuant to this paragraph or the certificate of incorporation or the bylaws of the corporation, the board of directors is authorized to determine the place of a meeting of stockholders, the board of directors may, in its sole discretion, determine that the meeting shall not be held at any place, but may instead be held solely by means of remote communication as authorized by paragraph (a)(2) of this section.

(2) If authorized by the board of directors in its sole discretion, and subject to such guidelines and procedures as the board of directors may adopt, stockholders and proxyholders not physically present at a meeting of stockholders may, by means of remote communication:

a. Participate in a meeting of stockholders; and

b. Be deemed present in person and vote at a meeting of stockholders, whether such meeting is to be held at a designated place or solely by means of remote communication, provided that (i) the corporation shall implement reasonable measures to verify that each person deemed present and permitted to vote at the meeting by means of remote communication is a stockholder or proxyholder, (ii) the corporation shall implement reasonable measures to provide such stockholders and proxyholders a reasonable opportunity to participate in the meeting and to vote on matters submitted to the stockholders, including an opportunity to read or hear the proceedings of the meeting substantially concurrently with such proceedings, and (iii) if any stockholder or proxyholder votes or takes other action at the meeting by means of remote communication, a record of such vote or other action shall be maintained by the corporation.

(b) Unless directors are elected by written consent in lieu of an annual meeting as permitted by this subsection, an annual meeting of stockholders shall be held for the election of directors on a date and at a time designated by or in the manner provided in the bylaws. Stockholders may, unless the certificate of incorporation otherwise provides, act by written consent to elect directors; provided, however, that, if such consent is less than unanimous, such action by written consent may be in lieu of holding an annual meeting only if all of the directorships to which directors could be elected at an annual meeting held at the effective time of such action are vacant and are filled by such action. Any other proper business may be transacted at the annual meeting.

(c) A failure to hold the annual meeting at the designated time or to elect a sufficient number of directors to conduct the business of the corporation shall not affect otherwise valid corporate acts or work a forfeiture or dissolution of the corporation except as may be otherwise specifically provided in this chapter. If the annual meeting for election of directors is not held on the date designated therefor or action by written consent to elect directors in lieu of an annual meeting has not been taken, the directors shall cause the meeting to be held as soon as is convenient. If there be a failure to hold the annual meeting or to take action by written consent to elect directors in lieu of an annual meeting for a period of 30 days after the date designated for the annual meeting, or if no date has been designated, for a period of 13 months after the latest to occur of the organization of the corporation, its last annual meeting or the last action by written consent to elect directors in lieu of an annual meeting, the Court of Chancery may summarily order a meeting to be held upon the application of any stockholder or director. The shares of stock represented at such meeting, either in person or by proxy, and entitled to vote thereat, shall constitute a quorum for the purpose of such meeting, notwithstanding any provision of the certificate of incorporation or bylaws to the contrary. The Court of Chancery may issue such orders as may be appropriate, including, without limitation, orders designating the time and place of such meeting, the record date or dates for determination of stockholders entitled to notice of the meeting and to vote thereat, and the form of notice of such meeting.

(d) Special meetings of the stockholders may be called by the board of directors or by such person or persons as may be authorized by the certificate of incorporation or by the bylaws.

(e) All elections of directors shall be by written ballot unless otherwise provided in the certificate of incorporation; if authorized by the board of directors, such requirement of a written ballot shall be satisfied by a ballot submitted by electronic transmission, provided that any such electronic transmission must either set forth or be submitted with information from which it can be determined that the electronic transmission was authorized by the stockholder or proxy holder.

§ 212. Voting Rights of Stockholders; Proxies; Limitations

(a) Unless otherwise provided in the certificate of incorporation and subject to § 213 of this title, each stockholder shall be entitled to 1 vote for each share of capital stock held by such stockholder. If the certificate of incorporation provides for more or less than 1 vote for any share, on any matter, every reference in this chapter to a majority or other proportion of stock, voting stock or shares shall refer to such majority or other proportion of the votes of such stock, voting stock or shares.

(b) Each stockholder entitled to vote at a meeting of stockholders or to express consent or dissent to corporate action in writing without a meeting may authorize another person or persons to act for such stockholder by proxy, but no such proxy shall be voted or acted upon after 3 years from its date, unless the proxy provides for a longer period.

(c) Without limiting the manner in which a stockholder may authorize another person or persons to act for such stockholder as proxy pursuant to subsection (b) of this section, the following shall constitute a valid means by which a stockholder may grant such authority:

(1) A stockholder may execute a writing authorizing another person or persons to act for such stockholder as proxy. Execution may be accomplished by the stockholder or such stockholder's authorized officer, director, employee or agent signing such writing or causing such person's signature to be affixed to such writing by any reasonable means including, but not limited to, by facsimile signature.

(2) A stockholder may authorize another person or persons to act for such stockholder as proxy by transmitting or authorizing the transmission of a telegram, cablegram, or other means of electronic transmission to the person who will be the holder of the proxy or to a proxy solicitation firm, proxy support service organization or like agent duly authorized by the person who will be the holder of the proxy to receive such transmission, provided that any such telegram, cablegram or other means of electronic transmission must either set forth or be submitted with information from which it can be determined that the telegram, cablegram or other electronic transmission was authorized by the stockholder. If it is determined that such telegrams, cablegrams or other electronic transmissions are valid, the inspectors or, if there are no inspectors, such other persons making that determination shall specify the information upon which they relied.

(d) Any copy, facsimile telecommunication or other reliable reproduction of the writing or transmission created pursuant to subsection (c) of this section may be substituted or used in lieu of the original writing or transmission for any and all purposes for which the original writing or transmission could be used, provided that such copy, facsimile telecommunication or other reproduction shall be a complete reproduction of the entire original writing or transmission.

(e) A duly executed proxy shall be irrevocable if it states that it is irrevocable and if, and only as long as, it is coupled with an interest sufficient in law to support an irrevocable power. A proxy may be made irrevocable regardless of whether the interest with which it is coupled is an interest in the stock itself or an interest in the corporation generally.

§ 213. Fixing Date for Determination of Stockholders of Record

(a) In order that the corporation may determine the stockholders entitled to notice of any meeting of stockholders or any adjournment thereof, the board of directors may fix a record date, which record date shall not precede the date upon which the resolution fixing the record date is adopted by the board of directors, and which record date shall not be more than 60 nor less than 10 days before the date of such meeting. If the board of directors so fixes a date, such date shall also be the record date for determining the stockholders entitled to vote at such meeting unless the board of directors determines, at the time it fixes such record date, that a later date on or before the date of the meeting shall be the date for making such determination. If no record date is fixed by the board of directors, the record date for determining stockholders entitled to notice of and to vote at a meeting of stockholders shall be at the close of business on the day next preceding the day on which notice is given, or, if notice is waived, at the close of business on the day next preceding the day on which the meeting is held. A determination of stockholders of record entitled to notice of or to vote at a meeting of stockholders shall apply to any adjournment of the meeting; provided, however, that the board of directors may fix a new record date for determination of stockholders entitled to vote at the adjourned meeting, and in such case shall also fix as the record date for stockholders entitled to notice of such adjourned meeting the same or an earlier date as that fixed for determination of stockholders entitled to vote in accordance with the foregoing provisions of this subsection (a) at the adjourned meeting.

(b) In order that the corporation may determine the stockholders entitled to consent to corporate action in writing without a meeting, the board of directors may fix a record date, which record date shall not precede the date upon which the resolution fixing the record date is adopted by the board of directors, and which date shall not be more than 10 days after the date upon which the resolution fixing the record date is adopted by the board of directors. If no record date has been fixed by the board of directors, the record date for determining stockholders entitled to consent to corporate action in writing without a meeting, when no prior action by the board of directors is required by this chapter, shall be the first date on which a signed written consent setting forth the action taken or proposed to be taken is delivered to the corporation by delivery to its registered office in this State, its principal place of business or an officer or agent of the corporation having custody of the book in which proceedings of meetings of stockholders are recorded. Delivery made to a corporation's registered office shall be by hand or by certified or registered mail, return receipt requested. If no record date has been fixed by the board of directors and prior action by the board of directors is required by this chapter, the record date for determining stockholders entitled to consent to corporate action in writing without a meeting shall be at the close of business on the day on which the board of directors adopts the resolution taking such prior action.

(c) In order that the corporation may determine the stockholders entitled to receive payment of any dividend or other distribution or allotment of any rights or the stockholders entitled to exercise any rights in respect of any change, conversion or exchange of stock, or for the purpose of any other lawful action, the board of directors may fix a record date, which record date shall not precede the date upon which the resolution fixing the record date is adopted, and which record date shall be not more than 60 days prior to such action. If no record date is fixed, the record date for determining stockholders for any such purpose shall be at the close of business on the day on which the board of directors adopts the resolution relating thereto.

§ 214. Cumulative Voting

The certificate of incorporation of any corporation may provide that at all elections of directors of the corporation, or at elections held under specified circumstances, each holder of stock or of any class or classes or of a series or series thereof shall be entitled to as many votes as shall equal the number of votes which (except for such provision as to cumulative voting) such holder would be entitled to cast for the election of directors with respect to such holder's shares of stock multiplied by the number of directors to be elected by such holder, and that such holder may cast all of such votes for a single director or may distribute them among the number to be voted for, or for any 2 or more of them as such holder may see fit.

§ 215. Voting Rights of Members of Nonstock Corporations; Quorum; Proxies

(a) Sections 211 through 214 and 216 of this title shall not apply to nonstock corporations, except that § 211(a) and (d) of this title and § 212(c), (d), and (e) of this title shall apply to such corporations, and, when so applied, all references therein to stockholders and to the board of directors shall be deemed to refer to the members and the governing body of a nonstock corporation, respectively; and all references to stock, capital stock, or shares thereof shall be deemed to refer to memberships of a nonprofit nonstock corporation and to membership interests of any other nonstock corporation.

(b) Unless otherwise provided in the certificate of incorporation or the bylaws of a nonstock corporation, and subject to subsection (f) of this section, each member shall be entitled at every meeting of members to 1 vote on each matter submitted to a vote of members. A member may exercise such voting rights in person or by proxy, but no proxy shall be voted on after 3 years from its date, unless the proxy provides for a longer period.

(c) Unless otherwise provided in this chapter, the certificate of incorporation or bylaws of a nonstock corporation may specify the number of members having voting power who shall be present or represented by proxy at any meeting in order to constitute a quorum for, and the votes that shall be necessary for, the transaction of any business. In the absence of such specification in the certificate of incorporation or bylaws of a nonstock corporation:

(1) One-third of the members of such corporation shall constitute a quorum at a meeting of such members;

(2) In all matters other than the election of the governing body of such corporation, the affirmative vote of a majority of such members present in person or represented by proxy at the meeting and entitled to vote on the subject matter shall be the act of the members, unless the vote of a greater number is required by this chapter;

(3) Members of the governing body shall be elected by a plurality of the votes of the members of the corporation present in person or represented by proxy at the meeting and entitled to vote thereon; and

(4) Where a separate vote by a class or group or classes or groups is required, a majority of the members of such class or group or classes or groups, present in person or represented by proxy, shall constitute a quorum entitled to take action with respect to that vote on that matter and, in all matters other than the election of members of the governing body, the affirmative vote of the majority of the members of such class or group or classes or groups present in person or represented by proxy at the meeting shall be the act of such class or group or classes or groups.

(d) If the election of the governing body of any nonstock corporation shall not be held on the day designated by the bylaws, the governing body shall cause the election to be held as soon thereafter as convenient. The failure to hold such an election at the designated time shall not work any forfeiture or dissolution of the corporation, but the Court of Chancery may summarily order such an election to be held upon the application of any member of the corporation. At any election pursuant to such order the persons entitled to vote in such election who shall be present at such meeting, either in person or by proxy, shall constitute a quorum for such meeting, notwithstanding any provision of the certificate of incorporation or the bylaws of the corporation to the contrary.

(e) If authorized by the governing body, any requirement of a written ballot shall be satisfied by a ballot submitted by electronic transmission, provided that any such electronic transmission must either set forth or be submitted with information from which it can be determined that the electronic transmission was authorized by the member or proxy holder.

(f) Except as otherwise provided in the certificate of incorporation, in the bylaws, or by resolution of the governing body, the record date for any meeting or corporate action shall be deemed to be the date of such meeting or corporate action; provided, however, that no record date may precede any action by the governing body fixing such record date.

§ 216. Quorum and Required Vote for Stock Corporations

Subject to this chapter in respect of the vote that shall be required for a specified action, the certificate of incorporation or bylaws of any corporation authorized to issue stock may specify the number of shares and/or the amount of other securities having voting power the holders of which shall be present or represented by proxy at any meeting in order to constitute a quorum for, and the votes that shall be necessary for, the transaction of any business, but in no event shall a quorum consist of less than 1/3 of the shares entitled to vote at the meeting, except that, where a separate vote by a class or series or classes or series is required, a quorum shall consist of no less than 1/3 of the shares of such class or series or classes or series. In the absence of such specification in the certificate of incorporation or bylaws of the corporation:

(1) A majority of the shares entitled to vote, present in person or represented by proxy, shall constitute a quorum at a meeting of stockholders;

(2) In all matters other than the election of directors, the affirmative vote of the majority of shares present in person or represented by proxy at the meeting and entitled to vote on the subject matter shall be the act of the stockholders;

(3) Directors shall be elected by a plurality of the votes of the shares present in person or represented by proxy at the meeting and entitled to vote on the election of directors; and

(4) Where a separate vote by a class or series or classes or series is required, a majority of the outstanding shares of such class or series or classes or series, present in person or represented by proxy, shall constitute a quorum entitled to take action with respect to that vote on that matter and, in all matters other than the election of directors, the affirmative vote of the majority of shares of such class or series or classes or series present in person or represented by proxy at the meeting shall be the act of such class or series or classes or series.

A bylaw amendment adopted by stockholders which specifies the votes that shall be necessary for the election of directors shall not be further amended or repealed by the board of directors.

§ 218. Voting Trusts and Other Voting Agreements

(a) One stockholder or 2 or more stockholders may by agreement in writing deposit capital stock of an original issue with or transfer capital stock to any person or persons, or entity or entities authorized to act as trustee, for the purpose of vesting in such person or persons, entity or entities, who may be designated voting trustee, or voting trustees, the right to vote thereon for any period of time determined by such agreement, upon the terms and conditions stated in such agreement. The agreement may contain any other lawful provisions not inconsistent with such purpose. After delivery of a copy of the agreement to the registered office of the corporation in this State or the principal place of business of the corporation, which copy shall be open to the inspection of any stockholder of the corporation or any beneficiary of the trust under the agreement daily during business hours, certificates of stock or uncertificated stock shall be issued to the voting trustee or trustees to represent any stock of an original issue so deposited with such voting trustee or trustees, and any certificates of stock or uncertificated stock so transferred to the voting trustee or trustees shall be surrendered and cancelled and new certificates or uncertificated stock shall be issued therefore to the voting trustee or trustees. In the certificate so issued, if any, it shall be stated that it is issued pursuant to such agreement, and that fact shall also be stated in the stock ledger of the corporation. The voting trustee or trustees may vote the stock so issued or transferred during the period specified in the agreement. Stock standing in the name of the voting trustee or trustees may be voted either in person or by proxy, and in voting the stock, the voting trustee or trustees shall incur no responsibility as stockholder, trustee or otherwise, except for their own individual malfeasance. In any case where 2 or more persons or entities are designated as voting trustees, and the right and method of voting any stock standing in their names at any meeting of the corporation are not fixed by the agreement appointing the trustees, the right to vote the stock and the manner of voting it at the meeting shall be determined by a majority of the trustees, or if they be equally divided as to the right and manner of voting the stock in any particular case, the vote of the stock in such case shall be divided equally among the trustees.

(b) Any amendment to a voting trust agreement shall be made by a written agreement, a copy of which shall be delivered to the registered office of the corporation in this State or principal place of business of the corporation.

(c) An agreement between 2 or more stockholders, if in writing and signed by the parties thereto, may provide that in exercising any voting rights, the shares held by them shall be voted as provided by the agreement, or as the parties may agree, or as determined in accordance with a procedure agreed upon by them.

(d) This section shall not be deemed to invalidate any voting or other agreement among stockholders or any irrevocable proxy which is not otherwise illegal.

§ 219. List of Stockholders Entitled to Vote; Penalty for Refusal to Produce; Stock Ledger

(a) The officer who has charge of the stock ledger of a corporation shall prepare and make, at least 10 days before every meeting of stockholders, a complete list of the stockholders entitled to vote at the meeting; provided, however, if the record date for determining the stockholders entitled to vote is less than 10 days before the meeting date, the list shall reflect the stockholders entitled to vote as of the tenth day before the meeting date, arranged in alphabetical order, and showing the address of each stockholder and the number of shares registered in the name of each stockholder. Nothing contained in this section shall require the corporation to include electronic mail addresses or other electronic contact information on such list. Such list shall be open to the examination of any stockholder for any purpose germane to the meeting for a period of at least 10 days prior to the meeting: (i) on a reasonably accessible electronic network, provided that the information required to gain access to such list is provided with the notice of the meeting, or (ii) during ordinary business hours, at the principal place of business of the corporation. In the event that the corporation determines to make the list available on an electronic network, the corporation may take reasonable steps to ensure that such information is available only to stockholders of the corporation. If the meeting is to be held at a place, then a list of stockholders entitled to vote at the meeting shall be produced and kept at the time and place of the meeting during the whole time thereof and may be examined by any stockholder who is present. If the meeting is to be held solely by means of remote communication, then such list shall also be open to the examination of any stockholder during the whole time of the meeting on a reasonably accessible electronic network, and the information required to access such list shall be provided with the notice of the meeting.

(b) If the corporation, or an officer or agent thereof, refuses to permit examination of the list by a stockholder, such stockholder may apply to the Court of Chancery for an order to compel the corporation to permit such examination. The burden of proof shall be on the corporation to establish that the examination such stockholder seeks is for a purpose not germane to the meeting. The Court may summarily order the corporation to permit examination of the list upon such conditions as the Court may deem appropriate, and may make such additional orders as may be appropriate, including, without limitation, postponing the meeting or voiding the results of the meeting.

(c) The stock ledger shall be the only evidence as to who are the stockholders entitled by this section to examine the list required by this section or to vote in person or by proxy at any meeting of stockholders.

§ 220. Inspection of Books and Records

. . .

(a) As used in this section:

(1) "Stockholder" means a holder of record of stock in a stock corporation, or a person who is the beneficial owner of shares of such

stock held either in a voting trust or by a nominee on behalf of such person.

(2) "Subsidiary" means any entity directly or indirectly owned, in whole or in part, by the corporation of which the stockholder is a stockholder and over the affairs of which the corporation directly or indirectly exercises control, and includes, without limitation, corporations, partnerships, limited partnerships, limited liability partnerships, limited liability companies, statutory trusts and/or joint ventures.

(3) "Under oath" includes statements the declarant affirms to be true under penalty of perjury under the laws of the United States or any state.

(b) Any stockholder, in person or by attorney or other agent, shall, upon written demand under oath stating the purpose thereof, have the right during the usual hours for business to inspect for any proper purpose, and to make copies and extracts from:

(1) The corporation's stock ledger, a list of its stockholders, and its other books and records; and

(2) A subsidiary's books and records, to the extent that:

a. The corporation has actual possession and control of such records of such subsidiary; or

b. The corporation could obtain such records through the exercise of control over such subsidiary, provided that as of the date of the making of the demand:

1. The stockholder inspection of such books and records of the subsidiary would not constitute a breach of an agreement between the corporation or the subsidiary and a person or persons not affiliated with the corporation; and

2. The subsidiary would not have the right under the law applicable to it to deny the corporation access to such books and records upon demand by the corporation.

In every instance where the stockholder is other than a record holder of stock in a stock corporation, or a member of a nonstock corporation, the demand under oath shall state the person's status as a stockholder, be accompanied by documentary evidence of beneficial ownership of the stock, and state that such documentary evidence is a true and correct copy of what it purports to be. A proper purpose shall mean a purpose reasonably related to such person's interest as a stockholder. In every instance where an attorney or other agent shall be the person who seeks the right to inspection, the demand under oath shall be accompanied by a power of attorney or such other writing which authorizes the attorney or other agent to so act on behalf of the stockholder. The demand under oath shall be directed to the corporation at its registered office in this State or at its principal place of business.

(c) If the corporation, or an officer or agent thereof, refuses to permit an inspection sought by a stockholder or attorney or other agent acting for the stockholder pursuant to subsection (b) of this section or does not reply to the demand within 5 business days after the demand has been made, the stockholder may apply to the Court of Chancery for an order to compel such inspection. The Court of Chancery is hereby vested with exclusive jurisdiction to determine whether or not the person seeking inspection is entitled to the inspection sought. The Court may summarily order the corporation to permit the stockholder to inspect the corporation's stock ledger, an existing list of stockholders, and its other books and records, and to make copies or extracts therefrom; or the Court may order the corporation to furnish to the stockholder a list of its stockholders as of a specific date on condition that the stockholder first pay to the corporation the reasonable cost of obtaining and furnishing such list and on such other conditions as the Court deems appropriate. Where the stockholder seeks to inspect the corporation's books and records, other than its stock ledger or list of stockholders, such stockholder shall first establish that:

(1) Such stockholder is a stockholder;

(2) Such stockholder has complied with this section respecting the form and manner of making demand for inspection of such documents; and

(3) The inspection such stockholder seeks is for a proper purpose.

Where the stockholder seeks to inspect the corporation's stock ledger or list of stockholders and establishes that such stockholder is a stockholder and has complied with this section respecting the form and manner of making demand for inspection of such documents, the burden of proof shall be upon the corporation to establish that the inspection such stockholder seeks is for an improper purpose. The Court may, in its discretion, prescribe any limitations or conditions with reference to the inspection, or award such other or further relief as the Court may deem just and proper. The Court may order books, documents and records, pertinent extracts therefrom, or duly authenticated copies thereof, to be brought within this State and kept in this State upon such terms and conditions as the order may prescribe.

(d) Any director shall have the right to examine the corporation's stock ledger, a list of its stockholders and its other books and records for a purpose reasonably related to the director's position as a director. The Court of Chancery is hereby vested with the exclusive jurisdiction to determine whether a director is entitled to the inspection sought. The Court may summarily order the corporation to permit the director to inspect any and all books and records, the stock ledger and the list of stockholders and to make copies or extracts therefrom. The burden of proof shall be upon the corporation to establish that the inspection such director seeks is for an improper purpose. The Court may, in its discretion, prescribe any limitations or conditions with reference to the inspection, or award such other and further relief as the Court may deem just and proper.

§ 221. Voting, Inspection and Other Rights of Bondholders and Debenture Holders

Every corporation may in its certificate of incorporation confer upon the holders of any bonds, debentures or other obligations issued or to be issued by the corporation the power to vote in respect to the corporate affairs and management of the corporation to the extent and in the manner provided in the certificate of incorporation and may confer upon such holders of bonds, debentures or other obligations the same right of inspection of its books, accounts and other records, and also any other rights, which the stockholders of the corporation have or may have by reason of this chapter or of its certificate of incorporation. If the certificate of incorporation so provides, such holders of bonds, debentures or other obligations shall be deemed to be stockholders, and their bonds, debentures or other obligations shall be deemed to be shares of stock, for the purpose of any provision of this chapter which requires the vote of stockholders as a prerequisite to any corporate action and the certificate of incorporation may divest the holders of capital stock, in whole or in part, of their right to vote on any corporate matter whatsoever, except as set forth in § 242(b)(2) of this title.

§ 222. Notice of Meetings and Adjourned Meetings

(a) Whenever stockholders are required or permitted to take any action at a meeting, a written notice of the meeting shall be given which shall state the place, if any, date and hour of the meeting, the means of remote communications, if any, by which stockholders and proxy holders may be deemed to be present in person and vote at such meeting, the record date for determining the stockholders entitled to vote at the meeting, if such date is different from the record date for determining stockholders entitled to notice of the meeting, and, in the case of a special meeting, the purpose or purposes for which the meeting is called.

(b) Unless otherwise provided in this chapter, the written notice of any meeting shall be given not less than 10 nor more than 60 days before the date of the meeting to each stockholder entitled to vote at such meeting as of the record date for determining the stockholders entitled to notice of the meeting. If mailed, notice is given when deposited in the United States mail, postage prepaid, directed to the stockholder at such stockholder's address as it appears on the records of the corporation. An affidavit of the secretary or an assistant secretary or of the transfer agent or other agent of the corporation that the notice has been given shall, in the absence of fraud, be prima facie evidence of the facts stated therein.

(c) When a meeting is adjourned to another time or place, unless the bylaws otherwise require, notice need not be given of the adjourned meeting if the time, place, if any, thereof, and the means of remote communications, if any, by which stockholders and proxy holders may be deemed to be present in person and vote at such adjourned meeting are announced at the meeting at which the adjournment is taken. At the adjourned meeting the corporation may transact any business which might have been transacted at the original meeting. If the adjournment is for more than 30 days, a notice of the adjourned meeting shall be given to each stockholder of record entitled to vote at the meeting. If after the adjournment a new record date for stockholders entitled to vote is fixed for the adjourned meeting, the board of directors shall fix a new record date for notice of such adjourned meeting in accordance with § 213(a) of this title, and shall give notice of the adjourned meeting to each stockholder of record entitled to vote at such adjourned meeting as of the record date fixed for notice of such adjourned meeting.

§ 223. Vacancies and Newly Created Directorships

(a) Unless otherwise provided in the certificate of incorporation or bylaws:

(1) Vacancies and newly created directorships resulting from any increase in the authorized number of directors elected by all of the stockholders having the right to vote as a single class may be filled by a majority of the directors then in office, although less than a quorum, or by a sole remaining director;

(2) Whenever the holders of any class or classes of stock or series thereof are entitled to elect 1 or more directors by the certificate of incorporation, vacancies and newly created directorships of such class or classes or series may be filled by a majority of the directors elected by such class or classes or series thereof then in office, or by a sole remaining director so elected.

If at any time, by reason of death or resignation or other cause, a corporation should have no directors in office, then any officer or any stockholder or an executor, administrator, trustee or guardian of a stockholder, or other fiduciary entrusted with like responsibility for the person or estate of a stockholder, may call a special meeting of stockholders in accordance with the certificate of incorporation or the bylaws, or may apply to the Court of Chancery for a decree summarily ordering an election as provided in § 211 or § 215 of this title.

(b) In the case of a corporation the directors of which are divided into classes, any directors chosen under subsection (a) of this section shall hold office until the next election of the class for which such directors shall have been chosen, and until their successors shall be elected and qualified.

(c) If, at the time of filling any vacancy or any newly created directorship, the directors then in office shall constitute less than a majority of the whole board (as constituted immediately prior to any such increase), the

Court of Chancery may, upon application of any stockholder or stockholders holding at least 10 percent of the voting stock at the time outstanding having the right to vote for such directors, summarily order an election to be held to fill any such vacancies or newly created directorships, or to replace the directors chosen by the directors then in office as aforesaid, which election shall be governed by § 211 or § 215 of this title as far as applicable.

(d) Unless otherwise provided in the certificate of incorporation or bylaws, when 1 or more directors shall resign from the board, effective at a future date, a majority of the directors then in office, including those who have so resigned, shall have power to fill such vacancy or vacancies, the vote thereon to take effect when such resignation or resignations shall become effective, and each director so chosen shall hold office as provided in this section in the filling of other vacancies.

§ 225. Contested Election of Directors; Proceedings to Determine Validity

(a) Upon application of any stockholder or director, or any officer whose title to office is contested, the Court of Chancery may hear and determine the validity of any election, appointment, removal or resignation of any director or officer of any corporation, and the right of any person to hold or continue to hold such office,

§ 226. Appointment of Custodian or Receiver of Corporation on Deadlock or for Other Cause

(a) The Court of Chancery, upon application of any stockholder, may appoint 1 or more persons to be custodians, and, if the corporation is insolvent, to be receivers, of and for any corporation when:

(1) At any meeting held for the election of directors the stockholders are so divided that they have failed to elect successors to directors whose terms have expired or would have expired upon qualification of their successors; or

(2) The business of the corporation is suffering or is threatened with irreparable injury because the directors are so divided respecting the management of the affairs of the corporation that the required vote for action by the board of directors cannot be obtained and the stockholders are unable to terminate this division; or

(3) The corporation has abandoned its business and has failed within a reasonable time to take steps to dissolve, liquidate or distribute its assets.

(b) A custodian appointed under this section shall have all the powers and title of a receiver appointed under § 291 of this title, but the authority of the custodian is to continue the business of the corporation and not to liquidate its affairs and distribute its assets, except when the Court shall otherwise order and except in cases arising under paragraph (a)(3) of this section or § 352(a)(2) of this title.

§ 227. Powers of Court in Elections of Directors

(a) The Court of Chancery, in any proceeding instituted under § 211, § 215 or § 225 of this title may determine the right and power of persons claiming to own stock to vote at any meeting of the stockholders.

(b) The Court of Chancery may appoint a Master to hold any election provided for in § 211, § 215 or § 225 of this title under such orders and powers as it deems proper; and it may punish any officer or director for contempt in case of disobedience of any order made by the Court; and, in case of disobedience by a corporation of any order made by the Court, may enter a decree against such corporation for a penalty of not more than $5,000.

§ 228. Consent of Stockholders or Members in Lieu of Meeting

(a) Unless otherwise provided in the certificate of incorporation, any action required by this chapter to be taken at any annual or special meeting of stockholders of a corporation, or any action which may be taken at any annual or special meeting of such stockholders, may be taken without a meeting, without prior notice and without a vote, if a consent or consents in writing, setting forth the action so taken, shall be signed by the holders of outstanding stock having not less than the minimum number of votes that would be necessary to authorize or take such action at a meeting at which all shares entitled to vote thereon were present and voted and shall be delivered to the corporation by delivery to its registered office in this State, its principal place of business or an officer or agent of the corporation having custody of the book in which proceedings of meetings of stockholders are recorded. Delivery made to a corporation's registered office shall be by hand or by certified or registered mail, return receipt requested.

(b) Unless otherwise provided in the certificate of incorporation, any action required by this chapter to be taken at a meeting of the members of a nonstock corporation, or any action which may be taken at any meeting of the members of a nonstock corporation, may be taken without a meeting, without prior notice and without a vote, if a consent or consents in writing, setting forth the action so taken, shall be signed by members having not less than the minimum number of votes that would be necessary to authorize or take such action at a meeting at which all members having a right to vote thereon were present and voted and shall be delivered to the corporation by delivery to its registered office in this State, its principal place of business or an officer or agent of the corporation having custody of the book in which proceedings of meetings of members are recorded. Delivery made to a corporation's registered office shall be by hand or by certified or registered mail, return receipt requested.

(c) Every written consent shall bear the date of signature of each stockholder or member who signs the consent, and no written consent shall be effective to take the corporate action referred to therein unless, within 60 days of the earliest dated consent delivered in the manner required by this section to the corporation, written consents signed by a sufficient number of holders or members to take action are delivered to the corporation by delivery to its registered office in this State, its principal place of business or an officer or agent of the corporation having custody of the book in which proceedings of meetings of stockholders or members are recorded. Delivery made to a corporation's registered office shall be by hand or by certified or registered mail, return receipt requested. Any person executing a consent may provide, whether through instruction to an agent or otherwise, that such a consent will be effective at a future time (including a time determined upon the happening of an event), no later than 60 days after such instruction is given or such provision is made, and, for the purposes of this section, if evidence of such instruction or provision is provided to the corporation, such later effective time shall serve as the date of signature. Unless otherwise provided, any such consent shall be revocable prior to its becoming effective.

(d)(1) A telegram, cablegram or other electronic transmission consenting to an action to be taken and transmitted by a stockholder, member or proxyholder, or by a person or persons authorized to act for a stockholder, member or proxyholder, shall be deemed to be written, signed and dated for the purposes of this section, provided that any such telegram, cablegram or other electronic transmission sets forth or is delivered with information from which the corporation can determine (A) that the telegram, cablegram or other electronic transmission was transmitted by the stockholder, member or proxyholder or by a person or persons authorized to act for the stockholder, member or proxyholder and (B) the date on which such stockholder, member or proxyholder or authorized person or persons transmitted such telegram, cablegram or electronic transmission. The date on which such telegram, cablegram or electronic transmission is transmitted shall be deemed to be the date on which such consent was signed. No consent given by telegram, cablegram or other electronic transmission shall be deemed to have been delivered until such consent is reproduced in paper form and until such paper form shall be delivered to the corporation by delivery to its registered office in this State, its principal place of business or an officer or agent of the corporation having custody of the book in which proceedings of meetings of stockholders or members are recorded.

Delivery made to a corporation's registered office shall be made by hand or by certified or registered mail, return receipt requested. Notwithstanding the foregoing limitations on delivery, consents given by telegram, cablegram or other electronic transmission, may be otherwise delivered to the principal place of business of the corporation or to an officer or agent of the corporation having custody of the book in which proceedings of meetings of stockholders or members are recorded if, to the extent and in the manner provided by resolution of the board of directors or governing body of the corporation.

(2) Any copy, facsimile or other reliable reproduction of a consent in writing may be substituted or used in lieu of the original writing for any and all purposes for which the original writing could be used, provided that such copy, facsimile or other reproduction shall be a complete reproduction of the entire original writing.

(e) Prompt notice of the taking of the corporate action without a meeting by less than unanimous written consent shall be given to those stockholders or members who have not consented in writing and who, if the action had been taken at a meeting, would have been entitled to notice of the meeting if the record date for notice of such meeting had been the date that written consents signed by a sufficient number of holders or members to take the action were delivered to the corporation as provided in subsection (c) of this section. In the event that the action which is consented to is such as would have required the filing of a certificate under any other section of this title, if such action had been voted on by stockholders or by members at a meeting thereof, the certificate filed under such other section shall state, in lieu of any statement required by such section concerning any vote of stockholders or members, that written consent has been given in accordance with this section.

§ 229. Waiver of Notice

Whenever notice is required to be given under any provision of this chapter or the certificate of incorporation or bylaws, a written waiver, signed by the person entitled to notice, or a waiver by electronic transmission by the person entitled to notice, whether before or after the time stated therein, shall be deemed equivalent to notice . . .

§ 231. Voting Procedures and Inspectors of Elections

(a) The corporation shall, in advance of any meeting of stockholders, appoint 1 or more inspectors to act at the meeting and make a written report thereof. The corporation may designate 1 or more persons as alternate inspectors to replace any inspector who fails to act. If no inspector or alternate is able to act at a meeting of stockholders, the person presiding at the meeting shall appoint 1 or more inspectors to act at the meeting. Each inspector, before entering upon the discharge of the duties of inspector, shall take and sign an oath faithfully to execute the duties of inspector with strict impartiality and according to the best of such inspector's ability.

(b) The inspectors shall:

(1) Ascertain the number of shares outstanding and the voting power of each;

(2) Determine the shares represented at a meeting and the validity of proxies and ballots;

(3) Count all votes and ballots;

(4) Determine and retain for a reasonable period a record of the disposition of any challenges made to any determination by the inspectors; and

(5) Certify their determination of the number of shares represented at the meeting, and their count of all votes and ballots.

The inspectors may appoint or retain other persons or entities to assist the inspectors in the performance of the duties of the inspectors.

(c) The date and time of the opening and the closing of the polls for each matter upon which the stockholders will vote at a meeting shall be announced at the meeting. No ballot, proxies or votes, nor any revocations thereof or changes thereto, shall be accepted by the inspectors after the closing of the polls unless the Court of Chancery upon application by a stockholder shall determine otherwise.

(d) In determining the validity and counting of proxies and ballots, the inspectors shall be limited to an examination of the proxies, any envelopes submitted with those proxies, any information provided in accordance with § 211(e) or § 212(c)(2) of this title, or any information provided pursuant to § 211(a)(2)b.(i) or (iii) of this title, ballots and the regular books and records of the corporation, except that the inspectors may consider other reliable information for the limited purpose of reconciling proxies and ballots submitted by or on behalf of banks, brokers, their nominees or similar persons which represent more votes than the holder of a proxy is authorized by the record owner to cast or more votes than the stockholder holds of record. If the inspectors consider other reliable information for the limited purpose permitted herein, the inspectors at the time they make their certification pursuant to paragraph (b)(5) of this section shall specify the precise information considered by them including the person or persons from whom they obtained the information, when the information was obtained, the means by which the information was obtained and the basis for the inspectors' belief that such information is accurate and reliable.

(e) Unless otherwise provided in the certificate of incorporation or bylaws, this section shall not apply to a corporation that does not have a class of voting stock that is:

(1) Listed on a national securities exchange;

(2) Authorized for quotation on an interdealer quotation system of a registered national securities association; or

(3) Held of record by more than 2,000 stockholders.

§ 232. Notice by Electronic Transmission

(a) Without limiting the manner by which notice otherwise may be given effectively to stockholders, any notice to stockholders given by the corporation under any provision of this chapter, the certificate of incorporation, or the bylaws shall be effective if given by a form of electronic transmission consented to by the stockholder to whom the notice is given . . .

Subchapter VIII. Amendment of Certificate of Incorporation; Changes in Capital and Capital Stock

§ 241. Amendment of Certificate of Incorporation Before Receipt of Payment for Stock

(a) Before a corporation has received any payment for any of its stock, it may amend its certificate of incorporation at any time or times, in any and as many respects as may be desired, so long as its certificate of incorporation as amended would contain only such provisions as it would be lawful and proper to insert in an original certificate of incorporation filed at the time of filing the amendment.

(b) The amendment of a certificate of incorporation authorized by this section shall be adopted by a majority of the incorporators, if directors were not named in the original certificate of incorporation or have not yet been elected, or, if directors were named in the original certificate of incorporation or have been elected and have qualified, by a majority of the directors. A certificate setting forth the amendment and certifying that the corporation has not received any payment for any of its stock, or that the corporation has no members, as applicable, and that the amendment has been duly adopted in accordance with this section shall be executed, acknowledged and filed in accordance with § 103 of this title. Upon such filing, the corporation's certificate of incorporation shall be deemed to be amended accordingly as of the date on which the original certificate of incorporation became effective, except as to those persons who are substantially and adversely affected by the amendment and as to those persons the amendment shall be effective from the filing date.

(c) This section will apply to a nonstock corporation before such a corporation has any members; provided, however, that all references to directors shall be deemed to be references to members of the governing body of the corporation.

§ 242. Amendment of Certificate of Incorporation After Receipt of Payment for Stock; Nonstock Corporations

(a) After a corporation has received payment for any of its capital stock, or after a nonstock corporation has members, it may amend its certificate of incorporation, from time to time, in any and as many respects as may be desired, so long as its certificate of incorporation as amended would contain only such provisions as it would be lawful and proper to insert in an original certificate of incorporation filed at the time of the filing of the amendment; and, if a change in stock or the rights of stockholders, or an exchange, reclassification, subdivision, combination or cancellation of stock or rights of stockholders is to be made, such provisions as may be necessary to effect such change, exchange, reclassification, subdivision, combination or cancellation. In particular, and without limitation upon such general power of amendment, a corporation may amend its certificate of incorporation, from time to time, so as:

(1) To change its corporate name; or

(2) To change, substitute, enlarge or diminish the nature of its business or its corporate powers and purposes; or

(3) To increase or decrease its authorized capital stock or to reclassify the same, by changing the number, par value, designations, preferences, or relative, participating, optional, or other special rights of the shares, or the qualifications, limitations or restrictions of such rights, or by changing shares with par value into shares without par value, or shares without par value into shares with par value either with or without increasing or decreasing the number of shares, or by subdividing or combining the outstanding shares of any class or series of a class of shares into a greater or lesser number of outstanding shares; or

(4) To cancel or otherwise affect the right of the holders of the shares of any class to receive dividends which have accrued but have not been declared; or

(5) To create new classes of stock having rights and preferences either prior and superior or subordinate and inferior to the stock of any class then authorized, whether issued or unissued; or

(6) To change the period of its duration; or

(7) To delete:

a. Such provisions of the original certificate of incorporation which named the incorporator or incorporators, the initial board of directors and the original subscribers for shares; and

b. Such provisions contained in any amendment to the certificate of incorporation as were necessary to effect a change, exchange, reclassification, subdivision, combination or cancellation of stock, if such change, exchange, reclassification, subdivision, combination or cancellation has become effective.

Any or all such changes or alterations may be effected by 1 certificate of amendment.

(b) Every amendment authorized by subsection (a) of this section shall be made and effected in the following manner:

(1) If the corporation has capital stock, its board of directors shall adopt a resolution setting forth the amendment proposed, declaring its advisability, and either calling a special meeting of the stockholders entitled to vote in respect thereof for the consideration of such amendment or directing that the amendment proposed be considered at the next annual meeting of the stockholders; provided, however, that unless otherwise expressly required by the certificate of incorporation, no meeting or vote of stockholders shall be required to adopt an amendment that effects only changes described in paragraph (a)(1) or (7) of this section. Such special or annual meeting shall be called and held upon notice in accordance with § 222 of this title. The notice shall set forth such amendment in full or a brief summary of the changes to be effected thereby unless such notice constitutes a notice of internet availability of proxy materials under the rules promulgated under the Securities Exchange Act of 1934 [15 U.S.C. § 78a et seq.]. At the meeting a vote of the stockholders entitled to vote thereon shall be taken for and against any proposed amendment that requires adoption by stockholders. If no vote of stockholders is required to effect such amendment, or if a majority of the outstanding stock entitled to vote thereon, and a majority of the outstanding stock of each class entitled to vote thereon as a class has been voted in favor of the amendment, a certificate setting forth the amendment and certifying that such amendment has been duly adopted in accordance with this section shall be executed, acknowledged and filed and shall become effective in accordance with § 103 of this title.

(2) The holders of the outstanding shares of a class shall be entitled to vote as a class upon a proposed amendment, whether or not entitled to vote thereon by the certificate of incorporation, if the amendment would increase or decrease the aggregate number of authorized shares of such class, increase or decrease the par value of the shares of such class, or alter or change the powers, preferences, or special rights of the shares of such class so as to affect them adversely. If any proposed amendment would alter or change the powers, preferences, or special rights of 1 or more series of any class so as to affect them adversely, but shall not so affect the entire class, then only the shares of the series so affected by the amendment shall be considered a separate class for the purposes of this paragraph. The number of authorized shares of any such class or classes of stock may be increased or decreased (but not below the number of shares thereof then outstanding) by the affirmative vote of the holders of a majority of the stock of the corporation entitled to vote irrespective of this subsection, if so provided in the original certificate of incorporation, in any amendment thereto which created

such class or classes of stock or which was adopted prior to the issuance of any shares of such class or classes of stock, or in any amendment thereto which was authorized by a resolution or resolutions adopted by the affirmative vote of the holders of a majority of such class or classes of stock.

(3) If the corporation is a nonstock corporation, then the governing body thereof shall adopt a resolution setting forth the amendment proposed and declaring its advisability. If a majority of all the members of the governing body shall vote in favor of such amendment, a certificate thereof shall be executed, acknowledged and filed and shall become effective in accordance with § 103 of this title. The certificate of incorporation of any nonstock corporation may contain a provision requiring any amendment thereto to be approved by a specified number or percentage of the members or of any specified class of members of such corporation in which event such proposed amendment shall be submitted to the members or to any specified class of members of such corporation in the same manner, so far as applicable, as is provided in this section for an amendment to the certificate of incorporation of a stock corporation; and in the event of the adoption thereof by such members, a certificate evidencing such amendment shall be executed, acknowledged and filed and shall become effective in accordance with § 103 of this title.

(4) Whenever the certificate of incorporation shall require for action by the board of directors of a corporation other than a nonstock corporation or by the governing body of a nonstock corporation, by the holders of any class or series of shares or by the members, or by the holders of any other securities having voting power the vote of a greater number or proportion than is required by any section of this title, the provision of the certificate of incorporation requiring such greater vote shall not be altered, amended or repealed except by such greater vote.

(c) The resolution authorizing a proposed amendment to the certificate of incorporation may provide that at any time prior to the effectiveness of the filing of the amendment with the Secretary of State, notwithstanding authorization of the proposed amendment by the stockholders of the corporation or by the members of a nonstock corporation, the board of directors or governing body may abandon such proposed amendment without further action by the stockholders or members.

§ 243 Retirement of Stock

(a) A corporation, by resolution of its board of directors, may retire any shares of its capital stock that are issued but are not outstanding.

(b) Whenever any shares of the capital stock of a corporation are retired, they shall resume the status of authorized and unissued shares of the class or series to which they belong unless the certificate of incorporation otherwise provides. If the certificate of incorporation prohibits the reissuance of such shares, or prohibits the reissuance of such shares as a part of a specific series only, a certificate stating that reissuance of the shares (as part of the class or series) is prohibited identifying the shares and reciting their retirement shall be executed, acknowledged and filed and shall become effective in accordance with § 103 of this title. When such certificate becomes effective, it shall have the effect of amending the certificate of incorporation so as to reduce accordingly the number of authorized shares of the class or series to which such shares belong or, if such retired shares constitute all of the authorized shares of the class or series to which they belong, of eliminating from the certificate of incorporation all reference to such class or series of stock.

(c) If the capital of the corporation will be reduced by or in connection with the retirement of shares, the reduction of capital shall be effected pursuant to § 244 of this title.

§ 244. Reduction of Capital

(a) A corporation, by resolution of its board of directors, may reduce its capital in any of the following ways:

(1) By reducing or eliminating the capital represented by shares of capital stock which have been retired;

(2) By applying to an otherwise authorized purchase or redemption of outstanding shares of its capital stock some or all of the capital represented by the shares being purchased or redeemed, or any capital that has not been allocated to any particular class of its capital stock;

(3) By applying to an otherwise authorized conversion or exchange of outstanding shares of its capital stock some or all of the capital represented by the shares being converted or exchanged, or some or all of any capital that has not been allocated to any particular class of its capital stock, or both, to the extent that such capital in the aggregate exceeds the total aggregate par value or the stated capital of any previously unissued shares issuable upon such conversion or exchange; or

(4) By transferring to surplus (i) some or all of the capital not represented by any particular class of its capital stock; (ii) some or all of the capital represented by issued shares of its par value capital stock, which capital is in excess of the aggregate par value of such shares; or (iii) some of the capital represented by issued shares of its capital stock without par value.

(b) Notwithstanding the other provisions of this section, no reduction of capital shall be made or effected unless the assets of the corporation remaining after such reduction shall be sufficient to pay any debts of the corporation for which payment has not been otherwise provided. No reduction of capital shall release any liability of any stockholder whose shares have not been fully paid.

Subchapter IX. Merger, Consolidation or Conversion

§ 251. Merger or Consolidation of Domestic Corporations

(a) Any 2 or more corporations existing under the laws of this State may merge into a single corporation, which may be any 1 of the constituent corporations or may consolidate into a new corporation formed by the consolidation, pursuant to an agreement of merger or consolidation, as the case may be, complying and approved in accordance with this section.

(b) The board of directors of each corporation which desires to merge or consolidate shall adopt a resolution approving an agreement of merger or consolidation and declaring its advisability. The agreement shall state:

(1) The terms and conditions of the merger or consolidation;

(2) The mode of carrying the same into effect;

(3) In the case of a merger, such amendments or changes in the certificate of incorporation of the surviving corporation as are desired to be effected by the merger (which amendments or changes may amend and restate the certificate of incorporation of the surviving corporation in its entirety), or, if no such amendments or changes are desired, a statement that the certificate of incorporation of the surviving corporation shall be its certificate of incorporation;

(4) In the case of a consolidation, that the certificate of incorporation of the resulting corporation shall be as is set forth in an attachment to the agreement;

(5) The manner, if any, of converting the shares of each of the constituent corporations into shares or other securities of the corporation surviving or resulting from the merger or consolidation, or of cancelling some or all of such shares, and, if any shares of any of the constituent corporations are not to remain outstanding, to be converted solely into shares or other securities of the surviving or resulting corporation or to be cancelled, the cash, property, rights or securities of any other corporation or entity which the holders of such shares are to receive in exchange for, or upon conversion of such shares and the surrender of any certificates evidencing them, which cash, property, rights or securities of any other corporation or entity may be in addition to or in lieu of shares or other securities of the surviving or resulting corporation; and

(6) Such other details or provisions as are deemed desirable, including, without limiting the generality of the foregoing, a provision for the payment of cash in lieu of the issuance or recognition of fractional shares, interests or rights, or for any other arrangement with respect thereto, consistent with § 155 of this title.

The agreement so adopted shall be executed and acknowledged in accordance with § 103 of this title. Any of the terms of the agreement of merger or consolidation may be made dependent upon facts ascertainable outside of such agreement, provided that the manner in which such facts shall operate upon the terms of the agreement is clearly and expressly set forth in the agreement of merger or consolidation. The term "facts," as used in the preceding sentence, includes, but is not limited to, the occurrence of any event, including a determination or action by any person or body, including the corporation.

(c) The agreement required by subsection (b) of this section shall be submitted to the stockholders of each constituent corporation at an annual or special meeting for the purpose of acting on the agreement. Due notice of the time, place and purpose of the meeting shall be mailed to each holder of stock, whether voting or nonvoting, of the corporation at the stockholder's address as it appears on the records of the corporation, at least 20 days prior to the date of the meeting. The notice shall contain a copy of the agreement or a brief summary thereof. At the meeting, the agreement shall be considered and a vote taken for its adoption or rejection. If a majority of the outstanding stock of the corporation entitled to vote thereon shall be voted for the adoption of the agreement, that fact shall be certified on the agreement by the secretary or assistant secretary of the corporation, provided that such certification on the agreement shall not be required if a certificate of merger or consolidation is filed in lieu of filing the agreement. If the agreement shall be so adopted and certified by each constituent corporation, it shall then be filed and shall become effective, in accordance with § 103 of this title. In lieu of filing the agreement of merger or consolidation required by this section, the surviving or resulting corporation may file a certificate of merger or consolidation, executed in accordance with § 103 of this title, which states:

(1) The name and state of incorporation of each of the constituent corporations;

(2) That an agreement of merger or consolidation has been approved, adopted, executed and acknowledged by each of the constituent corporations in accordance with this section;

(3) The name of the surviving or resulting corporation;

(4) In the case of a merger, such amendments or changes in the certificate of incorporation of the surviving corporation as are desired to be effected by the merger (which amendments or changes may amend and restate the certificate of incorporation of the surviving corporation in its entirety), or, if no such amendments or changes are desired, a statement that the certificate of incorporation of the surviving corporation shall be its certificate of incorporation;

(5) In the case of a consolidation, that the certificate of incorporation of the resulting corporation shall be as set forth in an attachment to the certificate;

(6) That the executed agreement of consolidation or merger is on file at an office of the surviving corporation, stating the address thereof; and

(7) That a copy of the agreement of consolidation or merger will be furnished by the surviving corporation, on request and without cost, to any stockholder of any constituent corporation.

(d) Any agreement of merger or consolidation may contain a provision that at any time prior to the time that the agreement (or a certificate in lieu thereof) filed with the Secretary of State becomes effective in accordance with § 103 of this title, the agreement may be terminated by the board of directors of any constituent corporation notwithstanding approval of the agreement by the stockholders of all or any of the constituent corporations; in the event the agreement of merger or consolidation is terminated after the filing of the agreement (or a certificate in lieu thereof) with the Secretary of State but before the agreement (or a certificate in lieu thereof) has become effective, a certificate of termination or merger or consolidation shall be filed in accordance with § 103 of this title. Any agreement of merger or consolidation may contain a provision that the boards of directors of the constituent corporations may amend the agreement at any time prior to the time that the agreement (or a certificate in lieu thereof) filed with the Secretary of State becomes effective in accordance with § 103 of this title, provided that an amendment made subsequent to the adoption of the agreement by the stockholders of any constituent corporation shall not (1) alter or change the amount or kind of shares, securities, cash, property and/or rights to be received in exchange for or on conversion of all or any of the shares of any class or series thereof of such constituent corporation, (2) alter or change any term of the certificate of incorporation of the surviving corporation to be effected by the merger or consolidation, or (3) alter or change any of the terms and conditions of the agreement if such alteration or change would adversely affect the holders of any class or series thereof of such constituent corporation; in the event the agreement of merger or consolidation is amended after the filing thereof with the Secretary of State but before the agreement has become effective, a certificate of amendment of merger or consolidation shall be filed in accordance with § 103 of this title.

(e) In the case of a merger, the certificate of incorporation of the surviving corporation shall automatically be amended to the extent, if any, that changes in the certificate of incorporation are set forth in the agreement of merger.

(f) Notwithstanding the requirements of subsection (c) of this section, unless required by its certificate of incorporation, no vote of stockholders of a constituent corporation surviving a merger shall be necessary to authorize a merger if (1) the agreement of merger does not amend in any respect the certificate of incorporation of such constituent corporation, (2) each share of stock of such constituent corporation outstanding immediately prior to the effective date of the merger is to be an identical outstanding or treasury share of the surviving corporation after the effective date of the merger, and (3) either no shares of common stock of the surviving corporation and no shares, securities or obligations convertible into such stock are to be issued or delivered under the plan of merger, or the authorized unissued shares or the treasury shares of common stock of the surviving corporation to be issued or delivered under the plan of merger plus those initially issuable upon conversion of any other shares, securities or obligations to be issued or delivered under such plan do not exceed 20% of the shares of common stock of such constituent corporation outstanding immediately prior to the effective date of the merger. No vote of stockholders of a constituent corporation shall be necessary to authorize a merger or consolidation if no shares of the stock of such corporation shall have been issued prior to the adoption by the board of directors of the resolution approving the agreement of merger or consolidation. If an agreement of merger is adopted by the constituent corporation surviving the merger, by action of its board of directors and without any vote of its stockholders pursuant to this subsection, the secretary or assistant secretary of that corporation shall certify on the agreement that the agreement has been adopted pursuant to this subsection and, (1) if it has been adopted pursuant to the first sentence of this subsection, that the conditions specified in that sentence have been satisfied, or (2) if it has been adopted pursuant to the second sentence of this subsection, that no shares of stock of such corporation were issued prior to the adoption by the board of directors of the resolution approving the agreement of merger or consolidation, provided that such certification on the agreement shall not be required if a certificate of merger or consolidation is filed in lieu of filing the agreement. The agreement so adopted and certified shall then be filed and shall become effective, in accordance with § 103 of this title. Such filing shall constitute a representation by the person who executes the agreement that the facts stated in the certificate remain true immediately prior to such filing.

(g) Notwithstanding the requirements of subsection (c) of this section, unless expressly required by its certificate of incorporation, no vote of stockholders of a constituent corporation shall be necessary to authorize a merger with or into a single direct or indirect wholly-owned subsidiary of such constituent corporation if: (1) such constituent corporation and the direct or indirect wholly-owned subsidiary of such constituent corporation are the only constituent entities to the merger; (2) each share or fraction of a share of the capital stock of the constituent corporation outstanding immediately prior to the effective time of the merger is converted in the merger into a share or equal fraction of share of capital stock of a holding company having the same designations, rights, powers and preferences, and the qualifications, limitations and restrictions thereof, as the share of stock of the constituent corporation being converted in the merger; (3) the holding company and the constituent corporation are corporations of this State and the direct or indirect wholly-owned subsidiary that is the other constituent entity to the merger is a corporation or limited liability company of this State; (4) the certificate of incorporation and by-laws of the holding company immediately following the effective time of the merger contain provisions identical to the certificate of incorporation and by-laws of the constituent corporation immediately prior to the effective time of the merger (other than provisions, if any, regarding the incorporator or incorporators, the corporate name, the registered office and agent, the initial board of directors and the initial subscribers for shares and such provisions contained in any amendment to the certificate of incorporation as were necessary to effect a change, exchange, reclassification, subdivision, combination or cancellation of stock, if such change, exchange, reclassification, subdivision, combination, or cancellation has become effective); (5) as a result of the merger the constituent corporation or its successor becomes or remains a direct or indirect wholly-owned subsidiary of the holding company; (6) the directors of the constituent corporation become or remain the directors of the holding company upon the effective time of the merger; (7) the organizational documents of the surviving entity immediately following the effective time of the merger contain provisions identical to the certificate of incorporation of the constituent corporation immediately prior to the effective time of the merger (other than provisions, if any, regarding the incorporator or incorporators, the corporate or entity name, the registered office and agent, the initial board of directors and the initial subscribers for shares, references to members rather than stockholders or shareholders, references to interests, units or the like rather than stock or shares, references to managers, managing members or other members of the governing body rather than directors and such provisions contained in any amendment to the certificate of incorporation as were necessary to effect a change, exchange, reclassification, subdivision, combination or cancellation of stock, if such change, exchange, reclassification, subdivision, combination or cancellation has become effective); provided, however, that (i) if the organizational documents of the surviving entity do not contain the following provisions, they shall be amended in the merger to contain provisions requiring that (A) any act or transaction by or involving the surviving entity, other than the election or removal of directors or managers, managing members or other members of the governing body of the surviving entity, that requires for its adoption under this chapter or its organizational documents the approval of the stockholders or members of the surviving entity shall, by specific reference to this subsection, require, in addition, the approval of the stockholders of the holding company (or any successor by merger), by the same vote as is required by this chapter and/or by the organizational documents of the surviving entity; provided, however, that for purposes of this clause (i)(A), any surviving entity that is not a corporation shall include in such amendment a requirement that the approval of the stockholders of the holding company be obtained for any act or transaction by or involving the surviving entity, other than the election or removal of directors or managers, managing members or other members of the governing body of the surviving entity, which would require the approval of the stockholders of the surviving entity if the surviving entity were a corporation subject to this chapter; (B) any amendment of the organizational documents of a surviving entity that is not a corporation, which amendment would, if adopted by a corporation subject to this chapter, be required to be included in the certificate of incorporation of such corporation, shall, by specific reference to this subsection, require, in addition, the approval of the stockholders of the holding company (or any successor by merger), by the same vote as is required by this chapter and/or by the organizational documents of the surviving entity; and (C) the business and affairs of a surviving entity that is not a corporation shall be managed by or under the direction of a board of directors, board of managers or other governing body consisting of individuals who are subject to the same fiduciary duties applicable to, and who are liable for breach of such duties to the same extent as, directors of a corporation subject to this chapter; and (ii) the organizational documents of the surviving entity may be amended in the merger (A) to reduce the number of classes and shares of capital stock or other equity interests or units that the surviving entity is authorized to issue and (B) to eliminate any provision authorized by § 141(d) of this title; and (8) the stockholders of the constituent corporation do not recognize gain or loss for United States federal income tax purposes as determined by the board of directors of the constituent corporation. Neither paragraph (g)(7)(i) of this section nor any provision of a surviving entity's organizational documents required by paragraph (g)(7)(i) of this section shall be deemed or construed to require approval of the stockholders of the holding company to elect or remove directors or managers, managing members or other members of the governing body of the surviving entity. The term "organizational documents", as used in paragraph (g)(7) of this section and in the preceding sentence, shall, when used in reference to a corporation, mean the certificate of incorporation of such corporation, and when used in reference to a limited liability company, mean the limited liability company agreement of such limited liability company.

As used in this subsection only, the term "holding company" means a corporation which, from its incorporation until consummation of a merger governed by this subsection, was at all times a direct or indirect wholly-owned subsidiary of the constituent corporation and whose capital stock is issued in such merger. From and after the effective time of a merger adopted by a constituent corporation by action of its board of directors and without any vote of stockholders pursuant to this subsection: (i) to the extent the restrictions of § 203 of this title applied to the constituent corporation and its stockholders at the effective time of the merger, such restrictions shall apply to the holding company and its stockholders immediately after the effective time of the merger as though it were the constituent corporation, and all shares of stock of the holding company acquired in the merger shall for purposes of § 203 of this title be deemed to have been acquired at the time that the shares of stock of the constituent corporation converted in the merger were acquired, and provided further that any stockholder who immediately prior to the effective time of the merger was not an interested stockholder within the meaning of § 203 of this title shall not solely by reason of the merger become an interested stockholder of the holding company, (ii) if the corporate name of the holding company immediately following the effective time of the merger is the same as the corporate name of the constituent corporation immediately prior to the effective time of the merger, the shares of capital stock of the holding company into which the shares of capital stock of the constituent corporation are converted in the merger shall be represented by the stock certificates that previously represented shares of capital stock of the constituent corporation and (iii) to the extent a stockholder of the constituent corporation immediately prior to the merger had standing to institute or maintain derivative litigation on behalf of the constituent corporation, nothing in this section shall be deemed to limit or extinguish such standing. If an agreement of merger is adopted by a constituent corporation by action of its board of directors and without any vote of stockholders pursuant to this subsection, the secretary or assistant secretary of the constituent corporation shall certify on the agreement that the agreement has been adopted pursuant to this subsection and that the conditions specified in the first sentence of this subsection have been satisfied, provided that such certification on the agreement shall not be required if a certificate of merger or consolidation is filed in lieu of filing the agreement. The agreement so adopted and certified shall then be filed and become effective, in accordance with § 103 of this title. Such filing shall constitute a representation by the person who executes the agreement that the facts stated in the certificate remain true immediately prior to such filing.

(h) Notwithstanding the requirements of subsection (c) of this section, unless expressly required by its certificate of incorporation, no vote of stockholders of a constituent corporation whose shares are listed on a national securities exchange or held of record by more than 2,000 holders immediately prior to the execution of the agreement of merger by such constituent corporation shall be necessary to authorize a merger if:

note: if private, still need vote

(1) The agreement of merger expressly:

a. Permits or requires such merger to be effected under this subsection; and

b. Provides that such merger shall be effected as soon as practicable following the consummation of the offer referred to in paragraph (h)(2) of this section if such merger is effected under this subsection;

(2) A corporation consummates a tender or exchange offer for any and all of the outstanding stock of such constituent corporation on the terms provided in such agreement of merger that, absent this subsection, would be entitled to vote on the adoption or rejection of the agreement of merger; provided, however, that such offer may exclude stock of such constituent corporation that is owned at the commencement of such offer by:

a. Such constituent corporation;

b. The corporation making such offer;

c. Any person that owns, directly or indirectly, all of the outstanding stock of the corporation making such offer; or

d. Any direct or indirect wholly-owned subsidiary of any of the foregoing;

(3) Following the consummation of the offer referred to in paragraph (h)(2) of this section, the stock irrevocably accepted for purchase or exchange pursuant to such offer and received by the depository prior to expiration of such offer, plus the stock otherwise owned by the consummating corporation equals at least such percentage of the stock, and of each class or series thereof, of such constituent corporation that, absent this subsection, would be required to adopt the agreement of merger by this chapter and by the certificate of incorporation of such constituent corporation;

(4) The corporation consummating the offer referred to in paragraph (h)(2) of this section merges with or into such constituent corporation pursuant to such agreement; and

(5) Each outstanding share of each class or series of stock of the constituent corporation that is the subject of and not irrevocably accepted for purchase or exchange in the offer referred to in paragraph (h)(2) of this section is to be converted in such merger into, or into the right to receive, the same amount and kind of cash, property, rights or securities to be paid for shares of such class or series of stock of such constituent corporation irrevocably accepted for purchase or exchange in such offer.

(6) As used in this section only, the term:

a. "Consummates" (and with correlative meaning, "consummation" and "consummating") means irrevocably accepts for purchase or exchange stock tendered pursuant to a tender or exchange offer;

b. "Depository" means an agent, including a depository, appointed to facilitate consummation of the offer referred to in paragraph (h)(2) of this section;

c. "Person" means any individual, corporation, partnership, limited liability company, unincorporated association or other entity; and

d. "Received" (solely for purposes of paragraph (h)(3) of this section) means physical receipt of a stock certificate in the case of certificated shares and transfer into the depository's account, or an agent's message being received by the depository, in the case of uncertificated shares.

If an agreement of merger is adopted without the vote of stockholders of a corporation pursuant to this subsection, the secretary or assistant secretary of the surviving corporation shall certify on the agreement that the agreement has been adopted pursuant to this subsection and that the conditions specified in this subsection (other than the condition listed in paragraph (h)(4) of this section) have been satisfied; provided that such certification on the agreement shall not be required if a certificate of merger is filed in lieu of filing the agreement. The agreement so adopted and certified shall then be filed and shall become effective, in accordance with § 103 of this title. Such filing shall constitute a representation by the person who executes the agreement that the facts stated in the certificate remain true immediately prior to such filing.

§ 252 Merger or Consolidation of Domestic and Foreign Corporations; Service of Process Upon Surviving or Resulting Corporation

(a) Any 1 or more corporations of this State may merge or consolidate with 1 or more other corporations of any other state or states of the United States, or of the District of Columbia if the laws of the other state or states, or of the District permit a corporation of such jurisdiction to merge or consolidate with a corporation of another jurisdiction. The constituent corporations may merge into a single corporation, which may be any 1 of the constituent corporations, or they may consolidate into a new corporation formed by the consolidation, which may be a corporation of the state of incorporation of any 1 of the constituent corporations, pursuant to an agreement of merger or consolidation, as the case may be, complying and approved in accordance with this section. In addition, any 1 or more corporations existing under the laws of this State may merge or consolidate with 1 or more corporations organized under the laws of any jurisdiction other than 1 of the United States if the laws under which the other corporation or corporations are organized permit a corporation of such jurisdiction to merge or consolidate with a corporation of another jurisdiction.

(b) All the constituent corporations shall enter into an agreement of merger or consolidation. The agreement shall state:

(1) The terms and conditions of the merger or consolidation;

(2) The mode of carrying the same into effect;

(3) The manner, if any, of converting the shares of each of the constituent corporations into shares or other securities of the corporation surviving or resulting from the merger or consolidation, or of cancelling some or all of such shares, and, if any shares of any of the constituent corporations are not to remain outstanding, to be converted solely into shares or other securities of the surviving or resulting corporation or to be cancelled, the cash, property, rights or securities of any other corporation or entity which the holders of such shares are to receive in exchange for, or upon conversion of, such shares and the surrender of any certificates evidencing them, which cash, property, rights or securities of any other corporation or entity may be in addition to or in lieu of the shares or other securities of the surviving or resulting corporation;

(4) Such other details or provisions as are deemed desirable, including, without limiting the generality of the foregoing, a provision for the payment of cash in lieu of the issuance or recognition of fractional shares of the surviving or resulting corporation or of any other corporation the securities of which are to be received in the merger or consolidation, or for some other arrangement with respect thereto consistent with § 155 of this title; and

(5) Such other provisions or facts as shall be required to be set forth in certificates of incorporation by the laws of the state which are stated in the agreement to be the laws that shall govern the surviving or resulting corporation and that can be stated in the case of a merger or consolidation.

Any of the terms of the agreement of merger or consolidation may be made dependent upon facts ascertainable outside of such agreement, provided that the manner in which such facts shall operate upon the terms of the agreement is clearly and expressly set forth in the agreement of merger or consolidation. The term "facts," as used in the preceding sentence, includes, but is not limited to, the occurrence of any event, including a determination or action by any person or body, including the corporation.

(c) The agreement shall be adopted, approved, certified, executed and acknowledged by each of the constituent corporations in accordance with the laws under which it is formed, and, in the case of a Delaware corporation, in the same manner as is provided in § 251 of this title. The agreement shall be filed and shall become effective for all purposes of the laws of this State when and as provided in § 251 of this title with respect to the merger or consolidation of corporations of this State. In lieu of filing the agreement of merger or consolidation, the surviving or resulting corporation may file a certificate of merger or consolidation, executed in accordance with § 103 of this title, which states:

(1) The name and state or jurisdiction of incorporation of each of the constituent corporations;

(2) That an agreement of merger or consolidation has been approved, adopted, certified, executed and acknowledged by each of the constituent corporations in accordance with this subsection;

(3) The name of the surviving or resulting corporation;

(4) In the case of a merger, such amendments or changes in the certificate of incorporation of the surviving corporation as are desired to be effected by the merger (which amendments or changes may amend and restate the certificate of incorporation of the surviving corporation in its entirety), or, if no such amendments or changes are desired, a statement that the certificate of incorporation of the surviving corporation shall be its certificate of incorporation;

(5) In the case of a consolidation, that the certificate of incorporation of the resulting corporation shall be as is set forth in an attachment to the certificate;

(6) That the executed agreement of consolidation or merger is on file at an office of the surviving corporation and the address thereof;

(7) That a copy of the agreement of consolidation or merger will be furnished by the surviving corporation, on request and without cost, to any stockholder of any constituent corporation;

(8) If the corporation surviving or resulting from the merger or consolidation is to be a corporation of this State, the authorized capital stock of each constituent corporation which is not a corporation of this State; and

(9) The agreement, if any, required by subsection (d) of this section.

(d) If the corporation surviving or resulting from the merger or consolidation is to be governed by the laws of the District of Columbia or any state or jurisdiction other than this State, it shall agree that it may be served with process in this State in any proceeding for enforcement of any obligation of any constituent corporation of this State, as well as for enforcement of any obligation of the surviving or resulting corporation arising from the merger or consolidation, including any suit or other proceeding to enforce the right of any stockholders as determined in appraisal proceedings pursuant to § 262 of this title, and shall irrevocably appoint the Secretary of State as its agent to accept service of process in any such suit or other proceedings and shall specify the address to which a copy of such process shall be mailed by the Secretary of State. Process may be served upon the Secretary of State under this subsection by means of electronic transmission but only as prescribed by the Secretary of State. The Secretary of State is authorized to issue such rules and regulations with respect to such service as the Secretary of State deems necessary or appropriate. In the event of such service upon the Secretary of State in accordance with this subsection, the Secretary of State shall forthwith notify such surviving or resulting corporation thereof by letter, directed to such surviving or resulting corporation at its address so specified, unless such surviving or resulting corporation shall have designated in writing to the Secretary of State a different address for such purpose, in which case it shall be mailed to the last address so designated. Such letter shall be sent by a mail or courier service that includes a record of mailing or deposit with the courier and a record of delivery evidenced by the signature of the recipient. Such letter shall enclose a copy of the process and any other papers served on the Secretary of State pursuant to this subsection. It shall be the duty of the plaintiff in the event of such service to serve process and any other papers in duplicate, to notify the Secretary of State that service is being effected pursuant to this subsection and to pay the Secretary of State the sum of $50 for the use of the State, which sum shall be taxed as part of the costs in the proceeding, if the plaintiff shall prevail therein. The Secretary of State shall maintain an alphabetical record of any such service setting forth the name of the plaintiff and the defendant, the title, docket number and nature of the proceeding in which process has been served, the fact that service has been effected pursuant to this subsection, the return date thereof, and the day and hour service was made. The Secretary of State shall not be required to retain such information longer than 5 years from receipt of the service of process.

(e) Section 251(d) of this title shall apply to any merger or consolidation under this section; § 251(e) of this title shall apply to a merger under this section in which the surviving corporation is a corporation of this State; and § 251(f) and (h) of this title shall apply to any merger under this section.

(d) — target has appraisal rights

§ 253. Merger of Parent Corporation and Subsidiary or Subsidiaries

(a) In any case in which at least 90% of the outstanding shares of each class of the stock of a corporation or corporations (other than a corporation which has in its certificate of incorporation the provision required by § 251(g)(7)(i) of this title), of which class there are outstanding shares that, absent this subsection, would be entitled to vote on such merger, is owned by another corporation and 1 of the corporations is a corporation of this State and the other or others are corporations of this State, or any other state or states, or the District of Columbia and the laws of the other state or states, or the District permit a corporation of such jurisdiction to merge with a corporation of another jurisdiction, the corporation having such stock ownership may either merge the other corporation or corporations into itself and assume all of its or their obligations, or merge itself, or itself and 1 or more of such other corporations, into 1 of the other corporations by executing, acknowledging and filing, in accordance with § 103 of this title, a certificate of such ownership and merger setting forth a copy of the resolution of its board of directors to so merge and the date of the adoption; provided, however, that in case the parent corporation shall not own all the outstanding stock of all the subsidiary corporations, parties to a merger as aforesaid, the resolution of the board of directors of the parent corporation shall state the terms and conditions of the merger, including the securities, cash, property, or rights to be issued, paid, delivered or granted by the surviving corporation upon surrender of each share of the subsidiary corporation or corporations not owned by the parent corporation, or the cancellation of some or all of such shares. Any of the terms of the resolution of the board of directors to so merge may be made dependent upon facts ascertainable outside of such resolution, provided that the manner in which such facts shall operate upon the terms of the resolution is clearly and expressly set forth in the resolution. The term "facts," as used in the preceding sentence, includes, but is not limited to, the occurrence of any event, including a determination or action by any person or body, including the corporation. If the parent corporation be not the surviving corporation, the resolution shall include provision for the pro rata issuance of stock of the surviving corporation to the holders of the stock of the parent corporation on surrender of any certificates therefor, and the certificate of ownership and merger shall state that the proposed merger has been approved by a majority of the outstanding stock of the parent corporation entitled to vote thereon at a meeting duly called and held after 20 days' notice of the purpose of the meeting mailed to each such stockholder at the stockholder's address as it appears on the records of the corporation if the parent corporation is a corporation of this State or state that the proposed merger has been adopted, approved, certified, executed and acknowledged by the parent corporation in accordance with the laws under which it is organized if the parent corporation is not a corporation of this State. If the surviving corporation exists under the laws of the District of Columbia or any state or jurisdiction other than this State:

(1) Section 252(d) of this title or § 258(c) of this title, as applicable, shall also apply to a merger under this section; and

(2) The terms and conditions of the merger shall obligate the surviving corporation to provide the agreement, and take the actions, required by § 252(d) of this title or § 258(c) of this title, as applicable.

(b) If the surviving corporation is a Delaware corporation, it may change its corporate name by the inclusion of a provision to that effect in the resolution of merger adopted by the directors of the parent corporation and set forth in the certificate of ownership and merger, and upon the effective date of the merger, the name of the corporation shall be so changed.

(c) Section § 251(d) of this title shall apply to a merger under this section, and § 251(e) of this title shall apply to a merger under this section in which the surviving corporation is the subsidiary corporation and is a corporation of this State. References to "agreement of merger" in § 251(d) and (e) of this title shall mean for purposes of this subsection the resolution of merger adopted by the board of directors of the parent corporation. Any merger which effects any changes other than those authorized by this section or made applicable by this subsection shall be accomplished under § 251, § 252, § 257, or § 258 of this title. Section 262 of this title shall not apply to any merger effected under this section, except as provided in subsection (d) of this section.

(d) In the event all of the stock of a subsidiary Delaware corporation party to a merger effected under this section is not owned by the parent corporation immediately prior to the merger, the stockholders of the subsidiary Delaware corporation party to the merger shall have appraisal rights as set forth in § 262 of this title.

(e) A merger may be effected under this section although 1 or more of the corporations parties to the merger is a corporation organized under the laws of a jurisdiction other than 1 of the United States; provided that the laws of such jurisdiction permit a corporation of such jurisdiction to merge with a corporation of another jurisdiction.

(f) This section shall apply to nonstock corporations if the parent corporation is such a corporation and is the surviving corporation of the merger; provided, however, that references to the directors of the parent corporation shall be deemed to be references to members of the governing body of the parent corporation, and references to the board of directors of the parent corporation shall be deemed to be references to the governing body of the parent corporation.

(g) Nothing in this section shall be deemed to authorize the merger of a corporation with a charitable nonstock corporation, if the charitable status of such charitable nonstock corporation would thereby be lost or impaired.

§ 259. Status, Rights, Liabilities, of Constituent and Surviving or Resulting Corporations Following Merger or Consolidation

(a) When any merger or consolidation shall have become effective under this chapter, for all purposes of the laws of this State the separate existence of all the constituent corporations, or of all such constituent corporations except the one into which the other or others of such constituent corporations have been merged, as the case may be, shall cease and the constituent corporations shall become a new corporation, or be merged into 1 of such corporations, as the case may be, possessing all the rights, privileges, powers and franchises as well of a public as of a private nature, and being subject to all the restrictions, disabilities and duties of each of such corporations so merged or consolidated; and all and singular, the rights, privileges, powers and franchises of each of said corporations, and all property, real, personal and mixed, and all debts due to any of said constituent corporations on whatever account, as well for stock subscriptions as all other things in action or belonging to each of such corporations shall be vested in the corporation surviving or resulting from such merger or consolidation; and all property, rights, privileges, powers and franchises, and all and every other interest shall be thereafter as effectually the property of the surviving or resulting corporation as they were of the several and respective constituent corporations, and the title to any real estate vested by deed or otherwise, under the laws of this State, in any of such constituent corporations, shall not revert or be in any way impaired by reason of this chapter; but all rights of creditors and all liens upon any property of any of said constituent corporations shall be preserved unimpaired, and all debts, liabilities and duties of the respective constituent corporations shall thenceforth attach to said surviving or resulting corporation, and may be enforced against it to the same extent as if said debts, liabilities and duties had been incurred or contracted by it.

(b) In the case of a merger of banks or trust companies, without any order or action on the part of any court or otherwise, all appointments, designations, and nominations, and all other rights and interests as trustee, executor, administrator, registrar of stocks and bonds, guardian of estates, assignee, receiver, trustee of estates of persons mentally ill and in every other fiduciary capacity, shall be automatically vested in the corporation resulting from or surviving such merger; provided, however, that any party in interest shall have the right to apply to an appropriate court or tribunal for a determination as to whether the surviving corporation shall continue to serve in the same fiduciary capacity as the merged corporation, or whether a new and different fiduciary should be appointed.

§ 260. Powers of Corporation Surviving or Resulting from Merger or Consolidation; Issuance of Stock, Bonds or Other Indebtedness

When 2 or more corporations are merged or consolidated, the corporation surviving or resulting from the merger may issue bonds or other obligations, negotiable or otherwise, and with or without coupons or interest certificates thereto attached, to an amount sufficient with its capital stock to provide for all the payments it will be required to make, or obligations it will be required to assume, in order to effect the merger or consolidation. For the purpose of securing the payment of any such bonds and obligations, it shall be lawful for the surviving or resulting corporation to mortgage its corporate franchise, rights, privileges and property, real, personal or mixed. The surviving or resulting corporation may issue certificates of its capital stock or uncertificated stock if authorized to do so and other securities to the stockholders of the constituent corporations in exchange or payment for the original shares, in such amount as shall be necessary in accordance with the terms of the agreement of merger or consolidation in order to effect such merger or consolidation in the manner and on the terms specified in the agreement.

§ 261. Effect of Merger Upon Pending Actions

Any action or proceeding, whether civil, criminal or administrative, pending by or against any corporation which is a party to a merger or consolidation shall be prosecuted as if such merger or consolidation had not taken place, or the corporation surviving or resulting from such merger or consolidation may be substituted in such action or proceeding.

§ 262. Appraisal Rights

(a) Any stockholder of a corporation of this State who holds shares of stock on the date of the making of a demand pursuant to subsection (d) of this section with respect to such shares, who continuously holds such shares through the effective date of the merger or consolidation, who has otherwise complied with subsection (d) of this section and who has neither voted in favor of the merger or consolidation nor consented thereto in writing pursuant to § 228 of this title shall be entitled to an appraisal by the Court of Chancery of the fair value of the stockholder's shares of stock under the circumstances described in subsections (b) and (c) of this section. As used in this section, the word "stockholder" means a holder of record of stock in a corporation; the words "stock" and "share" mean and include what is ordinarily meant by those words; and the words "depository receipt" mean a receipt or other instrument issued by a depository representing an interest in 1 or more shares, or fractions thereof, solely of stock of a corporation, which stock is deposited with the depository.

(b) Appraisal rights shall be available for the shares of any class or series of stock of a constituent corporation in a merger or consolidation to be effected pursuant to § 251 (other than a merger effected pursuant to § 251(g) of this title and, subject to paragraph (b)(3) of this section, § 251(h) of this title), § 252, § 254, § 255, § 256, § 257, § 258, § 263 or § 264 of this title:

(1) Provided, however, that, except as expressly provided in § 363(b) of this title, no appraisal rights under this section shall be available for the shares of any class or series of stock, which stock, or depository receipts in respect thereof, at the record date fixed to determine the stockholders entitled to receive notice of the meeting of stockholders to act upon the agreement of merger or consolidation, were either: (i) listed on a national securities exchange or (ii) held of record by more than 2,000 holders; and further provided that no appraisal rights shall be available for any shares of stock of the constituent corporation surviving a merger if the merger did not require for its approval the vote of the stockholders of the surviving corporation as provided in § 251(f) of this title.

(2) Notwithstanding paragraph (b)(1) of this section, appraisal rights under this section shall be available for the shares of any class or series of stock of a constituent corporation if the holders thereof are required by the terms of an agreement of merger or consolidation pursuant to §§ 251, 252, 254, 255, 256, 257, 258, 263 and 264 of this title to accept for such stock anything except:

a. Shares of stock of the corporation surviving or resulting from such merger or consolidation, or depository receipts in respect thereof;

b. Shares of stock of any other corporation, or depository receipts in respect thereof, which shares of stock (or depository receipts in respect thereof) or depository receipts at the effective date of the merger or consolidation will be either listed on a national securities exchange or held of record by more than 2,000 holders;

c. Cash in lieu of fractional shares or fractional depository receipts described in the foregoing paragraphs (b)(2)a. and b. of this section; or

d. Any combination of the shares of stock, depository receipts and cash in lieu of fractional shares or fractional depository receipts described in the foregoing paragraphs (b)(2)a., b. and c. of this section.

(3) In the event all of the stock of a subsidiary Delaware corporation party to a merger effected under § 251(h), § 253 or § 267 of this title is not owned by the parent immediately prior to the merger, appraisal rights shall be available for the shares of the subsidiary Delaware corporation.

(4) In the event of an amendment to a corporation's certificate of incorporation contemplated by § 363(a) of this title, appraisal rights shall be available as contemplated by § 363(b) of this title, and the procedures of this section, including those set forth in subsections (d) and (e) of this section, shall apply as nearly as practicable, with the word "amendment" substituted for the words "merger or consolidation," and the word "corporation" substituted for the words "constituent corporation" and/or "surviving or resulting corporation."

(c) Any corporation may provide in its certificate of incorporation that appraisal rights under this section shall be available for the shares of any class or series of its stock as a result of an amendment to its certificate of incorporation, any merger or consolidation in which the corporation is a constituent corporation or the sale of all or substantially all of the assets of the corporation. If the certificate of incorporation contains such a provision, the procedures of this section, including those set forth in subsections (d) and (e) of this section, shall apply as nearly as is practicable.

(d) Appraisal rights shall be perfected as follows:

(1) If a proposed merger or consolidation for which appraisal rights are provided under this section is to be submitted for approval at a meeting of stockholders, the corporation, not less than 20 days prior to the meeting, shall notify each of its stockholders who was such on the record date for notice of such meeting (or such members who received notice in accordance with § 255(c) of this title) with respect to shares for which appraisal rights are available pursuant to subsection (b) or (c) of this section that appraisal rights are available for any or all of the shares of the constituent corporations, and shall include in such notice a copy of this section and, if 1 of the constituent corporations is a nonstock corporation, a copy of § 114 of this title. Each stockholder electing to demand the appraisal of such stockholder's shares shall deliver to the corporation, before the taking of the vote on the merger or consolidation, a written demand for appraisal of such stockholder's shares. Such demand will be sufficient if it reasonably informs the corporation of the identity of the stockholder and that the stockholder intends thereby to demand the appraisal of such stockholder's shares. A proxy or vote against the merger or consolidation shall not constitute such a demand. A stockholder electing to take such action must do so by a separate written demand as herein provided. Within 10 days after the effective

date of such merger or consolidation, the surviving or resulting corporation shall notify each stockholder of each constituent corporation who has complied with this subsection and has not voted in favor of or consented to the merger or consolidation of the date that the merger or consolidation has become effective; or

(2) If the merger or consolidation was approved pursuant to § 228, § 251(h), § 253, or § 267 of this title, then either a constituent corporation before the effective date of the merger or consolidation or the surviving or resulting corporation within 10 days thereafter shall notify each of the holders of any class or series of stock of such constituent corporation who are entitled to appraisal rights of the approval of the merger or consolidation and that appraisal rights are available for any or all shares of such class or series of stock of such constituent corporation, and shall include in such notice a copy of this section and, if 1 of the constituent corporations is a nonstock corporation, a copy of § 114 of this title. Such notice may, and, if given on or after the effective date of the merger or consolidation, shall, also notify such stockholders of the effective date of the merger or consolidation. Any stockholder entitled to appraisal rights may, within 20 days after the date of mailing of such notice or, in the case of a merger approved pursuant to § 251(h) of this title, within the later of the consummation of the tender or exchange offer contemplated by § 251(h) of this title and 20 days after the date of mailing of such notice, demand in writing from the surviving or resulting corporation the appraisal of such holder's shares. Such demand will be sufficient if it reasonably informs the corporation of the identity of the stockholder and that the stockholder intends thereby to demand the appraisal of such holder's shares. If such notice did not notify stockholders of the effective date of the merger or consolidation, either (i) each such constituent corporation shall send a second notice before the effective date of the merger or consolidation notifying each of the holders of any class or series of stock of such constituent corporation that are entitled to appraisal rights of the effective date of the merger or consolidation or (ii) the surviving or resulting corporation shall send such a second notice to all such holders on or within 10 days after such effective date; provided, however, that if such second notice is sent more than 20 days following the sending of the first notice or, in the case of a merger approved pursuant to § 251(h) of this title, later than the later of the consummation of the tender or exchange offer contemplated by § 251(h) of this title and 20 days following the sending of the first notice, such second notice need only be sent to each stockholder who is entitled to appraisal rights and who has demanded appraisal of such holder's shares in accordance with this subsection. An affidavit of the secretary or assistant secretary or of the transfer agent of the corporation that is required to give either notice that such notice has been given shall, in the absence of fraud, be prima facie evidence of the facts stated therein. For purposes of determining the stockholders entitled to receive either

notice, each constituent corporation may fix, in advance, a record date that shall be not more than 10 days prior to the date the notice is given, provided, that if the notice is given on or after the effective date of the merger or consolidation, the record date shall be such effective date. If no record date is fixed and the notice is given prior to the effective date, the record date shall be the close of business on the day next preceding the day on which the notice is given.

(e) Within 120 days after the effective date of the merger or consolidation, the surviving or resulting corporation or any stockholder who has complied with subsections (a) and (d) of this section hereof and who is otherwise entitled to appraisal rights, may commence an appraisal proceeding by filing a petition in the Court of Chancery demanding a determination of the value of the stock of all such stockholders. Notwithstanding the foregoing, at any time within 60 days after the effective date of the merger or consolidation, any stockholder who has not commenced an appraisal proceeding or joined that proceeding as a named party shall have the right to withdraw such stockholder's demand for appraisal and to accept the terms offered upon the merger or consolidation. Within 120 days after the effective date of the merger or consolidation, any stockholder who has complied with the requirements of subsections (a) and (d) of this section hereof, upon written request, shall be entitled to receive from the corporation surviving the merger or resulting from the consolidation a statement setting forth the aggregate number of shares not voted in favor of the merger or consolidation and with respect to which demands for appraisal have been received and the aggregate number of holders of such shares. Such written statement shall be mailed to the stockholder within 10 days after such stockholder's written request for such a statement is received by the surviving or resulting corporation or within 10 days after expiration of the period for delivery of demands for appraisal under subsection (d) of this section hereof, whichever is later. Notwithstanding subsection (a) of this section, a person who is the beneficial owner of shares of such stock held either in a voting trust or by a nominee on behalf of such person may, in such person's own name, file a petition or request from the corporation the statement described in this subsection.

(f) Upon the filing of any such petition by a stockholder, service of a copy thereof shall be made upon the surviving or resulting corporation, which shall within 20 days after such service file in the office of the Register in Chancery in which the petition was filed a duly verified list containing the names and addresses of all stockholders who have demanded payment for their shares and with whom agreements as to the value of their shares have not been reached by the surviving or resulting corporation. If the petition shall be filed by the surviving or resulting corporation, the petition shall be accompanied by such a duly verified list. The Register in Chancery, if so ordered by the Court, shall give notice of the time and place fixed for the hearing of such petition by registered or certified mail to the surviving or resulting corporation and to the stockholders shown on the list at the addresses therein stated. Such notice shall also be given by 1 or more publications at least 1 week before the day of the hearing, in a newspaper of general circulation published in the City of Wilmington, Delaware or such publication as the Court deems advisable. The forms of the notices by mail and by publication shall be approved by the Court, and the costs thereof shall be borne by the surviving or resulting corporation.

(g) At the hearing on such petition, the Court shall determine the stockholders who have complied with this section and who have become entitled to appraisal rights. The Court may require the stockholders who have demanded an appraisal for their shares and who hold stock represented by certificates to submit their certificates of stock to the Register in Chancery for notation thereon of the pendency of the appraisal proceedings; and if any stockholder fails to comply with such direction, the Court may dismiss the proceedings as to such stockholder.

(h) After the Court determines the stockholders entitled to an appraisal, the appraisal proceeding shall be conducted in accordance with the rules of the Court of Chancery, including any rules specifically governing appraisal proceedings. Through such proceeding the Court shall determine the fair value of the shares exclusive of any element of value arising from the accomplishment or expectation of the merger or consolidation, together with interest, if any, to be paid upon the amount determined to be the fair value. In determining such fair value, the Court shall take into account all relevant factors. Unless the Court in its discretion determines otherwise for good cause shown, interest from the effective date of the merger through the date of payment of the judgment shall be compounded quarterly and shall accrue at 5% over the Federal Reserve discount rate (including any surcharge) as established from time to time during the period between the effective date of the merger and the date of payment of the judgment. Upon application by the surviving or resulting corporation or by any stockholder entitled to participate in the appraisal proceeding, the Court may, in its discretion, proceed to trial upon the appraisal prior to the final determination of the stockholders entitled to an appraisal. Any stockholder whose name appears on the list filed by the surviving or resulting corporation pursuant to subsection (f) of this section and who has submitted such stockholder's certificates of stock to the Register in Chancery, if such is required, may participate fully in all proceedings until it is finally determined that such stockholder is not entitled to appraisal rights under this section.

(i) The Court shall direct the payment of the fair value of the shares, together with interest, if any, by the surviving or resulting corporation to the stockholders entitled thereto. Payment shall be so made to each such stockholder, in the case of holders of uncertificated stock forthwith, and the case of holders of shares represented by certificates upon the surrender to the corporation of the certificates representing such stock. The Court's decree may be enforced as other decrees in the Court of Chancery may be enforced, whether such surviving or resulting corporation be a corporation of this State or of any state.

(j) The costs of the proceeding may be determined by the Court and taxed upon the parties as the Court deems equitable in the circumstances. Upon application of a stockholder, the Court may order all or a portion of the expenses incurred by any stockholder in connection with the appraisal proceeding, including, without limitation, reasonable attorney's fees and the fees and expenses of experts, to be charged pro rata against the value of all the shares entitled to an appraisal.

(k) From and after the effective date of the merger or consolidation, no stockholder who has demanded appraisal rights as provided in subsection (d) of this section shall be entitled to vote such stock for any purpose or to receive payment of dividends or other distributions on the stock (except dividends or other distributions payable to stockholders of record at a date which is prior to the effective date of the merger or consolidation); provided, however, that if no petition for an appraisal shall be filed within the time provided in subsection (e) of this section, or if such stockholder shall deliver to the surviving or resulting corporation a written withdrawal of such stockholder's demand for an appraisal and an acceptance of the merger or consolidation, either within 60 days after the effective date of the merger or consolidation as provided in subsection (e) of this section or thereafter with the written approval of the corporation, then the right of such stockholder to an appraisal shall cease. Notwithstanding the foregoing, no appraisal proceeding in the Court of Chancery shall be dismissed as to any stockholder without the approval of the Court, and such approval may be conditioned upon such terms as the Court deems just; provided, however that this provision shall not affect the right of any stockholder who has not commenced an appraisal proceeding or joined that proceeding as a named party to withdraw such stockholder's demand for appraisal and to accept the terms offered upon the merger or consolidation within 60 days after the effective date of the merger or consolidation, as set forth in subsection (e) of this section.

(*l*) The shares of the surviving or resulting corporation to which the shares of such objecting stockholders would have been converted had they assented to the merger or consolidation shall have the status of authorized and unissued shares of the surviving or resulting corporation.

§ 263. Merger or Consolidation of Domestic Corporations and Partnerships

(a) Any 1 or more corporations of this State may merge or consolidate with 1 or more partnerships (whether general (including a limited liability partnership) or limited (including a limited liability limited partnership)), of this State or of any other state or states of the United States, or of the District of Columbia, unless the laws of such other state or states or the District of Columbia forbid such merger or consolidation. Such corporation or corporations and such 1 or more partnerships may merge with or into a corporation, which may be any 1 of such corporations, or they may merge with or into a partnership, which may be any 1 of such partnerships, or they may consolidate into a new corporation or partnership formed by the consolidation, which shall be a corporation or partnership of this State or any other state of the United States, or the District of Columbia, which permits such merger or consolidation, pursuant to an agreement of merger or consolidation, as the case may be, complying and approved in accordance with this section.

(b) Each such corporation and partnership shall enter into a written agreement of merger or consolidation. The agreement shall state:

(1) The terms and conditions of the merger or consolidation;

(2) The mode of carrying the same into effect;

(3) The manner, if any, of converting the shares of stock of each such corporation and the partnership interests of each such partnership into shares, partnership interests or other securities of the entity surviving or resulting from such merger or consolidation or of cancelling some or all of such shares or interests, and if any shares of any such corporation or any partnership interests of any such partnership are not to remain outstanding, to be converted solely into shares, partnership interests or other securities of the entity surviving or resulting from such merger or consolidation or to be cancelled, the cash, property, rights or securities of any other corporation or entity which the holders of such shares or partnership interests are to receive in exchange for, or upon conversion of such shares or partnership interests and the surrender of any certificates evidencing them, which cash, property, rights or securities of any other corporation or entity may be in addition to or in lieu of shares, partnership interests or other securities of the entity surviving or resulting from such merger or consolidation; and

(4) Such other details or provisions as are deemed desirable, including, without limiting the generality of the foregoing, a provision for the payment of cash in lieu of the issuance of fractional shares or interests of the surviving or resulting corporation or partnership.

Any of the terms of the agreement of merger or consolidation may be made dependent upon facts ascertainable outside of such agreement, provided that the manner in which such facts shall operate upon the terms of the agreement is clearly and expressly set forth in the agreement of merger or consolidation. The term "facts," as used in the preceding sentence, includes, but is not limited to, the occurrence of any event, including a determination or action by any person or body, including the corporation.

(c) The agreement required by subsection (b) of this section shall be adopted, approved, certified, executed and acknowledged by each of the corporations in the same manner as is provided in § 251 or § 255 of this title and, in the case of the partnerships, in accordance with their partnership agreements and in accordance with the laws of the state under which they are formed, as the case may be. If the surviving or resulting entity is a partnership, in addition to any other approvals, each stockholder of a merging corporation who will become a general partner of the surviving or resulting partnership must approve the agreement of merger or consolidation. The agreement shall be filed and shall become effective for all purposes of the laws of this State when and as provided in § 251 or § 255 of this title with respect to the merger or consolidation of corporations of this State. In lieu of filing the agreement of merger or consolidation, the surviving or resulting corporation or partnership may file a certificate of merger or consolidation, executed in accordance with § 103 of this title, if the surviving or resulting entity is a corporation, or by a general partner, if the surviving or resulting entity is a partnership, which states:

(1) The name, state of domicile and type of entity of each of the constituent entities;

(2) That an agreement of merger or consolidation has been approved, adopted, certified, executed and acknowledged by each of the constituent entities in accordance with this subsection;

(3) The name of the surviving or resulting corporation or partnership;

(4) In the case of a merger in which a corporation is the surviving entity, such amendments or changes in the certificate of incorporation of the surviving corporation as are desired to be effected by the merger (which amendments or changes may amend and restate the certificate of incorporation of the surviving corporation in its entirety), or, if no such amendments or changes are desired, a statement that the certificate of incorporation of the surviving corporation shall be its certificate of incorporation;

(5) In the case of a consolidation in which a corporation is the resulting entity, that the certificate of incorporation of the resulting corporation shall be as is set forth in an attachment to the certificate;

(6) That the executed agreement of consolidation or merger is on file at an office of the surviving corporation or partnership and the address thereof;

(7) That a copy of the agreement of consolidation or merger will be furnished by the surviving or resulting entity, on request and without cost, to any stockholder of any constituent corporation or any partner of any constituent partnership; and

(8) The agreement, if any, required by subsection (d) of this section.

(d) If the entity surviving or resulting from the merger or consolidation is to be governed by the laws of the District of Columbia or any state other than this State, it shall agree that it may be served with process in this State in any proceeding for enforcement of any obligation of any constituent corporation or partnership of this State, as well as for enforcement of any obligation of the surviving or resulting corporation or partnership arising from the merger or consolidation, including any suit or other proceeding to enforce the right of any stockholders as determined in appraisal proceedings pursuant to § 262 of this title, and shall irrevocably appoint the Secretary of State as its agent to accept service of process in any such suit or other proceedings and shall specify the address to which a copy of such process shall be mailed by the Secretary of State. Process may be served upon the Secretary of State under this subsection by means of electronic transmission but only as prescribed by the Secretary of State. The Secretary of State is authorized to issue such rules and regulations with respect to such service as the Secretary of State deems necessary or appropriate. In the event of such service upon the Secretary of State in accordance with this subsection, the Secretary of State shall forthwith notify such surviving or resulting corporation or partnership thereof by letter, directed to such surviving or resulting corporation or partnership at its address so specified, unless such surviving or resulting corporation or partnership shall have designated in writing to the Secretary of State a different address for such purpose, in which case it shall be mailed to the last address so designated. Such letter shall be sent by a mail or courier service that includes a record of mailing or deposit with the courier and a record of delivery evidenced by the signature of the recipient. Such letter shall enclose a copy of the process and any other papers served on the Secretary of State pursuant to this subsection. It shall be the duty of the plaintiff in the event of such service to serve process and any other papers in duplicate, to notify the Secretary of State that service is being effected pursuant to this subsection and to pay the Secretary of State the sum of $50 for the use of the State, which sum shall be taxed as part of the costs in the proceeding, if the plaintiff shall prevail therein. The Secretary of State shall maintain an alphabetical record of any such service setting forth the name of the plaintiff and the defendant, the title, docket number and nature of the proceeding in which process has been served upon the Secretary of State, the fact that service has been effected pursuant to this subsection, the return date thereof, and the day and hour service was made. The Secretary of State shall not be required to retain such information longer than 5 years from receipt of the service of process.

(e) Sections 251(d)-(f), 255(c) (second sentence) and (d)-(f), 259-261 and 328 of this title shall, insofar as they are applicable, apply to mergers or consolidations between corporations and partnerships.

(f) Nothing in this section shall be deemed to authorize the merger of a charitable nonstock corporation into a partnership, if the charitable status of such nonstock corporation would thereby be lost or impaired; but a partnership may be merged into a charitable nonstock corporation which shall continue as the surviving corporation.

66 Del. Laws, c. 352, § 10; 67 Del. Laws, c. 190, § 6; 70 Del. Laws, c. 349, §§ 15, 20; 70 Del. Laws, c. 587, § 25; 71 Del. Laws, c. 339, §§ 53, 54; 73 Del. Laws, c. 82, §§ 22-26; 73 Del. Laws, c. 298, § 10; 74 Del. Laws, c. 84, § 18; 77 Del. Laws, c. 253, §§ 51-53; 77 Del. Laws, c. 290, §§ 18, 19; 78 Del. Laws, c. 273, § 2; 79 Del. Laws, c. 72, § 12.;

§ 264 Merger or Consolidation of Domestic Corporation and Limited Liability Company

(a) Any 1 or more corporations of this State may merge or consolidate with 1 or more limited liability companies, of this State or of any other state or states of the United States, or of the District of Columbia, unless the laws of such other state or states or the District of Columbia forbid such merger or consolidation. Such corporation or corporations and such 1 or more limited liability companies may merge with or into a corporation, which may be any 1 of such corporations, or they may merge with or into a limited liability company, which may be any 1 of such limited liability companies, or they may consolidate into a new corporation or limited liability company formed by the consolidation, which shall be a corporation or limited liability company of this State or any other state of the United States, or the District of Columbia, which permits such merger or consolidation, pursuant to an agreement of merger or consolidation, as the case may be, complying and approved in accordance with this section.

(b) Each such corporation and limited liability company shall enter into a written agreement of merger or consolidation. The agreement shall state:

(1) The terms and conditions of the merger or consolidation;

(2) The mode of carrying the same into effect;

(3) The manner, if any, of converting the shares of stock of each such corporation and the limited liability company interests of each such limited liability company into shares, limited liability company interests or other securities of the entity surviving or resulting from such merger or consolidation or of cancelling some or all of such shares or interests, and if any shares of any such corporation or any limited liability company interests of any such limited liability company are not to remain outstanding, to be converted solely into shares, limited liability company interests or other securities of the entity surviving or resulting from such merger or consolidation or to be cancelled, the cash, property, rights or securities of any other corporation or entity which the holders of such shares or limited liability company interests are to receive in exchange for, or upon conversion of such shares or limited liability company interests and the surrender of any certificates evidencing them, which cash, property, rights or securities of any other corporation or entity may be in addition to or in lieu of shares, limited liability company interests or other securities of the entity surviving or resulting from such merger or consolidation; and

(4) Such other details or provisions as are deemed desirable, including, without limiting the generality of the foregoing, a provision for the payment of cash in lieu of the issuance of fractional shares or interests of the surviving or resulting corporation or limited liability company. Any of the terms of the agreement of merger or consolidation may be made

dependent upon facts ascertainable outside of such agreement, provided that the manner in which such facts shall operate upon the terms of the agreement is clearly and expressly set forth in the agreement of merger or consolidation. The term "facts," as used in the preceding sentence, includes, but is not limited to, the occurrence of any event, including a determination or action by any person or body, including the corporation.

(c) The agreement required by subsection (b) of this section shall be adopted, approved, certified, executed and acknowledged by each of the corporations in the same manner as is provided in § 251 or § 255 of this title and, in the case of the limited liability companies, in accordance with their limited liability company agreements and in accordance with the laws of the state under which they are formed, as the case may be. The agreement shall be filed and shall become effective for all purposes of the laws of this State when and as provided in § 251 or § 255 of this title with respect to the merger or consolidation of corporations of this State. In lieu of filing the agreement of merger or consolidation, the surviving or resulting corporation or limited liability company may file a certificate of merger or consolidation, executed in accordance with § 103 of this title, if the surviving or resulting entity is a corporation, or by an authorized person, if the surviving or resulting entity is a limited liability company, which states:

(1) The name and state of domicile of each of the constituent entities;

(2) That an agreement of merger or consolidation has been approved, adopted, certified, executed and acknowledged by each of the constituent entities in accordance with this subsection;

(3) The name of the surviving or resulting corporation or limited liability company;

(4) In the case of a merger in which a corporation is the surviving entity, such amendments or changes in the certificate of incorporation of the surviving corporation as are desired to be effected by the merger (which amendments or changes may amend and restate the certificate of incorporation of the surviving corporation in its entirety), or, if no such amendments or changes are desired, a statement that the certificate of incorporation of the surviving corporation shall be its certificate of incorporation;

(5) In the case of a consolidation in which a corporation is the resulting entity, that the certificate of incorporation of the resulting corporation shall be as is set forth in an attachment to the certificate;

(6) That the executed agreement of consolidation or merger is on file at an office of the surviving corporation or limited liability company and the address thereof;

(7) That a copy of the agreement of consolidation or merger will be furnished by the surviving or resulting entity, on request and without cost, to any stockholder of any constituent corporation or any member of any constituent limited liability company; and

(8) The agreement, if any, required by subsection (d) of this section.

(d) If the entity surviving or resulting from the merger or consolidation is to be governed by the laws of the District of Columbia or any state other than this State, it shall agree that it may be served with process in this State in any proceeding for enforcement of any obligation of any constituent corporation or limited liability company of this State, as well as for enforcement of any obligation of the surviving or resulting corporation or limited liability company arising from the merger or consolidation, including any suit or other proceeding to enforce the right of any stockholders as determined in appraisal proceedings pursuant to the provisions of § 262 of this title, and shall irrevocably appoint the Secretary of State as its agent to accept service of process in any such suit or other proceedings and shall specify the address to which a copy of such process shall be mailed by the Secretary of State. Process may be served upon the Secretary of State under this subsection by means of electronic transmission but only as prescribed by the Secretary of State. The Secretary of State is authorized to issue such rules and regulations with respect to such service as the Secretary of State deems necessary or appropriate. In the event of such service upon the Secretary of State in accordance with this subsection, the Secretary of State shall forthwith notify such surviving or resulting corporation or limited liability company thereof by letter, directed to such surviving or resulting corporation or limited liability company at its address so specified, unless such surviving or resulting corporation or limited liability company shall have designated in writing to the Secretary of State a different address for such purpose, in which case it shall be mailed to the last address so designated. Such letter shall be sent by a mail or courier service that includes a record of mailing or deposit with the courier and a record of delivery evidenced by the signature of the recipient. Such letter shall enclose a copy of the process and any other papers served on the Secretary of State pursuant to this subsection. It shall be the duty of the plaintiff in the event of such service to serve process and any other papers in duplicate, to notify the Secretary of State that service is being effected pursuant to this subsection and to pay the Secretary of State the sum of $50 for the use of the State, which sum shall be taxed as part of the costs in the proceeding, if the plaintiff shall prevail therein. The Secretary of State shall maintain an alphabetical record of any such service setting forth the name of the plaintiff and the defendant, the title, docket number and nature of the proceeding in which process has been served upon the Secretary of State, the fact that service has been effected pursuant to this subsection, the return date thereof, and the day and hour service was made. The Secretary of State shall not be required to retain such information longer than 5 years from receipt of the service of process.

(e) Sections 251(d)-(f), 255(c) (second sentence) and (d)-(f), 259-261 and 328 of this title shall, insofar as they are applicable, apply to mergers or consolidations between corporations and limited liability companies.

(f) Nothing in this section shall be deemed to authorize the merger of a charitable nonstock corporation into a limited liability company, if the charitable status of such nonstock corporation would thereby be lost or impaired; but a limited liability company may be merged into a charitable nonstock corporation which shall continue as the surviving corporation.
69 Del. Laws, c. 61, § 11; 70 Del. Laws, c. 186, § 1; 70 Del. Laws, c. 349, §§ 16, 21; 70 Del. Laws, c. 587, § 26; 71 Del. Laws, c. 339, §§ 55, 56; 74 Del. Laws, c. 84, § 19; 77 Del. Laws, c. 253, §§ 54-56; 77 Del. Laws, c. 290, §§ 20, 21; 79 Del. Laws, c. 72, § 13.;

§ 265 Conversion of Other Entities to a Domestic Corporation

(a) As used in this section, the term "other entity"means a limited liability company, statutory trust, business trust or association, real estate investment trust, common-law trust or any other unincorporated business including a partnership (whether general (including a limited liability partnership) or limited (including a limited liability limited partnership)), or a foreign corporation.

(b) Any other entity may convert to a corporation of this State by complying with subsection (h) of this section and filing in the office of the Secretary of State:

(1) A certificate of conversion to corporation that has been executed in accordance with subsection (i) of this section and filed in accordance with § 103 of this title; and

(2) A certificate of incorporation that has been executed, acknowledged and filed in accordance with § 103 of this title.

Each of the certificates required by this subsection (b) shall be filed simultaneously in the office of the Secretary of State and, if such certificates are not to become effective upon their filing as permitted by § 103(d) of this title, then each such certificate shall provide for the same effective date or time in accordance with § 103(d) of this title.

(c) The certificate of conversion to corporation shall state:

(1) The date on which and jurisdiction where the other entity was first created, incorporated, formed or otherwise came into being and, if it has changed, its jurisdiction immediately prior to its conversion to a domestic corporation;

(2) The name and type of entity of the other entity immediately prior to the filing of the certificate of conversion to corporation; and

(3) The name of the corporation as set forth in its certificate of incorporation filed in accordance with subsection (b) of this section.

(4) [Repealed.]

(d) Upon the effective time of the certificate of conversion to corporation and the certificate of incorporation, the other entity shall be converted to a corporation of this State and the corporation shall thereafter be subject to all of the provisions of this title, except that notwithstanding § 106 of this title, the existence of the corporation shall be deemed to have commenced on the date the other entity commenced its existence in the jurisdiction in which the other entity was first created, formed, incorporated or otherwise came into being.

(e) The conversion of any other entity to a corporation of this State shall not be deemed to affect any obligations or liabilities of the other entity incurred prior to its conversion to a corporation of this State or the personal liability of any person incurred prior to such conversion.

(f) When an other entity has been converted to a corporation of this State pursuant to this section, the corporation of this State shall, for all purposes of the laws of the State of Delaware, be deemed to be the same entity as the converting other entity. When any conversion shall have become effective under this section, for all purposes of the laws of the State of Delaware, all of the rights, privileges and powers of the other entity that has converted, and all property, real, personal and mixed, and all debts due to such other entity, as well as all other things and causes of action belonging to such other entity, shall remain vested in the domestic corporation to which such other entity has converted and shall be the property of such domestic corporation and the title to any real property vested by deed or otherwise in such other entity shall not revert or be in any way impaired by reason of this chapter; but all rights of creditors and all liens upon any property of such other entity shall be preserved unimpaired, and all debts, liabilities and duties of the other entity that has converted shall remain attached to the corporation of this State to which such other entity has converted, and may be enforced against it to the same extent as if said debts, liabilities and duties had originally been incurred or contracted by it in its capacity as a corporation of this State. The rights, privileges, powers and interests in property of the other entity, as well as the debts, liabilities and duties of the other entity, shall not be deemed, as a consequence of the conversion, to have been transferred to the domestic corporation to which such other entity has converted for any purpose of the laws of the State of Delaware.

(g) Unless otherwise agreed for all purposes of the laws of the State of Delaware or as required under applicable non-Delaware law, the converting other entity shall not be required to wind up its affairs or pay its liabilities and distribute its assets, and the conversion shall not be deemed to constitute a dissolution of such other entity and shall constitute a continuation of the existence of the converting other entity in the form of a corporation of this State.

(h) Prior to filing a certificate of conversion to corporation with the office of the Secretary of State, the conversion shall be approved in the manner provided for by the document, instrument, agreement or other writing, as the case may be, governing the internal affairs of the other entity and the conduct of its business or by applicable law, as appropriate, and a certificate of incorporation shall be approved by the same authorization required to approve the conversion.

(i) The certificate of conversion to corporation shall be signed by any person who is authorized to sign the certificate of conversion to corporation on behalf of the other entity.

(j) In connection with a conversion hereunder, rights or securities of, or interests in, the other entity which is to be converted to a corporation of this State may be exchanged for or converted into cash, property, or shares of stock, rights or securities of such corporation of this State or, in addition to or in lieu thereof, may be exchanged for or converted into cash, property, or shares of stock, rights or securities of or interests in another domestic corporation or other entity or may be cancelled.

72 Del. Laws, c. 123, § 10; 73 Del. Laws, c. 82, §§ 27-29; 73 Del. Laws, c. 329, § 45; 75 Del. Laws, c. 30, §§ 4-18; 78 Del. Laws, c. 96, § 7; 78 Del. Laws, c. 273, § 3.;

§ 266 Conversion of a Domestic Corporation to Other Entities

(a) A corporation of this State may, upon the authorization of such conversion in accordance with this section, convert to a limited liability company, statutory trust, business trust or association, real estate investment trust, common-law trust or any other unincorporated business including a partnership (whether general (including a limited liability partnership) or limited (including a limited liability limited partnership)) or a foreign corporation.

(b) The board of directors of the corporation which desires to convert under this section shall adopt a resolution approving such conversion, specifying the type of entity into which the corporation shall be converted and recommending the approval of such conversion by the stockholders of the corporation. Such resolution shall be submitted to the stockholders of the corporation at an annual or special meeting. Due notice of the time, and purpose of the meeting shall be mailed to each holder of stock, whether voting or nonvoting, of the corporation at the address of the stockholder as it appears on the records of the corporation, at least 20 days prior to the date of the meeting. At the meeting, the resolution shall be considered and a vote taken for its adoption or rejection. If all outstanding shares of stock of the corporation, whether voting or nonvoting, shall be voted for the adoption of the resolution, the conversion shall be authorized.

(1)-(4) [Repealed.]

(c) If a corporation shall convert in accordance with this section to another entity organized, formed or created under the laws of a jurisdiction other than the State of Delaware, the corporation shall file with the Secretary of State a certificate of conversion executed in accordance with § 103 of this title, which certifies:

(1) The name of the corporation, and if it has been changed, the name under which it was originally incorporated;

(2) The date of filing of its original certificate of incorporation with the Secretary of State;

(3) The name and jurisdiction of the entity to which the corporation shall be converted;

(4) That the conversion has been approved in accordance with the provisions of this section;

(5) The agreement of the corporation that it may be served with process in the State of Delaware in any action, suit or proceeding for enforcement of any obligation of the corporation arising while it was a corporation of this State, and that it irrevocably appoints the Secretary of State as its agent to accept service of process in any such action, suit or proceeding; and

(6) The address to which a copy of the process referred to in paragraph (c)(5) of this section shall be mailed to it by the Secretary of State. Process may be served upon the Secretary of State in accordance with paragraph (c)(5) of this section by means of electronic transmission but only as prescribed by the Secretary of State. The Secretary of State is authorized to issue such rules and regulations with respect to such service as the Secretary of State deems necessary or appropriate. In the event of such service upon the Secretary of State in accordance with paragraph (c)(5) of this section, the Secretary of State shall forthwith notify such corporation that has converted out of the State of Delaware by letter, directed to such corporation that has converted out of the State of Delaware at the address so specified, unless such corporation shall have designated in writing to the Secretary of State a different address for such purpose, in which case it shall be mailed to the last address designated. Such letter shall be sent by a mail or courier service that includes a record of mailing or deposit with the courier and a record of delivery evidenced by the signature of the recipient. Such letter shall enclose a copy of the process and any other papers served on the Secretary of State pursuant to this subsection. It shall be the duty of the plaintiff in the event of such service to serve process and any other papers in duplicate, to notify the Secretary of State that service is being effected pursuant to this subsection and to pay the Secretary of State the sum of $50 for the use of the State, which sum shall be taxed as part of the costs in the proceeding, if the plaintiff shall prevail therein. The Secretary of State shall maintain an alphabetical record of any such service setting forth the name of the plaintiff and the defendant, the title, docket number and nature of the proceeding in which process has been served, the fact that service has been effected pursuant to this subsection, the return date thereof, and the day and hour service was made. The Secretary of State shall not be required to retain such information longer than 5 years from receipt of the service of process.

(d) Upon the filing in the Office of the Secretary of State of a certificate of conversion to non-Delaware entity in accordance with subsection (c) of this section or upon the future effective date or time of the certificate of conversion to non-Delaware entity and payment to the Secretary of State of all fees prescribed under this title, the Secretary of State shall certify that the corporation has filed all documents and paid all fees required by this title, and thereupon the corporation shall cease to exist as a corporation of this State at the time the certificate of conversion becomes effective in accordance with § 103 of this title. Such certificate of the Secretary of State shall be prima facie evidence of the conversion by such corporation out of the State of Delaware.

(e) The conversion of a corporation out of the State of Delaware in accordance with this section and the resulting cessation of its existence as a corporation of this State pursuant to a certificate of conversion to non-Delaware entity shall not be deemed to affect any obligations or liabilities of the corporation incurred prior to such conversion or the personal liability of any person incurred prior to such conversion, nor shall it be deemed to affect the choice of law applicable to the corporation with respect to matters arising prior to such conversion.

(f) Unless otherwise provided in a resolution of conversion adopted in accordance with this section, the converting corporation shall not be required to wind up its affairs or pay its liabilities and distribute its assets, and the conversion shall not constitute a dissolution of such corporation.

(g) In connection with a conversion of a domestic corporation to another entity pursuant to this section, shares of stock, of the corporation of this State which is to be converted may be exchanged for or converted into cash, property, rights or securities of, or interests in, the entity to which the corporation of this State is being converted or, in addition to or in lieu thereof, may be exchanged for or converted into cash, property, shares of stock, rights or securities of, or interests in, another domestic corporation or other entity or may be cancelled.

(h) When a corporation has been converted to another entity or business form pursuant to this section, the other entity or business form shall, for all purposes of the laws of the State of Delaware, be deemed to be the same entity as the corporation. When any conversion shall have become effective under this section, for all purposes of the laws of the State of Delaware, all of the rights, privileges and powers of the corporation that has converted, and all property, real, personal and mixed, and all debts due to such corporation, as well as all other things and causes of action belonging to such corporation, shall remain vested in the other entity or business form to which such corporation has converted and shall be the property of such other entity or business form, and the title to any real property vested by deed or otherwise in such corporation shall not revert or be in any way impaired by reason of this chapter; but all rights of creditors and all liens upon any property of such corporation shall be preserved unimpaired, and all debts, liabilities and duties of the corporation that has converted shall remain attached to the other entity or business form to which such corporation has converted, and may be enforced against it to the same extent as if said debts, liabilities and duties had originally been incurred or contracted by it in its capacity as such other entity or business form. The rights, privileges, powers and interest in property of the corporation that has converted, as well as the debts, liabilities and duties of such corporation, shall not be deemed, as a consequence of the conversion, to have been transferred to the other entity or business form to which such corporation has converted for any purpose of the laws of the State of Delaware.

(i) No vote of stockholders of a corporation shall be necessary to authorize a conversion if no shares of the stock of such corporation shall have been issued prior to the adoption by the board of directors of the resolution approving the conversion.

(j) Nothing in this section shall be deemed to authorize the conversion of a charitable nonstock corporation into another entity, if the charitable status of such charitable nonstock corporation would thereby be lost or impaired.

§ 267 Merger of Parent Entity and Subsidiary Corporation or Corporations

(a) In any case in which: (1) at least 90% of the outstanding shares of each class of the stock of a corporation or corporations (other than a corporation which has in its certificate of incorporation the provision required by § 251(g)(7)(i) of this title), of which class there are outstanding shares that, absent this subsection, would be entitled to vote on such merger, is owned by an entity, (2) 1 or more of such corporations is a corporation of this State, and (3) any entity or corporation that is not an entity or corporation of this State is an entity or corporation of any other state or the District of Columbia, the laws of which do not forbid such merger, the entity having such stock ownership may either merge the corporation or corporations into itself and assume all of its or their obligations, or merge itself, or itself and 1 or more of such corporations, into 1 of the other corporations by (a) authorizing such merger in accordance with such entity's governing documents and the laws of the jurisdiction under which such entity is formed or organized and (b) acknowledging and filing with the Secretary of State, in accordance with § 103 of this title, a certificate of such ownership and merger certifying (i) that such merger was authorized in accordance with such entity's governing documents and the laws of the jurisdiction under which such entity is formed or organized, such certificate executed in accordance with such entity's governing documents and in accordance with the laws of the jurisdiction under which such entity is formed or organized and (ii) the type of entity of each constituent entity to the merger; provided, however, that in case the entity shall not own all the outstanding stock of all the corporations, parties to a merger as aforesaid, (A) the certificate of ownership and merger shall state the terms and conditions of the merger, including the securities, cash, property, or rights to be issued, paid, delivered or granted by the surviving constituent party upon surrender of each share of the corporation or corporations not owned by the entity, or the cancellation of some or all of such shares and (B) such terms and conditions of the merger may not result in a holder of stock in a corporation becoming a general partner in a surviving entity that is a partnership (other than a limited liability partnership or a limited liability limited partnership). Any of the terms of the merger may be made dependent upon facts ascertainable outside of the certificate of ownership and merger, provided that the manner in which such facts shall operate upon the terms of the merger is clearly and expressly set forth in the certificate of ownership and merger. The term "facts," as used in the preceding sentence, includes, but is not limited to, the occurrence of any event, including a determination or action by any person or body, including the entity. If the surviving constituent party exists under the laws of the District of Columbia or any state or jurisdiction other than this State, (1) § 252(d) of this title shall also apply to a merger under this section; if the surviving constituent party is the entity, the word "corporation" where applicable, as used in § 252(d) of this title, shall be deemed to include an entity as defined herein; and (2) the terms and conditions of the merger shall obligate the surviving constituent party to provide the agreement, and take the actions, required by § 252(d) of this title.

(b) Sections 259, 261, and 328 of this title shall, insofar as they are applicable, apply to a merger under this section, and §§ 260 and 251(e) of this title shall apply to a merger under this section in which the surviving constituent party is a corporation of this State. For purposes of this subsection, references to "agreement of merger" in § 251(e) of this title shall mean the terms and conditions of the merger set forth in the certificate of ownership and merger, and references to "corporation" in §§ 259-261 of this title, and § 328 of this title shall be deemed to include the entity, as applicable. Section 262 of this title shall not apply to any merger effected under this section, except as provided in subsection (c) of this section.

(c) In the event all of the stock of a Delaware corporation party to a merger effected under this section is not owned by the entity immediately prior to the merger, the stockholders of such Delaware corporation party to the merger shall have appraisal rights as set forth in § 262 of this title.

(d) A merger may be effected under this section although 1 or more of the constituent parties is a corporation organized under the laws of a jurisdiction other than 1 of the United States; provided that the laws of such jurisdiction do not forbid such merger.

(e) As used in this section only, the term:

(1) "Constituent party" means an entity or corporation to be merged pursuant to this section;

(2) "Entity" means a partnership (whether general (including a limited liability partnership) or limited (including a limited liability limited partnership)), limited liability company, any association of the kind

commonly known as a joint-stock association or joint-stock company and any unincorporated association, trust or enterprise having members or having outstanding shares of stock or other evidences of financial or beneficial interest therein, whether formed by agreement or under statutory authority or otherwise; and

(3) "Governing documents" means a partnership agreement, limited liability company agreement, articles of association or any other instrument containing the provisions by which an entity is formed or organized.

Subchapter X. Sale of Assets, Dissolution and Winding Up

§ 271. Sale, Lease or Exchange of Assets; Consideration; Procedure

(a) Every corporation may at any meeting of its board of directors or governing body sell, lease or exchange all or substantially all of its property and assets, including its goodwill and its corporate franchises, upon such terms and conditions and for such consideration, which may consist in whole or in part of money or other property, including shares of stock in, and/or other securities of, any other corporation or corporations, as its board of directors or governing body deems expedient and for the best interests of the corporation, when and as authorized by a resolution adopted by the holders of a majority of the outstanding stock of the corporation entitled to vote thereon or, if the corporation is a nonstock corporation, by a majority of the members having the right to vote for the election of the members of the governing body and any other members entitled to vote thereon under the certificate of incorporation or the bylaws of such corporation, at a meeting duly called upon at least 20 days' notice. The notice of the meeting shall state that such a resolution will be considered.

(b) Notwithstanding authorization or consent to a proposed sale, lease or exchange of a corporation's property and assets by the stockholders or members, the board of directors or governing body may abandon such proposed sale, lease or exchange without further action by the stockholders or members, subject to the rights, if any, of third parties under any contract relating thereto.

(c) For purposes of this section only, the property and assets of the corporation include the property and assets of any subsidiary of the corporation. As used in this subsection, "subsidiary" means any entity wholly-owned and controlled, directly or indirectly, by the corporation and includes, without limitation, corporations, partnerships, limited partnerships, limited liability partnerships, limited liability companies, and/or statutory trusts. Notwithstanding subsection (a) of this section, except to the extent the certificate of incorporation otherwise provides, no resolution by stockholders or members shall be required for a sale, lease or exchange of property and assets of the corporation to a subsidiary.

§ 272. Mortgage or Pledge of Assets

The authorization or consent of stockholders to the mortgage or pledge of a corporation's property and assets shall not be necessary, except to the extent that the certificate of incorporation otherwise provides.

§ 273. Dissolution of Joint Venture Corporation Having 2 Stockholders

(a) If the stockholders of a corporation of this State, having only 2 stockholders each of which own 50% of the stock therein, shall be engaged in the prosecution of a joint venture and if such stockholders shall be unable to agree upon the desirability of discontinuing such joint venture and disposing of the assets used in such venture, either stockholder may, unless otherwise provided in the certificate of incorporation of the corporation or in a written agreement between the stockholders, file with the Court of Chancery a petition stating that it desires to discontinue such joint venture and to dispose of the assets used in such venture in accordance with a plan to be agreed upon by both stockholders or that, if no such plan shall be agreed upon by both stockholders, the corporation be dissolved. Such petition shall have attached thereto a copy of the proposed plan of discontinuance and distribution and a certificate stating that copies of such petition and plan have been transmitted in writing to the other stockholder and to the directors and officers of such corporation. The petition and certificate shall be executed and acknowledged in accordance with § 103 of this title.

(b) Unless both stockholders file with the Court of Chancery:

(1) Within 3 months of the date of the filing of such petition, a certificate similarly executed and acknowledged stating that they have agreed on such plan, or a modification thereof, and

(2) Within 1 year from the date of the filing of such petition, a certificate similarly executed and acknowledged stating that the distribution provided by such plan had been completed,

the Court of Chancery may dissolve such corporation and may by appointment of 1 or more trustees or receivers with all the powers and title of a trustee or receiver appointed under § 279 of this title, administer and wind up its affairs. Either or both of the above periods may be extended by agreement of the stockholders, evidenced by a certificate similarly executed, acknowledged and filed with the Court of Chancery prior to the expiration of such period.

(c) In the case of a charitable nonstock corporation, the petitioner shall provide a copy of any petition referred to in subsection (a) of this section to the Attorney General of the State of Delaware within 1 week of its filing with the Court of Chancery.

§ 274. Dissolution Before Issuance of Shares or Beginning of Business; Procedure

If a corporation has not issued shares or has not commenced the business for which the corporation was organized, a majority of the incorporators, or, if directors were named in the certificate of incorporation or have been elected, a majority of the directors, may surrender all of the corporation's rights and franchises by filing in the office of the Secretary of State a certificate, executed and acknowledged by a majority of the incorporators or directors, stating: that no shares of stock have been issued or that the business or activity for which the corporation was organized has not been begun; the date of filing of the corporation's original certificate of incorporation with the Secretary of State; that no part of the capital of the corporation has been paid, or, if some capital has been paid, that the amount actually paid in for the corporation's shares, less any part thereof disbursed for necessary expenses, has been returned to those entitled thereto; that if the corporation has begun business but it has not issued shares, all debts of the corporation have been paid; that if the corporation has not begun business but has issued stock certificates, all issued stock certificates, if any, have been surrendered and cancelled; and that all rights and franchises of the corporation are surrendered. Upon such certificate becoming effective in accordance with § 103 of this title, the corporation shall be dissolved.

§ 275. Dissolution Generally; Procedure

(a) If it should be deemed advisable in the judgment of the board of directors of any corporation that it should be dissolved, the board, after the adoption of a resolution to that effect by a majority of the whole board at any meeting called for that purpose, shall cause notice of the adoption of the resolution and of a meeting of stockholders to take action upon the resolution to be mailed to each stockholder entitled to vote thereon as of the record date for determining the stockholders entitled to notice of the meeting.

(b) At the meeting a vote shall be taken upon the proposed dissolution. If a majority of the outstanding stock of the corporation entitled to vote thereon shall vote for the proposed dissolution, a certification of dissolution shall be filed with the Secretary of State pursuant to subsection (d) of this section.

(c) Dissolution of a corporation may also be authorized without action of the directors if all the stockholders entitled to vote thereon shall consent in writing and a certificate of dissolution shall be filed with the Secretary of State pursuant to subsection (d) of this section.

(d) If dissolution is authorized in accordance with this section, a certificate of dissolution shall be executed, acknowledged and filed, and shall become effective, in accordance with § 103 of this title. Such certificate of dissolution shall set forth:

(1) The name of the corporation;

(2) The date dissolution was authorized;

(3) That the dissolution has been authorized by the board of directors and stockholders of the corporation, in accordance with subsections (a) and (b) of this section, or that the dissolution has been authorized by all of the stockholders of the corporation entitled to vote on a dissolution, in accordance with subsection (c) of this section;

(4) The names and addresses of the directors and officers of the corporation; and

(5) The date of filing of the corporation's original certificate of incorporation with the Secretary of State.

(e) The resolution authorizing a proposed dissolution may provide that notwithstanding authorization or consent to the proposed dissolution by the stockholders, or the members of a nonstock corporation pursuant to § 276 of this title, the board of directors or governing body may abandon such proposed dissolution without further action by the stockholders or members.

(f) Upon a certificate of dissolution becoming effective in accordance with § 103 of this title, the corporation shall be dissolved.

§ 277. Payment of Franchise Taxes Before Dissolution or Merger, Transfer or Conversion

No corporation shall be dissolved, merged, transferred (without continuing its existence as a corporation of this State) or converted under this chapter until:

(1) All franchise taxes due to or assessable by the State including all franchise taxes due or which would be due or assessable for the entire calendar month during which such dissolution, merger, transfer or conversion becomes effective have been paid by the corporation; and

(2) All annual franchise tax reports including a final annual franchise tax report for the year in which such dissolution, merger, transfer or conversion becomes effective have been filed by the corporation;

notwithstanding the foregoing, if the Secretary of State certifies that an instrument to effect a dissolution, merger, transfer or conversion has been filed in the Secretary of State's office, such corporation shall be dissolved, merged, transferred or converted at the effective time of such instrument.

§ 278. Continuation of Corporation After Dissolution for Purposes of Suit and Winding up Affairs

All corporations, whether they expire by their own limitation or are otherwise dissolved, shall nevertheless be continued, for the term of 3 years from such expiration or dissolution or for such longer period as the Court of Chancery shall in its discretion direct, bodies corporate for the purpose of prosecuting and defending suits, whether civil, criminal or administrative, by or against them, and of enabling them gradually to settle and close their business, to dispose of and convey their property, to discharge their liabilities and to distribute to their stockholders any remaining assets, but not for the purpose of continuing the business for which the corporation was organized. With respect to any action, suit or proceeding begun by or against the corporation either prior to or within 3 years after the date of its expiration or dissolution, the action shall not abate by reason of the dissolution of the corporation; the corporation shall, solely for the purpose of such action, suit or proceeding, be continued as a body corporate beyond the 3-year period and until any judgments, orders or decrees therein shall be fully executed, without the necessity for any special direction to that effect by the Court of Chancery.

Sections 279 through 282 of this title shall apply to any corporation that has expired by its own limitation, and when so applied, all references in those sections to a dissolved corporation or dissolution shall include a corporation that has expired by its own limitation and to such expiration, respectively.

§ 279. Trustees or Receivers for Dissolved Corporations; Appointment; Powers; Duties

When any corporation organized under this chapter shall be dissolved in any manner whatever, the Court of Chancery, on application of any creditor, stockholder or director of the corporation, or any other person who shows good cause therefor, at any time, may either appoint 1 or more of the directors of the corporation to be trustees, or appoint 1 or more persons to be receivers, of and for the corporation, to take charge of the corporation's property, and to collect the debts and property due and belonging to the corporation, with power to prosecute and defend, in the name of the corporation, or otherwise, all such suits as may be necessary or proper for the purposes aforesaid, and to appoint an agent or agents under them, and to do all other acts which might be done by the corporation, if in being, that may be necessary for the final settlement of the unfinished business of the corporation. The powers of the trustees or receivers may be continued as long as the Court of Chancery shall think necessary for the purposes aforesaid.

§ 280. Notice to Claimants; Filing of Claims

(a)(1) After a corporation has been dissolved in accordance with the procedures set forth in this chapter, the corporation or any successor entity may give notice of the dissolution, requiring all persons having a claim against the corporation other than a claim against the corporation in a pending action, suit or proceeding to which the corporation is a party to present their claims against the corporation in accordance with such notice. Such notice shall state:

a. That all such claims must be presented in writing and must contain sufficient information reasonably to inform the corporation or successor entity of the identity of the claimant and the substance of the claim;

b. The mailing address to which such a claim must be sent;

c. The date by which such a claim must be received by the corporation or successor entity, which date shall be no earlier than 60 days from the date thereof; and

d. That such claim will be barred if not received by the date referred to in paragraph (a)(1)c. of this section; and

e. That the corporation or a successor entity may make distributions to other claimants and the corporation's stockholders or persons interested as having been such without further notice to the claimant; and

f. The aggregate amount, on an annual basis, of all distributions made by the corporation to its stockholders for each of the 3 years prior to the date the corporation dissolved.

Such notice shall also be published at least once a week for 2 consecutive weeks in a newspaper of general circulation in the county in which the office of the corporation's last registered agent in this State is located and in the corporation's principal place of business and, in the case of a corporation having $10,000,000 or more in total assets at the time of its dissolution, at least once in all editions of a daily newspaper with a national circulation. On or before the date of the first publication of such notice, the corporation or successor entity shall mail a copy of such notice by certified or registered mail, return receipt requested, to each known claimant of the corporation including persons with claims asserted against the corporation in a pending action, suit or proceeding to which the corporation is a party.

(2) Any claim against the corporation required to be presented pursuant to this subsection is barred if a claimant who was given actual notice under this subsection does not present the claim to the dissolved corporation or successor entity by the date referred to in paragraph (a)(1)c. of this section.

(3) A corporation or successor entity may reject, in whole or in part, any claim made by a claimant pursuant to this subsection by mailing notice of such rejection by certified or registered mail, return receipt

requested, to the claimant within 90 days after receipt of such claim and, in all events, at least 150 days before the expiration of the period described in § 278 of this title; provided however, that in the case of a claim filed pursuant to § 295 of this title against a corporation or successor entity for which a receiver or trustee has been appointed by the Court of Chancery the time period shall be as provided in § 296 of this title, and the 30-day appeal period provided for in § 296 of this title shall be applicable. A notice sent by a corporation or successor entity pursuant to this subsection shall state that any claim rejected therein will be barred if an action, suit or proceeding with respect to the claim is not commenced within 120 days of the date thereof, and shall be accompanied by a copy of §§ 278-283 of this title and, in the case of a notice sent by a court-appointed receiver or trustee and as to which a claim has been filed pursuant to § 295 of this title, copies of §§ 295 and 296 of this title.

(4) A claim against a corporation is barred if a claimant whose claim is rejected pursuant to paragraph (a)(3) of this section does not commence an action, suit or proceeding with respect to the claim no later than 120 days after the mailing of the rejection notice.

(b)(1) A corporation or successor entity electing to follow the procedures described in subsection (a) of this section shall also give notice of the dissolution of the corporation to persons with contractual claims contingent upon the occurrence or nonoccurrence of future events or otherwise conditional or unmatured, and request that such persons present such claims in accordance with the terms of such notice. Provided however, that as used in this section and in § 281 of this title, the term "contractual claims" shall not include any implied warranty as to any product manufactured, sold, distributed or handled by the dissolved corporation. Such notice shall be in substantially the form, and sent and published in the same manner, as described in paragraph (a)(1) of this section.

(2) The corporation or successor entity shall offer any claimant on a contract whose claim is contingent, conditional or unmatured such security as the corporation or successor entity determines is sufficient to provide compensation to the claimant if the claim matures. The corporation or successor entity shall mail such offer to the claimant by certified or registered mail, return receipt requested, within 90 days of receipt of such claim and, in all events, at least 150 days before the expiration of the period described in § 278 of this title. If the claimant offered such security does not deliver in writing to the corporation or successor entity a notice rejecting the offer within 120 days after receipt of such offer for security, the claimant shall be deemed to have accepted such security as the sole source from which to satisfy the claim against the corporation.

(c)(1) A corporation or successor entity which has given notice in accordance with subsection (a) of this section shall petition the Court of Chancery to determine the amount and form of security that will be reasonably likely to be sufficient to provide compensation for any claim against the corporation which is the subject of a pending action, suit or proceeding to which the corporation is a party other than a claim barred pursuant to subsection (a) of this section.

(2) A corporation or successor entity which has given notice in accordance with subsections (a) and (b) of this section shall petition the Court of Chancery to determine the amount and form of security that will be sufficient to provide compensation to any claimant who has rejected the offer for security made pursuant to paragraph (b)(2) of this section.

(3) A corporation or successor entity which has given notice in accordance with subsection (a) of this section shall petition the Court of Chancery to determine the amount and form of security which will be reasonably likely to be sufficient to provide compensation for claims that have not been made known to the corporation or that have not arisen but that, based on facts known to the corporation or successor entity, are likely to arise or to become known to the corporation or successor entity within 5 years after the date of dissolution or such longer period of time as the Court of Chancery may determine not to exceed 10 years after the date of dissolution. The Court of Chancery may appoint a guardian ad litem in respect of any such proceeding brought under this subsection. The reasonable fees and expenses of such guardian, including all reasonable expert witness fees, shall be paid by the petitioner in such proceeding.

(d) The giving of any notice or making of any offer pursuant to this section shall not revive any claim then barred or constitute acknowledgment by the corporation or successor entity that any person to whom such notice is sent is a proper claimant and shall not operate as a waiver of any defense or counterclaim in respect of any claim asserted by any person to whom such notice is sent.

(e) As used in this section, the term "successor entity" shall include any trust, receivership or other legal entity governed by the laws of this State to which the remaining assets and liabilities of a dissolved corporation are transferred and which exists solely for the purposes of prosecuting and defending suits, by or against the dissolved corporation, enabling the dissolved corporation to settle and close the business of the dissolved corporation, to dispose of and convey the property of the dissolved corporation, to discharge the liabilities of the dissolved corporation and to distribute to the dissolved corporation's stockholders any remaining assets, but not for the purpose of continuing the business for which the dissolved corporation was organized.

(f) The time periods and notice requirements of this section shall, in the case of a corporation or successor entity for which a receiver or trustee has been appointed by the Court of Chancery, be subject to variation by, or in the manner provided in, the Rules of the Court of Chancery.

(g) In the case of a nonstock corporation, any notice referred to in the last sentence of paragraph (a)(3) of this section shall include a copy of § 114 of this title. In the case of a nonprofit nonstock corporation, provisions of this section regarding distributions to members shall not apply to the extent that those provisions conflict with any other applicable law or with that corporation's certificate of incorporation or bylaws.

§ 281. Payment and Distribution to Claimants and Stockholders

(a) A dissolved corporation or successor entity which has followed the procedures described in § 280 of this title:

(1) Shall pay the claims made and not rejected in accordance with § 280(a) of this title,

(2) Shall post the security offered and not rejected pursuant to § 280(b)(2) of this title,

(3) Shall post any security ordered by the Court of Chancery in any proceeding under § 280(c) of this title, and

(4) Shall pay or make provision for all other claims that are mature, known and uncontested or that have been finally determined to be owing by the corporation or such successor entity.

Such claims or obligations shall be paid in full and any such provision for payment shall be made in full if there are sufficient assets. If there are insufficient assets, such claims and obligations shall be paid or provided for according to their priority, and, among claims of equal priority, ratably to the extent of assets legally available therefor. Any remaining assets shall be distributed to the stockholders of the dissolved corporation; provided, however, that such distribution shall not be made before the expiration of 150 days from the date of the last notice of rejections given pursuant to § 280(a)(3) of this title. In the absence of actual fraud, the judgment of the directors of the dissolved corporation or the governing persons of such successor entity as to the provision made for the payment of all obligations under paragraph (a)(4) of this section shall be conclusive.

(b) A dissolved corporation or successor entity which has not followed the procedures described in § 280 of this title shall, prior to the expiration of the period described in § 278 of this title, adopt a plan of distribution pursuant to which the dissolved corporation or successor entity (i) shall pay or make reasonable provision to pay all claims and obligations, including all contingent, conditional or unmatured contractual claims known to the corporation or such successor entity, (ii) shall make such provision as will be reasonably likely to be sufficient to provide compensation for any claim against the corporation which is the subject of a pending action, suit or proceeding to which the corporation is a party and (iii) shall make such provision as will be reasonably likely to be sufficient to provide compensation for claims that have not been made known to the corporation or that have not arisen but that, based on facts known to the corporation or successor entity, are likely to arise or to become known to the corporation or successor entity within 10 years after the date of dissolution. The plan of distribution shall provide that such claims shall be paid in full and any such provision for payment made shall be made in full if there are sufficient assets. If there are insufficient assets, such plan shall provide that such claims and obligations shall be paid or provided for according to their priority and, among claims of equal priority, ratably to the extent of assets legally available therefor. Any remaining assets shall be distributed to the stockholders of the dissolved corporation.

(c) Directors of a dissolved corporation or governing persons of a successor entity which has complied with subsection (a) or (b) of this section shall not be personally liable to the claimants of the dissolved corporation.

(d) As used in this section, the term "successor entity" has the meaning set forth in § 280(e) of this title.

(e) The term "priority," as used in this section, does not refer either to the order of payments set forth in paragraph (a)(1)-(4) of this section or to the relative times at which any claims mature or are reduced to judgment.

(f) In the case of a nonprofit nonstock corporation, provisions of this section regarding distributions to members shall not apply to the extent that those provisions conflict with any other applicable law or with that corporation's certificate of incorporation or bylaws.

§ 282. Liability of Stockholders of Dissolved Corporations

(a) A stockholder of a dissolved corporation the assets of which were distributed pursuant to § 281(a) or (b) of this title shall not be liable for any claim against the corporation in an amount in excess of such stockholder's pro rata share of the claim or the amount so distributed to such stockholder, whichever is less.

(b) A stockholder of a dissolved corporation the assets of which were distributed pursuant to § 281(a) of this title shall not be liable for any claim against the corporation on which an action, suit or proceeding is not begun prior to the expiration of the period described in § 278 of this title.

(c) The aggregate liability of any stockholder of a dissolved corporation for claims against the dissolved corporation shall not exceed the amount distributed to such stockholder in dissolution.

MODEL BUSINESS CORPORATION ACT (1984)

Chapter 1. General Provisions

§ 1.02. Reservation of Power to Amend or Repeal

The [name of state legislature] has power to amend or repeal all or part of this Act at any time and all domestic and foreign corporations subject to this Act are governed by the amendment or repeal.

§ 1.40. Act Definitions

In this Act:

(1) "Articles of incorporation" means the original articles of incorporation, all amendments thereof, and any other documents permitted or required to be filed by a domestic business corporation with the secretary of state under any provision of this Act except section 16.21. If an amendment of the articles or any other document filed under this Act restates the articles in their entirety, thenceforth the "articles" shall not include any prior documents.

(2) "Authorized shares" means the shares of all classes a domestic or foreign corporation is authorized to issue....

CHAPTER 2. INCORPORATION

§ 2.01. Incorporators

One or more persons may act as the incorporator or incorporators of a corporation by delivering articles of incorporation to the secretary of state for filing.

§ 2.02. Articles of Incorporation

(a) The articles of incorporation must set forth:

(1) a corporate name for the corporation that satisfies the requirements of section 4.01;

(2) the number of shares the corporation is authorized to issue;

(3) the street address of the corporation's initial registered office and the name of its initial registered agent at that office; and

(4) the name and address of each incorporator.

(b) The articles of incorporation may set forth:

(1) the names and addresses of the individuals who are to serve as the initial directors;

(2) provisions not inconsistent with law regarding:

(i) the purpose or purposes for which the corporation is organized;

(ii) managing the business and regulating the affairs of the corporation;

(iii) defining, limiting, and regulating the powers of the corporation, its board of directors, and shareholders;

(iv) a par value for authorized shares or classes of shares;

(v) the imposition of personal liability on shareholders for the debts of the corporation to a specified extent and upon specified conditions;

(3) any provision that under this Act is required or permitted to be set forth in the bylaws;

(4) a provision eliminating or limiting the liability of a director to the corporation or its shareholders for money damages for any action taken, or any failure to take any action, as a director, except liability for (A) the amount of a financial benefit received by a director to which he is not entitled; (B) an intentional infliction of harm on the corporation or the shareholders; (C) a violation of section 8.33; or (D) an intentional violation of criminal law; and

(5) a provision permitting or making obligatory indemnification of a director for liability (as defined in section 8.50(5)) to any person for any action taken, or any failure to take any action, as a director, except liability for (A) receipt of a financial benefit to which he is not entitled, (B) an intentional infliction of harm on the corporation or its shareholders, (C) a violation of section 8.33, or (D) an intentional violation of criminal law.

(c) The articles of incorporation need not set forth any of the corporate powers enumerated in this Act.

(d) Provisions of the articles of incorporation may be made dependent upon facts objectively ascertainable outside the articles of incorporation in accordance with section 1.20(k).

§ 2.03. Incorporation

(a) Unless a delayed effective date is specified, the corporate existence begins when the articles of incorporation are filed.

(b) The secretary of state's filing of the articles of incorporation is conclusive proof that the incorporators satisfied all conditions precedent to incorporation except in a proceeding by the state to cancel or revoke the incorporation or involuntarily dissolve the corporation.

§ 2.04. Liability for Preincorporation Transactions

All persons purporting to act as or on behalf of a corporation, knowing there was no incorporation under this Act, are jointly and severally liable for all liabilities created while so acting.

§ 2.05. Organization of Corporation

(a) After incorporation:

(1) if initial directors are named in the articles of incorporation, the initial directors shall hold an organizational meeting, at the call of a majority of the directors, to complete the organization of the

corporation by appointing officers, adopting bylaws, and carrying on any other business brought before the meeting;

(2) if initial directors are not named in the articles, the incorporator or incorporators shall hold an organizational meeting at the call of a majority of the incorporators:

(i) to elect directors and complete the organization of the corporation; or

(ii) to elect a board of directors who shall complete the organization of the corporation.

(b) Action required or permitted by this Act to be taken by incorporators at an organizational meeting may be taken without a meeting if the action taken is evidenced by one or more written consents describing the action taken and signed by each incorporator.

(c) An organizational meeting may be held in or out of this state.

§ 2.06. Bylaws

(a) The incorporators or board of directors of a corporation shall adopt initial bylaws for the corporation.

(b) The bylaws of a corporation may contain any provision for managing the business and regulating the affairs of the corporation that is not inconsistent with law or the articles of incorporation.

CHAPTER 3. PURPOSES AND POWERS

§ 3.01. Purposes

(a) Every corporation incorporated under this Act has the purpose of engaging in any lawful business unless a more limited purpose is set forth in the articles of incorporation.

(b) A corporation engaging in a business that is subject to regulation under another statute of this state may incorporate under this Act only if permitted by, and subject to all limitations of, the other statute.

§ 3.02. General Powers

Unless its articles of incorporation provide otherwise, every corporation has perpetual duration and succession in its corporate name and has the same powers as an individual to do all things necessary or convenient to carry out its business and affairs, including without limitation power:

(1) to sue and be sued, complain and defend in its corporate name;

(2) to have a corporate seal, which may be altered at will, and to use it, or a facsimile of it, by impressing or affixing it or in any other manner reproducing it;

(3) to make and amend bylaws, not inconsistent with its articles of incorporation or with the laws of this state, for managing the business and regulating the affairs of the corporation;

(4) to purchase, receive, lease, or otherwise acquire, and own, hold, improve, use, and otherwise deal with, real or personal property, or any legal or equitable interest in property, wherever located;

(5) to sell, convey, mortgage, pledge, lease, exchange, and otherwise dispose of all or any part of its property;

(6) to purchase, receive, subscribe for, or otherwise acquire; own, hold, vote, use, sell, mortgage, lend, pledge, or otherwise dispose of; and deal in and with shares or other interests in, or obligations of, any other entity;

(7) to make contracts and guarantees, incur liabilities, borrow money, issue its notes, bonds, and other obligations (which may be convertible into or include the option to purchase other securities of the corporation), and secure any of its obligations by mortgage or pledge of any of its property, franchises, or income;

(8) to lend money, invest and reinvest its funds, and receive and hold real and personal property as security for repayment;

(9) to be a promoter, partner, member, associate, or manager of any partnership, joint venture, trust, or other entity;

(10) to conduct its business, locate offices, and exercise the powers granted by this Act within or without this state;

(11) to elect directors and appoint officers, employees, and agents of the corporation, define their duties, fix their compensation, and lend them money and credit;

(12) to pay pensions and establish pension plans, pension trusts, profit sharing plans, share bonus plans, share option plans, and benefit or incentive plans for any or all of its current or former directors, officers, employees, and agents;

(13) to make donations for the public welfare or for charitable, scientific, or educational purposes;

(14) to transact any lawful business that will aid governmental policy;

(15) to make payments or donations, or do any other act, not inconsistent with law, that furthers the business and affairs of the corporation.

§ 3.04. Ultra Vires

(a) Except as provided in subsection (b), the validity of corporate action may not be challenged on the ground that the corporation lacks or lacked power to act.

(b) A corporation's power to act may be challenged:

(1) in a proceeding by a shareholder against the corporation to enjoin the act;

(2) in a proceeding by the corporation, directly, derivatively, or through a receiver, trustee, or other legal representative, against an

incumbent or former director, officer, employee, or agent of the corporation; or

(3) in a proceeding by the attorney general under section 14.30.

(c) In a shareholder's proceeding under subsection (b)(1) to enjoin an unauthorized corporate act, the court may enjoin or set aside the act, if equitable and if all affected persons are parties to the proceeding, and may award damages for loss (other than anticipated profits) suffered by the corporation or another party because of enjoining the unauthorized act.

Chapter 4. Name

§ 4.01. Corporate Name

(a) A corporate name:

(1) must contain the word "corporation," "incorporated," "company," or "limited," or the abbreviation "corp.," "inc.," "co.," or "ltd.," or words or abbreviations of like import in another language; and

(2) may not contain language stating or implying that the corporation is organized for a purpose other than that permitted by section 3.01 and its articles of incorporation.

(b) Except as authorized by subsections (c) and (d), a corporate name must be distinguishable upon the records of the secretary of state from:

(1) the corporate name of a corporation incorporated or authorized to transact business in this state;

(2) a corporate name reserved or registered under section 4.02 or 4.03;

(3) the fictitious name adopted by a foreign corporation authorized to transact business in this state because its real name is unavailable; and

(4) the corporate name of a not-for-profit corporation incorporated or authorized to transact business in this state. . . .

Chapter 5. Office and Agent

§ 5.01. Registered Office and Registered Agent

Each corporation must continuously maintain in this state:

(1) a registered office that may be the same as any of its places of business; and

(2) a registered agent, who may be:

(i) an individual who resides in this state and whose business office is identical with the registered office;

(ii) a domestic corporation or not-for-profit domestic corporation whose business office is identical with the registered office; or

(iii) a foreign corporation or not-for-profit foreign corporation authorized to transact business in this state whose business office is identical with the registered office.

Chapter 6. Shares and Distributions

Subchapter A. Shares

§ 6.01. Authorized Shares

(a) The articles of incorporation must set forth any classes of shares and series of shares within a class, and the number of shares of each class and series, that the corporation is authorized to issue. If more than one class or series of shares is authorized, the articles of incorporation must prescribe a distinguishing designation for each class or series and must describe, prior to the issuance of shares of a class or series, the terms, including the preferences, rights, and limitations, of that class or series. Except to the extent varied as permitted by this section, all shares of a class or series must have terms, including preferences, rights and limitations, that are identical with those of other shares of the same class or series.

(b) The articles of incorporation must authorize:

(1) one or more classes or series of shares that together have unlimited voting rights, and

(2) one or more classes or series of shares (which may be the same class or classes as those with voting rights) that together are entitled to receive the net assets of the corporation upon dissolution.

(c) The articles of incorporation may authorize one or more classes or series of shares that:

(1) have special, conditional, or limited voting rights, or no right to vote, except to the extent otherwise provided by this Act;

(2) are redeemable or convertible as specified in the articles of incorporation:

(i) at the option of the corporation, the shareholder, or another person or upon the occurrence of a specified event;

(ii) for cash, indebtedness, securities, or other property; and

(iii) at prices and in amounts specified, or determined in accordance with a formula;

(3) entitle the holders to distributions calculated in any manner, including dividends that may be cumulative, noncumulative, or partially cumulative; or

(4) have preference over any other class or series of shares with respect to distributions, including distributions upon the dissolution of the corporation.

(d) Terms of shares may be made dependent upon facts objectively ascertainable outside the articles of incorporation in accordance with section 1.20(k).

(e) Any of the terms of shares may vary among holders of the same class or series so long as such variations are expressly set forth in the articles of incorporation.

(f) The description of the preferences, rights and limitations of classes or series of shares in subsection (c) is not exhaustive.

§ 6.02. Terms of Class or Series Determined by Board of Directors

(a) If the articles of incorporation so provide, the board of directors is authorized, without shareholder approval, to:

(1) classify any unissued shares into one or more classes or into one or more series within a class,

(2) reclassify any unissued shares of any class into one or more classes or into one or more series within one or more classes, or

(3) reclassify any unissued shares of any series of any class into one or more classes or into one or more series within a class.

(b) If the board of directors acts pursuant to subsection (a), it must determine the terms, including the preferences, rights and limitations, to the same extent permitted under section 6.01, of:

(1) any class of shares before the issuance of any shares of that class, or

(2) any series within a class before the issuance of any shares of that series.

(c) Before issuing any shares of a class or series created under this section, the corporation must deliver to the secretary of state for filing articles of amendment setting forth the terms determined under subsection (a).

§ 6.03. Issued and Outstanding Shares

(a) A corporation may issue the number of shares of each class or series authorized by the articles of incorporation. Shares that are issued are outstanding shares until they are reacquired, redeemed, converted, or cancelled.

(b) The reacquisition, redemption, or conversion of outstanding shares is subject to the limitations of subsection (c) of this section and to section 6.40.

(c) At all times that shares of the corporation are outstanding, one or more shares that together have unlimited voting rights and one or more shares that together are entitled to receive the net assets of the corporation upon dissolution must be outstanding.

Subchapter B. Issuance of Shares

§ 6.20. Subscription for Shares Before Incorporation

(a) A subscription for shares entered into before incorporation is irrevocable for six months unless the subscription agreement provides a longer or shorter period or all the subscribers agree to revocation.

(b) The board of directors may determine the payment terms of subscription for shares that were entered into before incorporation, unless the subscription agreement specifies them. A call for payment by the board of directors must be uniform so far as practicable as to all shares of the same class or series, unless the subscription agreement specifies otherwise.

(c) Shares issued pursuant to subscriptions entered into before incorporation are fully paid and nonassessable when the corporation receives the consideration specified in the subscription agreement.

(d) If a subscriber defaults in payment of money or property under a subscription agreement entered into before incorporation, the corporation may collect the amount owed as any other debt. Alternatively, unless the subscription agreement provides otherwise, the corporation may rescind the agreement and may sell the shares if the debt remains unpaid for more than 20 days after the corporation sends written demand for payment to the subscriber.

(e) A subscription agreement entered into after incorporation is a contract between the subscriber and the corporation subject to section 6.21.

§ 6.21. Issuance of Shares

(a) The powers granted in this section to the board of directors may be reserved to the shareholders by the articles of incorporation.

(b) The board of directors may authorize shares to be issued for consideration consisting of any tangible or intangible property or benefit to the corporation, including cash, promissory notes, services performed, contracts for services to be performed, or other securities of the corporation.

(c) Before the corporation issues shares, the board of directors must determine that the consideration received or to be received for shares to be issued is adequate. That determination by the board of directors is conclusive insofar as the adequacy of consideration for the issuance of shares relates to whether the shares are validly issued, fully paid, and nonassessable.

(d) When the corporation receives the consideration for which the board of directors authorized the issuance of shares, the shares issued therefor are fully paid and nonassessable.

(e) The corporation may place in escrow shares issued for a contract for future services or benefits or a promissory note, or make other arrangements to restrict the transfer of the shares, and may credit distributions in respect of the shares against their purchase price, until the services are performed, the note is paid, or the benefits received. If the services are not performed, the note is not paid, or the benefits are not received, the shares escrowed or restricted and the distributions credited may be cancelled in whole or part.

(f)(1) An issuance of shares or other securities convertible into or rights exercisable for shares, in a transaction or a series of integrated transactions, requires approval of the shareholders, at a meeting at which a quorum consisting of at least a majority of the votes entitled to be cast on the matter exists, if:

(i) the shares, other securities, or rights are issued for consideration other than cash or cash equivalents, and

(ii) the voting power of shares that are issued and issuable as a result of the transaction or series of integrated transactions will comprise more than 20 percent of the voting power of the shares of the corporation that were outstanding immediately before the transaction.

(2) In this subsection:

(i) For purposes of determining the voting power of shares issued and issuable as result of a transaction or series of integrated transactions, the voting power of shares shall be the greater of (A) the voting power of the shares to be issued, or (B) the voting power of the shares that would be outstanding after giving effect to the conversion of convertible shares and other securities and the exercise of rights to be issued.

(ii) A series of transactions is integrated if consummation of one transaction is made contingent on consummation of one or more of the other transactions.

§ 6.22. Liability of Shareholders

(a) A purchaser from a corporation of its own shares is not liable to the corporation or its creditors with respect to the shares except to pay the consideration for which the shares were authorized to be issued (section 6.21) or specified in the subscription agreement (section 6.20).

(b) Unless otherwise provided in the articles of incorporation, a shareholder of a corporation is not personally liable for the acts or debts of the corporation except that he may become personally liable by reason of his own acts or conduct.

§ 6.23. Share Dividends

(a) Unless the articles of incorporation provide otherwise, shares may be issued pro rata and without consideration to the corporation's shareholders or to the shareholders of one or more classes or series. An issuance of shares under this subsection is a share dividend.

(b) Shares of one class or series may not be issued as a share dividend in respect of shares of another class or series unless (1) the articles of incorporation so authorize, (2) a majority of the votes entitled to be cast by the class or series to be issued approve the issue, or (3) there are no outstanding shares of the class or series to be issued.

(c) If the board of directors does not fix the record date for determining shareholders entitled to a share dividend, it is the date the board of directors authorizes the share dividend.

§ 6.24. Share Options

(a) A corporation may issue rights, options, or warrants for the purchase of shares or other securities of the corporation. The board of directors shall determine (i) the terms upon which the rights, options, or warrants are issued and (ii) the terms, including the consideration for which the shares or other securities are to be issued. The authorization by the board of directors for the corporation to issue such rights, options, or warrants constitutes authorization of the issuance of the shares or other securities for which the rights, options or warrants are exercisable.

(b) The terms and conditions of such rights, options or warrants, including those outstanding on the effective date of this section, may include, without limitation, restrictions or conditions that:

(1) preclude or limit the exercise, transfer or receipt of such rights, options or warrants by any person or persons owning or offering to acquire a specified number or percentage of the outstanding shares or other securities of the corporation or by any transferee or transferees of any such person or persons, or

(2) invalidate or void such rights, options or warrants held by any such person or persons or any such transferee or transferees.

§ 6.27. Restriction on Transfer of Shares and Other Securities

(a) The articles of incorporation, bylaws, an agreement among shareholders, or an agreement between shareholders and the corporation may impose restrictions on the transfer or registration of transfer of shares of the corporation. A restriction does not affect shares issued before the restriction was adopted unless the holders of the shares are parties to the restriction agreement or voted in favor of the restriction.

(b) A restriction on the transfer or registration of transfer of shares is valid and enforceable against the holder or a transferee of the holder if the restriction is authorized by this section and its existence is noted conspicuously on the front or back of the certificate or is contained in the information statement required by section 6.26(b). Unless so noted, a restriction is not enforceable against a person without knowledge of the restriction.

(c) A restriction on the transfer or registration of transfer of shares is authorized:

(1) to maintain the corporation's status when it is dependent on the number or identity of its shareholders;

(2) to preserve exemptions under federal or state securities law;

(3) for any other reasonable purpose.

(d) A restriction on the transfer or registration of transfer of shares may:

(1) obligate the shareholder first to offer the corporation or other persons (separately, consecutively, or simultaneously) an opportunity to acquire the restricted shares;

(2) obligate the corporation or other persons (separately, consecutively, or simultaneously) to acquire the restricted shares;

(3) require the corporation, the holders of any class of its shares, or another person to approve the transfer of the restricted shares, if the requirement is not manifestly unreasonable;

(4) prohibit the transfer of the restricted shares to designated persons or classes of persons, if the prohibition is not manifestly unreasonable.

(e) For purposes of this section, "shares" includes a security convertible into or carrying a right to subscribe for or acquire shares.

Subchapter C. Subsequent Acquisition of Shares by Shareholders and Corporation

§ 6.30. Shareholders' Preemptive Rights

(a) The shareholders of a corporation do not have a preemptive right to acquire the corporation's unissued shares except to the extent the articles of incorporation so provide.

(b) A statement included in the articles of incorporation that "the corporation elects to have preemptive rights" (or words of similar import) means that the following principles apply except to the extent the articles of incorporation expressly provide otherwise:

(1) The shareholders of the corporation have a preemptive right, granted on uniform terms and conditions prescribed by the board of directors to provide a fair and reasonable opportunity to exercise the right, to acquire proportional amounts of the corporation's unissued shares upon the decision of the board of directors to issue them.

(2) A shareholder may waive his preemptive right. A waiver evidenced by a writing is irrevocable even though it is not supported by consideration.

(3) There is no preemptive right with respect to:

(i) shares issued as compensation to directors, officers, agents, or employees of the corporation, its subsidiaries or affiliates:

(ii) shares issued to satisfy conversion or option rights created to provide compensation to directors, officers, agents, or employees of the corporation, its subsidiaries or affiliates; . . .

§ 6.31. Corporation's Acquisition of Its Own Shares

(a) A corporation may acquire its own shares, and shares so acquired constitute authorized but unissued shares.

(b) If the articles of incorporation prohibit the reissue of the acquired shares, the number of authorized shares is reduced by the number of shares acquired.

Subchapter D. Distributions

§ 6.40. Distributions to Shareholders

(a) A board of directors may authorize and the corporation may make distributions to its shareholders subject to restriction by the articles of incorporation and the limitation in subsection (c).

(b) If the board of directors does not fix the record date for determining shareholders entitled to a distribution (other than one involving a purchase, redemption, or other acquisition of the corporation's shares), it is the date the board of directors authorizes the distribution.

(c) No distribution may be made if, after giving it effect:

(1) the corporation would not be able to pay its debts as they become due in the usual course of business; or

(2) the corporation's total assets would be less than the sum of its total liabilities plus (unless the articles of incorporation permit otherwise) the amount that would be needed, if the corporation were to be dissolved at the time of the distribution, to satisfy the preferential rights upon dissolution of shareholders whose preferential rights are superior to those receiving the distribution.

(d) The board of directors may base a determination that a distribution is not prohibited under subsection (c) either on financial statements prepared on the basis of accounting practices and principles that are reasonable in the circumstances or on a fair valuation or other method that is reasonable in the circumstances.

(e) Except as provided in subsection (g), the effect of a distribution under subsection (c) is measured:

(1) in the case of distribution by purchase, redemption, or other acquisition of the corporation's shares, as of the earlier of (i) the date money or other property is transferred or debt incurred by the corporation or (ii) the date the shareholder ceases to be a shareholder with respect to the acquired shares;

(2) in the case of any other distribution of indebtedness, as of the date the indebtedness is distributed; and

(3) in all other cases, as of (i) the date the distribution is authorized if the payment occurs within 120 days after the date of authorization or (ii) the date the payment is made if it occurs more than 120 days after the date of authorization.

(f) A corporation's indebtedness to a shareholder incurred by reason of a distribution made in accordance with this section is at parity with the corporation's indebtedness to its general, unsecured creditors except to the extent subordinated by agreement.

(g) Indebtedness of a corporation, including indebtedness issued as a distribution, is not considered a liability for purposes of determinations under subsection (c) if its terms provide that payment of principal and interest are made only if and to the extent that payment of a distribution to shareholders could then be made under this section. If the indebtedness is issued as a distribution, each payment of principal or interest is treated as a distribution, the effect of which is measured on the date the payment is actually made.

(h) This section shall not apply to distributions in liquidation under chapter 14.

CHAPTER 7. SHAREHOLDERS

Subchapter A. Meetings

§ 7.01. Annual Meeting

(a) A corporation shall hold a meeting of shareholders annually at a time stated in or fixed in accordance with the bylaws.

(b) Annual shareholders' meetings may be held in or out of this state at the place stated in or fixed in accordance with the bylaws. If no place is stated in or fixed in accordance with the bylaws, annual meetings shall be held at the corporation's principal office.

(c) The failure to hold an annual meeting at the time stated in or fixed in accordance with a corporation's bylaws does not affect the validity of any corporate action.

§ 7.02. Special Meeting

(a) A corporation shall hold a special meeting of shareholders:

(1) on call of its board of directors or the person or persons authorized to do so by the articles of incorporation or bylaws; or

(2) if the holders of at least 10 percent of all the votes entitled to be cast on an issue proposed to be considered at the proposed special meeting sign, date, and deliver to the corporation one or more written demands for the meeting describing the purpose or purposes for which it is to be held, provided that the articles of incorporation may fix a lower percentage or a higher percentage not exceeding 25 percent of all the votes entitled to be cast on any issue proposed to be considered. Unless otherwise provided in the articles of incorporation, a written demand for a special meeting may be revoked by a writing to that effect received by the corporation prior to the receipt by the corporation of demands sufficient in number to require the holding of a special meeting.

(b) If not otherwise fixed under section 7.03 or 7.07, the record date for determining shareholders entitled to demand a special meeting is the date the first shareholder signs the demand.

(c) Special shareholders' meetings may be held in or out of this state at the place stated in or fixed in accordance with the bylaws. If no place is stated or fixed in accordance with the bylaws, special meetings shall be held at the corporation's principal office.

(d) Only business within the purpose or purposes described in the meeting notice required by section 7.05(c) may be conducted at a special shareholders' meeting.

§ 7.04. Action Without Meeting

(a) Action required or permitted by this Act to be taken at a shareholders' meeting may be taken without a meeting if the action is taken by all the shareholders entitled to vote on the action. The action must be evidenced by one or more written consents bearing the date of signature and describing the action taken, signed by all the shareholders entitled to vote on the action, and delivered to the corporation for inclusion in the minutes or filing with the corporate records. . . .

§ 7.05. Notice of Meeting

(a) A corporation shall notify shareholders of the date, time, and place of each annual and special shareholders' meeting no fewer than 10 nor more than 60 days before the meeting date. Unless this Act or the articles of incorporation require otherwise, the corporation is required to give notice only to shareholders entitled to vote at the meeting.

(b) Unless this Act or the articles of incorporation require otherwise, notice of an annual meeting need not include a description of the purpose or purposes for which the meeting is called.

(c) Notice of a special meeting must include a description of the purpose or purposes for which the meeting is called.

(d) If not otherwise fixed under section 7.03 or 7.07, the record date for determining shareholders entitled to notice of and to vote at an annual or special shareholders' meeting is the day before the first notice is delivered to shareholders....

§ 7.06. Waiver of Notice

(a) A shareholder may waive any notice required by this Act, the articles of incorporation, or bylaws before or after the date and time stated in the notice. The waiver must be in writing, be signed by the shareholder entitled to the notice, and be delivered to the corporation for inclusion in the minutes or filing with the corporate records....

§ 7.07. Record Date

(a) The bylaws may fix or provide the manner of fixing the record date for one or more voting groups in order to determine the shareholders entitled to notice of a shareholders' meeting, to demand a special meeting, to vote, or to take any other action. If the bylaws do not fix or provide for fixing a record date, the board of directors of the corporation may fix a future date as the record date.

(b) A record date fixed under this section may not be more than 70 days before the meeting or action requiring a determination of shareholders....

§ 7.08. Conduct of the Meeting

(a) At each meeting of shareholders, a chair shall preside. The chair shall be appointed as provided in the bylaws or, in the absence of such provision, by the board.

(b) The chair, unless the articles of incorporation or bylaws provide otherwise, shall determine the order of business and shall have the authority to establish rules for the conduct of the meeting.

(c) Any rules adopted for, and the conduct of, the meeting shall be fair to shareholders.

(d) The chair of the meeting shall announce at the meeting when the polls close for each matter voted upon. If no announcement is made, the polls shall be deemed to have closed upon the final adjournment of the meeting. After the polls close, no ballots, proxies or votes nor any revocations or changes thereto may be accepted.

Subchapter B. Voting

§ 7.20. Shareholders' List for Meeting

(a) After fixing a record date for a meeting, a corporation shall prepare an alphabetical list of the names of all its shareholders who are entitled to notice of a shareholders' meeting. The list must be arranged by voting group (and within each voting group by class or series of shares) and show the address of and number of shares held by each shareholder.

(b) The shareholders' list must be available for inspection by any shareholder, beginning two business days after notice of the meeting is given for which the list was prepared and continuing through the meeting, at the corporation's principal office or at a place identified in the meeting notice in the city where the meeting will be held. A shareholder, his agent, or attorney is entitled on written demand to inspect and, subject to the requirements of section 16.02(c), to copy the list, during regular business hours and at his expense, during the period it is available for inspection.

(c) The corporation shall make the shareholders' list available at the meeting, and any shareholder, his agent, or attorney is entitled to inspect the list at any time during the meeting or any adjournment.

(d) If the corporation refuses to allow a shareholder, his agent, or attorney to inspect the shareholders' list before or at the meeting (or copy the list as permitted by subsection (b)), the [name or describe] court of the county where a corporation's principal office (or, if none in this state, its registered office) is located, on application of the shareholder, may summarily order the inspection or copying at the corporation's expense and may postpone the meeting for which the list was prepared until the inspection or copying is complete.

(e) Refusal or failure to prepare or make available the shareholders' list does not affect the validity of action taken at the meeting.

§ 7.21. Voting Entitlement of Shares

(a) Except as provided in subsections (b) and (d) or unless the articles of incorporation provide otherwise, each outstanding share, regardless of class, is entitled to one vote on each matter voted on at a shareholders' meeting. Only shares are entitled to vote.

(b) Absent special circumstances, the shares of a corporation are not entitled to vote if they are owned, directly or indirectly, by a second corporation, domestic or foreign, and the first corporation owns, directly or indirectly, a majority of the shares entitled to vote for directors of the second corporation.

(c) Subsection (b) does not limit the power of a corporation to vote any shares, including its own shares, held by it in a fiduciary capacity....

§ 7.22. Proxies

(a) A shareholder may vote his shares in person or by proxy.

(b) A shareholder or his agent or attorney-in-fact may appoint a proxy to vote or otherwise act for the shareholder by signing an appointment form, or by an electronic transmission. An electronic transmission must contain or be accompanied by information from which one can determine that the shareholder, the shareholder's agent, or the shareholder's attorney-in-fact authorized the transmission.

(c) An appointment of a proxy is effective when a signed appointment form or an electronic transmission of the appointment is received by the inspector of election or the officer or agent of the corporation authorized to tabulate votes. An appointment is valid for 11 months unless a longer period is expressly provided in the appointment form.

(d) An appointment of a proxy is revocable unless the appointment form or electronic transmission states that it is irrevocable and the appointment is coupled with an interest....

§ 7.25. Quorum and Voting Requirements for Voting Groups

(a) Shares entitled to vote as a separate voting group may take action on a matter at a meeting only if a quorum of those shares exists with respect to that matter. Unless the articles of incorporation or this Act provide otherwise, a majority of the votes entitled to be cast on the matter by the voting group constitutes a quorum of that voting group for action on that matter.

(b) Once a share is represented for any purpose at a meeting, it is deemed present for quorum purposes for the remainder of the meeting and for any adjournment of that meeting unless a new record date is or must be set for that adjourned meeting.

(c) If a quorum exists, action on a matter (other than the election of directors) by a voting group is approved if the votes cast within the voting group favoring the action exceed the votes cast opposing the action, unless the articles of incorporation or this Act require a greater number of affirmative votes.

(d) An amendment of articles of incorporation adding, changing, or deleting a quorum or voting requirement for a voting group greater than specified in subsection (a) or (c) is governed by section 7.27.

(e) The election of directors is governed by section 7.28.

§ 7.26. Action by Single and Multiple Voting Groups

(a) If the articles of incorporation or this Act provide for voting by a single voting group on a matter, action on that matter is taken when voted upon by that voting group as provided in section 7.25.

(b) If the articles of incorporation or this act provide for voting by two or more voting groups on a matter, action on that matter is taken only when voted upon by each of those voting groups counted separately as provided in section 7.25. Action may be taken by one voting group on a matter even though no action is taken by another voting group entitled to vote on the matter.

§ 7.27. Greater Quorum or Voting Requirements

(a) The articles of incorporation may provide for a greater quorum or voting requirement for shareholders (or voting groups of shareholders) than is provided for by this Act.

(b) An amendment to the articles of incorporation that adds, changes, or deletes a greater quorum or voting requirement must meet the same quorum requirement and be adopted by the same vote and voting groups required to take action under the quorum and voting requirements then in effect or proposed to be adopted, whichever is greater.

§ 7.28. Voting for Directors; Cumulative Voting

(a) Unless otherwise provided in the articles of incorporation, directors are elected by a plurality of the votes cast by the shares entitled to vote in the election at a meeting at which a quorum is present.

(b) Shareholders do not have a right to cumulate their votes for directors unless the articles of incorporation so provide.

(c) A statement included in the articles of incorporation that "[all] [a designated voting group of] shareholders are entitled to cumulate their votes for directors" (or words of similar import) means that the shareholders designated are entitled to multiply the number of votes they are entitled to cast by the number of directors for whom they are entitled to vote and cast the product for a single candidate or distribute the product among two or more candidates.

(d) Shares otherwise entitled to vote cumulatively may not be voted cumulatively at a particular meeting unless:

(1) the meeting notice or proxy statement accompanying the notice states conspicuously that cumulative voting is authorized; or

(2) a shareholder who has the right to cumulate his votes gives notice to the corporation not less than 48 hours before the time set for the meeting of his intent to cumulate his votes during the meeting, and if

one shareholder gives this notice all other shareholders in the same voting group participating in the election are entitled to cumulate their votes without giving further notice.

§ 7.29. Inspectors of Election

(a) A corporation having any shares listed on a national securities exchange or regularly traded in a market maintained by one or more members of a national or affiliated securities association shall, and any other corporation may, appoint one or more inspectors to act at a meeting of shareholders and make a written report of the inspectors' determinations. Each inspector shall take and sign an oath faithfully to execute the duties of inspector with strict impartiality and according to the best of the inspector's ability.

(b) The inspectors shall

(1) ascertain the number of shares outstanding and the voting power of each;

(2) determine the shares represented at a meeting;

(3) determine the validity of proxies and ballots;

(4) count all votes; and

(5) determine the result.

(c) An inspector may be an officer or employee of the corporation.

Subchapter C. Voting Trusts and Agreements

§ 7.30. Voting Trusts

(a) One or more shareholders may create a voting trust, conferring on a trustee the right to vote or otherwise act for them, by signing an agreement setting out the provisions of the trust (which may include anything consistent with its purpose) and transferring their shares to the trustee. When a voting trust agreement is signed, the trustee shall prepare a list of the names and addresses of all owners of beneficial interests in the trust, together with the number and class of shares each transferred to the trust, and deliver copies of the list and agreement to the corporation's principal office.

(b) A voting trust becomes effective on the date the first shares subject to the trust are registered in the trustee's name. A voting trust is valid for not more than 10 years after its effective date unless extended under subsection (c).

(c) All or some of the parties to a voting trust may extend it for additional terms of not more than 10 years each by signing written consent to the extension. An extension is valid for 10 years from the date the first shareholder signs the extension agreement. The voting trustee must deliver copies of the extension agreement and list of beneficial owners to the corporation's principal office. An extension agreement binds only those parties signing it.

§ 7.31. Voting Agreements

(a) Two or more shareholders may provide for the manner in which they will vote their shares by signing an agreement for that purpose. A voting agreement created under this section is not subject to the provisions of section 7.30.

(b) A voting agreement created under this section is specifically enforceable.

§ 7.32. Shareholder Agreements

(a) An agreement among the shareholders of a corporation that complies with this section is effective among the shareholders and the corporation even though it is inconsistent with one or more other provisions of this Act in that it:

(1) eliminates the board of directors or restricts the discretion or powers of the board of directors;

(2) governs the authorization or making of distributions whether or not in proportion to ownership of shares, subject to the limitations in section 6.40;

(3) establishes who shall be directors or officers of the corporation, or their terms of office or manner of selection or removal;

(4) governs, in general or in regard to specific matters, the exercise or division of voting power by or between the shareholders and directors or by or among any of them, including use of weighted voting rights or director proxies;

(5) establishes the terms and conditions of any agreement for the transfer or use of property or the provision of services between the corporation and any shareholder, director, officer or employee of the corporation or among any of them;

(6) transfers to one or more shareholders or other persons all or part of the authority to exercise the corporate powers or to manage the business and affairs of the corporation, including the resolution of any issue about which there exists a deadlock among directors or shareholders;

(7) requires dissolution of the corporation at the request of one or more of the shareholders or upon the occurrence of a specified event or contingency; or

(8) otherwise governs the exercise of the corporate powers or the management of the business and affairs of the corporation or the

relationship among the shareholders, the directors and the corporation, or among any of them, and is not contrary to public policy.

(b) An agreement authorized by this section shall be:

(1) set forth (A) in the articles of incorporation or bylaws and approved by all persons who are shareholders at the time of the agreement or (B) in a written agreement that is signed by all persons who are shareholders at the time of the agreement and is made known to the corporation;

(2) subject to amendment only by all persons who are shareholders at the time of the amendment, unless the agreement provides otherwise; and

(3) valid for 10 years, unless the agreement provides otherwise.

(c) The existence of an agreement authorized by this section shall be noted conspicuously on the front or back of each certificate for outstanding shares or on the information statement required by section 6.26(b). . . .

(d) An agreement authorized by this section shall cease to be effective when shares of the corporation are listed on a national securities exchange or regularly traded in a market maintained by one or more members of a national or affiliated securities association. . . .

(e) An agreement authorized by this section that limits the discretion or powers of the board of directors shall relieve the directors of, and impose upon the person or persons in whom such discretion or powers are vested, liability for acts or omissions imposed by law on directors to the extent that the discretion or powers of the directors are limited by the agreement.

(f) The existence or performance of an agreement authorized by this section shall not be a ground for imposing personal liability on any shareholder for the acts or debts of the corporation even if the agreement or its performance treats the corporation as if it were a partnership or results in failure to observe the corporate formalities otherwise applicable to the matters governed by the agreement.

(g) Incorporators or subscribers for shares may act as shareholders with respect to an agreement authorized by this section if no shares have been issued when the agreement is made.

Subchapter D. Derivative Proceedings

§ 7.40. Subchapter Definitions

In this subchapter:

(1) "Derivative proceeding" means a civil suit in the right of a domestic corporation or, to the extent provided in section 7.47, in the right of a foreign corporation.

(2) "Shareholder" includes a beneficial owner whose shares are held in a voting trust or held by a nominee on the beneficial owner's behalf.

§ 7.41. Standing

A shareholder may not commence or maintain a derivative proceeding unless the shareholder:

(1) was a shareholder of the corporation at the time of the act or omission complained of or became a shareholder through transfer by operation of law from one who was a shareholder at that time; and

(2) fairly and adequately represents the interests of the corporation in enforcing the right of the corporation.

§ 7.42. Demand

No shareholder may commence a derivative proceeding until:

(1) a written demand has been made upon the corporation to take suitable action; and

(2) 90 days have expired from the date the demand was made unless the shareholder has earlier been notified that the demand has been rejected by the corporation or unless irreparable injury to the corporation would result by waiting for the expiration of the 90-day period.

§ 7.43. Stay of Proceedings

If the corporation commences an inquiry into the allegations made in the demand or complaint, the court may stay any derivative proceeding for such period as the court deems appropriate.

§ 7.44. Dismissal

(a) A derivative proceeding shall be dismissed by the court on motion by the corporation if one of the groups specified in subsections (b) or (e) has determined in good faith after conducting a reasonable inquiry upon which its conclusions are based that the maintenance of the derivative proceeding is not in the best interests of the corporation.

(b) Unless a panel is appointed pursuant to subsection (e), the determination in subsection (a) shall be made by:

(1) a majority vote of independent directors present at a meeting of the board of directors if the independent directors constitute a quorum; or

(2) a majority vote of a committee consisting of two or more independent directors appointed by majority vote of independent directors present at a meeting of the board of directors, whether or not such independent directors constituted a quorum. . . .

(d) If a derivative proceeding is commenced after a determination has been made rejecting a demand by a shareholder, the complaint shall allege with particularity facts establishing either (1) that a majority of the board of directors did not consist of independent directors at the time the determination was made or (2) that the requirements of subsection (a) have not been met.

(e) If a majority of the board of directors does not consist of independent directors at the time the determination is made, the corporation shall have the burden of proving that the requirements of subsection (a) have been met. If a majority of the board of directors consists of independent directors at the time the determination is made, the plaintiff shall have the burden of proving that the requirements of subsection (a) have not been met.

(f) The court may appoint a panel of one or more independent persons upon motion by the corporation to make a determination whether the maintenance of the derivative proceeding is in the best interests of the corporation. In such case, the plaintiff shall have the burden of proving that the requirements of subsection (a) have not been met.

§ 7.45. Discontinuance or Settlement

A derivative proceeding may not be discontinued or settled without the court's approval. If the court determines that a proposed discontinuance or settlement will substantially affect the interests of the corporation's shareholders or a class of shareholders, the court shall direct that notice be given to the shareholders affected.

§ 7.46. Payment of Expenses

On termination of the derivative proceeding the court may:

(1) order the corporation to pay the plaintiff's reasonable expenses (including counsel fees) incurred in the proceeding if it finds that the proceeding has resulted in a substantial benefit to the corporation;

(2) order the plaintiff to pay any defendant's reasonable expenses (including counsel fees) incurred in defending the proceeding if it finds that the proceeding was commenced or maintained without reasonable cause or for an improper purpose; or

(3) order a party to pay an opposing party's reasonable expenses (including counsel fees) incurred because of the filing of a pleading, motion or other paper, if it finds that the pleading, motion or other paper was not well grounded in fact, after reasonable inquiry, or warranted by existing law or a good faith argument for the extension, modification or reversal of existing law and was interposed for an improper purpose, such as to harass or cause unnecessary delay or needless increase in the cost of litigation.

CHAPTER 8. DIRECTORS AND OFFICERS

Subchapter A. Board of Directors

§ 8.01. Requirement for and Duties of Board of Directors

(a) Except as provided in section 7.32, each corporation must have a board of directors.

(b) All corporate powers shall be exercised by or under the authority of, and the business and affairs of the corporation managed by or under the direction of, its board of directors, subject to any limitation set forth in the articles of incorporation or in an agreement authorized under section 7.32.

(c) In the case of a public corporation, the board's oversight responsibilities include attention to:

(1) business performance and plans;

(2) major risks to which the corporation is or may be exposed;

(3) the performance and compensation of senior officers;

(4) policies and practices to foster the corporation's compliance with law and ethical conduct;

(5) preparation of the company's financial statements;

(6) the effectiveness of the corporations internal controls;

(7) arrangements for providing adequate and timely information to directors; and

(8) the composition of the board and its committees, taking into account the important role of independent directors.

§ 8.03. Number and Election of Directors

(a) A board of directors must consist of one or more individuals, with the number specified in or fixed in accordance with the articles of incorporation or bylaws.

(b) The number of directors may be increased or decreased from time to time by amendment to, or in the manner provided in, the articles of incorporation or the bylaws.

(c) Directors are elected at the first annual shareholders' meeting and at each annual meeting thereafter unless their terms are staggered under section 8.06.

§ 8.04. Election of Directors by Certain Classes of Shareholders

If the articles of incorporation authorize dividing the shares into classes, the articles may also authorize the election of all or a specified number of directors by the holders of one or more authorized classes of shares. A class (or classes) of shares entitled to elect one or more directors is a separate voting group for purposes of the election of directors.

§ 8.05. Terms of Directors Generally

(a) The terms of the initial directors of a corporation expire at the first shareholders' meeting at which directors are elected.

(b) The terms of all other directors expire at the next, or if their terms are staggered in accordance with section 8.06, at the applicable second or third, annual shareholders' meeting following their election, except to the extent (i) provided in section 10.22 if a bylaw electing to be governed by that section is in effect or (ii) a shorter term is specified in the articles of incorporation in the event of a director nominee failing to receive a specified vote for election.

(c) A decrease in the number of directors does not shorten an incumbent director's term.

(d) The term of a director elected to fill a vacancy expires at the next shareholders' meeting at which directors are elected.

(e) Except to the extent otherwise provided in the articles of incorporation or under section 10.22 if a bylaw electing to be governed by that section is in effect, despite the expiration of a director's term, the director continues to serve until the director's successor is elected and qualifies or there is a decrease in the number of directors.

§ 8.06. Staggered Terms for Directors

The articles of incorporation may provide for staggering the terms of directors by dividing the total number of directors into two or three groups, with each group containing one-half or one-third of the total, as near as may be. In that event, the terms of directors in the first group expire at the first annual shareholders' meeting after their election, the terms of the second group expire at the second annual shareholders' meeting after their election, and the terms of the third group, if any, expire at the third annual shareholders' meeting after their election. At each annual shareholders' meeting held thereafter, directors shall be chosen for a term of two years or three years, as the case may be, to succeed those whose terms expire.

§ 8.07. Resignation of Directors

(a) A director may resign at any time by delivering a written resignation to the board of directors or its chair, or to the secretary of the corporation.

(b) A resignation is effective when the resignation is delivered unless the resignation specifies a later effective date or an effective date determined upon the happening of an event or events. A resignation that is conditioned upon failing to receive a specified vote for election as a director may provide that it is irrevocable.

§ 8.08. Removal of Directors by Shareholders

(a) The shareholders may remove one or more directors with or without cause unless the articles of incorporation provide that directors may be removed only for cause.

(b) If a director is elected by a voting group of shareholders, only the shareholders of that voting group may participate in the vote to remove him.

(c) If cumulative voting is authorized, a director may not be removed if the number of votes sufficient to elect him under cumulative voting is voted against his removal. If cumulative voting is not authorized, a director may be removed only if the number of votes cast to remove him exceeds the number of votes cast not to remove him.

(d) A director may be removed by the shareholders only at a meeting called for the purpose of removing him and the meeting notice must state that the purpose, or one of the purposes, of the meeting is removal of the director.

§ 8.09. Removal of Directors by Judicial Proceeding

(a) The [name or describe] court of the county where a corporation's principal office (or, if none in this state, its registered office) is located may remove a director of the corporation from office in a proceeding commenced by or in the right of the corporation if the court finds that (1) the director engaged in fraudulent conduct with respect to the corporation or its shareholders, grossly abused the position of director, or intentionally inflicted harm on the corporation; and (2) considering the director's course of conduct and the inadequacy of other available remedies, removal would be in the best interest of the corporation. . . .

§ 8.10. Vacancy on Board

(a) Unless the articles of incorporation provide otherwise, if a vacancy occurs on a board of directors, including a vacancy resulting from an increase in the number of directors:

(1) the shareholders may fill the vacancy;

(2) the board of directors may fill the vacancy; or

(3) if the directors remaining in office constitute fewer than a quorum of the board, they may fill the vacancy by the affirmative vote of a majority of all the directors remaining in office.

(b) If the vacant office was held by a director elected by a voting group of shareholders, only the holders of shares of that voting group are entitled to vote to fill the vacancy if it is filled by the shareholders, and only the directors elected by that voting group are entitled to fill the vacancy if it is filled by the directors.

(c) A vacancy that will occur at a specific later date (by reason of a resignation effective at a later date under section 8.07(b) or otherwise) may be filled before the vacancy occurs but the new director may not take office until the vacancy occurs.

§ 8.11. Compensation of Directors

Unless the articles of incorporation or bylaws provide otherwise, the board of directors may fix the compensation of directors.

Subchapter B. Meetings and Action of the Board

§ 8.20. Meetings

(a) The board of directors may hold regular or special meetings in or out of this state.

(b) Unless the articles of incorporation or bylaws provide otherwise, the board of directors may permit any or all directors to participate in a regular or special meeting by, or conduct the meeting through the use of, any means of communication by which all directors participating may simultaneously hear each other during the meeting. A director participating in a meeting by this means is deemed to be present in person at the meeting.

§ 8.21. Action Without Meeting

(a) Except to the extent that the articles of incorporation or bylaws require that action by the board of directors be taken at a meeting, action required or permitted by this Act to be taken by the board of directors may be taken without a meeting if each director signs a consent describing the action to be taken and delivers it to the corporation. . . .

§ 8.22. Notice of Meeting

(a) Unless the articles of incorporation or bylaws provide otherwise, regular meetings of the board of directors may be held without notice of the date, time, place, or purpose of the meeting.

(b) Unless the articles of incorporation or bylaws provide for a longer or shorter period, special meetings of the board of directors must be preceded by at least two days' notice of the date, time, and place of the meeting. The notice need not describe the purpose of the special meeting unless required by the articles of incorporation or bylaws.

§ 8.23. Waiver of Notice

(a) A director may waive any notice required by this Act, the articles of incorporation, or bylaws before or after the date and time stated in the notice. Except as provided by subsection (b), the waiver must be in writing, signed by the director entitled to the notice, and filed with the minutes or corporate records....

§ 8.24. Quorum and Voting

(a) Unless the articles of incorporation or bylaws require a greater number or unless otherwise specifically provided in this Act, a quorum of a board of directors consists of:

(1) a majority of the fixed number of directors if the corporation has a fixed board size; or

(2) a majority of the number of directors prescribed, or if no number is prescribed the number in office immediately before the meeting begins, if the corporation has a variable-range size board.

(b) The articles of incorporation or bylaws may authorize a quorum of a board of directors to consist of no fewer than one-third of the fixed or prescribed number of directors determined under subsection (a).

(c) If a quorum is present when a vote is taken, the affirmative vote of a majority of directors present is the act of the board of directors unless the articles of incorporation or bylaws require the vote of a greater number of directors.

(d) A director who is present at a meeting of the board of directors or a committee of the board of directors when corporate action is taken is deemed to have assented to the action taken unless: (1) he objects at the beginning of the meeting (or promptly upon his arrival) to holding it or transacting business at the meeting; (2) his dissent or abstention from the action taken is entered in the minutes of the meeting; or (3) he delivers written notice of his dissent or abstention to the presiding officer of the meeting before its adjournment or to the corporation immediately after adjournment of the meeting. The right of dissent or abstention is not available to a director who votes in favor of the action taken.

§ 8.25. Committees

(a) Unless this Act, the articles of incorporation or the bylaws provide otherwise, a board of directors may create one or more committees and appoint one or more members of the board of directors to serve on any such committee.

(b) Unless this Act otherwise provides, the creation of a committee and appointment of members to it must be approved by the greater of (1) a majority of all the directors in office when the action is taken or (2) the number of directors required by the articles of incorporation or bylaws to take action under section 8.24.

(c) Sections 8.20 through 8.24 apply both to committees of the board and to their members.

(d) To the extent specified by the board of directors or in the articles of incorporation or bylaws, each committee may exercise the powers of the board of directors under section 8.01.

(e) A committee may not, however:

(1) authorize or approve distributions, except according to a formula or method, or within limits, prescribed by the board of directors;

(2) approve or propose to shareholders action that this Act requires be approved by shareholders;

(3) fill vacancies on the board of directors or, subject to subsection (g), on any of its committees; or

(4) adopt, amend, or repeal bylaws.

(f) The creation of, delegation of authority to, or action by a committee does not alone constitute compliance by a director with the standards of conduct described in section 8.30.

(g) The board of directors may appoint one or more directors as alternate members of any committee to replace any absent or disqualified member during the member's absence or disqualification. Unless the articles of incorporation or the bylaws or the resolution creating the committee provide otherwise, in the event of the absence or disqualification of a member of a committee, the member or members present at any meeting and not disqualified from voting, unanimously, may appoint another director to act in place of the absent or disqualified member.

Subchapter C. Directors

§ 8.30. Standards of Conduct for Directors

(a) Each member of the board of directors, when discharging the duties of a director, shall act: (1) in good faith, and (2) in a manner the director reasonably believes to be in the best interests of the corporation.

(b) The members of the board of directors or a committee of the board, when becoming informed in connection with their decision-making function or devoting attention to their oversight function, shall discharge their duties with the care that a person in a like position would reasonably believe appropriate under similar circumstances.

(c) In discharging board or committee duties a director, who does not have knowledge that makes reliance unwarranted, is entitled to rely on the performance by any of the persons specified in subsection (e)(1) or subsection (e)(3) to whom the board may have delegated, formally or informally by course of conduct, the authority or duty to perform one or more of the board's functions that are delegable under applicable law.

(d) In discharging board or committee duties a director, who does not have knowledge that makes reliance unwarranted, is entitled to rely on information, opinions, reports or statements, including financial statements and other financial data, prepared or presented by any of the persons specified in subsection (e).

(e) A director is entitled to rely, in accordance with subsection (c) or (d), on:

(1) one or more officers or employees of the corporation whom the director reasonably believes to be reliable and competent in the functions performed or the information, opinions, reports or statements provided;

(2) legal counsel, public accountants, or other persons retained by the corporation as to matters involving skills or expertise the director reasonably believes are matters (i) within the particular person's professional or expert competence or (ii) as to which the particular person merits confidence; or

(3) a committee of the board of directors of which the director is not a member if the director reasonably believes the committee merits confidence.

§ 8.31. Standards of Liability for Directors

(a) A director shall not be liable to the corporation or its shareholders for any decision to take or not to take action, or any failure to take any action, as a director, unless the party asserting liability in a proceeding establishes that:

(1) any provision in the articles of incorporation authorized by section 2.02(b)(4) or the protection afforded by section 8.61 for action taken in compliance with section 8.62 or 8.63, if interposed as a bar to the proceeding by the director, does not preclude liability; and

(2) the challenged conduct consisted or was the result of:

(i) action not in good faith; or

(ii) a decision

(A) which the director did not reasonably believe to be in the best interests of the corporation, or

(B) as to which the director was not informed to an extent the director reasonably believed appropriate in the circumstances; or

(iii) a lack of objectivity due to the director's familial, financial or business relationship with, or a lack of independence due to the director's domination or control by, another person having a material interest in the challenged conduct

(A) which relationship or which domination or control could reasonably be expected to have affected the director's judgment respecting the challenged conduct in a manner adverse to the corporation, and

(B) after a reasonable expectation to such effect has been established, the director shall not have established that the challenged conduct was reasonably believed by the director to be in the best interests of the corporation; or

(iv) a sustained failure of the director to devote attention to ongoing oversight of the business and affairs of the corporation, or a failure to devote timely attention, by making (or causing to be made) appropriate inquiry, when particular facts and circumstances of significant concern materialize that would alert a reasonably attentive director to the need therefore; or

(v) receipt of a financial benefit to which the director was not entitled or any other breach of the director's duties to deal fairly with the corporation and its shareholders that is actionable under applicable law.

(b) The party seeking to hold the director liable:

(1) for money damages, shall also have the burden of establishing that:

(i) harm to the corporation or its shareholders has been suffered, and

(ii) the harm suffered was proximately caused by the director's challenged conduct; or

(2) for other money payment under a legal remedy, such as compensation for the unauthorized use of corporate assets, shall also have whatever persuasion burden may be called for to establish that the payment sought is appropriate in the circumstances; or

(3) for other money payment under an equitable remedy, such as profit recovery by or disgorgement to the corporation, shall also have whatever persuasion burden may be called for to establish that the equitable remedy sought is appropriate in the circumstances.

(c) Nothing contained in this section shall (1) in any instance where fairness is at issue, such as consideration of the fairness of a transaction to the corporation under section 8.61(b)(3), alter the burden of proving the fact or lack of fairness otherwise applicable, (2) alter the fact or lack of liability of a director under another section of this Act, such as the provisions governing the consequences of an unlawful distribution under section 8.33 or a transactional interest under section 8.61, or (3) affect any rights to which the corporation or a shareholder may be entitled under another statute of this state or the United States.

§ 8.33. Directors' Liability for Unlawful Distributions

(a) A director who votes for or assents to a distribution in excess of what may be authorized and made pursuant to section 6.40(a) or 14.09(a) is personally liable to the corporation for the amount of the distribution that exceeds what could have been distributed without violating section 6.40(a) or 14.09(a) if the party asserting liability establishes that when taking the action the director did not comply with section 8.30.

(b) A director held liable under subsection (a) for an unlawful distribution is entitled to:

(1) contribution from every other director who could be held liable under subsection (a) for the unlawful distribution; and

(2) recoupment from each shareholder of the pro-rata portion of the amount of the unlawful distribution the shareholder accepted, knowing the distribution was made in violation of section 6.40(a) or 14.09(a).

(c) A proceeding to enforce:

(1) the liability of a director under subsection (a) is barred unless it is commenced within two years after the date (i) on which the effect of the distribution was measured under section 6.40(e) or (g), (ii) as of which the violation of section 6.40(a) occurred as the consequence of disregard of a restriction in the articles of incorporation or (iii) on which the distribution of assets to Shareholders under section 14.09(a) was made; or

(2) contribution or recoupment under subsection (b) is barred unless it is commenced within one year after the liability of the claimant has been finally adjudicated under subsection (a).

Subchapter D. Officers

§ 8.40. Officers

(a) A corporation has the officers described in its bylaws or appointed by the board of directors in accordance with the bylaws.

(b) The board of directors may elect individuals to fill one or more offices of the corporation. An officer may appoint one or more officers if authorized by the bylaws or the board of directors.

(c) The bylaws or the board of directors shall assign to one of the officers responsibility for preparing the minutes of the directors' and shareholders' meetings and for maintaining and authenticating the records of the corporation required to be kept under sections 16.01(a) and 16.01(e).

(d) The same individual may simultaneously hold more than one office in a corporation.

§ 8.42. Standards of Conduct for Officers

(a) An officer, when performing in such capacity, shall act:

(1) in good faith;

(2) with the care that a person in a like position would reasonably exercise under similar circumstances; and

(3) in a manner the officer reasonably believes to be in the best interests of the corporation.

(b) The duty of the officer includes the obligation:

(1) to inform the superior officer to whom, or the board of directors of the committee thereof to which, the officer reports of information

about the affairs of the corporation known to the officer, within the scope of the officer's functions, and known to the officer to be material to such superior officer, board or committee; and

(2) to inform his or her superior officer, or other appropriate person within the corporation, or the board of directors, or a committee thereof, of any actual or probable material violation of law involving the corporation or material breach of duty to the corporation by an officer, employee, or agent of the corporation, that the officer believes has occurred or is likely to occur.

(c) In discharging those duties an officer, who does not have knowledge that makes reliance unwarranted, is entitled to rely on:

(1) the performance of properly delegated responsibilities by one or more employees of the corporation whom the officer reasonably believes to be reliable and competent in performing the responsibilities delegated; or

(2) information, opinions, reports or statements, including financial statements and other financial data, prepared or presented by one or more employees of the corporation whom the officer reasonably believes to be reliable and competent in the matters presented or by legal counsel, public accountants, or other persons retained by the corporation as to matters involving skills or expertise the officer reasonably believes are matters (i) within the particular person's professional or expert competence or (ii) as to which the particular person merits confidence.

(d) An officer shall not be liable to the corporation or its shareholders for any decision to take or not to take action, or any failure to take any action, as an officer, if the duties of the office are performed in compliance with this section. Whether an officer who does not comply with this section shall have liability will depend in such instance on applicable law, including those principles of Section 8.31 that have relevance.

§ 8.43. Resignation and Removal of Officers

...

(b) An officer may be removed at any time with or without cause by: (i) the board of directors; (ii) the officer who appointed such officer, unless the bylaws or the board of directors provide otherwise; or (iii) any other officer if authorized by the bylaws or the board of directors....

§ 8.44. Contract Rights of Officers

(a) The appointment of an officer does not itself create contract rights.

(b) An officer's removal does not affect the officer's contract rights, if any, with the corporation. An officer's resignation does not affect the corporation's contract rights, if any, with the officer.

Subchapter E. Indemnification and Advance for Expenses

§ 8.50. Subchapter Definitions

In this subchapter:

. . .

(3) "Disinterested director" means a director who, at the time of a vote referred to in section 8.53(c) or a vote or selection referred to in section 8.55(b) or (c), is not (i) a party to the proceeding, or (ii) an individual having a familial, financial, professional or employment relationship with the director whose indemnification or advance for expenses is the subject of the decision being made, which relationship would, in the circumstances, reasonably be expected to exert an influence on the director's judgment when voting on the decision being made.

(4) "Expenses" includes counsel fees.

(5) "Liability" means the obligation to pay a judgment, settlement, penalty, fine (including an excise tax assessed with respect to an employee benefit plan), or reasonable expenses incurred with respect to a proceeding.

(6) "Official capacity" means: (i) when used with respect to a director, the office of director in a corporation; and (ii) when used with respect to an officer, as contemplated in section 8.56, the office in a corporation held by the officer. "Official capacity" does not include service for any other domestic or foreign corporation or any partnership, joint venture, trust, employee benefit plan, or other entity.

(7) "Party" means an individual who was, is, or is threatened to be made, a defendant or respondent in a proceeding.

(8) "Proceeding" means any threatened, pending, or completed action, suit, or proceeding, whether civil, criminal, administrative, arbitrative, or investigative and whether formal or informal.

§ 8.51. Permissible Indemnification

(a) Except as otherwise provided in this section, a corporation may indemnify an individual who is a party to a proceeding because he is a director against liability incurred in the proceeding if:

(1)(i) he conducted himself in good faith; and

(ii) he reasonably believed:

(A) in the case of conduct in his official capacity, that his conduct was in the best interests of the corporation; and

(B) in all other cases, that his conduct was at least not opposed to the best interests of the corporation; and

(iii) in the case of any criminal proceeding, he had no reasonable cause to believe his conduct was unlawful; or

(2) he engaged in conduct for which broader indemnification has been made permissible or obligatory under a provision of the articles of incorporation (as authorized by section 2.02(b)(5)).

(b) A director's conduct with respect to an employee benefit plan for a purpose he reasonably believed to be in the interests of the participants in, and the beneficiaries of, the plan is conduct that satisfies the requirement of subsection (a)(1)(ii)(B).

(c) The termination of a proceeding by judgment, order, settlement, or conviction, or upon a plea of nolo contendere or its equivalent, is not, of itself, determinative that the director did not meet the relevant standard of conduct described in this section.

(d) Unless ordered by a court under section 8.54(a)(3), a corporation may not indemnify a director:

(1) in connection with a proceeding by or in the right of the corporation, except for reasonable expenses incurred in connection with the proceeding if it is determined that the director has met the relevant standard of conduct under subsection (a); or

(2) in connection with any proceeding with respect to conduct for which he was adjudged liable on the basis that he received a financial benefit to which he was not entitled, whether or not involving action in his official capacity.

§ 8.52. Mandatory Indemnification

A corporation shall indemnify a director who was wholly successful, on the merits or otherwise, in the defense of any proceeding to which he was a party because he was a director of the corporation against reasonable expenses incurred by him in connection with the proceeding.

§ 8.53. Advance for Expenses

(a) A corporation may, before final disposition of a proceeding, advance funds to pay for or reimburse the reasonable expenses incurred by a director who is a party to a proceeding because he is a director if he delivers to the corporation:

(1) a written affirmation of his good faith belief that he has met the relevant standard of conduct described in section 8.51 or that the proceeding involves conduct for which liability has been eliminated under a provision of the articles of incorporation as authorized by section 2.02(b)(4); and

(2) his written undertaking to repay any funds advanced if he is not entitled to mandatory indemnification under section 8.52 and it is ultimately determined under section 8.54 or section 8.55 that he has not met the relevant standard of conduct described in section 8.51.

(b) The undertaking required by subsection (a)(2) must be an unlimited general obligation of the director but need not be secured and may be accepted without reference to the financial ability of the director to make repayment.

(c) Authorizations under this section shall be made:

(1) by the board of directors:

(i) if there are two or more qualified directors, by a majority vote of all the qualified directors (a majority of whom shall for such purpose constitute a quorum) or by a majority of the members of a committee of two or more qualified directors appointed by such a vote; or

(ii) if there are fewer than two qualified directors, by the vote necessary for action by the board in accordance with section 8.24(c), in which authorization directors who are not qualified directors may participate; or

(2) by the shareholders, but shares owned by or voted under the control of a director who at the time is not a qualified director may not be voted on the authorization.

§ 8.54. Court-Ordered Indemnification and Advance for Expenses

(a) A director who is a party to a proceeding because he is a director may apply for indemnification or an advance for expenses to the court conducting the proceeding or to another court of competent jurisdiction. After receipt of an application and after giving any notice it considers necessary, the court shall:

(1) order indemnification if the court determines that the director is entitled to mandatory indemnification under section 8.52;

(2) order indemnification or advance for expenses if the court determines that the director is entitled to indemnification or advance for expenses pursuant to a provision authorized by section 8.58(a); or

(3) order indemnification or advance for expenses if the court determines, in view of all the relevant circumstances, that it is fair and reasonable

(i) to indemnify the director, or

(ii) to advance expenses to the director, even if he has not met the relevant standard of conduct set forth in section 8.51(a), failed to comply with section 8.53 or was adjudged liable in a proceeding referred to in subsection 8.51(d)(1) or (d)(2), but if he was adjudged so liable his indemnification shall be limited to reasonable expenses incurred in connection with the proceeding....

§ 8.55. Determination and Authorization of Indemnification

(a) A corporation may not indemnify a director under section 8.51 unless authorized for a specific proceeding after a determination has been made that indemnification of the director is permissible because he has met the relevant standard of conduct set forth in section 8.51.

(b) The determination shall be made:

(1) if there are two or more qualified directors, by the board of directors by a majority vote of all the qualified directors (a majority of whom shall for such purpose constitute a quorum), or by a majority of the members of a committee of two or more qualified directors appointed by such a vote;

(2) by special legal counsel:

(i) selected in the manner prescribed in subdivision (1); or

(ii) if there are fewer than two qualified directors, selected by the board of directors (in which selection directors who do not qualify as qualified directors may participate); or

(3) by the shareholders, but shares owned by or voted under the control of a director who at the time is not a qualified director may not be voted on the determination.

(c) Authorization of indemnification shall be made in the same manner as the determination that indemnification is permissible, except that if there are fewer than two qualified directors or if the determination is made by special legal counsel, authorization of indemnification shall be made by those entitled under subsection (b)(2)(ii) to select special legal counsel.

§ 8.56. Indemnification of Officers

(a) A corporation may indemnify and advance expenses under this subchapter to an officer of the corporation who is a party to a proceeding because he is an officer of the corporation

(1) to the same extent as a director; and

(2) if he is an officer but not a director, to such further extent as may be provided by the articles of incorporation, the bylaws, a resolution of the board of directors, or contract except for

(A) liability in connection with a proceeding by or in the right of the corporation other than for reasonable expenses incurred in connection with the proceeding or

(B) liability arising out of conduct that constitutes

(i) receipt by him of a financial benefit to which he is not entitled,

(ii) an intentional infliction of harm on the corporation or the shareholders, or

(iii) an intentional violation of criminal law.

(b) The provisions of subsection (a)(2) shall apply to an officer who is also a director if the basis on which he is made a party to the proceeding is an act or omission solely as an officer.

(c) An officer of a corporation who is not a director is entitled to mandatory indemnification under section 8.52, and may apply to a court under section 8.54 for indemnification or an advance for expenses, in each case to the same extent to which a director may be entitled to indemnification or advance for expenses under those provisions.

§ 8.57. Insurance

A corporation may purchase and maintain insurance on behalf of an individual who is a director or officer of the corporation, or who, while a director or officer of the corporation, serves at the corporation's request as a director, officer, partner, trustee, employee, or agent of another domestic or foreign corporation, partnership, joint venture, trust, employee benefit plan, or other entity, against liability asserted against or incurred by him in that capacity or arising from his status as a director or officer, whether or not the corporation would have power to indemnify or advance expenses to him against the same liability under this subchapter.

§ 8.58. Variation by Corporate Action; Application of Subchapter

(a) A corporation may, by a provision in its articles of incorporation or bylaws or in a resolution adopted or a contract approved by its board of directors or shareholders, obligate itself in advance of the act or omission giving rise to a proceeding to provide indemnification in accordance with section 8.51 or advance funds to pay for or reimburse expenses in accordance with section 8.53. Any such obligatory provision shall be deemed to satisfy the requirements for authorization referred to in section 8.53(c) and in section 8.55(c). Any such provision that obligates the corporation to provide indemnification to the fullest extent permitted by law shall be deemed to obligate the corporation to advance funds to pay for or reimburse expenses in accordance with section 8.53 to the fullest extent permitted by law, unless the provision specifically provides otherwise. . . .

§ 8.59. Exclusivity of Subchapter

A corporation may provide indemnification or advance expenses to a director or an officer only as permitted by this subchapter.

Subchapter F. Directors' Conflicting Interest Transactions Introductory Comment

§ 8.60. Subchapter Definitions

In this subchapter:

(1) Director's conflicting interest transaction" means a transaction effected or proposed to be effected by the corporation (or by an entity controlled by the corporation)

(i) to which, at the relevant time, the director is a party; or

(ii) respecting which, at the relevant time, the director had knowledge and a material financial interest known to the director; or

(iii) respecting which, at the relevant time, the director knew that a related person was a party or had a material financial interest.

(2) "Control" (including the term "controlled by" means (i) having the power, directly or indirectly, to elect or remove a majority of the members of the board of directors or other governing body of an entity, whether through the ownership of voting shares or interest, by contract, or otherwise, or (ii) being subject to a majority of the risk of loss from the entity's activities or entitled to receive a majority of the entity's residual returns.

(3) "Relevant time" means (i) the time at which the directors' action regarding the transaction is taken in compliance with 8.62, or (ii) if the transaction is not brought before the board of directors of the corporation (or its committee) for action under 8.62, at the time the corporation (or entity controlled by the corporation) becomes legally obligated to consummate the transaction.

(4) "Material financial interest" means a financial interest in a transaction that would reasonably be expected to impair the objectivity of the director's judgment when participating in action on the authorization of the transaction.

(5) "Related person" means

(i) the director's spouse;

(ii) a child, stepchild, grandchild, parent, step parent, grandparent, sibling, step sibling, half sibling, aunt, uncle, niece or nephew (or spouse of any thereof) of the director or the director's spouse;

(iii) an individual living in the same home as the director;

(iv) an entity (other than the corporation or an entity controlled by the corporation) controlled by the director or any person specified in this subdivision (5);

(v) a domestic or foreign (A) business or non-profit corporation (other than the corporation or an entity controlled by the corporation) of which the director is a director, (B) unincorporated entity of which the director is a general partner or a member of the governing body, or (C) individual, trust or estate for whom or of which the director is a trustee, guardian, personal representative or like fiduciary; or

(vi) a person that is, or an entity that is controlled by, an employer of the director.

(6) "Fair to the corporation" means, for purposes of section 8.61(B)(3) that the transaction as a whole was beneficial to the corporation, taking into appropriate account whether it was (i) fair in terms of the director's dealings with the corporation, and (ii) comparable to what might have been obtainable in an arm's length transaction, given the consideration paid or received by the corporation.

(7) "Required disclosure" means disclosure of (i) the existence and nature of the director's conflicting interest, and (ii) all facts known to the director respecting the subject matter of the transaction that a director

free of such conflicting interest would reasonably believe to be material in deciding whether to proceed with the transaction.

§ 8.61. Judicial Action

(a) A transaction effected or proposed to be effected by a corporation (or by an entity controlled by the corporation) may not be the subject of equitable relief, or give rise to an award of damages or other sanctions against a director of the corporation, in a proceeding by a shareholder or by or in the right of the corporation, on the ground that a director has an interest respecting the transaction, if it is not a director's conflicting interest transaction.

(b) A director's conflicting interest transaction may not be the subject of equitable relief, or give rise to an award of damages or other sanctions against a director, in a proceeding by a shareholder or by or in the right of the corporation, on the ground that the director has an interest respecting the transaction, if:

(1) directors' action respecting the transaction was at any time taken in compliance with section 8.62 at any time; or

(2) shareholders' action respecting the transaction was at any time taken in compliance with section 8.63 at any time; or

(3) the transaction, judged according to the circumstances at the relevant time, is established to have been fair to the corporation.

§ 8.62. Directors' Action

(a) Directors' action respecting a transaction is effective for purposes of section 8.61(b)(1) if the transaction received the affirmative vote of a majority (but no fewer than two) of those qualified directors on the board of directors or on a duly empowered committee of the board who voted on the transaction after either required disclosure to them (to the extent the information was not known by them) or compliance with subsection (b); provided that action by a committee is so effective only if:

(1) the qualified directors have deliberated and voted outside the presence of and without the participation by any other director

(2) where the action was taken by committee, all members of the committee were qualified directors and either (i) the committee was composed of all the qualified directors on the board of directors or (ii) the members of the committee were appointed by the affirmative vote of a majority of the qualified directors on the board.

(b) Notwithstanding subsection (a),when a transaction is a director's conflicting interest transaction only because a related person described in clause (v) or (vi) of section 8.60(5) is a party to or has a material financial interest in the transaction, the conflicted director is not obligated to make required disclosure to the extent that the director reasonably believes that doing so would violate a duty imposed under law, a legally enforceable obligation of confidentiality, or a professional ethics rule, provided that the conflicted director discloses to the qualified directors voting on the transaction:

(1) all information required to be disclosed that is not so volative,

(2) the existence and nature of the director's conflicting interest, and

(3) the nature of the conflicted director's duty not to disclose the confidential information.

(c) A majority (but no fewer than two) of all the qualified directors on the board of directors, or on the committee, constitutes a quorum for purposes of action that complies with this section.

(d) Where directors' action under this section does not satisfy a quorum or voting requirement applicable to the authorization of the transaction by reason of the articles of incorporation, the bylaws or a provision of law, independent action to satisfy those authorization requirements must be taken by the board of directors or a committee in which action directors who are not qualified directors may participate.

§ 8.63. Shareholders' Action

(a) Shareholders' action respecting a transaction is effective for purposes of section 8.61(b)(2) if a majority of the votes entitled to be cast by the holders of all qualified shares were cast in favor of the transaction after (1) notice to shareholders describing the director's conflicting interest transaction, (2) provision of the information referred to in subsection (d), and (3) required disclosure to the shareholders who voted on the transaction (to the extent the information was not known by them).

(b) For purposes of this section, "qualified shares" means any shares entitled to vote with respect to the director's conflicting interest transaction except shares that, to the knowledge, before the vote, of the secretary (or other officer or agent of the corporation authorized to tabulate votes), are beneficially owned (or the voting of which is controlled) by a director who has a conflicting interest respecting the transaction or by a related person of the director, or both.

(c) A majority of the votes entitled to be cast by the holders of all qualified shares constitutes a quorum for purposes of action that complies with this section. Subject to the provisions of subsections (d) and (e), shareholders' action that otherwise complies with this section is not affected by the presence of holders, or the voting, of shares that are not qualified shares.

(d) For purposes of compliance with subsection (a), a director who has a conflicting interest respecting the transaction shall, before the shareholders' vote, inform the secretary (or other office or agent of the corporation authorized to tabulate votes) of the number, and the identity of persons holding or controlling the vote, of all shares that the director knows are beneficially owned (or the voting of which is controlled) by the director or by a related person of the director, or both.

(e) If a shareholders' vote does not comply with subsection (a) solely because of a failure of a director to comply with subsection (d), and if the director establishes that his failure did not determine and was not intended by him to influence the outcome of the vote, the court may, with or without further proceedings respecting section 8.61(b)(3), take such action respecting the transaction and the director, and give such effect, if any, to the shareholders' vote, as it considers appropriate in the circumstances.

Chapter 10. Amendment of Articles of Incorporation and Bylaws

Subchapter A. Amendment of Articles of Incorporation

§ 10.01. Authority to Amend

(a) A corporation may amend its articles of incorporation at any time to add or change a provision that is required or permitted in the articles of incorporation as of the effective date of the amendment or to delete a provision that is not required to be contained in the articles of incorporation.

(b) A shareholder of the corporation does not have a vested property right resulting from any provision in the articles of incorporation, including provisions relating to management, control, capital structure, dividend entitlement, or purpose or duration of the corporation.

§ 10.02. Amendment Before Issuance of Shares

If a corporation has not yet issued shares, its board of directors, or its incorporators if it has no board of directors, may adopt one or more amendments to the corporation's articles of incorporation.

§ 10.03. Amendment by Board of Directors and Shareholders

If a corporation has issued shares, an amendment to the articles of incorporation shall be adopted in the following manner:

(a) The proposed amendment must be adopted by the board of directors.

(b) Except as provided in sections 10.05, 10.07, and 10.08, after adopting the proposed amendment the board of directors must submit the amendment to the shareholders for their approval. The board of directors must also transmit to the shareholders a recommendation that the shareholders approve the amendment, unless the board of directors makes a determination that because of conflicts of interest or other special circumstances it should not make such a recommendation, in which case the board of directors must transmit to the shareholders the basis for that determination.

(c) The board of directors may condition its submission of the amendment to the shareholders on any basis.

(d) If the amendment is required to be approved by the shareholders, and the approval is to be given at a meeting, the corporation must notify each shareholder, whether or not entitled to vote, of the meeting of shareholders at which the amendment is to be submitted for approval. The notice must state that the purpose, or one of the purposes, of the meeting is to consider the amendment and must contain or be accompanied by a copy of the amendment.

(e) Unless the articles of incorporation, or the board of directors acting pursuant to subsection (c), requires a greater vote or a greater number of shares to be present, approval of the amendment requires the approval of the shareholders at a meeting at which a quorum consisting of at least a majority of the votes entitled to be cast on the amendment exists, and, if any class or series of shares is entitled to vote as a separate group on the amendment, except as provided in section 10.04(c), the approval of each such separate voting group at a meeting at which a quorum of the voting group consisting of at least a majority of the votes entitled to be cast on the amendment by that voting group exists.

§ 10.04. Voting on Amendments by Voting Groups

(a) If a corporation has more than one class of shares outstanding, the holders of the outstanding shares of a class are entitled to vote as a separate voting group (if shareholder voting is otherwise required by this Act) on a proposed amendment to the articles of incorporation if the amendment would:

(1) effect an exchange or reclassification of all or part of the shares of the class into shares of another class;

(2) effect an exchange or reclassification, or create the right of exchange, of all or part of the shares of another class into shares of the class;

(3) change the rights, preferences, or limitations of all or part of the shares of the class;

(4) change the shares of all or part of the class into a different number of shares of the same class;

(5) create a new class of shares having rights or preferences with respect to distributions or to dissolution that are prior or superior to the shares of the class;

(6) increase the rights, preferences, or number of authorized shares of any class that, after giving effect to the amendment, have rights or preferences with respect to distributions or to dissolution that are prior or superior to the shares of the class;

(7) limit or deny an existing preemptive right of all or part of the shares of the class; or

(8) cancel or otherwise affect rights to distributions that have accumulated but not yet been authorized on all or part of the shares of the class.

(b) If a proposed amendment would affect a series of a class of shares in one or more of the ways described in subsection (a), the holders of shares of that series are entitled to vote as a separate voting group on the proposed amendment.

(c) If a proposed amendment that entitles the holders of two or more classes or series of shares to vote as separate voting groups under this section would affect those two or more classes or series in the same or a substantially similar way, the holders of shares of all the classes or series so affected must vote together as a single voting group on the proposed amendment, unless otherwise provided in the articles of incorporation or required by the board of directors.

(d) A class or series of shares is entitled to the voting rights granted by this section although the articles of incorporation provide that the shares are nonvoting shares.

§ 10.05. Amendment by Board of Directors

Unless the articles of incorporation provide otherwise, a corporation's board of directors may adopt amendments to the corporation's articles of incorporation without shareholder approval:

(1) to extend the duration of the corporation if it was incorporated at a time when limited duration was required by law;

(2) to delete the names and addresses of the initial directors;

(3) to delete the name and address of the initial registered agent or registered office, if a statement of change is on file with the secretary of state;

(4) if the corporation has only one class of shares outstanding:

(a) to change each issued and unissued authorized share of the class into a greater number of whole shares of that class; or

(b) to increase the number of authorized shares of the class to the extent necessary to permit the issuance of shares as a share dividend;

(5) to change the corporate name by substituting the word "corporation," "incorporated," "company," "limited," or the abbreviation "corp.," "inc.," "co.," or "ltd.," for a similar word or abbreviation in the name, or by adding, deleting, or changing a geographical attribution for the name;

(6) to reflect a reduction in authorized shares, as a result of the operation of section 6.31(b), when the corporation has acquired its own shares

and the articles of incorporation prohibit the reissue of the acquired shares;

(7) to delete a class of shares from the articles of incorporation, as a result of the operation of section 6.31(b), when there are no remaining shares of the class because the corporation has acquired all shares of the class and the articles of incorporation prohibit the reissue of the acquired shares; or

(8) to make any change expressly permitted by section 6.02(a) or (b) to be made without shareholder approval.

§ 10.06. Articles of Amendment

After an amendment to the articles of incorporation has been adopted and approved in the manner required by this Act and by the articles of incorporation, the corporation shall deliver to the secretary of state, for filing, articles of amendment, which shall set forth:

(1) the name of the corporation;

(2) the text of each amendment adopted, or the information required by section 1.20(k)(5);

(3) if an amendment provides for an exchange, reclassification, or cancellation of issued shares, provisions for implementing the amendment if not contained in the amendment itself, (which may be made dependent upon facts objectively ascertainable outside the articles of amendment in accordance with section 1.20(k)(5);

(4) the date of each amendment's adoption; and

(5) if an amendment:

(a) was adopted by the incorporators or board of directors without shareholder approval, a statement that the amendment was duly approved by the incorporators or by the board of directors, as the case may be, and that shareholder approval was not required;

(b) required approval by the shareholders, a statement that the amendment was duly approved by the shareholders in the manner required by this Act and by the articles of incorporation; or

(c) is being filed pursuant to section 1.20(k)(5), a statement to that effect.

§ 10.09. Effect of Amendment

An amendment to the articles of incorporation does not affect a cause of action existing against or in favor of the corporation, a proceeding to which the corporation is a party, or the existing rights of persons other than shareholders of the corporation. An amendment changing a corporation's name does not abate a proceeding brought by or against the corporation in its former name.

Subchapter B. Amendment of Bylaws

§ 10.20. Amendment by Board of Directors or Shareholders

(a) A corporation's shareholders may amend or repeal the corporation's bylaws.

(b) A corporation's board of directors may amend or repeal the corporation's bylaws, unless:

(1) the articles of incorporation, section 10.21 or, if applicable, section 10.22 reserve that power exclusively to the shareholders in whole or in part; or

(2) the shareholders in amending, repealing, or adopting a bylaw expressly provide that the board of directors may not amend, repeal, or reinstate that bylaw.

§ 10.21. Bylaw Increasing Quorum or Voting Requirement for Directors

(a) A bylaw that increases a quorum or voting requirement for the board of directors may be amended or repealed:

(1) if originally adopted by the shareholders, only by the shareholders, unless the bylaw otherwise provides;

(2) if adopted by the board of directors, either by the shareholders or by the board of directors.

(b) A bylaw adopted or amended by the shareholders that increases a quorum or voting requirement for the board of directors may provide that it can be amended or repealed only by a specified vote of either the shareholders or the board of directors.

(c) Action by the board of directors under subsection (a) to amend or repeal a bylaw that changes the quorum or voting requirement for the board of directors must meet the same quorum requirement and be adopted by the same vote required to take action under the quorum and voting requirement then in effect or proposed to be adopted, whichever is greater.

§ 10.22. Bylaw Provisions Relating to the Election of Directors

(a) Unless the articles of incorporation (i) specifically prohibit the adoption of a bylaw pursuant to this section, (ii) alter the vote specified in section 7.28(a), or (iii) provide for cumulative voting, a public corporation may elect in its bylaws to be governed in the election of directors as follows:

(1) each vote entitled to be cast may be voted for or against up to that number of candidates that is equal to the number of directors to be elected, or a shareholder may indicate an abstention, but without cumulating the votes;

(2) to be elected, a nominee must have received a plurality of the votes cast by holders of shares entitled to vote in the election at a meeting at which a quorum is present, provided that a nominee who is elected but receives more votes against than for election shall serve as a director for a term that shall terminate on the date that is the earlier of (i) 90 days from the date on which the voting results are determined pursuant to section 7.29(b)(5) or (ii) the date on which an individual is selected by the board of directors to fill the office held by such director, which selection shall be deemed to constitute the filling of a vacancy by the board to which section 8.10 applies. Subject to clause (3) of this section, a nominee who is elected but receives more votes against than for election shall not serve as a director beyond the 90-day period referenced above; and

(3) the board of directors may select any qualified individual to fill the office held by a director who received more votes against than for election.

(b) A bylaw electing to be governed by this section may be repealed:

(1) if originally adopted by the shareholders, only by the shareholders, unless the bylaw otherwise provides;

(2) if adopted by the board of directors, by the board of directors or the shareholders.

Chapter 11. Mergers and Share Exchanges

§ 11.01. Definitions

As used in this chapter:

(a) "Merger" means a business combination pursuant to section 11.02.

(b) "Party to a merger" or "party to a share exchange" means any domestic or foreign corporation or eligible entity that will:

(1) merge under a plan of merger;

(2) acquire shares or eligible interests of another corporation or an eligible entity in a share exchange; or

(3) have all of its shares or eligible interests or all of one or more classes or series of its shares or eligible interests acquired in a share exchange.

(c) "Share exchange" means a business combination pursuant to section 11.03.

(d) "Survivor" in a merger means the corporation or eligible entity into which one or more other corporations or eligible entities are merged. A survivor of a merger may preexist the merger or be created by the merger.

§ 11.02. Merger

(a) One or more domestic business corporations may merge with one or more domestic or foreign business corporations or eligible entities pursuant to a plan of merger, or two or more foreign business corporations or domestic or foreign eligible entities may merge into a new domestic business corporation to be created in the merger in the manner provided in this chapter.

(b) A foreign business corporation, or a foreign eligible entity, may be a party to a merger with a domestic business corporation, or may be created by the terms of the plan of merger, only if the merger is permitted by the foreign business corporation or eligible entity.

(b.1) If the organic law of a domestic eligible entity does not provide procedures for the approval of a merger, a plan of merger may be adopted and approved, the merger effectuated, and appraisal rights exercised in accordance with the procedures in this chapter and chapter 13. For the purposes of applying this chapter and chapter 13:

(1) the eligible entity, its members or interest holders, eligible interests and organic documents taken together shall be deemed to be a domestic business corporation, shareholders, shares and articles of incorporation, respectively and vice versa as the context may require; and

(2) if the business and affairs of the eligible entity are managed by a group of persons that is not identical to the members or interest holders, that group shall be deemed to be the board of directors.

(c) The plan of merger must include:

(1) the name of each domestic or foreign business corporation or eligible entity that will merge and the name of the domestic or foreign business corporation or eligible entity that will be the survivor of the merger;

(2) the terms and conditions of the merger;

(3) the manner and basis of converting the shares of each merging domestic or foreign business corporation and eligible interests of each merging domestic or foreign eligible entity into shares or other securities, eligible interests, obligations, rights to acquire shares, other securities or eligible interests, cash, other property, or any combination of the foregoing;

(4) the articles of incorporation of any domestic or foreign business or nonprofit corporation, or the organic documents of any domestic or foreign unincorporated entity, to be created by the merger, or if a new domestic or foreign business or nonprofit corporation or unincorporated entity is not to be created by the merger, any amendments to the survivor's articles of incorporation or organic documents; and

(5) any other provisions required by the laws under which any party to the merger is organized or by which it is governed, or by the articles of incorporation or organic document of any such party.

(d) Terms of a plan of merger may be made dependent on facts objectively ascertainable outside the plan in accordance with section 1.20(k).

(e) The plan of merger may also include a provision that the plan may be amended prior to filing articles of merger, but if the shareholders of a domestic corporation that is a party to the merger are required or permitted to vote on the plan, the plan must provide that subsequent to approval of the plan by such shareholders the plan may not be amended to change:

(1) the amount or kind of shares or other securities, eligible interests, obligations, rights to acquire shares, other securities or eligible interests, cash, or other property to be received under the plan by the shareholders of or owners of eligible interests in any party to the merger;

(2) the articles of incorporation of any corporation, or the organic documents of any unincorporated entity, that will survive or be created as a result of the merger, except for changes permitted by section 10.05 or by comparable provisions of the organic laws of any such foreign corporation or domestic or foreign unincorporated entity; or

(3) any of the other terms or conditions of the plan if the change would adversely affect such shareholders in any material respect.

(f) Property held in trust or for charitable purposes under the laws of this state by a domestic or foreign eligible entity shall not be diverted by a merger from the objects for which it was donated, granted or devised, unless and until the eligible entity obtains an order of [court] [the attorney general] specifying the disposition of the property to the extent required by and pursuant to [cite state statutory cy pres or other nondiversion statute].

§ 11.03. Share Exchange

(a) Through a share exchange:

(1) a domestic corporation may acquire all of the shares of one or more classes or series of shares of another domestic or foreign corporation, or all of the interests of one or more classes or series of interests of a domestic or foreign other entity, in exchange for shares or other securities, interests, obligations, rights to acquire shares or other securities, cash, other property, or any combination of the foregoing, pursuant to a plan of share exchange, or

(2) all of the shares of one or more classes or series of shares of a domestic corporation may be acquired by another domestic or foreign corporation or other entity, in exchange for shares or other securities, interests, obligations, rights to acquire shares or other securities, cash, other property, or any combination of the foregoing, pursuant to a plan of share exchange.

(b) A foreign corporation or eligible entity, may be a party to a share exchange only if the share exchange is permitted by the corporation or other entity is organized or by which it is governed.

(b.1) If the organic law of a domestic other entity does not provide procedures for the approval of a share exchange, a plan of share exchange may be adopted and approved, and the share exchange effectuated, in accordance with the procedures, if any, for a merger. If the organic law of a domestic other entity does not provide procedures for the approval of either a share exchange or a merger, a plan of share exchange may be adopted and approved, the share exchange effectuated, and appraisal rights exercised, in accordance with the procedures in this chapter and chapter 13. For the purposes of applying this chapter and chapter 13:

(1) the other entity, its interest holders, interests and organic documents taken together shall be deemed to be a domestic business corporation, shareholders, shares and articles of incorporation, respectively and vice versa as the context may require; and

(2) if the business and affairs of the other entity are managed by a group of persons that is not identical to the interest holders, that group shall be deemed to be the board of directors.

(c) The plan of share exchange must include:

(1) the name of each corporation or other entity whose shares or interests will be acquired and the name of the corporation or other entity that will acquire those shares or interests;

(2) the terms and conditions of the share exchange;

(3) the manner and basis of exchanging shares of a corporation or interests in an other entity whose shares or interests will be acquired under the share exchange into shares or other securities, interests, obligations, rights to acquire shares, other securities, or interests, cash, other property, or any combination of the foregoing; and

(4) any other provisions required by the laws under which any party to the share exchange is organized or by the articles of incorporation or organic document of any such party.

(d) Terms of a plan of share exchange may be made dependent on facts objectively ascertainable outside the plan in accordance with section 1.20(k).

(e) The plan of share exchange may also include a provision that the plan may be amended prior to filing articles of share exchange, but if the shareholders of a domestic corporation that is a party to the share exchange are required or permitted to vote on the plan, the plan must provide that subsequent to approval of the plan by such shareholders the plan may not be amended to change:

(1) the amount or kind of shares or other securities, interests, obligations, rights to acquire shares, other securities or interests, cash, or other property to be issued by the corporation or to be received under the plan by the shareholders of or owners of interests in any party to the share exchange; or

(2) any of the other terms or conditions of the plan if the change would adversely affect such shareholders in any material respect.

(f) Section 11.03 does not limit the power of a domestic corporation to acquire shares of another corporation or interests in another entity in a transaction other than a share exchange.

§ 11.04. Action on a Plan of Merger or Share Exchange

In the case of a domestic corporation that is a party to a merger or share exchange:

(a) The plan of merger or share exchange must be adopted by the board of directors.

(b) Except as provided in subsection (g) and in section 11.05, after adopting the plan of merger or share exchange the board of directors must submit the plan to the shareholders for their approval. The board of directors must also transmit to the shareholders a recommendation that the shareholders approve the plan, unless the board of directors makes a determination that because of conflicts of interest or other special circumstances it should not make such a recommendation, in which case the board of directors must transmit to the shareholders the basis for that determination.

(c) The board of directors may condition its submission of the plan of merger or share exchange to the shareholders on any basis.

(d) If the plan of merger or share exchange is required to be approved by the shareholders, and if the approval is to be given at a meeting, the corporation must notify each shareholder, whether or not entitled to vote, of the meeting of shareholders at which the plan is to be submitted for approval. The notice must state that the purpose, or one of the purposes, of the meeting is to consider the plan and must contain or be accompanied by a copy or summary of the plan. If the corporation is to be merged into an existing corporation or other entity, the notice shall also include or be accompanied by a copy or summary of the articles of incorporation or organizational documents of that corporation or other entity. If the corporation is to be merged into a corporation or other entity that is to be created pursuant to the merger, the notice shall include or be accompanied by a copy or a summary of the articles of incorporation or organizational documents of the new corporation or other entity.

(e) Unless the articles of incorporation, or the board of directors acting pursuant to subsection (c), requires a greater vote or a greater number of votes to be present, approval of the plan of merger or share exchange requires the approval of the shareholders at a meeting at which a quorum consisting of at least a majority of the votes entitled to be cast on the plan exists, and, if any class or series of shares is entitled to vote as a separate group on the plan of merger or share exchange, the approval of each such separate voting group at a meeting at which a quorum of the voting group consisting of at least a majority of the votes entitled to be cast on the merger or share exchange by that voting group is present.

(f) Separate voting by voting groups is required:

(1) on a plan of merger, by each class or series of shares that:

(i) are to be converted under the plan of merger into other securities, interests, obligations, rights to acquire shares, other securities or interests, cash, other property, or any combination of the foregoing; or

(ii) would be entitled to vote as a separate group on a provision in the plan that, if contained in a proposed amendment to articles of incorporation, would require action by separate voting groups under section 10.04;

(2) on a plan of share exchange, by each class or series of shares included in the exchange, with each class or series constituting a separate voting group; and

(3) on a plan of merger or share exchange, if the voting group is entitled under the articles of incorporation to vote as a voting group to approve a plan of merger or share exchange.

(g) Unless the articles of incorporation otherwise provide, approval by the corporation's shareholders of a plan of merger or share exchange is not required if:

(1) the corporation will survive the merger or is the acquiring corporation in a share exchange;

(2) except for amendments permitted by section 10.05, its articles of incorporation will not be changed;

(3) each shareholder of the corporation whose shares were outstanding immediately before the effective date of the merger or share exchange will hold the same number of shares, with identical preferences, limitations, and relative rights, immediately after the effective date of change; and

(4) the issuance in the merger or share exchange of shares or other securities convertible into or rights exercisable for shares does not require a vote under section 6.21(f).

(h) If as a result of a merger or share exchange one or more shareholders of a domestic corporation would become subject to owner liability for the debts, obligations or liabilities of any other person or entity, approval of the plan of merger or share exchange shall require the execution, by each such shareholder, of a separate written consent to become subject to such owner liability.

§ 11.05. Merger Between Parent and Subsidiary or Between Subsidiaries

(a) A domestic parent corporation that owns shares of a domestic or foreign subsidiary corporation that carry at least 90 percent of the voting power of each class and series of the outstanding shares of the subsidiary that have voting power may merge the subsidiary into itself or into another such subsidiary, or merge itself into the subsidiary, without the approval of the board of directors or shareholders of the subsidiary, unless the articles of incorporation of any of the corporations otherwise provide, and unless, in the case of a foreign subsidiary, approval by the subsidiary's board of directors or shareholders is required by the laws under which the subsidiary is organized.

(b) If under subsection (a) approval of a merger by the subsidiary's shareholders is not required, the parent corporation shall, within ten days after the effective date of the merger, notify each of the subsidiary's shareholders that the merger has become effective.

(c) Except as provided in subsections (a) and (b), a merger between a parent and a subsidiary shall be governed by the provisions of chapter 11 applicable to mergers generally.

§ 11.06. Articles of Merger or Share Exchange

(a) After a plan of merger or share exchange has been adopted and approved as required by this Act, articles of merger or share exchange shall be executed on behalf of each party to the merger or share exchange by any officer or other duly authorized representative. The articles shall set forth:

(1) the names of the parties to the merger or share exchange;

(2) if the articles of incorporation of the survivor of a merger are amended, or if a new corporation is created as a result of a merger, the amendments to the survivor's articles of incorporation or the articles of incorporation of the new corporation;

(3) if the plan of merger or share exchange required approval by the shareholders of a domestic corporation that was a party to the merger or share exchange, a statement that the plan was duly approved by the shareholders and, if voting by any separate voting group was required, by each such separate voting group, in the manner required by this Act and the articles of incorporation;

(4) if the plan of merger or share exchange did not require approval by the shareholders of a domestic corporation that was a party to the merger or share exchange, a statement to that effect; and

(5) as to each foreign corporation or eligible entity that was a party to the merger or share exchange, a statement that the participation of the foreign corporation or eligible entity was duly authorized as required by the organic law of the corporation or eligible entity.

(b) Articles of merger or share exchange shall be delivered to the secretary of state for filing by the survivor of the merger or the acquiring corporation in a share exchange, and shall take effect at the effective time provided in section 1.23. Articles of merger or share exchange filed under this section may be combined with any filing required under the organic law of any domestic eligible entity involved in the transaction if the combined filing satisfies the requirements of both this section and the other organic law.

§ 11.07. Effect of Merger or Share Exchange

(a) When a merger becomes effective:

(1) the corporation or eligible entity that is designated in the plan of merger as the survivor continues or comes into existence, as the case may be;

(2) the separate existence of every corporation or eligible entity that is merged into the survivor ceases;

(3) all property owned by, and every contract right possessed by, each corporation or eligible entity that merges into the survivor is vested in the survivor without reversion or impairment;

(4) all liabilities of each corporation or eligible entity that is merged into the survivor are vested in the survivor;

(5) the name of the survivor may, but need not be, substituted in any pending proceeding for the name of any party to the merger whose separate existence ceased in the merger;

(6) the articles of incorporation or organic documents of the survivor are amended to the extent provided in the plan of merger;

(7) the articles of incorporation or organic documents of a survivor that is created by the merger become effective; and

(8) the shares of each corporation that is a party to the merger, and the interests in an eligible entity that is a party to a merger, that are to be converted under the plan of merger into shares, eligible interests, obligations, rights to acquire securities, other securities, or eligible interests, cash, other property, or any combination of the foregoing, are converted, and the former holders of such shares or eligible interests are entitled only to the rights provided to them in the plan of merger or to any rights they may have under chapter 13 or the organic law of the eligible entity.

(b) When a share exchange becomes effective, the shares of each domestic corporation that are to be exchanged for shares or other securities, interests, obligations, rights to acquire shares or other securities, cash, other property, or any combination of the foregoing, are entitled only to the rights provided to them in the plan of share exchange or to any rights they may have under chapter 13.

(c) A person who becomes subject to owner liability for some or all of the debts, obligations or liabilities of any entity as a result of a merger or share exchange shall have owner liability only to the extent provided in the organic law of the entity and only for those debts, obligations and liabilities that arise after the effective time of the articles of merger or share exchange.

(d) Upon a merger becoming effective, a foreign corporation, or a foreign eligible entity, that is the survivor of the merger is deemed to:

(1) appoint the secretary of state as its agent for service of process in a proceeding to enforce the rights of shareholders of each domestic corporation that is a party to the merger who exercise appraisal rights, and

(2) agree that it will promptly pay the amount, if any, to which such shareholders are entitled under chapter 13.

(e) The effect of a merger or share exchange on the owner liability of a person who had owner liability for some or all of the debts, obligations or liabilities of a party to the merger or share exchange shall be as follows:

(1) The merger or share exchange does not discharge any owner liability under the organic law of the entity in which the person was a shareholder or interest holder to the extent any such owner liability arose before the effective time of the articles of merger or share exchange.

(2) The person shall not have owner liability under the organic law of the entity in which the person was a shareholder or interest holder prior to the merger or share exchange for any debt, obligation or liability that arises after the effective time of the articles of merger or share exchange.

(3) The provisions of the organic law of any entity for which the person had owner liability before the merger or share exchange shall continue to apply to the collection or discharge of any owner liability preserved by paragraph (1), as if the merger or share exchange had not occurred.

(4) The person shall have whatever rights of contribution from other persons are provided by the organic law of the entity for which the person had owner liability with respect to any owner liability preserved by paragraph (1), as if the merger or share exchange had not occurred.

CHAPTER 12. DISPOSITION OF ASSETS

§ 12.01. Disposition of Assets Not Requiring Shareholder Approval

No approval of the shareholders of a corporation is required, unless the articles of incorporation otherwise provide:

(1) to sell, lease, exchange, or otherwise dispose of any or all of the corporation's assets in the usual and regular course of business;

(2) to mortgage, pledge, dedicate to the repayment of indebtedness (whether with or without recourse), or otherwise encumber any or all of the corporation's assets, whether or not in the usual and regular course of business;

(3) to transfer any or all of the corporation's assets to one or more corporations or other entities all of the shares or interests of which are owned by the corporation; or

(4) to distribute assets pro rata to the holders of one or more classes or series of the corporation's shares.

§ 12.02. Shareholder Approval of Certain Dispositions

(a) A sale, lease, exchange, or other disposition of assets, other than a disposition described in section 12.01, requires approval of the corporation's shareholders if the disposition would leave the corporation without a significant continuing business activity. If a corporation retains a business activity that represented at least 25 percent of total assets at the end of the most recently completed fiscal year, and 25 percent of either income from continuing operations before taxes or revenues from continuing operations for that fiscal year, in each case of the corporation and its subsidiaries on a consolidated basis, the corporation will conclusively be deemed to have retained a significant continuing business activity.

(b) A disposition that requires approval of the shareholders under subsection (a) shall be initiated by a resolution by the board of directors authorizing the disposition. After adoption of such a resolution, the board of directors shall submit the proposed disposition to the shareholders for their approval. The board of directors shall also transmit to the shareholders a recommendation that the shareholders approve the proposed disposition, unless the board of directors makes a determination that because of conflicts of interest or other special circumstances it should not make such a recommendation, in which case the board of directors shall transmit to the shareholders the basis for that determination.

(c) The board of directors may condition its submission of a disposition to the shareholders under subsection (b) on any basis.

(d) If a disposition is required to be approved by the shareholders under subsection (a), and if the approval is to be given at a meeting, the corporation shall notify each shareholder, whether or not entitled to vote, of the meeting of shareholders at which the disposition is to be submitted for approval. The notice shall state that the purpose, or one of the purposes, of the meeting is to consider the disposition and shall contain a description of the disposition, including the terms and conditions thereof and the consideration to be received by the corporation.

(e) Unless the articles of incorporation or the board of directors acting pursuant to subsection (c) requires a greater vote, or a greater number of votes to be present, the approval of a disposition by the shareholders shall require the approval of the shareholders at a meeting at which a quorum consisting of at least a majority of the votes entitled to be cast on the disposition exists.

(f) After a disposition has been approved by the shareholders under subsection (b), and at any time before the disposition has been consummated, it may be abandoned by the corporation without action by the shareholders, subject to any contractual rights of other parties to the disposition.

(g) A disposition of assets in the course of dissolution under chapter 14 is not governed by this section.

(h) The assets of a direct or indirect consolidated subsidiary shall be deemed the assets of the parent corporation for the purposes of this section.

Chapter 13. Appraisal Rights

§ 13.01. Definitions

In this chapter: . . .

(4) "Fair value" means the value of the corporation's shares determined:

(i) immediately before the effectuation of the corporate action to which the shareholder objects;

(ii) using customary and current valuation concepts and techniques generally employed for similar businesses in the context of the transaction requiring appraisal; and

(iii) without discounting for lack of marketability or minority status except, if appropriate, for amendments to the articles pursuant to section 13.02(a)(5).

§ 13.02. Right to Appraisal

(a) A shareholder is entitled to appraisal rights, and to obtain payment of the fair value of that shareholder's shares, in the event of any of the following corporate actions:

(1) consummation of a merger to which the corporation is a party (i) if shareholder approval is required for the merger by section 11.04 and the shareholder is entitled to vote on the merger, except that appraisal rights shall not be available to any shareholder of the corporation with respect to shares of any class or series that remain outstanding after consummation of the merger, or (ii) if the corporation is a subsidiary and the merger is governed by section 11.05;

(2) consummation of a share exchange to which the corporation is a party as the corporation whose shares will be acquired if the shareholder is entitled to vote on the exchange, except that appraisal rights shall not be available to any shareholder of the corporation with respect to any class or series of shares of the corporation that is not exchanged;

(3) consummation of a disposition of assets pursuant to section 12.02 if the shareholder is entitled to vote on the disposition;

(4) an amendment of the articles of incorporation with respect to a class or series of shares that reduces the number of shares of a class or series owned by the shareholder to a fraction of a share if the corporation has the obligation or right to repurchase the fractional share so created;

(5) any other amendment to the articles of incorporation, merger, share exchange or disposition of assets to the extent provided by the articles of incorporation, bylaws or a resolution of the board of directors;

(6) consummation of a domestication if the shareholder does not receive shares in the foreign corporation resulting from the domestication that have terms as favorable to the shareholder in all material

respects, and represent at least the same percentage interest of the total voting rights of the outstanding shares of the corporation, as the shares held by the shareholder before the domestication;

(7) consummation of a conversion of the corporation to nonprofit status pursuant to subchapter 9C; or

(8) consummation of a conversion of the corporation to an unincorporated entity pursuant to subchapter 9E.

(b) Notwithstanding subsection (a), the availability of appraisal rights under subsections (a)(1), (2), (3), (4), (6) and (8) shall be limited in accordance with the following provisions:

(1) Appraisal rights shall not be available for the holders of shares of any class or series of shares which is:

(i) listed on the New York Stock Exchange or the American Stock Exchange or designated as a national market system security on an interdealer quotation system by the National Association of Securities Dealers, Inc.; or

(ii) not so listed or designated, but has at least 2,000 shareholders and the outstanding shares of such class or series has a market value of at least $20 million (exclusive of the value of such shares held by its subsidiaries, senior executives, directors and beneficial shareholders owning more than 10 percent of such shares).

(2) The applicability of subsection (b)(1) shall be determined as of:

(i) the record date fixed to determine the shareholders entitled to receive notice of, and to vote at, the meeting of shareholders to act upon the corporate action requiring appraisal rights; or

(ii) the day before the effective date of such corporate action if there is no meeting of shareholders.

(3) Subsection (b)(1) shall not be applicable and appraisal rights shall be available pursuant to subsection (a) for the holders of any class or series of shares who are required by the terms of the corporate action requiring appraisal rights to accept for such shares anything other than cash or shares of any class or any series of shares of any corporation, or any other proprietary interest of any other entity, that satisfies the standards set forth in subsection (b)(1) at the time the corporate action becomes effective.

(4) Subsection (b)(1) shall not be applicable and appraisal rights shall be available pursuant to subsection (a) for the holders of any class or series of shares where:

(i) any of the shares or assets of the corporation are being acquired or converted, whether by merger, share exchange or otherwise, pursuant to the corporate action by a person, or by an affiliate of a person, who:

(A) is, or at any time in the one-year period immediately preceding approval by the board of directors of the corporate action requiring appraisal rights was, the beneficial owner of 20 percent or more of the voting power of the corporation, excluding any shares acquired pursuant to an offer for all shares having voting power if such offer was made within one year prior to the corporate action requiring appraisal rights for consideration of the same kind and of a value equal to or less than that paid in connection with the corporate action; or

(B) directly or indirectly has, or at any time in the one-year period immediately preceding approval by the board of directors of the corporation of the corporate action requiring appraisal rights had, the power, contractually or otherwise, to cause the appointment or election of 25 percent or more of the directors to the board of directors of the corporation; or

(ii) any of the shares or assets of the corporation are being acquired or converted, whether by merger, share exchange or otherwise, pursuant to such corporate action by a person, or by an affiliate of a person, who is, or at any time in the one-year period immediately preceding approval by the board of directors of the corporate action requiring appraisal rights was, a senior executive or director of the corporation or a senior executive of any affiliate thereof, and that senior executive or director will receive, as a result of the corporate action, a financial benefit not generally available to other shareholders as such, other than:

(A) employment, consulting, retirement or similar benefits established separately and not as part of or in contemplation of the corporate action; or

(B) employment, consulting, retirement or similar benefits established in contemplation of, or as part of, the corporate action that are not more favorable than those existing before the corporate action or, if more favorable, that have been approved on behalf of the corporation in the same manner as is provided in section 8.62; or

(C) in the case of a director of the corporation who will, in the corporate action, become a director of the acquiring entity in the corporate action or one of its affiliates, rights and benefits as a director that are provided on the same basis as those afforded by the acquiring entity generally to other directors of such entity or such affiliate.

(5) For the purposes of paragraph (4) only, the term "beneficial owner" means any person who, directly or indirectly, through any contract, arrangement, or understanding, other than a revocable proxy, has or shares the power to vote, or to direct the voting of, shares, provided that a member of a national securities exchange shall not be deemed to be a beneficial owner of securities held directly or indirectly by it on behalf of another person solely because such member is the record holder of such securities if the member is precluded by the rules of such exchange from voting without instruction on contested matters or matters that may affect substantially the rights or privileges of the holders of the securities to be voted. When two or more persons agree to act together for the purpose of voting their shares of the corporation, each member

of the group formed thereby shall be deemed to have acquired beneficial ownership, as of the date of such agreement, of all voting shares of the corporation beneficially owned by any member of the group.

(c) Notwithstanding any other provision of section 13.02, the articles of incorporation as originally filed or any amendment thereto may limit or eliminate appraisal rights for any class or series of preferred shares, but any such limitation or elimination contained in an amendment to the articles of incorporation that limits or eliminates appraisal rights for any of such shares that are outstanding immediately prior to the effective date of such amendment or that the corporation is or may be required to issue or sell thereafter pursuant to any conversion, exchange or other right existing immediately before the effective date of such amendment shall not apply to any corporate action that becomes effective within one year of that date if such action would otherwise afford appraisal rights.

(d) A shareholder may not challenge a completed corporate action described in subsection (a), other than those subscribed in subsection (b)(3) and (4), unless such corporate action:

(1) was not effectuated in accordance with the applicable provisions of chapters 9, 10, 11 or 12 or the corporation's articles of incorporation, bylaws or board of directors' resolution authorizing the corporate action; or

(2) was procured as a result of fraud or material misrepresentation.

§ 13.03. Assertion of Rights by Nominees and Beneficial Owners

(a) A record shareholder may assert appraisal rights as to fewer than all the shares registered in the record shareholder's name but owned by a beneficial shareholder only if the record shareholder objects with respect to all shares of the class or series owned by the beneficial shareholder and notifies the corporation in writing of the name and address of each beneficial shareholder on whose behalf appraisal rights are being asserted. The rights of a record shareholder who asserts appraisal rights for only part of the shares held of record in the record shareholder's name under this subsection shall be determined as if the shares as to which the record shareholder objects and the record shareholder's other shares were registered in the names of different record shareholders.

(b) A beneficial shareholder may assert appraisal rights as to shares of any class or series held on behalf of the shareholder only if such shareholder:

(1) submits to the corporation the record shareholder's written consent to the assertion of such rights no later than the date referred to in section 13.22(b)(2)(ii); and

(2) does so with respect to all shares of the class or series that are beneficially owned by the beneficial shareholder.

Subchapter B. Procedure for Exercise of Appraisal Rights

§ 13.20. Notice of Appraisal Rights

(a) If proposed corporate action described in section 13.02(a) is to be submitted to a vote at a shareholders' meeting, the meeting notice must state that the corporation has concluded that shareholders are, are not or may be entitled to assert appraisal rights under this chapter. If the corporation concludes that appraisal rights are or may be available, a copy of this chapter must accompany the meeting notice sent to those record shareholders entitled to exercise appraisal rights.

(b) In a merger pursuant to section 11.05, the parent corporation must notify in writing all record shareholders of the subsidiary who are entitled to assert appraisal rights that the corporate action became effective. Such notice must be sent within ten days after the corporate action became effective and include the materials described in section 13.22.

§ 13.21. Notice of Intent to Demand Payment

(a) If proposed corporate action requiring appraisal rights under section 13.02 is submitted to a vote at a shareholders' meeting, a shareholder who wishes to assert appraisal rights with respect to any class or series of shares:

(1) must deliver to the corporation before the vote is taken written notice of the shareholder's intent to demand payment if the proposed action is effectuated; and

(2) must not vote, or cause or permit to be voted, any shares of such class or series in favor of the proposed action.

(b) A shareholder who does not satisfy the requirements of subsection (a) is not entitled to payment under this chapter.

§ 13.22. Appraisal Notice and Form

(a) If proposed corporate action requiring appraisal rights under section 13.02(a) becomes effective, the corporation must deliver a written appraisal notice and form required by subsection (b)(1) to all shareholders who satisfied the requirements of section 13.21. In the case of a merger under section 11.05, the parent must deliver a written appraisal notice and form to all record shareholders who may be entitled to assert appraisal rights.

(b) The appraisal notice must be sent no earlier than the date the corporate action became effective and no later than ten days after such date and must:

(1) supply a form that specifies the date of the first announcement to shareholders of the principal terms of the proposed corporate action and requires the shareholder asserting appraisal rights to certify (i) whether or not beneficial ownership of those shares for which appraisal rights are asserted was acquired before that date and (ii) that the shareholder did not vote for the transaction;

(2) state:

(i) where the form must be sent and where certificates for certificated shares must be deposited and the date by which those certificates must be deposited, which date may not be earlier than the date for receiving the required form under subsection (2)(ii);

(ii) a date by which the corporation must receive the form which date may not be fewer than 40 nor more than 60 days after the date the subsection (a) appraisal notice and form are sent, and state that the shareholder shall have waived the right to demand appraisal with respect to the shares unless the form is received by the corporation by such specified date;

(iii) the corporation's estimate of the fair value of the shares;

(iv) that, if requested in writing, the corporation will provide, to the shareholder so requesting, within ten days after the date specified in subsection (2)(ii) the number of shareholders who return the forms by the specified date and the total number of shares owned by them; and

(v) the date by which the notice to withdraw under section 13.23 must be received, which date must be within 20 days after the date specified in subsection (2)(ii); and

(3) be accompanied by a copy of this chapter.

§ 13.23. Perfection of Rights; Right to Withdraw

(a) A shareholder who receives notice pursuant to section 13.22 and who wishes to exercise appraisal rights must certify on the form sent by the corporation whether the beneficial owner of such shares acquired beneficial ownership of the shares before the date required to be set forth in the notice pursuant to section 13.22(b)(1). If a shareholder fails to make this certification, the corporation may elect to treat the shareholder's shares as after-acquired shares under section 13.25. In addition, a shareholder who wishes to exercise appraisal rights must execute and return the form and, in the case of certificated shares, deposit the shareholder's certificates in accordance with the terms of the notice by the date referred to in the notice pursuant to section 13.22(b)(2)(ii). Once a shareholder deposits that shareholder's certificates or, in the case of uncertificated shares, returns the executed forms, that shareholder loses all rights as a shareholder, unless the shareholder withdraws pursuant to subsection (b).

(b) A shareholder who has complied with subsection (a) may nevertheless decline to exercise appraisal rights and withdraw from the appraisal process by so notifying the corporation in writing by the date set forth in the appraisal notice pursuant to section 13.22(b)(2)(v). A shareholder who fails to so withdraw from the appraisal process may not thereafter withdraw without the corporation's written consent.

(c) A shareholder who does not execute and return the form and, in the case of certificated shares, deposit that shareholder's share certificates where required, each by the date set forth in the notice described in section 13.22(b), shall not be entitled to payment under this chapter.

§ 13.24. Payment

(a) Except as provided in section 13.25, within 30 days after the form required by section 13.22(b)(2)(ii) is due, the corporation shall pay in cash to those shareholders who complied with section 13.23(a) the amount the corporation estimates to be the fair value of their shares, plus interest.

(b) The payment to each shareholder pursuant to subsection (a) must be accompanied by:

(1) financial statements of the corporation that issued the shares to be appraised, consisting of a balance sheet as of the end of a fiscal year ending not more than 16 months before the date of payment, an income statement for that year, a statement of changes in shareholders' equity for that year, and the latest available interim financial statements, if any;

(2) a statement of the corporation's estimate of the fair value of the shares, which estimate must equal or exceed the corporation's estimate given pursuant to section 13.22(b)(2)(iii);

(3) a statement that shareholders described in subsection (a) have the right to demand further payment under section 13.26 and that if any such shareholder does not do so within the time period specified therein, such shareholder shall be deemed to have accepted such payment in full satisfaction of the corporation's obligations under this chapter.

§ 13.26. Procedure If Shareholder Dissatisfied with Payment or Offer

(a) A shareholder paid pursuant to section 13.24 who is dissatisfied with the amount of the payment must notify the corporation in writing of that shareholder's estimate of the fair value of the shares and demand payment of that estimate plus interest (less any payment under section 13.24). A shareholder offered payment under section 13.25 who is dissatisfied with that offer must reject the offer and demand payment of the shareholder's stated estimate of the fair value of the shares plus interest.

(b) A shareholder who fails to notify the corporation in writing of that shareholder's demand to be paid the shareholder's stated estimate of the fair value plus interest under subsection (a) within 30 days after receiving the corporation's payment or offer of payment under section 13.24 or section 13.25, respectively, waives the right to demand payment under this section and shall be entitled only to the payment made or offered pursuant to those respective sections.

Subchapter C. Judicial Appraisal of Shares

§ 13.30. Court Action

(a) If a shareholder makes demand for payment under section 13.26 which remains unsettled, the corporation shall commence a proceeding within 60 days after receiving the payment demand and petition the court to determine the fair value of the shares and accrued interest. If the corporation does not commence the proceeding within the 60-day period, it shall pay in cash to each shareholder the amount the shareholder demanded pursuant to section 13.26 plus interest.

(b) The corporation shall commence the proceeding in the appropriate court of the county where the corporation's principal office (or, if none, its registered office) in this state is located. If the corporation is a foreign corporation without a registered office in this state, it shall commence the proceeding in the county in this state where the principal office or registered office of the domestic corporation merged with the foreign corporation was located at the time of the transaction.

(c) The corporation shall make all shareholders (whether or not residents of this state) whose demands remain unsettled parties to the proceeding as in an action against their shares, and all parties must be served with a copy of the petition. Nonresidents may be served by registered or certified mail or by publication as provided by law.

(d) The jurisdiction of the court in which the proceeding is commenced under subsection (b) is plenary and exclusive. The court may appoint one or more persons as appraisers to receive evidence and recommend a decision on the question of fair value. The appraisers shall have the powers described in the order appointing them, or in any amendment to it. The shareholders demanding appraisal rights are entitled to the same discovery rights as parties in other civil proceedings. There shall be no right to a jury trial.

(e) Each shareholder made a party to the proceeding is entitled to judgment (i) for the amount, if any, by which the court finds the fair value of the shareholder's shares, plus interest, exceeds the amount paid by the corporation to the shareholder for such shares or (ii) for the fair value, plus interest, of the shareholder's shares for which the corporation elected to withhold payment under section 13.25.

§ 13.31. Court Costs and Counsel Fees

(a) The court in an appraisal proceeding commenced under section 13.30 shall determine all costs of the proceeding, including the reasonable compensation and expenses of appraisers appointed by the court. The court shall assess the costs against the corporation, except that the court may assess costs the extent the court finds such shareholders acted arbitrarily, vexatiously, or not in good faith with respect to the rights provided by this chapter.

(b) The court in an appraisal proceeding may also assess the fees and expenses of counsel and experts for the respective parties, in amounts the court finds equitable:

(1) against the corporation and in favor of any or all shareholders demanding appraisal if the court finds the corporation did not substantially comply with the requirements of sections 13.20, 13.22, 13.24 or 13.25; or

(2) against either the corporation or a shareholder demanding appraisal, in favor of any other party, if the court finds that the party against whom the fees and expenses are assessed acted arbitrarily, vexatiously, or not in good faith with respect to the rights provided by this chapter.

(c) If the court in an appraisal proceeding finds that the services of counsel for any shareholder were of substantial benefit to other shareholders similarly situated, and that the fees for those services should not be assessed against the corporation, the court may award to such counsel reasonable fees to be paid out of the amounts awarded the shareholders who were benefitted.

(d) To the extent the corporation fails to make a required payment pursuant to sections 13.24, 13.25, or 13.26, the shareholder may sue directly for the amount owed and, to the extent successful, shall be entitled to recover from the corporation all costs and expenses of the suit, including counsel fees.

Chapter 14. Dissolution

Subchapter A. Voluntary Dissolution

§ 14.02. Dissolution by Board of Directors and Shareholders

(a) A corporation's board of directors may propose dissolution for submission to the shareholders.

(b) For a proposal to dissolve to be adopted:

(1) the board of directors must recommend dissolution to the shareholders unless the board of directors determines that because of conflict of

interest or other special circumstances it should make no recommendation and communicates the basis for its determination to the shareholders; and

(2) the shareholders entitled to vote must approve the proposal to dissolve as provided in subsection (e).

(c) The board of directors may condition its submission of the proposal for dissolution on any basis.

(d) The corporation shall notify each shareholder, whether or not entitled to vote, of the proposed shareholders' meeting. The notice must also state that the purpose, or one of the purposes, of the meeting is to consider dissolving the corporation.

(e) Unless the articles of incorporation or the board of directors acting pursuant to subsection (c) require a greater vote, a greater number of shares to be present, or a vote by voting groups, adoption of the proposal to dissolve shall require the approval of the shareholders at a meeting at which a quorum consisting of at least a majority of the votes entitled to be cast exists.

§ 14.03. Articles of Dissolution

(a) At any time after dissolution is authorized, the corporation may dissolve by delivering to the secretary of state for filing articles of dissolution setting forth:

(1) the name of the corporation;

(2) the date dissolution was authorized; and

(3) if dissolution was approved by the shareholders, a statement that the proposal to dissolve was duly approved by the shareholders in the manner required by this Act and by the articles of incorporation....

§ 14.05. Effect of Dissolution

(a) A dissolved corporation continues its corporate existence but may not carry on any business except that appropriate to wind up and liquidate its business and affairs, including:

(1) collecting its assets;

(2) disposing of its properties that will not be distributed in kind to its shareholders;

(3) discharging or making provision for discharging its liabilities;

(4) distributing its remaining property among its shareholders according to their interests; and

(5) doing every other act necessary to wind up and liquidate its business and affairs.

(b) Dissolution of a corporation does not:

(1) transfer title to the corporation's property;

(2) prevent transfer of its shares or securities, although the authorization to dissolve may provide for closing the corporation's share transfer records;

(3) subject its directors or officers to standards of conduct different from those prescribed in chapter 8;

(4) change quorum or voting requirements for its board of directors or shareholders; change provisions for selection, resignation, or removal of its directors or officers or both; or change provisions for amending its bylaws;

(5) prevent commencement of a proceeding by or against the corporation in its corporate name;

(6) abate or suspend a proceeding pending by or against the corporation on the effective date of dissolution; or

(7) terminate the authority of the registered agent of the corporation.

§ 14.07. Unknown Claims Against Dissolved Corporation

(a) A dissolved corporation may also publish notice of its dissolution and request that persons with claims against the corporation present them in accordance with the notice.

(b) The notice must:

(1) be published one time in a newspaper of general circulation in the county where the dissolved corporation's principal office (or, if none in this state, its registered office) is or was last located;

(2) describe the information that must be included in a claim and provide a mailing address where the claim may be sent; and

(3) state that a claim against the corporation will be barred unless a proceeding to enforce the claim is commenced within five years after the publication of the notice.

(c) If the dissolved corporation publishes a newspaper notice in accordance with subsection (b), the claim of each of the following claimants is barred unless the claimant commences a proceeding to enforce the claim against the dissolved corporation within five years after the publication date of the newspaper notice:

(1) a claimant who did not receive written notice under section 14.06;

(2) a claimant whose claim was timely sent to the dissolved corporation but not acted on;

(3) a claimant whose claim is contingent or based on an event occurring after the effective date of dissolution.

(d) A claim may be enforced under this section:

(1) against the dissolved corporation, to the extent of its undistributed assets; or

(2) if the assets have been distributed in liquidation, against a shareholder of the dissolved corporation to the extent of his pro rata share of the claim or the corporate assets distributed to him in liquidation, whichever is less, but a shareholder's total liability for all claims under this section may not exceed the total amount of assets distributed to him.

Subchapter B. Administrative Dissolution

§ 14.20. Grounds for Administrative Dissolution

The secretary of state may commence a proceeding under section 14.21 to administratively dissolve a corporation if:

(1) the corporation does not pay within 60 days after they are due any franchise taxes or penalties imposed by this Act or other law;

(2) the corporation does not deliver its annual report to the secretary of state within 60 days after it is due;

(3) the corporation is without a registered agent or registered office in this state for 60 days or more;

(4) the corporation does not notify the secretary of state within 60 days that its registered agent or registered office has been changed, that its registered agent has resigned, or that its registered office has been discontinued; or

(5) the corporation's period of duration stated in its articles of incorporation expires.

Subchapter C. Judicial Dissolution

§ 14.30. Grounds for Judicial Dissolution

The [name or describe court or courts] may dissolve a corporation:

(1) in a proceeding by the attorney general if it is established that:

(i) the corporation obtained its articles of incorporation through fraud; or

(ii) the corporation has continued to exceed or abuse the authority conferred upon it by law;

(2) in a proceeding by a shareholder if it is established that:

(i) the directors are deadlocked in the management of the corporate affairs, the shareholders are unable to break the deadlock, and irreparable injury to the corporation is threatened or being suffered, or the business and affairs of the corporation can no longer be conducted to the advantage of the shareholders generally, because of the deadlock;

(ii) the directors or those in control of the corporation have acted, are acting, or will act in a manner that is illegal, oppressive, or fraudulent;

(iii) the shareholders are deadlocked in voting power and have failed, for a period that includes at least two consecutive annual meeting dates, to elect successors to directors whose terms have expired; or

(iv) the corporate assets are being misapplied or wasted;

(3) in a proceeding by a creditor if it is established that:

(i) the creditor's claim has been reduced to judgment, the execution on the judgment returned unsatisfied, and the corporation is insolvent; or

(ii) the corporation has admitted in writing that the creditor's claim is due and owing and the corporation is insolvent; or

(4) in a proceeding by the corporation to have its voluntary dissolution continued under court supervision.

§ 14.32. Receivership or Custodianship

(a) A court in a judicial proceeding brought to dissolve a corporation may appoint one or more receivers to wind up and liquidate, or one or more custodians to manage, the business and affairs of the corporation. The court shall hold a hearing, after notifying all parties to the proceeding and any interested persons designated by the court, before appointing a receiver or custodian. The court appointing a receiver or custodian has exclusive jurisdiction over the corporation and all of its property wherever located. . . .

§ 14.34. Election to Purchase in Lieu of Dissolution

(a) In a proceeding under section 14.30(2) to dissolve a corporation that has no shares listed on a national securities exchange or regularly traded in a market maintained by one or more members of a national or affiliated securities association, the corporation may elect or, if it fails to elect, one or more shareholders may elect to purchase all shares owned by the petitioning shareholder at the fair value of the shares. An election pursuant to this section shall be irrevocable unless the court determines that it is equitable to set aside or modify the election.

(b) An election to purchase pursuant to this section may be filed with the court at any time within 90 days after the filing of the petition under section 14.30(2) or at such later time as the court in its discretion may allow. . . .

(c) If, within 60 days of the filing of the first election, the parties reach agreement as to the fair value and terms of purchase of the petitioner's shares, the court shall enter an order directing the purchase of petitioner's shares upon the terms and conditions agreed to by the parties.

(d) If the parties are unable to reach an agreement as provided for in subsection (c), the court, upon application of any party, shall stay the section 14.30(2) proceedings and determine the fair value of the petitioner's shares as of the day before the date on which the petition under section 14.30(2) was filed or as of such other date as the court deems appropriate under the circumstances. . . .

CHAPTER 15. FOREIGN CORPORATIONS

Subchapter A. Certificate of Authority

§ 15.01. Authority to Transact Business Required

(a) A foreign corporation may not transact business in this state until it obtains a certificate of authority from the secretary of state.

(b) The following activities, among others, do not constitute transacting business within the meaning of subsection (a):

(1) maintaining, defending, or settling any proceeding;

(2) holding meetings of the board of directors or shareholders or carrying on other activities concerning internal corporate affairs;

(3) maintaining bank accounts;

(4) maintaining offices or agencies for the transfer, exchange, and registration of the corporation's own securities or maintaining trustees or depositaries with respect to those securities;

(5) selling through independent contractors;

(6) soliciting or obtaining orders, whether by mail or through employees or agents or otherwise, if the orders require acceptance outside this state before they become contracts;

(7) creating or acquiring indebtedness, mortgages, and security interests in real or personal property;

(8) securing or collecting debts or enforcing mortgages and security interests in property securing the debts;

(9) owning, without more, real or personal property;

(10) conducting an isolated transaction that is completed within 30 days and that is not one in the course of repeated transactions of a like nature;

(11) transacting business in interstate commerce.

(c) The list of activities in subsection (b) is not exhaustive.

§ 15.07. Registered Office and Registered Agent of Foreign Corporation

Each foreign corporation authorized to transact business in this state must continuously maintain in this state:

(1) a registered office that may be the same as any of its places of business; and

(2) a registered agent, who may be:

(i) an individual who resides in this state and whose business office is identical with the registered office;

(ii) a domestic corporation or not-for-profit domestic corporation whose business office is identical with the registered office; or

(iii) a foreign corporation or foreign not-for-profit corporation authorized to transact business in this state whose business office is identical with the registered office.

Chapter 16. Records and Reports

Subchapter A. Records

§ 16.01. Corporate Records

(a) A corporation shall keep as permanent records minutes of all meetings of its shareholders and board of directors, a record of all actions taken by the shareholders or board of directors without a meeting, and a record of all actions taken by a committee of the board of directors in place of the board of directors on behalf of the corporation.

(b) A corporation shall maintain appropriate accounting records.

(c) A corporation or its agent shall maintain a record of its shareholders, in a form that permits preparation of a list of the names and addresses of all shareholders, in alphabetical order by class of shares showing the number and class of shares held by each.

(d) A corporation shall maintain its records in written form or in another form capable of conversion into written form within a reasonable time.

(e) A corporation shall keep a copy of the following records at its principal office:

(1) its articles or restated articles of incorporation, all amendments to them currently in effect, and any notices to shareholders referred to in section 1.20(k)(5) regarding facts on which a filed document is dependent;

(2) its bylaws or restated bylaws and all amendments to them currently in effect;

(3) resolutions adopted by its board of directors creating one or more classes or series of shares, and fixing their relative rights, preferences, and limitations, if shares issued pursuant to those resolutions are outstanding;

(4) the minutes of all shareholders' meetings, and records of all action taken by shareholders without a meeting, for the past three years;

(5) all written communications to shareholders generally within the past three years, including the financial statements furnished for the past three years under section 16.20;

(6) a list of the names and business addresses of its current directors and officers; and

(7) its most recent annual report delivered to the secretary of state under section 16.21.

§ 16.02. Inspection of Records by Shareholders

(a) A shareholder of a corporation is entitled to inspect and copy, during regular business hours at the corporation's principal office, any of the records of the corporation described in section 16.01(e) if he gives the corporation written notice of his demand at least five business days before the date on which he wishes to inspect and copy.

(b) A shareholder of a corporation is entitled to inspect and copy, during regular business hours at a reasonable location specified by the corporation, any of the following records of the corporation if the shareholder meets the requirements of subsection (c) and gives the corporation written notice of his demand at least five business days before the date on which he wishes to inspect and copy:

(1) excerpts from minutes of any meeting of the board of directors, records of any action of a committee of the board of directors while acting in place of the board of directors on behalf of the corporation, minutes of any meeting of the shareholders, and records of action taken by the shareholders or board of directors without a meeting, to the extent not subject to inspection under section 16.02(a);

(2) accounting records of the corporation; and

(3) the record of shareholders.

(c) A shareholder may inspect and copy the records described in subsection (b) only if:

(1) his demand is made in good faith and for a proper purpose;

(2) he describes with reasonable particularity his purpose and the records he desires to inspect; and

(3) the records are directly connected with his purpose.

(d) The right of inspection granted by this section may not be abolished or limited by a corporation's articles of incorporation or bylaws.

(e) This section does not affect:

(1) the right of a shareholder to inspect records under section 7.20 or, if the shareholder is in litigation with the corporation, to the same extent as any other litigant;

(2) the power of a court, independently of this Act, to compel the production of corporate records for examination.

(f) For purposes of this section, "shareholder" includes a beneficial owner whose shares are held in a voting trust or by a nominee on his behalf.

§ 16.03. Scope of Inspection Right

(a) A shareholder's agent or attorney has the same inspection and copying rights as the shareholder represented.

(b) The right to copy records under section 16.02 includes, if reasonable, the right to receive copies by xerographic or other means, including copies through an electronic transmission if available and so requested by the shareholder.

(c) The corporation may comply at its expense with a shareholder's demand to inspect the record of shareholders under section 16.02(b)(3) by providing the shareholder with a list of shareholders that was compiled no earlier than the date of the shareholder's demand.

(d) The corporation may impose a reasonable charge, covering the costs of labor and material, for copies of any documents provided to the shareholder. The charge may not exceed the estimated cost of production, reproduction or transmission of the records.

§ 16.04. Court-Ordered Inspection

(a) If a corporation does not allow a shareholder who complies with section 16.02(a) to inspect and copy any records required by that subsection to be available for inspection, the [name or describe court] of the county where the corporation's principal office (or, if none in this state, its registered office) is located may summarily order inspection and copying of the records demanded at the corporation's expense upon application of the shareholder....

§ 16.05. Inspection of Records by Directors

(a) A director of a corporation is entitled to inspect and copy the books, records and documents of the corporation at any reasonable time to the extent reasonably related to the performance of the director's duties as a director, including duties as a member of a committee, but not for any other purpose or in any manner that would violate any duty to the corporation....

Subchapter B. Reports

§ 16.20. Financial Statements for Shareholders

(a) A corporation shall furnish its shareholders annual financial statements, which may be consolidated or combined statements of the corporation and one or more of its subsidiaries, as appropriate, that include a balance sheet as of the end of the fiscal year, an income statement for that year, and a statement of changes in shareholders' equity for the year unless that information appears elsewhere in the financial statements. If financial statements are prepared for the corporation on the basis of generally accepted accounting principles, the annual financial statements must also be prepared on that basis.

(b) If the annual financial statements are reported upon by a public accountant, his report must accompany them. If not, the statements must be accompanied by a statement of the president or the person responsible for the corporation's accounting records:

(1) stating his reasonable belief whether the statements were prepared on the basis of generally accepted accounting principles and, if not, describing the basis of preparation; and

(2) describing any respects in which the statements were not prepared on a basis of accounting consistent with the statements prepared for the preceding year.

(c) A corporation shall mail the annual financial statements to each shareholder within 120 days after the close of each fiscal year. Thereafter, on written request from a shareholder who was not mailed the statements, the corporation shall mail him the latest financial statements.

INDIANA CODE: STANDARD OF CONDUCT FOR DIRECTORS

Chapter 35. Standards of Conduct for Directors

IC 23-1-35-1. Good Faith Discharge of Duties; Liability; Reaffirmation of Corporate Governance Rules; Factors Considered

(a) A director shall, based on facts then known to the director, discharge the duties as a director, including the director's duties as a member of a committee:

(1) in good faith;

(2) with the care an ordinarily prudent person in a like position would exercise under similar circumstances; and

(3) in a manner the director reasonably believes to be in the best interests of the corporation.

(b) In discharging the director's duties a director is entitled to rely on information, opinions, reports, or statements, including financial statements and other financial data, if prepared or presented by:

(1) one (1) or more officers or employees of the corporation whom the director reasonably believes to be reliable and competent in the matters presented;

(2) legal counsel, public accountants, or other persons as to matters the director reasonably believes are within the person's professional or expert competence; or

(3) a committee of the board of directors of which the director is not a member if the director reasonably believes the committee merits confidence.

(c) A director is not acting in good faith if the director has knowledge concerning the matter in question that makes reliance otherwise permitted by subsection (b) unwarranted.

(d) A director may, in considering the best interests of a corporation, consider the effects of any action on shareholders, employees, suppliers, and customers of the corporation, and communities in which offices or other facilities of the corporation are located, and any other factors the director considers pertinent.

(e) A director is not liable for any action taken as a director, or any failure to take any action, regardless of the nature of the alleged breach of duty, including alleged breaches of the duty of care, the duty of loyalty, and the duty of good faith, unless:

(1) the director has breached or failed to perform the duties of the director's office in compliance with this section; and

(2) the breach or failure to perform constitutes willful misconduct or recklessness.

(f) In enacting this article, the general assembly established corporate governance rules for Indiana corporations, including in this chapter, the standards of conduct applicable to directors of Indiana corporations, and the corporate constituent groups and interests that a director may take into account in exercising the director's business judgment. The general assembly intends to reaffirm certain of these corporate governance rules to ensure that the directors of Indiana corporations, in exercising their business judgment, are not required to approve a proposed corporate action if the directors in good faith determine, after considering and weighing as they deem appropriate the effects of such action on the corporation's constituents, that such action is not in the best interests of the corporation. In making such determination, directors are not required to consider the effects of a proposed corporate action on any particular corporate constituent group or interest as a dominant or controlling factor. Without limiting the generality of the foregoing, directors are not required to render inapplicable any of the provisions of IC 23-1-43, to redeem any rights under or to render inapplicable a shareholder rights plan adopted pursuant to IC 23-1-26-5, or to take or decline to take any other action under this article, solely because of the effect such action might have on a proposed acquisition of control of the corporation or the amounts that might be paid to shareholders under such an acquisition. Certain judicial decisions in Delaware and other jurisdictions, which might otherwise be looked to for guidance in interpreting Indiana corporate law, including decisions relating to potential change of control transactions that impose a different or higher degree of scrutiny on actions taken by directors in response to a proposed acquisition of control of the corporation, are inconsistent with the proper application of the business judgment rule under this article. Therefore, the general assembly intends:

(1) to reaffirm that this section allows directors the full discretion to weigh the factors enumerated in subsection (d) as they deem appropriate; and

(2) to protect both directors and the validity of corporate action taken by them in the good faith exercise of their business judgment after reasonable investigation.

(g) In taking or declining to take any action, or in making or declining to make any recommendation to the shareholders of the corporation with respect to any matter, a board of directors may, in its discretion, consider both the short term and long term best interests of the corporation, taking into account, and weighing as the directors deem appropriate, the effects thereof on the corporation's shareholders and the other corporate constituent groups and interests listed or described in subsection (d), as well as any other factors deemed pertinent by the directors under subsection (d). If a determination is made with respect to the foregoing with the approval of a majority of the disinterested directors of the board of directors, that determination shall conclusively be presumed to be valid unless it can be demonstrated that the determination was not made in good faith after reasonable investigation.

(h) For the purposes of subsection (g), a director is disinterested if:

(1) the director does not have a conflict of interest, within the meaning of section 2 of this chapter, in connection with the action or recommendation in question;

(2) in connection with matters described in IC 23-1-32 the director is disinterested (as defined in IC 23-1-32-4(d));

(3) in connection with any matter involving or otherwise affecting:

(A) a control share acquisition (as defined in IC 23-1-42-2) or any matter related to a control share acquisition under IC 23-1-42 or other provisions of this article;

(B) a business combination (as defined in IC 23-1-43-5) or any matter related to a business combination under IC 23-1-43 (including a person becoming an interested shareholder) or other provisions of this article; or

(C) any transaction that may result in a change of control (as defined in IC 23-1-22-4) of the corporation;

the director is not an employee of the corporation; and

(4) in connection with any matter involving or otherwise affecting:

(A) a control share acquisition (as defined in IC 23-1-42-2) or any matter related to a control share acquisition under IC 23-1-42 or other provisions of this article;

(B) a business combination (as defined in IC 23-1-43-5) or any matter related to a business combination under IC 23-1-43 (including a person becoming an interested shareholder) or other provisions of this article; or

(C) any transaction that may result in a change of control (as defined in IC 23-1-22-4) of the corporation;

the director is not an affiliate or associate of, or was not nominated or designated as a director by, a person proposing any of the transactions described in clause (A), (B), or (C).

(i) A person may be disinterested under this section even though the person is a director or shareholder of the corporation.

As added by P.L.149-1986, Sec.19. Amended by P.L.227-1989, Sec. 2, P.L.133-2009, Sec. 27.

IC 23-1-35-2. Conflict of Interest Transaction

(a) A conflict of interest transaction is a transaction with the corporation in which a director of the corporation has a direct or indirect interest. A conflict of interest transaction is not voidable by the corporation solely because of the director's interest in the transaction if any one (1) of the following is true:

(1) The material facts of the transaction and the director's interest were disclosed or known to the board of directors or a committee of the board of directors and the board of directors or committee authorized, approved, or ratified the transaction.

(2) The material facts of the transaction and the director's interest were disclosed or known to the shareholders entitled to vote and they authorized, approved, or ratified the transaction.

(3) The transaction was fair to the corporation.

(b) For purposes of this section, a director of the corporation has an indirect interest in a transaction if:

(1) another entity in which the director has a material financial interest or in which the director is a general partner is a party to the transaction; or

(2) another entity of which the director is a director, officer, or trustee is a party to the transaction and the transaction is, or is required to be, considered by the board of directors of the corporation.

(c) For purposes of subsection (a)(1), a conflict of interest transaction is authorized, approved, or ratified if it receives the affirmative vote of a majority of the directors on the board of directors (or on the committee) who have no direct or indirect interest in the transaction, but a transaction may not be authorized, approved, or ratified under this section by a single director. If a majority of the directors who have no direct or indirect interest in the transaction vote to authorize, approve, or ratify the transaction, a quorum is present for the purpose of taking action under this section. The presence of, or a vote cast by, a director with a direct or indirect interest in the transaction does not affect the validity of any action taken under subsection (a)(1) if the transaction is otherwise authorized, approved, or ratified as provided in that subsection.

(d) For purposes of subsection (a)(2), shares owned by or voted under the control of a director who has a direct or indirect interest in the transaction, and shares owned by or voted under the control of an entity described in subsection (b), may be counted in a vote of shareholders to determine whether to authorize, approve, or ratify a conflict of interest transaction.

As added by P.L. 149-1986, Sec. 19. Amended by P.L. 107-1987, Sec. 12.

IC 23-1-35-3. Loan or Guarantee to Director

(a) Except as provided by subsection (c), a corporation may not lend money to or guarantee the obligation of a director of the corporation unless:

(1) the particular loan or guarantee is approved by a majority of the votes represented by the outstanding voting shares of all classes, voting as a single voting group, except the votes of shares owned by or voted under the control of the benefited director; or

(2) the corporation's board of directors determines that the loan or guarantee benefits the corporation and either approves the specific loan or guarantee or a general plan authorizing loans and guarantees.

(b) The fact that a loan or guarantee is made in violation of this section does not affect the borrower's liability on the loan.

(c) This section does not apply to loans and guarantees authorized by statute regulating any special class of corporations.

As added by P.L. 149-1986, Sec. 19.

IC 23-1-35-4. Unlawful Distribution; Liability; Contribution

Sec. 4. (a) Subject to section 1(e) of this chapter, a director who votes for or assents to a distribution made in violation of this article or the articles of incorporation is personally liable to the corporation for the amount of the distribution that exceeds what could have been distributed without violating this article or the articles of incorporation.

(b) A director held liable for an unlawful distribution under subsection (a) is entitled to contribution:

(1) from every other director who voted for or assented to the distribution, subject to section 1(e) of this chapter; and

(2) from each shareholder for the amount the shareholder accepted.

As added by P.L. 149-1986, Sec. 19. Amended by P.L. 107-1987, Sec. 13.

AMERICAN LAW INSTITUTE, PRINCIPLES OF CORPORATE GOVERNANCE: ANALYSIS AND RECOMMENDATIONS (1994)

Part II. The Objective and Conduct of the Corporation

§2.01. The Objective and Conduct of the Corporation

(a) Subject to the provisions of Subsection (b) and §6.02 (Action of Directors That Has the Foreseeable Effect of Blocking Unsolicited Tender Offers), a corporation [§1.12] should have as its objective the conduct of business activities with a view to enhancing corporate profit and shareholder gain.

(b) Even if corporate profit and shareholder gain are not thereby enhanced, the corporation, in the conduct of its business:

(1) Is obliged, to the same extent as a natural person, to act within the boundaries set by law;

(2) May take into account ethical considerations that are reasonably regarded as appropriate to the responsible conduct of business; and

(3) May devote a reasonable amount of resources to public welfare, humanitarian, educational, and philanthropic purposes.

Comment:

a. Comparison with present law. Present law on the matters within the scope of §2.01 cannot be stated with precision, because the case law is evolving and not entirely harmonious, while the statutes cover only some of the relevant issues and leave open significant questions even as to the issues they do cover. However, there is direct or indirect authoritative support for all of the principles embodied in §2.01....

f. The economic objective. In very general terms, Subsection (a) may be thought of as a broad injunction to enhance economic returns, while Subsection (b) makes clear that certain kinds of conduct must or may be pursued whether or not they enhance such returns (that is, even if the conduct either yields no economic return or entails a net economic loss). In most cases, however, the kinds of conduct described in Subsection (b) could be pursued even under the principle embodied in Subsection (a). Such conduct will usually be consistent with economic self-interest, because the principle embodied in Subsection (a) — that the objective of the corporation is to conduct business activities with a view to enhancing corporate profit and shareholder gain — does not mean that the objective of the corporation must be to realize corporate profit and shareholder gain in the short run. Indeed, the contrary is true: long-run profitability and shareholder gain are at the core of the economic objective. Activity that entails a short-run cost to achieve an appropriately greater long-run profit is therefore not a departure from the economic objective. An orientation toward lawful, ethical, and public-spirited activity will normally fall within this description....

g. Compliance with legal rules. Under §2.01(b)(1), the corporation is obliged, to the same extent as a natural person, to act within the boundaries set by law. It is sometimes maintained that whether a corporation should adhere to a given legal rule may properly depend on a kind of cost-benefit analysis, in which probable corporate gains are weighed against either probable social costs, measured by the dollar liability imposed for engaging in such conduct, or probable corporate losses, measured by potential dollar liability discounted for likelihood of detection. Section 2.01 does not adopt this position. With few exceptions, dollar liability is not a "price" that can properly be paid for the privilege of engaging in legally wrongful conduct. Cost-benefit analysis may have a place in the state's determination whether a given type of conduct should be deemed legally wrongful. Once that determination has been made, however, the resulting legal rule normally represents a community decision that the conduct is wrongful as such, so that cost-benefit analysis whether to obey the rule is out of place....

i. Public welfare, humanitarian, educational, and philanthropic purposes. Section 2.01(b)(3) permits the corporation to devote a reasonable amount of resources to public welfare, humanitarian, educational, and philanthropic purposes, even if corporate profit and shareholder gain are not thereby enhanced.... Section 2.01(b)(3)... allows corporate resources to be devoted to public welfare, humanitarian, educational, and philanthropic purposes even without a showing of expected profits or ethical norms. It is now widely accepted that the corporation should at least consider the social impact of its activities, so as to be aware of the social costs those activities entail. By implication, the corporation should be permitted to take such costs into account, within reason. For example, the corporation may take into account, within reason, public-welfare concerns relevant to groups with whom the corporation has a legitimate concern, such as employees, customers, suppliers, and members of the communities within which the corporation operates....

Part IV. Duty of Care and the Business Judgment Rule

§4.01. Duty of Care of Directors and Officers; the Business Judgment Rule

(a) A director or officer has a duty to the corporation to perform the director's or officer's functions in good faith, in a manner that he or she reasonably believes to be in the best interests of the corporation, and with the care that an ordinarily prudent person would reasonably be expected to exercise in a like position and under similar circumstances. This Subsection (a) is subject to the provisions of Subsection (c) (the business judgment rule) where applicable.

(1) The duty in Subsection (a) includes the obligation to make, or cause to be made, an inquiry when, but only when, the circumstances would alert a reasonable director or officer to the need therefor. The extent of such inquiry shall be such as the director or officer reasonably believes to be necessary.

(2) In performing any of his or her functions (including oversight functions), a director or officer is entitled to rely on materials and persons in accordance with §§4.02 and 4.03 (reliance on directors, officers, employees, experts, other persons, and committees of the board).

(b) Except as otherwise provided by statute or by a standard of the corporation [§1.36] and subject to the board's ultimate responsibility for oversight, in performing its functions (including oversight functions), the board may delegate, formally or informally by course of conduct, any function (including the function of identifying matters requiring the attention of the board) to committees of the board or to directors, officers, employees, experts, or other persons; a director may rely on such committees and persons in fulfilling the duty under this Section with respect to any delegated function if the reliance is in accordance with §§4.02 and 4.03.

(c) A director or officer who makes a business judgment in good faith fulfills the duty under this Section if the director or officer:

(1) is not interested [§1.23] in the subject of the business judgment;

(2) is informed with respect to the subject of the business judgment to the extent the director or officer reasonably believes to be appropriate under the circumstances; and

(3) rationally believes that the business judgment is in the best interests of the corporation.

(d) A person challenging the conduct of a director or officer under this Section has the burden of proving a breach of the duty of care, including the inapplicability of the provisions as to the fulfillment of duty under Subsection (b) or (c), and, in a damage action, the burden of proving that the breach was the legal cause of damage suffered by the corporation.

Comment to §4.01(c):

Section 4.01(c) affords protection only to a "business judgment." This means that to be afforded protection a decision must have been consciously made and judgment must, in fact, have been exercised. For efficiency reasons, corporate decisionmakers should be permitted to act decisively and with relative freedom from a judge's or jury's subsequent second-guessing. . . .

There is, however, no reason to provide special protection where no business decisionmaking is to be found. If, for example, directors have failed to oversee the conduct of the corporation's business (§3.02(a)(2)) by not even considering the need for an effective audit process, and this permits an executive to abscond with corporate funds, business judgment rule protection would be manifestly undesirable. The same would be true where a director received but did not read basic financial information, over a period of time, and thus allowed his corporation to be looted. . . .

e. Prerequisite of an informed decision. The great weight of case law and commentator authority supports the proposition that an informed decision (made, for example, on the basis of explanatory information presented to the board) is a prerequisite to the legal insulation afforded by the business judgment rule. . . .

The informed decision prerequisite in §4.01(c)(2) focuses on the preparedness of a director or officer in making a business decision as opposed to the quality of the decision itself. Fundamental to an understanding of the standard set forth in §4.01(c) is the recognition that the extent of the information required is that which the director or officer "reasonably believes to be appropriate under the circumstance." Here, as elsewhere in Part IV, the term "reasonably believes" has both an objective and a subjective content. See Comment b to §4.01(a)(1)-(a)(2). In evaluating what is a reasonable belief in a particular situation, the "informed" requirement in §4.01(c)(2) should be interpreted realistically and with an appreciation of the factual context in which the business judgment was made....

f. The "rationally believes" requirement. If the requirements of "good faith" and §4.01(c)(1)-(c)(2) are met, §4.01(c)(3) will protect a director or officer from liability for a business judgment if the director or officer "rationally believes that the business judgment is in the best interests of the corporation." The term "rationally believes" has both an objective and a subjective content. A director or officer must actually believe that the business judgment is in the best interests of the corporation and that belief must be rational....

There have been varying approaches taken in the cases and by commentators to the proper standard for judicial review of business judgments. Some courts have stated that a director's or officer's business judgment must be "reasonable" to be upheld.... On the other hand, a few cases have simply said that a director's or officer's judgment would be upheld if made with disinterest, in an informed manner, and in good faith. Both a "reasonableness" test and the "good faith alone" approach have been rejected in §4.01(c)....

§4.02. Reliance on Directors, Officers, Employees, Experts, and Other Persons

In performing his or her duties and functions, a director or officer who acts in good faith, and reasonably believes that reliance is warranted, is entitled to rely on information, opinions, reports, statements (including financial statements and other financial data), decisions, judgments, and performance (including decisions, judgments, and performance within the scope of §4.01(b)) prepared, presented, made, or performed by:

(a) One or more directors, officers, or employees of the corporation, or of a business organization [§1.04] under joint control or common control [§1.08] with the corporation, who the director or officer reasonably believes merit confidence; or

(b) Legal counsel, public accountants, engineers, or other persons who the director or officer reasonably believes merit confidence.

§4.03. Reliance on a Committee of the Board

In performing his or her duties and functions, a director who acts in good faith, and reasonably believes that reliance is warranted, is entitled to rely on:

(a) The decisions, judgments, and performance (including decisions, judgments, and performance within the scope of §4.01(b)), of a duly authorized committee of the board upon which the director does not serve, with respect to matters delegated to that committee, provided that the director reasonably believes the committee merits confidence.

(b) Information, opinions, reports, and statements (including financial statements and other financial data), prepared or presented by a duly authorized committee of the board upon which the director does not serve, provided that the director reasonably believes the committee merits confidence.

Part V. Duty of Fair Dealing

§5.02. [Senior Officer and Director] Transactions with the Corporation

(a) *General Rule.* A director [§1.13] or senior executive [§1.33] who enters into a transaction with the corporation (other than a transaction involving the payment of compensation) fulfills the duty of fair dealing with respect to the transaction if:

(1) Disclosure concerning the conflict of interest [§1.14(a)] and the transaction [§1.14(b)] is made to the corporate decisionmaker [§1.11] who authorizes in advance or ratifies the transaction; and

(2) Either:

(A) The transaction is fair to the corporation when entered into;

(B) The transaction is authorized in advance, following disclosure concerning the conflict of interest and the transaction, by disinterested directors [§1.15], or in the case of a senior executive who is not a director by a disinterested superior, who could reasonably have concluded that the transaction was fair to the corporation at the time of such authorization;

(C) The transaction is ratified, following such disclosure, by disinterested directors who could reasonably have concluded that the transaction was fair to the corporation at the time it was entered into, provided (i) a corporate decisionmaker who is not interested [§1.23] in the transaction acted for the corporation in the transaction and could reasonably have concluded that the transaction was fair to the corporation; (ii) the interested director or senior executive made disclosure to such decisionmaker pursuant to Subsection (a)(1) to the extent he or she then knew of the material facts; (iii) the interested director or senior executive did not act unreasonably in failing to seek advance authorization of the transaction by disinterested directors or a disinterested superior; and (iv) the failure to obtain advance authorization of the transaction by disinterested directors or a disinterested superior did not adversely affect the interests of the corporation in a significant way; or

(D) The transaction is authorized in advance or ratified, following such disclosure, by disinterested shareholders [§1.16], and does not constitute a waste of corporate assets [§1.42] at the time of the shareholder action.

(b) *Burden of Proof.* A party who challenges a transaction between a director or senior executive and the corporation has the burden of proof, except that if such party establishes that none of Subsections (a)(2)(B), (a)(2)(C), or (a)(2)(D) is satisfied, the director or senior executive has the burden of proving that the transaction was fair to the corporation.

(c) *Ratification of Disclosure or Nondisclosure.* The disclosure requirements of §5.02(a)(1) will be deemed to be satisfied if at any time (but no later than a reasonable time after suit is filed challenging the transaction) the transaction is ratified, following such disclosure, by the directors, the shareholders, or the corporate decisionmaker who initially approved the transaction or the decisionmaker's successor.

§5.03. Compensation of Directors and Senior Executives

(a) *General Rule.* A director or senior executive who receives compensation from the corporation for services in that capacity fulfills the duty of fair dealing with respect to the compensation if either:

(1) The compensation is fair to the corporation when approved;

(2) The compensation is authorized in advance by disinterested directors [§1.15] or, in the case of a senior executive who is not a director, authorized in advance by a disinterested superior, in a manner that satisfies the standards of the business judgment rule [§4.01(c)];

(3) The compensation is ratified by disinterested directors [§1.15] who satisfy the requirements of the business judgment rule [§4.01(c)], provided (i) a corporate decisionmaker who was not interested [§1.23] in receipt of the compensation acted for the corporation in determining the compensation and satisfied the requirements of the business judgment rule; (ii) the interested director or senior executive did not act unreasonably in failing to seek advance authorization of the compensation by disinterested directors or a disinterested superior; and (iii) the failure to obtain advance authorization of the compensation by disinterested directors or a disinterested superior did not adversely affect the interests of the corporation in a significant way; or

(4) The compensation is authorized in advance or ratified by disinterested shareholders [§1.16], and does not constitute a waste of corporate assets [§1.42] at the time of the shareholder action.

(b) *Burden of Proof.* A party who challenges a transaction involving the payment of compensation to a director or senior executive has the burden of proof, except that if such party establishes that the requirements of neither Subsections (a)(2), (a)(3), nor (a)(4) are met, the director or the senior executive has the burden of proving that the transaction was fair to the corporation.

§5.04. Use by a Director or Senior Executive of Corporate Property, Material Non-Public Corporate Information, or Corporate Position

(a) *General Rule.* A director [§1.13] or senior executive [§1.33] may not use corporate property, material non-public corporate information, or corporate position to secure a pecuniary benefit, unless either:

(1) Value is given for the use and the transaction meets the standards of §5.02 (Transactions with the Corporation);

(2) The use constitutes compensation and meets the standards of §5.03 (Compensation of Directors and Senior Executives);

(3) The use is solely of corporate information, and is not in connection with trading of the corporation's securities, is not a use of proprietary information of the corporation, and does not harm the corporation;

(4) The use is subject neither to §5.02 nor §5.03 but is authorized in advance or ratified by disinterested directors [§1.15] or disinterested shareholders [§1.16], and meets the requirements and standards of disclosure and review set forth in §5.02 as if that Section were applicable to the use; or

(5) The benefit is received as a shareholder and is made proportionately available to all other similarly situated shareholders,

and the use is not otherwise unlawful. . . .

§5.05. Taking of Corporate Opportunities by Directors or Senior Executives

(a) *General Rule.* A director [§1.13] or senior executive [§1.33] may not take advantage of a corporate opportunity unless:

(1) The director or senior executive first offers the corporate opportunity to the corporation and makes disclosure concerning the conflict of interest [§1.14(a)] and the corporate opportunity [§1.14(b)];

(2) The corporate opportunity is rejected by the corporation; and

(3) Either:

(A) The rejection of the opportunity is fair to the corporation;

(B) The opportunity is rejected in advance, following such disclosure, by disinterested directors [§1.15], or, in the case of a senior executive who is not a director, by a disinterested superior, in a manner that satisfies the standards of the business judgment rule [§4.01(c)]; or

(C) The rejection is authorized in advance or ratified, following such disclosure, by disinterested shareholders [§1.16], and the rejection is not equivalent to a waste of corporate assets [§1.42].

(b) *Definition of a Corporate Opportunity.* For purposes of this Section, a corporate opportunity means:

(1) Any opportunity to engage in a business activity of which a director or senior executive becomes aware, either:

(A) In connection with the performance of functions as a director or senior executive, or under circumstances that should reasonably lead the director or senior executive to believe that the person offering the opportunity expects it to be offered to the corporation; or

(B) Through the use of corporate information or property, if the resulting opportunity is one that the director or senior executive should reasonably be expected to believe would be of interest to the corporation; or

(2) Any opportunity to engage in a business activity of which a senior executive becomes aware and knows is closely related to a business in which the corporation is engaged or expects to engage.

(c) *Burden of Proof.* A party who challenges the taking of a corporate opportunity has the burden of proof, except that if such party establishes that the requirements of Subsection (a)(3)(B) or (C) are not met, the director or the senior executive has the burden of proving that the rejection and the taking of the opportunity were fair to the corporation.

(d) *Ratification of Defective Disclosure.* A good faith but defective disclosure of the facts concerning the corporate opportunity may be cured if at any time (but no later than a reasonable time after suit is filed challenging the taking of the corporate opportunity) the original rejection of the corporate opportunity is ratified, following the required disclosure, by the board, the shareholders, or the corporate decisionmaker who initially approved the rejection of the corporate opportunity, or such decisionmaker's successor. . . .

Comment:

a. Comparison with existing law. Existing judicial decisions offer a wide variety of tests for determining whether a director or a senior executive should be required to offer a corporate opportunity to the corporation. Some courts have given primary weight to whether the opportunity was related to or in the corporation's line of business. The doctrine has occasionally been limited to instances where the corporation has an interest already existing in the relevant property or an expectancy growing out of an existing right. Some courts have applied a so-called "two-step" approach, which seeks to combine the "line of business" test with a "fairness" test by first determining whether a corporate opportunity exists and then determining whether it is fair to require the director or senior executive to make it available to the corporation. Some courts have simply applied a general standard of fairness without articulating specific criteria to be utilized.

Section 5.05 sets forth a comprehensive statement of the doctrine of corporate opportunity that generally requires an opportunity to be offered to the corporation by a senior executive before it is taken by the senior executive. Directors other than those who are also senior executives are subjected to a significantly more limited duty to offer opportunities to the corporation than are senior executives. Section 5.05 reflects the general approach to what constitutes a corporate opportunity adopted by some courts and approved by the Corporate Directors' Guidebook (p. 6).

§5.06. Competition with the Corporation

(a) *General Rule.* Directors [§1.13] and senior executives [§1.33] may not advance their pecuniary interests by engaging in competition with the corporation unless either:

(1) Any reasonably foreseeable harm to the corporation from such competition is outweighed by the benefit that the corporation may reasonably be expected to derive from allowing the competition to take place, or there is no reasonably foreseeable harm to the corporation from such competition;

(2) The competition is authorized in advance or ratified, following disclosure concerning the conflict of interest [§1.14(a)] and the competition [§1.14(b)], by disinterested directors [§1.15], or in the case of a senior executive who is not a director, is authorized in advance by a disinterested superior, in a manner that satisfies the standards of the business judgment rule [§4.01(c)]; or

(3) The competition is authorized in advance or ratified, following such disclosure, by disinterested shareholders [§1.16], and the shareholders' action is not equivalent to a waste of corporate assets [§1.42]. . . .

§5.07. Transactions Between Corporations with Common Directors or Senior Executives

(a) A transaction between two corporations is not to be treated as a transaction subject to the provisions of §5.02 (Transactions with the Corporation) solely on the ground that the same person is a director [§1.13] or senior executive [§1.33] of both corporations unless:

(1) The director or senior executive participates personally and substantially in negotiating the transaction for either of the corporations; or

(2) The transaction is approved by the board of either corporation, and a director on that board who is also a director or senior executive of the other corporation casts a vote that is necessary to approve the transaction.

(b) If a transaction falls within Subsection (a)(1) or (a)(2), it will be reviewed under §5.02.

§5.10. Transactions by a Controlling Shareholder with the Corporation

(a) *General Rule.* A controlling shareholder [§1.10] who enters into a transaction with the corporation fulfills the duty of fair dealing to the corporation with respect to the transaction if:

(1) The transaction is fair to the corporation when entered into; or

(2) The transaction is authorized in advance or ratified by disinterested shareholders [§1.16], following disclosure concerning the conflict of interest [§1.14(a)] and the transaction [§1.14(b)], and does not constitute a waste of corporate assets [§1.42] at the time of the shareholder action.

(b) *Burden of Proof.* If the transaction was authorized in advance by disinterested directors [§1.15], or authorized in advance or ratified by disinterested shareholders, following such disclosure, the party challenging the transaction has the burden of proof. The party challenging the transaction also has the burden of proof if the transaction was ratified by disinterested directors and the failure to obtain advance authorization did not adversely affect the interests of the corporation in a significant way. If the transaction was not so authorized or ratified, the controlling shareholder has the burden of proof, except to the extent otherwise provided in Subsection (c).

(c) *Transactions in the Ordinary Course of Business.* In the case of a transaction between a controlling shareholder and the corporation that was in the ordinary course of the corporation's business, a party who challenges the transaction has the burden of coming forward with evidence that the transaction was unfair, whether or not the transaction was authorized in advance or ratified by disinterested directors or disinterested shareholders.

§5.11. Use by a Controlling Shareholder of Corporate Property, Material Non-Public Corporate Information, or Corporate Position

(a) *General Rule.* A controlling shareholder may not use corporate property, its controlling position, or (when trading in the corporation's securities) material non-public corporate information to secure a pecuniary benefit, unless:

(1) Value is given for the use and the transaction meets the standards of §5.10 (Transactions by a Controlling Shareholder with the Corporation), or

(2) Any resulting benefit to the controlling shareholder either is made proportionally available to the other similarly situated shareholders or is derived only from the use of controlling position and is not unfair to other shareholders, and the use is not otherwise unlawful.

(b) *Burden of Proof.* A party who challenges the conduct of a controlling shareholder under Subsection (a) has the burden of proof, except that if value was given for the benefit, the burden of proving whether the value was fair should be determined as provided in §5.10 in the case of a transaction with the corporation.

(c) *Special Rule on Remedies.* A controlling shareholder is subject to liability under this section only to the extent of any improper benefit received and retained, except to the extent that any foreseeable harm caused by the shareholder's conduct exceeds the value of the benefit received, and multiple liability based on receipt of the same benefit is not to be imposed.

§5.12. Taking of Corporate Opportunities by a Controlling Shareholder

(a) *General Rule.* A controlling shareholder [§1.10] may not take advantage of a corporate opportunity unless:

(1) The taking of the opportunity is fair to the corporation; or

(2) The taking of the opportunity is authorized in advance or ratified by disinterested shareholders [§1.16], following disclosure concerning the conflict of interest [§1.14(a)] and the corporate opportunity [§1.14(b)], and the taking of the opportunity is not equivalent to a waste of corporate assets [§1.42].

(b) *Definition of a Corporate Opportunity.* For purposes of this Section, a corporate opportunity means any opportunity to engage in a business activity that:

(1) Is developed or received by the corporation, or comes to the controlling shareholder primarily by virtue of its relationship to the corporation; or

(2) Is held out to shareholders of the corporation by the controlling shareholder, or by the corporation with the consent of the controlling shareholder, as being a type of business activity that will be within the scope of the business in which the corporation is engaged or expects to engage and will not be within the scope of the controlling shareholder's business.

(c) *Burden of Proof.* A party who challenges the taking of a corporate opportunity has the burden of proof, except that the controlling shareholder has the burden of proving that the taking of the opportunity is fair to the corporation if the taking of the opportunity was not authorized in advance or ratified by disinterested directors or disinterested shareholders, following the disclosure required by Subsection (a)(2).

§5.16. Disposition of Voting Equity Securities by a Controlling Shareholder to Third Parties

A controlling shareholder [§1.10] has the same right to dispose of voting equity securities [§1.40] as any other shareholder, including the right to dispose of those securities for a price that is not made proportionally available to other shareholders, but the controlling shareholder does not satisfy the duty of fair dealing to the other shareholders if:

(a) The controlling shareholder does not make disclosure concerning the transaction [§1.14(b)] to other shareholders with whom the controlling shareholder deals in connection with the transaction; or

(b) It is apparent from the circumstances that the purchaser is likely to violate the duty of fair dealing under Part V in such a way as to obtain a significant financial benefit for the purchaser or an associate [§1.03].

Comment:

a. Comparison with existing law. Judicial decisions generally have allowed controlling shareholders to sell their shares at a premium above the market price existing prior to disclosure of the transaction without having required either that the premium be shared with other shareholders or that the transaction be restructured so that all shareholders could participate on the same terms.... Section 5.16 follows these decisions and rejects the competing equal opportunity rule, which would require a premium to be initially offered to or later shared by all shareholders on a pro rata basis.

Part VII. Remedies

§7.01. Direct and Derivative Actions Distinguished

(a) A derivative action may be brought in the name or right of a corporation by a holder [§1.22], as provided in §7.02 (Standing to Commence and Maintain a Derivative Action), to redress an injury sustained by, or enforce a duty owed to, a corporation. An action in which the holder can prevail only by showing an injury or breach of duty to the corporation should be treated as a derivative action.

(b) A direct action may be brought in the name and right of a holder to redress an injury sustained by, or enforce a duty owed to, the holder. An action in which the holder can prevail without showing an injury or breach of duty to the corporation should be treated as a direct action that may be maintained by the holder in an individual capacity.

(c) If a transaction gives rise to both direct and derivative claims, a holder may commence and maintain direct and derivative actions simultaneously, and any special restrictions or defenses pertaining to the maintenance, settlement, or dismissal of either action should not apply to the other.

(d) In the case of a closely held corporation [§1.06],the court in its discretion may treat an action raising derivative claims as a direct action, exempt it from those restrictions and defenses applicable only to derivative actions, and order an individual recovery, if it finds that to do so will not (i) unfairly expose the corporation or the defendants to a multiplicity of actions, (ii) materially prejudice the interests of creditors of the corporation, or (iii) interfere with a fair distribution of the recovery among all interested persons.

§7.02. Standing to Commence and Maintain a Derivative Action

(a) A holder [§1.22] of an equity security [§1.20] has standing to commence and maintain a derivative action if the holder:

(1) Acquired the equity security either (A) before the material facts relating to the alleged wrong were publicly disclosed or were known by, or specifically communicated to, the holder, or (B) by devolution of law, directly or indirectly, from a prior holder who acquired the security as described in the preceding clause (A);

(2) Continues to hold the equity security until the time of judgment, unless the failure to do so is the result of corporate action in which the holder did not acquiesce, and either (A) the derivative action was commenced prior to the corporate action terminating the holder's status, or (B) the court finds that the holder is better able to represent the interests of the shareholders than any other holder who has brought suit;

(3) Has complied with the demand requirement of §7.03 (Exhaustion of Intracorporate Remedies: The Demand Rule) or was excused by its terms; and

(4) Is able to represent fairly and adequately the interests of the shareholders.

(b) On a timely motion, a holder of an equity security should be permitted to intervene in a derivative action, unless the court finds that the interests to be represented by the intervenor are already fairly and adequately represented or that the intervenor is unable to represent fairly and adequately the interests of the shareholders.

(c) A director [§1.13] of a corporation has standing to commence and maintain a derivative action unless the court finds that the director is unable to represent fairly and adequately the interests of the shareholders.

§7.03. Exhaustion of Intracorporate Remedies: The Demand Rule

(a) Before commencing a derivative action, a holder [§1.22] or a director [§1.13] should be required to make a written demand upon the board of directors of the corporation, requesting it to prosecute the action or take suitable corrective measures, unless demand is excused under §7.03(b). The demand should give notice to the board, with reasonable specificity, of the essential facts relied upon to support each of the claims made therein.

(b) Demand on the board should be excused only if the plaintiff makes a specific showing that irreparable injury to the corporation would otherwise result, and in such instances demand should be made promptly after commencement of the action.

(c) Demand on shareholders should not be required.

(d) Except as provided in §7.03(b), the court should dismiss a derivative action that is commenced prior to the response of the board or a committee thereof to the demand required by §7.03(a), unless the board or committee fails to respond within a reasonable time.

§7.04. Pleading, Demand Rejection, Procedure, and Costs in a Derivative Action

The legal standards applicable to a derivative action should provide that:

(a) *Particularity; Demand Rejection.*

(1) *In General.* The complaint shall plead with particularity facts that, if true, raise a significant prospect that the transaction or conduct complained of did not meet the applicable requirements of Parts IV (Duty of Care and the Business Judgment Rule), V (Duty of Fair Dealing), or VI (Role of Directors and Shareholders in Transactions in Control and Tender Offers), in light of any approvals of the transaction or conduct communicated to the plaintiff by the corporation.

(2) *Demand Rejection.* If the corporation rejects the demand made on the board pursuant to §7.03, and if, at or following the rejection, the corporation delivers to the plaintiff a written reply to the demand which states that the demand was rejected by directors who were not interested [§1.23] in the transaction or conduct described in and forming the basis for the demand and that those directors constituted a majority of the entire board and were capable as a group of objective judgment in the circumstances, and which provides specific reasons for those statements, then the complaint shall also plead with particularity facts that, if true, raise a significant prospect that either:

(A) The statements in the reply are not correct;

(B) If Part IV, V, or VI provides that the underlying transaction or conduct would be reviewed under the standard of the business judgment rule, that the rejection did not satisfy the requirements of the business judgment rule as specified in §4.01(c); or

(C) If Part IV, V, or VI provides that the underlying transaction or conduct would be reviewed under a standard other than the business judgment rule, either (i) that the disinterested directors who rejected the demand did not satisfy the good faith and informational requirements (§4.01(c)(2)) of the business judgment rule or (ii) that disinterested directors could not reasonably have determined that rejection of the demand was in the best interests of the corporation.

If the complaint fails to set forth sufficiently such particularized facts, defendants shall be entitled to dismissal of the complaint prior to discovery....

(d) *Award of Costs.* The court may award applicable costs, including reasonable attorney's fees and expenses, against a party, or a party's counsel:

(1) At any time, if the court finds that any specific claim for relief or defense was asserted or any pleading, motion, request for discovery, or

other action was made or taken in bad faith or without reasonable cause; or

(2) Upon final judgment, if the court finds, in light of all the evidence, and considering both the state and trend of the substantive law, that the action taken as a whole was brought, prosecuted, or defended in bad faith or in an unreasonable manner.

§7.05. Board or Committee Authority in Regard to a Derivative Action

(a) The board of a corporation in whose name or right a derivative action is brought has standing on behalf of the corporation to:

(1) Move to dismiss the action on account of the plaintiff's lack of standing under §7.02 (Standing to Commence and Maintain a Derivative Action) or the plaintiff's failure to comply with §7.03 (Exhaustion of Intracorporate Remedies: The Demand Rule) or §7.04(a) or (b) (Pleading, Demand Rejection, Procedure, and Costs in a Derivative Action) or move for dismissal of the complaint or for summary judgment;

(2) Move for a stay of the action, including discovery, as provided by §7.06 (Authority of Court to Stay a Derivative Action);

(3) Move to dismiss the action as contrary to the best interests of the corporation, as provided in §§7.07-7.12 (dismissal of a derivative action based on a motion requesting dismissal by the board, a board committee, the shareholders, or a special panel);

(4) Oppose injunctive or other relief materially affecting the corporation's interests;

(5) Adopt or pursue the action in the corporation's right;

(6) Comment on, object to, or recommend any proposed settlement, discontinuance, compromise, or voluntary dismissal by agreement between the plaintiff and any defendant under §7.14 (Settlement of a Derivative Action by Agreement Between the Plaintiff and a Defendant), or any award of attorney's fees and other expenses under §7.17 (Plaintiff's Attorney's Fees and Expenses); and

(7) Seek to settle the action without agreement of the plaintiff under §7.15 (Settlement of a Derivative Action Without the Agreement of the Plaintiff).

Except as provided above, the corporation may not otherwise defend the action in the place of, or raise defenses on behalf of, other defendants.

(b) The board of a corporation in whose name or right a derivative action is brought may:

(1) Delegate its authority to take any action specified in §7.05(a) to a committee of directors; or

(2) Request the court to appoint a special panel in lieu of a committee of directors, or a special member of a committee, under §7.12 (Special Panel or Special Committee Members).

§7.07. Dismissal of a Derivative Action Based on a Motion Requesting Dismissal by the Board or a Committee: General Statement

(a) The court having jurisdiction over a derivative action should dismiss the action as against one or more of the defendants based on a motion by the board or a properly delegated committee requesting dismissal of the action as in the best interests of the corporation, if:

(1) In the case of an action against a person [§1.28] other than a director [§1.13], senior executive [§1.33], or person in control [§1.08] of the corporation, or an associate [§1.03] of any such person, the determinations of the board or committee underlying the motion satisfy the requirements of the business judgment rule as specified in §4.01;

(2) In the case of an action against a director, senior executive, or person in control of the corporation, or an associate of any such person, the conditions specified in §7.08 (Dismissal of a Derivative Action Against Directors, Senior Executives, Controlling Persons, or Associates Based on a Motion Requesting Dismissal by the Board or a Committee) are satisfied; or

(3) In any case, the shareholders approve a resolution requesting dismissal of the action in the manner provided in §7.11 (Dismissal of a Derivative Action Based Upon Action by the Shareholders).

(b) Regardless of whether a corporation chooses to proceed under §7.08 or §7.11, it is free to make any other motion available to it under the law, including a motion to dismiss the complaint or for summary judgment.

§7.08. Dismissal of a Derivative Action Against Directors, Senior Executives, Controlling Persons, or Associates Based on a Motion Requesting Dismissal by the Board or a Committee

The court should, subject to the provisions of §7.10(b) (retention of significant improper benefit), dismiss a derivative action against a defendant who is a director [§1.13], a senior executive [§1.33], or a person [§1.28] in control [§1.08] of the corporation, or an associate [§1.03] of any such person, if:

(a) The board of directors or a properly delegated committee thereof (either in response to a demand or following commencement of the action) has determined that the action is contrary to the best interests of the corporation and has requested dismissal of the action;

(b) The procedures specified in §7.09 (Procedures for Requesting Dismissal of a Derivative Action) for the conduct of a review and evaluation of the action were substantially complied with (either in response to a demand or following commencement of the action), or any material departures therefrom were justified under the circumstances; and

(c) The determinations of the board or committee satisfy the applicable standard of review set forth in §7.10(a) (Standard of Judicial Review with Regard to a Board or Committee Motion Requesting Dismissal of a Derivative Action Under §7.08).

§7.09. Procedures for Requesting Dismissal of a Derivative Action

(a) The following procedural standards should apply to the review and evaluation of a derivative action by the board or committee under §7.08 (Dismissal of a Derivative Action Against Directors, Senior Executives, Controlling Persons, or Associates Based on a Motion Requesting Dismissal by the Board or a Committee) or §7.11 (Dismissal of a Derivative Action Based Upon Action by the Shareholders):

(1) The board or committee should be composed of two or more persons, no participating member of which was interested [§1.23] in the action, and should as a group be capable of objective judgment in the circumstances;

(2) The board or committee should be assisted by counsel of its choice and such other agents as it reasonably considers necessary;

(3) The determinations of the board or committee should be based upon a review and evaluation that was sufficiently informed to satisfy the standards applicable under §7.10(a); and

(4) If the board or committee determines to request dismissal of the derivative action, it shall prepare and file with the court a report or other written submission setting forth its determinations in a manner sufficient to enable the court to conduct the review required under §7.10 (Standard of Judicial Review with Regard to a Board or Committee Motion Requesting Dismissal of a Derivative Action Under §7.08).

(b) If the court is unwilling to grant a motion to dismiss under §7.08 or §7.11 because the procedures followed by the board or committee departed materially from the standards specified in §7.09(a), the court should permit the board or committee to supplement its procedures, and make such further reports or other written submissions, as will satisfy the standards specified in §7.09(a), unless the court decides that (i) the board or committee did not act on the basis of a good faith belief that its procedures and report were justified in the circumstances; (ii) unreasonable delay or prejudice would result; or (iii) there is no reasonable prospect that such further steps would support dismissal of the action.

§7.10. Standard of Judicial Review with Regard to a Board or Committee Motion Requesting Dismissal of a Derivative Action Under §7.08

(a) *Standard of Review.* In deciding whether an action should be dismissed under §7.08 (Dismissal of a Derivative Action Against Directors, Senior Executives, Controlling Persons, or Associates Based on a Motion Requesting Dismissal by the Board or a Committee), the court should apply the following standards of review:

(1) If the gravamen of the claim is that the defendant violated a duty set forth in Part IV (Duty of Care and the Business Judgment Rule), other than by committing a knowing and culpable violation of law that is alleged with particularity, or if the underlying transaction or conduct would be reviewed under the business judgment rule under §5.03, §5.04, §5.05, §5.06, §5.08, or §6.02, the court should dismiss the claim unless it finds that the board's or committee's determinations fail to satisfy the requirements of the business judgment rule as specified in §4.01(c).

(2) In other cases governed by Part V (Duty of Fair Dealing) or Part VI (Role of Directors and Shareholders in Transactions in Control and Tender Offers), or to which the business judgment rule is not applicable, including cases in which the gravamen of the claim is that defendant committed a knowing and culpable violation of law in breach of Part IV, the court should dismiss the action if the court finds, in light of the applicable standards under Part IV, V, or VI that the board or committee was adequately informed under the circumstances and reasonably determined that dismissal was in the best interests of the corporation, based on grounds that the court deems to warrant reliance.

(3) In cases arising under either Subsection (a)(1) or (a)(2), the court may substantively review and determine any issue of law.

(b) *Retention of Significant Improper Benefit.* The court shall not dismiss an action if the plaintiff establishes that dismissal would permit a defendant, or an associate [§1.03], to retain a significant improper benefit where:

(1) The defendant, either alone or collectively with others who are also found to have received a significant improper benefit arising out of the same transaction, possesses control [§1.08] of the corporation; or

(2) Such benefit was obtained:

(A) As the result of a knowing and material misrepresentation or omission or other fraudulent act; or

(B) Without advance authorization or the requisite ratification of such benefit by disinterested directors [§1.15] (or, in the case of a non-director senior executive, advance authorization by a disinterested superior), or authorization or ratification by disinterested shareholders [§1.16], and in breach of §5.02 (Transactions with the

Corporation) or §5.04 (Use by a Director or Senior Executive of Corporate Property, Material Non-Public Corporate Information, or Corporate Position);

unless the court determines, in light of specific reasons advanced by the board or committee, that the likely injury to the corporation from continuation of the action convincingly outweighs any adverse impact on the public interest from dismissal of the action....

§7.11. Dismissal of a Derivative Action Based Upon Action by the Shareholders

The court should dismiss a derivative action against any defendant upon approval by the shareholders of a resolution requesting dismissal of the action as in the best interests of the corporation if the court finds that:

(a) A resolution recommending such dismissal to the shareholders was adopted by the board of directors, or a properly delegated committee thereof, after a review and evaluation that substantially complied with the procedures specified in §7.09(a)(1)-(3) (Procedures for Requesting Dismissal of a Derivative Action) or in which any material departures from those procedures were justified under the circumstances;

(b) Disclosure was made to the shareholders of all material facts [§1.25] concerning the derivative action and the board's resolution recommending its dismissal to the shareholders and, if requested by plaintiff, the disclosure statement included a brief statement by the plaintiff summarizing the plaintiff's views of the action and of the board's or committee's resolutions;

(c) The resolution was approved by a vote of disinterested shareholders [§1.16]; and

(d) Dismissal would not constitute a waste of corporate assets [§1.42].

FEDERAL RULES OF CIVIL PROCEDURE

Rule 23. Class Actions

(a) PREREQUISITES. One or more members of a class may sue or be sued as representative parties on behalf of all members only if:

(1) the class is so numerous that joinder of all members is impracticable;

(2) there are questions of law or fact common to the class;

(3) the claims or defenses of the representative parties are typical of the claims or defenses of the class; and

(4) the representative parties will fairly and adequately protect the interests of the class.

(b) TYPES OF CLASS ACTIONS. A class action may be maintained if Rule 23(a) is satisfied and if:

(1) prosecuting separate actions by or against individual class members would create a risk of:

(A) inconsistent or varying adjudications with respect to individual class members that would establish incompatible standards of conduct for the party opposing the class; or

(B) adjudications with respect to individual class members that, as a practical matter, would be dispositive of the interests of the other members not parties to the individual adjudications or would substantially impair or impede their ability to protect their interests;

(2) the party opposing the class has acted or refused to act on grounds that apply generally to the class, so that final injunctive relief or corresponding declaratory relief is appropriate respecting the class as a whole; or

(3) the court finds that the questions of law or fact common to class members predominate over any questions affecting only individual members, and that a class action is superior to other available methods

for fairly and efficiently adjudicating the controversy. The matters pertinent to these findings include:

(A) the class members' interests in individually controlling the prosecution or defense of separate actions;

(B) the extent and nature of any litigation concerning the controversy already begun by or against class members;

(C) the desirability or undesirability of concentrating the litigation of the claims in the particular forum; and

(D) the likely difficulties in managing a class action.

(c) CERTIFICATION ORDER; NOTICE TO CLASS MEMBERS; JUDGMENT; ISSUES CLASSES; SUBCLASSES.

(1) *CERTIFICATION ORDER.*

(A) *TIME TO ISSUE.* At an early practicable time after a person sues or is sued as a class representative, the court must determine by order whether to certify the action as a class action.

(B) *DEFINING THE CLASS; Appointing Class Counsel.* An order that certifies a class action must define the class and the class claims, issues, or defenses, and must appoint class counsel under Rule 23(g).

(C) *ALTERING OR AMENDING THE ORDER.* An order that grants or denies class certification may be altered or amended before final judgment.

(2) *NOTICE.*

(A) *For (b)(1) or (b)(2) Classes.* For any class certified under Rule 23(b)(1) or (b)(2), the court may direct appropriate notice to the class.

(B) *For (b)(3) Classes.* For any class certified under Rule 23(b)(3), the court must direct to class members the best notice that is practicable under the circumstances, including individual notice to all members who can be identified through reasonable effort. The notice must clearly and concisely state in plain, easily understood language:

(i) the nature of the action;

(ii) the definition of the class certified;

(iii) the class claims, issues, or defenses;

(iv) that a class member may enter an appearance through an attorney if the member so desires;

(v) that the court will exclude from the class any member who requests exclusion;

(vi) the time and manner for requesting exclusion; and

(vii) the binding effect of a class judgment on members under Rule 23(c)(3).

(3) *JUDGMENT.* Whether or not favorable to the class, the judgment in a class action must:

(A) for any class certified under Rule 23(b)(1) or (b)(2), include and describe those whom the court finds to be class members; and

(B) for any class certified under Rule 23(b)(3), include and specify or describe those to whom the Rule 23(c)(2) notice was directed, who have not requested exclusion, and whom the court finds to be class members.

(4) *PARTICULAR ISSUES.* When appropriate, an action may be brought or maintained as a class action with respect to particular issues.

(5) *SUBCLASSES.* When appropriate, a class may be divided into subclasses that are each treated as a class under this rule.

(d) Conducting the Action.

(1) *IN GENERAL.* In conducting an action under this rule, the court may issue orders that:

(A) determine the course of proceedings or prescribe measures to prevent undue repetition or complication in presenting evidence or argument;

(B) require—to protect class members and fairly conduct the action – giving appropriate notice to some or all class members of:

(i) any step in the action;

(ii) the proposed extent of the judgment; or

(iii) the members' opportunity to signify whether they consider the representation fair and adequate, to intervene and present claims or defenses, or to otherwise come into the action;

(C) impose conditions on the representative parties or on intervenors;

(D) require that the pleadings be amended to eliminate allegations about representation of absent persons and that the action proceed accordingly; or

(E) deal with similar procedural matters.

(2) *COMBININGAND AMENDING ORDERS.* An order under Rule 23(d)(1) may be altered or amended from time to time and may be combined with an order under Rule 16.

(e) SETTLEMENT, VOLUNTARY DISMISSAL, OR COMPROMISE. The claims, issues, or defenses of a certified class may be settled, voluntarily dismissed, or compromised only with the court's approval. The following procedures apply to a proposed settlement, voluntary dismissal, or compromise:

(1) The court must direct notice in a reasonable manner to all class members who would be bound by the proposal.

(2) If the proposal would bind class members, the court may approve it only after a hearing and on finding that it is fair, reasonable, and adequate.

(3) The parties seeking approval must file a statement identifying any agreement made in connection with the proposal.

(4) If the class action was previously certified under Rule 23(b)(3), the court may refuse to approve a settlement unless it affords a new opportunity to request exclusion to individual class members who had an earlier opportunity to request exclusion but did not do so.

(5) Any class member may object to the proposal if it requires court approval under this subdivision (e); the objection may be withdrawn only with the court's approval.

(f) APPEALS. A court of appeals may permit an appeal from an order granting or denying class-action certification under this rule if a petition for permission to appeal is filed with the circuit clerk within 14 days after the order is entered. An appeal does not stay proceedings in the district court unless the district judge or the court of appeals so orders.

(g) CLASS COUNSEL.

(1) *APPOINTING CLASS COUNSEL.* Unless a statute provides otherwise, a court that certifies a class must appoint class counsel. In appointing class counsel, the court:

(A) must consider:

(i) the work counsel has done in identifying or investigating potential claims in the action;

(ii) counsel's experience in handling class actions, other complex litigation, and the types of claims asserted in the action;

(iii) counsel's knowledge of the applicable law; and

(iv) the resources that counsel will commit to representing the class;

(B) may consider any other matter pertinent to counsel's ability to fairly and adequately represent the interests of the class;

(C) may order potential class counsel to provide information on any subject pertinent to the appointment and to propose terms for attorney's fees and nontaxable costs;

(D) may include in the appointing order provisions about the award of attorney's fees or nontaxable costs under Rule 23(h); and

(E) may make further orders in connection with the appointment.

(2) *STANDARD FOR APPOINTING CLASS COUNSEL.* When one applicant seeks appointment as class counsel, the court may appoint that applicant only if the applicant is adequate under Rule 23(g)(1) and (4). If more than one adequate applicant seeks appointment, the court must appoint the applicant best able to represent the interests of the class.

(3) *INTERIM COUNSEL.* The court may designate interim counsel to act on behalf of a putative class before determining whether to certify the action as a class action.

(4) *DUTY OF CLASS COUNSEL.* Class counsel must fairly and adequately represent the interests of the class.

(h) Attorney's Fees and Nontaxable Costs. In a certified class action, the court may award reasonable attorney's fees and nontaxable costs that are authorized by law or by the parties' agreement. The following procedures apply:

(1) A claim for an award must be made by motion under Rule 54(d)(2), subject to the provisions of this subdivision (h), at a time the court sets. Notice of the motion must be served on all parties and, for motions by class counsel, directed to class members in a reasonable manner.

(2) A class member, or a party from whom payment is sought, may object to the motion.

(3) The court may hold a hearing and must find the facts and state its legal conclusions under Rule 52(a).

(4) The court may refer issues related to the amount of the award to a special master or a magistrate judge, as provided in Rule 54(d)(2)(D).

Rule 23.1. Derivative Actions by Shareholders

(a) PREREQUISITES. This rule applies when one or more shareholders or members of a corporation or an unincorporated association bring a derivative action to enforce a right that the corporation or association may properly assert but has failed to enforce. The derivative action may not be maintained if it appears that the plaintiff does not fairly and adequately represent the interests of shareholders or members who are similarly situated in enforcing the right of the corporation or association.

(b) PLEADING REQUIREMENTS. The complaint must be verified and must:

(1) allege that the plaintiff was a shareholder or member at the time of the transaction complained of, or that the plaintiff's share or membership later devolved on it by operation of law;

(2) allege that the action is not a collusive one to confer jurisdiction that the court would otherwise lack; and

(3) state with particularity:

(A) any effort by the plaintiff to obtain the desired action from the directors or comparable authority and, if necessary, from the shareholders or members; and

(B) the reasons for not obtaining the action or not making the effort.

(c) SETTLEMENT, DISMISSAL, AND COMPROMISE. A derivative action may be settled, voluntarily dismissed, or compromised only with the court's approval. Notice of a proposed settlement, voluntary dismissal, or compromise must be given to shareholders or members in the manner that the court orders.

UNIFORM FRAUDULENT TRANSFER ACT (1984)

§ 2. Insolvency

(a) A debtor is insolvent if the sum of the debtor's debts is greater than all of the debtor's assets at a fair valuation.

(b) A debtor who is generally not paying his [or her] debts as they become due is presumed to be insolvent.

(c) A partnership is insolvent under subsection (a) if the sum of the partnership's debts is greater than the aggregate, at a fair valuation, of all of the partnership's assets and the sum of the excess of the value of each general partner's non-partnership assets over the partner's non-partnership debts.

(d) Assets under this section do not include property that has been transferred, concealed, or removed with intent to hinder, delay, or defraud creditors or that has been transferred in a manner making the transfer voidable under this [Act].

(e) Debts under this section do not include an obligation to the extent it is secured by a valid lien on property of the debtor not included as an asset.

§ 3. Value

(a) Value is given for a transfer or an obligation if, in exchange for the transfer or obligation, property is transferred or an antecedent debt is secured or satisfied, but value does not include an unperformed promise made otherwise than in the ordinary course of the promisor's business to furnish support to the debtor or another person.

(b) For the purposes of Sections 4(a)(2) and 5, a person gives a reasonably equivalent value if the person acquires an interest of the debtor in an asset pursuant to a regularly conducted, noncollusive foreclosure sale or execution of a power of sale for the acquisition or disposition of the interest of the debtor upon default under a mortgage, deed of trust, or security agreement.

(c) A transfer is made for present value if the exchange between the debtor and the transferee is intended by them to be contemporaneous and is in fact substantially contemporaneous.

§ 4. Transfers Fraudulent as to Present and Future Creditors

(a) A transfer made or obligation incurred by a debtor is fraudulent as to a creditor, whether the creditor's claim arose before or after the transfer was made or the obligation was incurred, if the debtor made the transfer or incurred the obligation:

(1) with actual intent to hinder, delay, or defraud any creditor of the debtor; or

(2) without receiving a reasonably equivalent value in exchange for the transfer or obligation, and the debtor:

(i) was engaged or was about to engage in a business or a transaction for which the remaining assets of the debtor were unreasonably small in relation to the business or transaction; or

(ii) intended to incur, or believed or reasonably should have believed that he [or she] would incur, debts beyond his [or her] ability to pay as they became due.

(b) In determining actual intent under subsection (a)(1), consideration may be given, among other factors, to whether:

(1) the transfer or obligation was to an insider;

(2) the debtor retained possession or control of the property transferred after the transfer;

(3) the transfer or obligation was disclosed or concealed;

(4) before the transfer was made or obligation was incurred, the debtor had been sued or threatened with suit;

(5) the transfer was of substantially all the debtor's assets;

(6) the debtor absconded;

(7) the debtor removed or concealed assets;

(8) the value of the consideration received by the debtor was reasonably equivalent to the value of the asset transferred or the amount of the obligation incurred;

(9) the debtor was insolvent or became insolvent shortly after the transfer was made or the obligation was incurred;

(10) the transfer occurred shortly before or shortly after a substantial debt was incurred; and

(11) the debtor transferred the essential assets of the business to a lienor who transferred the assets to an insider of the debtor.

§ 5. Transfers Fraudulent as to Present Creditors

(a) A transfer made or obligation incurred by a debtor is fraudulent as to a creditor whose claim arose before the transfer was made or the obligation was incurred if the debtor made the transfer or incurred the obligation without receiving a reasonably equivalent value in exchange for the transfer or obligation and the debtor was insolvent at that time or the debtor became insolvent as a result of the transfer or obligation.

(b) A transfer made by a debtor is fraudulent as to a creditor whose claim arose before the transfer was made if the transfer was made to an insider for an antecedent debt, the debtor was insolvent at that time, and the insider had reasonable cause to believe that the debtor was insolvent.

§ 6. When Transfer Is Made or Obligation Is Incurred

For the purposes of this [Act]:

(1) a transfer is made:

(i) with respect to an asset that is real property other than a fixture, but including the interest of a seller or purchaser under a contract for the sale of the asset, when the transfer is so far perfected that a good-faith purchaser of the asset from the debtor against whom applicable law permits the transfer to be perfected cannot acquire an interest in the asset that is superior to the interest of the transferee; and

(ii) with respect to an asset that is not real property or that is a fixture, when the transfer is so far perfected that a creditor on a simple contract cannot acquire a judicial lien otherwise than under this [Act] that is superior to the interest of the transferee;

(2) if applicable law permits the transfer to be perfected as provided in paragraph (1) and the transfer is not so perfected before the commencement of an action for relief under this [Act], the transfer is deemed made immediately before the commencement of the action;

(3) if applicable law does not permit the transfer to be perfected as provided in paragraph (1), the transfer is made when it becomes effective between the debtor and the transferee;

(4) a transfer is not made until the debtor has acquired rights in the asset transferred;

(5) an obligation is incurred:

(i) if oral, when it becomes effective between the parties; or

(ii) if evidenced by a writing, when the writing executed by the obligor is delivered to or for the benefit of the obligee.

§ 7. Remedies of Creditors

(a) In an action for relief against a transfer or obligation under this [Act], a creditor, subject to the limitations in Section 8, may obtain:

(1) avoidance of the transfer or obligation to the extent necessary to satisfy the creditor's claim;

[(2) an attachment or other provisional remedy against the asset transferred or other property of the transferee in accordance with the procedure prescribed by [ ];]

(3) subject to applicable principles of equity and in accordance with applicable rules of civil procedure,

(i) an injunction against further disposition by the debtor or a transferee, or both, of the asset transferred or of other property;

(ii) appointment of a receiver to take charge of the asset transferred or of other property of the transferee; or

(iii) any other relief the circumstances may require.

(b) If a creditor has obtained a judgment on a claim against the debtor, the creditor, if the court so orders, may levy execution on the asset transferred or its proceeds.

§ 8. Defenses, Liability, and Protection of Transferee

(a) A transfer or obligation is not voidable under Section 4(a)(1) against a person who took in good faith and for a reasonably equivalent value or against any subsequent transferee or obligee.

(b) Except as otherwise provided in this section, to the extent a transfer is voidable in an action by a creditor under Section 7(a)(1), the creditor may recover judgment for the value of the asset transferred, as adjusted under subsection (c), or the amount necessary to satisfy the creditor's claim, whichever is less. The judgment may be entered against:

(1) the first transferee of the asset or the person for whose benefit the transfer was made; or

(2) any subsequent transferee other than a good faith transferee who took for value or from any subsequent transferee.

(c) If the judgment under subsection (b) is based upon the value of the asset transferred, the judgment must be for an amount equal to the value of the asset at the time of the transfer, subject to adjustment as the equities may require.

(d) Notwithstanding voidability of a transfer or an obligation under this [Act], a good-faith transferee or obligee is entitled, to the extent of the value given the debtor for the transfer or obligation, to

(1) a lien on or a right to retain any interest in the asset transferred;
(2) enforcement of any obligation incurred; or
(3) a reduction in the amount of the liability on the judgment.

(e) A transfer is not voidable under Section 4(a)(2) or Section 5 if the transfer results from:

(1) termination of a lease upon default by the debtor when the termination is pursuant to the lease and applicable law; or

(2) enforcement of a security interest in compliance with Article 9 of the Uniform Commercial Code.

(f) A transfer is not voidable under Section 5(b):

(1) to the extent the insider gave new value to or for the benefit of the debtor after the transfer was made unless the new value was secured by a valid lien;

(2) if made in the ordinary course of business or financial affairs of the debtor and the insider; or

(3) if made pursuant to a good-faith effort to rehabilitate the debtor and the transfer secured present value given for that purpose as well as an antecedent debt of the debtor.

§ 9. Extinguishment of [Claim for Relief] [Cause of Action]

A [claim for relief] [cause of action] with respect to a fraudulent transfer or obligation under this [Act] is extinguished unless action is brought:

(a) under Section 4(a)(1), within 4 years after the transfer was made or the obligation was incurred or, if later, within one year after the transfer or obligation was or could reasonably have been discovered by the claimant;

(b)under Section 4(a)(2) or 5(a), within 4 years after the transfer was made or the obligation was incurred; or

(c)under Section 5(b), within one year after the transfer was made or the obligation was incurred.

SECURITIES EXCHANGE ACT OF 1934

(15 U.S.C.A. § 78a) and Associated Rules

§ 78j Manipulative and Deceptive Devices [Section 10]

It shall be unlawful for any person, directly or indirectly, by the use of any means or instrumentality of interstate commerce or of the mails, or of any facility of any national securities exchange—

(a)(1) To effect a short sale, or to use or employ any stop-loss order in connection with the purchase or sale, of any security other than a government security, in contravention of such rules and regulations as the Commission may prescribe as necessary or appropriate in the public interest or for the protection of investors.

(2) Paragraph (1) of this subsection shall not apply to security futures products.

(b) To use or employ, in connection with the purchase or sale of any security registered on a national securities exchange or any security not so registered, or any securities-based swap agreement[1] any manipulative or deceptive device or contrivance in contravention of such rules and regulations as the Commission may prescribe as necessary or appropriate in the public interest or for the protection of investors.

(c)(1) To effect, accept, or facilitate a transaction involving the loan or borrowing of securities in contravention of such rules and regulations as the Commission may prescribe as necessary or appropriate in the public interest or for the protection of investors.

(2) Nothing in paragraph (1) may be construed to limit the authority of the appropriate Federal banking agency (as defined in section 1813(q) of Title 12), the National Credit Union Administration, or any other Federal department or agency having a responsibility under Federal law to prescribe rules or regulations restricting transactions involving the loan or borrowing of securities in order to protect the safety and soundness of a financial institution or to protect the financial system from systemic risk.

Rules promulgated under subsection (b) of this section that prohibit fraud, manipulation, or insider trading (but not rules imposing or specifying reporting or recordkeeping requirements, procedures, or standards as prophylactic measures against fraud, manipulation, or insider trading), and judicial precedents decided under subsection (b) of this section and rules promulgated thereunder that prohibit fraud, manipulation, or insider trading, shall apply to security-based swap agreements to the same extent as they apply to securities. Judicial precedents decided under section 77q(a) of this title and sections 78i, 78*o*, 78p, 78t, and 78u-1 of this title, and judicial precedents decided under applicable rules promulgated under such sections, shall apply to security-based swap agreements to the same extent as they apply to securities.

Rules Under Section 10

§ 240.10b-5 Employment of Manipulative and Deceptive Devices

It shall be unlawful for any person, directly or indirectly, by the use of any means or instrumentality of interstate commerce, or of the mails or of any facility of any national securities exchange,

(a) To employ any device, scheme, or artifice to defraud,

(b) To make any untrue statement of a material fact or to omit to state a material fact necessary in order to make the statements made, in the light of the circumstances under which they were made, not misleading, or

(c) To engage in any act, practice, or course of business which operates or would operate as a fraud or deceit upon any person, in connection with the purchase or sale of any security.

§ 240.10b5-1 Trading "on the Basis of" Material Nonpublic Information in Insider Trading Cases

Preliminary Note to § 240.10b5-1: This provision defines when a purchase or sale constitutes trading "on the basis of" material nonpublic information in insider trading cases brought under Section 10(b) of the Act and Rule 10b-5 thereunder. The law of insider trading is otherwise defined by judicial opinions construing Rule 10b-5, and Rule 10b5-1 does not modify the scope of insider trading law in any other respect.

(a) **General.** The "manipulative and deceptive devices" prohibited by Section 10(b) of the Act (15 U.S.C. 78j) and § 240.10b-5 thereunder include, among other things, the purchase or sale of a security of any issuer, on the basis of material nonpublic information about that security or issuer, in breach of a duty of trust or confidence that is owed directly, indirectly, or derivatively, to the issuer of that security or the shareholders of that issuer, or to any other person who is the source of the material nonpublic information.

(b) **Definition of "on the basis of."** Subject to the affirmative defenses in paragraph (c) of this section, a purchase or sale of a security of an issuer is "on the basis of" material nonpublic information about that security or issuer if the person making the purchase or sale was aware of the material nonpublic information when the person made the purchase or sale.

(c) **Affirmative defenses.**

(1)(i) Subject to paragraph (c)(1)(ii) of this section, a person's purchase or sale is not "on the basis of" material nonpublic information if the person making the purchase or sale demonstrates that:

(A) Before becoming aware of the information, the person had:

(1) Entered into a binding contract to purchase or sell the security,

(2) Instructed another person to purchase or sell the security for the instructing person's account, or

(3) Adopted a written plan for trading securities;

(B) The contract, instruction, or plan described in paragraph (c)(1)(i)(A) of this Section:

(1) Specified the amount of securities to be purchased or sold and the price at which and the date on which the securities were to be purchased or sold;

(2) Included a written formula or algorithm, or computer program, for determining the amount of securities to be purchased or sold and the price at which and the date on which the securities were to be purchased or sold; or

(3) Did not permit the person to exercise any subsequent influence over how, when, or whether to effect purchases or sales; provided, in addition, that any other person who, pursuant to the contract, instruction, or plan, did exercise such influence must not have been aware of the material nonpublic information when doing so; and

(C) The purchase or sale that occurred was pursuant to the contract, instruction, or plan. A purchase or sale is not "pursuant to a contract, instruction, or plan" if, among other things, the person who entered into the contract, instruction, or plan altered or deviated from the contract, instruction, or plan to purchase or sell securities (whether by changing the amount, price, or timing of the purchase or sale), or entered into or altered a corresponding or hedging transaction or position with respect to those securities.

(ii) Paragraph (c)(1)(i) of this section is applicable only when the contract, instruction, or plan to purchase or sell securities was given or entered into in good faith and not as part of a plan or scheme to evade the prohibitions of this section.

(iii) This paragraph (c)(1)(iii) defines certain terms as used in paragraph (c) of this Section.

(A) Amount. "Amount" means either a specified number of shares or other securities or a specified dollar value of securities.

(B) Price. "Price" means the market price on a particular date or a limit price, or a particular dollar price.

(C) Date. "Date" means, in the case of a market order, the specific day of the year on which the order is to be executed (or as soon thereafter as is practicable under ordinary principles of best execution). "Date" means, in the case of a limit order, a day of the year on which the limit order is in force.

(2) A person other than a natural person also may demonstrate that a purchase or sale of securities is not "on the basis of" material nonpublic information if the person demonstrates that:

(i) The individual making the investment decision on behalf of the person to purchase or sell the securities was not aware of the information; and

(ii) The person had implemented reasonable policies and procedures, taking into consideration the nature of the person's business, to ensure that individuals making investment decisions would not violate the laws prohibiting trading on the basis of material nonpublic information. These policies and procedures may include those that restrict any purchase, sale, and causing any purchase or sale of any security as to which the person has material nonpublic information, or those that prevent such individuals from becoming aware of such information.

§ 240.10b5-2 Duties of Trust or Confidence in Misappropriation Insider Trading Cases

Preliminary Note to § 240.10b5-2: This section provides a non-exclusive definition of circumstances in which a person has a duty of trust or confidence for purposes of the "misappropriation" theory of insider trading under Section 10(b) of the Act and Rule 10b-5. The law of insider trading is otherwise defined by judicial opinions construing Rule 10b-5, and Rule 10b5-2 does not modify the scope of insider trading law in any other respect.

(a) SCOPE OF RULE. This section shall apply to any violation of Section 10(b) of the Act (15 U.S.C. 78j(b)) and § 240.10b-5 thereunder that is based on the purchase or sale of securities on the basis of, or the communication of, material nonpublic information misappropriated in breach of a duty of trust or confidence.

(b) Enumerated "duties of trust or confidence." For purposes of this section, a "duty of trust or confidence" exists in the following circumstances, among others:

(1) Whenever a person agrees to maintain information in confidence;

(2) Whenever the person communicating the material nonpublic information and the person to whom it is communicated have a history, pattern, or practice of sharing confidences, such that the recipient of the information knows or reasonably should know that the person communicating the material nonpublic information expects that the recipient will maintain its confidentiality; or

(3) Whenever a person receives or obtains material nonpublic information from his or her spouse, parent, child, or sibling; provided, however, that the person receiving or obtaining the information may demonstrate that no duty of trust or confidence existed with respect to the information, by establishing that he or she neither knew nor reasonably should have known that the person who was the source of the information expected that the person would keep the information confidential, because of the parties' history, pattern, or practice of sharing and maintaining confidences, and because there was no agreement or understanding to maintain the confidentiality of the information.

SECTION 12. 1934 ACT ISSUER REGISTRATION REQUIREMENT

§ 78*l* Registration Requirements for Securities [Section 12]

(a) GENERAL REQUIREMENT OF REGISTRATION

It shall be unlawful for any member, broker, or dealer to effect any transaction in any security (other than an exempted security) on a national securities exchange unless a registration is effective as to such security for such exchange in accordance with the provisions of this chapter and the rules and regulations thereunder. The provisions of this subsection shall not apply in respect of a security futures product traded on a national securities exchange.

(b) PROCEDURE FOR REGISTRATION; INFORMATION A security may be registered on a national securities exchange by the issuer filing an application with the exchange (and filing with the Commission such duplicate originals thereof as the Commission may require), which application shall contain—

(1) Such information, in such detail, as to the issuer and any person directly or indirectly controlling or controlled by, or under direct or indirect common control with, the issuer, and any guarantor of the security as to principal or interest or both, as the Commission may by rules and regulations require, as necessary or appropriate in the public interest or for the protection of investors, in respect of the following:

(A) the organization, financial structure, and nature of the business;

(B) the terms, position, rights, and privileges of the different classes of securities outstanding;

(C) the terms on which their securities are to be, and during the preceding three years have been, offered to the public or otherwise;

(D) the directors, officers, and underwriters, and each security holder of record holding more than 10 per centum of any class of any equity security of the issuer (other than an exempted security), their remuneration and their interests in the securities of, and their material contracts with, the issuer and any person directly or indirectly controlling or controlled by, or under direct or indirect common control with, the issuer;

(E) remuneration to others than directors and officers exceeding $20,000 per annum;

(F) bonus and profit-sharing arrangements;

(G) management and service contracts;

(H) options existing or to be created in respect of their securities;

(I) material contracts, not made in the ordinary course of business, which are to be executed in whole or in part at or after the filing of the application or which were made not more than two years before such filing, and every material patent or contract for a material patent right shall be deemed a material contract;

(J) balance sheets for not more than the three preceding fiscal years, certified if required by the rules and regulations of the Commission by a registered public accounting firm;

(K) profit and loss statements for not more than the three preceding fiscal years, certified if required by the rules and regulations of the Commission by a registered public accounting firm; and

(L) any further financial statements which the Commission may deem necessary or appropriate for the protection of investors.

(2) Such copies of articles of incorporation, bylaws, trust indentures, or corresponding documents by whatever name known, underwriting arrangements, and other similar documents of, and voting trust agreements with respect to, the issuer and any person directly or indirectly controlling or controlled by, or under direct or indirect common control with, the issuer as the Commission may require as necessary or

appropriate for the proper protection of investors and to insure fair dealing in the security.

(3) Such copies of material contracts, referred to in paragraph (1)(I) above, as the Commission may require as necessary or appropriate for the proper protection of investors and to insure fair dealing in the security.

(c) ADDITIONAL OR ALTERNATIVE INFORMATION

If in the judgment of the Commission any information required under subsection (b) is inapplicable to any specified class or classes of issuers, the Commission shall require in lieu thereof the submission of such other information of comparable character as it may deem applicable to such class of issuers.

(d) EFFECTIVE DATE OF REGISTRATION; WITHDRAWAL OF REGISTRATION

If the exchange authorities certify to the Commission that the security has been approved by the exchange for listing and registration, the registration shall become effective thirty days after the receipt of such certification by the Commission or within such shorter period of time as the Commission may determine. A security registered with a national securities exchange may be withdrawn or stricken from listing and registration in accordance with the rules of the exchange and, upon such terms as the Commission may deem necessary to impose for the protection of investors, upon application by the issuer or the exchange to the Commission; whereupon the issuer shall be relieved from further compliance with the provisions of this section and section 78m of this title and any rules or regulations under such sections as to the securities so withdrawn or stricken. An unissued security may be registered only in accordance with such rules and regulations as the Commission may prescribe as necessary or appropriate in the public interest or for the protection of investors.

(e) EXEMPTION FROM PROVISIONS OF SECTION FOR PERIOD ENDING NOT LATER THAN JULY 1, 1935

Notwithstanding the foregoing provisions of this section, the Commission may by such rules and regulations as it deems necessary or appropriate in the public interest or for the protection of investors, permit securities listed on any exchange at the time the registration of such exchange as a national securities exchange becomes effective, to be registered for a period ending not later than July 1, 1935, without complying with the provisions of this section.

(f) UNLISTED TRADING PRIVILEGES FOR SECURITY ORIGINALLY LISTED ON ANOTHER NATIONAL EXCHANGE

(1)

(A) Notwithstanding the preceding subsections of this section, any national securities exchange, in accordance with the requirements of this subsection and the rules hereunder, may extend unlisted trading privileges to—

(i) any security that is listed and registered on a national securities exchange, subject to subparagraph (B); and

(ii) any security that is otherwise registered pursuant to this section, or that would be required to be so registered except for the exemption from registration provided in subparagraph (B) or (G) of subsection (g)(2), subject to subparagraph (E) of this paragraph.

(B) A national securities exchange may not extend unlisted trading privileges to a security described in subparagraph (A)(i) during such interval, if any, after the commencement of an initial public offering of such security, as is or may be required pursuant to subparagraph (C).

(C) Not later than 180 days after October 22, 1994, the Commission shall prescribe, by rule or regulation, the duration of the interval referred to in subparagraph (B), if any, as the Commission determines to be necessary or appropriate for the maintenance of fair and orderly markets, the protection of investors and the public interest, or otherwise in furtherance of the purposes of this chapter. Until the earlier of the effective date of such rule or regulation or 240 days after October 22, 1994, such interval shall begin at the opening of trading on the day on which such security commences trading on the national securities exchange with which such security is registered and end at the conclusion of the next day of trading.

(D) The Commission may prescribe, by rule or regulation such additional procedures or requirements for extending unlisted trading privileges to any security as the Commission deems necessary or appropriate for the maintenance of fair and orderly markets, the protection of investors and the public interest, or otherwise in furtherance of the purposes of this chapter.

(E) No extension of unlisted trading privileges to securities described in subparagraph (A)(ii) may occur except pursuant to a rule, regulation, or order of the Commission approving such extension or extensions. In promulgating such rule or regulation or in issuing such order, the Commission—

(i) shall find that such extension or extensions of unlisted trading privileges is consistent with the maintenance of fair and orderly markets, the protection of investors and the public interest, and otherwise in furtherance of the purposes of this chapter;

(ii) shall take account of the public trading activity in such securities, the character of such trading, the impact of such extension on the existing markets for such securities, and the desirability of removing impediments to and the progress that has been made toward the development of a national market system; and

(iii) shall not permit a national securities exchange to extend unlisted trading privileges to such securities if any rule of such national securities exchange would unreasonably impair the ability of a dealer to solicit or effect transactions in such securities for its own account, or would unreasonably restrict competition among dealers in such securities or between such dealers acting in the capacity of market makers who are specialists and such dealers who are not specialists.

(F) An exchange may continue to extend unlisted trading privileges in accordance with this paragraph only if the exchange and the subject security continue to satisfy the requirements for eligibility under this paragraph, including any rules and regulations issued by the Commission pursuant to this paragraph, except that unlisted trading privileges may continue with regard to securities which had been admitted on such exchange prior to July 1, 1964, notwithstanding the failure to satisfy such requirements. If unlisted trading privileges in a security are discontinued pursuant to this subparagraph, the exchange shall cease trading in that security, unless the exchange and the subject security thereafter satisfy the requirements of this paragraph and the rules issued hereunder.

(G) For purposes of this paragraph—

(i) a security is the subject of an initial public offering if—

(I) the offering of the subject security is registered under the Securities Act of 1933 [15 U.S.C. 77a et seq.]; and

(II) the issuer of the security, immediately prior to filing the registration statement with respect to the offering, was not subject to the reporting requirements of section 78m or 78o (d) of this title; and

(ii) an initial public offering of such security commences at the opening of trading on the day on which such security commences trading on the national securities exchange with which such security is registered.

(2) (A) At any time within 60 days of commencement of trading on an exchange of a security pursuant to unlisted trading privileges, the Commission may summarily suspend such unlisted trading privileges on the exchange. Such suspension shall not be reviewable under section 78y of this title and shall not be deemed to be a final agency action for purposes of section 704 of title 5. Upon such suspension—

(i) the exchange shall cease trading in the security by the close of business on the date of such suspension, or at such time as the Commission may prescribe by rule or order for the maintenance of fair and orderly markets, the protection of investors and the public interest, or otherwise in furtherance of the purposes of this chapter; and

(ii) if the exchange seeks to extend unlisted trading privileges to the security, the exchange shall file an application to reinstate its ability to do so with the Commission pursuant to such procedures as the Commission may prescribe by rule or order for the maintenance of fair and orderly markets, the protection of investors and the public interest, or otherwise in furtherance of the purposes of this chapter.

(B) A suspension under subparagraph (A) shall remain in effect until the Commission, by order, grants approval of an application to reinstate, as described in subparagraph (A)(ii).

(C) A suspension under subparagraph (A) shall not affect the validity or force of an extension of unlisted trading privileges in effect prior to such suspension.

(D) The Commission shall not approve an application by a national securities exchange to reinstate its ability to extend unlisted trading privileges to a security unless the Commission finds, after notice and opportunity for hearing, that the extension of unlisted trading privileges pursuant to such application is consistent with the maintenance of fair and orderly markets, the protection of investors and the public interest, and otherwise in furtherance of the purposes of this chapter. If the application is made to reinstate unlisted trading privileges to a security described in paragraph (1)(A)(ii), the Commission—

(i) shall take account of the public trading activity in such security, the character of such trading, the impact of such extension on the existing markets for such a security, and the desirability of removing impediments to and the progress that has been made toward the development of a national market system; and

(ii) shall not grant any such application if any rule of the national securities exchange making application under this subsection would unreasonably impair the ability of a dealer to solicit or effect transactions in such security for its own account, or would unreasonably restrict competition among dealers in such security or between such dealers acting in the capacity of marketmakers who are specialists and such dealers who are not specialists.

(3) Notwithstanding paragraph (2), the Commission shall by rules and regulations suspend unlisted trading privileges in whole or in part for any or all classes of securities for a period not exceeding twelve months, if it deems such suspension necessary or appropriate in the public interest or for the protection of investors or to prevent evasion of the purposes of this chapter.

(4) On the application of the issuer of any security for which unlisted trading privileges on any exchange have been continued or extended pursuant to this subsection, or of any broker or dealer who makes or creates a market for such security, or of any other person having a bona fide interest in the question of termination or suspension of such unlisted trading privileges, or on its own motion, the Commission shall by order terminate, or suspend for a period not exceeding twelve months, such unlisted trading privileges for such security if the Commission finds, after appropriate notice and opportunity for hearing, that such termination or suspension is necessary or appropriate in the public interest or for the protection of investors.

(5) In any proceeding under this subsection in which appropriate notice and opportunity for hearing are required, notice of not less than ten days to the applicant in such proceeding, to the issuer of the security involved, to the exchange which is seeking to continue or extend or has continued or extended unlisted trading privileges for such security, and to the exchange, if any, on which such security is listed and registered, shall be deemed adequate notice, and any broker or dealer who makes or creates a market for such security, and any other person having a bona fide interest in such proceeding, shall upon application be entitled to be heard.

(6) Any security for which unlisted trading privileges are continued or extended pursuant to this subsection shall be deemed to be registered on a national securities exchange within the meaning of this chapter. The powers and duties of the Commission under this chapter shall be applicable to the rules of an exchange in respect of any such security. The Commission may, by such rules and regulations as it deems necessary or appropriate in the public interest or for the protection of investors, either unconditionally or upon specified terms and conditions, or for stated periods, exempt such securities from the operation of any provision of section 78m,78n, or 78p of this title.

(g) REGISTRATION OF SECURITIES BY ISSUER; EXEMPTIONS

(1) Every issuer which is engaged in interstate commerce, or in a business affecting interstate commerce, or whose securities are traded by use of the mails or any means or instrumentality of interstate commerce shall—

(A) within 120 days after the last day of its first fiscal year ended on which the issuer has total assets exceeding $10,000,000 and a class of equity security (other than an exempted security) held of record by either—

(i) 2,000 persons, or

(ii) 500 persons who are not accredited investors (as such term is defined by the Commission), and

(B) in the case of an issuer that is a bank or a bank holding company, as such term is defined in section 1841 of title 12, not later than 120 days after the last day of its first fiscal year ended after the effective date of this subsection, on which the issuer has total assets exceeding $10,000,000 and a class of equity security (other than an exempted security) held of record by 2,000 or more persons,

register such security by filing with the Commission a registration statement (and such copies thereof as the Commission may require) with respect to such security containing such information and documents as the Commission may specify comparable to that which is required in an application to register a security pursuant to subsection (b) of this section. Each such registration statement shall become effective sixty days after filing with the Commission or within such shorter period as the Commission may direct. Until such registration statement becomes effective it shall not be deemed filed for the purposes ofsection 78r of this title. Any issuer may register any class of equity security not required to be registered by filing a registration statement pursuant to the provisions of this paragraph. The Commission is authorized to extend the date upon which any issuer or class of issuers is required to register a security pursuant to the provisions of this paragraph.

(2) The provisions of this subsection shall not apply in respect of—

(A) any security listed and registered on a national securities exchange.

(B) any security issued by an investment company registered pursuant to section 80a-8 of this title.

(C) any security, other than permanent stock, guaranty stock, permanent reserve stock, or any similar certificate evidencing nonwithdrawable capital, issued by a savings and loan association, building and loan association, cooperative bank, homestead association, or similar institution, which is supervised and examined by State or Federal authority having supervision over any such institution.

(D) any security of an issuer organized and operated exclusively for religious, educational, benevolent, fraternal, charitable, or reformatory purposes and not for pecuniary profit, and no part of the net earnings of which inures to the benefit of any private shareholder or individual; or any security of a fund that is excluded from the definition of an investment company under section 80a-3(c)(10)(B) of this title.

(E) any security of an issuer which is a "cooperative association" as defined in the Agricultural Marketing Act, approved June 15, 1929, as amended [12 U.S.C. 1141 et seq.], or a federation of such cooperative associations, if such federation possesses no greater powers or purposes than cooperative associations so defined.

(F) any security issued by a mutual or cooperative organization which supplies a commodity or service primarily for the benefit of its members and operates not for pecuniary profit, but only if the security is part of a class issuable only to persons who purchase commodities or services from the issuer, the security is transferable only to a successor in interest or occupancy of premises serviced or to be served by the issuer, and no dividends are payable to the holder of the security.

(G) any security issued by an insurance company if all of the following conditions are met:

(i) Such insurance company is required to and does file an annual statement with the Commissioner of Insurance (or other officer or agency performing a similar function) of its domiciliary State, and such annual statement conforms to that prescribed by the National Association of Insurance Commissioners or in the determination of such State commissioner, officer or agency substantially conforms to that so prescribed.

(ii) Such insurance company is subject to regulation by its domiciliary State of proxies, consents, or authorizations in respect of securities issued by such company and such regulation conforms to that prescribed by the National Association of Insurance Commissioners.

(iii) After July 1, 1966, the purchase and sales of securities issued by such insurance company by beneficial owners, directors, or officers of such company are subject to regulation (including reporting) by its domiciliary State substantially in the manner provided in section 78p of this title.

(H) any interest or participation in any collective trust funds maintained by a bank or in a separate account maintained by an insurance company which interest or participation is issued in connection with (i) a stock-bonus, pension, or profit-sharing plan which meets the requirements for qualification under section 401 of title 26, (ii) an annuity plan which meets the requirements for deduction of the employer's contribution under section 404(a)(2) of title 26, or (iii) a church plan, company, or account that is excluded from the definition of an investment company under section 80a-3(c)(14) of this title.

(3) The Commission may by rules or regulations or, on its own motion, after notice and opportunity for hearing, by order, exempt from this subsection any security of a foreign issuer, including any certificate of deposit for such a security, if the Commission finds that such exemption is in the public interest and is consistent with the protection of investors.

(4) Registration of any class of security pursuant to this subsection shall be terminated ninety days, or such shorter period as the Commission may determine, after the issuer files a certification with the Commission that the number of holders of record of such class of security is reduced to less than 300 persons, or, in the case of a bank or a bank holding company, as such term is defined in section 1841 of title 12, 1,200 persons persons.[1] The Commission shall after notice and opportunity for hearing deny termination of registration if it finds that the certification is untrue. Termination of registration shall be deferred pending final determination on the question of denial.

(5) For the purposes of this subsection the term "class" shall include all securities of an issuer which are of substantially similar character and the holders of which enjoy substantially similar rights and privileges. The Commission may for the purpose of this subsection define by rules and regulations the terms "total assets" and "held of record" as it deems necessary or appropriate in the public interest or for the protection of investors in order to prevent circumvention of the provisions of this subsection. For purposes of this subsection, a security futures product shall not be considered a class of equity security of the issuer of the securities underlying the security futures product. For purposes of

determining whether an issuer is required to register a security with the Commission pursuant to paragraph (1), the definition of "held of record" shall not include securities held by persons who received the securities pursuant to an employee compensation plan in transactions exempted from the registration requirements of section 5 of the Securities Act of 1933 [15 U.S.C. 77e].

(6) EXCLUSION FOR PERSONS HOLDING CERTAIN SECURITIES.—

The Commission shall, by rule, exempt, conditionally or unconditionally, securities acquired pursuant to an offering made under section 4(6) [2] of the Securities Act of 1933 [15 U.S.C. 77d(a)(6)] from the provisions of this subsection.

(h) EXEMPTION BY RULES AND REGULATIONS FROM CERTAIN PROVISIONS OF SECTION

The Commission may by rules and regulations, or upon application of an interested person, by order, after notice and opportunity for hearing, exempt in whole or in part any issuer or class of issuers from the provisions of subsection (g) of this section or from section 78m, 78n, or 78*o*(d) of this title or may exempt from section 78p of this title any officer, director, or beneficial owner of securities of any issuer, any security of which is required to be registered pursuant to subsection (g) hereof, upon such terms and conditions and for such period as it deems necessary or appropriate, if the Commission finds, by reason of the number of public investors, amount of trading interest in the securities, the nature and extent of the activities of the issuer, income or assets of the issuer, or otherwise, that such action is not inconsistent with the public interest or the protection of investors. The Commission may, for the purposes of any of the above-mentioned sections or subsections of this chapter, classify issuers and prescribe requirements appropriate for each such class.

(i) SECURITIES ISSUED BY BANKS

In respect of any securities issued by banks and savings associations the deposits of which are insured in accordance with the Federal Deposit Insurance Act [12 U.S.C. 1811et seq.], the powers, functions, and duties vested in the Commission to administer and enforce this section and sections 78j-1(m), 78m, 78n(a), 78n(c), 78n(d), 78n(f), and 78p of this title, and sections 7241, 7242, 7243, 7244, 7261(b), 7262, 7264, and 7265 of this title, (1) with respect to national banks and Federal savings associations, the accounts of which are insured by the Federal Deposit Insurance Corporation [3] are vested in the Comptroller of the Currency, (2) with respect to all other member banks of the Federal Reserve System are vested in the Board of Governors of the Federal Reserve System, and (3) with respect to all other insured banks and State savings associations, the accounts of which are insured by the Federal Deposit Insurance Corporation, are vested in the Federal Deposit Insurance Corporation. The Comptroller of the Currency, the Board of Governors of the Federal Reserve System, and the Federal Deposit Insurance Corporation shall have the power to make such rules and regulations as may be necessary for the execution of the functions vested in them as provided in this subsection. In carrying out their responsibilities under this subsection, the agencies named in the first sentence of this subsection shall issue substantially similar regulations to regulations and rules issued by the Commission under this section and sections 78j-1(m), 78m, 78n(a), 78n(c), 78n(d), 78n(f), and 78p of this title, and sections 7241, 7242, 7243, 7244, 7261(b), 7262, 7264, and 7265 of this title, unless they find that implementation of substantially similar regulations with respect to insured banks and insured institutions are not necessary or appropriate in the public interest or for protection of investors, and publish such findings, and the detailed reasons therefor, in the Federal Register. Such regulations of the above-named agencies, or the reasons for failure to publish such substantially similar regulations to those of the Commission, shall be published in the Federal Register within 120 days of October 28, 1974 are vested in the Comptroller of the Currency, (2) with respect to all other member banks of the Federal Reserve System are vested in the Board of Governors of the Federal Reserve System, and (3) with respect to all other insured banks and State savings associations, the accounts of which are insured by the Federal Deposit Insurance Corporation, are vested in the Federal Deposit Insurance Corporation. The Comptroller of the Currency, the Board of Governors of the Federal Reserve System, and the Federal Deposit Insurance Corporation shall have the power to make such rules and regulations as may be necessary for the execution of the functions vested in them as provided in this subsection. In carrying out their responsibilities under this subsection, the agencies named in the first sentence of this subsection shall issue substantially similar regulations to regulations and rules issued by the Commission under this section and sections 78j-1(m), 78m, 78n(a), 78n(c), 78n(d), 78n(f), and 78p of this title, andsections7241, 7242, 7243, 7244, 7261(b), 7262, 7264, and 7265 of this title, unless they find that implementation of substantially similar regulations with respect to insured banks and insured institutions are not necessary or appropriate in the public interest or for protection of investors, and publish such findings, and the detailed reasons therefor, in the Federal Register. Such regulations of the above-named agencies, or the reasons for failure to publish such substantially similar regulations to those of the Commission, shall be published in the Federal Register within 120 days of

(j) DENIAL, SUSPENSION, OR REVOCATION OF REGISTRATION; NOTICE AND HEARING

The Commission is authorized, by order, as it deems necessary or appropriate for the protection of investors to deny, to suspend the effective date of, to suspend for a period not exceeding twelve months, or to revoke the registration of a security, if the Commission finds, on the record after notice and opportunity for hearing, that the issuer, of such security has failed to comply with any provision of this chapter or the rules and regulations thereunder. No member of a national securities exchange, broker, or dealer shall make use of the mails or any means or instrumentality of interstate commerce to effect any transaction in, or to induce the purchase or sale of, any security the registration of which has been and is suspended or revoked pursuant to the preceding sentence.

(k) TRADING SUSPENSIONS; EMERGENCY AUTHORITY

(1) TRADING SUSPENSIONS If in its opinion the public interest and the protection of investors so require, the Commission is authorized by order—

(A) summarily to suspend trading in any security (other than an exempted security) for a period not exceeding 10 business days, and

(B) summarily to suspend all trading on any national securities exchange or otherwise, in securities other than exempted securities, for a period not exceeding 90 calendar days.

The action described in subparagraph (B) shall not take effect unless the Commission notifies the President of its decision and the President notifies the Commission that the President does not disapprove of such decision. If the actions described in subparagraph (A) or (B) involve a security futures product, the Commission shall consult with and consider the views of the Commodity Futures Trading Commission.

(2) EMERGENCY ORDERS

(A) In general

The Commission, in an emergency, may by order summarily take such action to alter, supplement, suspend, or impose requirements or restrictions with respect to any matter or action subject to regulation by the Commission or a self-regulatory organization under the securities laws, as the Commission determines is necessary in the public interest and for the protection of investors—

(i) to maintain or restore fair and orderly securities markets (other than markets in exempted securities);

(ii) to ensure prompt, accurate, and safe clearance and settlement of transactions in securities (other than exempted securities); or

(iii) to reduce, eliminate, or prevent the substantial disruption by the emergency of—

(I) securities markets (other than markets in exempted securities), investment companies, or any other significant portion or segment of such markets; or

(II) the transmission or processing of securities transactions (other than transactions in exempted securities).

(B) Effective period

An order of the Commission under this paragraph shall continue in effect for the period specified by the Commission, and may be extended. Except as provided in subparagraph (C), an order of the Commission under this paragraph may not continue in effect for more than 10 business days, including extensions.

(C) Extension

An order of the Commission under this paragraph may be extended to continue in effect for more than 10 business days if, at the time of the extension, the Commission finds that the emergency still exists and determines that the continuation of the order beyond 10 business days is necessary in the public interest and for the protection of investors to attain an objective described in clause (i), (ii), or (iii) of subparagraph (A). In no event shall an order of the Commission under this paragraph continue in effect for more than 30 calendar days.

(D) Security futures

If the actions described in subparagraph (A) involve a security futures product, the Commission shall consult with and consider the views of the Commodity Futures Trading Commission.

(E) ExemptionIn exercising its authority under this paragraph, the Commission shall not be required to comply with the provisions of—

(i) section 78s(c) of this title; or

(ii) section 553 of title 5.

(3) TERMINATION OF EMERGENCY ACTIONS BY PRESIDENT

The President may direct that action taken by the Commission under paragraph (1)(B) or paragraph (2) of this subsection shall not continue in effect.

(4) COMPLIANCE WITH ORDERS

No member of a national securities exchange, broker, or dealer shall make use of the mails or any means or instrumentality of interstate commerce to effect any transaction in, or to induce the purchase or sale of, any security in contravention of an order of the Commission under this subsection unless such order has been stayed, modified, or set aside as provided in paragraph (5) of this subsection or has ceased to be effective upon direction of the President as provided in paragraph (3).

(5) LIMITATIONS ON REVIEW OF ORDERS

An order of the Commission pursuant to this subsection shall be subject to review only as provided in section 78y(a) of this title. Review shall be based on an examination of all the information before the Commission at the time such order was issued. The reviewing court shall not enter a stay, writ of mandamus, or similar relief unless the court finds, after notice and hearing before a panel of the court, that the Commission's action is arbitrary, capricious, an abuse of discretion, or otherwise not in accordance with law.

(6) CONSULTATION

Prior to taking any action described in paragraph (1)(B), the Commission shall consult with and consider the views of the Secretary of the Treasury, the Board of Governors of the Federal Reserve System, and the Commodity Futures Trading Commission, unless such consultation is impracticable in light of the emergency.

(7) DEFINITION

For purposes of this subsection, the term "emergency" means—

(A) a major market disturbance characterized by or constituting—

(i) sudden and excessive fluctuations of securities prices generally, or a substantial threat thereof, that threaten fair and orderly markets; or

(ii) a substantial disruption of the safe or efficient operation of the national system for clearance and settlement of transactions in securities, or a substantial threat thereof; or

(B) a major disturbance that substantially disrupts, or threatens to substantially disrupt—

(i) the functioning of securities markets, investment companies, or any other significant portion or segment of the securities markets; or

(ii) the transmission or processing of securities transactions.

(*l*) ISSUANCE OF ANY SECURITY IN CONTRAVENTION OF RULES AND REGULATIONS; APPLICATION TO ANNUITY CONTRACTS AND VARIABLE LIFE POLICIES

It shall be unlawful for an issuer, any class of whose securities is registered pursuant to this section or would be required to be so registered except for the exemption from registration provided by subsection (g)(2)(B) or (g)(2)(G) of this section, by the use of any means or instrumentality of interstate commerce, or of the mails, to issue, either originally or upon transfer, any of such securities in a form or with a format which contravenes such rules and regulations as the Commission may prescribe as necessary or appropriate for the prompt and accurate clearance and settlement of transactions in securities. The provisions of this subsection shall not apply to variable annuity contracts or variable life policies issued by an insurance company or its separate accounts.

SECTION 13(a)-(b). ISSUER REPORTING REQUIREMENTS

§ 78m Periodical and Other Reports [Section 13]

(a) REPORTS BY ISSUER OF SECURITY; CONTENTS

Every issuer of a security registered pursuant to section 78 of this title shall file with the Commission, in accordance with such rules and regulations as the Commission may prescribe as necessary or appropriate for the proper protection of investors and to insure fair dealing in the security—

(1) such information and documents (and such copies thereof) as the Commission shall require to keep reasonably current the information and documents required to be included in or filed with an application or registration statement filed pursuant to section 78 of this title, except

that the Commission may not require the filing of any material contract wholly executed before July 1, 1962.

(2) such annual reports (and such copies thereof), certified if required by the rules and regulations of the Commission by independent public accountants, and such quarterly reports (and such copies thereof), as the Commission may prescribe.

Every issuer of a security registered on a national securities exchange shall also file a duplicate original of such information, documents, and reports with the exchange. In any registration statement, periodic report, or other reports to be filed with the Commission, an emerging growth company need not present selected financial data in accordance with section 229.301 of title 17, Code of Federal Regulations, for any period prior to the earliest audited period presented in connection with its first registration statement that became effective under this chapter or the Securities Act of 1933 [15 U.S.C. 77a et seq.] and, with respect to any such statement or reports, an emerging growth company may not be required to comply with any new or revised financial accounting standard until such date that a company that is not an issuer (as defined under section 7201 of this title) is required to comply with such new or revised accounting standard, if such standard applies to companies that are not issuers.

(b) FORM OF REPORT; BOOKS, RECORDS, AND INTERNAL ACCOUNTING; DIRECTIVES

(1) The Commission may prescribe, in regard to reports made pursuant to this chapter, the form or forms in which the required information shall be set forth, the items or details to be shown in the balance sheet and the earnings statement, and the methods to be followed in the preparation of reports, in the appraisal or valuation of assets and liabilities, in the determination of depreciation and depletion, in the differentiation of recurring and nonrecurring income, in the differentiation of investment and operating income, and in the preparation, where the Commission deems it necessary or desirable, of separate and/or consolidated balance sheets or income accounts of any person directly or indirectly controlling or controlled by the issuer, or any person under direct or indirect common control with the issuer; but in the case of the reports of any person whose methods of accounting are prescribed under the provisions of any law of the United States, or any rule or regulation thereunder, the rules and regulations of the Commission with respect to reports shall not be inconsistent with the requirements imposed by such law or rule or regulation in respect of the same subject matter (except that such rules and regulations of the Commission may be inconsistent with such requirements to the extent that the Commission determines that the public interest or the protection of investors so requires).

(2) Every issuer which has a class of securities registered pursuant to section 78 of this title and every issuer which is required to file reports pursuant to section 78o (d) of this title shall—

(A) make and keep books, records, and accounts, which, in reasonable detail, accurately and fairly reflect the transactions and dispositions of the assets of the issuer;

(B) devise and maintain a system of internal accounting controls sufficient to provide reasonable assurances that—

(i) transactions are executed in accordance with management's general or specific authorization;

(ii) transactions are recorded as necessary (I) to permit preparation of financial statements in conformity with generally accepted accounting principles or any other criteria applicable to such statements, and (II) to maintain accountability for assets;

(iii) access to assets is permitted only in accordance with management's general or specific authorization; and

(iv) the recorded accountability for assets is compared with the existing assets at reasonable intervals and appropriate action is taken with respect to any differences; and

(C) notwithstanding any other provision of law, pay the allocable share of such issuer of a reasonable annual accounting support fee or fees, determined in accordance with section 7219 of this title.

(3)(A) With respect to matters concerning the national security of the United States, no duty or liability under paragraph (2) of this subsection shall be imposed upon any person acting in cooperation with the head of any Federal department or agency responsible for such matters if such act in cooperation with such head of a department or agency was done upon the specific, written directive of the head of such department or agency pursuant to Presidential authority to issue such directives. Each directive issued under this paragraph shall set forth the specific facts and circumstances with respect to which the provisions of this paragraph are to be invoked. Each such directive shall, unless renewed in writing, expire one year after the date of issuance.

(B) Each head of a Federal department or agency of the United States who issues a directive pursuant to this paragraph shall maintain a complete file of all such directives and shall, on October 1 of each year, transmit a summary of matters covered by such directives in force at any time during the previous year to the Permanent Select Committee on Intelligence of the House of Representatives and the Select Committee on Intelligence of the Senate.

(4) No criminal liability shall be imposed for failing to comply with the requirements of paragraph (2) of this subsection except as provided in paragraph (5) of this subsection.

(5) No person shall knowingly circumvent or knowingly fail to implement a system of internal accounting controls or knowingly falsify any book, record, or account described in paragraph (2).

(6) Where an issuer which has a class of securities registered pursuant to section 78*l* of this title or an issuer which is required to file

reports pursuant to section 78*o*(d) of this title holds 50 per centum or less of the voting power with respect to a domestic or foreign firm, the provisions of paragraph (2) require only that the issuer proceed in good faith to use its influence, to the extent reasonable under the issuer's circumstances, to cause such domestic or foreign firm to devise and maintain a system of internal accounting controls consistent with paragraph (2). Such circumstances include the relative degree of the issuer's ownership of the domestic or foreign firm and the laws and practices governing the business operations of the country in which such firm is located. An issuer which demonstrates good faith efforts to use such influence shall be conclusively presumed to have complied with the requirements of paragraph (2).

(7) For the purpose of paragraph (2) of this subsection, the terms "reasonable assurances" and "reasonable detail" mean such level of detail and degree of assurance as would satisfy prudent officials in the conduct of their own affairs.

(c) ALTERNATIVE REPORTS

If in the judgment of the Commission any report required under subsection (a) is inapplicable to any specified class or classes of issuers, the Commission shall require in lieu thereof the submission of such reports of comparable character as it may deem applicable to such class or classes of issuers.

(d) REPORTS BY PERSONS ACQUIRING MORE THAN FIVE PER CENTUM OF CERTAIN CLASSES OF SECURITIES

(1) Any person who, after acquiring directly or indirectly the beneficial ownership of any equity security of a class which is registered pursuant to section 78*l* of this title, or any equity security of an insurance company which would have been required to be so registered except for the exemption contained in section 781 (g)(2)(G) of this title, or any equity security issued by a closed-end investment company registered under the Investment Company Act of 1940 [15 U.S.C. 80a-1 et seq.] or any equity security issued by a Native Corporation pursuant to section 1629c(d)(6) of title 43, or otherwise becomes or is deemed to become a beneficial owner of any of the foregoing upon the purchase or sale of a security-based swap that the Commission may define by rule, and is directly or indirectly the beneficial owner of more than 5 per centum of such class shall, within ten days after such acquisition or within such shorter time as the Commission may establish by rule, file with the Commission, a statement containing such of the following information, and such additional information, as the Commission may by rules and regulations, prescribe as necessary or appropriate in the public interest or for the protection of investors—

(A) the background, and identity, residence, and citizenship of, and the nature of such beneficial ownership by, such person and all other persons by whom or on whose behalf the purchases have been or are to be effected;

(B) the source and amount of the funds or other consideration used or to be used in making the purchases, and if any part of the purchase price is represented or is to be represented by funds or other consideration borrowed or otherwise obtained for the purpose of acquiring, holding, or trading such security, a description of the transaction and the names of the parties thereto, except that where a source of funds is a loan made in the ordinary course of business by a bank, as defined in section 78c(a)(6) of this title, if the person filing such statement so requests, the name of the bank shall not be made available to the public;

(C) if the purpose of the purchases or prospective purchases is to acquire control of the business of the issuer of the securities, any plans or proposals which such persons may have to liquidate such issuer, to sell its assets to or merge it with any other persons, or to make any other major change in its business or corporate structure;

(D) the number of shares of such security which are beneficially owned, and the number of shares concerning which there is a right to acquire, directly or indirectly, by (i) such person, and (ii) by each associate of such person, giving the background, identity, residence, and citizenship of each such associate; and

(E) information as to any contracts, arrangements, or understandings with any person with respect to any securities of the issuer, including but not limited to transfer of any of the securities, joint ventures, loan or option arrangements, puts or calls, guaranties of loans, guaranties against loss or guaranties of profits, division of losses or profits, or the giving or withholding of proxies, naming the persons with whom such contracts, arrangements, or understandings have been entered into, and giving the details thereof.

(2) If any material change occurs in the facts set forth in the statement filed with the Commission, an amendment shall be filed with the Commission, in accordance with such rules and regulations as the Commission may prescribe as necessary or appropriate in the public interest or for the protection of investors.

(3) When two or more persons act as a partnership, limited partnership, syndicate, or other group for the purpose of acquiring, holding, or disposing of securities of an issuer, such syndicate or group shall be deemed a "person" for the purposes of this subsection.

(4) In determining, for purposes of this subsection, any percentage of a class of any security, such class shall be deemed to consist of the amount of the outstanding securities of such class, exclusive of any securities of such class held by or for the account of the issuer or a subsidiary of the issuer.

(5) The Commission, by rule or regulation or by order, may permit any person to file in lieu of the statement required by paragraph (1) of this subsection or the rules and regulations thereunder, a notice stating the name of such person, the number of shares of any equity securities

subject to paragraph (1) which are owned by him, the date of their acquisition and such other information as the Commission may specify, if it appears to the Commission that such securities were acquired by such person in the ordinary course of his business and were not acquired for the purpose of and do not have the effect of changing or influencing the control of the issuer nor in connection with or as a participant in any transaction having such purpose or effect.

(6) The provisions of this subsection shall not apply to—

(A) any acquisition or offer to acquire securities made or proposed to be made by means of a registration statement under the Securities Act of 1933 [15 U.S.C. 77a et seq.];

(B) any acquisition of the beneficial ownership of a security which, together with all other acquisitions by the same person of securities of the same class during the preceding twelve months, does not exceed 2 per centum of that class;

(C) any acquisition of an equity security by the issuer of such security;

(D) any acquisition or proposed acquisition of a security which the Commission, by rules or regulations or by order, shall exempt from the provisions of this subsection as not entered into for the purpose of, and not having the effect of, changing or influencing the control of the issuer or otherwise as not comprehended within the purposes of this subsection.

(e) PURCHASE OF SECURITIES BY ISSUER

(1) It shall be unlawful for an issuer which has a class of equity securities registered pursuant to section 78*l* of this title, or which is a closed-end investment company registered under the Investment Company Act of 1940 [15 U.S.C. 80a-1 et seq.], to purchase any equity security issued by it if such purchase is in contravention of such rules and regulations as the Commission, in the public interest or for the protection of investors, may adopt (A) to define acts and practices which are fraudulent, deceptive, or manipulative, and (B) to prescribe means reasonably designed to prevent such acts and practices. Such rules and regulations may require such issuer to provide holders of equity securities of such class with such information relating to the reasons for such purchase, the source of funds, the number of shares to be purchased, the price to be paid for such securities, the method of purchase, and such additional information, as the Commission deems necessary or appropriate in the public interest or for the protection of investors, or which the Commission deems to be material to a determination whether such security should be sold.

(2) For the purpose of this subsection, a purchase by or for the issuer or any person controlling, controlled by, or under common control with the issuer, or a purchase subject to control of the issuer or any such person, shall be deemed to be a purchase by the issuer. The Commission shall have power to make rules and regulations implementing this

paragraph in the public interest and for the protection of investors, including exemptive rules and regulations covering situations in which the Commission deems it unnecessary or inappropriate that a purchase of the type described in this paragraph shall be deemed to be a purchase by the issuer for purposes of some or all of the provisions of paragraph (1) of this subsection.

(3) At the time of filing such statement as the Commission may require by rule pursuant to paragraph (1) of this subsection, the person making the filing shall pay to the Commission a fee at a rate that, subject to paragraph (4), is equal to $92 per $1,000,000 of the value of securities proposed to be purchased. The fee shall be reduced with respect to securities in an amount equal to any fee paid with respect to any securities issued in connection with the proposed transaction under section 6(b) of the Securities Act of 1933 [15 U.S.C. 77f(b)], or the fee paid under that section shall be reduced in an amount equal to the fee paid to the Commission in connection with such transaction under this paragraph.

(4) ANNUAL ADJUSTMENT.—

For each fiscal year, the Commission shall by order adjust the rate required by paragraph (3) for such fiscal year to a rate that is equal to the rate (expressed in dollars per million) that is applicable under section 6(b) of the Securities Act of 1933 [15 U.S.C. 77f(b)] for such fiscal year.

(5) FEE COLLECTIONS.—

Fees collected pursuant to this subsection for fiscal year 2012 and each fiscal year thereafter shall be deposited and credited as general revenue of the Treasury and shall not be available for obligation.

(6) EFFECTIVE DATE; PUBLICATION.—

In exercising its authority under this subsection, the Commission shall not be required to comply with the provisions of section 553 of title 5. An adjusted rate prescribed under paragraph (4) shall be published and take effect in accordance with section 6(b) of the Securities Act of 1933 (15 U.S.C. 77f(b)).

(7) PRO RATA APPLICATION.—

The rates per $1,000,000 required by this subsection shall be applied pro rata to amounts and balances of less than $1,000,000.

(f) REPORTS BY INSTITUTIONAL INVESTMENT MANAGERS

(1) Every institutional investment manager which uses the mails, or any means or instrumentality of interstate commerce in the course of its business as an institutional investment manager and which exercises investment discretion with respect to accounts holding equity securities of a class described in subsection (d)(1) or otherwise becomes or is deemed to become a beneficial owner of any security of a class described in subsection (d)(1) upon the purchase or sale of a security-based swap that the Commission may define by rule, having an aggregate fair market value on the last trading day in any of the preceding twelve months of at least $100,000,000 or such lesser amount (but in no case less than

$10,000,000) as the Commission, by rule, may determine, shall file reports with the Commission in such form, for such periods, and at such times after the end of such periods as the Commission, by rule, may prescribe, but in no event shall such reports be filed for periods longer than one year or shorter than one quarter. Such reports shall include for each such equity security held on the last day of the reporting period by accounts (in aggregate or by type as the Commission, by rule, may prescribe) with respect to which the institutional investment manager exercises investment discretion (other than securities held in amounts which the Commission, by rule, determines to be insignificant for purposes of this subsection), the name of the issuer and the title, class, CUSIP number, number of shares or principal amount, and aggregate fair market value of each such security. Such reports may also include for accounts (in aggregate or by type) with respect to which the institutional investment manager exercises investment discretion such of the following information as the Commission, by rule, prescribes—

(A) the name of the issuer and the title, class, CUSIP number, number of shares or principal amount, and aggregate fair market value or cost or amortized cost of each other security (other than an exempted security) held on the last day of the reporting period by such accounts;

(B) the aggregate fair market value or cost or amortized cost of exempted securities (in aggregate or by class) held on the last day of the reporting period by such accounts;

(C) the number of shares of each equity security of a class described in subsection (d)(1) held on the last day of the reporting period by such accounts with respect to which the institutional investment manager possesses sole or shared authority to exercise the voting rights evidenced by such securities;

(D) the aggregate purchases and aggregate sales during the reporting period of each security (other than an exempted security) effected by or for such accounts; and

(E) with respect to any transaction or series of transactions having a market value of at least $500,000 or such other amount as the Commission, by rule, may determine, effected during the reporting period by or for such accounts in any equity security of a class described in subsection (d)(1)—

(i) the name of the issuer and the title, class, and CUSIP number of the security;

(ii) the number of shares or principal amount of the security involved in the transaction;

(iii) whether the transaction was a purchase or sale;

(iv) the per share price or prices at which the transaction was effected;

(v) the date or dates of the transaction;

(vi) the date or dates of the settlement of the transaction;

(vii) the broker or dealer through whom the transaction was effected;

(viii) the market or markets in which the transaction was effected; and

(ix) such other related information as the Commission, by rule, may prescribe.

(2) The Commission shall prescribe rules providing for the public disclosure of the name of the issuer and the title, class, CUSIP number, aggregate amount of the number of short sales of each security, and any additional information determined by the Commission following the end of the reporting period. At a minimum, such public disclosure shall occur every month.

(3) The Commission, by rule, or order, may exempt, conditionally or unconditionally, any institutional investment manager or security or any class of institutional investment managers or securities from any or all of the provisions of this subsection or the rules thereunder.

(4) The Commission shall make available to the public for a reasonable fee a list of all equity securities of a class described in subsection (d)(1), updated no less frequently than reports are required to be filed pursuant to paragraph (1) of this subsection. The Commission shall tabulate the information contained in any report filed pursuant to this subsection in a manner which will, in the view of the Commission, maximize the usefulness of the information to other Federal and State authorities and the public. Promptly after the filing of any such report, the Commission shall make the information contained therein conveniently available to the public for a reasonable fee in such form as the Commission, by rule, may prescribe, except that the Commission, as it determines to be necessary or appropriate in the public interest or for the protection of investors, may delay or prevent public disclosure of any such information in accordance with section 552 of title 5. Notwithstanding the preceding sentence, any such information identifying the securities held by the account of a natural person or an estate or trust (other than a business trust or investment company) shall not be disclosed to the public.

(5) In exercising its authority under this subsection, the Commission shall determine (and so state) that its action is necessary or appropriate in the public interest and for the protection of investors or to maintain fair and orderly markets or, in granting an exemption, that its action is consistent with the protection of investors and the purposes of this subsection. In exercising such authority the Commission shall take such steps as are within its power, including consulting with the Comptroller General of the United States, the Director of the Office of Management and Budget, the appropriate regulatory agencies, Federal and State authorities which, directly or indirectly, require reports from institutional investment managers of information substantially similar to

that called for by this subsection, national securities exchanges, and registered securities associations, (A) to achieve uniform, centralized reporting of information concerning the securities holdings of and transactions by or for accounts with respect to which institutional investment managers exercise investment discretion, and (B) consistently with the objective set forth in the preceding subparagraph, to avoid unnecessarily duplicative reporting by, and minimize the compliance burden on, institutional investment managers. Federal authorities which, directly or indirectly, require reports from institutional investment managers of information substantially similar to that called for by this subsection shall cooperate with the Commission in the performance of its responsibilities under the preceding sentence. An institutional investment manager which is a bank, the deposits of which are insured in accordance with the Federal Deposit Insurance Act [12 U.S.C. 1811 et seq.], shall file with the appropriate regulatory agency a copy of every report filed with the Commission pursuant to this subsection.

(6)(A) For purposes of this subsection the term "institutional investment manager" includes any person, other than a natural person, investing in or buying and selling securities for its own account, and any person exercising investment discretion with respect to the account of any other person.

(B) The Commission shall adopt such rules as it deems necessary or appropriate to prevent duplicative reporting pursuant to this subsection by two or more institutional investment managers exercising investment discretion with respect to the same amount.[1]

(g) STATEMENT OF EQUITY SECURITY OWNERSHIP

(1)Any person who is directly or indirectly the beneficial owner of more than 5 per centum of any security of a class described in subsection (d)(1) of this section or otherwise becomes or is deemed to become a beneficial owner of any security of a class described in subsection (d)(1) upon the purchase or sale of a security-based swap that the Commission may define by rule shall file with the Commission a statement setting forth, in such form and at such time as the Commission may, by rule, prescribe—

(A) such person's identity, residence, and citizenship; and

(B) the number and description of the shares in which such person has an interest and the nature of such interest.

(2) If any material change occurs in the facts set forth in the statement filed with the Commission, an amendment shall be filed with the Commission, in accordance with such rules and regulations as the Commission may prescribe as necessary or appropriate in the public interest or for the protection of investors.

(3) When two or more persons act as a partnership, limited partnership, syndicate, or other group for the purpose of acquiring, holding, or disposing of securities of an issuer, such syndicate or group shall be deemed a "person" for the purposes of this subsection.

(4) In determining, for purposes of this subsection, any percentage of a class of any security, such class shall be deemed to consist of the amount of the outstanding securities of such class, exclusive of any securities of such class held by or for the account of the issuer or a subsidiary of the issuer.

(5) In exercising its authority under this subsection, the Commission shall take such steps as it deems necessary or appropriate in the public interest or for the protection of investors (A) to achieve centralized reporting of information regarding ownership, (B) to avoid unnecessarily duplicative reporting by and minimize the compliance burden on persons required to report, and (C) to tabulate and promptly make available the information contained in any report filed pursuant to this subsection in a manner which will, in the view of the Commission, maximize the usefulness of the information to other Federal and State agencies and the public.

(6) The Commission may, by rule or order, exempt, in whole or in part, any person or class of persons from any or all of the reporting requirements of this subsection as it deems necessary or appropriate in the public interest or for the protection of investors.

(h) LARGE TRADER REPORTING

(1) IDENTIFICATION REQUIREMENTS FOR LARGE TRADERS For the purpose of monitoring the impact on the securities markets of securities transactions involving a substantial volume or a large fair market value or exercise value and for the purpose of otherwise assisting the Commission in the enforcement of this chapter, each large trader shall—

(A) provide such information to the Commission as the Commission may by rule or regulation prescribe as necessary or appropriate, identifying such large trader and all accounts in or through which such large trader effects such transactions; and

(B) identify, in accordance with such rules or regulations as the Commission may prescribe as necessary or appropriate, to any registered broker or dealer by or through whom such large trader directly or indirectly effects securities transactions, such large trader and all accounts directly or indirectly maintained with such broker or dealer by such large trader in or through which such transactions are effected.

(2) RECORDKEEPING AND REPORTING REQUIREMENTS FOR BROKERS AND DEALERS

Every registered broker or dealer shall make and keep for prescribed periods such records as the Commission by rule or regulation prescribes as necessary or appropriate in the public interest, for the protection of investors, or otherwise in furtherance of the purposes of this chapter, with respect to securities transactions that equal or exceed the reporting activity level effected directly or indirectly by or through such registered broker or dealer of or for any person that such broker or dealer knows is a large trader, or any person that such broker or dealer has reason to know is a large trader on the basis of transactions in securities effected by or through such broker or dealer. Such records shall be available for reporting to the Commission, or any self-regulatory organization that the Commission shall designate to receive such reports, on the morning of the day following the day the transactions were effected, and shall be reported to the Commission or a self-regulatory organization designated by the Commission immediately upon request by the Commission or such a self-regulatory organization. Such records and reports shall be in a format and transmitted in a manner prescribed by the Commission (including, but not limited to, machine readable form).

(3) AGGREGATION RULES

The Commission may prescribe rules or regulations governing the manner in which transactions and accounts shall be aggregated for the purpose of this subsection, including aggregation on the basis of common ownership or control.

(4) EXAMINATION OF BROKER AND DEALER RECORDS

All records required to be made and kept by registered brokers and dealers pursuant to this subsection with respect to transactions effected by large traders are subject at any time, or from time to time, to such reasonable periodic, special, or other examinations by representatives of the Commission as the Commission deems necessary or appropriate in the public interest, for the protection of investors, or otherwise in furtherance of the purposes of this chapter.

(5) FACTORS TO BE CONSIDERED IN COMMISSION ACTIONS In exercising its authority under this subsection, the Commission shall take into account—

(A) existing reporting systems;

(B) the costs associated with maintaining information with respect to transactions effected by large traders and reporting such information to the Commission or self-regulatory organizations; and

(C) the relationship between the United States and international securities markets.

(6) EXEMPTIONS

The Commission, by rule, regulation, or order, consistent with the purposes of this chapter, may exempt any person or class of persons or any transaction or class of transactions, either conditionally or upon specified terms and conditions or for stated periods, from the operation of this subsection, and the rules and regulations thereunder.

(7) AUTHORITY OF COMMISSION TO LIMIT DISCLOSURE OF INFORMATION

Notwithstanding any other provision of law, the Commission shall not be compelled to disclose any information required to be kept or reported under this subsection. Nothing in this subsection shall authorize the Commission to withhold information from Congress, or prevent the Commission from complying with a request for information from any other Federal department or agency requesting information for purposes within the scope of its jurisdiction, or complying with an order of a court of the United States in an action brought by the United States or the Commission. For purposes of section 552 of title 5, this subsection shall be considered a statute described in subsection (b)(3)(B) of such section 552.

(8) DEFINITIONS For purposes of this subsection—

(A) the term "large trader" means every person who, for his own account or an account for which he exercises investment discretion, effects transactions for the purchase or sale of any publicly traded security or securities by use of any means or instrumentality of interstate commerce or of the mails, or of any facility of a national securities exchange, directly or indirectly by or through a registered broker or dealer in an aggregate amount equal to or in excess of the identifying activity level;

(B) the term "publicly traded security" means any equity security (including an option on individual equity securities, and an option on a group or index of such securities) listed, or admitted to unlisted trading privileges, on a national securities exchange, or quoted in an automated interdealer quotation system;

(C) the term "identifying activity level" means transactions in publicly traded securities at or above a level of volume, fair market value, or exercise value as shall be fixed from time to time by the Commission by rule or regulation, specifying the time interval during which such transactions shall be aggregated;

(D) the term "reporting activity level" means transactions in publicly traded securities at or above a level of volume, fair market value, or exercise value as shall be fixed from time to time by the Commission by rule, regulation, or order, specifying the time interval during which such transactions shall be aggregated; and

(E) the term "person" has the meaning given in section 78c(a)(9) of this title and also includes two or more persons acting as a partnership, limited partnership, syndicate, or other group, but does not include a foreign central bank.

(i) ACCURACY OF FINANCIAL REPORTS

Each financial report that contains financial statements, and that is required to be prepared in accordance with (or reconciled to) generally accepted accounting principles under this chapter and filed with the Commission shall reflect all material correcting adjustments that have been identified by a registered public accounting firm in accordance with generally accepted accounting principles and the rules and regulations of the Commission.

(j) OFF-BALANCE SHEET TRANSACTIONS

Not later than 180 days after July 30, 2002, the Commission shall issue final rules providing that each annual and quarterly financial report required to be filed with the Commission shall disclose all material off-balance sheet transactions, arrangements, obligations (including contingent obligations), and other relationships of the issuer with unconsolidated entities or other persons, that may have a material current or future effect on financial condition, changes in financial condition, results of operations, liquidity, capital expenditures, capital resources, or significant components of revenues or expenses.

(k) PROHIBITION ON PERSONAL LOANS TO EXECUTIVES

(1) IN GENERAL

It shall be unlawful for any issuer (as defined in section 7201 of this title), directly or indirectly, including through any subsidiary, to extend or maintain credit, to arrange for the extension of credit, or to renew an extension of credit, in the form of a personal loan to or for any director or executive officer (or equivalent thereof) of that issuer. An extension of credit maintained by the issuer on July 30, 2002, shall not be subject to the provisions of this subsection, provided that there is no material modification to any term of any such extension of credit or any renewal of any such extension of credit on or after July 30, 2002.

(2) LIMITATION

Paragraph (1) does not preclude any home improvement and manufactured home loans (as that term is defined in section 1464 of title 12), consumer credit (as defined in section 1602 of this title), or any extension of credit under an open end credit plan (as defined in section 1602 of this title), or a charge card (as defined in section 1637(c)(4)(e) of this title), or any extension of credit by a broker or dealer registered under section 78*o* of this title to an employee of that broker or dealer to buy, trade, or carry securities, that is permitted under rules or regulations of the Board of Governors of the Federal Reserve System pursuant to section 78g of this title (other than an extension of credit that would be used to purchase the stock of that issuer), that is—

(A) made or provided in the ordinary course of the consumer credit business of such issuer;

(B) of a type that is generally made available by such issuer to the public; and

(C) made by such issuer on market terms, or terms that are no more favorable than those offered by the issuer to the general public for such extensions of credit.

(3) RULE OF CONSTRUCTION FOR CERTAIN LOANS

Paragraph (1) does not apply to any loan made or maintained by an insured depository institution (as defined in section 3 of the Federal Deposit Insurance Act (12 U.S.C. 1813)), if the loan is subject to the insider lending restrictions of section 375b of title 12.

(*l*) REAL TIME ISSUER DISCLOSURES

Each issuer reporting under subsec. (a) or section 78*o*(d) of this title shall disclose to the public on a rapid and current basis such additional information concerning material changes in the financial condition or operations of the issuer, in plain English, which may include trend and qualitative information and graphic presentations, as the Commission determines, by rule, is necessary or useful for the protection of investors and in the public interest.

(m) PUBLIC AVAILABILITY OF SECURITY-BASED SWAP TRANSACTION DATA

(1) IN GENERAL

(A) Definition of real-time public reporting

In this paragraph, the term "real-time public reporting" means to report data relating to a security-based swap transaction, including price and volume, as soon as technologically practicable after the time at which the security-based swap transaction has been executed.

(B) Purpose

The purpose of this subsection is to authorize the Commission to make security-based swap transaction and pricing data available to the public in such form and at such times as the Commission determines appropriate to enhance price discovery.

(C) General rule

The Commission is authorized to provide by rule for the public availability of security-based swap transaction, volume, and pricing data as follows:

(i) With respect to those security-based swaps that are subject to the mandatory clearing requirement described in section 78c-3(a)(1) of this title(including those security-based swaps that are excepted from the requirement pursuant to section 78c-3(g) of this title), the Commission shall require real-time public reporting for such transactions.

(ii) With respect to those security-based swaps that are not subject to the mandatory clearing requirement described in section 78c-3(a)(1) of this title, but are cleared at a registered clearing agency, the Commission shall require real-time public reporting for such transactions.

(iii) With respect to security-based swaps that are not cleared at a registered clearing agency and which are reported to a security-based swap data repository or the Commission under section 78c-3 (a)(6) of this title,[2] the Commission shall require real-time public reporting for such transactions, in a manner that does not disclose the business transactions and market positions of any person.

(iv) With respect to security-based swaps that are determined to be required to be cleared under section 78c-3(b) of this title but are not cleared, the Commission shall require real-time public reporting for such transactions.

(D) Registered entities and public reporting

The Commission may require registered entities to publicly disseminate the security-based swap transaction and pricing data required to be reported under this paragraph.

(E) Rulemaking required

With respect to the rule providing for the public availability of transaction and pricing data for security-based swaps described in clauses (i) and (ii) of subparagraph (C), the rule promulgated by the Commission shall contain provisions—

(i) to ensure such information does not identify the participants;

(ii) to specify the criteria for determining what constitutes a large notional security-based swap transaction (block trade) for particular markets and contracts;

(iii) to specify the appropriate time delay for reporting large notional security-based swap transactions (block trades) to the public; and

(iv) that take into account whether the public disclosure will materially reduce market liquidity.

(F) Timeliness of reporting

Parties to a security-based swap (including agents of the parties to a security-based swap) shall be responsible for reporting security-based swap transaction information to the appropriate registered entity in a timely manner as may be prescribed by the Commission.

(G) Reporting of swaps to registered security-based swap data repositories

Each security-based swap (whether cleared or uncleared) shall be reported to a registered security-based swap data repository.

(H)Registration of clearing agencies

A clearing agency may register as a security-based swap data repository.

(2) SEMIANNUAL AND ANNUAL PUBLIC REPORTING OF AGGREGATE SECURITY-BASED SWAP DATA

(A) In general In accordance with subparagraph (B), the Commission shall issue a written report on a semiannual and annual basis to make available to the public information relating to—

(i) the trading and clearing in the major security-based swap categories; and

(ii) the market participants and developments in new products.

(B) Use; consultation In preparing a report under subparagraph (A), the Commission shall—

(i) use information from security-based swap data repositories and clearing agencies; and

(ii) consult with the Office of the Comptroller of the Currency, the Bank for International Settlements, and such other regulatory bodies as may be necessary.

(C) Authority of Commission

The Commission may, by rule, regulation, or order, delegate the public reporting responsibilities of the Commission under this paragraph in accordance with such terms and conditions as the Commission determines to be appropriate and in the public interest.

(n) SECURITY-BASED SWAP DATA REPOSITORIES

(1) Registration requirement

It shall be unlawful for any person, unless registered with the Commission, directly or indirectly, to make use of the mails or any means or instrumentality of interstate commerce to perform the functions of a security-based swap data repository.

(2) Inspection and examination

Each registered security-based swap data repository shall be subject to inspection and examination by any representative of the Commission.

(3) Compliance with core principles

(A) In general

To be registered, and maintain registration, as a security-based swap data repository, the security-based swap data repository shall comply with—

(i) the requirements and core principles described in this subsection; and

(ii) any requirement that the Commission may impose by rule or regulation.

(B) Reasonable discretion of security-based swap data repository

Unless otherwise determined by the Commission, by rule or regulation, a security-based swap data repository described in subparagraph (A) shall have reasonable discretion in establishing the manner in which the security-based swap data repository complies with the core principles described in this subsection.

(4) Standard setting

(A) Data identification

(i) In general

In accordance with clause (ii), the Commission shall prescribe standards that specify the data elements for each security-based swap that shall be collected and maintained by each registered security-based swap data repository.

(ii) Requirement

In carrying out clause (i), the Commission shall prescribe consistent data element standards applicable to registered entities and reporting counterparties.

(B) Data collection and maintenance

The Commission shall prescribe data collection and data maintenance standards for security-based swap data repositories.

(C) Comparability

The standards prescribed by the Commission under this subsection shall be comparable to the data standards imposed by the Commission on clearing agencies in connection with their clearing of security-based swaps.

(5) Duties

A security-based swap data repository shall—

(A) accept data prescribed by the Commission for each security-based swap under subsection (b);

(B) confirm with both counterparties to the security-based swap the accuracy of the data that was submitted;

(C) maintain the data described in subparagraph (A) in such form, in such manner, and for such period as may be required by the Commission;

(D)(i) provide direct electronic access to the Commission (or any designee of the Commission, including another registered entity); and

(ii) provide the information described in subparagraph (A) in such form and at such frequency as the Commission may require to comply with the public reporting requirements set forth in subsection (m);

(E) at the direction of the Commission, establish automated systems for monitoring, screening, and analyzing security-based swap data;

(F) maintain the privacy of any and all security-based swap transaction information that the security-based swap data repository receives from a security-based swap dealer, counterparty, or any other registered entity; and

(G) on a confidential basis pursuant to section 78x of this title, upon request, and after notifying the Commission of the request, make available all data obtained by the security-based swap data repository, including individual counterparty trade and position data, to—

(i) each appropriate prudential regulator;

(ii) the Financial Stability Oversight Council;

(iii) the Commodity Futures Trading Commission;

(iv) the Department of Justice; and

(v) any other person that the Commission determines to be appropriate, including—

(I) foreign financial supervisors (including foreign futures authorities);

(II) foreign central banks; and

(III) foreign ministries.

(H) Confidentiality and indemnification agreement.—Before the security-based swap data repository may share information with any entity described in subparagraph (G)—

(i) the security-based swap data repository shall receive a written agreement from each entity stating that the entity shall abide by the confidentiality requirements described in section 78x of this title relating to the information on security-based swap transactions that is provided; and

(ii) each entity shall agree to indemnify the security-based swap data repository and the Commission for any expenses arising from litigation relating to the information provided under section 78x of this title.

(6) DESIGNATION OF CHIEF COMPLIANCE OFFICER

(A) In general

Each security-based swap data repository shall designate an individual to serve as a chief compliance officer.

(B) Duties

The chief compliance officer shall—

(i) report directly to the board or to the senior officer of the security-based swap data repository;

(ii) review the compliance of the security-based swap data repository with respect to the requirements and core principles described in this subsection;

(iii) in consultation with the board of the security-based swap data repository, a body performing a function similar to the board of the security-based swap data repository, or the senior officer of the security-based swap data repository, resolve any conflicts of interest that may arise;

(iv) be responsible for administering each policy and procedure that is required to be established pursuant to this section;

(v) ensure compliance with this chapter (including regulations) relating to agreements, contracts, or transactions, including each rule prescribed by the Commission under this section;

(vi) establish procedures for the remediation of noncompliance issues identified by the chief compliance officer through any—

(I) compliance office review;

(II) look-back;

(III) internal or external audit finding;

(IV) self-reported error; or

(V) validated complaint; and

(vii) establish and follow appropriate procedures for the handling, management response, remediation, retesting, and closing of noncompliance issues.

(C) Annual reports

(i) In general

In accordance with rules prescribed by the Commission, the chief compliance officer shall annually prepare and sign a report that contains a description of—

(I) the compliance of the security-based swap data repository of the chief compliance officer with respect to this chapter (including regulations); and

(II) each policy and procedure of the security-based swap data repository of the chief compliance officer (including the code of ethics and conflict of interest policies of the security-based swap data repository).

(ii) Requirements

A compliance report under clause (i) shall—

(I) accompany each appropriate financial report of the security-based swap data repository that is required to be furnished to the Commission pursuant to this section; and

(II) include a certification that, under penalty of law, the compliance report is accurate and complete.

(7) CORE PRINCIPLES APPLICABLE TO SECURITY-BASED SWAP DATA REPOSITORIES

(A) Antitrust considerations

Unless necessary or appropriate to achieve the purposes of this chapter, the swap data repository shall not—

(i) adopt any rule or take any action that results in any unreasonable restraint of trade; or

(ii) impose any material anticompetitive burden on the trading, clearing, or reporting of transactions.

(B) Governance arrangements

Each security-based swap data repository shall establish governance arrangements that are transparent—

(i) to fulfill public interest requirements; and

(ii) to support the objectives of the Federal Government, owners, and participants.

(C) Conflicts of interest

Each security-based swap data repository shall—

(i) establish and enforce rules to minimize conflicts of interest in the decision-making process of the security-based swap data repository; and

(ii) establish a process for resolving any conflicts of interest described in clause (i).

(D) Additional duties developed by Commission

(i) In general

The Commission may develop 1 or more additional duties applicable to security-based swap data repositories.

(ii) Consideration of evolving standards

In developing additional duties under subparagraph (A),[3] the Commission may take into consideration any evolving standard of the United States or the international community.

(iii) Additional duties for Commission designees

The Commission shall establish additional duties for any registrant described in subsection (m)(2)(C) in order to minimize conflicts of interest, protect data, ensure compliance, and guarantee the safety and security of the security-based swap data repository.

(8) REQUIRED REGISTRATION FOR SECURITY-BASED SWAP DATA REPOSITORIES

Any person that is required to be registered as a security-based swap data repository under this subsection shall register with the Commission, regardless of whether that person is also licensed under the Commodity Exchange Act [7 U.S.C. 1 et seq.] as a swap data repository.

(9) RULES

The Commission shall adopt rules governing persons that are registered under this subsection.

(*o*) BENEFICIAL OWNERSHIP

For purposes of this section and section 78p of this title, a person shall be deemed to acquire beneficial ownership of an equity security based on the purchase or sale of a security-based swap, only to the extent that the Commission, by rule, determines after consultation with the prudential regulators and the Secretary of the Treasury, that the purchase or sale of the security-based swap, or class of security-based swap, provides incidents of ownership comparable to direct ownership of the equity security, and that it is necessary to achieve the purposes of this section that the purchase or sale of the security-based swaps, or class of security-based swap, be deemed the acquisition of beneficial ownership of the equity security.

(p) DISCLOSURES RELATING TO CONFLICT MINERALS ORIGINATING IN THE DEMOCRATIC REPUBLIC OF THE CONGO

(1) REGULATIONS

(A) In general

Not later than 270 days after July 21, 2010, the Commission shall promulgate regulations requiring any person described in paragraph (2) to disclose annually, beginning with the person's first full fiscal year that begins after the date of promulgation of such regulations, whether conflict minerals that are necessary as described in paragraph (2)(B), in the year for which such reporting is required, did originate in the Democratic Republic of the Congo or an adjoining country and, in cases in which such conflict minerals did originate in any such country, submit to the Commission a report that includes, with respect to the period covered by the report—

(i) a description of the measures taken by the person to exercise due diligence on the source and chain of custody of such minerals, which measures shall include an independent private sector audit of such report submitted through the Commission that is conducted in accordance with standards established by the Comptroller General of the United States, in accordance with rules promulgated by the Commission, in consultation with the Secretary of State; and

(ii) a description of the products manufactured or contracted to be manufactured that are not DRC conflict free ("DRC conflict free" is defined to mean the products that do not contain minerals that directly or indirectly finance or benefit armed groups in the Democratic Republic of the Congo or an adjoining country), the entity that conducted the independent private sector audit in accordance with clause (i), the facilities used to process the conflict minerals, the country of origin of the conflict minerals, and the efforts to determine the mine or location of origin with the greatest possible specificity.

(B) Certification

The person submitting a report under subparagraph (A) shall certify the audit described in clause (i) of such subparagraph that is included in such report. Such a certified audit shall constitute a critical component of due diligence in establishing the source and chain of custody of such minerals.

(C) Unreliable determination

If a report required to be submitted by a person under subparagraph (A) relies on a determination of an independent private sector audit, as described under subparagraph (A)(i), or other due diligence processes previously determined by the Commission to be unreliable, the report shall not satisfy the requirements of the regulations promulgated under subparagraph (A)(i).

(D) DRC conflict free

For purposes of this paragraph, a product may be labeled as "DRC conflict free" if the product does not contain conflict minerals that directly or indirectly finance or benefit armed groups in the Democratic Republic of the Congo or an adjoining country.

(E) Information available to the public

Each person described under paragraph (2) shall make available to the public on the Internet website of such person the information disclosed by such person under subparagraph (A).

(2) PERSON DESCRIBED

A person is described in this paragraph if—

(A) the person is required to file reports with the Commission pursuant to paragraph (1)(A); and

(B) conflict minerals are necessary to the functionality or production of a product manufactured by such person.

(3) REVISIONS AND WAIVERS

The Commission shall revise or temporarily waive the requirements described in paragraph (1) if the President transmits to the Commission a determination that—

(A) such revision or waiver is in the national security interest of the United States and the President includes the reasons therefor; and

(B) establishes a date, not later than 2 years after the initial publication of such exemption, on which such exemption shall expire.

(4) TERMINATION OF DISCLOSURE REQUIREMENTS

The requirements of paragraph (1) shall terminate on the date on which the President determines and certifies to the appropriate congressional committees, but in no case earlier than the date that is one day after the end of the 5-year period beginning on July 21, 2010, that no armed groups continue to be directly involved and benefitting from commercial activity involving conflict minerals.

(5) DEFINITIONS

For purposes of this subsection, the terms "adjoining country", "appropriate congressional committees", "armed group", and "conflict mineral" have the meaning given those terms under section 1502 of the Dodd-Frank Wall Street Reform and Consumer Protection Act.

(q) DISCLOSURE OF PAYMENTS BY RESOURCE EXTRACTION ISSUERS

(1) DEFINITIONS

In this subsection—

(A) the term "commercial development of oil, natural gas, or minerals" includes exploration, extraction, processing, export, and other significant actions relating to oil, natural gas, or minerals, or the acquisition of a license for any such activity, as determined by the Commission;

(B) the term "foreign government" means a foreign government, a department, agency, or instrumentality of a foreign government, or a company owned by a foreign government, as determined by the Commission;

(C) the term "payment"—

(i) means a payment that is—

(I) made to further the commercial development of oil, natural gas, or minerals; and

(II) not de minimis; and

(ii) includes taxes, royalties, fees (including license fees), production entitlements, bonuses, and other material benefits, that the Commission, consistent with the guidelines of the Extractive Industries Transparency Initiative (to the extent practicable), determines are part of the commonly recognized revenue stream for the commercial development of oil, natural gas, or minerals;

(D) the term "resource extraction issuer" means an issuer that—

(i) is required to file an annual report with the Commission; and

(ii) engages in the commercial development of oil, natural gas, or minerals;

(E) the term "interactive data format" means an electronic data format in which pieces of information are identified using an interactive data standard; and

(F) the term "interactive data standard" means [4] standardized list of electronic tags that mark information included in the annual report of a resource extraction issuer.

(2) DISCLOSURE

(A) Information requiredNot later than 270 days after July 21, 2010, the Commission shall issue final rules that require each resource extraction issuer to include in an annual report of the resource extraction issuer information relating to any payment made by the resource extraction issuer, a subsidiary of the resource extraction issuer, or an entity under the control of the resource extraction issuer to a foreign government or the Federal

Government for the purpose of the commercial development of oil, natural gas, or minerals, including—

(i) the type and total amount of such payments made for each project of the resource extraction issuer relating to the commercial development of oil, natural gas, or minerals; and

(ii) the type and total amount of such payments made to each government.

(B) Consultation in rulemaking

In issuing rules under subparagraph (A), the Commission may consult with any agency or entity that the Commission determines is relevant.

(C) Interactive data format

The rules issued under subparagraph (A) shall require that the information included in the annual report of a resource extraction issuer be submitted in an interactive data format.

(D) Interactive data standard

(i) In general

The rules issued under subparagraph (A) shall establish an interactive data standard for the information included in the annual report of a resource extraction issuer.

(ii) Electronic tags

The interactive data standard shall include electronic tags that identify, for any payments made by a resource extraction issuer to a foreign government or the Federal Government—

(I) the total amounts of the payments, by category;

(II) the currency used to make the payments;

(III) the financial period in which the payments were made;

(IV) the business segment of the resource extraction issuer that made the payments;

(V) the government that received the payments, and the country in which the government is located;

(VI) the project of the resource extraction issuer to which the payments relate; and

(VII) such other information as the Commission may determine is necessary or appropriate in the public interest or for the protection of investors.

(E) International transparency efforts

To the extent practicable, the rules issued under subparagraph (A) shall support the commitment of the Federal Government to international transparency promotion efforts relating to the commercial development of oil, natural gas, or minerals.

(F) Effective date

With respect to each resource extraction issuer, the final rules issued under subparagraph (A) shall take effect on the date on which the resource extraction issuer is required to submit an annual report relating to the fiscal year of the resource extraction issuer that ends not earlier than 1 year after the date on which the Commission issues final rules under subparagraph (A).

(3) PUBLIC AVAILABILITY OF INFORMATION

(A) In general

To the extent practicable, the Commission shall make available online, to the public, a compilation of the information required to be submitted under the rules issued under paragraph (2)(A).

(B) Other information

Nothing in this paragraph shall require the Commission to make available online information other than the information required to be submitted under the rules issued under paragraph (2)(A).

(4) AUTHORIZATION OF APPROPRIATIONS

There are authorized to be appropriated to the Commission such sums as may be necessary to carry out this subsection.

(r) DISCLOSURE OF CERTAIN ACTIVITIES RELATING TO IRAN

(1) IN GENERAL

Each issuer required to file an annual or quarterly report under subsection (a) shall disclose in that report the information required by paragraph (2) if, during the period covered by the report, the issuer or any affiliate of the issuer—

(A) knowingly engaged in an activity described in subsection (a) or (b) of section 5 of the Iran Sanctions Act of 1996 (Public Law 104-172; 50 U.S.C. 1701 note);

(B) knowingly engaged in an activity described in subsection (c)(2) of section 8513 of title 22 or a transaction described in subsection (d)(1) of that section;

(C) knowingly engaged in an activity described in section 8514a(b)(2) of title 22; or

(D) knowingly conducted any transaction or dealing with—

(i) any person the property and interests in property of which are blocked pursuant to Executive Order No. 13224 (66 Fed. Reg. 49079; relating to blocking property and prohibiting transactions with persons who commit, threaten to commit, or support terrorism);

(ii) any person the property and interests in property of which are blocked pursuant to Executive Order No. 13382 (70 Fed. Reg. 38567; relating to blocking of property of weapons of mass destruction proliferators and their supporters); or

(iii) any person or entity identified under section 560.304 of title 31, Code of Federal Regulations (relating to the definition of the Government of Iran) without the specific authorization of a Federal department or agency.

(2) INFORMATION REQUIRED

If an issuer or an affiliate of the issuer has engaged in any activity described in paragraph (1), the issuer shall disclose a detailed description of each such activity, including—

(A) the nature and extent of the activity;

(B) the gross revenues and net profits, if any, attributable to the activity; and

(C) whether the issuer or the affiliate of the issuer (as the case may be) intends to continue the activity.

(3) NOTICE OF DISCLOSURES

If an issuer reports under paragraph (1) that the issuer or an affiliate of the issuer has knowingly engaged in any activity described in that paragraph, the issuer shall separately file with the Commission, concurrently with the annual or quarterly report under subsection (a), a notice that the disclosure of that activity has been included in that annual or quarterly report that identifies the issuer and contains the information required by paragraph (2).

(4) PUBLIC DISCLOSURE OF INFORMATION

Upon receiving a notice under paragraph (3) that an annual or quarterly report includes a disclosure of an activity described in paragraph (1), the Commission shall promptly—

(A) transmit the report to—

(i) the President;

(ii) the Committee on Foreign Affairs and the Committee on Financial Services of the House of Representatives; and

(iii) the Committee on Foreign Relations and the Committee on Banking, Housing, and Urban Affairs of the Senate; and

(B) make the information provided in the disclosure and the notice available to the public by posting the information on the Internet website of the Commission.

(5) INVESTIGATIONS

Upon receiving a report under paragraph (4) that includes a disclosure of an activity described in paragraph (1) (other than an activity described in subparagraph (D)(iii) of that paragraph), the President shall—

(A) initiate an investigation into the possible imposition of sanctions under the Iran Sanctions Act of 1996 (Public Law 104-172; 50 U.S.C. 1701 note), section 8513 or 8514a of title 22, an Executive order specified in clause (i) or (ii) of paragraph (1)(D), or any other provision of law relating to the imposition of sanctions with respect to Iran, as applicable; and

(B) not later than 180 days after initiating such an investigation, make a determination with respect to whether sanctions should be imposed with respect to the issuer or the affiliate of the issuer (as the case may be).

(6) SUNSET

The provisions of this subsection shall terminate on the date that is 30 days after the date on which the President makes the certification described in section 8551(a) of title 22.

SECTION 13(d). 5% BLOCK REPORTING REQUIREMENT

(d) *Reports by persons acquiring more than five per centum of certain classes of securities*

(1) Any person who, after acquiring directly or indirectly the beneficial ownership of any equity security of a class which is registered pursuant to section 78*l* of this title, or any equity security of an insurance company which would have been required to be so registered except for the exemption contained in section 78*l*(g)(2)(G) of this title, or any equity security issued by a closed-end investment company registered under the Investment Company Act of 1940 [15 U.S.C.A. § 80a-1 et seq.] or any equity security issued by a Native Corporation pursuant to section 1629c(d)(6) of Title 43, or otherwise becomes or is deemed to become a beneficial owner of any of the foregoing upon the purchase or sale of a security-based swap that the Commission may define by rule, and is directly or indirectly the beneficial owner of more than 5 per centum of such class shall, within ten days after such acquisition or within such shorter time as the Commission may establish by rule, file with the Commission, a statement containing such of the following information, and such additional information, as the Commission may by rules and regulations, prescribe as necessary or appropriate in the public interest or for the protection of investors—

(A) the background, and identity, residence, and citizenship of, and the nature of such beneficial ownership by, such person and all other persons by whom or on whose behalf the purchases have been or are to be effected;

(B) the source and amount of the funds or other consideration used or to be used in making the purchases, and if any part of the purchase price is represented or is to be represented by funds or other consideration borrowed or otherwise obtained for the purpose of acquiring, holding, or trading such security, a description of the transaction and the names of the parties thereto, except that where a source of funds is a loan made in the ordinary course of business by a bank, as defined in section 78c(a)(6) of this title, if the person filing such statement so requests, the name of the bank shall not be made available to the public;

(C) if the purpose of the purchases or prospective purchases is to acquire control of the business of the issuer of the securities, any plans or proposals which such persons may have to liquidate such issuer, to sell its assets to or merge it with any other persons, or to make any other major change in its business or corporate structure;

(D) the number of shares of such security which are beneficially owned, and the number of shares concerning which there is a right to acquire, directly or indirectly, by (i) such person, and (ii) by each associate of such person, giving the background, identity, residence, and citizenship of each such associate; and

(E) information as to any contracts, arrangements, or understandings with any person with respect to any securities of the issuer, including but not limited to transfer of any of the securities, joint ventures, loan or option arrangements, puts or calls, guaranties of loans, guaranties against loss or guaranties of profits, division of losses or profits, or the giving or withholding of proxies, naming the persons with whom such contracts, arrangements, or understandings have been entered into, and giving the details thereof.

(2) If any material change occurs in the facts set forth in the statement filed with the Commission, an amendment shall be filed with the Commission, in accordance with such rules and regulations as the Commission may prescribe as necessary or appropriate in the public interest or for the protection of investors.

(3) When two or more persons act as a partnership, limited partnership, syndicate, or other group for the purpose of acquiring, holding, or disposing of securities of an issuer, such syndicate or group shall be deemed a "person" for the purposes of this subsection.

(4) In determining, for purposes of this subsection, any percentage of a class of any security, such class shall be deemed to consist of the amount of the outstanding securities of such class, exclusive of any securities of such class held by or for the account of the issuer or a subsidiary of the issuer.

(5) The Commission, by rule or regulation or by order, may permit any person to file in lieu of the statement required by paragraph (1) of this subsection or the rules and regulations thereunder, a notice stating the name of such person, the number of shares of any equity securities subject to paragraph (1) which are owned by him, the date of their acquisition and such other information as the Commission may specify, if it appears to the Commission that such securities were acquired by such person in the ordinary course of his business and were not acquired for the purpose of and do not have the effect of changing or influencing the control of the issuer nor in connection with or as a participant in any transaction having such purpose or effect.

(6) The provisions of this subsection shall not apply to—

(A) any acquisition or offer to acquire securities made or proposed to be made by means of a registration statement under the Securities Act of 1933 [15 U.S.C.A. 77a et seq.];

(B) any acquisition of the beneficial ownership of a security which, together with all other acquisitions by the same person of securities of the same class during the preceding twelve months, does not exceed 2 per centum of that class;

(C) any acquisition of an equity security by the issuer of such security;

(D) any acquisition or proposed acquisition of a security which the Commission, by rules or regulations or by order, shall exempt from the provisions of this subsection as not entered into for the purpose of, and not having the effect of, changing or influencing the control of the issuer or otherwise as not comprehended within the purposes of this subsection.

Rules Under Section 13(d)

§ 240.13d-1 Filing of Schedules 13D and 13G

(a) Any person who, after acquiring directly or indirectly the beneficial ownership of any equity security of a class which is specified in paragraph (i) of this section, is directly or indirectly the beneficial owner of more than five percent of the class shall, within 10 days after the acquisition, file with the Commission, a statement containing the information required by Schedule 13D (§ 240.13d-101).

file a statement when >5%

(b)(1) A person who would otherwise be obligated under paragraph (a) of this section to file a statement on Schedule 13D (§ 240.13d-101) may, in lieu thereof, file with the Commission, a short-form statement on Schedule 13G (§ 240.13d-102), *Provided*, That:

(i) Such person has acquired such securities in the ordinary course of his business and not with the purpose nor with the effect of changing or influencing the control of the issuer, nor in connection with or as a participant in any transaction having such purpose or effect, including any transaction subject to § 240.13d-3(b), other than activities solely in connection with a nomination under § 240.14a-11; and

(ii) Such person is:

(A) A broker or dealer registered under section 15 of the Act (15 U.S.C. 78*o*);

(B) A bank as defined in section 3(a)(6) of the Act (15 U.S.C. 78c);

(C) An insurance company as defined in section 3(a)(19) of the Act (15 U.S.C. 78c);

(D) An investment company registered under section 8 of the Investment Company Act of 1940 (15 U.S.C. 80a-8);

(E) Any person registered as an investment adviser under Section 203 of the Investment Advisers Act of 1940 (15 U.S.C. 80b-3) or under the laws of any state;

(F) An employee benefit plan as defined in Section 3(3) of the Employee Retirement Income Security Act of 1974, as amended, 29 U.S.C. 1001 et seq. ("ERISA") that is subject to the provisions of ERISA, or any such plan that is not subject to ERISA that is maintained primarily for the benefit of the employees of a state or local government or instrumentality, or an endowment fund;

(G) A parent holding company or control person, provided the aggregate amount held directly by the parent or control person, and directly and indirectly by their subsidiaries or affiliates that are not persons specified in § 240.13d-1(b)(1)(ii)(A) through (J), does not exceed one percent of the securities of the subject class;

(H) A savings association as defined in Section 3(b) of the Federal Deposit Insurance Act (12 U.S.C. 1813);

(I) A church plan that is excluded from the definition of an investment company under section 3(c)(14) of the Investment Company Act of 1940 (15 U.S.C. 80a-3);

(J) A non-U.S. institution that is the functional equivalent of any of the institutions listed in § 240.13d-1 (b)(1)(ii)(A) through (I), so long as the non-U.S. institution is subject to a regulatory scheme that is substantially comparable to the regulatory scheme applicable to the equivalent U.S. institution; and

(K) A group, provided that all the members are persons specified in § 240.13d-1(b)(1)(ii)(A) through (J).

(iii) Such person has promptly notified any other person (or group within the meaning of section 13(d)(3) of the Act) on whose behalf it holds, on a discretionary basis, securities exceeding five percent of the class, of any acquisition or transaction on behalf of such other person which might be reportable by that person under section 13(d) of the Act. This paragraph only requires notice to the account owner of information which the filing person reasonably should be expected to know and which would advise the account owner of an obligation he may have to file a statement pursuant to section 13(d) of the Act or an amendment thereto.

Instruction 1 to paragraph (b)(1). For purposes of paragraph (b)(1)(i) of this section, the exception for activities solely in connection with a nomination under § 240.14a-11 will not be available after the election of directors.

(2) The Schedule 13G filed pursuant to paragraph (b)(1) of this section shall be filed within 45 days after the end of the calendar year in which the person became obligated under paragraph (b)(1) of this section to report the person's beneficial ownership as of the last day of the calendar year,*Provided,* That it shall not be necessary to file a Schedule 13G unless the percentage of the class of equity security specified in paragraph (i) of this section beneficially owned as of the end of the calendar year is more than five percent; *However,* if the person's direct or indirect beneficial ownership exceeds 10 percent of the class of equity securities prior to the end of the calendar year, the initial Schedule 13G shall be filed within 10 days after the end of the first month in which the person's direct or indirect beneficial ownership exceeds 10 percent of the class of equity securities, computed as of the last day of the month.

(c) A person who would otherwise be obligated under paragraph (a) of this section to file a statement on Schedule 13D (§ 240.13d-101) may, in lieu thereof, file with the Commission, within 10 days after an acquisition described in paragraph (a) of this section, a short-form statement on Schedule 13G (§ 240.13d-102). *Provided,* That the person:

(1) Has not acquired the securities with any purpose, or with the effect, of changing or influencing the control of the issuer, or in connection with or as a participant in any transaction having that purpose or effect, including any transaction subject to § 240.13d-3(b), other than activities solely in connection with a nomination under § 240.14a-11;

Instruction 1 to paragraph (c)(1). For purposes of paragraph (c)(1) of this section, the exception for activities solely in connection with a nomination under § 240.14a-11 will not be available after the election of directors.

(2) Is not a person reporting pursuant to paragraph (b)(1) of this section; and

(3) Is not directly or indirectly the beneficial owner of 20 percent or more of the class.

(d) Any person who, as of the end of any calendar year, is or becomes directly or indirectly the beneficial owner of more than five percent of any equity security of a class specified in paragraph (i) of this section and who is not required to file a statement under paragraph (a) of this section by virtue of the exemption provided by Section 13(d)(6)(A) or (B) of the Act (15 U.S.C. 78m(d)(6)(A) or 78m(d)(6)(B)), or because the beneficial ownership was acquired prior to December 22, 1970, or because the person otherwise (except for the exemption provided by Section 13(d)(6)(C) of the Act (15 U.S.C. 78m(d)(6)(C))) is not required to file a statement, shall file with the Commission, within 45 days after the end of the calendar year in which the person became obligated to report under this paragraph (d), a statement containing the information required by Schedule 13G (§ 240.13d-102).

(e)(1) Notwithstanding paragraphs (b) and (c) of this section and § 240.13d-2(b), a person that has reported that it is the beneficial owner of more than five percent of a class of equity securities in a statement on Schedule 13G (§ 240.13d-102) pursuant to paragraph (b) or (c) of this section, or is required to report the acquisition but has not yet filed the schedule, shall immediately become subject to §§ 240.13d-1(a) and 240.13d-2(a) and shall file a statement on Schedule 13D (§ 240.13d-101) within 10 days if, and shall remain subject to those requirements for so long as, the person:

(i) Has acquired or holds the securities with a purpose or effect of changing or influencing control of the issuer, or in connection with or as a participant in any transaction having that purpose or effect, including any transaction subject to § 240.13d-3(b); and

(ii) Is at that time the beneficial owner of more than five percent of a class of equity securities described in § 240.13d-1(i).

(2) From the time the person has acquired or holds the securities with a purpose or effect of changing or influencing control of the issuer, or in connection with or as a participant in any transaction having that purpose or effect until the expiration of the tenth day from the date of the filing of the Schedule 13D (§ 240.13d-101) pursuant to this section, that person shall not:

(i) Vote or direct the voting of the securities described therein; or

(ii) Acquire an additional beneficial ownership interest in any equity securities of the issuer of the securities, nor of any person controlling the issuer.

(f)(1) Notwithstanding paragraph (c) of this section and § 240.13d-2(b), persons reporting on Schedule 13G (§ 240.13d-102) pursuant to paragraph (c) of this section shall immediately become subject to §§ 240.13d-1(a) and 240.13d-2(a) and shall remain subject to those requirements for so long as, and shall file a statement on Schedule 13D (§ 240.13d-101) within 10 days of the date on which, the person's beneficial ownership equals or exceeds 20 percent of the class of equity securities.

(2) From the time of the acquisition of 20 percent or more of the class of equity securities until the expiration of the tenth day from the date of the filing of the Schedule 13D (§ 240.13d-101) pursuant to this section, the person shall not:

(i) Vote or direct the voting of the securities described therein, or

(ii) Acquire an additional beneficial ownership interest in any equity securities of the issuer of the securities, nor of any person controlling the issuer.

(g) Any person who has reported an acquisition of securities in a statement on Schedule 13G (§ 240.13d-102) pursuant to paragraph (b) of this section, or has become obligated to report on the Schedule 13G (§ 240.13d-102) but has not yet filed the Schedule, and thereafter ceases to be a person specified in paragraph (b)(1)(ii) of this section or determines that it no longer has acquired or holds the securities in the ordinary course of business shall immediately become subject to § 240.13d-1(a) or § 240.13d-1(c) (if the person satisfies the requirements specified in § 240.13d-1(c)), and §§ 240.13d-2 (a), (b) or (d), and shall file, within 10 days thereafter, a statement on Schedule 13D (§ 240.13d-101) or amendment to Schedule 13G, as applicable, if the person is a beneficial owner at that time of more than five percent of the class of equity securities.

(h) Any person who has filed a Schedule 13D (§ 240.13d-101) pursuant to paragraph (e), (f) or (g) of this section may again report its beneficial ownership on Schedule 13G (§ 240.13d-102) pursuant to paragraphs (b) or (c) of this section provided the person qualifies thereunder, as applicable, by filing a Schedule 13G (§ 240.13d-102) once the person determines that the provisions of paragraph (e), (f) or (g) of this section no longer apply.

(i) For the purpose of this regulation, the term "equity security" means any equity security of a class which is registered pursuant to section 12 of that Act, or any equity security of any insurance company which would have been required to be so registered except for the exemption contained in section 12(g)(2)(G) of the Act, or any equity security issued by a closed-end investment company registered under the Investment Company Act of 1940; *Provided*, Such term shall not include securities of a class of non-voting securities.

(j) For the purpose of sections 13(d) and 13(g), any person, in determining the amount of outstanding securities of a class of equity securities, may rely upon information set forth in the issuer's most recent quarterly or annual report, and any current report subsequent thereto, filed with the Commission pursuant to this Act, unless he knows or has reason to believe that the information contained therein is inaccurate.

(k)(1) Whenever two or more persons are required to file a statement containing the information required by Schedule 13D or Schedule 13G with respect to the same securities, only one statement need be filed:*Provided*, That:

(i) Each person on whose behalf the statement is filed is individually eligible to use the Schedule on which the information is filed;

(ii) Each person on whose behalf the statement is filed is responsible for the timely filing of such statement and any amendments thereto, and for the completeness and accuracy of the information concerning such person contained therein; such person is not responsible for the completeness or accuracy of the information concerning the other persons making the filing, unless such person knows or has reason to believe that such information is inaccurate; and

(iii) Such statement identifies all such persons, contains the required information with regard to each such person, indicates that such statement is filed on behalf of all such persons, and includes, as an exhibit, their agreement in writing that such a statement is filed on behalf of each of them.

(2) A group's filing obligation may be satisfied either by a single joint filing or by each of the group's members making an individual filing. If the group's members elect to make their own filings, each such filing should identify all members of the group but the information provided concerning the other persons making the filing need only reflect information which the filing person knows or has reason to know.

§ 240.13d-2 Filing of Amendments to Schedules 13D or 13G

(a) If any material change occurs in the facts set forth in the Schedule 13D (§ 240.13d-101) required by § 240.13d-1(a), including, but not limited to, any material increase or decrease in the percentage of the class beneficially owned, the person or persons who were required to file the statement shall promptly file or cause to be filed with the Commission an amendment disclosing that change. An acquisition or disposition of beneficial ownership of securities in an amount equal to one percent or more of the class of securities shall be deemed "material" for purposes of this section; acquisitions or dispositions of less than those amounts may be material, depending upon the facts and circumstances.

(b) Notwithstanding paragraph (a) of this section, and provided that the person filing a Schedule 13G (§ 240.13d-102) pursuant to § 240.13d-1(b) or § 240.13d-1(c) continues to meet the requirements set forth therein, any person who has filed a Schedule 13G (§ 240.13d-102) pursuant to § 240.13d-1(b), § 240.13d-1(c) or § 240.13d-1(d) shall amend the statement within forty-five days after the end of each calendar year if, as of the end of the calendar year, there are any changes in the information reported in the previous filing on that Schedule: Provided, however, That an amendment need not be filed with respect to a change in the percent of class outstanding previously reported if the change results solely from a change in the aggregate number of securities outstanding. Once an amendment has been filed reflecting beneficial ownership of five percent or less of the class of securities, no additional filings are required unless the person thereafter becomes the beneficial owner of more than five percent of the class and is required to file pursuant to § 240.13d-1.

(c) Any person relying on § 240.13d-1(b) that has filed its initial Schedule 13G (§ 240.13d-102) pursuant to that paragraph shall, in addition to filing any amendments pursuant to § 240.13d-2(b), file an amendment on Schedule 13G (§ 240.13d-102) within 10 days after the end of the first month in which the person's direct or indirect beneficial ownership, computed as of the last day of the month, exceeds 10 percent of the class of equity securities. Thereafter, that person shall, in addition to filing any amendments pursuant to § 240.13d-2(b), file an amendment on Schedule 13G (§ 240.13d-102) within 10 days after the end of the first month in which the person's direct or indirect beneficial ownership, computed as of the last day of the month, increases or decreases by more than five percent of the class of equity securities. Once an amendment has been filed reflecting beneficial ownership of five percent or less of the class of securities, no additional filings are required by this paragraph (c).

(d) Any person relying on § 240.13d-1(c) and has filed its initial Schedule 13G (§ 240.13d-102) pursuant to that paragraph shall, in addition to filing any amendments pursuant to § 240.13d-2(b), file an amendment on Schedule 13G (§ 240.13d-102) promptly upon acquiring, directly or indirectly, greater than 10 percent of a class of equity securities specified in § 240.13d-1(d), and thereafter promptly upon increasing or decreasing its beneficial ownership by more than five percent of the class of equity securities. Once an amendment has been filed reflecting beneficial ownership of five percent or less of the class of securities, no additional filings are required by this paragraph (d).

(e) The first electronic amendment to a paper format Schedule 13D (§ 240.13d-101 of this chapter) or Schedule 13G (§ 240.13d-102 of this chapter) shall restate the entire text of the Schedule 13D or 13G, but previously filed paper exhibits to such Schedules are not required to be restated electronically. See Rule 102 of Regulation S-T (§ 232.102 of this chapter) regarding amendments to exhibits previously filed in paper format. Notwithstanding the foregoing, if the sole purpose of filing the first electronic Schedule 13D or 13G amendment is to report a change in beneficial ownership that would terminate the filer's obligation to report, the amendment need not include a restatement of the entire text of the Schedule being amended.

§ 240.13d-5 Acquisition of Securities

(a) A person who becomes a beneficial owner of securities shall be deemed to have acquired such securities for purposes of section 13(d)(1) of the Act, whether such acquisition was through purchase or otherwise. However, executors or administrators of a decedent's estate generally will be presumed not to have acquired beneficial ownership of the securities in the decedent's estate until such time as such executors or administrators are qualified under local law to perform their duties.

(b)(1) When two or more persons agree to act together for the purpose of acquiring, holding, voting or disposing of equity securities of an issuer, the group formed thereby shall be deemed to have acquired beneficial ownership, for purposes of sections 13(d) and (g) of the Act, as of the date of such agreement, of all equity securities of that issuer beneficially owned by any such persons.

(2) Notwithstanding the previous paragraph, a group shall be deemed not to have acquired any equity securities beneficially owned by the other members of the group solely by virtue of their concerted actions relating to the purchase of equity securities directly from an issuer in a transaction not involving a public offering: Provided, That:

(i) All the members of the group are persons specified in Rule 13d-1(b)(1)(ii);

(ii) The purchase is in the ordinary course of each member's business and not with the purpose nor with the effect of changing or influencing control of the issuer, nor in connection with or as a participant in any transaction having such purpose or effect, including any transaction subject to Rule 13d-3(b);

(iii) There is no agreement among, or between any members of the group to act together with respect to the issuer or its securities except for the purpose of facilitating the specific purchase involved; and

(iv) The only actions among or between any members of the group with respect to the issuer or its securities subsequent to the closing date of the non-public offering are those which are necessary to conclude ministerial matters directly related to the completion of the offer or sale of the securities.

Section 13(e). SEC Rule-Making Authority over Issuer Self-Purchases

(e) *Purchase of securities by issuer.*

(1) It shall be unlawful for an issuer which has a class of equity securities registered pursuant to section 78*l* of this title, or which is a closed-end investment company registered under the Investment Company Act of 1940 [15 U.S.C.A. § 80a-1 et seq.], to purchase any equity security issued by it if such purchase is in contravention of such rules and regulations as the Commission, in the public interest or for the protection of investors, may adopt (A) to define acts and practices which are fraudulent, deceptive, or manipulative, and (B) to prescribe means reasonably designed to prevent such acts and practices. Such rules and regulations may require such issuer to provide holders of equity securities of such class with such information relating to the reasons for such purchase, the source of funds, the number of shares to be purchased, the price to be paid for such securities, the method of purchase, and such additional information, as the Commission deems necessary or appropriate in the public interest or for the protection of investors, or which the Commission deems to be material to a determination whether such security should be sold.

(2) For the purpose of this subsection, a purchase by or for the issuer or any person controlling, controlled by, or under common control with the issuer, or a purchase subject to control of the issuer or any such person, shall be deemed to be a purchase by the issuer. The Commission shall have power to make rules and regulations implementing this paragraph in the public interest and for the protection of investors, including exemptive rules and regulations covering situations in which the Commission deems it unnecessary or inappropriate that a purchase of the type described in this paragraph shall be deemed to be a purchase by the issuer for purposes of some or all of the provisions of paragraph (1) of this subsection.

(3) At the time of filing such statement as the Commission may require by rule pursuant to paragraph (1) of this subsection, the person making the filing shall pay to the Commission a fee at a rate that, subject to paragraph (4), is equal to $92 per $1,000,000 of the value of securities proposed to be purchased. The fee shall be reduced with respect to securities in an amount equal to any fee paid with respect to any securities issued in connection with the proposed transaction under section 77f(b) of this title, or the fee paid under that section shall be reduced in an amount equal to the fee paid to the Commission in connection with such transaction under this paragraph.

(4) Annual adjustment

For each fiscal year, the Commission shall by order adjust the rate required by paragraph (3) for such fiscal year to a rate that is equal to the rate (expressed in dollars per million) that is applicable under section 6(b) of the Securities Act of 1933 for such fiscal year.

(5) Fee collections

Fees collected pursuant to this subsection for fiscal year 2012 and each fiscal year thereafter shall be deposited and credited as general revenue of the Treasury and shall not be available for obligation.

(6) Effective date; publication

In exercising its authority under this subsection, the Commission shall not be required to comply with the provisions of section 553 of Title 5. An adjusted rate prescribed under paragraph (4) shall be published and take effect in accordance with section 6(b) of the Securities Act of 1933 (15 U.S.C. 77f(b)).

(7) Pro rata application

The rates per $1,000,000 required by this subsection shall be applied pro rata to amounts and balances of less than $1,000,000.

Rules Under Section 13(e)

§ 240.13e-1 Purchase of Securities by the Issuer During a Third-Party Tender Offer

An issuer that has received notice that it is the subject of a tender offer made under Section 14(d)(1) of the Act (15 U.S.C. 78n), that has commenced under § 240.14d-2 must not purchase any of its equity securities during the tender offer unless the issuer first:

(a) Files a statement with the Commission containing the following information:

(1) The title and number of securities to be purchased;

(2) The names of the persons or classes of persons from whom the issuer will purchase the securities;

(3) The name of any exchange, inter-dealer quotation system or any other market on or through which the securities will be purchased;

(4) The purpose of the purchase;

(5) Whether the issuer will retire the securities, hold the securities in its treasury, or dispose of the securities. If the issuer intends to dispose of the securities, describe how it intends to do so; and

(6) The source and amount of funds or other consideration to be used to make the purchase. If the issuer borrows any funds or other consideration to make the purchase or enters any agreement for the purpose of acquiring, holding, or trading the securities, describe the transaction and agreement and identify the parties; and

(b) Pays the fee required by § 240.0-11 when it files the initial statement.

(c) This section does not apply to periodic repurchases in connection with an employee benefit plan or other similar plan of the issuer so long as the purchases are made in the ordinary course and not in response to the tender offer.

§ 240.13e-3 Going Private Transactions by Certain Issuers or Their Affiliates

(a) Definitions. Unless indicated otherwise or the context otherwise requires, all terms used in this section and in Schedule 13E-3 [§ 240.13e-100] shall have the same meaning as in the Act or elsewhere in the General Rules and Regulations thereunder. In addition, the following definitions apply:

(1) An affiliate of an issuer is a person that directly or indirectly through one or more intermediaries controls, is controlled by, or is under common control with such issuer. For the purposes of this section only, a person who is not an affiliate of an issuer at the commencement of such person's tender offer for a class of equity securities of such issuer will not be deemed an affiliate of such issuer prior to the stated termination of such tender offer and any extensions thereof;

(2) The term purchase means any acquisition for value including, but not limited to, (i) any acquisition pursuant to the dissolution of an issuer subsequent to the sale or other disposition of substantially all the assets of such issuer to its affiliate, (ii) any acquisition pursuant to a merger, (iii) any acquisition of fractional interests in connection with a reverse stock split, and (iv) any acquisition subject to the control of an issuer or an affiliate of such issuer;

(3) A Rule 13e-3 transaction is any transaction or series of transactions involving one or more of the transactions described in paragraph (a)(3)(i) of this section which has either a reasonable likelihood or a purpose of producing, either directly or indirectly, any of the effects described in paragraph (a)(3)(ii) of this section;

(i) The transactions referred to in paragraph (a)(3) of this section are:

(A) A purchase of any equity security by the issuer of such security or by an affiliate of such issuer;

(B) A tender offer for or request or invitation for tenders of any equity security made by the issuer of such class of securities or by an affiliate of such issuer; or

(C) A solicitation subject to Regulation 14A [§§ 240.14a-1 to 240.14b-1] of any proxy, consent or authorization of, or a distribution subject to Regulation 14C [§§ 240.14c-1 to 14c-101] of information statements to, any equity security holder by the issuer of the class of securities or by an affiliate of such issuer, in connection with: a merger, consolidation, reclassification, recapitalization, reorganization or similar corporate transaction of an issuer or between an issuer (or its subsidiaries) and its affiliate; a sale of substantially all the assets of an issuer to its affiliate or group of affiliates; or a reverse stock split of any class of equity securities of the issuer involving the purchase of fractional interests.

(ii) The effects referred to in paragraph (a)(3) of this section are:

(A) Causing any class of equity securities of the issuer which is subject to section 12(g) or section 15(d) of the Act to become eligible for termination of registration under Rule 12g-4 (§ 240.12g-4) or Rule 12h-6 (§ 240.12h-6), or causing the reporting obligations with respect to such class to become eligible for termination under Rule 12h-6 (§ 240.12h-6); or suspension under Rule 12h-3 (§ 240.12h-3) or section 15(d); or

(B) Causing any class of equity securities of the issuer which is either listed on a national securities exchange or authorized to be quoted in an inter-dealer quotation system of a registered national securities association to be neither listed on any national securities exchange nor authorized to be quoted on an inter-dealer quotation system of any registered national securities association.

(4) An unaffiliated security holder is any security holder of an equity security subject to a Rule 13e-3 transaction who is not an affiliate of the issuer of such security.

(b) Application of section to an issuer (or an affiliate of such issuer) subject to section 12 of the Act.

(1) It shall be a fraudulent, deceptive or manipulative act or practice, in connection with a Rule 13e-3 transaction, for an issuer which has a class of equity securities registered pursuant to section 12 of the Act or which is a closed-end investment company registered under the Investment Company Act of 1940, or an affiliate of such issuer, directly or indirectly

(i) To employ any device, scheme or artifice to defraud any person;

(ii) To make any untrue statement of a material fact or to omit to state a material fact necessary in order to make the statements made, in light of the circumstances under which they were made, not misleading; or

(iii) To engage in any act, practice or course of business which operates or would operate as a fraud or deceit upon any person.

(2) As a means reasonably designed to prevent fraudulent, deceptive or manipulative acts or practices in connection with any Rule 13e-3 transaction, it shall be unlawful for an issuer which has a class of equity securities registered pursuant to section 12 of the Act, or an affiliate of such issuer, to engage, directly or indirectly, in a Rule 13e-3 transaction unless:

(i) Such issuer or affiliate complies with the requirements of paragraphs (d), (e) and (f) of this section; and

(ii) The Rule 13e-3 transaction is not in violation of paragraph (b)(1) of this section.

(c) Application of section to an issuer (or an affiliate of such issuer) subject to section 15(d) of the Act.

(1) It shall be unlawful as a fraudulent, deceptive or manipulative act or practice for an issuer which is required to file periodic reports pursuant to Section 15(d) of the Act, or an affiliate of such issuer, to engage, directly or indirectly, in a Rule 13e-3 transaction unless such issuer or affiliate complies with the requirements of paragraphs (d), (e) and (f) of this section.

(2) An issuer or affiliate which is subject to paragraph (c)(1) of this section and which is soliciting proxies or distributing information statements in connection with a transaction described in paragraph (a)(3)(i)(A) of this section may elect to use the timing procedures for conducting a solicitation subject to Regulation 14A (§§ 240.14a-1 to 240.14b-1) or a distribution subject to Regulation 14C (§§ 240.14c-1 to 240.14c-101) in complying with paragraphs (d), (e) and (f) of this section, provided that if an election is made, such solicitation or distribution is conducted in accordance with the requirements of the respective regulations, including the filing of preliminary copies of soliciting materials or an information statement at the time specified in Regulation 14A or 14C, respectively.

(d) Material required to be filed. The issuer or affiliate engaging in a Rule 13e-3 transaction must file with the Commission:

(1) A Schedule 13E-3 (§ 240.13e-100), including all exhibits;

(2) An amendment to Schedule 13E-3 reporting promptly any material changes in the information set forth in the schedule previously filed; and

(3) A final amendment to Schedule 13E-3 reporting promptly the results of the Rule 13e-3 transaction.

(e) Disclosure of information to security holders.

(1) In addition to disclosing the information required by any other applicable rule or regulation under the federal securities laws, the issuer or affiliate engaging in a § 240.13e-3 transaction must disclose to security holders of the class that is the subject of the transaction, as specified in paragraph (f) of this section, the following:

(i) The information required by Item 1 of Schedule 13E-3 (§ 240.13e-100) (Summary Term Sheet);

(ii) The information required by Items 7, 8 and 9 of Schedule 13E-3, which must be prominently disclosed in a "Special Factors" section in the front of the disclosure document;

(iii) A prominent legend on the outside front cover page that indicates that neither the Securities and Exchange Commission nor any state securities commission has: approved or disapproved of the transaction; passed upon the merits or fairness of the transaction; or passed upon the adequacy or accuracy of the disclosure in the document. The legend also must make it clear that any representation to the contrary is a criminal offense;

(iv) The information concerning appraisal rights required by § 229.1016(f) of this chapter; and

(v) The information required by the remaining items of Schedule 13E-3, except for § 229.1016 of this chapter (exhibits), or a fair and adequate summary of the information.

Instructions to paragraph (e)(1):

1. If the Rule 13e-3 transaction also is subject to Regulation 14A (§§ 240.14a-1 through 240.14b-2) or 14C (§§ 240.14c-1 through 240.14c-101), the registration provisions and rules of the Securities Act of 1933, Regulation 14D or § 240.13e-4, the information required by paragraph (e)(1) of this section must be combined with the proxy statement, information statement, prospectus or tender offer material sent or given to security holders.
2. If the Rule 13e-3 transaction involves a registered securities offering, the legend required by § 229.501(b)(7) of this chapter must be combined with the legend required by paragraph (e)(1)(iii) of this section.
3. The required legend must be written in clear, plain language.

(2) If there is any material change in the information previously disclosed to security holders, the issuer or affiliate must disclose the change promptly to security holders as specified in paragraph (f)(1)(iii) of this section.

(f) Dissemination of information to security holders.

(1) If the Rule 13e-3 transaction involves a purchase as described in paragraph (a)(3)(i)(A) of this section or a vote, consent, authorization, or distribution of information statements as described in paragraph (a)(3)(i)(C) of this section, the issuer or affiliate engaging in the Rule 13e-3 transaction shall:

(i) Provide the information required by paragraph (e) of this section: (A) In accordance with the provisions of any applicable Federal or State law, but in no event later than 20 days prior to: any such purchase; any such vote, consent or authorization; or with respect to the distribution of information statements, the meeting date, or if corporate action is to be taken by means of the written authorization or consent of security holders, the earliest date on which corporate action may be taken: *Provided, however,* That if the purchase subject to this section is pursuant to a tender offer excepted from Rule 13e-4 by paragraph (g)(5) of Rule 13e-4, the information required by paragraph (e) of this section shall be disseminated in accordance with paragraph (e) of Rule 13e-4 no later than 10 business days prior to any purchase pursuant to such tender offer, (B) to each person who is a record holder of a class of equity securities subject to the Rule 13e-3 transaction as of a date not more than 20 days prior to the date of dissemination of such information.

(ii) If the issuer or affiliate knows that securities of the class of securities subject to the Rule 13e-3 transaction are held of record by a broker, dealer, bank or voting trustee or their nominees, such issuer or affiliate shall (unless Rule 14a-13(a) [§ 240.14a-13(a)] or 14c-7 [§ 240.14c-7] is applicable) furnish the number of copies of the information required by paragraph (e) of this section that are requested by such persons (pursuant to inquiries by or on behalf of the issuer or affiliate), instruct such persons to forward such information to the beneficial owners of such securities in a timely manner and undertake to pay the reasonable expenses incurred by such persons in forwarding such information; and

(iii) Promptly disseminate disclosure of material changes to the information required by paragraph (d) of this section in a manner reasonably calculated to inform security holders.

(2) If the Rule 13e-3 transaction is a tender offer or a request or invitation for tenders of equity securities which is subject to Regulation 14D [§§ 240.14d-1 to 240.14d-101] or Rule 13e-4 [§ 240.13e-4], the tender offer containing the information required by paragraph (e) of this section, and any material change with respect thereto, shall be published, sent or given in accordance with Regulation 14D or Rule 13e-4, respectively, to security holders of the class of securities being sought by the issuer or affiliate.

(g) Exceptions. This section shall not apply to:

(1) Any Rule 13e-3 transaction by or on behalf of a person which occurs within one year of the date of termination of a tender offer in which such person was the bidder and became an affiliate of the issuer as a result of such tender offer: *Provided,* That the consideration offered to unaffiliated security holders in such Rule 13e-3 transaction is at least equal to the highest consideration offered during such tender offer and *Provided further,* That:

(i) If such tender offer was made for any or all securities of a class of the issuer;

(A) Such tender offer fully disclosed such person's intention to engage in a Rule 13e-3 transaction, the form and effect of such transaction and, to the extent known, the proposed terms thereof; and

(B) Such Rule 13e-3 transaction is substantially similar to that described in such tender offer; or

(ii) If such tender offer was made for less than all the securities of a class of the issuer:

(A) Such tender offer fully disclosed a plan of merger, a plan of liquidation or a similar binding agreement between such person and the issuer with respect to a Rule 13e-3 transaction; and

(B) Such Rule 13e-3 transaction occurs pursuant to the plan of merger, plan of liquidation or similar binding agreement disclosed in the bidder's tender offer.

(2) Any Rule 13e-3 transaction in which the security holders are offered or receive only an equity security Provided, That:

(i) Such equity security has substantially the same rights as the equity security which is the subject of the Rule 13e-3 transaction including, but not limited to, voting, dividends, redemption and liquidation rights except that this requirement shall be deemed to be satisfied if unaffiliated security holders are offered common stock;

(ii) Such equity security is registered pursuant to section 12 of the Act or reports are required to be filed by the issuer thereof pursuant to section 15(d) of the Act; and

(iii) If the security which is the subject of the Rule 13e-3 transaction was either listed on a national securities exchange or authorized to be quoted in an interdealer quotation system of a registered national securities association, such equity security is either listed on a national securities exchange or authorized to be quoted in an inter-dealer quotation system of a registered national securities association.

(3) [Reserved by 73 FR 17813]

(4) Redemptions, calls or similar purchases of an equity security by an issuer pursuant to specific provisions set forth in the instrument(s) creating or governing that class of equity securities; or

(5) Any solicitation by an issuer with respect to a plan of reorganization under Chapter XI of the Bankruptcy Act, as amended, if made after the entry of an order approving such plan pursuant to section 1125(b) of that Act and after, or concurrently with, the transmittal of information concerning such plan as required by section 1125(b) of that Act.

(6) Any tender offer or business combination made in compliance with § 230.802 of this chapter, § 240.13e-4(h)(8) or § 240.14d-1(c) or any other kind of transaction that otherwise meets the conditions for reliance on the cross-border exemptions set forth in § 240.13e-4(h)(8), § 240.14d-1(c)or § 230.802 of this chapter except for the fact that it is not technically subject to those rules.

Instruction to § 240.13e-3(g)(6): To the extent applicable, the acquiror must comply with the conditions set forth in § 230.802 of this chapter, and §§ 240.13e-4(h)(8) and 14d-1(c). If the acquiror publishes or otherwise disseminates an informational document to the holders of the subject securities in connection with the transaction, the acquiror must furnish an English translation of that informational document, including any amendments thereto, to the Commission under cover of Form CB (§ 239.800 of this chapter) by the first business day after publication or dissemination. If the acquiror is a foreign entity, it must also file a Form F-X (§ 239.42 of this chapter) with the Commission at the same time as the submission of the Form CB to appoint an agent for service in the United States.

§ 240.13e-4 Tender Offers by Issuers

(a) Definitions. Unless the context otherwise requires, all terms used in this section and in Schedule TO (§ 240.14d-100) shall have the same meaning as in the Act or elsewhere in the General Rules and Regulations thereunder. In addition, the following definitions shall apply:

(1) The term issuer means any issuer which has a class of equity security registered pursuant to section 12 of the Act, or which is required to file periodic reports pursuant to section 15(d) of the Act, or which is a closed-end investment company registered under the Investment Company Act of 1940.

(2) The term issuer tender offer refers to a tender offer for, or a request or invitation for tenders of, any class of equity security, made by the issuer of such class of equity security or by an affiliate of such issuer.

(3) As used in this section and in Schedule TO (§ 240.14d-100), the term business day means any day, other than Saturday, Sunday, or a Federal holiday, and shall consist of the time period from 12:01 a.m. through 12:00 midnight Eastern Time. In computing any time period under this Rule or Schedule TO, the date of the event that begins the running of such time period shall be included except that if such event occurs on other than a business day such period shall begin to run on and shall include the first business day thereafter.

(4) The term commencement means 12:01 a.m. on the date that the issuer or affiliate has first published, sent or given the means to tender to security holders. For purposes of this section, the means to tender includes the transmittal form or a statement regarding how the transmittal form may be obtained.

(5) The term termination means the date after which securities may not be tendered pursuant to an issuer tender offer.

(6) The term security holders means holders of record and beneficial owners of securities of the class of equity security which is the subject of an issuer tender offer.

(7) The term security position listing means, with respect to the securities of any issuer held by a registered clearing agency in the name of the clearing agency or its nominee, a list of those participants in the clearing agency on whose behalf the clearing agency holds the issuer's securities and of the participants' respective positions in such securities as of a specified date.

(b) Filing, disclosure and dissemination. As soon as practicable on the date of commencement of the issuer tender offer, the issuer or affiliate making the issuer tender offer must comply with:

(1) The filing requirements of paragraph (c)(2) of this section;

(2) The disclosure requirements of paragraph (d)(1) of this section; and

(3) The dissemination requirements of paragraph (e) of this section.

(c) Material required to be filed. The issuer or affiliate making the issuer tender offer must file with the Commission:

(1) All written communications made by the issuer or affiliate relating to the issuer tender offer, from and including the first public announcement, as soon as practicable on the date of the communication;

(2) A Schedule TO (§ 240.14d-100), including all exhibits;

(3) An amendment to Schedule TO (§ 240.14d-100) reporting promptly any material changes in the information set forth in the schedule previously filed; and

(4) A final amendment to Schedule TO (§ 240.14d-100) reporting promptly the results of the issuer tender offer.

Instructions to § 240.13e-4(c):

1. Pre-commencement communications must be filed under cover of Schedule TO (§ 240.14d-100) and the box on the cover page of the schedule must be marked.

2. Any communications made in connection with an exchange offer registered under the Securities Act of 1933 need only be filed under § 230.425 of this chapter and will be deemed filed under this section.

3. Each pre-commencement written communication must include a prominent legend in clear, plain language advising security holders to read the tender offer statement when it is available because it contains important information. The legend also must advise investors that they can get the tender offer statement and other filed documents for free at the Commission's web site and explain which documents are free from the issuer.

4. See §§ 230.135, 230.165 and 230.166 of this chapter for pre-commencement communications made in connection with registered exchange offers.

5. "Public announcement" is any oral or written communication by the issuer, affiliate or any person authorized to act on their behalf that is reasonably designed to, or has the effect of, informing the public or security holders in general about the issuer tender offer.

(d) Disclosure of tender offer information to security holders.

(1) The issuer or affiliate making the issuer tender offer must disclose, in a manner prescribed by paragraph (e)(1) of this section, the following:

(i) The information required by Item 1 of Schedule TO (§ 240.14d-100) (summary term sheet); and

(ii) The information required by the remaining items of Schedule TO for issuer tender offers, except for Item 12 (exhibits), or a fair and adequate summary of the information.

(2) If there are any material changes in the information previously disclosed to security holders, the issuer or affiliate must disclose the changes promptly to security holders in a manner specified in paragraph (e)(3) of this section.

(3) If the issuer or affiliate disseminates the issuer tender offer by means of summary publication as described in paragraph (e)(1)(iii) of this section, the summary advertisement must not include a transmittal letter that would permit security holders to tender securities sought in the offer and must disclose at least the following information:

(i) The identity of the issuer or affiliate making the issuer tender offer;

(ii) The information required by § 229.1004(a)(1) and § 229.1006(a) of this chapter;

(iii) Instructions on how security holders can obtain promptly a copy of the statement required by paragraph (d)(1) of this section, at the issuer or affiliate's expense; and

(iv) A statement that the information contained in the statement required by paragraph (d)(1) of this section is incorporated by reference.

(e) Dissemination of tender offers to security holders. An issuer tender offer will be deemed to be published, sent or given to security holders if the issuer or affiliate making the issuer tender offer complies fully with one or more of the methods described in this section.

(1) For issuer tender offers in which the consideration offered consists solely of cash and/or securities exempt from registration under section 3 of the Securities Act of 1933 (15 U.S.C. 77c):

(i) Dissemination of cash issuer tender offers by long-form publication: By making adequate publication of the information required by paragraph (d)(1) of this section in a newspaper or newspapers, on the date of commencement of the issuer tender offer.

(ii) Dissemination of any issuer tender offer by use of stockholder and other lists:

(A) By mailing or otherwise furnishing promptly a statement containing the information required by paragraph (d)(1) of this section to each security holder whose name appears on the most recent stockholder list of the issuer;

(B) By contacting each participant on the most recent security position listing of any clearing agency within the possession or access of the issuer or affiliate making the issuer tender offer, and making inquiry of each participant as to the approximate number of beneficial owners of the securities sought in the offer that are held by the participant;

(C) By furnishing to each participant a sufficient number of copies of the statement required by paragraph (d)(1) of this section for transmittal to the beneficial owners; and

(D) By agreeing to reimburse each participant promptly for its reasonable expenses incurred in forwarding the statement to beneficial owners.

(iii) Dissemination of certain cash issuer tender offers by summary publication:

(A) If the issuer tender offer is not subject to § 240.13e-3, by making adequate publication of a summary advertisement containing the information required by paragraph (d)(3) of this section in a newspaper or newspapers, on the date of commencement of the issuer tender offer; and

(B) By mailing or otherwise furnishing promptly the statement required by paragraph (d)(1) of this section and a transmittal letter to any security holder who requests a copy of the statement or transmittal letter.

Instruction to paragraph (e)(1): For purposes of paragraphs (e)(1)(i) and (e)(1)(iii) of this section, adequate publication of the issuer tender offer may require publication in a newspaper with a national circulation, a newspaper with metropolitan or regional circulation, or a combination of the two, depending upon the facts and circumstances involved.

(2) For tender offers in which the consideration consists solely or partially of securities registered under the Securities Act of 1933, a registration statement containing all of the required information, including pricing information, has been filed and a preliminary prospectus or a prospectus that meets the requirements of Section 10(a) of the Securities Act (15 U.S.C. 77j(a)), including a letter of transmittal, is delivered to security holders. However, for going-private transactions (as defined by § 240.13e-3) and roll-up transactions (as described by Item 901 of Regulation S-K (§ 229.901 of this chapter)), a registration statement registering the securities to be offered must have become effective and only a prospectus that meets the requirements of Section 10(a) of the Securities Act may be delivered to security holders on the date of commencement.

Instructions to paragraph (e)(2):

1. If the prospectus is being delivered by mail, mailing on the date of commencement is sufficient.

2. A preliminary prospectus used under this section may not omit information under § 230.430 or § 230.430A of this chapter.

3. If a preliminary prospectus is used under this section and the issuer must disseminate material changes, the tender offer must remain open for the period specified in paragraph (e)(3) of this section.

4. If a preliminary prospectus is used under this section, tenders may be requested in accordance with § 230.162(a) of this chapter.

(3) If a material change occurs in the information published, sent or given to security holders, the issuer or affiliate must disseminate promptly disclosure of the change in a manner reasonably calculated to inform security holders of the change. In a registered securities offer where the issuer or affiliate disseminates the preliminary prospectus as permitted by paragraph (e)(2) of this section, the offer must remain open from the date that material changes to the tender offer materials are disseminated to security holders, as follows:

(i) Five business days for a prospectus supplement containing a material change other than price or share levels;

(ii) Ten business days for a prospectus supplement containing a change in price, the amount of securities sought, the dealer's soliciting fee, or other similarly significant change;

(iii) Ten business days for a prospectus supplement included as part of a post-effective amendment; and

(iv) Twenty business days for a revised prospectus when the initial prospectus was materially deficient.

(f) Manner of making tender offer.

(1) The issuer tender offer, unless withdrawn, shall remain open until the expiration of:

(i) At least twenty business days from its commencement; and

(ii) At least ten business days from the date that notice of an increase or decrease in the percentage of the class of securities being sought or the consideration offered or the dealer's soliciting fee to be given is first published, sent or given to security holders.

Provided, however, That, for purposes of this paragraph, the acceptance for payment by the issuer or affiliate of an additional amount of securities not to exceed two percent of the class of securities that is the subject of the tender offer shall not be deemed to be an increase. For purposes of this paragraph, the percentage of a class of securities shall be calculated in accordance with section 14(d)(3) of the Act.

(2) The issuer or affiliate making the issuer tender offer shall permit securities tendered pursuant to the issuer tender offer to be withdrawn:

(i) At any time during the period such issuer tender offer remains open; and

(ii) If not yet accepted for payment, after the expiration of forty business days from the commencement of the issuer tender offer.

(3) If the issuer or affiliate makes a tender offer for less than all of the outstanding equity securities of a class, and if a greater number of securities is tendered pursuant thereto than the issuer or affiliate is bound or willing to take up and pay for, the securities taken up and paid for shall be taken up and paid for as nearly as may be pro rata, disregarding fractions, according to the number of securities tendered by each security holder during the period such offer remains open; *Provided, however,*

That this provision shall not prohibit the issuer or affiliate making the issuer tender offer from:

(i) Accepting all securities tendered by persons who own, beneficially or of record, an aggregate of not more than a specified number which is less than one hundred shares of such security and who tender all their securities, before prorating securities tendered by others; or

(ii) Accepting by lot securities tendered by security holders who tender all securities held by them and who, when tendering their securities, elect to have either all or none or at least a minimum amount or none accepted, if the issuer or affiliate first accepts all securities tendered by security holders who do not so elect;

(4) In the event the issuer or affiliate making the issuer tender increases the consideration offered after the issuer tender offer has commenced, such issuer or affiliate shall pay such increased consideration to all security holders whose tendered securities are accepted for payment by such issuer or affiliate.

(5) The issuer or affiliate making the tender offer shall either pay the consideration offered, or return the tendered securities, promptly after the termination or withdrawal of the tender offer.

(6) Until the expiration of at least ten business days after the date of termination of the issuer tender offer, neither the issuer nor any affiliate shall make any purchases, otherwise than pursuant to the tender offer, of:

(i) Any security which is the subject of the issuer tender offer, or any security of the same class and series, or any right to purchase any such securities; and

(ii) In the case of an issuer tender offer which is an exchange offer, any security being offered pursuant to such exchange offer, or any security of the same class and series, or any right to purchase any such security.

(7) The time periods for the minimum offering periods pursuant to this section shall be computed on a concurrent as opposed to a consecutive basis.

(8) No issuer or affiliate shall make a tender offer unless:

(i) The tender offer is open to all security holders of the class of securities subject to the tender offer; and

(ii) The consideration paid to any security holder for securities tendered in the tender offer is the highest consideration paid to any other security holder for securities tendered in the tender offer.

(9) Paragraph (f)(8)(i) of this section shall not:

(i) Affect dissemination under paragraph (e) of this section; or

(ii) Prohibit an issuer or affiliate from making a tender offer excluding all security holders in a state where the issuer or affiliate is prohibited from making the tender offer by administrative or judicial action pursuant to a state statute after a good faith effort by the issuer or affiliate to comply with such statute.

(10) Paragraph (f)(8)(ii) of this section shall not prohibit the offer of more than one type of consideration in a tender offer, provided that:

(i) Security holders are afforded equal right to elect among each of the types of consideration offered; and

(ii) The highest consideration of each type paid to any security holder is paid to any other security holder receiving that type of consideration.

(11) If the offer and sale of securities constituting consideration offered in an issuer tender offer is prohibited by the appropriate authority of a state after a good faith effort by the issuer or affiliate to register or qualify the offer and sale of such securities in such state:

(i) The issuer or affiliate may offer security holders in such state an alternative form of consideration; and

(ii) Paragraph (f)(10) of this section shall not operate to require the issuer or affiliate to offer or pay the alternative form of consideration to security holders in any other state.

(12)(i) Paragraph (f)(8)(ii) of this section shall not prohibit the negotiation, execution or amendment of an employment compensation, severance or other employee benefit arrangement, or payments made or to be made or benefits granted or to be granted according to such an arrangement, with respect to any security holder of the issuer, where the amount payable under the arrangement:

(A) Is being paid or granted as compensation for past services performed, future services to be performed, or future services to be refrained from performing, by the security holder (and matters incidental thereto); and

(B) Is not calculated based on the number of securities tendered or to be tendered in the tender offer by the security holder.

(ii) The provisions of paragraph (f)(12)(i) of this section shall be satisfied and, therefore, pursuant to this non-exclusive safe harbor, the negotiation, execution or amendment of an arrangement and any payments made or to be made or benefits granted or to be granted according to that arrangement shall not be prohibited by paragraph (f)(8)(ii) of this section, if the arrangement is approved as an employment compensation, severance or other employee benefit arrangement solely by independent directors as follows:

(A) The compensation committee or a committee of the board of directors that performs functions similar to a compensation committee of the issuer approves the arrangement, regardless of whether the issuer is a party to the arrangement, or, if an affiliate is a party to the arrangement, the compensation committee or a committee of the board of directors that performs functions similar to a compensation committee of the affiliate approves the arrangement; or

(B) If the issuer's or affiliate's board of directors, as applicable, does not have a compensation committee or a committee of the board of directors that performs functions similar to a compensation committee or if none of the members of the issuer's or affiliate's compensation committee or committee that performs functions similar to a compensation committee is independent, a special committee of the board of directors formed to consider and approve the arrangement approves the arrangement; or

(C) If the issuer or affiliate, as applicable, is a foreign private issuer, any or all members of the board of directors or any committee of the board of directors authorized to approve employment compensation, severance or other employee benefit arrangements under the laws or regulations of the home country approves the arrangement.

Instructions to paragraph (f)(12)(ii): For purposes of determining whether the members of the committee approving an arrangement in accordance with the provisions of paragraph (f)(12)(ii) of this section are independent, the following provisions shall apply:

1. If the issuer or affiliate, as applicable, is a listed issuer (as defined in § 240.10A-3 of this chapter) whose securities are listed either on a national securities exchange registered pursuant to section 6(a) of the Exchange Act (15 U.S.C. 78f(a)) or in an inter-dealer quotation system of a national securities association registered pursuant to section 15A(a) of the Exchange Act (15 U.S.C. 78*o*-3(a)) that has independence requirements for compensation committee members that have been approved by the Commission (as those requirements may be modified or supplemented), apply the issuer's or affiliate's definition of independence that it uses for determining that the members of the compensation committee are independent in compliance with the listing standards applicable to compensation committee members of the listed issuer.

2. If the issuer or affiliate, as applicable, is not a listed issuer (as defined in § 240.10A-3 of this chapter), apply the independence requirements for compensation committee members of a national securities exchange registered pursuant to section 6(a) of the Exchange Act (15 U.S.C. 78f(a)) or an inter-dealer quotation system of a national securities association registered pursuant to section 15A(a) of the Exchange Act (15 U.S.C. 78*o*-3(a)) that have been approved by the Commission (as those requirements may be modified or supplemented). Whatever definition the issuer or affiliate, as applicable, chooses, it must apply that definition consistently to all members of the committee approving the arrangement.

3. Notwithstanding Instructions 1 and 2 to paragraph (f)(12)(ii), if the issuer or affiliate, as applicable, is a closed-end investment company registered under the Investment Company Act of 1940, a director is considered to be independent if the director is not, other than in his or her capacity as a member of the board of directors or any board committee, an "interested person" of the investment company, as defined in section 2(a)(19) of the Investment Company Act of 1940 (15 U.S.C. 80a-2(a)(19)).

4. If the issuer or affiliate, as applicable, is a foreign private issuer, apply either the independence standards set forth in Instructions 1 and 2 to paragraph (f)(12)(ii) or the independence requirements of the laws, regulations, codes or standards of the home country of the issuer or affiliate, as applicable, for members of the board of directors or the committee of the board of directors approving the arrangement.

5. A determination by the issuer's or affiliate's board of directors, as applicable, that the members of the board of directors or the committee of the board of directors, as applicable, approving an arrangement in accordance with the provisions of paragraph (f)(12)(ii) are independent in accordance with the provisions of this instruction to paragraph (f)(12)(ii) shall satisfy the independence requirements of paragraph (f)(12)(ii).

Instruction to paragraph (f)(12): The fact that the provisions of paragraph (f)(12) of this section extend only to employment compensation, severance and other employee benefit arrangements and not to other arrangements, such as commercial arrangements, does not raise any inference that a payment under any such other arrangement constitutes consideration paid for securities in a tender offer.

(13) Electronic filings. If the issuer or affiliate is an electronic filer, the minimum offering periods set forth in paragraph (f)(1) of this section shall be tolled for any period during which it fails to file in electronic format, absent a hardship exemption (§§ 232.201 and 232.202 of this chapter), the Schedule TO (§ 240.14d-100), the tender offer material specified in Item 1016(a)(1) of Regulation M-A (§ 229.1016(a)(1) of this chapter), and any amendments thereto. If such documents were filed in paper pursuant to a hardship exemption (see § 232.201 and § 232.202 of this chapter), the minimum offering periods shall be tolled for any period during which a required confirming electronic copy of such Schedule and tender offer material is delinquent.

(g) The requirements of section 13(e) (1) of the Act and Rule 13e-4 and Schedule TO (§ 240.14d-100) thereunder shall be deemed satisfied with respect to any issuer tender offer, including any exchange offer, where the issuer is incorporated or organized under the laws of Canada or any Canadian province or territory, is a foreign private issuer, and is not an investment company registered or required to be registered under the Investment Company Act of 1940, if less than 40 percent of the class of securities that is the subject of the tender offer is held by U.S. holders, and the tender offer is subject to, and the issuer complies with, the laws, regulations and policies of Canada and/or any of its provinces or territories governing the conduct of the offer (unless the issuer has received an exemption(s) from, and the issuer tender offer does not comply with, requirements that otherwise would be prescribed by this section), provided that:

(1) Where the consideration for an issuer tender offer subject to this paragraph consists solely of cash, the entire disclosure document or documents required to be furnished to holders of the class of securities to be acquired shall be filed with the Commission on Schedule 13E-4F (§ 240.13e-102) and disseminated to shareholders residing in the United States in accordance with such Canadian laws, regulations and policies; or

(2) Where the consideration for an issuer tender offer subject to this paragraph includes securities to be issued pursuant to the offer, any registration statement and/or prospectus relating thereto shall be filed with the Commission along with the Schedule 13E-4F referred to in paragraph (g)(1) of this section, and shall be disseminated, together with the home jurisdiction document(s) accompanying such Schedule, to shareholders of the issuer residing in the United States in accordance with such Canadian laws, regulations and policies.

Note: Notwithstanding the grant of an exemption from one or more of the applicable Canadian regulatory provisions imposing requirements that otherwise would be prescribed by this section, the issuer tender offer will be eligible to proceed in accordance with the requirements of this section if the Commission by order determines that the applicable Canadian regulatory provisions are adequate to protect the interest of investors.

(h) This section shall not apply to:

(1) Calls or redemptions of any security in accordance with the terms and conditions of its governing instruments;

(2) Offers to purchase securities evidenced by a scrip certificate, order form or similar document which represents a fractional interest in a share of stock or similar security;

(3) Offers to purchase securities pursuant to a statutory procedure for the purchase of dissenting security holders' securities;

(4) Any tender offer which is subject to section 14(d) of the Act;

(5) Offers to purchase from security holders who own an aggregate of not more than a specified number of shares that is less than one hundred: *Provided, however,* That:

(i) The offer complies with paragraph (f)(8)(i) of this section with respect to security holders who own a number of shares equal to or less than the specified number of shares, except that an issuer can elect to exclude participants in a plan as that term is defined in § 242.100 of this chapter, or to exclude security holders who do not own their shares as of a specified date determined by the issuer; and

(ii) The offer complies with paragraph (f)(8)(ii) of this section or the consideration paid pursuant to the offer is determined on the basis of a uniformly applied formula based on the market price of the subject security;

(6) An issuer tender offer made solely to effect a rescission offer: *Provided, however,* That the offer is registered under the Securities Act of 1933 (15 U.S.C. 77a et seq.), and the consideration is equal to the price paid by each security holder, plus legal interest if the issuer elects to or is required to pay legal interest;

(7) Offers by closed-end management investment companies to repurchase equity securities pursuant to § 270.23c-3 of this chapter;

(8) Cross-border tender offers (Tier I). Any issuer tender offer (including any exchange offer) where the issuer is a foreign private issuer as defined in § 240.3b-4 if the following conditions are satisfied.

(i) Except in the case of an issuer tender offer that is commenced during the pendency of a tender offer made by a third party in reliance on § 240.14d-1(c), U.S. holders do not hold more than 10 percent of the subject class sought in the offer (as determined under Instructions 2 or 3 to paragraph (h)(8) and paragraph (i) of this section);

(ii) The issuer or affiliate must permit U.S. holders to participate in the offer on terms at least as favorable as those offered any other holder of the same class of securities that is the subject of the offer; however:

(A) Registered exchange offers. If the issuer or affiliate offers securities registered under the Securities Act of 1933 (15 U.S.C. 77a et seq.), the issuer or affiliate need not extend the offer to security holders in those states or jurisdictions that prohibit the offer or sale of the securities after the issuer or affiliate has made a good faith effort to register or qualify the offer and sale of securities in that state or jurisdiction, except that the issuer or affiliate must offer the same cash alternative to security holders in any such state or jurisdiction that it has offered to security holders in any other state or jurisdiction.

(B) Exempt exchange offers. If the issuer or affiliate offers securities exempt from registration under § 230.802 of this chapter, the issuer or affiliate need not extend the offer to security holders in those states or jurisdictions that require registration or qualification, except that the issuer or affiliate must offer the same cash alternative to security holders in any such state or jurisdiction that it has offered to security holders in any other state or jurisdiction.

(C) Cash only consideration. The issuer or affiliate may offer U.S. holders cash only consideration for the tender of the subject securities, notwithstanding the fact that the issuer or affiliate is offering security holders outside the United States a consideration that consists in whole or in part of securities of the issuer or affiliate, if the issuer or affiliate has a reasonable basis for believing that the amount of cash is substantially equivalent to the value of the consideration offered to non-U.S. holders, and either of the following conditions are satisfied:

(*1*) The offered security is a "margin security" within the meaning of Regulation T (12 CFR 220.2) and the issuer or affiliate undertakes to provide, upon the request of any U.S. holder or the Commission staff, the closing price and daily trading volume of the security on the principal trading market for the security as of the last trading day of each of the six months preceding the announcement of the offer and each of the trading days thereafter; or

(*2*) If the offered security is not a "margin security" within the meaning of Regulation T (12 CFR 220.2), the issuer or affiliate undertakes to provide, upon the request of any U.S. holder or the Commission staff, an opinion of an independent expert stating that the cash consideration offered to U.S. holders is substantially equivalent to the value of the consideration offered security holders outside the United States.

(D) Disparate tax treatment. If the issuer or affiliate offers "loan notes" solely to offer sellers tax advantages not available in the United States and these notes are neither listed on any organized securities market nor registered under the Securities Act of 1933 (15 U.S.C. 77a et seq.), the loan notes need not be offered to U.S. holders.

(iii) Informational documents.

(A) If the issuer or affiliate publishes or otherwise disseminates an informational document to the holders of the securities in connection with the issuer tender offer (including any exchange offer), the issuer or affiliate must furnish that informational document, including any amendments thereto, in English, to the Commission on Form CB (§ 249.480 of this chapter) by the first business day after publication or dissemination. If the issuer or affiliate is a foreign company, it must also file a Form F-X (§ 239.42 of this chapter) with the Commission at the same time as the submission of Form CB to appoint an agent for service in the United States.

(B) The issuer or affiliate must disseminate any informational document to U.S. holders, including any amendments thereto, in English, on a comparable basis to that provided to security holders in the home jurisdiction.

(C) If the issuer or affiliate disseminates by publication in its home jurisdiction, the issuer or affiliate must publish the information in the United States in a manner reasonably calculated to inform U.S. holders of the offer.

(iv) An investment company registered or required to be registered under the Investment Company Act of 1940 (15 U.S.C. 80a-1 et seq.), other than a registered closed-end investment company, may not use this paragraph (h)(8); or

(9) Any other transaction or transactions, if the Commission, upon written request or upon its own motion, exempts such transaction or

transactions, either unconditionally, or on specified terms and conditions, as not constituting a fraudulent, deceptive or manipulative act or practice comprehended within the purpose of this section.

(i) Cross-border tender offers (Tier II). Any issuer tender offer (including any exchange offer) that meets the conditions in paragraph (i)(1) of this section shall be entitled to the exemptive relief specified in paragraph (i)(2) of this section, provided that such issuer tender offer complies with all the requirements of this section other than those for which an exemption has been specifically provided in paragraph (i)(2) of this section. In addition, any issuer tender offer (including any exchange offer) subject only to the requirements of section 14(e) of the Act and Regulation 14E (§§ 240.14e-1 through 240.14e-8) thereunder that meets the conditions in paragraph (i)(1) of this section also shall be entitled to the exemptive relief specified in paragraph (i)(2) of this section, to the extent needed under the requirements of Regulation 14E, so long as the tender offer complies with all requirements of Regulation 14E other than those for which an exemption has been specifically provided in paragraph (i)(2) of this section:

(1) Conditions.

(i) The issuer is a foreign private issuer as defined in § 240.3b-4 and is not an investment company registered or required to be registered under the Investment Company Act of 1940 (15 U.S.C. 80a-1 et seq.), other than a registered closed-end investment company; and

(ii) Except in the case of an issuer tender offer commenced during the pendency of a tender offer made by a third party in reliance on § 240.14d-1(d), U.S. holders do not hold more than 40 percent of the class of securities sought in the offer (as determined in accordance with Instructions 2 or 3 to paragraphs (h)(8) and (i) of this section).

(2) Exemptions. The issuer tender offer shall comply with all requirements of this section other than the following:

(i) Equal treatment—loan notes. If the issuer or affiliate offers loan notes solely to offer sellers tax advantages not available in the United States and these notes are neither listed on any organized securities market nor registered under the Securities Act (15 U.S.C. 77a et seq.), the loan notes need not be offered to U.S. holders, notwithstanding paragraph (f)(8) and (h)(9) of this section.

(ii) Equal treatment—separate U.S. and foreign offers. Notwithstanding the provisions of paragraph (f)(8) of this section, an issuer or affiliate conducting an issuer tender offer meeting the conditions of paragraph (i)(1) of this section may separate the offer into multiple offers: one offer made to U.S. holders, which also may include all holders of American Depositary Shares representing interests in the subject securities, and one or more offers made to non-U.S. holders. The U.S. offer must be made on terms at least as favorable as those offered any other holder of the same class of securities that is the subject of the tender offers. U.S. holders may be included in the foreign offer(s) only where the laws of the jurisdiction governing such foreign offer(s) expressly preclude the exclusion of U.S. holders from the foreign offer(s) and where the offer materials distributed to U.S. holders fully and adequately disclose the risks of participating in the foreign offer(s).

(iii) Notice of extensions. Notice of extensions made in accordance with the requirements of the home jurisdiction law or practice will satisfy the requirements of § 240.14e-1(d).

(iv) Prompt payment. Payment made in accordance with the requirements of the home jurisdiction law or practice will satisfy the requirements of § 240.14e-1(c).

(v) Suspension of withdrawal rights during counting of tendered securities. The issuer or affiliate may suspend withdrawal rights required under paragraph (f)(2) of this section at the end of the offer and during the period that securities tendered into the offer are being counted, provided that:

(A) The issuer or affiliate has provided an offer period, including withdrawal rights, for a period of at least 20 U.S. business days;

(B) At the time withdrawal rights are suspended, all offer conditions have been satisfied or waived, except to the extent that the issuer or affiliate is in the process of determining whether a minimum acceptance condition included in the terms of the offer has been satisfied by counting tendered securities; and

(C) Withdrawal rights are suspended only during the counting process and are reinstated immediately thereafter, except to the extent that they are terminated through the acceptance of tendered securities.

(vi) Early termination of an initial offering period. An issuer or affiliate conducting an issuer tender offer may terminate an initial offering period, including a voluntary extension of that period, if at the time the initial offering period and withdrawal rights terminate, the following conditions are met:

(A) The initial offering period has been open for at least 20 U.S. business days;

(B) The issuer or affiliate has adequately discussed the possibility of and the impact of the early termination in the original offer materials;

(C) The issuer or affiliate provides a subsequent offering period after the termination of the initial offering period;

(D) All offer conditions are satisfied as of the time when the initial offering period ends; and

(E) The issuer or affiliate does not terminate the initial offering period or any extension of that period during any mandatory extension required under U.S. tender offer rules.

Instructions to paragraph (h)(8) and (i) of this section:

1. Home jurisdiction means both the jurisdiction of the issuer's incorporation, organization or chartering and the principal foreign market where the issuer's securities are listed or quoted.

2. U.S. holder means any security holder resident in the United States. To determine the percentage of outstanding securities held by U.S. holders:

i. Calculate the U.S. ownership as of a date no more than 60 days before and no more than 30 days after the public announcement of the tender offer. If you are unable to calculate as of a date within these time frames, the calculation may be made as of the most recent practicable date before public announcement, but in no event earlier than 120 days before announcement;

ii. Include securities underlying American Depositary Shares convertible or exchangeable into the securities that are the subject of the tender offer when calculating the number of subject securities outstanding, as well as the number held by U.S. holders. Exclude from the calculations other types of securities that are convertible or exchangeable into the securities that are the subject of the tender offer, such as warrants, options and convertible securities;

iii. Use the method of calculating record ownership in § 240.12g3-2(a), except that your inquiry as to the amount of securities represented by accounts of customers resident in the United States may be limited to brokers, dealers, banks and other nominees located in the United States, your jurisdiction of incorporation, and the jurisdiction that is the primary trading market for the subject securities, if different than your jurisdiction of incorporation;

iv. If, after reasonable inquiry, you are unable to obtain information about the amount of securities represented by accounts of customers resident in the United States, you may assume, for purposes of this definition, that the customers are residents of the jurisdiction in which the nominee has its principal place of business; and

v. Count securities as beneficially owned by residents of the United States as reported on reports of beneficial ownership that are provided to you or publicly filed and based on information otherwise provided to you.

3. If you are unable to conduct the analysis of U.S. ownership set forth in Instruction 2 above, U.S. holders will be presumed to hold 10 percent or less of the outstanding subject securities (40 percent for Tier II) so long as there is a primary trading market outside the United States, as defined in § 240.12h-6(f)(5) of this chapter, unless:

i. Average daily trading volume of the subject securities in the United States for a recent twelve-month period ending on a date no more than 60 days before the public announcement of the tender offer exceeds 10 percent (or 40 percent) of the average daily trading volume of that class of securities on a worldwide basis for the same period; or

ii. The most recent annual report or annual information filed or submitted by the issuer with securities regulators of the home jurisdiction or with the Commission or any jurisdiction in which the subject securities trade before the public announcement of the offer indicates that U.S. holders hold more than 10 percent (or 40 percent) of the outstanding subject class of securities; or

iii. You know or have reason to know, before the public announcement of the offer, that the level of U.S. ownership of the subject securities exceeds 10 percent (or 40 percent) of such securities. As an example, you are deemed to know information about U.S. ownership of the subject class of securities that is publicly available and that appears in any filing with the Commission or any regulatory body in the home jurisdiction and, if different, the non-U.S. jurisdiction in which the primary trading market for the subject class of securities is located. You are also deemed to know information obtained or readily available from any other source that is reasonably reliable, including from persons you have retained to advise you about the transaction, as well as from third-party information providers. These examples are not intended to be exclusive.

4. United States means the United States of America, its territories and possessions, any State of the United States, and the District of Columbia.

5. The exemptions provided by paragraphs (h)(8) and (i) of this section are not available for any securities transaction or series of transactions that technically complies with paragraph (h)(8) and (i) of this section but are part of a plan or scheme to evade the provisions of this section.

(j)(1) It shall be a fraudulent, deceptive or manipulative act or practice, in connection with an issuer tender offer, for an issuer or an affiliate of such issuer, in connection with an issuer tender offer:

(i) To employ any device, scheme or artifice to defraud any person;

(ii) To make any untrue statement of a material fact or to omit to state a material fact necessary in order to make the statements made, in the light of the circumstances under which they were made, not misleading; or

(iii) To engage in any act, practice or course of business which operates or would operate as a fraud or deceit upon any person.

(2) As a means reasonably designed to prevent fraudulent, deceptive or manipulative acts or practices in connection with any issuer tender offer, it shall be unlawful for an issuer or an affiliate of such issuer to make an issuer tender offer unless:

(i) Such issuer or affiliate complies with the requirements of paragraphs (b), (c), (d), (e) and (f) of this section; and

(ii) The issuer tender offer is not in violation of paragraph (j)(1) of this section.

Section 14(a). The Solicitation of Proxies

§ 78n Proxies [Section 14]

(a) Solicitation of proxies in violation of rules and regulations

(1) It shall be unlawful for any person, by the use of the mails or by any means or instrumentality of interstate commerce or of any facility of a national securities exchange or otherwise, in contravention of such rules and regulations as the Commission may prescribe as necessary or appropriate in the public interest or for the protection of investors, to solicit or to permit the use of his name to solicit any proxy or consent or authorization in respect of any security (other than an exempted security) registered pursuant to section 78*l* of this title.

(2) The rules and regulations prescribed by the Commission under paragraph (1) may include—

(A) a requirement that a solicitation of proxy, consent, or authorization by (or on behalf of) an issuer include a nominee submitted by a shareholder to serve on the board of directors of the issuer; and

(B) a requirement that an issuer follow a certain procedure in relation to a solicitation described in subparagraph (A).

(b) Giving or refraining from giving proxy in respect of any security carried for account of customer

(1) It shall be unlawful for any member of a national securities exchange, or any broker or dealer registered under this chapter, or any bank, association, or other entity that exercises fiduciary powers, in contravention of such rules and regulations as the Commission may prescribe as necessary or appropriate in the public interest or for the protection of investors, to give, or to refrain from giving a proxy, consent, authorization, or information statement in respect of any security registered pursuant to section 78*l* of this title, or any security issued by an investment company registered under the Investment Company Act of 1940 [15 U.S.C. 80a-1 et seq.], and carried for the account of a customer.

(2) With respect to banks, the rules and regulations prescribed by the Commission under paragraph (1) shall not require the disclosure of the names of beneficial owners of securities in an account held by the bank on December 28, 1985, unless the beneficial owner consents to the disclosure. The provisions of this paragraph shall not apply in the case of a bank which the Commission finds has not made a good faith effort to obtain such consent from such beneficial owners.

(c) Information to holders of record prior to annual or other meeting

Unless proxies, consents, or authorizations in respect of a security registered pursuant to section 78*l* of this title, or a security issued by an investment company registered under the Investment Company Act of

1940 [15 U.S.C. 80a-1 et seq.], are solicited by or on behalf of the management of the issuer from the holders of record of such security in accordance with the rules and regulations prescribed under subsection (a) of this section, prior to any annual or other meeting of the holders of such security, such issuer shall, in accordance with rules and regulations prescribed by the Commission, file with the Commission and transmit to all holders of record of such security information substantially equivalent to the information which would be required to be transmitted if a solicitation were made, but no information shall be required to be filed or transmitted pursuant to this subsection before July 1, 1964.

(d) TENDER OFFER BY OWNER OF MORE THAN FIVE PER CENTUM OF CLASS OF SECURITIES; EXCEPTIONS

(1) It shall be unlawful for any person, directly or indirectly, by use of the mails or by any means or instrumentality of interstate commerce or of any facility of a national securities exchange or otherwise, to make a tender offer for, or a request or invitation for tenders of, any class of any equity security which is registered pursuant to section 78*l* of this title, or any equity security of an insurance company which would have been required to be so registered except for the exemption contained in section 78*l*(g)(2)(G) of this title, or any equity security issued by a a closed-end investment company registered under the Investment Company Act of 1940 [15 U.S.C. 80a-1 et seq.], if, after consummation thereof, such person would, directly or indirectly, be the beneficial owner of more than 5 per centum of such class, unless at the time copies of the offer or request or invitation are first published or sent or given to security holders such person has filed with the Commission a statement containing such of the information specified in section 78m(d) of this title, and such additional information as the Commission may by rules and regulations prescribe as necessary or appropriate in the public interest or for the protection of investors. All requests or invitations for tenders or advertisements making a tender offer or requesting or inviting tenders of such a security shall be filed as a part of such statement and shall contain such of the information contained in such statement as the Commission may by rules and regulations prescribe. Copies of any additional material soliciting or requesting such tender offers subsequent to the initial solicitation or request shall contain such information as the Commission may by rules and regulations prescribe as necessary or appropriate in the public interest or for the protection of investors, and shall be filed with the Commission not later than the time copies of such material are first published or sent or given to security holders. Copies of all statements, in the form in which such material is furnished to security holders and the Commission, shall be sent to the issuer not later than the date such material is first published or sent or given to any security holders.

(2) When two or more persons act as a partnership, limited partnership, syndicate, or other group for the purpose of acquiring, holding, or

disposing of securities of an issuer, such syndicate or group shall be deemed a "person" for purposes of this subsection.

(3) In determining, for purposes of this subsection, any percentage of a class of any security, such class shall be deemed to consist of the amount of the outstanding securities of such class, exclusive of any securities of such class held by or for the account of the issuer or a subsidiary of the issuer.

(4) Any solicitation or recommendation to the holders of such a security to accept or reject a tender offer or request or invitation for tenders shall be made in accordance with such rules and regulations as the Commission may prescribe as necessary or appropriate in the public interest or for the protection of investors.

(5) Securities deposited pursuant to a tender offer or request or invitation for tenders may be withdrawn by or on behalf of the depositor at any time until the expiration of seven days after the time definitive copies of the offer or request or invitation are first published or sent or given to security holders, and at any time after sixty days from the date of the original tender offer or request or invitation, except as the Commission may otherwise prescribe by rules, regulations, or order as necessary or appropriate in the public interest or for the protection of investors.

(6) Where any person makes a tender offer, or request or invitation for tenders, for less than all the outstanding equity securities of a class, and where a greater number of securities is deposited pursuant thereto within ten days after copies of the offer or request or invitation are first published or sent or given to security holders than such person is bound or willing to take up and pay for, the securities taken up shall be taken up as nearly as may be pro rata, disregarding fractions, according to the number of securities deposited by each depositor. The provisions of this subsection shall also apply to securities deposited within ten days after notice of an increase in the consideration offered to security holders, as described in paragraph (7), is first published or sent or given to security holders.

(7) Where any person varies the terms of a tender offer or request or invitation for tenders before the expiration thereof by increasing the consideration offered to holders of such securities, such person shall pay the increased consideration to each security holder whose securities are taken up and paid for pursuant to the tender offer or request or invitation for tenders whether or not such securities have been taken up by such person before the variation of the tender offer or request or invitation.

(8) The provisions of this subsection shall not apply to any offer for, or request or invitation for tenders of, any security—

(A) if the acquisition of such security, together with all other acquisitions by the same person of securities of the same class during the preceding twelve months, would not exceed 2 per centum of that class;

(B) by the issuer of such security; or

(C) which the Commission, by rules or regulations or by order, shall exempt from the provisions of this subsection as not entered into for the purpose of, and not having the effect of, changing or influencing the control of the issuer or otherwise as not comprehended within the purposes of this subsection.

(e) UNTRUE STATEMENT OF MATERIAL FACT OR OMISSION OF FACT WITH RESPECT TO TENDER OFFER

It shall be unlawful for any person to make any untrue statement of a material fact or omit to state any material fact necessary in order to make the statements made, in the light of the circumstances under which they are made, not misleading, or to engage in any fraudulent, deceptive, or manipulative acts or practices, in connection with any tender offer or request or invitation for tenders, or any solicitation of security holders in opposition to or in favor of any such offer, request, or invitation. The Commission shall, for the purposes of this subsection, by rules and regulations define, and prescribe means reasonably designed to prevent, such acts and practices as are fraudulent, deceptive, or manipulative.

(f) ELECTION OR DESIGNATION OF MAJORITY OF DIRECTORS OF ISSUER BY OWNER OF MORE THAN FIVE PER CENTUM OF CLASS OF SECURITIES AT OTHER THAN MEETING OF SECURITY HOLDERS

If, pursuant to any arrangement or understanding with the person or persons acquiring securities in a transaction subject to subsection (d) of this section or subsection (d) ofsection 78m of this title, any persons are to be elected or designated as directors of the issuer, otherwise than at a meeting of security holders, and the persons so elected or designated will constitute a majority of the directors of the issuer, then, prior to the time any such person takes office as a director, and in accordance with rules and regulations prescribed by the Commission, the issuer shall file with the Commission, and transmit to all holders of record of securities of the issuer who would be entitled to vote at a meeting for election of directors, information substantially equivalent to the information which would be required by subsection (a) or (c) of this section to be transmitted if such person or persons were nominees for election as directors at a meeting of such security holders.

(g) FILING FEES

(1)(A) At the time of filing such preliminary proxy solicitation material as the Commission may require by rule pursuant to subsection (a) of this section that concerns an acquisition, merger, consolidation, or proposed sale or other disposition of substantially all the assets of a company, the person making such filing, other than a company registered under the Investment Company Act of 1940 [15 U.S.C. 80a-1 et seq.], shall pay to the Commission the following fees:

(i) for preliminary proxy solicitation material involving an acquisition, merger, or consolidation, if there is a proposed payment of cash or transfer of securities or property to shareholders, a fee at a rate that, subject to paragraph (4), is equal to $92 per $1,000,000 of such proposed payment, or of the value of such securities or other property proposed to be transferred; and

(ii) for preliminary proxy solicitation material involving a proposed sale or other disposition of substantially all of the assets of a company, a fee at a rate that, subject to paragraph (4), is equal to $92 per $1,000,000 of the cash or of the value of any securities or other property proposed to be received upon such sale or disposition.

(B) The fee imposed under subparagraph (A) shall be reduced with respect to securities in an amount equal to any fee paid to the Commission with respect to such securities in connection with the proposed transaction under section 77f(b) of this title, or the fee paid under that section shall be reduced in an amount equal to the fee paid to the Commission in connection with such transaction under this subsection. Where two or more companies involved in an acquisition, merger, consolidation, sale, or other disposition of substantially all the assets of a company must file such proxy material with the Commission, each shall pay a proportionate share of such fee.

(2) At the time of filing such preliminary information statement as the Commission may require by rule pursuant to subsection (c) of this section, the issuer shall pay to the Commission the same fee as required for preliminary proxy solicitation material under paragraph (1) of this subsection.

(3) At the time of filing such statement as the Commission may require by rule pursuant to subsection (d)(1) of this section, the person making the filing shall pay to the Commission a fee at a rate that, subject to paragraph (4), is equal to $92 per $1,000,000 of the aggregate amount of cash or of the value of securities or other property proposed to be offered. The fee shall be reduced with respect to securities in an amount equal to any fee paid with respect to such securities in connection with the proposed transaction under section 6(b) of the Securities Act of 1933 (15 U.S.C. 77f(b)), or the fee paid under that section shall be reduced in an amount equal to the fee paid to the Commission in connection with such transaction under this subsection.

(4) ANNUAL ADJUSTMENT.—

For each fiscal year, the Commission shall by order adjust the rate required by paragraphs (1) and (3) for such fiscal year to a rate that is equal to the rate (expressed in dollars per million) that is applicable under section 6(b) of the Securities Act of 1933 (15 U.S.C. 77f(b)) for such fiscal year.

(5) FEE COLLECTION.—

Fees collected pursuant to this subsection for fiscal year 2012 and each fiscal year thereafter shall be deposited and credited as general revenue of the Treasury and shall not be available for obligation.

(6) REVIEW; EFFECTIVE DATE; PUBLICATION.—

In exercising its authority under this subsection, the Commission shall not be required to comply with the provisions of section 553 of title 5. An adjusted rate prescribed under paragraph (4) shall be published and take effect in accordance with section 6(b) of the Securities Act of 1933 (15 U.S.C. 77f(b)).

(7) PRO RATA APPLICATION.—

The rates per $1,000,000 required by this subsection shall be applied pro rata to amounts and balances of less than $1,000,000.

(8) Notwithstanding any other provision of law, the Commission may impose fees, charges, or prices for matters not involving any acquisition, merger, consolidation, sale, or other disposition of assets described in this subsection, as authorized bysection 9701 of title 31, or otherwise.

(h) PROXY SOLICITATIONS AND TENDER OFFERS IN CONNECTION WITH LIMITED PARTNERSHIP ROLLUP TRANSACTIONS

(1) PROXY RULES TO CONTAIN SPECIAL PROVISIONS It shall be unlawful for any person to solicit any proxy, consent, or authorization concerning a limited partnership rollup transaction, or to make any tender offer in furtherance of a limited partnership rollup transaction, unless such transaction is conducted in accordance with rules prescribed by the Commission under subsections (a) and (d) as required by this subsection. Such rules shall—

(A) permit any holder of a security that is the subject of the proposed limited partnership rollup transaction to engage in preliminary communications for the purpose of determining whether to solicit proxies, consents, or authorizations in opposition to the proposed limited partnership rollup transaction, without regard to whether any such communication would otherwise be considered a solicitation of proxies, and without being required to file soliciting material with the Commission prior to making that determination, except that—

(i) nothing in this subparagraph shall be construed to limit the application of any provision of this chapter prohibiting, or reasonably designed to prevent, fraudulent, deceptive, or manipulative acts or practices under this chapter; and

(ii) any holder of not less than 5 percent of the outstanding securities that are the subject of the proposed limited partnership rollup transaction who engages in the business of buying and selling limited partnership interests in the secondary market shall be required to disclose such ownership interests and any potential conflicts of interests in such preliminary communications;

(B) require the issuer to provide to holders of the securities that are the subject of the limited partnership rollup transaction such list of the holders of the issuer's securities as the Commission may determine in such form and subject to such terms and conditions as the Commission may specify;

(C) prohibit compensating any person soliciting proxies, consents, or authorizations directly from security holders concerning such a limited partnership rollup transaction—

(i) on the basis of whether the solicited proxy, consent, or authorization either approves or disapproves the proposed limited partnership rollup transaction; or

(ii) contingent on the approval, disapproval, or completion of the limited partnership rollup transaction;

(D) set forth disclosure requirements for soliciting material distributed in connection with a limited partnership rollup transaction, including requirements for clear, concise, and comprehensible disclosure with respect to—

(i) any changes in the business plan, voting rights, form of ownership interest, or the compensation of the general partner in the proposed limited partnership rollup transaction from each of the original limited partnerships;

(ii) the conflicts of interest, if any, of the general partner;

(iii) whether it is expected that there will be a significant difference between the exchange values of the limited partnerships and the trading price of the securities to be issued in the limited partnership rollup transaction;

(iv) the valuation of the limited partnerships and the method used to determine the value of the interests of the limited partners to be exchanged for the securities in the limited partnership rollup transaction;

(v) the differing risks and effects of the limited partnership rollup transaction for investors in different limited partnerships proposed to be included, and the risks and effects of completing the limited partnership rollup transaction with less than all limited partnerships;

(vi) the statement by the general partner required under subparagraph (E);

(vii) such other matters deemed necessary or appropriate by the Commission;

(E) require a statement by the general partner as to whether the proposed limited partnership rollup transaction is fair or unfair to investors in each limited partnership, a discussion of the basis for that conclusion, and an evaluation and a description by the general partner of alternatives to the limited partnership rollup transaction, such as liquidation;

(F) provide that, if the general partner or sponsor has obtained any opinion (other than an opinion of counsel), appraisal, or report that is prepared by an outside party and that is materially related to the limited partnership rollup transaction, such soliciting materials shall contain or be accompanied by clear, concise, and comprehensible disclosure with respect to—

(i) the analysis of the transaction, scope of review, preparation of the opinion, and basis for and methods of arriving at conclusions, and any representations and undertakings with respect thereto;

(ii) the identity and qualifications of the person who prepared the opinion, the method of selection of such person, and any material past, existing, or contemplated relationships between the person or any of its affiliates and the general partner, sponsor, successor, or any other affiliate;

(iii) any compensation of the preparer of such opinion, appraisal, or report that is contingent on the transaction's approval or completion; and

(iv) any limitations imposed by the issuer on the access afforded to such preparer to the issuer's personnel, premises, and relevant books and records;

(G) provide that, if the general partner or sponsor has obtained any opinion, appraisal, or report as described in subparagraph (F) from any person whose compensation is contingent on the transaction's approval or completion or who has not been given access by the issuer to its personnel and premises and relevant books and records, the general partner or sponsor shall state the reasons therefor;

(H) provide that, if the general partner or sponsor has not obtained any opinion on the fairness of the proposed limited partnership rollup transaction to investors in each of the affected partnerships, such soliciting materials shall contain or be accompanied by a statement of such partner's or sponsor's reasons for concluding that such an opinion is not necessary in order to permit the limited partners to make an informed decision on the proposed transaction;

(I) require that the soliciting material include a clear, concise, and comprehensible summary of the limited partnership rollup transaction (including a summary of the matters referred to in clauses (i) through (vii) of subparagraph (D) and a summary of the matter referred to in subparagraphs (F), (G), and (H)), with the risks of the limited partnership rollup transaction set forth prominently in the fore part thereof;

(J) provide that any solicitation or offering period with respect to any proxy solicitation, tender offer, or information statement in a limited partnership rollup transaction shall be for not less than the lesser of 60 calendar days or the maximum number of days permitted under applicable State law; and

(K) contain such other provisions as the Commission determines to be necessary or appropriate for the protection of investors in limited partnership rollup transactions.

(2) Exemptions

The Commission may, consistent with the public interest, the protection of investors, and the purposes of this chapter, exempt by rule or order any security or class of securities, any transaction or class of transactions, or any person or class of persons, in whole or in part, conditionally or unconditionally, from the requirements imposed pursuant to paragraph (1) or from the definition contained in paragraph (4).

(3) Effect on commission authority

Nothing in this subsection limits the authority of the Commission under subsection (a) or (d) or any other provision of this chapter or precludes the Commission from imposing, under subsection (a) or (d) or any other provision of this chapter, a remedy or procedure required to be imposed under this subsection.

(4) "Limited partnership rollup transaction" defined Except as provided in paragraph (5), as used in this subsection, the term "limited partnership rollup transaction" means a transaction involving the combination or reorganization of one or more limited partnerships, directly or indirectly, in which—

(A) some or all of the investors in any of such limited partnerships will receive new securities, or securities in another entity, that will be reported under a transaction reporting plan declared effective before December 17, 1993, by the Commission under section 78k-1 of this title;

(B) any of the investors' limited partnership securities are not, as of the date of filing, reported under a transaction reporting plan declared effective beforeDecember 17, 1993, by the Commission under section 78k-1 of this title;

(C) investors in any of the limited partnerships involved in the transaction are subject to a significant adverse change with respect to voting rights, the term of existence of the entity, management compensation, or investment objectives; and

(D) any of such investors are not provided an option to receive or retain a security under substantially the same terms and conditions as the original issue.

(5) Exclusions from definition

Notwithstanding paragraph (4), the term "limited partnership rollup transaction" does not include—

(A) a transaction that involves only a limited partnership or partnerships having an operating policy or practice of retaining cash available for distribution and reinvesting proceeds from the sale, financing, or refinancing of assets in accordance with such criteria as the Commission determines appropriate;

(B) a transaction involving only limited partnerships wherein the interests of the limited partners are repurchased, recalled, or exchanged in accordance with the terms of the preexisting limited partnership agreements for securities in an operating company specifically identified at the time of the formation of the original limited partnership;

(C) a transaction in which the securities to be issued or exchanged are not required to be and are not registered under the Securities Act of 1933 [15 U.S.C. 77a et seq.];

(D) a transaction that involves only issuers that are not required to register or report under section 78*l* of this title, both before and after the transaction;

(E) a transaction, except as the Commission may otherwise provide by rule for the protection of investors, involving the combination or reorganization of one or more limited partnerships in which a non-affiliated party succeeds to the interests of a general partner or sponsor, if—

(i) such action is approved by not less than $66\frac{2}{3}$ percent of the outstanding units of each of the participating limited partnerships; and

(ii) as a result of the transaction, the existing general partners will receive only compensation to which they are entitled as expressly provided for in the preexisting limited partnership agreements; or

(F) a transaction, except as the Commission may otherwise provide by rule for the protection of investors, in which the securities offered to investors are securities of another entity that are reported under a transaction reporting plan declared effective before December 17, 1993, by the Commission under section 78k-1 of this title, if—

(i) such other entity was formed, and such class of securities was reported and regularly traded, not less than 12 months before the date on which soliciting material is mailed to investors; and

(ii) the securities of that entity issued to investors in the transaction do not exceed 20 percent of the total outstanding securities of the entity, exclusive of any securities of such class held by or for the account of the entity or a subsidiary of the entity.

(i) DISCLOSURE OF PAY VERSUS PERFORMANCE

The Commission shall, by rule, require each issuer to disclose in any proxy or consent solicitation material for an annual meeting of the shareholders of the issuer a clear description of any compensation required to be disclosed by the issuer under section 229.402 of title 17, Code of Federal Regulations (or any successor thereto), including, for any issuer other than an emerging growth company, information that shows the relationship between executive compensation actually paid and the financial performance of the issuer, taking into account any change in the value of the shares of stock and dividends of the issuer and any distributions. The disclosure under this subsection may include a graphic representation of the information required to be disclosed.

(j) DISCLOSURE OF HEDGING BY EMPLOYEES AND DIRECTORS

The Commission shall, by rule, require each issuer to disclose in any proxy or consent solicitation material for an annual meeting of the shareholders of the issuer whether any employee or member of the board of directors of the issuer, or any designee of such employee or member, is permitted to purchase financial instruments (including prepaid variable forward contracts, equity swaps, collars, and exchange funds) that are designed to hedge or offset any decrease in the market value of equity securities—

(1) granted to the employee or member of the board of directors by the issuer as part of the compensation of the employee or member of the board of directors; or

(2) held, directly or indirectly, by the employee or member of the board of directors.

§ 240.14a-2 Solicitations to Which § 240.14a-3 to § 240.14a-15 Apply

Sections 240.14a-3 to 240.14a-15, except as specified, apply to every solicitation of a proxy with respect to securities registered pursuant to section 12 of the Act (15 U.S.C. 78*l*), whether or not trading in such securities has been suspended. To the extent specified below, certain of these sections also apply to roll-up transactions that do not involve an entity with securities registered pursuant to section 12 of the Act.

(a) Sections 240.14a-3 to 240.14a-15 do not apply to the following:

(1) Any solicitation by a person in respect to securities carried in his name or in the name of his nominee (otherwise than as voting trustee) or held in his custody, if such person—

(i) Receives no commission or remuneration for such solicitation, directly or indirectly, other than reimbursement of reasonable expenses,

(ii) Furnishes promptly to the person solicited (or such person's household in accordance with § 240.14a-3(e)(1)) a copy of all soliciting material with respect to the same subject matter or meeting received from all persons who shall furnish copies thereof for such purpose and who shall, if requested, defray the reasonable expenses to be incurred in forwarding such material, and

(iii) In addition, does no more than impartially instruct the person solicited to forward a proxy to the person, if any, to whom the person solicited desires to give a proxy, or impartially request from the person solicited instructions as to the authority to be conferred by the proxy and state that a proxy will be given if no instructions are received by a certain date.

(2) Any solicitation by a person in respect of securities of which he is the beneficial owner;

(3) Any solicitation involved in the offer and sale of securities registered under the Securities Act of 1933: *Provided*, That this paragraph shall not apply to securities to be issued in any transaction of the character specified in paragraph (a) of Rule 145 under that Act;

(4) Any solicitation with respect to a plan of reorganization under Chapter 11 of the Bankruptcy Reform Act of 1978, as amended, if made after the entry of an order approving the written disclosure statement concerning a plan of reorganization pursuant to section 1125 of said Act and after, or concurrently with, the transmittal of such disclosure statement as required by section 1125 of said Act;

(5) [Reserved by 73 FR 17814;]

(6) Any solicitation through the medium of a newspaper advertisement which informs security holders of a source from which they may obtain copies of a proxy statement, form of proxy and any other soliciting material and does no more than:

(i) Name the registrant,

(ii) State the reason for the advertisement, and

(iii) Identify the proposal or proposals to be acted upon by security holders.

(b) Sections 240.14a-3 to 240.14a-6 (other than paragraphs 14a-6(g) and 14a-6(p)), § 240.14a-8, § 240.14a-10, and §§ 240.14a-12 to 240.14a-15 do not apply to the following:

(1) Any solicitation by or on behalf of any person who does not, at any time during such solicitation, seek directly or indirectly, either on its own or another's behalf, the power to act as proxy for a security holder and does not furnish or otherwise request, or act on behalf of a person who furnishes or requests, a form of revocation, abstention, consent or authorization. *Provided, however*, That the exemption set forth in this paragraph shall not apply to:

(i) The registrant or an affiliate or associate of the registrant (other than an officer or director or any person serving in a similar capacity);

(ii) An officer or director of the registrant or any person serving in a similar capacity engaging in a solicitation financed directly or indirectly by the registrant;

(iii) An officer, director, affiliate or associate of a person that is ineligible to rely on the exemption set forth in this paragraph (other than persons specified in paragraph (b)(1)(i) of this section), or any person serving in a similar capacity;

(iv) Any nominee for whose election as a director proxies are solicited;

(v) Any person soliciting in opposition to a merger, recapitalization, reorganization, sale of assets or other extraordinary transaction recommended or approved by the board of directors of the registrant who is proposing or intends to propose an alternative transaction to which such person or one of its affiliates is a party;

(vi) Any person who is required to report beneficial ownership of the registrant's equity securities on a Schedule 13D (§ 240.13d-101), unless such person has filed a Schedule 13D and has not disclosed pursuant to Item 4 thereto an intent, or reserved the right, to engage in a control transaction, or any contested solicitation for the election of directors;

(vii) Any person who receives compensation from an ineligible person directly related to the solicitation of proxies, other than pursuant to § 240.14a-13;

(viii) Where the registrant is an investment company registered under the Investment Company Act of 1940 (15 U.S.C. 80a-1 et seq.), an "interested person" of that investment company, as that term is defined in section 2(a)(19) of the Investment Company Act (15 U.S.C. 80a-2);

(ix) Any person who, because of a substantial interest in the subject matter of the solicitation, is likely to receive a benefit from a successful solicitation that would not be shared pro rata by all other holders of the same class of securities, other than a benefit arising from the person's employment with the registrant; and

(x) Any person acting on behalf of any of the foregoing.

(2) Any solicitation made otherwise than on behalf of the registrant where the total number of persons solicited is not more than ten;

(3) The furnishing of proxy voting advice by any person (the "advisor") to any other person with whom the advisor has a business relationship, if:

(i) The advisor renders financial advice in the ordinary course of his business;

(ii) The advisor discloses to the recipient of the advice any significant relationship with the registrant or any of its affiliates, or a security holder proponent of the matter on which advice is given, as well as any material interests of the advisor in such matter;

(iii) The advisor receives no special commission or remuneration for furnishing the proxy voting advice from any person other than a recipient of the advice and other persons who receive similar advice under this subsection; and

(iv) The proxy voting advice is not furnished on behalf of any person soliciting proxies or on behalf of a participant in an election subject to the provisions of § 240.14a-12(c); and

(4) Any solicitation in connection with a roll-up transaction as defined in Item 901(c) of Regulation S-K (§ 229.901 of this chapter) in which the holder of a security that is the subject of a proposed roll-up

transaction engages in preliminary communications with other holders of securities that are the subject of the same limited partnership roll-up transaction for the purpose of determining whether to solicit proxies, consents, or authorizations in opposition to the proposed limited partnership roll-up transaction; *provided, however*, that:

(i) This exemption shall not apply to a security holder who is an affiliate of the registrant or general partner or sponsor; and

(ii) This exemption shall not apply to a holder of five percent (5%) or more of the outstanding securities of a class that is the subject of the proposed roll-up transaction who engages in the business of buying and selling limited partnership interests in the secondary market unless that holder discloses to the persons to whom the communications are made such ownership interest and any relations of the holder to the parties of the transaction or to the transaction itself, as required by § 240.14a-6(n)(1) and specified in the Notice of Exempt Preliminary Roll-up Communication (§ 240.14a-104). If the communication is oral, this disclosure may be provided to the security holder orally. Whether the communication is written or oral, the notice required by § 240.14a-6(n) and § 240.14a-104 shall be furnished to the Commission.

(5) Publication or distribution by a broker or a dealer of a research report in accordance with Rule 138 (§ 230.138 of this chapter) or Rule 139 (§ 230.139 of this chapter) during a transaction in which the broker or dealer or its affiliate participates or acts in a an advisory role.

(6) Any solicitation by or on behalf of any person who does not seek directly or indirectly, either on its own or another's behalf, the power to act as proxy for a shareholder and does not furnish or otherwise request, or act on behalf of a person who furnishes or requests, a form of revocation, abstention, consent, or authorization in an electronic shareholder forum that is established, maintained or operated pursuant to the provisions of § 240.14a-17, provided that the solicitation is made more than 60 days prior to the date announced by a registrant for its next annual or special meeting of shareholders. If the registrant announces the date of its next annual or special meeting of shareholders less than 60 days before the meeting date, then the solicitation may not be made more than two days following the date of the registrant's announcement of the meeting date. Participation in an electronic shareholder forum does not eliminate a person's eligibility to solicit proxies after the date that this exemption is no longer available, or is no longer being relied upon, provided that any such solicitation is conducted in accordance with this regulation.

(7) Any solicitation by or on behalf of any shareholder in connection with the formation of a nominating shareholder group pursuant to § 240.14a-11, provided that:

(i) The soliciting shareholder is not holding the registrant's securities with the purpose, or with the effect, of changing control of the registrant or to gain a number of seats on the board of directors that exceeds the maximum number of nominees that the registrant could be required to include under § 240.14a-11(d);

(ii) Each written communication includes no more than:

(A) A statement of each soliciting shareholder's intent to form a nominating shareholder group in order to nominate one or more directors under § 240.14a-11;

(B) Identification of, and a brief statement regarding, the potential nominee or nominees or, where no nominee or nominees have been identified, the characteristics of the nominee or nominees that the shareholder intends to nominate, if any;

(C) The percentage of voting power of the registrant's securities that are entitled to be voted on the election of directors that each soliciting shareholder holds or the aggregate percentage held by any group to which the shareholder belongs; and

(D) The means by which shareholders may contact the soliciting party.

(iii) Any written soliciting material published, sent or given to shareholders in accordance with this paragraph must be filed by the shareholder with the Commission, under the registrant's Exchange Act file number, or, in the case of a registrant that is an investment company registered under the Investment Company Act of 1940 (15 U.S.C. 80a-1 et seq.), under the registrant's Investment Company Act file number, no later than the date the material is first published, sent or given to shareholders. Three copies of the material must at the same time be filed with, or mailed for filing to, each national securities exchange upon which any class of securities of the registrant is listed and registered. The soliciting material must include a cover page in the form set forth in Schedule 14N (§ 240.14n-101) and the appropriate box on the cover page must be marked.

(iv) In the case of an oral solicitation made in accordance with the terms of this section, the nominating shareholder must file a cover page in the form set forth in Schedule 14N (§ 240.14n-101), with the appropriate box on the cover page marked, under the registrant's Exchange Act file number (or in the case of an investment company registered under the Investment Company Act of 1940 (15 U.S.C. 80a-1 et seq.), under the registrant's Investment Company Act file number), no later than the date of the first such communication.

Instruction to paragraph (b)(7). The exemption provided in paragraph (b)(7) of this section shall not apply to a shareholder that subsequently engages in soliciting or other nominating activities outside the scope of § 240.14a-2(b)(8) and § 240.14a-11 in connection with the subject election of directors or is or becomes a member of any other group, as determined under section 13(d)(3) of the Act (15 U.S.C. 78m(d)(3) and § 240.13d-5(b)), or otherwise, with persons engaged in soliciting or other nominating activities in connection with the subject election of directors.

(8) Any solicitation by or on behalf of a nominating shareholder or nominating shareholder group in support of its nominee that is included or that will be included on the registrant's form of proxy in accordance with § 240.14a-11 or for or against the registrant's nominee or nominees, provided that:

(i) The soliciting party does not, at any time during such solicitation, seek directly or indirectly, either on its own or another's behalf, the power to act as proxy for a shareholder and does not furnish or otherwise request, or act on behalf of a person who furnishes or requests, a form of revocation, abstention, consent or authorization;

(ii) Any written communication includes:

(A) The identity of each nominating shareholder and a description of his or her direct or indirect interests, by security holdings or otherwise;

(B) A prominent legend in clear, plain language advising shareholders that a shareholder nominee is or will be included in the registrant's proxy statement and that they should read the registrant's proxy statement when available because it includes important information (or, if the registrant's proxy statement is publicly available, advising shareholders of that fact and encouraging shareholders to read the registrant's proxy statement because it includes important information). The legend also must explain to shareholders that they can find the registrant's proxy statement, other soliciting material, and any other relevant documents at no charge on the Commission's Web site; and

(iii) Any written soliciting material published, sent or given to shareholders in accordance with this paragraph must be filed by the nominating shareholder or nominating shareholder group with the Commission, under the registrant's Exchange Act file number, or, in the case of a registrant that is an investment company registered under the Investment Company Act of 1940 (15 U.S.C. 80a-1 et seq.), under the registrant's Investment Company Act file number, no later than the date the material is first published, sent or given to shareholders. Three copies of the material must at the same time be filed with, or mailed for filing to, each national securities exchange upon which any class of securities of the registrant is listed and registered. The soliciting material must include a cover page in the form set forth in Schedule 14N (§ 240.14n-101) and the appropriate box on the cover page must be marked.

Instruction 1 to paragraph (b)(8). A nominating shareholder or nominating shareholder group may rely on the exemption provided in paragraph (b)(8) of this section only after receiving notice from the registrant in accordance with § 240.14a-11(g)(1) or § 240.14a-11(g)(3)(iv) that the registrant will include the nominating shareholder's or nominating shareholder group's nominee or nominees in its form of proxy.

Instruction 2 to paragraph (b)(8). Any solicitation by or on behalf of a nominating shareholder or nominating shareholder group in support of its nominee included or to be included on the registrant's form of proxy in accordance with § 240.14a-11 or for or against the registrant's nominee or nominees must be made in reliance on the exemption provided in paragraph (b)(8) of this section and not on any other exemption.

Instruction 3 to paragraph (b)(8). The exemption provided in paragraph (b)(8) of this section shall not apply to a person that subsequently engages in soliciting or other nominating activities outside the scope of § 240.14a-11 in connection with the subject election of directors or is or becomes a member of any other group, as determined under section 13(d)(3) of the Act (15 U.S.C. 78m(d)(3) and § 240.13d-5(b)), or otherwise, with persons engaged in soliciting or other nominating activities in connection with the subject election of directors.

§ 240.14a-3 Information to Be Furnished to Security Holders

(a) No solicitation subject to this regulation shall be made unless each person solicited is concurrently furnished or has previously been furnished with:

(1) A publicly-filed preliminary or definitive proxy statement, in the form and manner described in § 240.14a-16, containing the information specified in Schedule 14A (§ 240.14a-101);

(2) A preliminary or definitive written proxy statement included in a registration statement filed under the Securities Act of 1933 on Form S-4 or F-4 (§ 239.25 or § 239.34 of this chapter) or Form N-14 (§ 239.23 of this chapter) and containing the information specified in such Form; or

(3) A publicly-filed preliminary or definitive proxy statement, not in the form and manner described in § 240.14a-16, containing the information specified in Schedule 14A (§ 240.14a-101), if:

(i) The solicitation relates to a business combination transaction as defined in § 230.165 of this chapter, as well as transactions for cash consideration requiring disclosure under Item 14 of § 240.14a-101.

(ii) The solicitation may not follow the form and manner described in § 240.14a-16 pursuant to the laws of the state of incorporation of the registrant;

(b) If the solicitation is made on behalf of the registrant, other than an investment company registered under the Investment Company Act of

1940, and relates to an annual (or special meeting in lieu of the annual) meeting of security holders, or written consent in lieu of such meeting, at which directors are to be elected, each proxy statement furnished pursuant to paragraph (a) of this section shall be accompanied or preceded by an annual report to security holders as follows:

(1) The report shall include, for the registrant and its subsidiaries, consolidated and audited balance sheets as of the end of the two most recent fiscal years and audited statements of income and cash flows for each of the three most recent fiscal years prepared in accordance with Regulation S-X (part 210 of this chapter), except that the provisions of Article 3 (other than §§ 210.3-03(e), 210.3-04 and 210.3-20) and Article 11 shall not apply. Any financial statement schedules or exhibits or separate financial statements which may otherwise be required in filings with the Commission may be omitted. If the financial statements of the registrant and its subsidiaries consolidated in the annual report filed or to be filed with the Commission are not required to be audited, the financial statements required by this paragraph may be unaudited. A smaller reporting company may provide the information in Article 8 of Regulation S-X (§ 210.8 of this chapter) in lieu of the financial information required by this paragraph 9(b)(1).

Note 1 to paragraph (b)(1): If the financial statements for a period prior to the most recently completed fiscal year have been examined by a predecessor accountant, the separate report of the predecessor accountant may be omitted in the report to security holders, provided the registrant has obtained from the predecessor accountant a reissued report covering the prior period presented and the successor accountant clearly indicates in the scope paragraph of his or her report (a) that the financial statements of the prior period were examined by other accountants, (b) the date of their report, (c) the type of opinion expressed by the predecessor accountant and (d) the substantive reasons therefore, if it was other than unqualified. It should be noted, however, that the separate report of any predecessor accountant is required in filings with the Commission. If, for instance, the financial statements in the annual report to security holders are incorporated by reference in a Form 10-K, the separate report of a predecessor accountant shall be filed in Part II or in Part IV as a financial statement schedule.

Note 2 to paragraph (b)(1): For purposes of complying with § 240.14a-3, if the registrant has changed its fiscal closing date, financial statements covering two years and one period of 9 to 12 months shall be deemed to satisfy the requirements for statements of income and cash flows for the three most recent fiscal years.

(2)(i) Financial statements and notes thereto shall be presented in roman type at least as large and as legible as 10-point modern type. If necessary for convenient presentation, the financial statements may be in roman type as large and as legible as 8-point modern type. All type shall be leaded at least 2 points.

(ii) Where the annual report to security holders is delivered through an electronic medium, issuers may satisfy legibility requirements applicable to printed documents, such as type size and font, by presenting all required information in a format readily communicated to investors.

(3) The report shall contain the supplementary financial information required by item 302 of Regulation S-K (§ 229.302 of this chapter).

(4) The report shall contain information concerning changes in and disagreements with accountants on accounting and financial disclosure required by Item 304 of Regulation S-K (§ 229.304 of this chapter).

(5)(i) The report shall contain the selected financial data required by Item 301 of Regulation S-K (§ 229.301 of this chapter).

(ii) The report shall contain management's discussion and analysis of financial condition and results of operations required by Item 303 of Regulation S-K (§ 229.303 of this chapter).

(iii) The report shall contain the quantitative and qualitative disclosures about market risk required by Item 305 of Regulation S-K (§ 229.305 of this chapter).

(6) The report shall contain a brief description of the business done by the registrant and its subsidiaries during the most recent fiscal year which will, in the opinion of management, indicate the general nature and scope of the business of the registrant and its subsidiaries.

(7) The report shall contain information relating to the registrant's industry segments, classes of similar products or services, foreign and domestic operations and exports sales required by paragraphs (b), (c)(1)(i) and (d) of Item 101 of Regulation S-K (§ 229.101 of this chapter).

(8) The report shall identify each of the registrant's directors and executive officers, and shall indicate the principal occupation or employment of each such person and the name and principal business of any organization by which such person is employed.

(9) The report shall contain the market price of and dividends on the registrant's common equity and related security holder matters required by Items 201(a), (b) and (c) of Regulation S-K (§ 229.201(a), (b) and (c) of this chapter). If the report precedes or accompanies a proxy statement or information statement relating to an annual meeting of security holders at which directors are to be elected (or special meeting or written consents in lieu of such meeting), furnish the performance graph required by Item 201(e) (§ 229.201(e) of this chapter).

(10) The registrant's proxy statement, or the report, shall contain an undertaking in bold face or otherwise reasonably prominent type to provide without charge to each person solicited upon the written request of any such person, a copy of the registrant's annual report

on Form 10-K, including the financial statements and the financial statement schedules, required to be filed with the Commission pursuant to Rule 13a-1 (§ 240.13a-1 of this chapter) under the Act for the registrant's most recent fiscal year, and shall indicate the name and address (including title or department) of the person to whom such a written request is to be directed. In the discretion of management, a registrant need not undertake to furnish without charge copies of all exhibits to its Form 10-K, provided that the copy of the annual report on Form 10-K furnished without charge to requesting security holders is accompanied by a list briefly describing all the exhibits not contained therein and indicating that the registrant will furnish any exhibit upon the payment of a specified reasonable fee, which fee shall be limited to the registrant's reasonable expenses in furnishing such exhibit. If the registrant's annual report to security holders complies with all of the disclosure requirements of Form 10-K and is filed with the Commission in satisfaction of its Form 10-K filing requirements, such registrant need not furnish a separate Form 10-K to security holders who receive a copy of such annual report.

Note to paragraph (b)(10): Pursuant to the undertaking required by paragraph (b)(10) of this section, a registrant shall furnish a copy of its annual report on Form 10-K (§ 249.310 of this chapter) to a beneficial owner of its securities upon receipt of a written request from such person. Each request must set forth a good faith representation that, as of the record date for the solicitation requiring the furnishing of the annual report to security holders pursuant to paragraph (b) of this section, the person making the request was a beneficial owner of securities entitled to vote.

(11) Subject to the foregoing requirements, the report may be in any form deemed suitable by management and the information required by paragraphs (b)(5) to (10) of this section may be presented in an appendix or other separate section of the report, provided that the attention of security holders is called to such presentation.

Note: Registrants are encouraged to utilize tables, schedules, charts and graphic illustrations of present financial information in an understandable manner. Any presentation of financial information must be consistent with the data in the financial statements contained in the report and, if appropriate, should refer to relevant portions of the financial statements and notes thereto.

(12) [Reserved]

(13) Paragraph (b) of this section shall not apply, however, to solicitations made on behalf of the registrant before the financial state-

ments are available if a solicitation is being made at the same time in opposition to the registrant and if the registrant's proxy statement includes an undertaking in bold face type to furnish such annual report to security holders to all persons being solicited at least 20 calendar days before the date of the meeting or, if the solicitation refers to a written consent or authorization in lieu of a meeting, at least 20 calendar days prior to the earliest date on which it may be used to effect corporate action.

(c) Seven copies of the report sent to security holders pursuant to this rule shall be mailed to the Commission, solely for its information, not later than the date on which such report is first sent or given to security holders or the date on which preliminary copies, or definitive copies, if preliminary filing was not required, of solicitation material are filed with the Commission pursuant to Rule 14a-6, whichever date is later. The report is not deemed to be "soliciting material" or to be "filed" with the Commission or subject to this regulation otherwise than as provided in this Rule, or to the liabilities of section 18 of the Act, except to the extent that the registrant specifically requests that it be treated as a part of the proxy soliciting material or incorporates it in the proxy statement or other filed report by reference.

(d) An annual report to security holders prepared on an integrated basis pursuant to General Instruction H to Form 10-K (§ 249.310 of this chapter) may also be submitted in satisfaction of this section. When filed as the annual report on Form 10-K, responses to the Items of that form are subject to section 18 of the Act notwithstanding paragraph (c) of this section.

(e)(1)(i) A registrant will be considered to have delivered an annual report to security holders, proxy statement or Notice of Internet Availability of Proxy Materials, as described in § 240.14a-16, to all security holders of record who share an address if:

> (A) The registrant delivers one annual report to security holders, proxy statement or Notice of Internet Availability of Proxy Materials, as applicable, to the shared address;
>
> (B) The registrant addresses the annual report to security holders, proxy statement or Notice of Internet Availability of Proxy Materials, as applicable, to the security holders as a group (for example, "ABC Fund [or Corporation] Security Holders," "Jane Doe and Household," "The Smith Family"), to each of the security holders individually (for example, "John Doe and Richard Jones") or to the security holders in a form to which each of the security holders has consented in writing;

Note to paragraph (e)(1)(i)(B): Unless the registrant addresses the annual report to security holders, proxy statement or Notice of Internet Availability of Proxy Materials to the security holders as a group or to each of the security holders individually, it must obtain, from each security holder to be included in the household group, a separate affirmative written consent to the specific form of address the registrant will use.

(C) The security holders consent, in accordance with paragraph (e)(1)(ii) of this section, to delivery of one annual report to security holders or proxy statement, as applicable;

(D) With respect to delivery of the proxy statement or Notice of Internet Availability of Proxy Materials, the registrant delivers, together with or subsequent to delivery of the proxy statement, a separate proxy card for each security holder at the shared address; and

(E) The registrant includes an undertaking in the proxy statement to deliver promptly upon written or oral request a separate copy of the annual report to security holders, proxy statement or Notice of Internet Availability of Proxy Materials, as applicable, to a security holder at a shared address to which a single copy of the document was delivered.

(ii) Consent—

(A) Affirmative written consent. Each security holder must affirmatively consent, in writing, to delivery of one annual report to security holders or proxy statement, as applicable. A security holder's affirmative written consent will be considered valid only if the security holder has been informed of:

(*1*) The duration of the consent;

(*2*) The specific types of documents to which the consent will apply;

(*3*) The procedures the security holder must follow to revoke consent; and

(*4*) The registrant's obligation to begin sending individual copies to a security holder within thirty days after the security holder revokes consent.

(B) Implied consent. The registrant need not obtain affirmative written consent from a security holder for purposes of paragraph (e)(1)(ii)(A) of this section if all of the following conditions are met:

(*1*) The security holder has the same last name as the other security holders at the shared address or the registrant reasonably believes that the security holders are members of the same family;

(*2*) The registrant has sent the security holder a notice at least 60 days before the registrant begins to rely on this section concerning delivery of annual reports to security holders, proxy statements or Notices of Internet Availability of Proxy Materials to that security holder. The notice must:

(*i*) Be a separate written document;

(*ii*) State that only one annual report to security holders, proxy statement or Notice of Internet Availability of Proxy

Materials, as applicable, will be delivered to the shared address unless the registrant receives contrary instructions;

(*iii*) Include a toll-free telephone number, or be accompanied by a reply form that is pre-addressed with postage provided, that the security holder can use to notify the registrant that the security holder wishes to receive a separate annual report to security holders, proxy statement or Notice of Internet Availability of Proxy Materials;

(*iv*) State the duration of the consent;

(*v*) Explain how a security holder can revoke consent;

(*vi*) State that the registrant will begin sending individual copies to a security holder within thirty days after the security holder revokes consent; and

(*vii*) Contain the following prominent statement, or similar clear and understandable statement, in bold-face type: "Important Notice Regarding Delivery of Security Holder Documents." This statement also must appear on the envelope in which the notice is delivered. Alternatively, if the notice is delivered separately from other communications to security holders, this statement may appear either on the notice or on the envelope in which the notice is delivered.

Note to paragraph (e)(1)(ii)(B)(2): The notice should be written in plain English. See § 230.421(d)(2) of this chapter for a discussion of plain English principles.

(*3*) The registrant has not received the reply form or other notification indicating that the security holder wishes to continue to receive an individual copy of the annual report to security holders, proxy statement or Notice of Internet Availability of Proxy Materials, as applicable, within 60 days after the registrant sent the notice required by paragraph (e)(1)(ii)(B)(2) of this section; and

(*4*) The registrant delivers the document to a post office box or residential street address.

Note to paragraph (e)(1)(ii)(B)(4): The registrant can assume that a street address is residential unless the registrant has information that indicates the street address is a business.

(iii) Revocation of consent. If a security holder, orally or in writing, revokes consent to delivery of one annual report to security holders, proxy statement or Notice of Internet Availability of Proxy Materials to a shared address, the registrant must begin sending individual copies to that security holder within 30 days after the registrant receives revocation of the security holder's consent.

(iv) Definition of address. Unless otherwise indicated, for purposes of this section, address means a street address, a post office box number, an electronic mail address, a facsimile telephone number or other similar destination to which paper or electronic documents are delivered, unless otherwise provided in this section. If the registrant has reason to believe that the address is a street address of a multi-unit building, the address must include the unit number.

Note to paragraph (e)(1): A person other than the registrant making a proxy solicitation may deliver a single proxy statement to security holders of record or beneficial owners who have separate accounts and share an address if: (a) the registrant or intermediary has followed the procedures in this section; and (b) the registrant or intermediary makes available the shared address information to the person in accordance with § 240.14a-7(a)(2)(i) and (ii).

(2) Notwithstanding paragraphs (a) and (b) of this section, unless state law requires otherwise, a registrant is not required to send an annual report to security holders, proxy statement or Notice of Internet Availability of Proxy Materials to a security holder if:

(i) An annual report to security holders and a proxy statement, or a Notice of Internet Availability of Proxy Materials, for two consecutive annual meetings; or

(ii) All, and at least two, payments (if sent by first class mail) of dividends or interest on securities, or dividend reinvestment confirmations, during a twelve month period, have been mailed to such security holder's address and have been returned as undeliverable. If any such security holder delivers or causes to be delivered to the registrant written notice setting forth his then current address for security holder communications purposes, the registrant's obligation to deliver an annual report to security holders, a proxy statement or a Notice of Internet Availability of Proxy Materials under this section is reinstated.

(f) The provisions of paragraph (a) of this section shall not apply to a communication made by means of speeches in public forums, press releases, published or broadcast opinions, statements, or advertisements appearing in a broadcast media, newspaper, magazine or other bona fide publication disseminated on a regular basis, provided that:

(1) No form of proxy, consent or authorization or means to execute the same is provided to a security holder in connection with the communication; and

(2) At the time the communication is made, a definitive proxy statement is on file with the Commission pursuant to § 240.14a-6(b).

§ 240.14a-4 Requirements as to Proxy

(a) The form of proxy

(1) shall indicate in bold-face type whether or not the proxy is solicited on behalf of the registrant's board of directors or, if provided other than by a majority of the board of directors, shall indicate in bold-face type on whose behalf the solicitation is made;

(2) Shall provide a specifically designated blank space for dating the proxy card; and

(3) Shall identify clearly and impartially each separate matter intended to be acted upon, whether or not related to or conditioned on the approval of other matters, and whether proposed by the registrant or by security holders. No reference need be made, however, to proposals as to which discretionary authority is conferred pursuant to paragraph (c) of this section.

Note to paragraph (a)(3) (Electronic filers): Electronic filers shall satisfy the filing requirements of Rule 14a-6(a) or (b) (§ 240.14a-6(a) or (b)) with respect to the form of proxy by filing the form of proxy as an appendix at the end of the proxy statement. Forms of proxy shall not be filed as exhibits or separate documents within an electronic submission.

(b)(1) Means shall be provided in the form of proxy whereby the person solicited is afforded an opportunity to specify by boxes a choice between approval or disapproval of, or abstention with respect to each separate matter referred to therein as intended to be acted upon, other than elections to office and votes to determine the frequency of shareholder votes on executive compensation pursuant to § 240.14a-21(b) of this chapter. A proxy may confer discretionary authority with respect to matters as to which a choice is not specified by the security holder provided that the form of proxy states in bold-face type how it is intended to vote the shares represented by the proxy in each such case.

(2) A form of proxy that provides for the election of directors shall set forth the names of persons nominated for election as directors, including any person whose nomination by a shareholder or shareholder group satisfies the requirements of § 240.14a-11, an applicable state or foreign law provision, or a registrant's governing documents as they relate to the inclusion of shareholder director nominees in the registrant's proxy materials. Such form of proxy shall clearly provide any of the following means for security holders to withhold authority to vote for each nominee: Means to grant authority to vote for any nominees as a group or to withhold authority for any nominees as a group may not be provided if the form of proxy includes one or more shareholder nominees in accordance with § 240.14a-11, an applicable state or foreign law provision, or a registrant's governing documents as they

relate to the inclusion of shareholder director nominees in the registrant's proxy materials.

(i) A box opposite the name of each nominee which may be marked to indicate that authority to vote for such nominee is withheld; or

(ii) An instruction in bold-face type which indicates that the security holder may withhold authority to vote for any nominee by lining through or otherwise striking out the name of any nominee; or

(iii) Designated blank spaces in which the security holder may enter the names of nominees with respect to whom the security holder chooses to withhold authority to vote; or

(iv) Any other similar means, provided that clear instructions are furnished indicating how the security holder may withhold authority to vote for any nominee.

Such form of proxy also may provide a means for the security holder to grant authority to vote for the nominees set forth, as a group, provided that there is a similar means for the security holder to withhold authority to vote for such group of nominees. Any such form of proxy which is executed by the security holder in such manner as not to withhold authority to vote for the election of any nominee shall be deemed to grant such authority, provided that the form of proxy so states in bold-face type. Means to grant authority to vote for any nominees as a group or to withhold authority for any nominees as a group may not be provided if the form of proxy includes one or more shareholder nominees in accordance with § 240.14a-11, an applicable state or foreign law provision, or a registrant's governing documents as they relate to the inclusion of shareholder director nominees in the registrant's proxy materials.

Instructions.

1. Paragraph (2) does not apply in the case of a merger, consolidation or other plan if the election of directors is an integral part of the plan.

2. If applicable state law gives legal effect to votes cast against a nominee, then in lieu of, or in addition to, providing a means for security holders to withhold authority to vote, the registrant should provide a similar means for security holders to vote against each nominee.

(3) A form of proxy which provides for a shareholder vote on the frequency of shareholder votes to approve the compensation of executives required by section 14A(a)(2) of the Securities Exchange Act of 1934 (15 U.S.C. 78n-1(a)(2)) shall provide means whereby the person solicited is afforded an opportunity to specify by boxes a choice among 1, 2 or 3 years, or abstain.

(c) A proxy may confer discretionary authority to vote on any of the following matters:

(1) For an annual meeting of shareholders, if the registrant did not have notice of the matter at least 45 days before the date on which the registrant first sent its proxy materials for the prior year's annual meeting of shareholders (or date specified by an advance notice provision), and a specific statement to that effect is made in the proxy statement or form of proxy. If during the prior year the registrant did not hold an annual meeting, or if the date of the meeting has changed more than 30 days from the prior year, then notice must not have been received a reasonable time before the registrant sends its proxy materials for the current year.

(2) In the case in which the registrant has received timely notice in connection with an annual meeting of shareholders (as determined under paragraph (c)(1) of this section), if the registrant includes, in the proxy statement, advice on the nature of the matter and how the registrant intends to exercise its discretion to vote on each matter. However, even if the registrant includes this information in its proxy statement, it may not exercise discretionary voting authority on a particular proposal if the proponent:

(i) Provides the registrant with a written statement, within the time-frame determined under paragraph (c)(1) of this section, that the proponent intends to deliver a proxy statement and form of proxy to holders of at least the percentage of the company's voting shares required under applicable law to carry the proposal;

(ii) Includes the same statement in its proxy materials filed under § 240.14a-6; and

(iii) Immediately after soliciting the percentage of shareholders required to carry the proposal, provides the registrant with a statement from any solicitor or other person with knowledge that the necessary steps have been taken to deliver a proxy statement and form of proxy to holders of at least the percentage of the company's voting shares required under applicable law to carry the proposal.

(3) For solicitations other than for annual meetings or for solicitations by persons other than the registrant, matters which the persons making the solicitation do not know, a reasonable time before the solicitation, are to be presented at the meeting, if a specific statement to that effect is made in the proxy statement or form of proxy.

(4) Approval of the minutes of the prior meeting if such approval does not amount to ratification of the action taken at that meeting;

(5) The election of any person to any office for which a bona fide nominee is named in the proxy statement and such nominee is unable to serve or for good cause will not serve.

(6) Any proposal omitted from the proxy statement and form of proxy pursuant to § 240.14a-8 or § 240.14a-9 of this chapter.

(7) Matters incident to the conduct of the meeting.

(d) No proxy shall confer authority:

14a-4(d) = no proxy shall confer authority

(1) To vote for the election of any person to any office for which a bona fide nominee is not named in the proxy statement,

(2) To vote at any annual meeting other than the next annual meeting (or any adjournment thereof) to be held after the date on which the proxy statement and form of proxy are first sent or given to security holders,

(3) To vote with respect to more than one meeting (and any adjournment thereof) or more than one consent solicitation or

(4) To consent to or authorize any action other than the action proposed to be taken in the proxy statement, or matters referred to in paragraph (c) of this rule. A person shall not be deemed to be a bona fide nominee and he shall not be named as such unless he has consented to being named in the proxy statement and to serve if elected. *Provided, however,* That nothing in this section 240.14a-4 shall prevent any person soliciting in support of nominees who, if elected, would constitute a minority of the board of directors, from seeking authority to vote for nominees named in the registrant's proxy statement, so long as the soliciting party:

(i) Seeks authority to vote in the aggregate for the number of director positions then subject to election;

(ii) Represents that it will vote for all the registrant nominees, other than those registrant nominees specified by the soliciting party;

(iii) Provides the security holder an opportunity to withhold authority with respect to any other registrant nominee by writing the name of that nominee on the form of proxy; and

(iv) States on the form of proxy and in the proxy statement that there is no assurance that the registrant's nominees will serve if elected with any of the soliciting party's nominees.

(e) The proxy statement or form of proxy shall provide, subject to reasonable specified conditions, that the shares represented by the proxy will be voted and that where the person solicited specifies by means of a ballot provided pursuant to paragraph (b) of this section a choice with respect to any matter to be acted upon, the shares will be voted in accordance with the specifications so made.

(f) No person conducting a solicitation subject to this regulation shall deliver a form of proxy, consent or authorization to any security holder unless the security holder concurrently receives, or has previously received, a definitive proxy statement that has been filed with the Commission pursuant to § 240.14a-6(b).

§ 240.14a-6 Filing Requirements

(a) Preliminary proxy statement. Five preliminary copies of the proxy statement and form of proxy shall be filed with the Commission at least 10 calendar days prior to the date definitive copies of such material are first sent or given to security holders, or such shorter period prior to that date as the

Commission may authorize upon a showing of good cause thereunder. A registrant, however, shall not file with the Commission a preliminary proxy statement, form of proxy or other soliciting material to be furnished to security holders concurrently therewith if the solicitation relates to an annual (or special meeting in lieu of the annual) meeting, or for an investment company registered under the Investment Company Act of 1940 (15 U.S.C. 80a-1 et seq.) or a business development company, if the solicitation relates to any meeting of security holders at which the only matters to be acted upon are:

(1) The election of directors;

(2) The election, approval or ratification of accountant(s);

(3) A security holder proposal included pursuant to Rule 14a-8 (§ 240.14a-8 of this chapter);

(4) A shareholder nominee for director included pursuant to § 240.14a-11, an applicable state or foreign law provision, or a registrant's governing documents as they relate to the inclusion of shareholder director nominees in the registrant's proxy materials.

(5) The approval or ratification of a plan as defined in paragraph (a)(6)(ii) of Item 402 of Regulation S-K (§ 229.402(a)(6)(ii) of this chapter) or amendments to such a plan;

(6) With respect to an investment company registered under the Investment Company Act of 1940 or a business development company, a proposal to continue, without change, any advisory or other contract or agreement that previously has been the subject of a proxy solicitation for which proxy material was filed with the Commission pursuant to this section;

(7) With respect to an open-end investment company registered under the Investment Company Act of 1940, a proposal to increase the number of shares authorized to be issued; and/or

(8) A vote to approve the compensation of executives as required pursuant to section 14A(a)(1) of the Securities Exchange Act of 1934 (15 U.S.C. 78n-1(a)(1)) and § 240.14a-21(a) of this chapter, or pursuant to section 111(e)(1) of the Emergency Economic Stabilization Act of 2008 (12 U.S.C. 5221(e)(1)) and § 240.14a-20 of this chapter, a vote to determine the frequency of shareholder votes to approve the compensation of executives as required pursuant to Section 14A(a)(2) of the Securities Exchange Act of 1934 (15 U.S.C. 78n-1(a)(2)) and § 240.14a-21(b) of this chapter, or any other shareholder advisory vote on executive compensation.

This exclusion from filing preliminary proxy material does not apply if the registrant comments upon or refers to a solicitation in opposition in connection with the meeting in its proxy material.

Note 1 to paragraph (a): The filing of revised material does not recommence the ten day time period unless the revised material contains material revisions or material new proposal(s) that constitute a fundamental change in the proxy material.

Note 2 to paragraph (a): The official responsible for the preparation of the proxy material should make every effort to verify the accuracy and completeness of the information required by the applicable rules. The preliminary material should be filed with the Commission at the earliest practicable date.

Note 3 to paragraph (a): Solicitation in Opposition. For purposes of the exclusion from filing preliminary proxy material, a "solicitation in opposition" includes: (a) Any solicitation opposing a proposal supported by the registrant; and (b) any solicitation supporting a proposal that the registrant does not expressly support, other than a security holder proposal included in the registrant's proxy material pursuant to Rule 14a-8 (§ 240.14a-8 of this chapter). The inclusion of a security holder proposal in the registrant's proxy material pursuant to Rule 14a-8 does not constitute a "solicitation in opposition," even if the registrant opposes the proposal and/or includes a statement in opposition to the proposal. The inclusion of a shareholder nominee in the registrant's proxy materials pursuant to § 240.14a-11, an applicable state or foreign law provision, or a registrant's governing documents as they relate to the inclusion of shareholder director nominees in the registrant's proxy materials does not constitute a "solicitation in opposition" for purposes of Rule 14a-6(a) (§ 240.14a-6(a)), even if the registrant opposes the shareholder nominee and solicits against the shareholder nominee and in favor of a registrant nominee.

Note 4 to paragraph (a): A registrant that is filing proxy material in preliminary form only because the registrant has commented on or referred to a solicitation in opposition should indicate that fact in a transmittal letter when filing the preliminary material with the Commission.

(b) Definitive proxy statement and other soliciting material. Eight definitive copies of the proxy statement, form of proxy and all other soliciting materials, in the same form as the materials sent to security holders, must be filed with the Commission no later than the date they are first sent or given to security holders. Three copies of these materials also must be filed with, or mailed for filing to, each national securities exchange on which the registrant has a class of securities listed and registered.

(c) Personal solicitation materials. If part or all of the solicitation involves personal solicitation, then eight copies of all written instructions or other materials that discuss, review or comment on the merits of any matter to be acted on, that are furnished to persons making the actual solicitation for their use directly or indirectly in connection with the solicitation, must be filed with the Commission no later than the date the materials are first sent or given to these persons.

(d) Release dates. All preliminary proxy statements and forms of proxy filed pursuant to paragraph (a) of this section shall be accompanied by a statement of the date on which definitive copies thereof filed pursuant to paragraph (b) of this section are intended to be released to security holders. All definitive material filed pursuant to paragraph (b) of this section shall be accompanied by a statement of the date on which copies of such material were released to security holders, or, if not released, the date on which copies thereof are intended to be released. All material filed pursuant to paragraph (c) of this section shall be accompanied by a statement of the date on which copies thereof were released to the individual who will make the actual solicitation or if not released, the date on which copies thereof are intended to be released.

(e)(1) Public availability of information. All copies of preliminary proxy statements and forms of proxy filed pursuant to paragraph (a) of this section shall be clearly marked "Preliminary Copies," and shall be deemed immediately available for public inspection unless confidential treatment is obtained pursuant to paragraph (e)(2) of this section.

(2) Confidential treatment. If action will be taken on any matter specified in Item 14 of Schedule 14A (§ 240.14a-101), all copies of the preliminary proxy statement and form of proxy filed under paragraph (a) of this section will be for the information of the Commission only and will not be deemed available for public inspection until filed with the Commission in definitive form so long as:

(i) The proxy statement does not relate to a matter or proposal subject to § 240.13e-3 or a roll-up transaction as defined in Item 901(c) of Regulation S-K (§ 229.901(c) of this chapter);

(ii) Neither the parties to the transaction nor any persons authorized to act on their behalf have made any public communications relating to the transaction except for statements where the content is limited to the information specified in § 230.135 of this chapter; and

(iii) The materials are filed in paper and marked "Confidential, For Use of the Commission Only." In all cases, the materials may be disclosed to any department or agency of the United States Government and to the Congress, and the Commission may make any inquiries or investigation into the materials as may be necessary to conduct an adequate review by the Commission.

Instruction to paragraph (e)(2): If communications are made publicly that go beyond the information specified in § 230.135of this chapter, the preliminary proxy materials must be re-filed promptly with the Commission as public materials.

(f) Communications not required to be filed. Copies of replies to inquiries from security holders requesting further information and copies of communications which do no more than request that forms of proxy theretofore solicited be signed and returned need not be filed pursuant to this section.

(g) Solicitations subject to § 240.14a-2(b)(1).

(1) Any person who:

(i) Engages in a solicitation pursuant to § 240.14a-2(b)(1), and

(ii) At the commencement of that solicitation owns beneficially securities of the class which is the subject of the solicitation with a market value of over $5 million,

shall furnish or mail to the Commission, not later than three days after the date the written solicitation is first sent or given to any security holder, five copies of a statement containing the information specified in the Notice of Exempt Solicitation (§ 240.14a-103) which statement shall attach as an exhibit all written soliciting materials. Five copies of an amendment to such statement shall be furnished or mailed to the Commission, in connection with dissemination of any additional communications, not later than three days after the date the additional material is first sent or given to any security holder. Three copies of the Notice of Exempt Solicitation and amendments thereto shall, at the same time the materials are furnished or mailed to the Commission, be furnished or mailed to each national securities exchange upon which any class of securities of the registrant is listed and registered.

(2) Notwithstanding paragraph (g)(1) of this section, no such submission need be made with respect to oral solicitations (other than with respect to scripts used in connection with such oral solicitations), speeches delivered in a public forum, press releases, published or broadcast opinions, statements, and advertisements appearing in a broadcast media, or a newspaper, magazine or other bona fide publication disseminated on a regular basis.

(h) Revised material. Where any proxy statement, form of proxy or other material filed pursuant to this section is amended or revised, two of the copies of such amended or revised material filed pursuant to this section (or in the case of investment companies registered under the Investment Company Act of 1940, three of such copies) shall be marked to indicate clearly and precisely the changes effected therein. If the amendment or revision alters the text of the material the changes in such text shall be indicated by means of underscoring or in some other appropriate manner.

(i) Fees. At the time of filing the proxy solicitation material, the persons upon whose behalf the solicitation is made, other than investment companies registered under the Investment Company Act of 1940, shall pay to the Commission the following applicable fee:

(1) For preliminary proxy material involving acquisitions, mergers, spinoffs, consolidations or proposed sales or other dispositions of substantially all the assets of the company, a fee established in accordance with Rule 0-11 (§ 240.0-11 of this chapter) shall be paid. No refund shall be given.

(2) For all other proxy submissions and submissions made pursuant to § 240.14a-6(g), no fee shall be required.

(j) Merger proxy materials.

(1) Any proxy statement, form of proxy or other soliciting material required to be filed by this section that also is either

(i) Included in a registration statement filed under the Securities Act of 1933 on Forms S-4 (§ 239.25 of this chapter), F-4 (§ 239.34 of this chapter) or N-14 (§ 239.23 of this chapter); or

(ii) Filed under § 230.424, § 230.425 or § 230.497 of this chapter is required to be filed only under the Securities Act, and is deemed filed under this section.

(2) Under paragraph (j)(1) of this section, the fee required by paragraph (i) of this section need not be paid.

(k) Computing time periods. In computing time periods beginning with the filing date specified in Regulation 14A (§§ 240.14a-1 to 240.14b-1 of this chapter), the filing date shall be counted as the first day of the time period and midnight of the last day shall constitute the end of the specified time period.

(*l*) Roll-up transactions. If a transaction is a roll-up transaction as defined in Item 901(c) of Regulation S-K (17 CFR 229.901(c)) and is registered (or authorized to be registered) on Form S-4 (17 CFR 229.25) or Form F-4 (17 CFR 229.34), the proxy statement of the sponsor or the general partner as defined in Item 901(d) and Item 901(a), respectively, of Regulation S-K (17 CFR 229.901) must be distributed to security holders no later than the lesser of 60 calendar days prior to the date on which the meeting of security holders is held or action is taken, or the maximum number of days permitted for giving notice under applicable state law.

(m) Cover page. Proxy materials filed with the Commission shall include a cover page in the form set forth in Schedule 14A (§ 240.14a-101 of this chapter). The cover page required by this paragraph need not be distributed to security holders.

(n) Solicitations subject to § 240.14a-2(b)(4). Any person who:

(1) Engages in a solicitation pursuant to § 240.14a-2(b)(4); and

(2) At the commencement of that solicitation both owns five percent (5%) or more of the outstanding securities of a class that is the subject of the proposed roll-up transaction, and engages in the business of buying and selling limited partnership interests in the secondary market, shall furnish or mail to the Commission, not later than three days after the date an oral or written solicitation by that person is first made, sent or provided to any security holder, five copies of a statement containing the information specified in the Notice of Exempt Preliminary Roll-up Communication (§ 240.14a-104). Five copies of any amendment to such statement shall be furnished or mailed to the Commission not later than three days after a communication containing revised material is first made, sent or provided to any security holder.

(*o*) Solicitations before furnishing a definitive proxy statement. Solicitations that are published, sent or given to security holders before they have been furnished a definitive proxy statement must be made in accordance with § 240.14a-12 unless there is an exemption available under § 240.14a-2.

(p) Solicitations subject to § 240.14a-11. Any soliciting material that is published, sent or given to shareholders in connection with § 240.14a-2(b)(7) or (b)(8) must be filed with the Commission as specified in that section.

§ 240.14a-7 Obligations of Registrants to Provide a List of, or Mail Soliciting Material to, Security Holders

(a) If the registrant has made or intends to make a proxy solicitation in connection with a security holder meeting or action by consent or authorization, upon the written request by any record or beneficial holder of securities of the class entitled to vote at the meeting or to execute a consent or authorization to provide a list of security holders or to mail the requesting security holder's materials, regardless of whether the request references this section, the registrant shall:

(1) Deliver to the requesting security holder within five business days after receipt of the request:

(i) Notification as to whether the registrant has elected to mail the security holder's soliciting materials or provide a security holder list if the election under paragraph (b) of this section is to be made by the registrant;

(ii) A statement of the approximate number of record holders and beneficial holders, separated by type of holder and class, owning securities in the same class or classes as holders which have been or are to be solicited on management's behalf, or any more limited group of such holders designated by the security holder if available or retrievable under the registrant's or its transfer agent's security holder data systems; and

(iii) The estimated cost of mailing a proxy statement, form of proxy or other communication to such holders, including to the extent known or reasonably available, the estimated costs of any bank, broker, and similar person through whom the registrant has solicited or intends to solicit beneficial owners in connection with the security holder meeting or action;

(2) Perform the acts set forth in either paragraphs (a)(2)(i) or (a)(2)(ii) of this section, at the registrant's or requesting security holder's option, as specified in paragraph (b) of this section:

(i) Send copies of any proxy statement, form of proxy, or other soliciting material, including a Notice of Internet Availability of Proxy Materials (as described in § 240.14a-16), furnished by the security holder to the record holders, including banks, brokers, and similar entities, designated by the security holder. A sufficient number of copies must be sent to the banks, brokers, and similar entities for distribution to all beneficial owners designated by the security holder. The security holder may designate only record holders and/or beneficial owners who have not requested paper and/ or e-mail copies of the proxy statement. If the registrant has received affirmative written or implied consent to deliver a single proxy statement to security holders at a shared address in accordance with the procedures in § 240.14a-3(e)(1), a single copy of the proxy statement or Notice of Internet Availability of Proxy Materials furnished by the security holder shall be sent to that address, provided that if multiple copies of the Notice of Internet Availability of Proxy Materials are furnished by the security holder for that address, the registrant shall deliver those copies in a single envelope to that address. The registrant shall send the security holder material with reasonable promptness after tender of the material to be sent, envelopes or other containers therefore, postage or payment for postage and other reasonable expenses of effecting such distribution. The registrant shall not be responsible for the content of the material; or

(ii) Deliver the following information to the requesting security holder within five business days of receipt of the request:

(A) A reasonably current list of the names, addresses and security positions of the record holders, including banks, brokers and similar entities holding securities in the same class or classes as holders which have been or are to be solicited on management's behalf, or any more limited group of such holders designated by the security holder if available or retrievable under the registrant's or its transfer agent's security holder data systems;

(B) The most recent list of names, addresses and security positions of beneficial owners as specified in § 240.14a-13(b), in the possession, or which subsequently comes into the possession, of the registrant;

(C) The names of security holders at a shared address that have consented to delivery of a single copy of proxy materials to a shared address, if the registrant has received written or implied consent in accordance with § 240.14a-3(e)(1); and

(D) If the registrant has relied on § 240.14a-16, the names of security holders who have requested paper copies of the proxy materials for all meetings and the names of security holders who, as of the date that the registrant receives the request, have requested paper copies of the proxy materials only for the meeting to which the solicitation relates.

(iii) All security holder list information shall be in the form requested by the security holder to the extent that such form is available to the registrant without undue burden or expense. The registrant shall furnish the security holder with updated record holder information on a daily basis or, if not available on a daily basis, at the shortest reasonable intervals; provided, however, the registrant need not provide beneficial or record holder information more current than the record date for the meeting or action.

(b)(1) The requesting security holder shall have the options set forth in paragraph (a)(2) of this section, and the registrant shall have corresponding obligations, if the registrant or general partner or sponsor is soliciting or intends to solicit with respect to:

(i) A proposal that is subject to § 240.13e-3;

(ii) A roll-up transaction as defined in Item 901(c) of Regulation S-K (§ 229.901(c) of this chapter) that involves an entity with securities registered pursuant to Section 12 of the Act (15 U.S.C. 78*l*); or

(iii) A roll-up transaction as defined in Item 901(c) of Regulation S-K (§ 229.901(c) of this chapter) that involves a limited partnership, unless the transaction involves only:

(A) Partnerships whose investors will receive new securities or securities in another entity that are not reported under a transaction reporting plan declared effective before December 17, 1993 by the Commission under Section 11A of the Act (15 U.S.C. 78k-1); or

(B) Partnerships whose investors' securities are reported under a transaction reporting plan declared effective before December 17, 1993 by the Commission under Section 11A of the Act (15 U.S.C. 78k-1).

(2) With respect to all other requests pursuant to this section, the registrant shall have the option to either mail the security holder's material or furnish the security holder list as set forth in this section.

(c) At the time of a list request, the security holder making the request shall:

(1) If holding the registrant's securities through a nominee, provide the registrant with a statement by the nominee or other independent third party, or a copy of a current filing made with the Commission and furnished to the registrant, confirming such holder's beneficial ownership; and

(2) Provide the registrant with an affidavit, declaration, affirmation or other similar document provided for under applicable state law identifying the proposal or other corporate action that will be the subject of the security holder's solicitation or communication and attesting that:

(i) The security holder will not use the list information for any purpose other than to solicit security holders with respect to the same meeting or action by consent or authorization for which the registrant is soliciting or intends to solicit or to communicate with security holders with respect to a solicitation commenced by the registrant; and

(ii) The security holder will not disclose such information to any person other than a beneficial owner for whom the request was made and an employee or agent to the extent necessary to effectuate the communication or solicitation.

(d) The security holder shall not use the information furnished by the registrant pursuant to paragraph (a)(2)(ii) of this section for any purpose other than to solicit security holders with respect to the same meeting or action by consent or authorization for which the registrant is soliciting or intends to solicit or to communicate with security holders with respect to a solicitation commenced by the registrant; or disclose such information to any person other than an employee, agent, or beneficial owner for whom a request was made to the extent necessary to effectuate the communication or solicitation. The security holder shall return the information provided pursuant to paragraph (a)(2)(ii) of this section and shall not retain any copies thereof or of any information derived from such information after the termination of the solicitation.

(e) The security holder shall reimburse the reasonable expenses incurred by the registrant in performing the acts requested pursuant to paragraph (a) of this section.

Note 1 to § 240.14a-7. Reasonably prompt methods of distribution to security holders may be used instead of mailing. If an alternative distribution method is chosen, the costs of that method should be considered where necessary rather than the costs of mailing.

Note 2 to § 240.14a-7. When providing the information required by § 240.14a-7(a)(1)(ii), if the registrant has received affirmative written or implied consent to delivery of a single copy of proxy materials to a shared address in accordance with § 240.14a-3(e)(1), it shall exclude from the number of record holders those to whom it does not have to deliver a separate proxy statement.

§ 240.14a-8 Shareholder Proposals

This section addresses when a company must include a shareholder's proposal in its proxy statement and identify the proposal in its form of proxy when the company holds an annual or special meeting of shareholders. In summary, in order to have your shareholder proposal included on a company's proxy card, and included along with any supporting statement in its proxy statement, you must be eligible and follow certain procedures. Under a few specific circumstances, the company is permitted to exclude your proposal, but only after submitting its reasons to the Commission. We structured this section in a question-and-answer format so that it is easier to understand. The references to "you" are to a shareholder seeking to submit the proposal.

(a) Question 1: What is a proposal? A shareholder proposal is your recommendation or requirement that the company and/or its board of directors take action, which you intend to present at a meeting of the company's shareholders. Your proposal should state as clearly as possible

Vagueness

the course of action that you believe the company should follow. If your proposal is placed on the company's proxy card, the company must also provide in the form of proxy means for shareholders to specify by boxes a choice between approval or disapproval, or abstention. Unless otherwise indicated, the word "proposal" as used in this section refers both to your proposal, and to your corresponding statement in support of your proposal (if any).

(b) Question 2: Who is eligible to submit a proposal, and how do I demonstrate to the company that I am eligible?

(1) In order to be eligible to submit a proposal, you must have continuously held at least $2,000 in market value, or 1%, of the company's securities entitled to be voted on the proposal at the meeting for at least one year by the date you submit the proposal. You must continue to hold those securities through the date of the meeting.

(2) If you are the registered holder of your securities, which means that your name appears in the company's records as a shareholder, the company can verify your eligibility on its own, although you will still have to provide the company with a written statement that you intend to continue to hold the securities through the date of the meeting of shareholders. However, if like many shareholders you are not a registered holder, the company likely does not know that you are a shareholder, or how many shares you own. In this case, at the time you submit your proposal, you must prove your eligibility to the company in one of two ways:

(i) The first way is to submit to the company a written statement from the "record" holder of your securities (usually a broker or bank) verifying that, at the time you submitted your proposal, you continuously held the securities for at least one year. You must also include your own written statement that you intend to continue to hold the securities through the date of the meeting of shareholders; or

(ii) The second way to prove ownership applies only if you have filed a Schedule 13D (§ 240.13d-101), Schedule 13G (§ 240.13d-102), Form 3 (§ 249.103 of this chapter), Form 4 (§ 249.104 of this chapter) and/or Form 5 (§ 249.105 of this chapter), or amendments to those documents or updated forms, reflecting your ownership of the shares as of or before the date on which the one-year eligibility period begins. If you have filed one of these documents with the SEC, you may demonstrate your eligibility by submitting to the company:

(A) A copy of the schedule and/or form, and any subsequent amendments reporting a change in your ownership level;

(B) Your written statement that you continuously held the required number of shares for the one-year period as of the date of the statement; and

(C) Your written statement that you intend to continue ownership of the shares through the date of the company's annual or special meeting.

(c) Question 3: How many proposals may I submit? Each shareholder may submit no more than one proposal to a company for a particular shareholders' meeting.

(d) Question 4: How long can my proposal be? The proposal, including any accompanying supporting statement, may not exceed 500 words.

(e) Question 5: What is the deadline for submitting a proposal?

(1) If you are submitting your proposal for the company's annual meeting, you can in most cases find the deadline in last year's proxy statement. However, if the company did not hold an annual meeting last year, or has changed the date of its meeting for this year more than 30 days from last year's meeting, you can usually find the deadline in one of the company's quarterly reports on Form 10-Q (§ 249.308a of this chapter), or in shareholder reports of investment companies under § 270.30d-1 of this chapter of the Investment Company Act of 1940. In order to avoid controversy, shareholders should submit their proposals by means, including electronic means, that permit them to prove the date of delivery.

(2) The deadline is calculated in the following manner if the proposal is submitted for a regularly scheduled annual meeting. The proposal must be received at the company's principal executive offices not less than 120 calendar days before the date of the company's proxy statement released to shareholders in connection with the previous year's annual meeting. However, if the company did not hold an annual meeting the previous year, or if the date of this year's annual meeting has been changed by more than 30 days from the date of the previous year's meeting, then the deadline is a reasonable time before the company begins to print and send its proxy materials.

(3) If you are submitting your proposal for a meeting of shareholders other than a regularly scheduled annual meeting, the deadline is a reasonable time before the company begins to print and send its proxy materials.

(f) Question 6: What if I fail to follow one of the eligibility or procedural requirements explained in answers to Questions 1 through 4 of this section?

(1) The company may exclude your proposal, but only after it has notified you of the problem, and you have failed adequately to correct it. Within 14 calendar days of receiving your proposal, the company must notify you in writing of any procedural or eligibility deficiencies, as well as of the time frame for your response. Your response must be postmarked, or transmitted electronically, no later than 14 days from the date you received the company's notification. A company need not provide you such notice of a deficiency if the deficiency cannot be remedied, such as if you fail to submit a proposal by the company's properly determined deadline. If the company intends to exclude the proposal, it will later have to make a submission under § 240.14a-8 and provide you with a copy under Question 10 below, § 240.14a-8(j).

(2) If you fail in your promise to hold the required number of securities through the date of the meeting of shareholders, then the company will be permitted to exclude all of your proposals from its proxy materials for any meeting held in the following two calendar years.

(g) Question 7: Who has the burden of persuading the Commission or its staff that my proposal can be excluded? Except as otherwise noted, the burden is on the company to demonstrate that it is entitled to exclude a proposal.

(h) Question 8: Must I appear personally at the shareholders' meeting to present the proposal?

(1) Either you, or your representative who is qualified under state law to present the proposal on your behalf, must attend the meeting to present the proposal. Whether you attend the meeting yourself or send a qualified representative to the meeting in your place, you should make sure that you, or your representative, follow the proper state law procedures for attending the meeting and/or presenting your proposal.

(2) If the company holds its shareholder meeting in whole or in part via electronic media, and the company permits you or your representative to present your proposal via such media, then you may appear through electronic media rather than traveling to the meeting to appear in person.

(3) If you or your qualified representative fail to appear and present the proposal, without good cause, the company will be permitted to exclude all of your proposals from its proxy materials for any meetings held in the following two calendar years.

(i) Question 9: If I have complied with the procedural requirements, on what other bases may a company rely to exclude my proposal?

(1) Improper under state law: If the proposal is not a proper subject for action by shareholders under the laws of the jurisdiction of the company's organization;

Note to paragraph (i)(1): Depending on the subject matter, some proposals are not considered proper under state law if they would be binding on the company if approved by shareholders. In our experience, most proposals that are cast as recommendations or requests that the board of directors take specified action are proper under state law. Accordingly, we will assume that a proposal drafted as a recommendation or suggestion is proper unless the company demonstrates otherwise.

(2) Violation of law: If the proposal would, if implemented, cause the company to violate any state, federal, or foreign law to which it is subject;

Note to paragraph (i)(2): We will not apply this basis for exclusion to permit exclusion of a proposal on grounds that it would violate foreign law if compliance with the foreign law would result in a violation of any state or federal law.

(3) Violation of proxy rules: If the proposal or supporting statement is contrary to any of the Commission's proxy rules, including § 240.14a-9, which prohibits materially false or misleading statements in proxy soliciting materials;

(4) Personal grievance; special interest: If the proposal relates to the redress of a personal claim or grievance against the company or any other person, or if it is designed to result in a benefit to you, or to further a personal interest, which is not shared by the other shareholders at large;

(5) Relevance: If the proposal relates to operations which account for less than 5 percent of the company's total assets at the end of its most recent fiscal year, and for less than 5 percent of its net earnings and gross sales for its most recent fiscal year, and is not otherwise significantly related to the company's business;

(6) Absence of power/authority: If the company would lack the power or authority to implement the proposal;

(7) Management functions: If the proposal deals with a matter relating to the company's ordinary business operations;

(8) Director elections: If the proposal:

(i) Would disqualify a nominee who is standing for election;

(ii) Would remove a director from office before his or her term expired;

(iii) Questions the competence, business judgment, or character of one or more nominees or directors;

(iv) Seeks to include a specific individual in the company's proxy materials for election to the board of directors; or

(v) Otherwise could affect the outcome of the upcoming election of directors.

(9) Conflicts with company's proposal: If the proposal directly conflicts with one of the company's own proposals to be submitted to shareholders at the same meeting;

Note to paragraph (i)(9): A company's submission to the Commission under this section should specify the points of conflict with the company's proposal.

(10) Substantially implemented: If the company has already substantially implemented the proposal;

Note to paragraph (i)(10): A company may exclude a shareholder proposal that would provide an advisory vote or seek future advisory votes to approve the compensation of executives as disclosed pursuant to Item 402 of Regulation S-K (§ 229.402 of this chapter) or any successor to Item 402 (a "say-on-pay vote") or that relates to the frequency of say-on-pay votes, provided that in the most recent shareholder vote required by § 240.14a-21(b) of this chapter a single year (i.e., one, two, or three years) received approval of a majority of votes cast on the matter and the company has adopted a policy on the frequency of say-on-pay votes that is consistent with the choice of the majority of votes cast in the most recent shareholder vote required by § 240.14a-21(b) of this chapter.

(11) Duplication: If the proposal substantially duplicates another proposal previously submitted to the company by another proponent that will be included in the company's proxy materials for the same meeting;

(12) Resubmissions: If the proposal deals with substantially the same subject matter as another proposal or proposals that has or have been previously included in the company's proxy materials within the preceding 5 calendar years, a company may exclude it from its proxy materials for any meeting held within 3 calendar years of the last time it was included if the proposal received:

(i) Less than 3% of the vote if proposed once within the preceding 5 calendar years;

(ii) Less than 6% of the vote on its last submission to shareholders if proposed twice previously within the preceding 5 calendar years; or

(iii) Less than 10% of the vote on its last submission to shareholders if proposed three times or more previously within the preceding 5 calendar years; and

(13) Specific amount of dividends: If the proposal relates to specific amounts of cash or stock dividends.

(j) Question 10: What procedures must the company follow if it intends to exclude my proposal?

(1) If the company intends to exclude a proposal from its proxy materials, it must file its reasons with the Commission no later than 80 calendar days before it files its definitive proxy statement and form of proxy with the Commission. The company must simultaneously provide you with a copy of its submission. The Commission staff may permit the company to make its submission later than 80 days before the company files its definitive proxy statement and form of proxy, if the company demonstrates good cause for missing the deadline.

(2) The company must file six paper copies of the following:

(i) The proposal;

(ii) An explanation of why the company believes that it may exclude the proposal, which should, if possible, refer to the most recent applicable authority, such as prior Division letters issued under the rule; and

(iii) A supporting opinion of counsel when such reasons are based on matters of state or foreign law.

(k) Question 11: May I submit my own statement to the Commission responding to the company's arguments?

Yes, you may submit a response, but it is not required. You should try to submit any response to us, with a copy to the company, as soon as possible after the company makes its submission. This way, the Commission staff will have time to consider fully your submission before it issues its response. You should submit six paper copies of your response.

(*l*) Question 12: If the company includes my shareholder proposal in its proxy materials, what information about me must it include along with the proposal itself?

(1) The company's proxy statement must include your name and address, as well as the number of the company's voting securities that you hold. However, instead of providing that information, the company may instead include a statement that it will provide the information to shareholders promptly upon receiving an oral or written request.

(2) The company is not responsible for the contents of your proposal or supporting statement.

(m) Question 13: What can I do if the company includes in its proxy statement reasons why it believes shareholders should not vote in favor of my proposal, and I disagree with some of its statements?

(1) The company may elect to include in its proxy statement reasons why it believes shareholders should vote against your proposal. The company is allowed to make arguments reflecting its own point of view, just as you may express your own point of view in your proposal's supporting statement.

(2) However, if you believe that the company's opposition to your proposal contains materially false or misleading statements that may violate our anti-fraud rule, § 240.14a-9, you should promptly send to the Commission staff and the company a letter explaining the reasons for your view, along with a copy of the company's statements opposing your proposal. To the extent possible, your letter should include specific factual information demonstrating the inaccuracy of the company's claims. Time permitting, you may wish to try to work out your differences with the company by yourself before contacting the Commission staff.

(3) We require the company to send you a copy of its statements opposing your proposal before it sends its proxy materials, so that you may bring to our attention any materially false or misleading statements, under the following timeframes:

(i) If our no-action response requires that you make revisions to your proposal or supporting statement as a condition to requiring the company to include it in its proxy materials, then the company must provide you with a copy of its opposition statements no later than 5 calendar days after the company receives a copy of your revised proposal; or

(ii) In all other cases, the company must provide you with a copy of its opposition statements no later than 30 calendar days before its files definitive copies of its proxy statement and form of proxy under § 240.14a-6.

§ 240.14a-9 False or Misleading Statements

(a) No solicitation subject to this regulation shall be made by means of any proxy statement, form of proxy, notice of meeting or other communication, written or oral, containing any statement which, at the time and in the light of the circumstances under which it is made, is false or misleading with respect to any material fact, or which omits to state any material fact necessary in order to make the statements therein not false or misleading or necessary to correct any statement in any earlier communication with respect to the solicitation of a proxy for the same meeting or subject matter which has become false or misleading.

(b) The fact that a proxy statement, form of proxy or other soliciting material has been filed with or examined by the Commission shall not be deemed a finding by the Commission that such material is accurate or complete or not false or misleading, or that the Commission has passed upon the merits of or approved any statement contained therein or any matter to be acted upon by security holders. No representation contrary to the foregoing shall be made.

(c) No nominee, nominating shareholder or nominating shareholder group, or any member thereof, shall cause to be included in a registrant's proxy materials, either pursuant to the Federal proxy rules, an applicable state or foreign law provision, or a registrant's governing documents as they relate to including shareholder nominees for director in a registrant's proxy materials, include in a notice on Schedule 14N (§ 240.14n-101), or include in any other related communication, any statement which, at the time and in the light of the circumstances under which it is made, is false or misleading with respect to any material fact, or which omits to state any material fact necessary in order to make the statements therein not false or misleading or necessary to correct any statement in any earlier communication with respect to a solicitation for the same meeting or subject matter which has become false or misleading.

Note: The following are some examples of what, depending upon particular facts and circumstances, may be misleading within the meaning of this section.

a. Predictions as to specific future market values.

b. Material which directly or indirectly impugns character, integrity or personal reputation, or directly or indirectly makes charges concerning improper, illegal or immoral conduct or associations, without factual foundation.

c. Failure to so identify a proxy statement, form of proxy and other soliciting material as to clearly distinguish it from the soliciting material of any other person or persons soliciting for the same meeting or subject matter.

d. Claims made prior to a meeting regarding the results of a solicitation.

§ 240.14a-12 Solicitation Before Furnishing a Proxy Statement

(a) Notwithstanding the provisions of § 240.14a-3(a), a solicitation may be made before furnishing security holders with a proxy statement meeting the requirements of § 240.14a-3(a) if:

(1) Each written communication includes:

(i) The identity of the participants in the solicitation (as defined in Instruction 3 to Item 4 of Schedule 14A (§ 240.14a-101)) and a description of their direct or indirect interests, by security holdings or otherwise, or a prominent legend in clear, plain language advising security holders where they can obtain that information; and

(ii) A prominent legend in clear, plain language advising security holders to read the proxy statement when it is available because it contains important information. The legend also must explain to investors that they can get the proxy statement, and any other relevant documents, for free at the Commission's web site and describe which documents are available free from the participants; and

(2) A definitive proxy statement meeting the requirements of § 240.14a-3(a) is sent or given to security holders solicited in reliance on this section before or at the same time as the forms of proxy, consent or authorization are furnished to or requested from security holders.

(b) Any soliciting material published, sent or given to security holders in accordance with paragraph (a) of this section must be filed with the Commission no later than the date the material is first published, sent or given to security holders. Three copies of the material must at the same time be filed with, or mailed for filing to, each national securities exchange upon which any class of securities of the registrant is listed and registered. The soliciting material must include a cover page in the form set forth in Schedule 14A (§ 240.14a-101) and the appropriate box on the cover page must be marked. Soliciting material in connection with a registered offering is required to be filed only under § 230.424 or § 230.425 of this chapter, and will be deemed filed under this section.

(c) Solicitations by any person or group of persons for the purpose of opposing a solicitation subject to this regulation by any other person or group of persons with respect to the election or removal of directors at any annual or special meeting of security holders also are subject to the following provisions:

(1) Application of this rule to annual report to security holders. Notwithstanding the provisions of § 240.14a-3(b) and (c), any portion of the annual report to security holders referred to in § 240.14a-3(b) that comments upon or refers to any solicitation subject to this rule, or to any participant in the solicitation, other than the solicitation by the management, must be filed with the Commission as proxy material subject to this regulation. This must be filed in electronic format unless an exemption is available under Rules 201 or 202 of Regulation S-T (§ 232.201 or § 232.202 of this chapter).

(2) Use of reprints or reproductions. In any solicitation subject to this § 240.14a-12(c), soliciting material that includes, in whole or part, any reprints or reproductions of any previously published material must:

(i) State the name of the author and publication, the date of prior publication, and identify any person who is quoted without being named in the previously published material.

(ii) Except in the case of a public or official document or statement, state whether or not the consent of the author and publication has been obtained to the use of the previously published material as proxy soliciting material.

(iii) If any participant using the previously published material, or anyone on his or her behalf, paid, directly or indirectly, for the preparation or prior publication of the previously published material, or has made or proposes to make any payments or give any other consideration in connection with the publication or republication of the material, state the circumstances.

Instruction 1 to § 240.14a-12. If paper filing is permitted, file eight copies of the soliciting material with the Commission, except that only three copies of the material specified by § 240.14a-12(c)(1) need be filed.

Instruction 2 to § 240.14a-12. Any communications made under this section after the definitive proxy statement is on file but before it is disseminated also must specify that the proxy statement is publicly available and the anticipated date of dissemination.

Instruction 3 to § 240.14a-12. Inclusion of a nominee pursuant to § 240.14a-11, an applicable state or foreign law provision, or a registrant's governing documents as they relate to the inclusion of shareholder director nominees in the registrant's proxy materials, or solicitations by a nominating shareholder or nominating shareholder group that are made in connection with that nomination constitute solicitations in opposition subject to § 240.14a-12(c), except for purposes of § 240.14a-6(a).

§ 240.14a-16 Internet Availability of Proxy Materials

(a)(1) A registrant shall furnish a proxy statement pursuant to § 240.14a-3(a), or an annual report to security holders pursuant to § 240.14a-3(b), to a security holder by sending the security holder a Notice of Internet Availability of Proxy Materials, as described in this section, 40 calendar days or more prior to the security holder meeting date, or if no meeting is to be held, 40 calendar days or more prior to the date the votes, consents or authorizations may be used to effect the corporate action, and complying with all other requirements of this section.

(2) Unless the registrant chooses to follow the full set delivery option set forth in paragraph (n) of this section, it must provide the record holder or respondent bank with all information listed in paragraph (d) of this section in sufficient time for the record holder or respondent bank to prepare, print and send a Notice of Internet Availability of Proxy Materials to beneficial owners at least 40 calendar days before the meeting date.

(b)(1) All materials identified in the Notice of Internet Availability of Proxy Materials must be publicly accessible, free of charge, at the Web site address specified in the notice on or before the time that the notice is sent to the security holder and such materials must remain available on that Web site through the conclusion of the meeting of security holders.

(2) All additional soliciting materials sent to security holders or made public after the Notice of Internet Availability of Proxy Materials has been sent must be made publicly accessible at the specified Web site address no later than the day on which such materials are first sent to security holders or made public.

(3) The Web site address relied upon for compliance under this section may not be the address of the Commission's electronic filing system.

(4) The registrant must provide security holders with a means to execute a proxy as of the time the Notice of Internet Availability of Proxy Materials is first sent to security holders.

(c) The materials must be presented on the Web site in a format, or formats, convenient for both reading online and printing on paper.

(d) The Notice of Internet Availability of Proxy Materials must contain the following:

(1) A prominent legend in bold-face type that states "Important Notice Regarding the Availability of Proxy Materials for the Shareholder Meeting To Be Held on [insert meeting date]";

(2) An indication that the communication is not a form for voting and presents only an overview of the more complete proxy materials, which contain important information and are available on the Internet or by mail, and encouraging a security holder to access and review the proxy materials before voting;

(3) The Internet Web site address where the proxy materials are available;

(4) Instructions regarding how a security holder may request a paper or e-mail copy of the proxy materials at no charge, including the date by which they should make the request to facilitate timely delivery, and an indication that they will not otherwise receive a paper or e-mail copy;

(5) The date, time, and location of the meeting, or if corporate action is to be taken by written consent, the earliest date on which the corporate action may be effected;

(6) A clear and impartial identification of each separate matter intended to be acted on and the soliciting person's recommendations, if any, regarding those matters, but no supporting statements;

(7) A list of the materials being made available at the specified Web site;

(8) A toll-free telephone number, an e-mail address, and an Internet Web site where the security holder can request a copy of the proxy statement, annual report to security holders, and form of proxy, relating to all of the registrant's future security holder meetings and for the particular meeting to which the proxy materials being furnished relate;

(9) Any control/identification numbers that the security holder needs to access his or her form of proxy;

(10) Instructions on how to access the form of proxy, provided that such instructions do not enable a security holder to execute a proxy without having access to the proxy statement and, if required by § 240.14a-3(b), the annual report to security holders; and

(11) Information on how to obtain directions to be able to attend the meeting and vote in person.

(e)(1) The Notice of Internet Availability of Proxy Materials may not be incorporated into, or combined with, another document, except that it may be incorporated into, or combined with, a notice of security holder meeting required under state law, unless state law prohibits such incorporation or combination.

(2) The Notice of Internet Availability of Proxy Materials may contain only the information required by paragraph (d) of this section and any additional information required to be included in a notice of security holders meeting under state law; provided that:

(i) The registrant must revise the information on the Notice of Internet Availability of Proxy Materials, including any title to the document, to reflect the fact that:

(A) The registrant is conducting a consent solicitation rather than a proxy solicitation; or

(B) The registrant is not soliciting proxy or consent authority, but is furnishing an information statement pursuant to § 240.14c-2; and

(ii) The registrant may include a statement on the Notice to educate security holders that no personal information other than the identification or control number is necessary to execute a proxy.

(f)(1) Except as provided in paragraph (h) of this section, the Notice of Internet Availability of Proxy Materials must be sent separately from other types of security holder communications and may not accompany any other document or materials, including the form of proxy.

(2) Notwithstanding paragraph (f)(1) of this section, the registrant may accompany the Notice of Internet Availability of Proxy Materials with:

(i) A pre-addressed, postage-paid reply card for requesting a copy of the proxy materials;

(ii) A copy of any notice of security holder meeting required under state law if that notice is not combined with the Notice of Internet Availability of Proxy Materials;

(iii) In the case of an investment company registered under the Investment Company Act of 1940, the company's prospectus, a summary prospectus that satisfies the requirements of § 230.498(b)of this chapter, or a report that is required to be transmitted to stockholders by section 30(e) of the Investment Company Act (15 U.S.C. 80a-29(e)) and the rules thereunder; and

(iv) An explanation of the reasons for a registrant's use of the rules detailed in this section and the process of receiving and reviewing the proxy materials and voting as detailed in this section.

(g) Plain English.

(1) To enhance the readability of the Notice of Internet Availability of Proxy Materials, the registrant must use plain English principles in the organization, language, and design of the notice.

(2) The registrant must draft the language in the Notice of Internet Availability of Proxy Materials so that, at a minimum, it substantially complies with each of the following plain English writing principles:

(i) Short sentences;

(ii) Definite, concrete, everyday words;

(iii) Active voice;

(iv) Tabular presentation or bullet lists for complex material, whenever possible;

(v) No legal jargon or highly technical business terms; and

(vi) No multiple negatives.

(3) In designing the Notice of Internet Availability of Proxy Materials, the registrant may include pictures, logos, or similar design elements so long as the design is not misleading and the required information is clear.

(h) The registrant may send a form of proxy to security holders if:

(1) At least 10 calendar days or more have passed since the date it first sent the Notice of Internet Availability of Proxy Materials to security holders and the form of proxy is accompanied by a copy of the Notice of Internet Availability of Proxy Materials; or

(2) The form of proxy is accompanied or preceded by a copy, via the same medium, of the proxy statement and any annual report to security holders that is required by § 240.14a-3(b).

(i) The registrant must file a form of the Notice of Internet Availability of Proxy Materials with the Commission pursuant to § 240.14a-6(b) no later than the date that the registrant first sends the notice to security holders.

(j) Obligation to provide copies.

(1) The registrant must send, at no cost to the record holder or respondent bank and by U.S. first class mail or other reasonably prompt means, a paper copy of the proxy statement, information statement, annual report to security holders, and form of proxy (to the extent each of those documents is applicable) to any record holder or respondent bank requesting

such a copy within three business days after receiving a request for a paper copy.

(2) The registrant must send, at no cost to the record holder or respondent bank and via e-mail, an electronic copy of the proxy statement, information statement, annual report to security holders, and form of proxy (to the extent each of those documents is applicable) to any record holder or respondent bank requesting such a copy within three business days after receiving a request for an electronic copy via e-mail.

(3) The registrant must provide copies of the proxy materials for one year after the conclusion of the meeting or corporate action to which the proxy materials relate, provided that, if the registrant receives the request after the conclusion of the meeting or corporate action to which the proxy materials relate, the registrant need not send copies via First Class mail and need not respond to such request within three business days.

(4) The registrant must maintain records of security holder requests to receive materials in paper or via e-mail for future solicitations and must continue to provide copies of the materials to a security holder who has made such a request until the security holder revokes such request.

(k) Security holder information.

(1) A registrant or its agent shall maintain the Internet Web site on which it posts its proxy materials in a manner that does not infringe on the anonymity of a person accessing such Web site.

(2) The registrant and its agents shall not use any e-mail address obtained from a security holder solely for the purpose of requesting a copy of proxy materials pursuant to paragraph (j) of this section for any purpose other than to send a copy of those materials to that security holder. The registrant shall not disclose such information to any person other than an employee or agent to the extent necessary to send a copy of the proxy materials pursuant to paragraph (j) of this section.

(*l*) A person other than the registrant may solicit proxies pursuant to the conditions imposed on registrants by this section, provided that:

(1) A soliciting person other than the registrant is required to provide copies of its proxy materials only to security holders to whom it has sent a Notice of Internet Availability of Proxy Materials; and

(2) A soliciting person other than the registrant must send its Notice of Internet Availability of Proxy Materials by the later of:

(i) 40 Calendar days prior to the security holder meeting date or, if no meeting is to be held, 40 calendar days prior to the date the votes, consents, or authorizations may be used to effect the corporate action; or

(ii) The date on which it files its definitive proxy statement with the Commission, provided its preliminary proxy statement is filed no later than 10 calendar days after the date that the registrant files its definitive proxy statement.

(3) Content of the soliciting person's Notice of Internet Availability of Proxy Materials.

(i) If, at the time a soliciting person other than the registrant sends its Notice of Internet Availability of Proxy Materials, the soliciting person is not aware of all matters on the registrant's agenda for the meeting of security holders, the soliciting person's Notice on Internet Availability of Proxy Materials must provide a clear and impartial identification of each separate matter on the agenda to the extent known by the soliciting person at that time. The soliciting person's notice also must include a clear statement indicating that there may be additional agenda items of which the soliciting person is not aware and that the security holder cannot direct a vote for those items on the soliciting person's proxy card provided at that time.

(ii) If a soliciting person other than the registrant sends a form of proxy not containing all matters intended to be acted upon, the Notice of Internet Availability of Proxy Materials must clearly state whether execution of the form of proxy will invalidate a security holder's prior vote on matters not presented on the form of proxy.

(m) This section shall not apply to a proxy solicitation in connection with a business combination transaction, as defined in § 230.165 of this chapter, as well as transactions for cash consideration requiring disclosure under Item 14 of § 240.14a-101.

(n) Full Set Delivery Option.

(1) For purposes of this paragraph (n), the term full set of proxy materials shall include all of the following documents:

(i) A copy of the proxy statement;

(ii) A copy of the annual report to security holders if required by § 240.14a-3(b); and

(iii) A form of proxy.

(2) Notwithstanding paragraphs (e) and (f)(2) of this section, a registrant or other soliciting person may:

(i) Accompany the Notice of Internet Availability of Proxy Materials with a full set of proxy materials; or

(ii) Send a full set of proxy materials without a Notice of Internet Availability of Proxy Materials if all of the information required in a Notice of Internet Availability of Proxy Materials pursuant to paragraphs (d) and (n)(4) of this section is incorporated in the proxy statement and the form of proxy.

(3) A registrant or other soliciting person that sends a full set of proxy materials to a security holder pursuant to this paragraph (n) need not comply with

(i) The timing provisions of paragraphs (a) and (l)(2) of this section; and

(ii) The obligation to provide copies pursuant to paragraph (j) of this section.

(4) A registrant or other soliciting person that sends a full set of proxy materials to a security holder pursuant to this paragraph (n) need not include in its Notice of Internet Availability of Proxy Materials, proxy statement, or form of proxy the following disclosures:

(i) Instructions regarding the nature of the communication pursuant to paragraph (d)(2) of this section;

(ii) Instructions on how to request a copy of the proxy materials; and

(iii) Instructions on how to access the form of proxy pursuant to paragraph (d)(10) of this section.

Tender Offer Rules Under Sections 14(d) and 14(e)

SECTIONS 14(D)-(E). TENDER OFFERS

(a) Scope. Regulation 14D (§§ 240.14d-1 through 240.14d-101) shall apply to any tender offer that is subject to section 14(d)(1) of the Act (15 U.S.C. 78n(d)(1)), including, but not limited to, any tender offer for securities of a class described in that section that is made by an affiliate of the issuer of such class. Regulation 14E (§§ 240.14e-1 through 240.14e-8) shall apply to any tender offer for securities (other than exempted securities) unless otherwise noted therein . . .

§ 240.14d-2 Commencement of a Tender Offer

(a) Date of commencement. A bidder will have commenced its tender offer for purposes of section 14(d) of the Act (15 U.S.C. 78n) and the rules under that section at 12:01 a.m. on the date when the bidder has first published, sent or given the means to tender to security holders. For purposes of this section, the means to tender includes the transmittal form or a statement regarding how the transmittal form may be obtained.

(b) Pre-commencement communications. A communication by the bidder will not be deemed to constitute commencement of a tender offer if:

(1) It does not include the means for security holders to tender their shares into the offer; and

(2) All written communications relating to the tender offer, from and including the first public announcement, are filed under cover of Schedule TO (§ 240.14d-100) with the Commission no later than the date of the communication. The bidder also must deliver to the subject company and any other bidder for the same class of securities the first communication relating to the transaction that is filed, or required to be filed, with the Commission . . .

§ 240.14d-3 Filing and Transmission of Tender Offer Statement

(a) Filing and transmittal. No bidder shall make a tender offer if, after consummation thereof, such bidder would be the beneficial owner of more than 5 percent of the class of the subject company's securities for which the tender offer is made, unless as soon as practicable on the date of the commencement of the tender offer such bidder:

(1) Files with the Commission a Tender Offer Statement on Schedule TO (§ 240.14d-100), including all exhibits thereto;

(2) Delivers a copy of such Schedule TO, including all exhibits thereto:

(i) To the subject company at its principal executive office; and

(ii) To any other bidder, which has filed a Schedule TO with the Commission relating to a tender offer which has not yet terminated for the same class of securities of the subject company, at such bidder's principal executive office or at the address of the person authorized to receive notices and communications (which is disclosed on the cover sheet of such other bidder's Schedule TO);

(3) Gives telephonic notice of the information required by Rule 14d-6(d)(2)(i) and (ii) (§ 240.14d-6(d)(2)(i) and (ii)) and mails by means of first class mail a copy of such Schedule TO, including all exhibits thereto:

(i) To each national securities exchange where such class of the subject company's securities is registered and listed for trading (which may be based upon information contained in the subject company's most recent Annual Report on Form 10-K (§ 249.310 of this chapter) filed with the Commission unless the bidder has reason to believe that such information is not current), which telephonic notice shall be made when practicable before the opening of each such exchange; and

(ii) To the National Association of Securities Dealers, Inc. ("NASD") if such class of the subject company's securities is authorized for quotation in the NASDAQ interdealer quotation system . . .

§ 240.14d-4 Dissemination of Tender Offers to Security Holders

As soon as practicable on the date of commencement of a tender offer, the bidder must publish, send or give the disclosure required by § 240.14d-6 to security holders of the class of securities that is the subject of the offer, by complying with all of the requirements of any of the following:

(a) Cash tender offers and exempt securities offers. For tender offers in which the consideration consists solely of cash and/or securities exempt from registration under section 3 of the Securities Act of 1933 (15 U.S.C. 77c):

(1) Long-form publication. The bidder makes adequate publication in a newspaper or newspapers of long-form publication of the tender offer.

(2) Summary publication.

(i) If the tender offer is not subject to Rule 13e-3 (§ 240.13e-3), the bidder makes adequate publication in a newspaper or newspapers of a summary advertisement of the tender offer; and

(ii) Mails by first class mail or otherwise furnishes with reasonable promptness the bidder's tender offer materials to any security holder who requests such tender offer materials pursuant to the summary advertisement or otherwise.

(3) Use of stockholder lists and security position listings. Any bidder using stockholder lists and security position listings under § 240.14d-5 must comply with paragraph (a)(1) or (2) of this section on or before the date of the bidder's request under § 240.14d-5(a).

Instruction to paragraph (a): Tender offers may be published or sent or given to security holders by other methods, but with respect to summary publication and the use of stockholder lists and security position listings under § 240.14d-5, paragraphs (a)(2) and (a)(3) of this section are exclusive.

(b) Registered securities offers. For tender offers in which the consideration consists solely or partially of securities registered under the Securities Act of 1933, a registration statement containing all of the required information, including pricing information, has been filed and a preliminary prospectus or a prospectus that meets the requirements of section 10(a) of the Securities Act (15 U.S.C. 77j(a)), including a letter of transmittal, is delivered to security holders. However, for going-private transactions (as defined by § 240.13e-3) and roll-up transactions (as described by Item 901 of Regulation S-K (§ 229.901 of this chapter)), a registration statement registering the securities to be offered must have become effective and only a prospectus that meets the requirements of section 10(a) of the Securities Act may be delivered to security holders on the date of commencement.

Instructions to paragraph (b):

1. If the prospectus is being delivered by mail, mailing on the date of commencement is sufficient.

2. A preliminary prospectus used under this section may not omit information under §§ 230.430or 230.430A of this chapter.

3. If a preliminary prospectus is used under this section and the bidder must disseminate material changes, the tender offer must remain open for the period specified in paragraph (d)(2) of this section.

4. If a preliminary prospectus is used under this section, tenders may be requested in accordance with § 230.162(a) of this chapter.

(c) Adequate publication. Depending on the facts and circumstances involved, adequate publication of a tender offer pursuant to this section may require publication in a newspaper with a national circulation or may only require publication in a newspaper with metropolitan or regional circulation or may require publication in a combination thereof: Provided, however, That publication in all editions of a daily newspaper with a national circulation shall be deemed to constitute adequate publication.

(d) Publication of changes and extension of the offer.

(1) If a tender offer has been published or sent or given to security holders by one or more of the methods enumerated in this section, a material change in the information published or sent or given to security holders shall be promptly disseminated to security holders in a manner reasonably designed to inform security holders of such change; Provided, however, That if the bidder has elected pursuant to rule 14d-5 (f)(1) of this section to require the subject company to disseminate amendments disclosing material changes to the tender offer materials pursuant to Rule 14d-5, the bidder shall disseminate material changes in the information published or sent or given to security holders at least pursuant to Rule 14d-5.

(2) In a registered securities offer where the bidder disseminates the preliminary prospectus as permitted by paragraph (b) of this section, the offer must remain open from the date that material changes to the tender offer materials are disseminated to security holders, as follows:

(i) Five business days for a prospectus supplement containing a material change other than price or share levels;

(ii) Ten business days for a prospectus supplement containing a change in price, the amount of securities sought, the dealer's soliciting fee, or other similarly significant change;

(iii) Ten business days for a prospectus supplement included as part of a post-effective amendment; and

(iv) Twenty business days for a revised prospectus when the initial prospectus was materially deficient.

§ 240.14d-5 Dissemination of Certain Tender Offers by the Use of Stockholder Lists and Security Position Listings

comp. can mail tender offer itself or furnish stockholder list

(a) Obligations of the subject company. Upon receipt by a subject company at its principal executive offices of a bidder's written request, meeting the requirements of paragraph (e) of this section, the subject company shall comply with the following sub-paragraphs.

(1) The subject company shall notify promptly transfer agents and any other person who will assist the subject company in complying with the requirements of this section of the receipt by the subject company of a request by a bidder pursuant to this section.

(2) The subject company shall promptly ascertain whether the most recently prepared stockholder list, written or otherwise, within the access of the subject company was prepared as of a date earlier than ten business days before the date of the bidder's request and, if so, the subject company shall promptly prepare or cause to be prepared a stockholder list as of the most recent practicable date which shall not be more than ten business days before the date of the bidder's request.

need most up-to-date stockholder list

(3) The subject company shall make an election to comply and shall comply with all of the provisions of either paragraph (b) or paragraph (c) of this section. The subject company's election once made shall not be modified or revoked during the bidder's tender offer and extensions thereof.

(4) No later than the second business day after the date of the bidder's request, the subject company shall orally notify the bidder, which notification shall be confirmed in writing, of the subject company's election made pursuant to paragraph (a)(3) of this section. Such notification shall indicate (i) the approximate number of security holders of the class of securities being sought by the bidder and, (ii) if the subject company elects to comply with paragraph (b) of this section, appropriate information concerning the location for delivery of the bidder's tender offer materials and the approximate direct costs incidental to the mailing to security holders of the bidder's tender offer materials computed in accordance with paragraph (g)(2) of this section.

(b) Mailing of tender offer materials by the subject company. A subject company which elects pursuant to paragraph (a)(3) of this section to comply with the provisions of this paragraph shall perform the acts prescribed by the following paragraphs.

(1) The subject company shall promptly contact each participant named on the most recent security position listing of any clearing agency within the access of the subject company and make inquiry of each such participant as to the approximate number of beneficial owners of the subject company securities being sought in the tender offer held by each such participant.

(2) No later than the third business day after delivery of the bidder's tender offer materials pursuant to paragraph (g)(1) of this section, the subject company shall begin to mail or cause to be mailed by means of first class mail a copy of the bidder's tender offer materials to each person whose name appears as a record holder of the class of securities for which the offer is made on the most recent stockholder list referred to in paragraph (a)(2) of this section. The subject company shall use its best efforts to complete the mailing in a timely manner but in no event shall such mailing be completed in a substantially greater period of time than the subject company would complete a mailing to security holders of its own materials relating to the tender offer.

(3) No later than the third business day after the delivery of the bidder's tender offer materials pursuant to paragraph (g)(1) of this sec-

tion, the subject company shall begin to transmit or cause to be transmitted a sufficient number of sets of the bidder's tender offer materials to the participants named on the security position listings described in paragraph (b)(1) of this section. The subject company shall use its best efforts to complete the transmittal in a timely manner but in no event shall such transmittal be completed in a substantially greater period of time than the subject company would complete a transmittal to such participants pursuant to security position listings of clearing agencies of its own material relating to the tender offer.

(4) The subject company shall promptly give oral notification to the bidder, which notification shall be confirmed in writing, of the commencement of the mailing pursuant to paragraph (b)(2) of this section and of the transmittal pursuant to paragraph (b)(3) of this section.

(5) During the tender offer and any extension thereof the subject company shall use reasonable efforts to update the stockholder list and shall mail or cause to be mailed promptly following each update a copy of the bidder's tender offer materials (to the extent sufficient sets of such materials have been furnished by the bidder) to each person who has become a record holder since the later of (i) the date of preparation of the most recent stockholder list referred to in paragraph (a)(2) of this section or (ii) the last preceding update.

(6) If the bidder has elected pursuant to paragraph (f)(1) of this section to require the subject company to disseminate amendments disclosing material changes to the tender offer materials pursuant to this section, the subject company, promptly following delivery of each such amendment, shall mail or cause to be mailed a copy of each such amendment to each record holder whose name appears on the shareholder list described in paragraphs (a)(2) and (b)(5) of this section and shall transmit or cause to be transmitted sufficient copies of such amendment to each participant named on security position listings who received sets of the bidder's tender offer materials pursuant to paragraph (b)(3) of this section.

(7) The subject company shall not include any communication other than the bidder's tender offer materials or amendments thereto in the envelopes or other containers furnished by the bidder.

(8) Promptly following the termination of the tender offer, the subject company shall reimburse the bidder the excess, if any, of the amounts advanced pursuant to paragraph (f)(3)(iii) over the direct costs incidental to compliance by the subject company and its agents in performing the acts required by this section computed in accordance with paragraph (g)(2) of this section.

(c) Delivery of stockholder lists and security position listings. A subject company which elects pursuant to paragraph (a)(3) of this section to comply with the provisions of this paragraph shall perform the acts prescribed by the following paragraphs.

(1) No later than the third business day after the date of the bidder's request, the subject company must furnish to the bidder at the subject company's principal executive office a copy of the names and addresses of the record holders on the most recent stockholder list referred to in paragraph (a)(2) of this section; the names and addresses of participants identified on the most recent security position listing of any clearing agency that is within the access of the subject company; and the most recent list of names, addresses and security positions of beneficial owners as specified in § 240.14a-13(b), in the possession of the subject company, or that subsequently comes into its possession. All security holder list information must be in the format requested by the bidder to the extent the format is available to the subject company without undue burden or expense.

(2) If the bidder has elected pursuant to paragraph (f)(1) of this section to require the subject company to disseminate amendments disclosing material changes to the tender offer materials, the subject company shall update the stockholder list by furnishing the bidder with the name and address of each record holder named on the stockholder list, and not previously furnished to the bidder, promptly after such information becomes available to the subject company during the tender offer and any extensions thereof.

...

Note to § 240.14d-5. Reasonably prompt methods of distribution to security holders may be used instead of mailing. If alternative methods are chosen, the approximate direct costs of distribution shall be computed by adding the estimated direct costs of preparing the document for distribution through the chosen medium (including updating of shareholder lists) plus the estimated reasonable cost of distribution through that medium. Direct costs incidental to the distribution of tender offer materials and amendments thereto may include all reasonable charges paid by the subject company to third parties for supplies or services, including costs attendant to preparing shareholder lists, handling the bidder's materials, and contacting participants named on security position listings, but shall not include indirect costs, such as employee time which is devoted to either contesting or supporting the tender offer on behalf of the subject company.

§ 240.14d-6 Disclosure of Tender Offer Information to Security Holders

(a) Information required on date of commencement—

(1) Long-form publication. If a tender offer is published, sent or given to security holders on the date of commencement by means of long-form publication under § 240.14d-4(a)(1), the long-form publication must include the information required by paragraph (d)(1) of this section.

(2) Summary publication. If a tender offer is published, sent or given to security holders on the date of commencement by means of summary publication under § 240.14d-4(a)(2):

(i) The summary advertisement must contain at least the information required by paragraph (d)(2) of this section; and

(ii) The tender offer materials furnished by the bidder upon request of any security holder must include the information required by paragraph (d)(1) of this section.

(3) Use of stockholder lists and security position listings. If a tender offer is published, sent or given to security holders on the date of commencement by the use of stockholder lists and security position listings under § 240.14d-4(a)(3):

(i) The summary advertisement must contain at least the information required by paragraph (d)(2) of this section; and

(ii) The tender offer materials transmitted to security holders pursuant to such lists and security position listings and furnished by the bidder upon the request of any security holder must include the information required by paragraph (d)(1) of this section.

(4) Other tender offers. If a tender offer is published or sent or given to security holders other than pursuant to § 240.14d-4(a), the tender offer materials that are published or sent or given to security holders on the date of commencement of such offer must include the information required by paragraph (d)(1) of this section.

(b) Information required in other tender offer materials published after commencement. Except for tender offer materials described in paragraphs (a)(2)(ii) and (a)(3)(ii) of this section, additional tender offer materials published, sent or given to security holders after commencement must include:

(1) The identities of the bidder and subject company;

(2) The amount and class of securities being sought;

(3) The type and amount of consideration being offered; and

(4) The scheduled expiration date of the tender offer, whether the tender offer may be extended and, if so, the procedures for extension of the tender offer.

Instruction to paragraph (b): If the additional tender offer materials are summary advertisements, they also must include the information required by paragraphs (d)(2)(v) of this section.

(c) Material changes. A material change in the information published or sent or given to security holders must be promptly disclosed to security holders in additional tender offer materials.

(d) Information to be included—

(1) Tender offer materials other than summary publication. The following information is required by paragraphs (a)(1), (a)(2)(ii), (a)(3)(ii) and (a)(4) of this section:

(i) The information required by Item 1 of Schedule TO (§ 240.14d-100) (Summary Term Sheet); and

(ii) The information required by the remaining items of Schedule TO (§ 240.14d-100) for third-party tender offers, except for Item 12 (exhibits) of Schedule TO (§ 240.14d-100), or a fair and adequate summary of the information.

(2) Summary Publication. The following information is required in a summary advertisement under paragraphs (a)(2)(i) and (a)(3)(i) of this section:

(i) The identity of the bidder and the subject company;

(ii) The information required by Item 1004(a)(1) of Regulation M-A (§ 229.1004(a)(1) of this chapter);

(iii) If the tender offer is for less than all of the outstanding securities of a class of equity securities, a statement as to whether the purpose or one of the purposes of the tender offer is to acquire or influence control of the business of the subject company;

(iv) A statement that the information required by paragraph (d)(1) of this section is incorporated by reference into the summary advertisement;

(v) Appropriate instructions as to how security holders may obtain promptly, at the bidder's expense, the bidder's tender offer materials; and

(vi) In a tender offer published or sent or given to security holders by use of stockholder lists and security position listings under § 240.14d-4(a)(3), a statement that a request is being made for such lists and listings. The summary publication also must state that tender offer materials will be mailed to record holders and will be furnished to brokers, banks and similar persons whose name appears or whose nominee appears on the list of security holders or, if applicable, who are listed as participants in a clearing agency's security position listing for subsequent transmittal to beneficial owners of such securities. If the list furnished to the bidder also included beneficial owners pursuant to § 240.14d-5(c)(1) and tender offer materials will be mailed directly to beneficial holders, include a statement to that effect.

(3) No transmittal letter. Neither the initial summary advertisement nor any subsequent summary advertisement may include a transmittal letter (the letter furnished to security holders for transmission of securities sought in the tender offer) or any amendment to the transmittal letter.

§ 240.14d-7 Additional Withdrawal Rights

(a) Rights.

(1) In addition to the provisions of section 14(d)(5) of the Act, any person who has deposited securities pursuant to a tender offer has the

right to withdraw any such securities during the period such offer request or invitation remains open.

(2) Exemption during subsequent offering period. Notwithstanding the provisions of section 14(d)(5) of the Act (15 U.S.C. 78n(d)(5)) and paragraph (a) of this section, the bidder need not offer withdrawal rights during a subsequent offering period.

(b) Notice of withdrawal. Notice of withdrawal pursuant to this section shall be deemed to be timely upon the receipt by the bidder's depositary of a written notice of withdrawal specifying the name(s) of the tendering stockholder(s), the number or amount of the securities to be withdrawn and the name(s) in which the certificate(s) is (are) registered, if different from that of the tendering security holder(s). A bidder may impose other reasonable requirements, including certificate numbers and a signed request for withdrawal accompanied by a signature guarantee, as conditions precedent to the physical release of withdrawn securities.

§ 240.14d-8 Exemption from Statutory Pro Rata Requirements

Notwithstanding the pro rata provisions of section 14(d)(6) of the Act, if any person makes a tender offer or request or invitation for tenders, for less than all of the outstanding equity securities of a class, and if a greater number of securities are deposited pursuant thereto than such person is bound or willing to take up and pay for, the securities taken up and paid for shall be taken up and paid for as nearly as may be pro rata, disregarding fractions, according to the number of securities deposited by each depositor during the period such offer, request or invitation remains open.

§ 240.14d-9 Recommendation or Solicitation by the Subject Company and Others

(a) Pre-commencement communications. A communication by a person described in paragraph (e) of this section with respect to a tender offer will not be deemed to constitute a recommendation or solicitation under this section if:

(1) The tender offer has not commenced under § 240.14d-2; and

(2) The communication is filed under cover of Schedule 14D-9 (§ 240.14d-101) with the Commission no later than the date of the communication.

Instructions to paragraph (a)(2):

1. The box on the front of Schedule 14D-9 (§ 240.14d-101) indicating that the filing contains pre-commencement communications must be checked.

2. Any communications made in connection with an exchange offer registered under the Securities Act of 1933 need only be filed under § 230.425 of this chapter and will be deemed filed under this section.

3. Each pre-commencement written communication must include a prominent legend in clear, plain language advising security holders to read the company's solicitation/recommendation statement when it is available because it contains important information. The legend also must advise investors that they can get the recommendation and other filed documents for free at the Commission's web site and explain which documents are free from the filer.

4. See §§ 230.135, 230.165 and 230.166 of this chapter for pre-commencement communications made in connection with registered exchange offers.

(b) Post-commencement communications. After commencement by a bidder under § 240.14d-2, no solicitation or recommendation to security holders may be made by any person described in paragraph (e) of this section with respect to a tender offer for such securities unless as soon as practicable on the date such solicitation or recommendation is first published or sent or given to security holders such person complies with the following:

(1) Such person shall file with the Commission a Tender Offer Solicitation/Recommendation Statement on Schedule 14D-9 (§ 240.14d-101), including all exhibits thereto; and

(2) If such person is either the subject company or an affiliate of the subject company,

(i) Such person shall hand deliver a copy of the Schedule 14D-9 to the bidder at its principal office or at the address of the person authorized to receive notices and communications (which[1] is set forth on the cover sheet of the bidder's Schedule TO (§ 240.14d-100) filed with the Commission; and

(ii) Such person shall give telephonic notice (which notice to the extent possible shall be given prior to the opening of the market) of the information required by Items 1003(d) and 1012(a) of Regulation M-A (§ 229.1003(d) and § 229.1012(a)) and shall mail a copy of the Schedule to each national securities exchange where the class of securities is registered and listed for trading and, if the class is authorized for quotation in the NASDAQ interdealer quotation system, to the National Association of Securities Dealers, Inc. ("NASD").

(3) If such person is neither the subject company nor an affiliate of the subject company,

(i) Such person shall mail a copy of the schedule to the bidder at its principal office or at the address of the person authorized to receive notices and communications (which is set forth on the cover sheet of the bidder's Schedule TO (§ 240.14d-100) filed with the Commission); and

(ii) Such person shall mail a copy of the Schedule to the subject company at its principal office.

(c) Amendments. If any material change occurs in the information set forth in the Schedule 14D-9 (§ 240.14d-101) required by this section, the person who filed such Schedule 14D-9 shall:

(1) File with the Commission an amendment on Schedule 14D-9 (§ 240.14d-101) disclosing such change promptly, but not later than the date such material is first published, sent or given to security holders; and

(2) Promptly deliver copies and give notice of the amendment in the same manner as that specified in paragraph (b)(2) or (3) of this section, whichever is applicable; and

(3) Promptly disclose and disseminate such change in a manner reasonably designed to inform security holders of such change.

(d) Information required in solicitation or recommendation. Any solicitation or recommendation to holders of a class of securities referred to in section 14(d)(1) of the Act with respect to a tender offer for such securities shall include the name of the person making such solicitation or recommendation and the information required by Items 1 through 8 of Schedule 14D-9 (§ 240.14d-101) or a fair and adequate summary thereof: *Provided, however,* That such solicitation or recommendation may omit any of such information previously furnished to security holders of such class of securities by such person with respect to such tender offer.

(e) Applicability.

(1) Except as is provided in paragraphs (e)(2) and (f) of this section, this section shall only apply to the following persons:

(i) The subject company, any director, officer, employee, affiliate or subsidiary of the subject company;

(ii) Any record holder or beneficial owner of any security issued by the subject company, by the bidder, or by any affiliate of either the subject company or the bidder; and

(iii) Any person who makes a solicitation or recommendation to security holders on behalf of any of the foregoing or on behalf of the bidder other than by means of a solicitation or recommendation to security holders which has been filed with the Commission pursuant to this section or Rule 14d-3 (§ 240.14d-3).

(2) Notwithstanding paragraph (e)(1) of this section, this section shall not apply to the following persons:

(i) A bidder who has filed a Schedule TO (§ 240.14d-100) pursuant to Rule 14d-3 (§ 240.14d-3);

(ii) Attorneys, banks, brokers, fiduciaries or investment advisers who are not participating in a tender offer in more than a ministerial capacity and who furnish information and/or advice regarding such tender offer to their customers or clients on the unsolicited request of such customers or clients or solely pursuant to a contract or a relationship providing for advice to the customer or client to whom the information and/or advice is given.

(iii) Any person specified in paragraph (e)(1) of this section if:

(A) The subject company is the subject of a tender offer conducted under § 240.14d-1(c);

(B) Any person specified in paragraph (e)(1) of this section furnishes to the Commission on Form CB (§ 249.480 of this chapter) the entire informational document it publishes or otherwise disseminates to holders of the class of securities in connection with the tender offer no later than the next business day after publication or dissemination;

(C) Any person specified in paragraph (e)(1) of this section disseminates any informational document to U.S. holders, including any amendments thereto, in English, on a comparable basis to that provided to security holders in the issuer's home jurisdiction; and

(D) Any person specified in paragraph (e)(1) of this section disseminates by publication in its home jurisdiction, such person must publish the information in the United States in a manner reasonably calculated to inform U.S. security holders of the offer.

(f) Stop-look-and-listen communication. This section shall not apply to the subject company with respect to a communication by the subject company to its security holders which only:

(1) Identifies the tender offer by the bidder;

(2) States that such tender offer is under consideration by the subject company's board of directors and/or management;

(3) States that on or before a specified date (which shall be no later than 10 business days from the date of commencement of such tender offer) the subject company will advise such security holders of (i) whether the subject company recommends acceptance or rejection of such tender offer; expresses no opinion and remains neutral toward such tender offer; or is unable to take a position with respect to such tender offer and (ii) the reason(s) for the position taken by the subject company with respect to the tender offer (including the inability to take a position); and

(4) Requests such security holders to defer making a determination whether to accept or reject such tender offer until they have been advised of the subject company's position with respect thereto pursuant to paragraph (f)(3) of this section.

(g) Statement of management's position. A statement by the subject company's of its position with respect to a tender offer which is required to be published or sent or given to security holders pursuant to Rule 14e-2 shall be deemed to constitute a solicitation or recommendation within the meaning of this section and section 14(d)(4) of the Act.

§ 240.14d-10 Equal Treatment of Security Holders

(a) No bidder shall make a tender offer unless:

(1) The tender offer is open to all security holders of the class of securities subject to the tender offer; and

(2) The consideration paid to any security holder for securities tendered in the tender offer is the highest consideration paid to any other security holder for securities tendered in the tender offer.

(b) Paragraph (a)(1) of this section shall not:

(1) Affect dissemination under Rule 14d-4 (§ 240.14d-4); or

(2) Prohibit a bidder from making a tender offer excluding all security holders in a state where the bidder is prohibited from making the tender offer by administrative or judicial action pursuant to a state statute after a good faith effort by the bidder to comply with such statute.

(c) Paragraph (a)(2) of this section shall not prohibit the offer of more than one type of consideration in a tender offer, *Provided*, That:

(1) Security holders are afforded equal right to elect among each of the types of consideration offered; and

(2) The highest consideration of each type paid to any security holder is paid to any other security holder receiving that type of consideration.

(d)(1) Paragraph (a)(2) of this section shall not prohibit the negotiation, execution or amendment of an employment compensation, severance or other employee benefit arrangement, or payments made or to be made or benefits granted or to be granted according to such an arrangement, with respect to any security holder of the subject company, where the amount payable under the arrangement:

(i) Is being paid or granted as compensation for past services performed, future services to be performed, or future services to be refrained from performing, by the security holder (and matters incidental thereto); and

(ii) Is not calculated based on the number of securities tendered or to be tendered in the tender offer by the security holder.

(2) The provisions of paragraph (d)(1) of this section shall be satisfied and, therefore, pursuant to this non-exclusive safe harbor, the negotiation, execution or amendment of an arrangement and any payments made or to be made or benefits granted or to be granted according to that arrangement shall not be prohibited by paragraph (a)(2) of this section, if the arrangement is approved as an employment compensation, severance or other employee benefit arrangement solely by independent directors as follows:

(i) The compensation committee or a committee of the board of directors that performs functions similar to a compensation committee of the subject company approves the arrangement, regardless of whether the subject company is a party to the arrangement, or, if the bidder is a party to the arrangement, the compensation committee or a committee of the board of directors that performs functions similar to a compensation committee of the bidder approves the arrangement; or

(ii) If the subject company's or bidder's board of directors, as applicable, does not have a compensation committee or a committee of the board of directors that performs functions similar to a compensation committee or if none of the members of the subject company's or bidder's compensation committee or committee that performs functions similar to a compensation committee is independent, a special committee of the board of directors formed to consider and approve the arrangement approves the arrangement; or

(iii) If the subject company or bidder, as applicable, is a foreign private issuer, any or all members of the board of directors or any committee of the board of directors authorized to approve employment compensation, severance or other employee benefit arrangements under the laws or regulations of the home country approves the arrangement.

Instructions to paragraph (d)(2): For purposes of determining whether the members of the committee approving an arrangement in accordance with the provisions of paragraph (d)(2) of this section are independent, the following provisions shall apply:

1. If the bidder or subject company, as applicable, is a listed issuer (as defined in § 240.10A-3 of this chapter) whose securities are listed either on a national securities exchange registered pursuant to section 6(a) of the Exchange Act (15 U.S.C. 78f(a)) or in an inter-dealer quotation system of a national securities association registered pursuant to section 15A(a) of the Exchange Act (15 U.S.C. 78*o*-3(a)) that has independence requirements for compensation committee members that have been approved by the Commission (as those requirements may be modified or supplemented), apply the bidder's or subject company's definition of independence that it uses for determining that the members of the compensation committee are independent in compliance with the listing standards applicable to compensation committee members of the listed issuer.

2. If the bidder or subject company, as applicable, is not a listed issuer (as defined in § 240.10A-3 of this chapter), apply the independence requirements for compensation committee members of a national securities exchange registered pursuant to section 6(a) of the Exchange Act (15 U.S.C. 78f(a)) or an inter-dealer quotation system of a national securities association registered pursuant to section 15A(a) of the Exchange Act (15 U.S.C. 78*o*-3(a)) that have been approved by the Commission (as those requirements may be modified or supplemented). Whatever definition the bidder or subject company, as applicable, chooses, it must apply that

definition consistently to all members of the committee approving the arrangement.

3. Notwithstanding Instructions 1 and 2 to paragraph (d)(2), if the bidder or subject company, as applicable, is a closed-end investment company registered under the Investment Company Act of 1940, a director is considered to be independent if the director is not, other than in his or her capacity as a member of the board of directors or any board committee, an "interested person" of the investment company, as defined in section 2(a)(19) of the Investment Company Act of 1940 (15 U.S.C. 80a-2(a)(19)).

4. If the bidder or the subject company, as applicable, is a foreign private issuer, apply either the independence standards set forth in Instructions 1 and 2 to paragraph (d)(2) or the independence requirements of the laws, regulations, codes or standards of the home country of the bidder or subject company, as applicable, for members of the board of directors or the committee of the board of directors approving the arrangement.

5. A determination by the bidder's or the subject company's board of directors, as applicable, that the members of the board of directors or the committee of the board of directors, as applicable, approving an arrangement in accordance with the provisions of paragraph (d)(2) are independent in accordance with the provisions of this instruction to paragraph (d)(2) shall satisfy the independence requirements of paragraph (d)(2).

Instruction to paragraph (d): The fact that the provisions of paragraph (d) of this section extend only to employment compensation, severance and other employee benefit arrangements and not to other arrangements, such as commercial arrangements, does not raise any inference that a payment under any such other arrangement constitutes consideration paid for securities in a tender offer.

(e) If the offer and sale of securities constituting consideration offered in a tender offer is prohibited by the appropriate authority of a state after a good faith effort by the bidder to register or qualify the offer and sale of such securities in such state:

(1) The bidder may offer security holders in such state an alternative form of consideration; and

(2) Paragraph (c) of this section shall not operate to require the bidder to offer or pay the alternative form of consideration to security holders in any other state.

(f) This section shall not apply to any tender offer with respect to which the Commission, upon written request or upon its own motion, either unconditionally or on specified terms and conditions, determines that compliance with this section is not necessary or appropriate in the public interest or for the protection of investors.

§ 240.14e-1 Unlawful Tender Offer Practices

As a means reasonably designed to prevent fraudulent, deceptive or manipulative acts or practices within the meaning of section 14(e) of the Act, no person who makes a tender offer shall:

(a) Hold such tender offer open for less than twenty business days from the date such tender offer is first published or sent to security holders; provided, however, that if the tender offer involves a roll-up transaction as defined in Item 901(c) of Regulation S-K (17 CFR 229.901(c)) and the securities being offered are registered (or authorized to be registered) on Form S-4 (17 CFR 229.25) or Form F-4 (17 CFR 229.34), the offer shall not be open for less than sixty calendar days from the date the tender offer is first published or sent to security holders;

(b) Increase or decrease the percentage of the class of securities being sought or the consideration offered or the dealer's soliciting fee to be given in a tender offer unless such tender offer remains open for at least ten business days from the date that notice of such increase or decrease is first published or sent or given to security holders . . .

§ 240.14e-2 Position of Subject Company with Respect to a Tender Offer

(a) Position of subject company. As a means reasonably designed to prevent fraudulent, deceptive or manipulative acts or practices within the meaning of section 14(e) of the Act, the subject company, no later than 10 business days from the date the tender offer is first published or sent or given, shall publish, send or give to security holders a statement disclosing that the subject company:

(1) Recommends acceptance or rejection of the bidder's tender offer;

(2) Expresses no opinion and is remaining neutral toward the bidder's tender offer; or

(3) Is unable to take a position with respect to the bidder's tender offer. Such statement shall also include the reason(s) for the position (including the inability to take a position) disclosed therein.

(b) Material change. If any material change occurs in the disclosure required by paragraph (a) of this section, the subject company shall promptly publish or send or give a statement disclosing such material change to security holders.

(c) Any issuer, a class of the securities of which is the subject of a tender offer filed with the Commission on Schedule 14D-1F and conducted in reliance upon and in conformity with Rule 14d-1(b) under the Act, and any director or officer of such issuer where so required by the laws, regulations and policies of Canada and/or any of its provinces or territories, in lieu of the statements called for by paragraph (a) of this section and Rule

14d-9 under the Act, shall file with the Commission on Schedule 14D-9F the entire disclosure document(s) required to be furnished to holders of securities of the subject issuer by the laws, regulations and policies of Canada and/or any of its provinces or territories governing the conduct of the tender offer, and shall disseminate such document(s) in the United States in accordance with such laws, regulations and policies.

(d) Exemption for cross-border tender offers. The subject company shall be exempt from this section with respect to a tender offer conducted under § 240.14d-1(c).

§ 240.14e-3 Transactions in Securities on the Basis of Material, Nonpublic Information in the Context of Tender Offers

(a) If any person has taken a substantial step or steps to commence, or has commenced, a tender offer (the "offering person"), it shall constitute a fraudulent, deceptive or manipulative act or practice within the meaning of section 14(e) of the Act for any other person who is in possession of material information relating to such tender offer which information he knows or has reason to know is nonpublic and which he knows or has reason to know has been acquired directly or indirectly from:

(1) The offering person,

(2) The issuer of the securities sought or to be sought by such tender offer, or

(3) Any officer, director, partner or employee or any other person acting on behalf of the offering person or such issuer, to purchase or sell or cause to be purchased or sold any of such securities or any securities convertible into or exchangeable for any such securities or any option or right to obtain or to dispose of any of the foregoing securities, unless within a reasonable time prior to any purchase or sale such information and its source are publicly disclosed by press release or otherwise.

(b) A person other than a natural person shall not violate paragraph (a) of this section if such person shows that:

(1) The individual(s) making the investment decision on behalf of such person to purchase or sell any security described in paragraph (a) of this section or to cause any such security to be purchased or sold by or on behalf of others did not know the material, nonpublic information; and

(2) Such person had implemented one or a combination of policies and procedures, reasonable under the circumstances, taking into consideration the nature of the person's business, to ensure that individual (s) making investment decision(s) would not violate paragraph (a) of this section, which policies and procedures may include, but are not limited to, (i) those which restrict any purchase, sale and causing any purchase and sale of any such security or (ii) those which prevent such individual (s) from knowing such information.

(c) Notwithstanding anything in paragraph (a) of this section to contrary, the following transactions shall not be violations of paragraph (a) of this section:

(1) Purchase(s) of any security described in paragraph (a) of this section by a broker or by another agent on behalf of an offering person; or

(2) Sale(s) by any person of any security described in paragraph (a) of this section to the offering person.

(d)(1) As a means reasonably designed to prevent fraudulent, deceptive or manipulative acts or practices within the meaning of section 14(e) of the Act, it shall be unlawful for any person described in paragraph (d)(2) of this section to communicate material, nonpublic information relating to a tender offer to any other person under circumstances in which it is reasonably foreseeable that such communication is likely to result in a violation of this section except that this paragraph shall not apply to a communication made in good faith,

(i) To the officers, directors, partners or employees of the offering person, to its advisors or to other persons, involved in the planning, financing, preparation or execution of such tender offer;

(ii) To the issuer whose securities are sought or to be sought by such tender offer, to its officers, directors, partners, employees or advisors or to other persons, involved in the planning, financing, preparation or execution of the activities of the issuer with respect to such tender offer; or

(iii) To any person pursuant to a requirement of any statute or rule or regulation promulgated thereunder.

(2) The persons referred to in paragraph (d)(1) of this section are:

(i) The offering person or its officers, directors, partners, employees or advisors;

(ii) The issuer of the securities sought or to be sought by such tender offer or its officers, directors, partners, employees or advisors;

(iii) Anyone acting on behalf of the persons in paragraph (d)(2)(i) of this section or the issuer or persons in paragraph (d)(2)(ii) of this section; and

(iv) Any person in possession of material information relating to a tender offer which information he knows or has reason to know is nonpublic and which he knows or has reason to know has been acquired directly or indirectly from any of the above.

SECTION 16. BAN ON SHORT-SWING PROFITS

§ 78p Directors, Officers, and Principal Stockholders [Section 16]

(a) Disclosures required

(1) Directors, officers, and principal stockholders required to file

Every person who is directly or indirectly the beneficial owner of more than 10 percent of any class of any equity security (other than an exempted security) which is registered pursuant tosection 78*l* of this title, or who is a director or an officer of the issuer of such security, shall file the statements required by this subsection with the Commission.

(2) Time of filing

The statements required by this subsection shall be filed—

(A) at the time of the registration of such security on a national securities exchange or by the effective date of a registration statement filed pursuant to section 78*l*(g) of this title;

(B) within 10 days after he or she becomes such beneficial owner, director, or officer, or within such shorter time as the Commission may establish by rule;

(C) if there has been a change in such ownership, or if such person shall have purchased or sold a security-based swap agreement involving such equity security, before the end of the second business day following the day on which the subject transaction has been executed, or at such other time as the Commission shall establish, by rule, in any case in which the Commission determines that such 2-day period is not feasible.

(3) Contents of statements

A statement filed—

(A) under subparagraph (A) or (B) of paragraph (2) shall contain a statement of the amount of all equity securities of such issuer of which the filing person is the beneficial owner; and

(B) under subparagraph (C) of such paragraph shall indicate ownership by the filing person at the date of filing, any such changes in such ownership, and such purchases and sales of the security-based swap agreements or security-based swaps as have occurred since the most recent such filing under such subparagraph.

(4) Electronic filing and availability

Beginning not later than 1 year after July 30, 2002—

(A) a statement filed under subparagraph (C) of paragraph (2) shall be filed electronically;

(B) the Commission shall provide each such statement on a publicly accessible Internet site not later than the end of the business day following that filing; and

(C) the issuer (if the issuer maintains a corporate website) shall provide that statement on that corporate website, not later than the end of the business day following that filing.

(b) Profits from purchase and sale of security within six months

For the purpose of preventing the unfair use of information which may have been obtained by such beneficial owner, director, or officer by reason of his relationship to the issuer, any profit realized by him from any purchase and sale, or any sale and purchase, of any equity security of such issuer (other than an exempted security) or a security-based swap agreement involving any such equity security within any period of less than six months, unless such security or security-based swap agreement was acquired in good faith in connection with a debt previously contracted, shall inure to and be recoverable by the issuer, irrespective of any intention on the part of such beneficial owner, director, or officer in entering into such transaction of holding the security or security-based swap agreement purchased or of not repurchasing the security or security-based swap agreement sold for a period exceeding six months. Suit to recover such profit may be instituted at law or in equity in any court of competent jurisdiction by the issuer, or by the owner of any security of the issuer in the name and in behalf of the issuer if the issuer shall fail or refuse to bring such suit within sixty days after request or shall fail diligently to prosecute the same thereafter; but no such suit shall be brought more than two years after the date such profit was realized. This subsection shall not be construed to cover any transaction where such beneficial owner was not such both at the time of the purchase and sale, or the sale and purchase, of the security or security-based swap agreement or a security-based swap involved, or any transaction or transactions which the Commission by rules and regulations may exempt as not comprehended within the purpose of this subsection.

(c) Conditions for sale of security by beneficial owner, director, or officer

It shall be unlawful for any such beneficial owner, director, or officer, directly or indirectly, to sell any equity security of such issuer (other than an exempted security), if the person selling the security or his principal (1) does not own the security sold, or (2) if owning the security, does not deliver it against such sale within twenty days thereafter, or does not within five days after such sale deposit it in the mails or other usual channels of transportation; but no person shall be deemed to have violated this subsection if he proves that notwithstanding the exercise of good faith he was unable to make such delivery or deposit within such time, or that to do so would cause undue inconvenience or expense.

(d) Securities held in investment account, transactions in ordinary course of business, and establishment of primary or secondary market

The provisions of subsection (b) of this section shall not apply to any purchase and sale, or sale and purchase, and the provisions of subsection (c) of this section shall not apply to any sale, of an equity security not then or theretofore held by him in an investment account, by a dealer in the ordinary course of his business and incident to the establishment or maintenance by him of a primary or secondary market (otherwise than on a national securities exchange or an exchange exempted from registration under section 78e of this title) for such security. The Commission may, by such rules and regulations as it deems necessary or appropriate in the public interest, define and prescribe terms and conditions with respect to securities held in an investment account and transactions made in the ordinary course of business and incident to the establishment or maintenance of a primary or secondary market.

(e) Application of section to foreign or domestic arbitrage transactions

The provisions of this section shall not apply to foreign or domestic arbitrage transactions unless made in contravention of such rules and regulations as the Commission may adopt in order to carry out the purposes of this section.

(f) Treatment of transactions in security futures products

The provisions of this section shall apply to ownership of and transactions in security futures products.

(g) Limitation on Commission authority

The authority of the Commission under this section with respect to security-based swap agreements shall be subject to the restrictions and limitations of section 78c-1(b) of this title.

§ 78t-1 Liability to Contemporaneous Traders for Insider Trading [Section 20(a)]

(a) Private rights of action based on contemporaneous trading

Any person who violates any provision of this chapter or the rules or regulations thereunder by purchasing or selling a security while in possession of material, nonpublic information shall be liable in an action in any court of competent jurisdiction to any person who, contemporaneously with the purchase or sale of securities that is the subject of such violation, has purchased (where such violation is based on a sale of securities) or sold (where such violation is based on a purchase of securities) securities of the same class.

(b) Limitations on liability

(1) Contemporaneous trading actions limited to profit gained or loss avoided

The total amount of damages imposed under subsection (a) of this section shall not exceed the profit gained or loss avoided in the transaction or transactions that are the subject of the violation.

(2) Offsetting disgorgements against liability

The total amount of damages imposed against any person under subsection (a) of this section shall be diminished by the amounts, if any, that such person may be required to disgorge, pursuant to a court order obtained at the instance of the Commission, in a proceeding brought under section 78u(d) of this title relating to the same transaction or transactions.

(3) Controlling person liability

No person shall be liable under this section solely by reason of employing another person who is liable under this section, but the liability of a controlling person under this section shall be subject to section 78t(a) of this title.

(4) Statute of limitations

No action may be brought under this section more than 5 years after the date of the last transaction that is the subject of the violation.

(c) Joint and several liability for communicating

Any person who violates any provision of this chapter or the rules or regulations thereunder by communicating material, nonpublic information shall be jointly and severally liable under subsection (a) of this section with, and to the same extent as, any person or persons liable under subsection (a) of this section to whom the communication was directed.

(d) Authority not to restrict other express or implied rights of action

Nothing in this section shall be construed to limit or condition the right of any person to bring an action to enforce a requirement of this chapter or the availability of any cause of action implied from a provision of this chapter.

(e) Provisions not to affect public prosecutions

This section shall not be construed to bar or limit in any manner any action by the Commission or the Attorney General under any other provision of this chapter, nor shall it bar or limit in any manner any action to recover penalties, or to seek any other order regarding penalties.

Short-Swing Profit Rules Under Section 16

§ 240.16a-1 Definition of Terms

Terms defined in this rule shall apply solely to section 16 of the Act and the rules thereunder. These terms shall not be limited to section 16(a) of the Act but also shall apply to all other subsections under section 16 of the Act.

(a) The term beneficial owner shall have the following applications:

(1) Solely for purposes of determining whether a person is a beneficial owner of more than ten percent of any class of equity securities registered pursuant to section 12 of the Act, the term "beneficial owner" shall mean any person who is deemed a beneficial owner pursuant to section 13(d) of the Act and the rules thereunder...

...

Note to paragraph (a): Pursuant to this section, a person deemed a beneficial owner of more than ten percent of any class of equity securities registered under section 12 of the Act would file a Form 3 (§ 249.103), but the securities holdings disclosed on Form 3, and changes in beneficial ownership reported on subsequent Forms 4 (§ 249.104) or 5 (§ 249.105), would be determined by the definition of "beneficial owner" in paragraph (a)(2) of this section.

(2) Other than for purposes of determining whether a person is a beneficial owner of more than ten percent of any class of equity securities registered under Section 12 of the Act, the term beneficial owner

shall mean any person who, directly or indirectly, through any contract, arrangement, understanding, relationship or otherwise, has or shares a direct or indirect pecuniary interest in the equity securities, subject to the following:

(i) The term pecuniary interest in any class of equity securities shall mean the opportunity, directly or indirectly, to profit or share in any profit derived from a transaction in the subject securities.

(ii) The term indirect pecuniary interest in any class of equity securities shall include, but not be limited to:

(A) Securities held by members of a person's immediate family sharing the same household; provided, however, that the presumption of such beneficial ownership may be rebutted; see also § 240.16a-1(a)(4);

(B) A general partner's proportionate interest in the portfolio securities held by a general or limited partnership. The general partner's proportionate interest, as evidenced by the partnership agreement in effect at the time of the transaction and the partnership's most recent financial statements, shall be the greater of:

(*1*) The general partner's share of the partnership's profits, including profits attributed to any limited partnership interests held by the general partner and any other interests in profits that arise from the purchase and sale of the partnership's portfolio securities; or

(*2*) The general partner's share of the partnership capital account, including the share attributable to any limited partnership interest held by the general partner.

(C) A performance-related fee, other than an asset-based fee, received by any broker, dealer, bank, insurance company, investment company, investment adviser, investment manager, trustee or person or entity performing a similar function; provided, however, that no pecuniary interest shall be present where:

(*1*) The performance-related fee, regardless of when payable, is calculated based upon net capital gains and/or net capital appreciation generated from the portfolio or from the fiduciary's overall performance over a period of one year or more; and

(*2*) Equity securities of the issuer do not account for more than ten percent of the market value of the portfolio. A right to a nonperformance-related fee alone shall not represent a pecuniary interest in the securities;

(D) A person's right to dividends that is separated or separable from the underlying securities. Otherwise, a right to dividends alone shall not represent a pecuniary interest in the securities;

(E) A person's interest in securities held by a trust, as specified in § 240.16a-8(b); and

(F) A person's right to acquire equity securities through the exercise or conversion of any derivative security, whether or not presently exercisable.

(iii) A shareholder shall not be deemed to have a pecuniary interest in the portfolio securities held by a corporation or similar entity in which the person owns securities if the shareholder is not a controlling shareholder of the entity and does not have or share investment control over the entity's portfolio.

(3) Where more than one person subject to section 16 of the Act is deemed to be a beneficial owner of the same equity securities, all such persons must report as beneficial owners of the securities, either separately or jointly, as provided in § 240.16a-3(j). In such cases, the amount of short-swing profit recoverable shall not be increased above the amount recoverable if there were only one beneficial owner.

(4) Any person filing a statement pursuant to section 16(a) of the Act may state that the filing shall not be deemed an admission that such person is, for purposes of section 16 of the Act or otherwise, the beneficial owner of any equity securities covered by the statement.

(5) The following interests are deemed not to confer beneficial ownership for purposes of section 16 of the Act:

(i) Interests in portfolio securities held by any investment company registered under the Investment Company Act of 1940 (15 U.S.C. 80a-1 et seq.); and

(ii) Interests in securities comprising part of a broad-based, publicly traded market basket or index of stocks, approved for trading by the appropriate federal governmental authority.

(b) The term call equivalent position shall mean a derivative security position that increases in value as the value of the underlying equity increases, including, but not limited to, a long convertible security, a long call option, and a short put option position.

(c) The term derivative securities shall mean any option, warrant, convertible security, stock appreciation right, or similar right with an exercise or conversion privilege at a price related to an equity security, or similar securities with a value derived from the value of an equity security, but shall not include:

(1) Rights of a pledgee of securities to sell the pledged securities;

(2) Rights of all holders of a class of securities of an issuer to receive securities pro rata, or obligations to dispose of securities, as a result of a merger, exchange offer, or consolidation involving the issuer of the securities;

(3) Rights or obligations to surrender a security, or have a security withheld, upon the receipt or exercise of a derivative security or the receipt or vesting of equity securities, in order to satisfy the exercise price or the tax withholding consequences of receipt, exercise or vesting;

(4) Interests in broad-based index options, broad-based index futures, and broad-based publicly traded market baskets of stocks approved for trading by the appropriate federal governmental authority;

(5) Interests or rights to participate in employee benefit plans of the issuer;

(6) Rights with an exercise or conversion privilege at a price that is not fixed; or

(7) Options granted to an underwriter in a registered public offering for the purpose of satisfying over-allotments in such offering.

(d) The term equity security of such issuer shall mean any equity security or derivative security relating to an issuer, whether or not issued by that issuer.

(e) The term immediate family shall mean any child, stepchild, grandchild, parent, stepparent, grandparent, spouse, sibling, mother-in-law, father-in-law, son-in-law, daughter-in-law, brother-in-law, or sister-in-law, and shall include adoptive relationships.

(f) The term "officer" shall mean an issuer's president, principal financial officer, principal accounting officer (or, if there is no such accounting officer, the controller), any vice-president of the issuer in charge of a principal business unit, division or function (such as sales, administration or finance), any other officer who performs a policy-making function, or any other person who performs similar policy-making functions for the issuer. Officers of the issuer's parent(s) or subsidiaries shall be deemed officers of the issuer if they perform such policy-making functions for the issuer. In addition, when the issuer is a limited partnership, officers or employees of the general partner(s) who perform policy-making functions for the limited partnership are deemed officers of the limited partnership. When the issuer is a trust, officers or employees of the trustee(s) who perform policy-making functions for the trust are deemed officers of the trust.

Note: "Policy-making function" is not intended to include policy-making functions that are not significant. If pursuant to Item 401(b) of Regulation S-K (§ 229.401(b)) the issuer identifies a person as an "executive officer," it is presumed that the Board of Directors has made that judgment and that the persons so identified are the officers for purposes of Section 16 of the Act, as are such other persons enumerated in this paragraph (f) but not in Item 401(b).

(g) The term portfolio securities shall mean all securities owned by an entity, other than securities issued by the entity.

(h) The term put equivalent position shall mean a derivative security position that increases in value as the value of the underlying equity decreases, including, but not limited to, a long put option and a short call option position.

§ 240.16a-2 Persons and Transactions Subject to Section 16

Any person who is the beneficial owner, directly or indirectly, of more than ten percent of any class of equity securities ("ten percent beneficial owner") registered pursuant to section 12 of the Act (15 U.S.C. 78l), any director or officer of the issuer of such securities, and any person specified in section 30(h) of the Investment Company Act of 1940 (15 U.S.C. 80a-29(h)), including any person specified in § 240.16a-8, shall be subject to the provisions of section 16 of the Act (15 U.S.C. 78p). The rules under section 16 of the Act apply to any class of equity securities of an issuer whether or not registered under section 12 of the Act. The rules under section 16 of the Act also apply to non-equity securities as provided by the Investment Company Act of 1940. With respect to transactions by persons subject to section 16 of the Act:

(a) A transaction(s) carried out by a director or officer in the six months prior to the director or officer becoming subject to section 16 of the Act shall be subject to section 16 of the Act and reported on the first required Form 4 only if the transaction(s) occurred within six months of the transaction giving rise to the Form 4 filing obligation and the director or officer became subject to section 16 of the Act solely as a result of the issuer registering a class of equity securities pursuant to section 12 of the Act.

(b) A transaction(s) following the cessation of director or officer status shall be subject to section 16 of the Act only if:

(1) Executed within a period of less than six months of an opposite transaction subject to section 16(b) of the Act that occurred while that person was a director or officer; and

(2) Not otherwise exempted from section 16(b) of the Act pursuant to the provisions of this chapter.

Note to paragraph (b): For purposes of this paragraph, an acquisition and a disposition each shall be an opposite transaction with respect to the other.

(c) The transaction that results in a person becoming a ten percent beneficial owner is not subject to section 16 of the Act unless the person otherwise is subject to section 16 of the Act. A ten percent beneficial owner not otherwise subject to section 16 of the Act must report only those transactions conducted while the beneficial owner of more than ten percent of a class of equity securities of the issuer registered pursuant to section 12 of the Act.

(d)(1) Transactions by a person or entity shall be exempt from the provisions of section 16 of the Act for the 12 months following appointment and qualification, to the extent such person or entity is acting as:

(i) Executor or administrator of the estate of a decedent;

(ii) Guardian or member of a committee for an incompetent;

(iii) Receiver, trustee in bankruptcy, assignee for the benefit of creditors, conservator, liquidating agent, or other similar person duly authorized by law to administer the estate or assets of another person; or

(iv) Fiduciary in a similar capacity.

(2) Transactions by such person or entity acting in a capacity specified in paragraph (d)(1) of this section after the period specified in that paragraph shall be subject to section 16 of the Act only where the estate, trust or other entity is a beneficial owner of more than ten percent of any class of equity security registered pursuant to section 12 of the Act.

§ 240.16a-3 Reporting Transactions and Holdings

(a) Initial statements of beneficial ownership of equity securities required by section 16(a) of the Act shall be filed on Form 3. Statements of changes in beneficial ownership required by that section shall be filed on Form 4. Annual statements shall be filed on Form 5. At the election of the reporting person, any transaction required to be reported on Form 5 may be reported on an earlier filed Form 4. All such statements shall be prepared and filed in accordance with the requirements of the applicable form.

(b) A person filing statements pursuant to section 16(a) of the Act with respect to any class of equity securities registered pursuant to section 12 of the Act need not file an additional statement on Form 3:

(1) When an additional class of equity securities of the same issuer becomes registered pursuant to section 12 of the Act; or

(2) When such person assumes a different or an additional relationship to the same issuer (for example, when an officer becomes a director).

(c) Any issuer that has equity securities listed on more than one national securities exchange may designate one exchange as the only exchange with which reports pursuant to section 16(a) of the Act need be filed. Such designation shall be made in writing and shall be filed with the Commission and with each national securities exchange on which any equity security of the issuer is listed at the time of such election. The reporting person's obligation to file reports with each national securities exchange on which any equity security of the issuer is listed shall be satisfied by filing with the exchange so designated.

(d) Any person required to file a statement with respect to securities of a single issuer under both section 16(a) of the Act (15 U.S.C. 78p(a)) and section 30(h) of the Investment Company Act of 1940 (15 U.S.C. 80a-29(h)) may file a single statement containing the required information, which will be deemed to be filed under both Acts.

(e) Any person required to file a statement under section 16(a) of the Act shall, not later than the time the statement is transmitted for filing with the Commission, send or deliver a duplicate to the person designated by the issuer to receive such statements, or, in the absence of such a designation, to the issuer's corporate secretary or person performing equivalent functions.

(f)(1) A Form 5 shall be filed by every person who at any time during the issuer's fiscal year was subject to section 16 of the Act with respect to such issuer, except as provided in paragraph (f)(2) of this section. The Form shall be filed within 45 days after the issuer's fiscal year end, and shall disclose the following holdings and transactions not reported previously on Forms 3, 4 or 5:

(i) All transactions during the most recent fiscal year that were exempt from section 16(b) of the Act, except:

(A) Exercises and conversions of derivative securities exempt under either § 240.16b-3 or § 240.16b-6(b), and any transaction exempt under § 240.16b-3(d), § 240.16b-3(e), or § 240.16b-3(f) (these are required to be reported on Form 4);

(B) Transactions exempt from section 16(b) of the Act pursuant to § 240.16b-3(c), which shall be exempt from section 16(a) of the Act; and

(C) Transactions exempt from section 16(a) of the Act pursuant to another rule;

(ii) Transactions that constituted small acquisitions pursuant to § 240.16a-6(a);

(iii) All holdings and transactions that should have been reported during the most recent fiscal year, but were not; and

(iv) With respect to the first Form 5 requirement for a reporting person, all holdings and transactions that should have been reported in each of the issuer's last two fiscal years but were not, based on the reporting person's reasonable belief in good faith in the completeness and accuracy of the information.

(2) Notwithstanding the above, no Form 5 shall be required where all transactions otherwise required to be reported on the Form 5 have been reported before the due date of the Form 5.

Persons no longer subject to section 16 of the Act, but who were subject to the Section at any time during the issuer's fiscal year, must file a Form 5 unless paragraph (f)(2) is satisfied. See also § 240.16a-2(b) regarding the reporting obligations of persons ceasing to be officers or directors.

(g)(1) A Form 4 must be filed to report: All transactions not exempt from section 16(b) of the Act; All transactions exempt from section 16(b) of the Act pursuant to § 240.16b-3(d), § 240.16b-3(e), or § 240.16b-3(f); and all exercises and conversions of derivative securities, regardless of whether exempt from section 16(b) of the Act. Form 4 must be filed before the end of the second business day following the day on which the subject transaction has been executed.

(2) Solely for purposes of section 16(a)(2)(C) of the Act and paragraph (g)(1) of this section, the date on which the executing broker,

dealer or plan administrator notifies the reporting person of the execution of the transaction is deemed the date of execution for a transaction where the following conditions are satisfied:

(i) the transaction is pursuant to a contract, instruction or written plan for the purchase or sale of equity securities of the issuer (as defined in § 16a-1(d)) that satisfies the affirmative defense conditions of § 240.10b5-1(c) of this chapter; and

(ii) the reporting person does not select the date of execution.

(3) Solely for purposes of section 16(a)(2)(C) of the Act and paragraph (g)(1) of this section, the date on which the plan administrator notifies the reporting person that the transaction has been executed is deemed the date of execution for a discretionary transaction (as defined in § 16b-3(b)(1)) for which the reporting person does not select the date of execution.

(4) In the case of the transactions described in paragraphs (g)(2) and (g)(3) of this section, if the notification date is later than the third business day following the trade date of the transaction, the date of execution is deemed to be the third business day following the trade date of the transaction.

(5) At the option of the reporting person, transactions that are reportable on Form 5 may be reported on Form 4, so long as the Form 4 is filed no later than the due date of the Form 5 on which the transaction is otherwise required to be reported.

(h) The date of filing with the Commission shall be the date of receipt by the Commission.

(i) Signatures. Where Section 16 of the Act, or the rules or forms thereunder, require a document filed with or furnished to the Commission to be signed, such document shall be manually signed, or signed using either typed signatures or duplicated or facsimile versions of manual signatures. Where typed, duplicated or facsimile signatures are used, each signatory to the filing shall manually sign a signature page or other document authenticating, acknowledging or otherwise adopting his or her signature that appears in the filing. Such document shall be executed before or at the time the filing is made and shall be retained by the filer for a period of five years. Upon request, the filer shall furnish to the Commission or its staff a copy of any or all documents retained pursuant to this section.

(j) Where more than one person subject to section 16 of the Act is deemed to be a beneficial owner of the same equity securities, all such persons must report as beneficial owners of the securities, either separately or jointly. Where persons in a group are deemed to be beneficial owners of equity securities pursuant to § 240.16a-1(a)(1) due to the aggregation of holdings, a single Form 3, 4 or 5 may be filed on behalf of all persons in the group. Joint and group filings must include all required information for each beneficial owner, and such filings must be signed by each beneficial owner, or on behalf of such owner by an authorized person.

(k) Any issuer that maintains a corporate Web site shall post on that Web site by the end of the business day after filing any Form 3, 4 or 5 filed under section 16(a) of the Act as to the equity securities of that issuer. Each such form shall remain accessible on such issuer's Web site for at least a 12-month period. In the case of an issuer that is an investment company and that does not maintain its own Web site, if any of the issuer's investment adviser, sponsor, depositor, trustee, administrator, principal underwriter, or any affiliated person of the investment company maintains a Web site that includes the name of the issuer, the issuer shall comply with the posting requirements by posting the forms on one such Web site.

Section 21(a). Authority to Impose Civil Penalties for Insider Trading

§ 78u-1 Civil Penalties for Insider Trading [Section 21(a)]

(a) Authority to impose civil penalties

(1) Judicial actions by Commission authorized

Whenever it shall appear to the Commission that any person has violated any provision of this chapter or the rules or regulations thereunder by purchasing or selling a security or security-based swap agreement while in possession of material, nonpublic information in, or has violated any such provision by communicating such information in connection with, a transaction on or through the facilities of a national securities exchange or from or through a broker or dealer, and which is not part of a public offering by an issuer of securities other than standardized options or security futures products, the Commission—

(A) may bring an action in a United States district court to seek, and the court shall have jurisdiction to impose, a civil penalty to be paid by the person who committed such violation; and

(B) may, subject to subsection (b)(1) of this section, bring an action in a United States district court to seek, and the court shall have jurisdiction to impose, a civil penalty to be paid by a person who, at the time of the violation, directly or indirectly controlled the person who committed such violation.

(2) Amount of penalty for person who committed violation

The amount of the penalty which may be imposed on the person who committed such violation shall be determined by the court in light of the facts and circumstances, but shall not exceed three times the profit gained or loss avoided as a result of such unlawful purchase, sale, or communication.

(3) Amount of penalty for controlling person

The amount of the penalty which may be imposed on any person who, at the time of the violation, directly or indirectly controlled the person who committed such violation, shall be determined by the court in light of the facts and circumstances, but shall not exceed the greater of $1,000,000, or three times the amount of the profit gained or loss avoided as a result of such controlled person's violation. If such controlled person's violation was a violation by communication, the profit gained or loss avoided as a result of the violation shall, for purposes of this paragraph only, be deemed to be limited to the profit gained or loss avoided by the person or persons to whom the controlled person directed such communication.

(b) Limitations on liability

(1) Liability of controlling persons

No controlling person shall be subject to a penalty under subsection (a)(1)(B) of this section unless the Commission establishes that—

(A) such controlling person knew or recklessly disregarded the fact that such controlled person was likely to engage in the act or acts constituting the violation and failed to take appropriate steps to prevent such act or acts before they occurred; or

(B) such controlling person knowingly or recklessly failed to establish, maintain, or enforce any policy or procedure required under section 78*o*(f) of this title or section 80b-4a of this title and such failure substantially contributed to or permitted the occurrence of the act or acts constituting the violation.

(2) Additional restrictions on liability

No person shall be subject to a penalty under subsection (a) of this section solely by reason of employing another person who is subject to a penalty under such subsection, unless such employing person is liable as a controlling person under paragraph (1) of this subsection.Section 78t(a) of this title shall not apply to actions under subsection (a) of this section.

(c) Authority of Commission

The Commission, by such rules, regulations, and orders as it considers necessary or appropriate in the public interest or for the protection of investors, may exempt, in whole or in part, either unconditionally or upon specific terms and conditions, any person or transaction or class of persons or transactions from this section.

(d) Procedures for collection

(1) Payment of penalty to Treasury

A penalty imposed under this section shall be payable into the Treasury of the United States, except as otherwise provided in section 7246 of this title and section 78u-6 of this title.

(2) Collection of penalties

If a person upon whom such a penalty is imposed shall fail to pay such penalty within the time prescribed in the court's order, the Commission may refer the matter to the Attorney General who shall recover such penalty by action in the appropriate United States district court.

(3) Remedy not exclusive

The actions authorized by this section may be brought in addition to any other actions that the Commission or the Attorney General are entitled to bring.

(4) Jurisdiction and venue

For purposes of section 78aa of this title, actions under this section shall be actions to enforce a liability or a duty created by this chapter.

(5) Statute of limitations

No action may be brought under this section more than 5 years after the date of the purchase or sale. This section shall not be construed to bar or limit in any manner any action by the Commission or the Attorney General under any other provision of this chapter, nor shall it bar or limit in any manner any action to recover penalties, or to seek any other order regarding penalties, imposed in an action commenced within 5 years of such transaction.

(e) Definition

For purposes of this section, "profit gained" or "loss avoided" is the difference between the purchase or sale price of the security and the value of that security as measured by the trading price of the security a reasonable period after public dissemination of the nonpublic information.

(f) Limitation

The authority of the Commission under this section with respect to security-based swap agreements shall be subject to the restrictions and limitations of section 78c-1(b) of this title.

(g) Duty of members and employees of Congress

(1) In general

Subject to the rule of construction under section 10 of the STOCK Act and solely for purposes of the insider trading prohibitions arising under this chapter, including section 78j(b)of this title and Rule 10b-5 thereunder, each Member of Congress or employee of Congress owes a duty arising from a relationship of trust and confidence to the Congress, the United States Government, and the citizens of the United States with respect to material, nonpublic information derived from such person's position as a Member of Congress or employee of Congress or gained from the performance of such person's official responsibilities.

(2) Definitions

In this subsection—

(A) the term "Member of Congress" means a member of the Senate or House of Representatives, a Delegate to the House of Representatives, and the Resident Commissioner from Puerto Rico; and

(B) the term "employee of Congress" means—

(i) any individual (other than a Member of Congress), whose compensation is disbursed by the Secretary of the Senate or the Chief Administrative Officer of the House of Representatives; and

(ii) any other officer or employee of the legislative branch (as defined in section 109(11) of the Ethics in Government Act of 1978 (5 U.S.C. App. 109(11))).

(3) Rule of construction

Nothing in this subsection shall be construed to impair or limit the construction of the existing antifraud provisions of the securities laws or the authority of the Commission under those provisions.

(h) Duty of other Federal officials

(1) In general

Subject to the rule of construction under section 10 of the STOCK Act and solely for purposes of the insider trading prohibitions arising under this chapter, including section 78j(b)of this title, and Rule 10b-5 thereunder, each executive branch employee, each judicial officer, and each judicial employee owes a duty arising from a relationship of trust and confidence to the United States Government and the citizens of the United States with respect to material, nonpublic information derived from such person's position as an executive branch employee, judicial officer, or judicial employee or gained from the performance of such person's official responsibilities.

(2) Definitions

In this subsection—

(A) the term "executive branch employee"—

(i) has the meaning given the term "employee" under section 2105 of Title 5;

(ii) includes—

(I) the President;

(II) the Vice President; and

(III) an employee of the United States Postal Service or the Postal Regulatory Commission;

(B) the term "judicial employee" has the meaning given that term in section 109(8) of the Ethics in Government Act of 1978 (5 U.S.C. App. 109(8)) ; and

(C) the term "judicial officer" has the meaning given that term under section 109(10) of the Ethics in Government Act of 1978 (5 U.S.C. App. 109(10)).

(3) Rule of construction

Nothing in this subsection shall be construed to impair or limit the construction of the existing antifraud provisions of the securities laws or the authority of the Commission under those provisions.

(i) Participation in initial public offerings

An individual described in section 101(f) of the Ethics in Government Act of 1978 may not purchase securities that are the subject of an initial public offering (within the meaning given such term in section 78*l* (f)(1)(G)(i)) of this title in any manner other than is available to members of the public generally.

REGULATION FD

17 C.F.R. § 243.100

§ 243.100 General Rule Regarding Selective Disclosure

(a) Whenever an issuer, or any person acting on its behalf, discloses any material nonpublic information regarding that issuer or its securities to any person described in paragraph (b)(1) of this section, the issuer shall make public disclosure of that information as provided in § 243.101(e):

(1) Simultaneously, in the case of an intentional disclosure; and

(2) Promptly, in the case of a non-intentional disclosure.

(b)(1) Except as provided in paragraph (b)(2) of this section, paragraph (a) of this section shall apply to a disclosure made to any person outside the issuer:

(i) Who is a broker or dealer, or a person associated with a broker or dealer, as those terms are defined in Section 3(a) of the Securities Exchange Act of 1934 (15 U.S.C. 78c(a));

(ii) Who is an investment adviser, as that term is defined in Section 202(a)(11) of the Investment Advisers Act of 1940 (15 U.S.C. 80b-2(a)(11)); an institutional investment manager, as that term is defined in Section 13(f)(6) of the Securities Exchange Act of 1934 (15 U.S.C. 78m(f)(6)), that filed a report on Form 13F (17 CFR 249.325) with the Commission for the most recent quarter ended prior to the date of the disclosure; or a person associated with either of the foregoing. For purposes of this paragraph, a "person associated with an investment adviser or institutional investment manager" has the meaning set forth in Section 202(a)(17) of the Investment Advisers Act of 1940 (15 U.S.C. 80b-2(a)(17)), assuming for these purposes that an institutional investment manager is an investment adviser;

(iii) Who is an investment company, as defined in Section 3 of the Investment Company Act of 1940 (15 U.S.C. 80a–3), or who would be an investment company but for Section 3(c)(1) (15 U.S.C. 80a–3(c)(1)) or Section 3(c)(7) (15 U.S.C. 80a–3(c)(7)) thereof, or an affiliated person of either of the foregoing. For purposes of this paragraph, "affiliated person" means only those persons described in Section 2(a)(3)(C), (D), (E), and (F) of the Investment Company Act of 1940 (15 U.S.C. 80a–2(a)(3)(C), (D), (E), and (F)), assuming for these purposes that a person who would be an investment company but for Section 3(c)(1) (15 U.S.C. 80a–3(c)(1)) or Section 3(c)(7) (15 U.S.C. 80a–3(c)(7)) of the Investment Company Act of 1940 is an investment company; or

(iv) Who is a holder of the issuer's securities, under circumstances in which it is reasonably foreseeable that the person will purchase or sell the issuer's securities on the basis of the information.

(2) Paragraph (a) of this section shall not apply to a disclosure made:

(i) To a person who owes a duty of trust or confidence to the issuer (such as an attorney, investment banker, or accountant);

(ii) To a person who expressly agrees to maintain the disclosed information in confidence;

(iii) In connection with a securities offering registered under the Securities Act, other than an offering of the type described in any of Rule 415(a)(1)(i) through (vi) under the Securities Act (§ 230.415(a)(1)(i) through (vi) of this chapter) (except an offering of the type described in Rule 415(a)(1)(i) under the Securities Act (§ 230.415(a)(1)(i) of this chapter) also involving a registered offering, whether or not underwritten, for capital formation purposes for the account of the issuer (unless the issuer's offering is being registered for the purpose of evading the requirements of this section)), if the disclosure is by any of the following means:

(A) A registration statement filed under the Securities Act, including a prospectus contained therein;

(B) A free writing prospectus used after filing of the registration statement for the offering or a communication falling within the exception to the definition of prospectus contained in clause (a) of section 2(a)(10) of the Securities Act;

(C) Any other Section 10(b) prospectus;

(D) A notice permitted by Rule 135 under the Securities Act (§ 230.135 of this chapter);

(E) A communication permitted by Rule 134 under the Securities Act (§ 230.134 of this chapter); or

(F) An oral communication made in connection with the registered securities offering after filing of the registration statement for the offering under the Securities Act.

§ 243.101 Definitions

(a) Intentional. A selective disclosure of material nonpublic information is "intentional" when the person making the disclosure either knows, or is reckless in not knowing, that the information he or she is communicating is both material and nonpublic.

(b) Issuer. An "issuer" subject to this regulation is one that has a class of securities registered under Section 12 of the Securities Exchange Act of 1934 (15 U.S.C. 78*l*), or is required to file reports under Section 15(d) of the Securities Exchange Act of 1934 (15 U.S.C. 78*o*(d)), including any closed-end investment company (as defined in Section 5(a)(2) of the Investment Company Act of 1940) (15 U.S.C. 80a–5(a)(2)), but not including any other investment company or any foreign government or foreign private issuer, as those terms are defined in Rule 405 under the Securities Act (§ 230.405 of this chapter).

(c) Person acting on behalf of an issuer. "Person acting on behalf of an issuer" means any senior official of the issuer (or, in the case of a closed-end investment company, a senior official of the issuer's investment adviser), or any other officer, employee, or agent of an issuer who regularly communicates with any person described in § 243.100(b)(1)(i), (ii), or (iii), or with holders of the issuer's securities. An officer, director, employee, or agent of an issuer who discloses material nonpublic information in breach of a duty of trust or confidence to the issuer shall not be considered to be acting on behalf of the issuer.

(d) Promptly. "Promptly" means as soon as reasonably practicable (but in no event after the later of 24 hours or the commencement of the next day's trading on the New York Stock Exchange) after a senior official of the issuer (or, in the case of a closed-end investment company, a senior official of the issuer's investment adviser) learns that there has been a non-intentional disclosure by the issuer or person acting on behalf of the issuer of information that the senior official knows, or is reckless in not knowing, is both material and nonpublic.

(e) Public disclosure.

(1) Except as provided in paragraph (e)(2) of this section, an issuer shall make the "public disclosure" of information required by § 243.100(a) by furnishing to or filing with the Commission a Form 8–K (17 CFR 249.308) disclosing that information.

(2) An issuer shall be exempt from the requirement to furnish or file a Form 8–K if it instead disseminates the information through another method (or combination of methods) of disclosure that is reasonably designed to provide broad, non-exclusionary distribution of the information to the public.

(f) Senior official. "Senior official" means any director, executive officer (as defined in § 240.3b–7 of this chapter), investor relations or public relations officer, or other person with similar functions.

(g) Securities offering. For purposes of § 243.100(b)(2)(iv):

(1) Underwritten offerings. A securities offering that is underwritten commences when the issuer reaches an understanding with the broker-dealer that is to act as managing underwriter and continues until the later of the end of the period during which a dealer must deliver a prospectus or the sale of the securities (unless the offering is sooner terminated);

(2) Non-underwritten offerings. A securities offering that is not underwritten:

(i) If covered by Rule 415(a)(1)(x) (§ 230.415(a)(1)(x) of this chapter), commences when the issuer makes its first bona fide offer in a takedown of securities and continues until the later of the end of the period during which each dealer must deliver a prospectus or the sale of the securities in that takedown (unless the takedown is sooner terminated);

(ii) If a business combination as defined in Rule 165(f)(1) (§ 230.165(f)(1) of this chapter), commences when the first public announcement of the transaction is made and continues until the completion of the vote or the expiration of the tender offer, as applicable (unless the transaction is sooner terminated);

(iii) If an offering other than those specified in paragraphs (a) and (b) of this section, commences when the issuer files a registration statement and continues until the later of the end of the period during which each dealer must deliver a prospectus or the sale of the securities (unless the offering is sooner terminated).

§ 243.102 No Effect on Antifraud Liability

No failure to make a public disclosure required solely by § 243.100 shall be deemed to be a violation of Rule 10b–5 (17 CFR 240.10b–5) under the Securities Exchange Act.

REGULATION S-K—STANDARD INSTRUCTIONS FOR FILING FORMS UNDER SECURITIES ACT OF 1933, SECURITIES EXCHANGE ACT OF 1934 AND ENERGY POLICY AND CONSERVATION ACT OF 1975

17 C.F.R. §229.10 et seq.

Subpart I—General

§ 229.10 (Item 10) General

(a) *Application of Regulation S-K.* This part (together with the General Rules and Regulations under the Securities Act of 1933, 15 U.S.C. 77a *et seq.*, as amended (*Securities Act*), and the Securities Exchange Act of 1934, 15 U.S.C. 78a *et seq.*, as amended (*Exchange Act*) (parts 230 and 240 of this chapter), the Interpretative Releases under these Acts (parts 231 and 241 of this chapter) and the forms under these Acts (parts 239 and 249 of this chapter)) states the requirements applicable to the content of the non-financial statement portions of:

(1) Registration statements under the Securities Act (part 239 of this chapter) to the extent provided in the forms to be used for registration under such Act; and

(2) Registration statements under section 12 (subpart C of part 249 of this chapter), annual or other reports under sections 13 and 15(d) (subparts D and E of part 249 of this chapter), going-private transaction statements under section 13 (part 240 of this chapter), tender offer statements under sections 13 and 14 (part 240 of this chapter), annual reports to security holders and proxy and information statements under section 14 (part 240 of this chapter), and any other documents required to be filed under the Exchange Act, to the extent provided in the forms and rules under that Act.

(b) *Commission policy on projections.* The Commission encourages the use in documents specified in Rule 175 under the Securities Act (§ 230.175 of this chapter) and Rule 3b-6 under the Exchange Act (§ 240.3b-6 of this chapter) of management's projections of future economic performance that have a reasonable basis and are presented in an appropriate format. The guidelines set forth herein represent the Commission's views on important factors to be considered in formulating and disclosing such projections.

Subpart 100—Business

§ 229.101 (Item 101) Description of Business

(a) *General development of business.* Describe the general development of the business of the registrant, its subsidiaries and any predecessor(s) during the past five years, or such shorter period as the registrant may have been engaged in business. Information shall be disclosed for earlier periods if material to an understanding of the general development of the business.

(1) In describing developments, information shall be given as to matters such as the following: the year in which the registrant was organized and its form of organization; the nature and results of any bankruptcy, receivership or similar proceedings with respect to the registrant or any of its significant subsidiaries; the nature and results of any other material reclassification, merger or consolidation of the registrant or any of its significant subsidiaries; the acquisition or disposition of any material amount of assets otherwise than in the ordinary course of business; and any material changes in the mode of conducting the business.

(2) Registrants:

(i) Filing a registration statement on Form S-1 (§ 239.11 of this chapter) under the Securities Act or on Form 10 (§ 249.210 of this chapter) under the Exchange Act;

(ii) Not subject to the reporting requirements of section 13(a) or 15(d) of the Exchange Act immediately before the filing of such registration statement; and

(iii) That (including predecessors) have not received revenue from operations during each of the three fiscal years immediately before the filing of such registration statement, shall provide the following information:

(A) If the registration statement is filed prior to the end of the registrant's second fiscal quarter, a description of the registrant's plan of operation for the remainder of the fiscal year; or

(B) If the registration statement is filed subsequent to the end of the registrant's second fiscal quarter, a descripition of the registrant's plan of operation for the remainder of the fiscal year and for the first six months of the next fiscal year. If such information is not available, the reasons for its not being available shall be stated. Disclosure relating to any plan shall include such matters as:

(*1*) In the case of a registration statement on Form S-1, a statement in narrative form indicating the registrant's opinion as to the period of time that the proceeds from the offering will satisfy cash requirements and whether in the next six months it will be necessary to raise additional funds to meet the expenditures required for operating the business of the registrant; the specific reasons for such opinion shall be set forth and categories of expenditures and sources of cash resources shall be identified; however, amounts of expenditures and cash resources need not be provided; in addition, if the narrative statement is based on a cash budget, such budget shall be furnished to the Commission as supplemental information, but not as part of the registration statement;

(*2*) An explanation of material product research and development to be performed during the period covered in the plan;

(*3*) Any anticipated material acquisition of plant and equipment and the capacity thereof;

(*4*) Any anticipated material changes in number of employees in the various departments such as research and development, production, sales or administration; and

(*5*) Other material areas which may be peculiar to the registrant's business.

(b) *Financial information about segments.* Report for each segment, as defined by generally accepted accounting principles, revenues from external customers, a measure of profit or loss and total assets. A registrant must report this information for each of the last three fiscal years or for as long as it has been in business, whichever period is shorter. If the information provided in response to this paragraph (b) conforms with generally accepted accounting principles, a registrant may include in its financial statements a cross reference to this data in lieu of presenting duplicative information in the financial statements; conversely, a registrant may cross reference to the financial statements.

(1) If a registrant changes the structure of its internal organization in a manner that causes the composition of its reportable segments to change, the registrant must restate the corresponding information for earlier periods, including interim periods, unless it is impracticable to do so. Following a change in the composition of its reportable segments, a registrant shall disclose whether it has restated the corresponding items of segment information for earlier periods. If it has not restated the items from earlier periods, the registrant shall disclose in the year in which the change occurs segment information for the current period under both the old basis and the new basis of segmentation, unless it is impracticable to do so.

(2) If the registrant includes, or is required by Article 3 of Regulation S-X (17 CFR 210) to include, interim financial statements, discuss any facts relating to the performance of any of the segments during the

period which, in the opinion of management, indicate that the three year segment financial data may not be indicative of current or future operations of the segment. Comparative financial information shall be included to the extent necessary to the discussion.

(c) *Narrative description of business.*

(1) Describe the business done and intended to be done by the registrant and its subsidiaries, focusing upon the registrant's dominant segment or each reportable segment about which financial information is presented in the financial statements. To the extent material to an understanding of the registrant's business taken as a whole, the description of each such segment shall include the information specified in paragraphs (c)(1)(i) through (x) of this section. The matters specified in paragraphs (c)(1)(xi) through (xiii) of this section shall be discussed with respect to the registrant's business in general; where material, the segments to which these matters are significant shall be identified.

(i) The principal products produced and services rendered by the registrant in the segment and the principal markets for, and methods of distribution of, the segment's principal products and services. In addition, state for each of the last three fiscal years the amount or percentage of total revenue contributed by any class of similar products or services which accounted for 10 percent or more of consolidated revenue in any of the last three fiscal years or 15 percent or more of consolidated revenue, if total revenue did not exceed $50,000,000 during any of such fiscal years.

(ii) A description of the status of a product or segment (e.g. whether in the planning stage, whether prototypes exist, the degree to which product design has progressed or whether further engineering is necessary), if there has been a public announcement of, or if the registrant otherwise has made public information about, a new product or segment that would require the investment of a material amount of the assets of the registrant or that otherwise is material. This paragraph is not intended to require disclosure of otherwise nonpublic corporate information the disclosure of which would affect adversely the registrant's competitive position.

(iii) The sources and availability of raw materials.

(iv) The importance to the segment and the duration and effect of all patents, trademarks, licenses, franchises and concessions held.

(v) The extent to which the business of the segment is or may be seasonal.

(vi) The practices of the registrant and the industry (respective industries) relating to working capital items (e.g., where the registrant is required to carry significant amounts of inventory to meet rapid delivery requirements of customers or to assure itself of a continuous allotment of goods from suppliers; where the registrant provides rights to return merchandise; or where the registrant has provided extended payment terms to customers).

(vii) The dependence of the segment upon a single customer, or a few customers, the loss of any one or more of which would have a material adverse effect on the segment. The name of any customer and its relationship, if any, with the registrant or its subsidiaries shall be disclosed if sales to the customer by one or more segments are made in an aggregate amount equal to 10 percent or more of the registrant's consolidated revenues and the loss of such customer would have a material adverse effect on the registrant and its subsidiaries taken as a whole. The names of other customers may be included, unless in the particular case the effect of including the names would be misleading. For purposes of this paragraph, a group of customers under common control or customers that are affiliates of each other shall be regarded as a single customer.

(viii) The dollar amount of backlog orders believed to be firm, as of a recent date and as of a comparable date in the preceding fiscal year, together with an indication of the portion thereof not reasonably expected to be filled within the current fiscal year, and seasonal or other material aspects of the backlog. (There may be included as firm orders government orders that are firm but not yet funded and contracts awarded but not yet signed, provided an appropriate statement is added to explain the nature of such orders and the amount thereof. The portion of orders already included in sales or operating revenues on the basis of percentage of completion or program accounting shall be excluded.)

(ix) A description of any material portion of the business that may be subject to renegotiation of profits or termination of contracts or subcontracts at the election of the Government.

(x) Competitive conditions in the business involved including, where material, the identity of the particular markets in which the registrant competes, an estimate of the number of competitors and the registrant's competitive position, if known or reasonably available to the registrant. Separate consideration shall be given to the principal products or services or classes of products or services of the segment, if any. Generally, the names of competitors need not be disclosed. The registrant may include such names, unless in the particular case the effect of including the names would be misleading. Where, however, the registrant knows or has reason to know that one or a small number of competitors is dominant in the industry it shall be identified. The principal methods of competition (e.g., price, service, warranty or product performance) shall be identified, and positive and negative factors pertaining to the competitive position of the registrant, to the extent that they exist, shall be explained if known or reasonably available to the registrant.

(xi) If material, the estimated amount spent during each of the last three fiscal years on company-sponsored research and development activities determined in accordance with generally accepted accounting principles. In addition, state, if material, the estimated dollar amount spent during each of such years on customer-sponsored research activities relating to the development of new products, services or techniques or the improvement of existing products, services or techniques.

(xii) Appropriate disclosure also shall be made as to the material effects that compliance with Federal, State and local provisions which have been enacted or adopted regulating the discharge of materials into the environment, or otherwise relating to the protection of the environment, may have upon the capital expenditures, earnings and competitive position of the registrant and its subsidiaries. The registrant shall disclose any material estimated capital expenditures for environmental control facilities for the remainder of its current fiscal year and its succeeding fiscal year and for such further periods as the registrant may deem materials.

(xiii) The number of persons employed by the registrant.

(d) *Financial information about geographic areas.*

(1) State for each of the registrant's last three fiscal years, or for each fiscal year the registrant has been engaged in business, whichever period is shorter:

(i) Revenues from external customers attributed to:

(A) The registrant's country of domicile;

(B) All foreign countries, in total, from which the registrant derives revenues; and

(C) Any individual foreign country, if material. Disclose the basis for attributing revenues from external customers to individual countries.

(ii) Long-lived assets, other than financial instruments, long-term customer relationships of a financial institution, mortgage and other servicing rights, deferred policy acquisition costs, and deferred tax assets, located in:

(A) The registrant's country of domicile;

(B) All foreign countries, in total, in which the registrant holds assets; and

(C) Any individual foreign country, if material.

(2) A registrant shall report the amounts based on the financial information that it uses to produce the general-purpose financial statements. If providing the geographic information is impracticable, the registrant shall disclose that fact. A registrant may wish to provide, in addition to the information required by paragraph (d)(1) of this section, subtotals of geographic information about groups of countries. To the extent that the disclosed information conforms with generally accepted accounting principles, the registrant may include in its financial statements a cross reference to this data in lieu of presenting duplicative data in its financial statements; conversely, a registrant may cross-reference to the financial statements.

(3) A registrant shall describe any risks attendant to the foreign operations and any dependence on one or more of the registrant's segments upon such foreign operations, unless it would be more appropriate to discuss this information in connection with the description of one or more of the registrant's segments under paragraph (c) of this item.

(4) If the registrant includes, or is required by Article 3 of Regulation S-X (17 CFR 210), to include, interim financial statements, discuss any facts relating to the information furnished under this paragraph (d) that, in the opinion of management, indicate that the three year financial data for geographic areas may not be indicative of current or future operations. To the extent necessary to the discussion, include comparative information . . .

§ 229.102 (Item 102) Description of Property

State briefly the location and general character of the principal plants, mines and other materially important physical properties of the registrant and its subsidiaries. In addition, identify the segment(s), as reported in the financial statements, that use the properties described. If any such property is not held in fee or is held subject to any major encumbrance, so state and describe briefly how held.

Instructions to Item 102: 1. What is required is such information as reasonably will inform investors as to the suitability, adequacy, productive capacity and extent of utilization of the facilities by the registrant. Detailed descriptions of the physical characteristics of individual properties or legal descriptions by metes and bounds are not required. . . .

§ 229.103 (Item 103) Legal Proceedings

Describe briefly any material pending legal proceedings, other than ordinary routine litigation incidental to the business, to which the registrant or any of its subsidiaries is a party or of which any of their property is the subject. Include the name of the court or agency in which the proceedings are pending, the date instituted, the principal parties thereto, a description of the factual basis alleged to underlie the proceeding and the relief sought. Include similar information as to any such proceedings known to be contemplated by governmental authorities.

Instructions to Item 103:

1. If the business ordinarily results in actions for negligence or other claims, no such action or claim need be described unless it departs from the normal kind of such actions.

2. No information need be given with respect to any proceeding that involves primarily a claim for damages if the amount involved, exclusive of interest and costs, does not exceed 10 percent of the current assets of the registrant and its subsidiaries . . .

4. Any material proceedings to which any director, officer or affiliate of the registrant, any owner of record or beneficially of more than five percent of any class of voting securities of the registrant, or any associate of any such director, officer, affiliate of the registrant, or security holder is a party adverse to the registrant or any of its subsidiaries or has a material interest adverse to the registrant or any of its subsidiaries also shall be described.

5. Notwithstanding the foregoing, an administrative or judicial proceeding (including, for purposes of A and B of this Instruction, proceedings which present in large degree the same issues) arising under any Federal, State or local provisions that have been enacted or adopted . . . primary for the purpose of protecting the environment shall not be deemed "ordinary routine litigation incidental to the business" and shall be described if:

A. Such proceeding is . . . ;

B. Such proceeding involves primarily a claim for damages, or involves potential monetary sanctions, capital expenditures, deferred charges or charges to income and the amount involved, exclusive of interest and costs, exceeds 10 percent of the current assets of the registrant and its subsidiaries on a consolidated basis; or

C. A governmental authority is a party to such proceeding and such proceeding involves potential monetary sanctions, unless the registrant reasonably believes that such proceeding will result in no monetary sanctions, or in monetary sanctions, exclusive of interest and costs, of less than $100,000. . . .

Subpart 200 — Securities of the Registrant

§ 229.201 (Item 201) Market Price of and Dividends on the Registrant's Common Equity and Related Stockholder Matters

(a) *Market information.*

(1)(i) Identify the principal United States market or markets in which each class of the registrant's common equity is being traded. . . .

(ii) If the principal United States market for such common equity is an exchange, state the high and low sales prices for the equity for each full quarterly period within the two most recent fiscal years and any subsequent interim period for which financial statements are included, or are required to be included by Article 3-01 through 3-04 of Regulation S-X (§ 210.3-01 through 3-04 of this chapter), or Article 8-02 through 8-03 of Regulation S-X (§ 210.8-02 through 8-03 of this chapter) in the case of smaller reporting companies, as reported in the consolidated transaction reporting system or, if not so reported, as reported on the principal exchange market for such equity....

(b) *Holders.*

(1) Set forth the approximate number of holders of each class of common equity of the registrant as of the latest practicable date....

(c) *Dividends.*

(1) State the frequency and amount of any cash dividends declared on each class of its common equity by the registrant for the two most recent fiscal years and any subsequent interim period for which financial statements are required to be presented by § 210.3 of Regulation S-X....

(d) *Securities authorized for issuance under equity compensation plans.*

(1)..., [P]rovide the information specified in paragraph (d)(2) of this Item as of the end of the most recently completed fiscal year with respect to compensation plans (including individual compensation arrangements) under which equity securities of the registrant are authorized for issuance, aggregated as follows:

(i) All compensation plans previously approved by security holders; and

(ii) All compensation plans not previously approved by security holders.

(2)... [I]nclude the following information as of the end of the most recently completed fiscal year for each category of equity compensation plan described in paragraph (d)(1) of this Item:

(i) The number of securities to be issued upon the exercise of outstanding options, warrants and rights (column (a));

(ii) The weighted-average exercise price of the outstanding options, warrants and rights disclosed pursuant to paragraph (d)(2)(i) of this Item (column (b)); and

(iii) Other than securities to be issued upon the exercise of the outstanding options, warrants and rights disclosed in paragraph (d)(2)(i) of this Item, the number of securities remaining available for future issuance under the plan (column (c)).

(3) For each compensation plan under which equity securities of the registrant are authorized for issuance that was adopted without the approval of security holders, describe briefly, in narrative form, the material features of the plan....

Subpart 300—Financial Information

§ 229.301 (Item 301) Selected Financial Data

Furnish in comparative columnar form the selected financial data for the registrant referred to below, for

(a) Each of the last five fiscal years of the registrant (or for the life of the registrant and its predecessors, if less), and

(b) Any additional fiscal years necessary to keep the information from being misleading

Instructions to Item 301:

1. The purpose of the selected financial data shall be to supply in a convenient and readable format selected financial data which highlight certain significant trends in the registrant's financial condition and results of operations.

2. Subject to appropriate variation to conform to the nature of the registrant's business, the following items shall be included in the table of financial data: net sales or operating revenues; income (loss) from continuing operations; income (loss) from continuing operations per common share; total assets; long-term obligations and redeemable preferred stock . . . and cash dividends declared per common share. Registrants may include additional items which they believe would enhance an understanding of and would highlight other trends in their financial condition and results of operations.

§ 229.303 (Item 303) Management's Discussion and Analysis of Financial Condition and Results of Operations

(a) *Full fiscal years.* Discuss registrant's financial condition, changes in financial condition and results of operations. The discussion shall provide information as specified in paragraphs (a)(1) through (5) of this Item and also shall provide such other information that the registrant believes to be necessary to an understanding of its financial condition, changes in financial condition and results of operations. Discussions of liquidity and capital resources may be combined whenever the two topics are interrelated. Where in the registrant's judgment a discussion of segment information or of other subdivisions of the registrant's business would be appropriate to an understanding of such business, the discussion shall focus on each relevant, reportable segment or other subdivision of the business and on the registrant as a whole.

(1) *Liquidity.* Identify any known trends or any known demands, commitments, events or uncertainties that will result in or that are reasonably likely to result in the registrant's liquidity increasing or decreasing in any material way. If a material deficiency is identified, indicate the course of action that the registrant has taken or proposes to take to remedy the deficiency. Also identify and separately describe internal and external sources of liquidity, and briefly discuss any material unused sources of liquid assets.

(2) *Capital resources.*

(i) Describe the registrant's material commitments for capital expenditures as of the end of the latest fiscal period, and indicate the general purpose of such commitments and the anticipated source of funds needed to fulfill such commitments.

(ii) Describe any known material trends, favorable or unfavorable, in the registrant's capital resources. Indicate any expected material changes in the mix and relative cost of such resources. The discussion shall consider changes between equity, debt and any off-balance sheet financing arrangements.

(3) *Results of operations.*

(i) Describe any unusual or infrequent events or transactions or any significant economic changes that materially affected the amount of reported income from continuing operations and, in each case, indicate the extent to which income was so affected. In addition, describe any other significant components of revenues or expenses that, in the registrant's judgment, should be described in order to understand the registrant's results of operations.

(ii) Describe any known trends or uncertainties that have had or that the registrant reasonably expects will have a material favorable or unfavorable impact on net sales or revenues or income from continuing operations. If the registrant knows of events that will cause a material change in the relationship between costs and revenues (such as known future increases in costs of labor or materials or price increases or inventory adjustments), the change in the relationship shall be disclosed.

(iii) To the extent that the financial statements disclose material increases in net sales or revenues, provide a narrative discussion of the extent to which such increases are attributable to increases in prices or to increases in the volume or amount of goods or services being sold or to the introduction of new products or services.

(iv) For the three most recent fiscal years of the registrant or for those fiscal years in which the registrant has been engaged in business, whichever period is shortest, discuss the impact of inflation and changing prices on the registrant's net sales and revenues and on income from continuing operations.

(4) *Off-balance sheet arrangements.*

(i) In a separately-captioned section, discuss the registrant's off-balance sheet arrangements that have or are reasonably likely to have a current or future effect on the registrant's financial condition, changes in financial condition, revenues or expenses, results of operations, liquidity, capital expenditures or capital resources that is material to investors. The disclosure shall include the items specified in paragraphs (a)(4)(i)(A), (B), (C) and (D) of this Item to the extent necessary to an understanding of such arrangements and effect and shall also include such other information that the registrant believes is necessary for such an understanding.

(A) The nature and business purpose to the registrant of such off-balance sheet arrangements;

(B) The importance to the registrant of such off-balance sheet arrangements in respect of its liquidity, capital resources, market risk support, credit risk support or other benefits;

(C) The amounts of revenues, expenses and cash flows of the registrant arising from such arrangements; the nature and amounts of any interests retained, securities issued and other indebtedness incurred by the registrant in connection with such arrangements; and the nature and amounts of any other obligations or liabilities (including contingent obligations or liabilities) of the registrant arising from such arrangements that are or are reasonably likely to become material and the triggering events or circumstances that could cause them to arise; and

(D) Any known event, demand, commitment, trend or uncertainty that will result in or is reasonably likely to result in the termination, or material reduction in availability to the registrant, of its off-balance sheet arrangements that provide material benefits to it, and the course of action that the registrant has taken or proposes to take in response to any such circumstances.

(ii) As used in this paragraph (a)(4), the term off-balance sheet arrangement means any transaction, agreement or other contractual arrangement to which an entity unconsolidated with the registrant is a party, under which the registrant has:

(A) Any obligation under a guarantee contract that has any of the characteristics identified in FASB ASC paragraph 460-10-15-4 (Guarantees Topic), as may be modified or supplemented, and that is not excluded from the initial recognition and measurement provisions of FASB ASC paragraphs 460-10-15-7, 460-10-25-1, and 460-10-30-1.

(B) A retained or contingent interest in assets transferred to an unconsolidated entity or similar arrangement that serves as credit, liquidity or market risk support to such entity for such assets;

(C) Any obligation, including a contingent obligation, under a contract that would be accounted for as a derivative instrument, except that it is both indexed to the registrant's own stock and classified in stockholders' equity in the registrant's statement of financial position, and therefore excluded from the scope of FASB ASC Topic 815, Derivatives and Hedging, pursuant to FASB ASC subparagraph 815-10-15-74(a), as may be modified or supplemented; or

(D) Any obligation, including a contingent obligation, arising out of a variable interest (as defined in the FASB ASC Master Glossary), as may be modified or supplemented) in an unconsolidated entity that is held by, and material to, the registrant, where such entity provides financing, liquidity, market risk or credit risk support to, or engages in leasing, hedging or research and development services with, the registrant.

(5) *Tabular disclosure of contractual obligations.*

(i) In a tabular format, provide the information specified in this paragraph (a)(5) as of the latest fiscal year end balance sheet date with respect to the registrant's known contractual obligations specified in the table that follows this paragraph (a)(5)(i). The registrant shall provide amounts, aggregated by type of contractual obligation. The registrant may disaggregate the specified categories of contractual obligations using other categories suitable to its business, but the presentation must include all of the obligations of the registrant that fall within the specified categories. A presentation covering at least the periods specified shall be included. The tabular presentation may be accompanied by footnotes to describe provisions that create, increase or accelerate obligations, or other pertinent data to the extent necessary for an understanding of the timing and amount of the registrant's specified contractual obligations.

Contractual obligations	*Payments due by period*				
	Total	*Less than 1 year*	*1-3 years*	*3-5 years*	*More than 5 years*
[Long-Term Debt Obligations]					
[Capital Lease Obligations]					
[Operating Lease Obligations]					
[Purchase Obligations]					
[Other Long-Term Liabilities Reflected on the Registrant's Balance Sheet under GAAP]					
Total					

§ 229.304 (Item 304) Changes in and Disagreements with Accountants on Accounting and Financial Disclosure

(a)(1) If during the registrant's two most recent fiscal years or any subsequent interim period, an independent accountant who was previously engaged as the principal accountant to audit the registrant's financial statements, or an independent accountant who was previously engaged to audit a significant subsidiary and on whom the principal accountant expressed reliance in its report, has resigned (or indicated it has declined to stand for re-election after the completion of the current audit) or was dismissed, then the registrant shall:

(i) State whether the former accountant resigned, declined to stand for re-election or was dismissed and the date thereof.

(ii) State whether the principal accountant's report on the financial statements for either of the past two years contained an adverse opinion or a disclaimer of opinion, or was qualified or modified as to uncertainty, audit scope, or accounting principles; and also describe the nature of each such adverse opinion, disclaimer of opinion, modification, or qualification.

(iii) State whether the decision to change accountants was recommended or approved by:

(A) Any audit or similar committee of the board of directors, if the issuer has such a committee; or

(B) The board of directors, if the issuer has no such committee.

(iv) State whether during the registrant's two most recent fiscal years and any subsequent interim period preceding such resignation, declination or dismissal there were any disagreements with the former accountant on any matter of accounting principles or practices, financial statement disclosure, or auditing scope or procedure, which disagreement(s), if not resolved to the satisfaction of the former accountant, would have caused it to make reference to the subject matter of the disagreement(s) in connection with its report. Also, (A) describe each such disagreement; (B) state whether any audit or similar committee of the board of directors, or the board of directors, discussed the subject matter of each of such disagreements with the former accountant; and (C) state whether the registrant has authorized the former accountant to respond fully to the inquiries of the successor accountant concerning the subject matter of each of such disagreements and, if not, describe the nature of any limitation thereon and the reason therefore. The disagreements required to be reported in response to this Item include both those resolved to the former accountant's satisfaction and those not resolved to the former accountant's satisfaction. Disagreements contemplated by this Item are those that occur at the decision-making level, *i.e.*, between personnel of the registrant responsible for presentation of its financial statements and personnel of the accounting firm responsible for rendering its report.

(v) Provide the information required by paragraph (a)(1)(iv) of this Item for each of the kinds of events (even though the registrant and the former accountant did not express a difference of opinion regarding the event) listed in paragraphs (a)(1)(v) (A) through (D) of this section, that occurred within the registrant's two most recent fiscal years and any subsequent interim period preceding the former accountant's resignation, declination to stand for re-election, or dismissal ("reportable events"). If the event led to a disagreement or difference of opinion, then the event should be reported as a disagreement under paragraph (a)(1)(iv) and need not be repeated under this paragraph.

(A) The accountant's having advised the registrant that the internal controls necessary for the registrant to develop reliable financial statements do not exist;

(B) The accountant's having advised the registrant that information has come to the accountant's attention that has led it to no longer be able to rely on management's representations, or that has made it unwilling to be associated with the financial statements prepared by management;

(C)(*1*) The accountant's having advised the registrant of the need to expand significantly the scope of its audit, or that information has come to the accountant's attention during the time period covered by Item 304(a)(1)(iv), that if further investigated may:

(*i*) Materially impact the fairness or reliability of either: a previously issued audit report or the underlying financial statements; or the financial statements issued or to be issued covering the fiscal period(s) subsequent to the date of the most recent financial statements covered by an audit report (including information that may prevent it from rendering an unqualified audit report on those financial statements), or

(*ii*) Cause it to be unwilling to rely on management's representations or be associated with the registrant's financial statements, and

(*2*) Due to the accountant's resignation (due to audit scope limitations or otherwise) or dismissal, or for any other reason, the accountant did not so expand the scope of its audit or conduct such further investigation; or

(D)(*1*) The accountant's having advised the registrant that information has come to the accountant's attention that it has concluded materially impacts the fairness or reliability of either (*i*) a previously issued audit report or the underlying financial statements, or (*ii*) the financial statements issued or to be issued covering the fiscal period(s) subsequent to the date of the most recent financial statements covered by an audit report (including information that, unless resolved to the accountant's satisfaction, would prevent it from rendering an unqualified audit report on those financial statements), and

(*2*) Due to the accountant's resignation, dismissal or declination to stand for re-election, or for any other reason, the issue has not been resolved to the accountant's satisfaction prior to its resignation, dismissal or declination to stand for re-election.

(2) If during the registrant's two most recent fiscal years or any subsequent interim period, a new independent accountant has been engaged as either the principal accountant to audit the registrant's financial statements, or as an independent accountant to audit a significant subsidiary and on whom the principal accountant is expected to express reliance in its report, then the registrant shall identify the newly engaged accountant and indicate the date of such accountant's engagement. In addition, if during the registrant's two most recent fiscal years, and any subsequent interim period prior to engaging that accountant, the registrant (or someone on its behalf) consulted the newly engaged accountant regarding:

(i) Either: The application of accounting principles to a specified transaction, either completed or proposed; or the type of audit opinion that might be rendered on the registrant's financial statements, and either a written report was provided to the registrant or oral advice was provided that the new accountant concluded was an important factor considered by the registrant in reaching a decision as to the accounting, auditing or financial reporting issue; or

(ii) Any matter that was either the subject of a disagreement (as defined in paragraph 304(a)(1)(iv) and the related instructions to this item) or a reportable event (as described in paragraph 304(a)(1)(v)), then the registrant shall:

(A) So state and identify the issues that were the subjects of those consultations;

(B) Briefly describe the views of the newly engaged accountant as expressed orally or in writing to the registrant on each such issue and, if written views were received by the registrant, file them as an exhibit to the report or registration statement requiring compliance with this Item 304(a);

(C) State whether the former accountant was consulted by the registrant regarding any such issues, and if so, provide a summary of the former accountant's views; and

(D) Request the newly engaged accountant to review the disclosure required by this Item 304(a) before it is filed with the Commission and provide the new accountant the opportunity to furnish the registrant with a letter addressed to the Commission containing any new information, clarification of the registrant's expression of its views, or the respects in which it does not agree with the statements made by the registrant in response to Item 304(a). The registrant shall file any such letter as an exhibit to the report or registration statement containing the disclosure required by this Item.

(3) The registrant shall provide the former accountant with a copy of the disclosures it is making in response to this Item 304(a) that the

former accountant shall receive no later than the day that the disclosures are filed with the Commission. The registrant shall request the former accountant to furnish the registrant with a letter addressed to the Commission stating whether it agrees with the statements made by the registrant in response to this Item 304(a) and, if not, stating the respects in which it does not agree. The registrant shall file the former accountant's letter as an exhibit to the report on registration statement containing this disclosure. If the former accountant's letter is unavailable at the time of filing such report or registration statement, then the registrant shall request the former accountant to provide the letter as promptly as possible so that the registrant can file the letter with the Commission within ten business days after the filing of the report or registration statement. Notwithstanding the ten business day period, the registrant shall file the letter by amendment within two business days of receipt; if the letter is received on a Saturday, Sunday or holiday on which the Commission is not open for business, then the two business day period shall begin to run on and shall include the first business day thereafter. The former accountant may provide the registrant with an interim letter highlighting specific areas of concern and indicating that a more detailed letter will be forthcoming within the ten business day period noted above. If not filed with the report or registration statement containing the registrant's disclosure under this Item 304(a), then the interim letter, if any, shall be filed by the registrant by amendment within two business days of receipt.

(b) If: (1) In connection with a change in accountants subject to paragraph (a) of this Item 304, there was any disagreement of the type described in paragraph (a)(1)(iv) or any reportable event as described in paragraph (a)(1)(v) of this Item;

(2) During the fiscal year in which the change in accountants took place or during the subsequent fiscal year, there have been any transactions or events similar to those which involved such disagreement or reportable event; and

(3) Such transactions or events were material and were accounted for or disclosed in a manner different from that which the former accountants apparently would have concluded was required, the registrant shall state the existence and nature of the disagreement or reportable event and also state the effect on the financial statements if the method had been followed which the former accountants apparently would have concluded was required.

These disclosures need not be made if the method asserted by the former accountants ceases to be generally accepted because of authoritative standards or interpretations subsequently issued.

Instructions to Item 304:

4. The term "disagreements" as used in this Item shall be interpreted broadly, to include any difference of opinion concerning any matter of

accounting principles or practices, financial statement disclosure, or auditing scope or procedure which (if not resolved to the satisfaction of the former accountant) would have caused it to make reference to the subject matter of the disagreement in connection with its report. It is not necessary for there to have been an argument to have had a disagreement, merely a difference of opinion. For purposes of this Item, however, the term disagreements does not include initial differences of opinion based on incomplete facts or preliminary information that were later resolved to the former accountant's satisfaction by, and providing the registrant and the accountant do not continue to have a difference of opinion upon, obtaining additional relevant facts or information.

5. In determining whether any disagreement or reportable event has occurred, an oral communication from the engagement partner or another person responsible for rendering the accounting firm's opinion (or their designee) will generally suffice as the accountant advising the registrant of a reportable event or as a statement of a disagreement at the "decision-making level" within the accounting firm and require disclosure under this Item.

§ 229.307 (Item 307) Disclosure Controls and Procedures

Disclose the conclusions of the registrant's principal executive and principal financial officers, or persons performing similar functions, regarding the effectiveness of the registrant's disclosure controls and procedures (as defined in § 240.13a-15(e) or § 240.15d-15(e) of this chapter) as of the end of the period covered by the report, based on the evaluation of these controls and procedures required by paragraph (b) of § 240.13a-15 or § 240.15d-15 of this chapter

§ 229.308 (Item 308) Internal Control over Financial Reporting

(a) *Management's annual report on internal control over financial reporting.* Provide a report of management on the registrant's internal control over financial reporting (as defined in § 240.13a-15(f) or § 240.15d-15(f) of this chapter) that contains:

(1) A statement of management's responsibility for establishing and maintaining adequate internal control over financial reporting for the registrant;

(2) A statement identifying the framework used by management to evaluate the effectiveness of the registrant's internal control over financial reporting as required by paragraph (c) of § 240.13a-15 or § 240.15d-15 of this chapter;

(3) Management's assessment of the effectiveness of the registrant's internal control over financial reporting as of the end of the registrant's

most recent fiscal year, including a statement as to whether or not internal control over financial reporting is effective. This discussion must include disclosure of any material weakness in the registrant's internal control over financial reporting identified by management. Management is not permitted to conclude that the registrant's internal control over financial reporting is effective if there are one or more material weaknesses in the registrant's internal control over financial reporting; and

(4) If the registrant is an accelerated filer or a large accelerated filer (as defined in § 240.12b-2 of this chapter), or otherwise includes in its annual report a registered public accounting firm's attestation report on internal control over financial reporting, a statement that the registered public accounting firm that audited the financial statements included in the annual report containing the disclosure required by this Item has issued an attestation report on the registrant's internal control over financial reporting.

(b) *Attestation report of the registered public accounting firm.* If the registrant is an accelerated filer or a large accelerated filer (as defined in § 240.12b-2 of this chapter), provide the registered public accounting firm's attestation report on the registrant's internal control over financial reporting in the registrant's annual report containing the disclosure required by this Item.

(c) *Changes in internal control over financial reporting.* Disclose any change in the registrant's internal control over financial reporting identified in connection with the evaluation required by paragraph (d) of § 240.13a-15 or 240.15d-15 of this chapter that occurred during the registrant's last fiscal quarter (the registrant's fourth fiscal quarter in the case of an annual report) that has materially affected, or is reasonably likely to materially affect, the registrant's internal control over financial reporting.

Subpart 400— Management and Certain Securities Holders

§ 229.401 (Item 401) Directors, Executive Officers, Promoters and Control Persons

(a) *Identification of directors.* List the names and ages of all directors of the registrant and all persons nominated or chosen to become directors; indicate all positions and offices with the registrant held by each such person; state his term of office as director and any period(s) during which he has served as such; describe briefly any arrangement or understanding between him and any other person(s) (naming such person(s)) pursuant to which he was or is to be selected as a director or nominee.

. . .

(b) *Identification of executive officers*. List the names and ages of all executive officers of the registrant and all persons chosen to become executive officers; indicate all positions and offices with the registrant held by each such person; state his term of office as officer and the period during which he has served as such and describe briefly any arrangement or understanding between him and any other person(s) (naming such person) pursuant to which he was or is to be selected as an officer.

. . .

(c) *Identification of certain significant employees*. Where the registrant employs persons such as production managers, sales managers, or research scientists who are not executive officers but who make or are expected to make significant contributions to the business of the registrant, such persons shall be identified and their background disclosed to the same extent as in the case of executive officers. Such disclosure need not be made if the registrant was subject to section 13(a) or 15(d) of the Exchange Act or was exempt from section 13(a) by section 12(g)(2)(G) of such Act immediately prior to the filing of the registration statement, report, or statement to which this Item is applicable.

(d) *Family relationships*. State the nature of any family relationship between any director, executive officer, or person nominated or chosen by the registrant to become a director or executive officer . . .

(e) Business experience —

(1) *Background.* Briefly describe the business experience during the past five years of each director, executive officer, person nominated or chosen to become a director or executive officer, and each person named in answer to paragraph (c) of Item 401 . . .

(2) *Directorships.* Indicate any other directorships held, including any other directorships held during the past five years, held by each director or person nominated or chosen to become a director in any company with a class of securities registered pursuant to section 12 of the Exchange Act or subject to the requirements of section 15(d) of such Act or any company registered as an investment company under the Investment Company Act of 1940, 15 U.S.C. 80a-1, *et seq.*, as amended, naming such company . . .

(f) *Involvement in certain legal proceedings*. Describe any of the following events that occurred during the past ten years and that are material to an evaluation of the ability or integrity of any director, person nominated to become a director or executive officer of the registrant:

(1) A petition under the Federal bankruptcy laws or any state insolvency law was filed by or against, or a receiver, fiscal agent or similar officer was appointed by a court for the business or property of such person, or any partnership in which he was a general partner at or within two years before the time of such filing, or any corporation or

business association of which he was an executive officer at or within two years before the time of such filing;

(2) Such person was convicted in a criminal proceeding or is a named subject of a pending criminal proceeding (excluding traffic violations and other minor offenses)...

§ 229.402 (Item 402) Executive Compensation

(a) General—

(1) *Treatment of foreign private issuers.* A foreign private issuer will be deemed to comply with this Item if it provides the information required by Items 6.B and 6.E.2 of Form 20–F (17 CFR 249.220f), with more detailed information provided if otherwise made publicly available or required to be disclosed by the issuer's home jurisdiction or a market in which its securities are listed or traded.

(2) *All compensation covered.* This Item requires clear, concise and understandable disclosure of all plan and non-plan compensation awarded to, earned by, or paid to the named executive officers designated under paragraph (a)(3) of this Item, and directors covered by paragraph (k) of this Item, by any person for all services rendered in all capacities to the registrant and its subsidiaries, unless otherwise specifically excluded from disclosure in this Item...

(3) *Persons covered.* Disclosure shall be provided pursuant to this item for each of the following (the "named executive officers"):

(i) All individuals serving as the registrant's principal executive officer or acting in a similar capacity during the last completed fiscal year ("PEO"), regardless of compensation level;

(ii) All individuals serving as the registrant's principal financial officer or acting in a similar capacity during the last completed fiscal year ("PFO"), regardless of compensation level;

(iii) The registrant's three most highly compensated executive officers other than the PEO and PFO who were serving as executive officers at the end of the last completed fiscal year; and

(iv) Up to two additional individuals for whom disclosure would have been provided pursuant to paragraph (a)(3)(iii) of this Item but for the fact that the individual was not serving as an executive officer of the registrant at the end of the last completed fiscal year.

Instructions to Item 402(a)(3). 1. *Determination of most highly compensated executive officers.* The determination as to which executive officers are most highly compensated shall be made by reference to total compensation for the last completed fiscal year (as required to be disclosed pursuant to paragraph (c)(2)(x) of this Item) reduced by the amount required to be disclosed pursuant to paragraph (c)(2)(viii) of this Item, *provided, however,* that no disclosure need be provided for any executive officer, other than the PEO and PFO, whose total compensation, as so reduced, does not exceed $100,000.

(6) Definitions. For purposes of this item:

(i) The term stock means instruments such as common stock, restricted stock, restricted stock units, phantom stock, phantom stock units, common stock equivalent units or any similar instruments that do not have option-like features, and the term option means instruments such as stock options, stock appreciation rights and similar instruments with option-like features. The term stock appreciation rights ("SARs") refers to SARs payable in cash or stock, including SARs payable in cash or stock at the election of the registrant or a named executive officer. The term equity is used to refer generally to stock and/or options.

(ii) The term plan includes, but is not limited to, the following: Any plan, contract, authorization or arrangement, whether or not set forth in any formal document, pursuant to which cash, securities, similar instruments, or any other property may be received. A plan may be applicable to one person. Except with respect to the disclosure required by paragraph (t) of this Item, registrants may omit information regarding group life, health, hospitalization, or medical reimbursement plans that do not discriminate in scope, terms or operation, in favor of executive officers or directors of the registrant and that are available generally to all salaried employees.

(iii) The term incentive plan means any plan providing compensation intended to serve as incentive for performance to occur over a specified period, whether such performance is measured by reference to financial performance of the registrant or an affiliate, the registrant's stock price, or any other performance measure. An equity incentive plan is an incentive plan or portion of an incentive plan under which awards are granted that fall within the scope of FASB ASC Topic 718, Compensation—Stock Compensation. A non-equity incentive plan is an incentive plan or portion of an incentive plan that is not an equity incentive plan. The term incentive plan award means an award provided under an incentive plan.

(iv) The terms date of grant or grant date refer to the grant date determined for financial statement reporting purposes pursuant to FASB ASC Topic 718.

(v) Closing market price is defined as the price at which the registrant's security was last sold in the principal United States market for such security as of the date for which the closing market price is determined.

(b) *Compensation discussion and analysis.* (1) Discuss the compensation awarded to, earned by, or paid to the named executive officers. The discussion shall explain all material elements of the registrant's compensation of the named executive officers. The discussion shall describe the following:

(i) The objectives of the registrant's compensation programs;

(ii) What the compensation program is designed to reward;

(iii) Each element of compensation;

(iv) Why the registrant chooses to pay each element;

(v) How the registrant determines the amount (and, where applicable, the formula) for each element to pay;

(vi) How each compensation element and the registrant's decisions regarding that element fit into the registrant's overall compensation objectives and affect decisions regarding other elements; and

(vii) Whether and, if so, how the registrant has considered the results of the most recent shareholder advisory vote on executive compensation required by section 14A of the Exchange Act (15 U.S.C. 78n-1) or § 240.14a-20 of this chapter in determining compensation policies and decisions and, if so, how that consideration has affected the registrant's executive compensation decisions and policies.

(2) While the material information to be disclosed under Compensation Discussion and Analysis will vary depending upon the facts and circumstances, examples of such information may include, in a given case, among other things, the following:

(i) The policies for allocating between long-term and currently paid out compensation;

(ii) The policies for allocating between cash and non-cash compensation, and among different forms of non-cash compensation;

(iii) For long-term compensation, the basis for allocating compensation to each different form of award (such as relationship of the award to the achievement of the registrant's long-term goals, management's exposure to downside equity performance risk, correlation between cost to registrant and expected benefits to the registrant);

(iv) How the determination is made as to when awards are granted, including awards of equity-based compensation such as options;

(v) What specific items of corporate performance are taken into account in setting compensation policies and making compensation decisions;

(vi) How specific forms of compensation are structured and implemented to reflect these items of the registrant's performance, including whether discretion can be or has been exercised (either to award compensation absent attainment of the relevant performance goal(s) or to reduce or increase the size of any award or payout), identifying any particular exercise of discretion, and stating whether it applied to one or more specified named executive officers or to all compensation subject to the relevant performance goal(s);

(vii) How specific forms of compensation are structured and implemented to reflect the named executive officer's individual performance and/or individual contribution to these items of the registrant's performance, describing the elements of individual performance and/or contribution that are taken into account;

(viii) Registrant policies and decisions regarding the adjustment or recovery of awards or payments if the relevant registrant performance measures upon which they are based are restated or otherwise adjusted in a manner that would reduce the size of an award or payment;

(ix) The factors considered in decisions to increase or decrease compensation materially;

(x) How compensation or amounts realizable from prior compensation are considered in setting other elements of compensation (e. g., how gains from prior option or stock awards are considered in setting retirement benefits);

(xi) With respect to any contract, agreement, plan or arrangement, whether written or unwritten, that provides for payment(s) at, following, or in connection with any termination or change-in-control, the basis for selecting particular events as triggering payment (e.g., the rationale for providing a single trigger for payment in the event of a change-in-control);

(xii) The impact of the accounting and tax treatments of the particular form of compensation;

(xiii) The registrant's equity or other security ownership requirements or guidelines (specifying applicable amounts and forms of ownership), and any registrant policies regarding hedging the economic risk of such ownership;

(xiv) Whether the registrant engaged in any benchmarking of total compensation, or any material element of compensation, identifying the benchmark and, if applicable, its components (including component companies); and

(xv) The role of executive officers in determining executive compensation.

(c) *Summary compensation table —*

(1) *General.* Provide the information specified in paragraph (c)(2) of this Item, concerning the compensation of the named executive officers for each of the registrant's last three completed fiscal years, in a Summary Compensation Table in the tabular format specified below.

SUMMARY COMPENSATION TABLE

Name and principal position (a)	*Year (b)*	*Salary ($) (c)*	*Bonus ($) (d)*	*Stock awards ($) (e)*	*Option awards ($) (f)*	*Non-equity incentive plan compensa-tion ($) (g)*	*Change in pension value and nonqualified deferred compensation earnings ($) (h)*	*All other compensa-tion ($) (i)*	*Total ($) (j)*
PEO									
PFO									
A									
B									
C									

(2) The Table shall include:

(i) The name and principal position of the named executive officer (column (a));

(ii) The fiscal year covered (column (b));

(iii) The dollar value of base salary (cash and non-cash) earned by the named executive officer during the fiscal year covered (column (c));

(iv) The dollar value of bonus (cash and non-cash) earned by the named executive officer during the fiscal year covered (column (d));

(v) For awards of stock, the aggregate grant date fair value computed in accordance with FASB ASC Topic 718 (column (e));

(vi) For awards of options, with or without tandem SARs (including awards that subsequently have been transferred), the aggregate grant date fair value computed in accordance with FASB ASC Topic 718 (column (f));

(vii) The dollar value of all earnings for services performed during the fiscal year pursuant to awards under non-equity incentive plans as defined in paragraph (a)(6)(iii) of this Item, and all earnings on any outstanding awards (column (g));

(viii) The sum of the amounts specified in paragraphs (c)(2)(viii)(A) and (B) of this Item (column (h)) as follows:

(A) The aggregate change in the actuarial present value of the named executive officer's accumulated benefit under all defined benefit and actuarial pension plans (including supplemental plans) from the pension plan measurement date used for financial statement reporting purposes with respect to the registrant's audited financial statements for the prior completed fiscal year to the pension plan measurement date used for financial statement reporting purposes with respect to the registrant's audited financial statements for the covered fiscal year; and

(B) Above-market or preferential earnings on compensation that is deferred on a basis that is not tax-qualified, including such earnings on nonqualified defined contribution plans;

(ix) All other compensation for the covered fiscal year that the registrant could not properly report in any other column of the Summary Compensation Table (column (i)). Each compensation item that is not properly reportable in columns (c)-(h), regardless of the amount of the compensation item, must be included in column (i). Such compensation must include, but is not limited to:

(A) Perquisites and other personal benefits, or property, unless the aggregate amount of such compensation is less than $10,000;

(B) All "gross-ups" or other amounts reimbursed during the fiscal year for the payment of taxes;

(C) For any security of the registrant or its subsidiaries purchased from the registrant or its subsidiaries (through deferral of salary or bonus, or otherwise) at a discount from the market price of such security at the date of purchase, unless that discount is available generally, either to all security holders or to all salaried employees of the registrant, the compensation cost, if any, computed in accordance with FASB ASC Topic 718;

(D) The amount paid or accrued to any named executive officer pursuant to a plan or arrangement in connection with:

(*1*) Any termination, including without limitation through retirement, resignation, severance or constructive termination (including a change in responsibilities) of such executive officer's employment with the registrant and its subsidiaries; or

(*2*) A change in control of the registrant;

(E) Registrant contributions or other allocations to vested and unvested defined contribution plans;

(F) The dollar value of any insurance premiums paid by, or on behalf of, the registrant during the covered fiscal year with respect to life insurance for the benefit of a named executive officer; and

(G) The dollar value of any dividends or other earnings paid on stock or option awards, when those amounts were not factored into the grant date fair value required to be reported for the stock or option award in column (e) or (f); and

(x) The dollar value of total compensation for the covered fiscal year (column (j)). With respect to each named executive officer, disclose the sum of all amounts reported in columns (c) through (i).

(d) *Grants of plan-based awards table.* (1) Provide the information specified in paragraph (d)(2) of this Item, concerning each grant of an award made to a named executive officer in the last completed fiscal year under any plan, including awards that subsequently have been transferred, in the following tabular format:

Grants of Plan-Based Awards

		Estimated future payouts under non-equity incentive plan awards			Estimated future payouts under equity incentive plan awards						
Name (a)	*Grant date (b)*	*Threshold ($) (c)*	*Target ($) (d)*	*Maximum ($) (e)*	*Threshold ($) (f)*	*Target ($) (g)*	*Maximum ($) (h)*	*All other stock awards: Number of shares of stock or units (#) (i)*	*All other option awards: Number of securities underlying options (#) (j)*	*Exercise or base price of option awards ($/Sh) (k)*	*Grant date fair value of stock and option awards (l)*
PEO											
PFO											
A											
B											
C											

(2) The Table shall include:

(i) The name of the named executive officer (column (a));

(ii) The grant date for equity-based awards reported in the table (column (b)). If such grant date is different than the date on which the compensation committee (or a committee of the board of directors performing a similar function or the full board of directors) takes action or is deemed to take action to grant such awards, a separate, adjoining column shall be added between columns (b) and (c) showing such date;

(iii) The dollar value of the estimated future payout upon satisfaction of the conditions in question under non-equity incentive plan awards granted in the fiscal year, or the applicable range of estimated payouts denominated in dollars (threshold, target and maximum amount) (columns (c) through (e));

(iv) The number of shares of stock, or the number of shares underlying options to be paid out or vested upon satisfaction of the conditions in question under equity incentive plan awards granted in the fiscal year, or the applicable range of estimated payouts denominated in the number of shares of stock, or the number of shares underlying options under the award (threshold, target and maximum amount) (columns (f) through (h));

(v) The number of shares of stock granted in the fiscal year that are not required to be disclosed in columns (f) through (h) (column (i));

(vi) The number of securities underlying options granted in the fiscal year that are not required to be disclosed in columns (f) through (h) (column (j));

(vii) The per-share exercise or base price of the options granted in the fiscal year (column (k)). If such exercise or base price is less than the closing market price of the underlying security on the date of the grant, a separate, adjoining column showing the closing market price on the date of the grant shall be added after column (k) and

(viii) The grant date fair value of each equity award computed in accordance with FASB ASC Topic 718 (column (*l*)). If at any time during the last completed fiscal year, the registrant has adjusted or amended the exercise or base price of options, SARs or similar option-like instruments previously awarded to a named executive officer, whether through amendment, cancellation or replacement grants, or any other means ("repriced"), or otherwise has materially modified such awards, the incremental fair value, computed as of the repricing or modification date in accordance with FASB ASC Topic 718, with respect to that repriced or modified award, shall be reported.

(e) *Narrative disclosure to summary compensation table and grants of plan-based awards table.* (1) Provide a narrative description of any material factors necessary to an understanding of the information disclosed in the tables required by paragraphs (c) and (d) of this Item. Examples of such factors may include, in given cases, among other things:

(i) The material terms of each named executive officer's employment agreement or arrangement, whether written or unwritten;

(ii) If at any time during the last fiscal year, any outstanding option or other equity-based award was repriced or otherwise materially modified (such as by extension of exercise periods, the change of vesting or forfeiture conditions, the change or elimination of applicable performance criteria, or the change of the bases upon which returns are determined), a description of each such repricing or other material modification;

(iii) The material terms of any award reported in response to paragraph (d) of this Item, including a general description of the formula or criteria to be applied in determining the amounts payable, and the vesting schedule. For example, state where applicable that dividends will be paid on stock, and if so, the applicable dividend rate and whether that rate is preferential. Describe any performance-based conditions, and any other material conditions, that are applicable to the award. For purposes of the Table required by paragraph (d) of this Item and the narrative disclosure required by paragraph (e) of this Item, performance-based conditions include both performance conditions and market conditions, as those terms are defined in FASB ASC Topic 718; and

(iv) An explanation of the amount of salary and bonus in proportion to total compensation.

(2) [Reserved]

(f) *Outstanding equity awards at fiscal year-end table.* (1) Provide the information specified in paragraph (f)(2) of this Item, concerning unexercised options; stock that has not vested; and equity incentive plan awards for each named executive officer outstanding as of the end of the registrant's last completed fiscal year in the following tabular format:

(2) The Table shall include:

(i) The name of the named executive officer (column (a));

(ii) On an award-by-award basis, the number of securities underlying unexercised options, including awards that have been transferred other than for value, that are exercisable and that are not reported in column (d) (column (b));

(iii) On an award-by-award basis, the number of securities underlying unexercised options, including awards that have been transferred other than for value, that are unexercisable and that are not reported in column (d) (column (c));

(iv) On an award-by-award basis, the total number of shares underlying unexercised options awarded under any equity incentive plan that have not been earned (column (d));

(v) For each instrument reported in columns (b), (c) and (d), as applicable, the exercise or base price (column (e));

OUTSTANDING EQUITY AWARDS AT FISCAL YEAR-END

	OPTION AWARDS					*STOCK AWARDS*			
Name (a)	*Number of securities underlying unexercised options (#) exercisable (b)*	*Number of securities underlying unexercised options (#) unexercisable (c)*	*Equity incentive plan awards: number of securities underlying unexercised unearned options (#) (d)*	*Option exercise price ($) (e)*	*Option expiration date (f)*	*Number of shares or units of stock that have not vested (#) (g)*	*Market value of shares or units of stock that have not vested ($) (h)*	*Equity incentive plan awards: number of unearned shares, units or other rights that have not vested (#) (i)*	*Equity incentive plan awards: market or payout value of unearned shares, units or other rights that have not vested (#) (j)*
PEO									
PFO									
A									
B									
C									

(vi) For each instrument reported in columns (b), (c) and (d), as applicable, the expiration date (column (f));

(vii) The total number of shares of stock that have not vested and that are not reported in column (i) (column (g));

(viii) The aggregate market value of shares of stock that have not vested and that are not reported in column (j) (column (h));

(ix) The total number of shares of stock, units or other rights awarded under any equity incentive plan that have not vested and that have not been earned, and, if applicable the number of shares underlying any such unit or right (column (i)); and

(x) The aggregate market or payout value of shares of stock, units or other rights awarded under any equity incentive plan that have not vested and that have not been earned (column (j))

(g) *Option exercises and stock vested table.* (1) Provide the information specified in paragraph (g)(2) of this Item, concerning each exercise of stock options, SARs and similar instruments, and each vesting of stock, including restricted stock, restricted stock units and similar instruments, during the last completed fiscal year for each of the named executive officers on an aggregated basis in the following tabular format:

OPTION EXERCISES AND STOCK VESTED

	OPTION AWARDS		*STOCK AWARDS*	
Name (a)	*Number of shares acquired on exercise (#) (b)*	*Value realized on exercise ($) (c)*	*Number of shares acquired on vesting (#) (d)*	*Value realized on vesting ($) (e)*
PEO				
PFO				
A				
B				
C				

(2) The Table shall include:

(i) The name of the executive officer (column (a));

(ii) The number of securities for which the options were exercised (column (b));

(iii) The aggregate dollar value realized upon exercise of options, or upon the transfer of an award for value (column (c));

(iv) The number of shares of stock that have vested (column (d)); and

(v) The aggregate dollar value realized upon vesting of stock, or upon the transfer of an award for value (column (e)).

(h) *Pension benefits.* (1) Provide the information specified in paragraph (h)(2) of this Item with respect to each plan that provides for payments or other benefits at, following, or in connection with retirement, in the following tabular format:

PENSION BENEFITS

Name *(a)*	*Plan name* *(b)*	*Number of years credited service (#)* *(c)*	*Present value of accumulated benefit ($)* *(d)*	*Payments during last fiscal year ($)* *(e)*
PEO				
PFO				
A				
B				
C				

(2) The Table shall include:

(i) The name of the executive officer (column (a));

(ii) The name of the plan (column (b));

(iii) The number of years of service credited to the named executive officer under the plan, computed as of the same pension plan measurement date used for financial statement reporting purposes with respect to the registrant's audited financial statements for the last completed fiscal year (column (c));

(iv) The actuarial present value of the named executive officer's accumulated benefit under the plan, computed as of the same pension plan measurement date used for financial statement reporting purposes with respect to the registrant's audited financial statements for the last completed fiscal year (column (d)); and

(v) The dollar amount of any payments and benefits paid to the named executive officer during the registrant's last completed fiscal year (column (e)).

(3) Provide a succinct narrative description of any material factors necessary to an understanding of each plan covered by the tabular disclosure required by this paragraph. While material factors will vary depending upon the facts, examples of such factors may include, in given cases, among other things:

(i) The material terms and conditions of payments and benefits available under the plan, including the plan's normal retirement payment and benefit formula and eligibility standards, and the effect of the form of benefit elected on the amount of annual benefits. For this purpose, normal retirement means retirement at the normal retirement age as defined in the plan, or if not so defined, the earliest time at which a participant may retire under the plan without any benefit reduction due to age;

(ii) If any named executive officer is currently eligible for early retirement under any plan, identify that named executive officer and the plan, and describe the plan's early retirement payment and benefit formula and eligibility standards. For this purpose, early retirement means retirement at the early retirement age as defined in the plan, or otherwise available to the executive under the plan;

(iii) The specific elements of compensation (e.g., salary, bonus, etc.) included in applying the payment and benefit formula, identifying each such element;

(iv) With respect to named executive officers' participation in multiple plans, the different purposes for each plan; and

(v) Registrant policies with regard to such matters as granting extra years of credited service.

(i) *Nonqualified defined contribution and other nonqualified deferred compensation plans.* (1) Provide the information specified in paragraph (i)(2) of this Item with respect to each defined contribution or other plan that provides for the deferral of compensation on a basis that is not tax-qualified in the following tabular format:

NONQUALIFIED DEFERRED COMPENSATION

Name (a)	*Executive contributions in last FY ($) (b)*	*Registrant contributions in last FY ($) (c)*	*Aggregate earnings in last FY ($) (d)*	*Aggregate withdrawals/ distributions ($) (e)*	*Aggregate balance at last FYE ($) (f)*
PEO					
PFO					
A					
B					
C					

(2) The Table shall include:

(i) The name of the executive officer (column (a));

(ii) The dollar amount of aggregate executive contributions during the registrant's last fiscal year (column (b));

(iii) The dollar amount of aggregate registrant contributions during the registrant's last fiscal year (column (c));

(iv) The dollar amount of aggregate interest or other earnings accrued during the registrant's last fiscal year (column (d));

(v) The aggregate dollar amount of all withdrawals by and distributions to the executive during the registrant's last fiscal year (column (e)); and

(vi) The dollar amount of total balance of the executive's account as of the end of the registrant's last fiscal year (column (f)).

(3) Provide a succinct narrative description of any material factors necessary to an understanding of each plan covered by tabular disclosure required by this paragraph. While material factors will vary depending upon the facts, examples of such factors may include, in given cases, among other things:

(i) The type(s) of compensation permitted to be deferred, and any limitations (by percentage of compensation or otherwise) on the extent to which deferral is permitted;

(ii) The measures for calculating interest or other plan earnings (including whether such measure(s) are selected by the executive or the registrant and the frequency and manner in which selections may be changed), quantifying interest rates and other earnings measures applicable during the registrant's last fiscal year; and

(iii) Material terms with respect to payouts, withdrawals and other distributions.

(j) *Potential payments upon termination or change-in-control.* Regarding each contract, agreement, plan or arrangement, whether written or unwritten, that provides for payment(s) to a named executive officer at, following, or in connection with any termination, including without limitation resignation, severance, retirement or a constructive termination of a named executive officer, or a change in control of the registrant or a change in the named executive officer's responsibilities, with respect to each named executive officer:

(1) Describe and explain the specific circumstances that would trigger payment(s) or the provision of other benefits, including perquisites and health care benefits;

(2) Describe and quantify the estimated payments and benefits that would be provided in each covered circumstance, whether they would or could be lump sum, or annual, disclosing the duration, and by whom they would be provided;

(3) Describe and explain how the appropriate payment and benefit levels are determined under the various circumstances that trigger payments or provision of benefits;

(4) Describe and explain any material conditions or obligations applicable to the receipt of payments or benefits, including but not limited to non-compete, non-solicitation, non-disparagement or confidentiality agreements, including the duration of such agreements and provisions regarding waiver of breach of such agreements; and

(5) Describe any other material factors regarding each such contract, agreement, plan or arrangement.

(k) *Compensation of directors.* (1) Provide the information specified in paragraph (k)(2) of this Item, concerning the compensation of the directors for the registrant's last completed fiscal year, in the following tabular format:

DIRECTOR COMPENSATION

Name (a)	*Fees earned or paid in cash ($) (b)*	*Stock awards ($) (c)*	*Option awards ($) (d)*	*Non-equity incentive plan compensation ($) (e)*	*Change in pension value and nonqualified deferred compensation earnings (f)*	*All other compensation ($) (g)*	*Total ($) (j)*
A							
B							
C							
D							
E							

(2) The Table shall include:

(i) The name of each director unless such director is also a named executive officer under paragraph (a) of this Item and his or her compensation for service as a director is fully reflected in the Summary Compensation Table pursuant to paragraph (c) of this Item and otherwise as required pursuant to paragraphs (d) through (j) of this Item (column (a));

(ii) The aggregate dollar amount of all fees earned or paid in cash for services as a director, including annual retainer fees, committee and/or chairmanship fees, and meeting fees (column (b));

(iii) For awards of stock, the aggregate grant date fair value computed in accordance with FASB ASC Topic 718 (column (c));

(iv) For awards of options, with or without tandem SARs (including awards that subsequently have been transferred), the aggregate grant date fair value computed in accordance with FASB ASC Topic 718 (column (d));

(v) The dollar value of all earnings for services performed during the fiscal year pursuant to non-equity incentive plans as defined in paragraph (a)(6)(iii) of this Item, and all earnings on any outstanding awards (column (e));

(vi) The sum of the amounts specified in paragraphs (k)(2)(vi)(A) and (B) of this Item (column (f)) as follows:

(A) The aggregate change in the actuarial present value of the director's accumulated benefit under all defined benefit and actuarial pension plans (including supplemental plans) from the pension plan measurement date used for financial statement reporting purposes with respect to the registrant's audited financial statements for the prior completed fiscal year to the pension plan measurement date used for financial statement reporting purposes with respect to the registrant's audited financial statements for the covered fiscal year; and

(B) Above-market or preferential earnings on compensation that is deferred on a basis that is not tax-qualified, including such earnings on nonqualified defined contribution plans;

(vii) All other compensation for the covered fiscal year that the registrant could not properly report in any other column of the Director Compensation Table (column (g)). Each compensation item that is not properly reportable in columns (b)-(f), regardless of the amount of the compensation item, must be included in column (g). Such compensation must include, but is not limited to:

(A) Perquisites and other personal benefits, or property, unless the aggregate amount of such compensation is less than $10,000;

(B) All "gross-ups" or other amounts reimbursed during the fiscal year for the payment of taxes;

(C) For any security of the registrant or its subsidiaries purchased from the registrant or its subsidiaries (through deferral of salary or bonus, or otherwise) at a discount from the market price of such security at the date of purchase, unless that discount is available generally, either to all security holders or to all salaried employees of the registrant, the compensation cost, if any, computed in accordance with FASB ASC Topic 718;

(D) The amount paid or accrued to any director pursuant to a plan or arrangement in connection with:

(*1*) The resignation, retirement or any other termination of such director; or

(*2*) A change in control of the registrant;

(E) Registrant contributions or other allocations to vested and unvested defined contribution plans;

(F) Consulting fees earned from, or paid or payable by the registrant and/or its subsidiaries (including joint ventures);

(G) The annual costs of payments and promises of payments pursuant to director legacy programs and similar charitable award programs;

(H) The dollar value of any insurance premiums paid by, or on behalf of, the registrant during the covered fiscal year with respect to life insurance for the benefit of a director; and

(I) The dollar value of any dividends or other earnings paid on stock or option awards, when those amounts were not factored into the grant date fair value required to be reported for the stock or option award in column (c) or (d); and

(3) *Narrative to director compensation table.* Provide a narrative description of any material factors necessary to an understanding of the director compensation disclosed in this Table. While material factors will vary depending upon the facts, examples of such factors may include, in given cases, among other things:

(i) A description of standard compensation arrangements (such as fees for retainer, committee service, service as chairman of the board or a committee, and meeting attendance); and

(ii) Whether any director has a different compensation arrangement, identifying that director and describing the terms of that arrangement.

§ 229.403 (Item 403) Security Ownership of Certain Beneficial Owners and Management

(a) *Security ownership of certain beneficial owners.* Furnish the following information, as of the most recent practicable date, substantially in the tabular form indicated, with respect to any person (including any "group" as that term is used in section 13(d)(3) of the Exchange Act) who is known to the registrant to be the beneficial owner of more than five percent of any class of the registrant's voting securities...

(1) Title of Class	*(2) Name and address of beneficial owner*	*(3) Amount and nature of beneficial ownership*	*(4) Percent of class*

(b) *Security ownership of management.* Furnish the following information, as of the most recent practicable date, in substantially the tabular form indicated, as to each class of equity securities of the registrant or any of its parents or subsidiaries, including directors' qualifying shares, beneficially owned by all directors and nominees, naming them, each of the named executive officers as defined in Item 402(a)(3) (§ 229.402(a)(3)), and directors and executive officers of the registrant as a group, without naming them. Show in column (3) the total number of shares beneficially owned and in column (4) the percent of the class so owned...

(1) Title of class	*(2) Name of beneficial owner*	*(3) Amount of nature of beneficial ownership*	*(4) Percent of class*

(c) *Changes in control.* Describe any arrangements, known to the registrant, including any pledge by any person of securities of the registrant or any of its parents, the operation of which may at a subsequent date result in a change in control of the registrant.

§ 229.404 (Item 404) Transactions with Related Persons, Promoters and Certain Control Persons

(a) *Transactions with related persons.* Describe any transaction, since the beginning of the registrant's last fiscal year, or any currently proposed transaction, in which the registrant was or is to be a participant and the amount involved exceeds $120,000, and in which any related person had or will have a direct or indirect material interest. Disclose the following information regarding the transaction:

(1) The name of the related person and the basis on which the person is a related person.

(2) The related person's interest in the transaction with the registrant, including the related person's position(s) or relationship(s) with, or ownership in, a firm, corporation, or other entity that is a party to, or has an interest in, the transaction.

(3) The approximate dollar value of the amount involved in the transaction.

(4) The approximate dollar value of the amount of the related person's interest in the transaction, which shall be computed without regard to the amount of profit or loss.

(5) In the case of indebtedness, disclosure of the amount involved in the transaction shall include the largest aggregate amount of principal outstanding during the period for which disclosure is provided, the amount thereof outstanding as of the latest practicable date, the amount of principal paid during the periods for which disclosure is provided, the amount of interest paid during the period for which disclosure is provided, and the rate or amount of interest payable on the indebtedness.

(6) Any other information regarding the transaction or the related person in the context of the transaction that is material to investors in light of the circumstances of the particular transaction.

Instructions to Item 404(a):

. . .

1. For the purposes of paragraph (a) of this Item, the term related person means:

a. Any person who was in any of the following categories at any time during the specified period for which disclosure under paragraph (a) of this Item is required:

i. Any director or executive officer of the registrant;

ii. Any nominee for director, when the information called for by paragraph (a) of this Item is being presented in a proxy or information statement relating to the election of that nominee for director; or

iii. Any immediate family member of a director or executive officer of the registrant, or of any nominee for director when the information called for by paragraph (a) of this Item is being presented in a proxy or information statement relating to the election of that nominee for director, which means any child, stepchild, parent, stepparent, spouse, sibling, mother-in-law, father-in-law, son-in-law, daughter-in-law, brother-in-law, or sister-in-law of such director, executive officer or nominee for director, and any person (other than a tenant or employee) sharing the household of such director, executive officer or nominee for director; and

b. Any person who was in any of the following categories when a transaction in which such person had a direct or indirect material interest occurred or existed:

i. A security holder covered by Item 403(a) (§ 229.403(a)); or

ii. Any immediate family member of any such security holder, which means any child, stepchild, parent, stepparent, spouse, sibling, mother-in-law, father-in-law, son-in-law, daughter-in-law, brother-in-law, or sister-in-law of such security holder, and any person (other than a tenant or employee) sharing the household of such security holder.

2. For purposes of paragraph (a) of this Item, a transaction includes, but is not limited to, any financial transaction, arrangement or relationship (including any indebtedness or guarantee of indebtedness) or any series of similar transactions, arrangements or relationships.

3. The amount involved in the transaction shall be computed by determining the dollar value of the amount involved in the transaction in question, which shall include:

a. In the case of any lease or other transaction providing for periodic payments or installments, the aggregate amount of all periodic payments or installments due on or after the beginning of the registrant's last fiscal year, including any required or optional payments due during or at the conclusion of the lease or other transaction providing for periodic payments or installments; and

b. In the case of indebtedness, the largest aggregate amount of all indebtedness outstanding at any time since the beginning of the registrant's last fiscal year and all amounts of interest payable on it during the last fiscal year.

4. In the case of a transaction involving indebtedness:

a. The following items of indebtedness may be excluded from the calculation of the amount of indebtedness and need not be disclosed: Amounts due from the related person for purchases of goods and services subject to usual trade terms, for ordinary business travel and expense payments and for other transactions in the ordinary course of business;

b. Disclosure need not be provided of any indebtedness transaction for the related persons specified in Instruction 1.b. to paragraph (a) of this Item; and

c. If the lender is a bank, savings and loan association, or broker-dealer extending credit under Federal Reserve Regulation T (12 CFR part 220) and the loans are not disclosed as nonaccrual, past due, restructured or potential problems (see Item III.C.1. and 2. of Industry Guide 3, Statistical Disclosure by Bank Holding Companies (17 CFR 229.802(c))), disclosure under paragraph (a) of this Item may consist of a statement, if such is the case, that the loans to such persons:

i. Were made in the ordinary course of business;

ii. Were made on substantially the same terms, including interest rates and collateral, as those prevailing at the time for comparable loans with persons not related to the lender; and

iii. Did not involve more than the normal risk of collectibility or present other unfavorable features.

5.a. Disclosure of an employment relationship or transaction involving an executive officer and any related compensation solely resulting from that employment relationship or transaction need not be provided pursuant to paragraph (a) of this Item if:

i. The compensation arising from the relationship or transaction is reported pursuant to Item 402 (§ 229.402); or

ii. The executive officer is not an immediate family member (as specified in Instruction 1 to paragraph (a) of this Item) and such compensation would have been reported under Item 402 (§ 229.402) as compensation earned for services to the registrant if the executive officer was a named executive officer as that term is defined in Item 402(a)(3) (§ 229.402(a)(3)), and such compensation had been approved, or recommended to the board of directors of the registrant for approval, by the compensation committee of the board of directors (or group of independent directors performing a similar function) of the registrant.

b. Disclosure of compensation to a director need not be provided pursuant to paragraph (a) of this Item if the compensation is reported pursuant to Item 402(k) (§ 229.402(k)).

6. A person who has a position or relationship with a firm, corporation, or other entity that engages in a transaction with the registrant shall not be deemed to have an indirect material interest within the meaning of paragraph (a) of this Item where:

a. The interest arises only:

i. From such person's position as a director of another corporation or organization that is a party to the transaction; or

ii. From the direct or indirect ownership by such person and all other persons specified in Instruction 1 to paragraph (a) of this Item, in the aggregate, of less than a ten percent equity interest in another person (other than a partnership) which is a party to the transaction; or

iii. From both such position and ownership; or

b. The interest arises only from such person's position as a limited partner in a partnership in which the person and all other persons specified in Instruction 1 to paragraph (a) of this Item, have an interest of less than ten percent, and the person is not a general partner of and does not hold another position in the partnership.

7. Disclosure need not be provided pursuant to paragraph (a) of this Item if:

a. The transaction is one where the rates or charges involved in the transaction are determined by competitive bids, or the transaction involves the rendering of services as a common or contract carrier, or public utility, at rates or charges fixed in conformity with law or governmental authority;

b. The transaction involves services as a bank depositary of funds, transfer agent, registrar, trustee under a trust indenture, or similar services; or

c. The interest of the related person arises solely from the ownership of a class of equity securities of the registrant and all holders of that class of equity securities of the registrant received the same benefit on a pro rata basis.

(b) *Review, approval or ratification of transactions with related persons.* (1) Describe the registrant's policies and procedures for the review, approval, or ratification of any transaction required to be reported under paragraph (a) of this Item. While the material features of such policies and procedures will vary depending on the particular circumstances, examples of such features may include, in given cases, among other things:

(i) The types of transactions that are covered by such policies and procedures;

(ii) The standards to be applied pursuant to such policies and procedures;

(iii) The persons or groups of persons on the board of directors or otherwise who are responsible for applying such policies and procedures; and

(iv) A statement of whether such policies and procedures are in writing and, if not, how such policies and procedures are evidenced.

(2) Identify any transaction required to be reported under paragraph (a) of this Item since the beginning of the registrant's last fiscal year where such policies and procedures did not require review, approval or ratification or where such policies and procedures were not followed.

§ 229.405 (Item 405) Compliance with Section 16(a) of the Exchange Act

Every registrant having a class of equity securities registered pursuant to section 12 of the Exchange Act (15 U.S.C. 78*l*) and every closed-end investment company registered under the Investment Company Act of 1940 (15 U.S.C. 80a-1 *et seq.*) shall:

(a) Based solely upon a review of Forms 3 and 4 (17 CFR 249.103 and 249.104) and amendments thereto furnished to the registrant under 17 CFR 240.16a-3(e) during its most recent fiscal year and Forms 5 and amendments thereto (17 CFR 249.105) furnished to the registrant with respect to its most recent fiscal year, and any written representation referred to in paragraph (b)(1) of this section.

(1) Under the caption "Section 16(a) Beneficial Ownership Reporting Compliance," identify each person who, at any time during the fiscal year, was a director, officer, beneficial owner of more than ten percent of any class of equity securities of the registrant registered pursuant to section 12 of the Exchange Act, or any other person subject to section 16 of the Exchange Act with respect to the registrant because of the requirements of section 30 of the Investment Company Act ("reporting person") that failed to file on a timely basis, as disclosed in the above Forms, reports required by section 16(a) of the Exchange Act during the most recent fiscal year or prior fiscal years.

(2) For each such person, set forth the number of late reports, the number of transactions that were not reported on a timely basis, and any known failure to file a required Form. A known failure to file would include, but not be limited to, a failure to file a Form 3, which is required of all reporting persons, and a failure to file a Form 5 in the absence of the written representation referred to in paragraph (b)(1) of this section, unless the registrant otherwise knows that no Form 5 is required.

§ 229.406 (Item 406) Code of Ethics

(a) Disclose whether the registrant has adopted a code of ethics that applies to the registrant's principal executive officer, principal financial officer, principal accounting officer or controller, or persons performing similar functions. If the registrant has not adopted such a code of ethics, explain why it has not done so.

(b) For purposes of this Item 406, the term *code of ethics* means written standards that are reasonably designed to deter wrongdoing and to promote:

(1) Honest and ethical conduct, including the ethical handling of actual or apparent conflicts of interest between personal and professional relationships;

(2) Full, fair, accurate, timely, and understandable disclosure in reports and documents that a registrant files with, or submits to, the Commission and in other public communications made by the registrant;

(3) Compliance with applicable governmental laws, rules and regulations;

(4) The prompt internal reporting of violations of the code to an appropriate person or persons identified in the code; and

(5) Accountability for adherence to the code.

(c) The registrant must:

(1) File with the Commission a copy of its code of ethics that applies to the registrant's principal executive officer, principal financial officer, principal accounting officer or controller, or persons performing similar functions, as an exhibit to its annual report;

(2) Post the text of such code of ethics on its Internet website and disclose, in its annual report, its Internet address and the fact that it has posted such code of ethics on its Internet Web site; or

(3) Undertake in its annual report filed with the Commission to provide to any person without charge, upon request, a copy of such code of ethics and explain the manner in which such request may be made.

(d) If the registrant intends to satisfy the disclosure requirement under Item 10 of Form 8-K regarding an amendment to, or a waiver from, a provision of its code of ethics that applies to the registrant's principal executive officer, principal financial officer, principal accounting officer or controller, or persons performing similar functions and that relates to any element of the code of ethics definition enumerated in paragraph (b) of this Item by posting such information on its Internet website, disclose the registrant's Internet address and such intention.

§ 229.407 (Item 407) Corporate Governance

(a) *Director independence.* Identify each director and, when the disclosure called for by this paragraph is being presented in a proxy or information statement relating to the election of directors, each nominee for director, that is independent under the independence standards applicable to the registrant under paragraph (a)(1) of this Item. In addition, if such independence standards contain independence requirements for committees of the board of directors, identify each director that is a member of the compensation, nominating or audit committee that is not independent under such committee independence standards. If the registrant does not have a separately designated audit, nominating or compensation committee or committee performing similar functions, the registrant must provide the disclosure of directors that are not independent with respect to all members of the board of directors applying such committee independence standards.

(1) In determining whether or not the director or nominee for director is independent for the purposes of paragraph (a) of this Item, the registrant shall use the applicable definition of independence, as follows:

(i) If the registrant is a listed issuer whose securities are listed on a national securities exchange or in an inter-dealer quotation system which has requirements that a majority of the board of directors be independent, the registrant's definition of independence that it uses for determining if a majority of the board of directors is independent in compliance with the listing standards applicable to the registrant. When determining whether the members of a committee of the board of directors are independent, the registrant's definition of independence that it uses for determining if the members of that specific committee are independent in compliance with the independence standards applicable for the members of the specific committee in the listing standards of the national securities exchange or inter-dealer quotation system that the registrant uses for determining if a majority of the board of directors are independent. If the registrant does not have independence standards for a committee, the independence standards for that specific committee in the listing standards of the national securities exchange or inter-dealer quotation system that the registrant uses for determining if a majority of the board of directors are independent.

(ii) If the registrant is not a listed issuer, a definition of independence of a national securities exchange or of an inter-dealer quotation system which has requirements that a majority of the board of directors be independent, and state which definition is used. Whatever such definition the registrant chooses, it must use the same definition with respect to all directors and nominees for director. When determining whether the members of a specific committee of the board of directors are independent, if the national securities exchange or national securities association whose standards are used has independence standards for the members of a specific committee, use those committee specific standards.

(iii) If the information called for by paragraph (a) of this Item is being presented in a registration statement on Form S-1 (§ 239.11 of this chapter) under the Securities Act or on a Form 10 (§ 249.210 of this chapter) under the Exchange Act where the registrant has applied for listing with a national securities exchange or in an inter-dealer quotation system that has requirements that a majority of the board of directors be independent, the definition of independence that the registrant uses for determining if a majority of the board of directors is independent, and the definition of independence that the registrant uses for determining if members of the specific committee of the board of directors are independent, that is in compliance with the independence listing standards of the national securities exchange or inter-dealer quotation system on which it has applied for listing, or if the registrant has not adopted such definitions, the independence standards for determining if the majority of the board of directors is independent and if members of the committee of the board of directors are independent of that national securities exchange or inter-dealer quotation system.

(2) If the registrant uses its own definitions for determining whether its directors and nominees for director, and members of specific committees of the board of directors, are independent, disclose whether these definitions are available to security holders on the registrant's Web site. If so, provide the registrant's Web site address. If not, include a copy of these policies in an appendix to the registrant's proxy statement or information statement that is provided to security holders at least once every three fiscal years or if the policies have been materially amended since the beginning of the registrant's last fiscal year. If a current copy of the policies is not available to security holders on the registrant's Web site, and is not included as an appendix to the registrant's proxy statement or information statement, identify the most recent fiscal year in which the policies were so included in satisfaction of this requirement.

(3) For each director and nominee for director that is identified as independent, describe, by specific category or type, any transactions, relationships or arrangements not disclosed pursuant to Item 404(a) (§ 229.404(a)), or for investment companies, Item 22(b) of Schedule 14A (§ 240.14a-101 of this chapter), that were considered by the board of directors under the applicable independence definitions in determining that the director is independent.

Instructions to Item 407(a):

1. If the registrant is a listed issuer whose securities are listed on a national securities exchange or in an inter-dealer quotation system which has requirements that a majority of the board of directors be independent, and also has exemptions to those requirements (for independence of a majority of the board of directors or committee member independence) upon which the registrant relied, disclose the exemption relied upon and explain the basis for the registrant's conclusion that such exemption is applicable. The same disclosure should be provided if the registrant is not a listed issuer and the national securities exchange or inter-dealer quotation system selected by the registrant has exemptions that are applicable to the registrant. Any national securities exchange or inter-dealer quotation system which has requirements that at least 50 percent of the members of a small business issuer's board of directors must be independent shall be considered a national securities exchange or inter-dealer quotation system which has requirements that a majority of the

board of directors be independent for the purposes of the disclosure required by paragraph (a) of this Item.

2. Registrants shall provide the disclosure required by paragraph (a) of this Item for any person who served as a director during any part of the last completed fiscal year, except that no information called for by paragraph (a) of this Item need be given in a registration statement filed at a time when the registrant is not subject to the reporting requirements of section 13(a) or 15(d) of the Exchange Act (15 U.S.C. 78m(a) or 78*o*(d)) respecting any director who is no longer a director at the time of effectiveness of the registration statement.

3. The description of the specific categories or types of transactions, relationships or arrangements required by paragraph (a)(3) of this Item must be provided in such detail as is necessary to fully describe the nature of the transactions, relationships or arrangements.

(b) *Board meetings and committees; annual meeting attendance.* (1) State the total number of meetings of the board of directors (including regularly scheduled and special meetings) which were held during the last full fiscal year. Name each incumbent director who during the last full fiscal year attended fewer than 75 percent of the aggregate of:

(i) The total number of meetings of the board of directors (held during the period for which he has been a director); and

(ii) The total number of meetings held by all committees of the board on which he served (during the periods that he served).

(2) Describe the registrant's policy, if any, with regard to board members' attendance at annual meetings of security holders and state the number of board members who attended the prior year's annual meeting.

(3) State whether or not the registrant has standing audit, nominating and compensation committees of the board of directors, or committees performing similar functions. If the registrant has such committees, however designated, identify each committee member, state the number of committee meetings held by each such committee during the last fiscal year and describe briefly the functions performed by each such committee. Such disclosure need not be provided to the extent it is duplicative of disclosure provided in accordance with paragraph (c), (d) or (e) of this Item.

(c) *Nominating committee.* (1) If the registrant does not have a standing nominating committee or committee performing similar functions, state the basis for the view of the board of directors that it is appropriate for the registrant not to have such a committee and identify each director who participates in the consideration of director nominees.

(2) Provide the following information regarding the registrant's director nomination process:

(i) State whether or not the nominating committee has a charter. If the nominating committee has a charter, provide the disclosure required by Instruction 2 to this Item regarding the nominating committee charter;

(ii) If the nominating committee has a policy with regard to the consideration of any director candidates recommended by security holders, provide a description of the material elements of that policy, which shall include, but need not be limited to, a statement as to whether the committee will consider director candidates recommended by security holders;

(iii) If the nominating committee does not have a policy with regard to the consideration of any director candidates recommended by security holders, state that fact and state the basis for the view of the board of directors that it is appropriate for the registrant not to have such a policy;

(iv) If the nominating committee will consider candidates recommended by security holders, describe the procedures to be followed by security holders in submitting such recommendations;

(v) Describe any specific minimum qualifications that the nominating committee believes must be met by a nominating committee-recommended nominee for a position on the registrant's board of directors, and describe any specific qualities or skills that the nominating committee believes are necessary for one or more of the registrant's directors to possess;

(vi) Describe the nominating committee's process for identifying and evaluating nominees for director, including nominees recommended by security holders, and any differences in the manner in which the nominating committee evaluates nominees for director based on whether the nominee is recommended by a security holder, and whether, and if so how, the nominating committee (or the board) considers diversity in identifying nominees for director. If the nominating committee (or the board) has a policy with regard to the consideration of diversity in identifying director nominees, describe how this policy is implemented, as well as how the nominating committee (or the board) assesses the effectiveness of its policy;

(vii) With regard to each nominee approved by the nominating committee for inclusion on the registrant's proxy card (other than nominees who are executive officers or who are directors standing for re-election), state which one or more of the following categories of persons or entities recommended that nominee: Security holder, non-management director, chief executive officer, other executive officer, third-party search firm, or other specified source. With regard to each such nominee approved by a nominating committee of an investment company, state which one or more of the following additional categories of persons or entities recommended that nominee: Security holder, director, chief executive officer, other executive officer, or employee of the investment company's investment adviser, principal underwriter, or any affiliated person of the investment adviser or principal underwriter;

(viii) If the registrant pays a fee to any third party or parties to identify or evaluate or assist in identifying or evaluating potential nominees, disclose the function performed by each such third party; and

(ix) If the registrant's nominating committee received, by a date not later than the 120th calendar day before the date of the registrant's proxy statement released to security holders in connection with the previous year's annual meeting, a recommended nominee from a security holder that beneficially owned more than 5% of the registrant's voting common stock for at least one year as of the date the recommendation was made, or from a group of security holders that beneficially owned, in the aggregate, more than 5% of the registrant's voting common stock, with each of the securities used to calculate that ownership held for at least one year as of the date the recommendation was made, identify the candidate and the security holder or security holder group that recommended the candidate and disclose whether the nominating committee chose to nominate the candidate, *provided, however,* that no such identification or disclosure is required without the written consent of both the security holder or security holder group and the candidate to be so identified.

Instructions to Item 407(c)(2)(ix):

. . .

2. For purposes of the registrant's obligation to provide the disclosure specified in paragraph (c)(2)(ix) of this Item, where the date of the annual meeting has been changed by more than 30 days from the date of the previous year's meeting, the obligation under that Item will arise where the registrant receives the security holder recommendation a reasonable time before the registrant begins to print and mail its proxy materials.

3. For purposes of paragraph (c)(2)(ix) of this Item, the percentage of securities held by a recommending security holder, as well as the holding period of those securities, may be determined by the registrant if the security holder is the registered holder of the securities. If the security holder is not the registered owner of the securities, he or she can submit one of the following to the registrant to evidence the required ownership percentage and holding period:

a. A written statement from the "record" holder of the securities (usually a broker or bank) verifying that, at the time the security holder made the recommendation, he or she had held the required securities for at least one year; or

b. If the security holder has filed a Schedule 13D (§ 240.13d-101 of this chapter), Schedule 13G (§ 240.13d-102 of this chapter), Form 3

(§ 249.103 of this chapter), Form 4 (§ 249.104 of this chapter), and/or Form 5 (§ 249.105 of this chapter), or amendments to those documents or updated forms, reflecting ownership of the securities as of or before the date of the recommendation, a copy of the schedule and/or form, and any subsequent amendments reporting a change in ownership level, as well as a written statement that the security holder continuously held the securities for the one-year period as of the date of the recommendation.

4. For purposes of the registrant's obligation to provide the disclosure specified in paragraph (c)(2)(ix) of this Item, the security holder or group must have provided to the registrant, at the time of the recommendation, the written consent of all parties to be identified and, where the security holder or group members are not registered holders, proof that the security holder or group satisfied the required ownership percentage and holding period as of the date of the recommendation.

(3) Describe any material changes to the procedures by which security holders may recommend nominees to the registrant's board of directors, where those changes were implemented after the registrant last provided disclosure in response to the requirements of paragraph (c)(2)(iv) of this Item, or paragraph (c)(3) of this Item.

(d) *Audit committee.* (1) State whether or not the audit committee has a charter. If the audit committee has a charter, provide the disclosure required by Instruction 2 to this Item regarding the audit committee charter.

(2) If a listed issuer's board of directors determines, in accordance with the listing standards applicable to the issuer, to appoint a director to the audit committee who is not independent (apart from the requirements in § 240.10A-3 of this chapter), including as a result of exceptional or limited or similar circumstances, disclose the nature of the relationship that makes that individual not independent and the reasons for the board of directors' determination.

(3)(i) The audit committee must state whether:

(A) The audit committee has reviewed and discussed the audited financial statements with management;

(B) The audit committee has discussed with the independent auditors the matters required to be discussed by the statement on Auditing Standards No. 61, as amended (AICPA, *Professional Standards*, Vol. 1. AU section 380),[1] as adopted by the Public Company Accounting Oversight Board in Rule 3200T;

(C) The audit committee has received the written disclosures and the letter from the independent accountant required by applicable requirements of the Public Company Accounting Oversight Board regarding the independent accountant's communications with the audit committee concerning independence, and has discussed with the independent accountant the independent accountant's independence; and

(D) Based on the review and discussions referred to in paragraphs (d)(3)(i)(A) through (d)(3)(i)(C) of this Item, the audit committee recommended to the board of directors that the audited financial statements be included in the company's annual report on Form 10-K (17 CFR 249.310) (or, for closed-end investment companies registered under the Investment Company Act of 1940 (15 U.S.C. 80a-1 *et seq.*), the annual report to shareholders required by section 30(e) of the Investment Company Act of 1940 (15 U.S.C. 80a-29(e)) and Rule 30d-1 (17 CFR 270.30d-1) thereunder) for the last fiscal year for filing with the Commission.

(ii) The name of each member of the company's audit committee (or, in the absence of an audit committee, the board committee performing equivalent functions or the entire board of directors) must appear below the disclosure required by paragraph (d)(3)(i) of this Item.

(4)(i) If the registrant meets the following requirements, provide the disclosure in paragraph (d)(4)(ii) of this Item:

(A) The registrant is a listed issuer, as defined in § 240.10A-3 of this chapter;

(B) The registrant is filing an annual report on Form 10-K (§ 249.310 of this chapter) or a proxy statement or information statement pursuant to the Exchange Act (15 U.S.C. 78a *et seq.*) if action is to be taken with respect to the election of directors; and

(C) The registrant is neither:

(*1*) A subsidiary of another listed issuer that is relying on the exemption in § 240.10A-3(c)(2) of this chapter; nor

(*2*) Relying on any of the exemptions in § 240.10A-3(c)(4) through (c)(7) of this chapter.

(ii)(A) State whether or not the registrant has a separately-designated standing audit committee established in accordance with section 3(a)(58)(A) of the Exchange Act (15 U.S.C. 78c(a)(58)(A)), or a committee performing similar functions. If the registrant has such a committee, however designated, identify each committee member. If the entire board of directors is acting as the registrant's audit committee as specified in section 3(a)(58)(B) of the Exchange Act (15 U.S. C. 78c(a)(58)(B)), so state.

(B) If applicable, provide the disclosure required by § 240.10A-3(d) of this chapter regarding an exemption from the listing standards for audit committees.

(5) *Audit committee financial expert.* (i)(A) Disclose that the registrant's board of directors has determined that the registrant either:

(*1*) Has at least one audit committee financial expert serving on its audit committee; or

(*2*) Does not have an audit committee financial expert serving on its audit committee.

(B) If the registrant provides the disclosure required by paragraph (d)(5)(i)(A)(*1*) of this Item, it must disclose the name of the audit committee financial expert and whether that person is independent, as *independence* for audit committee members is defined in the listing standards applicable to the listed issuer.

(C) If the registrant provides the disclosure required by paragraph (d)(5)(i)(A)(*2*) of this Item, it must explain why it does not have an audit committee financial expert.

(ii) For purposes of this Item, an *audit committee financial expert* means a person who has the following attributes:

(A) An understanding of generally accepted accounting principles and financial statements;

(B) The ability to assess the general application of such principles in connection with the accounting for estimates, accruals and reserves;

(C) Experience preparing, auditing, analyzing or evaluating financial statements that present a breadth and level of complexity of accounting issues that are generally comparable to the breadth and complexity of issues that can reasonably be expected to be raised by the registrant's financial statements, or experience actively supervising one or more persons engaged in such activities;

(D) An understanding of internal control over financial reporting; and

(E) An understanding of audit committee functions.

(iii) A person shall have acquired such attributes through:

(A) Education and experience as a principal financial officer, principal accounting officer, controller, public accountant or auditor or experience in one or more positions that involve the performance of similar functions;

(B) Experience actively supervising a principal financial officer, principal accounting officer, controller, public accountant, auditor or person performing similar functions;

(C) Experience overseeing or assessing the performance of companies or public accountants with respect to the preparation, auditing or evaluation of financial statements; or

(D) Other relevant experience.

(iv) *Safe harbor.* (A) A person who is determined to be an audit committee financial expert will not be deemed an *expert* for any purpose, including without limitation for purposes of section 11 of the Securities Act (15 U.S.C. 77k), as a result of being designated or identified as an audit committee financial expert pursuant to this Item 407.

(B) The designation or identification of a person as an audit committee financial expert pursuant to this Item 407 does not impose on such person any duties, obligations or liability that are greater than the duties, obligations and liability imposed on such person as a member of the audit committee and board of directors in the absence of such designation or identification.

(C) The designation or identification of a person as an audit committee financial expert pursuant to this Item does not affect the duties, obligations or liability of any other member of the audit committee or board of directors.

Instructions to Item 407(d)(5):

...

2. If a person qualifies as an audit committee financial expert by means of having held a position described in paragraph (d)(5)(iii)(D) of this Item, the registrant shall provide a brief listing of that person's relevant experience. Such disclosure may be made by reference to disclosures required under Item 401(e) (§ 229.401(e)).

3. In the case of a foreign private issuer with a two-tier board of directors, for purposes of paragraph (d)(5) of this Item, the term*board of directors* means the supervisory or non-management board. In the case of a foreign private issuer meeting the requirements of § 240.10A-3(c)(3) of this chapter, for purposes of paragraph (d)(5) of this Item, the term *board of directors* means the issuer's board of auditors (or similar body) or statutory auditors, as applicable. Also, in the case of a foreign private issuer, the term *generally accepted accounting principles* in paragraph (d)(5)(ii)(A) of this Item means the body of generally accepted accounting principles used by that issuer in its primary financial statements filed with the Commission.

(e) *Compensation committee.* (1) If the registrant does not have a standing compensation committee or committee performing similar functions, state the basis for the view of the board of directors that it is appropriate for the registrant not to have such a committee and identify each director who participates in the consideration of executive officer and director compensation.

(2) State whether or not the compensation committee has a charter. If the compensation committee has a charter, provide the disclosure required by Instruction 2 to this Item regarding the compensation committee charter.

(3) Provide a narrative description of the registrant's processes and procedures for the consideration and determination of executive and director compensation, including:

(i)(A) The scope of authority of the compensation committee (or persons performing the equivalent functions); and

(B) The extent to which the compensation committee (or persons performing the equivalent functions) may delegate any authority described in paragraph (e)(3)(i)(A) of this Item to other persons, specifying what authority may be so delegated and to whom;

(ii) Any role of executive officers in determining or recommending the amount or form of executive and director compensation; and

(iii) Any role of compensation consultants in determining or recommending the amount or form of executive and director compensation (other than any role *limited* to consulting on any broad-based plan that does not discriminate in scope, terms, or operation, in favor of executive officers or directors of the registrant, and that is available generally to all salaried employees; or providing information that either is not customized for a particular registrant or that is customized based on parameters that are not developed by the compensation consultant, and about which the compensation consultant does not provide advice) during the registrant's last completed fiscal year, identifying such consultants, stating whether such consultants were engaged directly by the compensation committee (or persons performing the equivalent functions) or any other person, describing the nature and scope of their assignment, and the material elements of the instructions or directions given to the consultants with respect to the performance of their duties under the engagement.

(4) Under the caption "Compensation Committee Interlocks and Insider Participation":

(i) Identify each person who served as a member of the compensation committee of the registrant's board of directors (or board committee performing equivalent functions) during the last completed fiscal year, indicating each committee member who:

(A) Was, during the fiscal year, an officer or employee of the registrant;

(B) Was formerly an officer of the registrant; or

(C) Had any relationship requiring disclosure by the registrant under any paragraph of Item 404 (§ 229.404). In this event, the disclosure required by Item 404 (§ 229.404) shall accompany such identification.

(ii) If the registrant has no compensation committee (or other board committee performing equivalent functions), the registrant shall identify each officer and employee of the registrant, and any former officer of the registrant, who, during the last completed fiscal year, participated in deliberations of the registrant's board of directors concerning executive officer compensation.

(iii) Describe any of the following relationships that existed during the last completed fiscal year:

(A) An executive officer of the registrant served as a member of the compensation committee (or other board committee performing equivalent functions or, in the absence of any such committee, the entire board of directors) of another entity, one of whose executive officers served on the compensation committee (or other board committee performing equivalent functions or, in the absence of any such committee, the entire board of directors) of the registrant;

(B) An executive officer of the registrant served as a director of another entity, one of whose executive officers served on the compensation committee (or other board committee performing equivalent functions or, in the absence of any such committee, the entire board of directors) of the registrant; and

(C) An executive officer of the registrant served as a member of the compensation committee (or other board committee performing equivalent functions or, in the absence of any such committee, the entire board of directors) of another entity, one of whose executive officers served as a director of the registrant.

(iv) Disclosure required under paragraph (e)(4)(iii) of this Item regarding a compensation committee member or other director of the registrant who also served as an executive officer of another entity shall be accompanied by the disclosure called for by Item 404 with respect to that person

(5) Under the caption "Compensation Committee Report":

(i) The compensation committee (or other board committee performing equivalent functions or, in the absence of any such committee, the entire board of directors) must state whether:

(A) The compensation committee has reviewed and discussed the Compensation Discussion and Analysis required by Item 402(b) (§ 229.402(b)) with management; and

(B) Based on the review and discussions referred to in paragraph (e)(5)(i)(A) of this Item, the compensation committee recommended to the board of directors that the Compensation Discussion and Analysis be included in the registrant's annual report on Form 10-K (§ 249.310 of this chapter), proxy statement on Schedule 14A (§ 240.14a-101 of this chapter) or information statement on Schedule 14C (§ 240.14c-101 of this chapter).

(ii) The name of each member of the registrant's compensation committee (or other board committee performing equivalent functions or, in the absence of any such committee, the entire board of directors) must appear below the disclosure required by paragraph (e)(5)(i) of this Item.

(f) *Shareholder communications.* (1) State whether or not the registrant's board of directors provides a process for security holders to send communications to the board of directors and, if the registrant does not have such a process for security holders to send communications to the board of directors, state the basis for the view of the board of directors that it is appropriate for the registrant not to have such a process.

(2) If the registrant has a process for security holders to send communications to the board of directors:

(i) Describe the manner in which security holders can send communications to the board and, if applicable, to specified individual directors; and

(ii) If all security holder communications are not sent directly to board members, describe the registrant's process for determining which communications will be relayed to board members.

Subpart 229.1000—Mergers and Acquisitions (Regulation M-A)

§ 229.1000 (Item 1000) Definitions

The following definitions apply . . .

(f) *Subject company* means the company or entity whose securities are sought to be acquired in the transaction (e.g., the target), or that is otherwise the subject of the transaction;

(g) *Subject securities* means the securities or class of securities that are sought to be acquired in the transaction or that are otherwise the subject of the transaction; and

(h) *Third-party tender offer* means a tender offer that is not an issuer tender offer.

§ 229.1001 (Item 1001) Summary Term Sheet

Summary term sheet. Provide security holders with a summary term sheet that is written in plain English. The summary term sheet must briefly describe in bullet point format the most material terms of the proposed transaction . . .

§ 229.1002 (Item 1002) Subject Company Information

(a) *Name and address.* State the name of the subject company (or the issuer in the case of an issuer tender offer), and the address and telephone number of its principal executive offices.

(b) *Securities.* State the exact title and number of shares outstanding of the subject class of equity securities as of the most recent practicable date. This may be based upon information in the most recently available filing with the Commission by the subject company unless the filing person has more current information.

(c) *Trading market and price.* Identify the principal market in which the subject securities are traded and state the high and low sales prices for the subject securities in the principal market (or, if there is no principal market, the range of high and low bid quotations and the source of the quotations) for each quarter during the past two years. If there is no established trading market for the securities (except for limited or sporadic quotations), so state.

(d) *Dividends.* State the frequency and amount of any dividends paid during the past two years with respect to the subject securities. Briefly describe any restriction on the subject company's current or future ability to pay dividends. If the filing person is not the subject company, furnish this information to the extent known after making reasonable inquiry.

(e) *Prior public offerings.* If the filing person has made an underwritten public offering of the subject securities for cash during the past three years that was registered under the Securities Act of 1933 or exempt from registration under Regulation A (§ 230.251 through § 230.263 of this chapter), state the date of the offering, the amount of securities offered, the offering price per share (adjusted for stock splits, stock dividends, etc. as appropriate) and the aggregate proceeds received by the filing person.

(f) *Prior stock purchases.* If the filing person purchased any subject securities during the past two years, state the amount of the securities purchased, the range of prices paid and the average purchase price for each quarter during that period. Affiliates need not give information for purchases made before becoming an affiliate

§ 229.1003 (Item 1003) Identity and Background of Filing Person

(a) *Name and address.* State the name, business address and business telephone number of each filing person. Also state the name and address of each person specified in Instruction C to the schedule (except for Schedule 14D-9 (§ 240.14d-101 of this chapter)). If the filing person is an affiliate of the subject company, state the nature of the affiliation. If the filing person is the subject company, so state.

(b) *Business and background of entities.* If any filing person (other than the subject company) or any person specified in Instruction C to the schedule is not a natural person, state the person's principal business, state or other place of organization, and the information required by paragraphs (c)(3) and (c)(4) of this section for each person.

(c) *Business and background of natural persons.* If any filing person or any person specified in Instruction C to the schedule is a natural person, provide the following information for each person:

(1) Current principal occupation or employment and the name, principal business and address of any corporation or other organization in which the employment or occupation is conducted;

(2) Material occupations, positions, offices or employment during the past five years, giving the starting and ending dates of each and the name, principal business and address of any corporation or other

organization in which the occupation, position, office or employment was carried on;

(3) A statement whether or not the person was convicted in a criminal proceeding during the past five years (excluding traffic violations or similar misdemeanors). If the person was convicted, describe the criminal proceeding, including the dates, nature of conviction, name and location of court, and penalty imposed or other disposition of the case;

(4) A statement whether or not the person was a party to any judicial or administrative proceeding during the past five years (except for matters that were dismissed without sanction or settlement) that resulted in a judgment, decree or final order enjoining the person from future violations of, or prohibiting activities subject to, federal or state securities laws, or a finding of any violation of federal or state securities laws. Describe the proceeding, including a summary of the terms of the judgment, decree or final order; and

(5) Country of citizenship.

(d) *Tender offer.* Identify the tender offer and the class of securities to which the offer relates, the name of the offeror and its address (which may be based on the offeror's Schedule TO (§ 240.14d-100 of this chapter) filed with the Commission).

§ 229.1004 (Item 1004) Terms of the Transaction

(a) *Material terms.* State the material terms of the transaction.

(1) *Tender offers.* In the case of a tender offer, the information must include:

(i) The total number and class of securities sought in the offer;

(ii) The type and amount of consideration offered to security holders;

(iii) The scheduled expiration date;

(iv) Whether a subsequent offering period will be available, if the transaction is a third-party tender offer;

(v) Whether the offer may be extended, and if so, how it could be extended;

(vi) The dates before and after which security holders may withdraw securities tendered in the offer;

(vii) The procedures for tendering and withdrawing securities;

(viii) The manner in which securities will be accepted for payment;

(ix) If the offer is for less than all securities of a class, the periods for accepting securities on a pro rata basis and the offeror's present intentions in the event that the offer is oversubscribed;

(x) An explanation of any material differences in the rights of security holders as a result of the transaction, if material;

(xi) A brief statement as to the accounting treatment of the transaction, if material; and

(xii) The federal income tax consequences of the transaction, if material.

(2) *Mergers or similar transactions.* In the case of a merger or similar transaction, the information must include:

(i) A brief description of the transaction;

(ii) The consideration offered to security holders;

(iii) The reasons for engaging in the transaction;

(iv) The vote required for approval of the transaction;

(v) An explanation of any material differences in the rights of security holders as a result of the transaction, if material;

(vi) A brief statement as to the accounting treatment of the transaction, if material; and

(vii) The federal income tax consequences of the transaction, if material.

...

(b) *Purchases.* State whether any securities are to be purchased from any officer, director or affiliate of the subject company and provide the details of each transaction.

(c) *Different terms.* Describe any term or arrangement in the Rule 13e-3 transaction that treats any subject security holders differently from other subject security holders.

(d) *Appraisal rights.* State whether or not dissenting security holders are entitled to any appraisal rights. If so, summarize the appraisal rights. If there are no appraisal rights available under state law for security holders who object to the transaction, briefly outline any other rights that may be available to security holders under the law.

(e) *Provisions for unaffiliated security holders.* Describe any provision made by the filing person in connection with the transaction to grant unaffiliated security holders access to the corporate files of the filing person or to obtain counsel or appraisal services at the expense of the filing person. If none, so state.

(f) *Eligibility for listing or trading.* If the transaction involves the offer of securities of the filing person in exchange for equity securities held by unaffiliated security holders of the subject company, describe whether or not the filing person will take steps to assure that the securities offered are or will be eligible for trading on an automated quotations system operated by a national securities association.

§ 229.1005 (Item 1005) Past Contacts, Transactions, Negotiations and Agreements

(a) *Transactions.* Briefly state the nature and approximate dollar amount of any transaction, other than those described in paragraphs (b) or (c) of this section, that occurred during the past two years, between the filing person (including any person specified in Instruction C of the schedule) and;

(1) The subject company or any of its affiliates that are not natural persons if the aggregate value of the transactions is more than one percent of the subject company's consolidated revenues for:

(i) The fiscal year when the transaction occurred; or

(ii) The past portion of the current fiscal year, if the transaction occurred in the current year; and

Instruction to Item 1005(a)(1): The information required by this Item may be based on information in the subject company's most recent filing with the Commission, unless the filing person has reason to believe the information is not accurate.

(2) Any executive officer, director or affiliate of the subject company that is a natural person if the aggregate value of the transaction or series of similar transactions with that person exceeds $60,000.

(b) *Significant corporate events.* Describe any negotiations, transactions or material contacts during the past two years between the filing person (including subsidiaries of the filing person and any person specified in Instruction C of the schedule) and the subject company or its affiliates concerning any:

(1) Merger;

(2) Consolidation;

(3) Acquisition;

(4) Tender offer for or other acquisition of any class of the subject company's securities;

(5) Election of the subject company's directors; or

(6) Sale or other transfer of a material amount of assets of the subject company.

(c) *Negotiations or contacts.* Describe any negotiations or material contacts concerning the matters referred to in paragraph (b) of this section during the past two years between:

(1) Any affiliates of the subject company; or

(2) The subject company or any of its affiliates and any person not affiliated with the subject company who would have a direct interest in such matters.

Instruction to paragraphs (b) and (c) of Item 1005: Identify the person who initiated the contacts or negotiations.

(d) *Conflicts of interest.* If material, describe any agreement, arrangement or understanding and any actual or potential conflict of interest between the filing person or its affiliates and:

(1) The subject company, its executive officers, directors or affiliates; or

(2) The offeror, its executive officers, directors or affiliates.

Instruction to Item 1005(d): If the filing person is the subject company, no disclosure called for by this paragraph is required in the document disseminated to security holders, so long as substantially the same information was filed with the Commission previously and disclosed in a proxy statement, report or other communication sent to security holders by the subject company in the past year. The document disseminated to security holders, however, must refer specifically to the discussion in the proxy statement, report or other communication that was sent to security holders previously. The information also must be filed as an exhibit to the schedule.

(e) *Agreements involving the subject company's securities.* Describe any agreement, arrangement, or understanding, whether or not legally enforceable, between the filing person (including any person specified in Instruction C of the schedule) and any other person with respect to any securities of the subject company. Name all persons that are a party to the agreements, arrangements, or understandings and describe all material provisions.

§ 229.1006 (Item 1006) Purposes of the Transaction and Plans or Proposals

(a) *Purposes.* State the purposes of the transaction.

(b) *Use of securities acquired.* Indicate whether the securities acquired in the transaction will be retained, retired, held in treasury, or otherwise disposed of.

(c) *Plans.* Describe any plans, proposals or negotiations that relate to or would result in:

(1) Any extraordinary transaction, such as a merger, reorganization or liquidation, involving the subject company or any of its subsidiaries;

(2) Any purchase, sale or transfer of a material amount of assets of the subject company or any of its subsidiaries;

(3) Any material change in the present dividend rate or policy, or indebtedness or capitalization of the subject company;

(4) Any change in the present board of directors or management of the subject company, including, but not limited to, any plans or proposals to change the number or the term of directors or to fill any existing vacancies on the board or to change any material term of the employment contract of any executive officer;

(5) Any other material change in the subject company's corporate structure or business, including, if the subject company is a registered

closed-end investment company, any plans or proposals to make any changes in its investment policy for which a vote would be required by Section 13 of the Investment Company Act of 1940 (15 U.S.C. 80a-13);

(6) Any class of equity securities of the subject company to be delisted from a national securities exchange or cease to be authorized to be quoted in an automated quotations system operated by a national securities association;

(7) Any class of equity securities of the subject company becoming eligible for termination of registration under section 12(g)(4) of the Act (15 U.S.C. 78*l*);

(8) The suspension of the subject company's obligation to file reports under Section 15(d) of the Act (15 U.S.C. 78*o*);

(9) The acquisition by any person of additional securities of the subject company, or the disposition of securities of the subject company; or (10) Any changes in the subject company's charter, bylaws or other governing instruments or other actions that could impede the acquisition of control of the subject company.

(d) *Subject company negotiations.* If the filing person is the subject company:

(1) State whether or not that person is undertaking or engaged in any negotiations in response to the tender offer that relate to:

(i) A tender offer or other acquisition of the subject company's securities by the filing person, any of its subsidiaries, or any other person; or

(ii) Any of the matters referred to in paragraphs (c)(1) through (c)(3) of this section; and

(2) Describe any transaction, board resolution, agreement in principle, or signed contract that is entered into in response to the tender offer that relates to one or more of the matters referred to in paragraph (d)(1) of this section.

Instruction to Item 1006(d)(1): If an agreement in principle has not been reached at the time of filing, no disclosure under paragraph (d)(1) of this section is required of the possible terms of or the parties to the transaction if in the opinion of the board of directors of the subject company disclosure would jeopardize continuation of the negotiations. In that case, disclosure indicating that negotiations are being undertaken or are underway and are in the preliminary stages is sufficient.

§ 229.1007 (Item 1007) Source and Amount of Funds or Other Consideration

(a) *Source of funds.* State the specific sources and total amount of funds or other consideration to be used in the transaction. If the transaction involves a tender offer, disclose the amount of funds or other consideration required to purchase the maximum amount of securities sought in the offer.

(b) *Conditions.* State any material conditions to the financing discussed in response to paragraph (a) of this section. Disclose any alternative financing arrangements or alternative financing plans in the event the primary financing plans fall through. If none, so state.

(c) *Expenses.* Furnish a reasonably itemized statement of all expenses incurred or estimated to be incurred in connection with the transaction including, but not limited to, filing, legal, accounting and appraisal fees, solicitation expenses and printing costs and state whether or not the subject company has paid or will be responsible for paying any or all expenses.

(d) *Borrowed funds.* If all or any part of the funds or other consideration required is, or is expected, to be borrowed, directly or indirectly, for the purpose of the transaction:

(1) Provide a summary of each loan agreement or arrangement containing the identity of the parties, the term, the collateral, the stated and effective interest rates, and any other material terms or conditions of the loan; and

(2) Briefly describe any plans or arrangements to finance or repay the loan, or, if no plans or arrangements have been made, so state.

§ 229.1008 (Item 1008) Interest in Securities of the Subject Company

(a) *Securities ownership.* State the aggregate number and percentage of subject securities that are beneficially owned by each person named in response to Item 1003 of Regulation M-A (§ 229.1003) and by each associate and majority-owned subsidiary of those persons. Give the name and address of any associate or subsidiary.

Instructions to Item 1008(a). 1. For purposes of this section, beneficial ownership is determined in accordance with Rule 13d-3 (§ 240.13d-3 of this chapter) under the Exchange Act. Identify the shares that the person has a right to acquire.

2. The information required by this section may be based on the number of outstanding securities disclosed in the subject company's most recently available filing with the Commission, unless the filing person has more current information.

3. The information required by this section with respect to officers, directors and associates of the subject company must be given to the extent known after making reasonable inquiry.

(b) *Securities transactions.* Describe any transaction in the subject securities during the past 60 days. The description of transactions required must include, but not necessarily be limited to:

(1) The identity of the persons specified in the Instruction to this section who effected the transaction;

(2) The date of the transaction;

(3) The amount of securities involved;

(4) The price per share; and

(5) Where and how the transaction was effected.

§ 229.1009 (Item 1009) Persons/Assets, Retained, Employed, Compensated or Used

(a) *Solicitations or recommendations.* Identify all persons and classes of persons that are directly or indirectly employed, retained, or to be compensated to make solicitations or recommendations in connection with the transaction. Provide a summary of all material terms of employment, retainer or other arrangement for compensation.

(b) *Employees and corporate assets.* Identify any officer, class of employees or corporate assets of the subject company that has been or will be employed or used by the filing person in connection with the transaction. Describe the purpose for their employment or use.

Instruction to Item 1009(b): Provide all information required by this Item except for the information required by paragraph (a) of this section and Item 1007 of Regulation M-A (§ 229.1007).

§ 229.1010 (Item 1010) Financial Statements

(a) *Financial information.* Furnish the following financial information:

(1) Audited financial statements for the two fiscal years required to be filed with the company's most recent annual report under sections 13 and 15(d) of the Exchange Act (15 U.S.C. 78m; 15 U.S.C. 78o);

(2) Unaudited balance sheets, comparative year-to-date income statements and related earnings per share data, statements of cash flows, and comprehensive income required to be included in the company's most recent quarterly report filed under the Exchange Act;

(3) Ratio of earnings to fixed charges, computed in a manner consistent with Item 503(d) of Regulation S-K (§ 229.503(d)), for the two most recent fiscal years and the interim periods provided under paragraph (a)(2) of this section; and

(4) Book value per share as of the date of the most recent balance sheet presented.

(b) *Pro forma information.* If material, furnish pro forma information disclosing the effect of the transaction on:

(1) The company's balance sheet as of the date of the most recent balance sheet presented under paragraph (a) of this section;

(2) The company's statement of income, earnings per share, and ratio of earnings to fixed charges for the most recent fiscal year and the latest interim period provided under paragraph (a)(2) of this section; and

(3) The company's book value per share as of the date of the most recent balance sheet presented under paragraph (a) of this section.

(c) *Summary information.* Furnish a fair and adequate summary of the information specified in paragraphs (a) and (b) of this section for the same periods specified. A fair and adequate summary includes:

(1) The summarized financial information specified in § 210.1-02(bb)(1) of this chapter;

(2) Income per common share from continuing operations (basic and diluted, if applicable);

(3) Net income per common share (basic and diluted, if applicable);

(4) Ratio of earnings to fixed charges, computed in a manner consistent with Item 503(d) of Regulation S-K (§ 229.503(d));

(5) Book value per share as of the date of the most recent balance sheet; and

(6) If material, pro forma data for the summarized financial information specified in paragraphs (c)(1) through (c)(5) of this section disclosing the effect of the transaction.

§ 229.1011 (Item 1011) Additional Information

(a) *Agreements, regulatory requirements and legal proceedings.* If material to a security holder's decision whether to sell, tender or hold the securities sought in the tender offer, furnish the following information:

(1) Any present or proposed material agreement, arrangement, understanding or relationship between the offeror or any of its executive officers, directors, controlling persons or subsidiaries and the subject company or any of its executive officers, directors, controlling persons or subsidiaries (other than any agreement, arrangement or understanding disclosed under any other sections of Regulation M-A (§ § 229.1000 through 229.1016));

Instruction to paragraph (a)(1): In an issuer tender offer disclose any material agreement, arrangement, understanding or relationship between the offeror and any of its executive officers, directors, controlling persons or subsidiaries.

(2) To the extent known by the offeror after reasonable investigation, the applicable regulatory requirements which must be complied

with or approvals which must be obtained in connection with the tender offer;

(3) The applicability of any anti-trust laws;

(4) The applicability of margin requirements under section 7 of the Act (15 U.S.C. 78g) and the applicable regulations; and

(5) Any material pending legal proceedings relating to the tender offer, including the name and location of the court or agency in which the proceedings are pending, the date instituted, the principal parties, and a brief summary of the proceedings and the relief sought.

(b) Furnish the information required by Item 402(t)(2) and (3) of this part (§ 229.402(t)(2) and (3)) and in the tabular format set forth in Item 402(t)(1) of this part (§ 229.402(t)(1)) with respect to each named executive officer

(c) *Other material information.* Furnish such additional material information, if any, as may be necessary to make the required statements, in light of the circumstances under which they are made, not materially misleading.

§ 229.1012 (Item 1012) The Solicitation or Recommendation

(a) *Solicitation or recommendation.* State the nature of the solicitation or the recommendation. If this statement relates to a recommendation, state whether the filing person is advising holders of the subject securities to accept or reject the tender offer or to take other action with respect to the tender offer and, if so, describe the other action recommended. If the filing person is the subject company and is not making a recommendation, state whether the subject company is expressing no opinion and is remaining neutral toward the tender offer or is unable to take a position with respect to the tender offer.

(b) *Reasons.* State the reasons for the position (including the inability to take a position) stated in paragraph (a) of this section. Conclusory statements such as "The tender offer is in the best interests of shareholders" are not considered sufficient disclosure.

(c) *Intent to tender.* To the extent known by the filing person after making reasonable inquiry, state whether the filing person or any executive officer, director, affiliate or subsidiary of the filing person currently intends to tender, sell or hold the subject securities that are held of record or beneficially owned by that person.

(d) *Intent to tender or vote in a going-private transaction.* To the extent known by the filing person after making reasonable inquiry, state whether or not any executive officer, director or affiliate of the issuer (or any person specified in Instruction C to the schedule) currently intends to tender or sell subject securities owned or held by that person and/or how each person currently intends to vote subject securities, including any securities the person has proxy authority for. State the reasons for the intended action.

Instruction to Item 1012(d): Provide the information required by this section if it is available to the filing person at the time the statement is initially filed with the Commission. If the information is not available, it must be filed with the Commission promptly, but in no event later than three business days after the date of the initial filing, and if material, disclosed in a manner reasonably designed to inform security holders.

(e) *Recommendations of others.* To the extent known by the filing person after making reasonable inquiry, state whether or not any person specified in paragraph (d) of this section has made a recommendation either in support of or opposed to the transaction and the reasons for the recommendation.

§ 229.1013 (Item 1013) Purposes, Alternatives, Reasons and Effects in a Going-Private Transaction

(a) *Purposes.* State the purposes for the Rule 13e-3 transaction.

(b) *Alternatives.* If the subject company or affiliate considered alternative means to accomplish the stated purposes, briefly describe the alternatives and state the reasons for their rejection.

(c) *Reasons.* State the reasons for the structure of the Rule 13e-3 transaction and for undertaking the transaction at this time.

(d) *Effects.* Describe the effects of the Rule 13e-3 transaction on the subject company, its affiliates and unaffiliated security holders, including the federal tax consequences of the transaction.

Instructions to Item 1013: 1. Conclusory statements will not be considered sufficient disclosure in response to this section.

2. The description required by paragraph (d) of this section must include a reasonably detailed discussion of both the benefits and detriments of the Rule 13e-3 transaction to the subject company, its affiliates and unaffiliated security holders. The benefits and detriments of the Rule 13e-3 transaction must be quantified to the extent practicable.

3. If this statement is filed by an affiliate of the subject company, the description required by paragraph (d) of this section must include, but not be limited to, the effect of the Rule 13e-3 transaction on the affiliate's interest in the net book value and net earnings of the subject company in terms of both dollar amounts and percentages.

§ 229.1014 (Item 1014) Fairness of the Going-Private Transaction

(a) *Fairness.* State whether the subject company or affiliate filing the statement reasonably believes that the Rule 13e-3 transaction is fair or unfair to unaffiliated security holders. If any director dissented to or abstained from voting on the Rule 13e-3 transaction, identify the director, and indicate, if known, after making reasonable inquiry, the reasons for the dissent or abstention.

(b) *Factors considered in determining fairness.* Discuss in reasonable detail the material factors upon which the belief stated in paragraph (a) of this section is based and, to the extent practicable, the weight assigned to each factor. The discussion must include an analysis of the extent, if any, to which the filing person's beliefs are based on the factors described in Instruction 2 of this section, paragraphs (c), (d) and (e) of this section and Item 1015 of Regulation M-A (§ 229.1015).

(c) *Approval of security holders.* State whether or not the transaction is structured so that approval of at least a majority of unaffiliated security holders is required.

(d) *Unaffiliated representative.* State whether or not a majority of directors who are not employees of the subject company has retained an unaffiliated representative to act solely on behalf of unaffiliated security holders for purposes of negotiating the terms of the Rule 13e-3 transaction and/or preparing a report concerning the fairness of the transaction.

(e) *Approval of directors.* State whether or not the Rule 13e-3 transaction was approved by a majority of the directors of the subject company who are not employees of the subject company.

(f) *Other offers.* If any offer of the type described in paragraph (viii) of Instruction 2 to this section has been received, describe the offer and state the reasons for its rejection.

Instructions to Item 1014: 1. A statement that the issuer or affiliate has no reasonable belief as to the fairness of the Rule 13e-3 transaction to unaffiliated security holders will not be considered sufficient disclosure in response to paragraph (a) of this section.

2. The factors that are important in determining the fairness of a transaction to unaffiliated security holders and the weight, if any, that should be given to them in a particular context will vary. Normally such factors will include, among others, those referred to in paragraphs (c), (d) and (e) of this section and whether the consideration offered to unaffiliated security holders constitutes fair value in relation to:

(i) Current market prices;

(ii) Historical market prices;

(iii) Net book value;

(iv) Going concern value;

(v) Liquidation value;

(vi) Purchase prices paid in previous purchases disclosed in response to Item 1002(f) of Regulation M-A (§ 229.1002(f));

(vii) Any report, opinion, or appraisal described in Item 1015 of Regulation M-A (§ 229.1015); and

(viii) Firm offers of which the subject company or affiliate is aware made by any unaffiliated person, other than the filing persons, during the past two years for:

(A) The merger or consolidation of the subject company with or into another company, or *vice versa;*

(B) The sale or other transfer of all or any substantial part of the assets of the subject company; or

(C) A purchase of the subject company's securities that would enable the holder to exercise control of the subject company.

3. Conclusory statements, such as "The Rule 13e-3 transaction is fair to unaffiliated security holders in relation to net book value, going concern value and future prospects of the issuer" will not be considered sufficient disclosure in response to paragraph (b) of this section.

§ 229.1015 (Item 1015) Reports, Opinions, Appraisals and Negotiations

(a) *Report, opinion or appraisal.* State whether or not the subject company or affiliate has received any report, opinion (other than an opinion of counsel) or appraisal from an outside party that is materially related to the Rule 13e-3 transaction, including, but not limited to: Any report, opinion or appraisal relating to the consideration or the fairness of the consideration to be offered to security holders or the fairness of the transaction to the issuer or affiliate or to security holders who are not affiliates.

(b) *Preparer and summary of the report, opinion or appraisal.* For each report, opinion or appraisal described in response to paragraph (a) of this section or any negotiation or report described in response to Item 1014(d) of Regulation M-A (§ 229.1014) or Item 14(b)(6) of Schedule 14A (§ 240.14a-101 of this chapter) concerning the terms of the transaction:

(1) Identify the outside party and/or unaffiliated representative;

(2) Briefly describe the qualifications of the outside party and/or unaffiliated representative;

(3) Describe the method of selection of the outside party and/or unaffiliated representative;

(4) Describe any material relationship that existed during the past two years or is mutually understood to be contemplated and any compensation received or to be received as a result of the relationship between:

(i) The outside party, its affiliates, and/or unaffiliated representative; and

(ii) The subject company or its affiliates;

(5) If the report, opinion or appraisal relates to the fairness of the consideration, state whether the subject company or affiliate determined the amount of consideration to be paid or whether the outside party recommended the amount of consideration to be paid; and

(6) Furnish a summary concerning the negotiation, report, opinion or appraisal. The summary must include, but need not be limited to, the procedures followed; the findings and recommendations; the bases for and methods of arriving at such findings and recommendations; instructions received from the subject company or affiliate; and any limitation imposed by the subject company or affiliate on the scope of the investigation.

Instruction to Item 1015(b): The information called for by paragraphs (b)(1), (2) and (3) of this section must be given with respect to the firm that provides the report, opinion or appraisal rather than the employees of the firm that prepared the report.

(c) *Availability of documents.* Furnish a statement to the effect that the report, opinion or appraisal will be made available for inspection and copying at the principal executive offices of the subject company or affiliate during its regular business hours by any interested equity security holder of the subject company or representative who has been so designated in writing. This statement also may provide that a copy of the report, opinion or appraisal will be transmitted by the subject company or affiliate to any interested equity security holder of the subject company or representative who has been so designated in writing upon written request and at the expense of the requesting security holder.

SARBANES-OXLEY ACT OF 2002

Pub. L. No. 107-204

Title I — Public Company Accounting Oversight Board

§ 101. Establishment; Administrative Provisions

(a) *Establishment of Board*

There is established the Public Company Accounting Oversight Board, to oversee the audit of companies that are subject to the securities laws, and related matters, in order to protect the interests of investors and further the public interest in the preparation of informative, accurate, and independent audit reports. The Board shall be a body corporate, operate as a nonprofit corporation, and have succession until dissolved by an Act of Congress.

(b) *Status*

The Board shall not be an agency or establishment of the United States Government, and, except as otherwise provided in this Act, shall be subject to, and have all the powers conferred upon a nonprofit corporation by, the District of Columbia Nonprofit Corporation Act. No member or person employed by, or agent for, the Board shall be deemed to be an officer or employee of or agent for the Federal Government by reason of such service.

(c) *Duties of the Board*

The Board shall, subject to action by the Commission under section 7217 of this title, and once a determination is made by the Commission under subsection (d) of this section–

(1) register public accounting firms that prepare audit reports for issuers, brokers, and dealers, in accordance with section 7212 of this title;

(2) establish or adopt, or both, by rule, auditing, quality control, ethics, independence, and other standards relating to the preparation of audit reports for issuers, brokers, and dealers, in accordance with section 7213 of this title;

(3) conduct inspections of registered public accounting firms, in accordance with section 7214of this title and the rules of the Board;

(4) conduct investigations and disciplinary proceedings concerning, and impose appropriate sanctions where justified upon, registered public accounting firms and associated persons of such firms, in accordance with section 7215 of this title;

(5) perform such other duties or functions as the Board (or the Commission, by rule or order) determines are necessary or appropriate to promote high professional standards among, and improve the quality of audit services offered by, registered public accounting firms and associated persons thereof, or otherwise to carry out this Act, in order to protect investors, or to further the public interest;

(6) enforce compliance with this Act, the rules of the Board, professional standards, and the securities laws relating to the preparation and issuance of audit reports and the obligations and liabilities of accountants with respect thereto, by registered public accounting firms and associated persons thereof; and

(7) set the budget and manage the operations of the Board and the staff of the Board.

§ 103. Auditing, Quality Control, and Independence Standards and Rules

(a) *Auditing, quality control, and ethics standards*

(1) In general

The Board shall, by rule, establish, including, to the extent it determines appropriate, through adoption of standards proposed by 1 or more professional groups of accountants designated pursuant to paragraph (3)(A) or advisory groups convened pursuant to paragraph (4), and amend or otherwise modify or alter, such auditing and related attestation standards, such quality control standards, such ethics standards, and such independence standards to be used by registered public accounting firms in the preparation and issuance of audit reports, as required by this Act or the rules of the Commission, or as may be necessary or appropriate in the public interest or for the protection of investors.

(2) *Rule requirements*

In carrying out paragraph (1), the Board—

(A) shall include in the auditing standards that it adopts, requirements that each registered public accounting firm shall—

(i) prepare, and maintain for a period of not less than 7 years, audit work papers, and other information related to any audit report, in sufficient detail to support the conclusions reached in such report;

(ii) provide a concurring or second partner review and approval of such audit report (and other related information), and concurring approval in its issuance, by a qualified person (as prescribed by the Board) associated with the public accounting firm, other than the person in charge of the audit, or by an independent reviewer (as prescribed by the Board); and

(iii) in each audit report for an issuer, describe the scope of the auditor's testing of the internal control structure and procedures of the issuer, required by section 404(b)...

§ 104. Inspections of Registered Public Accounting Firms

(a) *In general*

(1) Inspections generally

The Board shall conduct a continuing program of inspections to assess the degree of compliance of each registered public accounting firm and associated persons of that firm with this Act, the rules of the Board, the rules of the Commission, or professional standards, in connection with its performance of audits, issuance of audit reports, and related matters involving issuers.

(2) Inspections of audit reports for brokers and dealers

(A) The Board may, by rule, conduct and require a program of inspection in accordance with paragraph (1), on a basis to be determined by the Board, of registered public accounting firms that provide one or more audit reports for a broker or dealer. The Board, in establishing such a program, may allow for differentiation among classes of brokers and dealers, as appropriate.

(B) If the Board determines to establish a program of inspection pursuant to subparagraph (A), the Board shall consider in establishing any inspection schedules whether differing schedules would be appropriate with respect to registered public accounting firms that issue audit reports only for one or more brokers or dealers that do not receive, handle, or hold customer securities or cash or are not a member of the Securities Investor Protection Corporation.

(C) Any rules of the Board pursuant to this paragraph shall be subject to prior approval by the Commission pursuant to section 7217(b) of this title before the rules become effective, including an opportunity for public notice and comment.

(D) Notwithstanding anything to the contrary in section 7212 of this title, a public accounting firm shall not be required to register with the Board if the public accounting firm is exempt from the inspection program which may be established by the Board under subparagraph (A).

(b) *Inspection frequency*

(1) In general

Subject to paragraph (2), inspections required by this section shall be conducted–

(A) annually with respect to each registered public accounting firm that regularly provides audit reports for more than 100 issuers; and

(B) not less frequently than once every 3 years with respect to each registered public accounting firm that regularly provides audit reports for 100 or fewer issuers.

(2) Adjustments to schedules

The Board may, by rule, adjust the inspection schedules set under paragraph (1) if the Board finds that different inspection schedules are consistent with the purposes of this Act, the public interest, and the protection of investors. The Board may conduct special inspections at the request of the Commission or upon its own motion.

(c) *Procedures*

The Board shall, in each inspection under this section, and in accordance with its rules for such inspections—

(1) identify any act or practice or omission to act by the registered public accounting firm, or by any associated person thereof, revealed by such inspection that may be in violation of this Act, the rules of the Board, the rules of the Commission, the firm's own quality control policies, or professional standards;

(2) report any such act, practice, or omission, if appropriate, to the Commission and each appropriate State regulatory authority; and

(3) begin a formal investigation or take disciplinary action, if appropriate, with respect to any such violation, in accordance with this Act and the rules of the Board.

(d) *Conduct of inspections*

In conducting an inspection of a registered public accounting firm under this section, the Board shall—

(1) inspect and review selected audit and review engagements of the firm (which may include audit engagements that are the subject of ongoing litigation or other controversy between the firm and 1 or

more third parties), performed at various offices and by various associated persons of the firm, as selected by the Board;

(2) evaluate the sufficiency of the quality control system of the firm, and the manner of the documentation and communication of that system by the firm; and

(3) perform such other testing of the audit, supervisory, and quality control procedures of the firm as are necessary or appropriate in light of the purpose of the inspection and the responsibilities of the Board.

Title II—Auditor Independence

§ 201. Services Outside the Scope of Practice of Auditors

(a) PROHIBITED ACTIVITIES—Section 10A of the Securities Exchange Act of 1934 (15 U.S.C. 78j-1) is amended by adding at the end the following:

'(g) PROHIBITED ACTIVITIES—Except as provided in subsection (h), it shall be unlawful for a registered public accounting firm (and any associated person of that firm, to the extent determined appropriate by the Commission) that performs for any issuer any audit required by this title or the rules of the Commission under this title or, beginning 180 days after the date of commencement of the operations of the Public Company Accounting Oversight Board established under section 101 of the Sarbanes-Oxley Act of 2002 (in this section referred to as the 'Board'), the rules of the Board, to provide to that issuer, contemporaneously with the audit, any non-audit service, including—

(1) bookkeeping or other services related to the accounting records or financial statements of the audit client;

(2) financial information systems design and implementation;

(3) appraisal or valuation services, fairness opinions, or contribution-in-kind reports;

(4) actuarial services;

(5) internal audit outsourcing services;

(6) management functions or human resources;

(7) broker or dealer, investment adviser, or investment banking services;

(8) legal services and expert services unrelated to the audit; and

(9) any other service that the Board determines, by regulation, is impermissible.

(h) PREAPPROVAL REQUIRED FOR NON-AUDIT SERVICES—A registered public accounting firm may engage in any non-audit service, including tax services, that is not described in any of paragraphs (1) through (9) of subsection (g) for an audit client, only if the activity is approved in advance by the audit committee of the issuer, in accordance with subsection (i).'.

(b) EXEMPTION AUTHORITY—The Board may, on a case by case basis, exempt any person, issuer, public accounting firm, or transaction from the prohibition on the provision of services under section 10A(g) of the Securities Exchange Act of 1934 (as added by this section), to the extent that such exemption is necessary or appropriate in the public interest and is consistent with the protection of investors, and subject to review by the Commission in the same manner as for rules of the Board under section 107.

§ 203. Audit Partner Rotation

Section 10A of the Securities Exchange Act of 1934 (15 U.S.C. 78j-1), as amended by this Act, is amended by adding at the end the following:

'(j) AUDIT PARTNER ROTATION—It shall be unlawful for a registered public accounting firm to provide audit services to an issuer if the lead (or coordinating) audit partner (having primary responsibility for the audit), or the audit partner responsible for reviewing the audit, has performed audit services for that issuer in each of the 5 previous fiscal years of that issuer.'.

§ 204. Auditor Reports to Audit Committees

Section 10A of the Securities Exchange Act of 1934 (15 U.S.C. 78j-1), as amended by this Act, is amended by adding at the end the following:

'(k) REPORTS TO AUDIT COMMITTEES—Each registered public accounting firm that performs for any issuer any audit required by this title shall timely report to the audit committee of the issuer—

'(1) all critical accounting policies and practices to be used;

'(2) all alternative treatments of financial information within generally accepted accounting principles that have been discussed with management officials of the issuer, ramifications of the use of such alternative disclosures and treatments, and the treatment preferred by the registered public accounting firm; and

'(3) other material written communications between the registered public accounting firm and the management of the issuer, such as any management letter or schedule of unadjusted differences.'.

Title III—Corporate Responsibility

§ 301. Public Company Audit Committees

Section 10A of the Securities Exchange Act of 1934 (15 U.S.C. 78f) is amended by adding at the end the following:

'(m) STANDARDS RELATING TO AUDIT COMMITTEES—

'(1) COMMISSION RULES—

'(A) IN GENERAL—Effective not later than 270 days after the date of enactment of this subsection, the Commission shall, by rule, direct the national securities exchanges and national securities associations to prohibit the listing of any security of an issuer that is not in compliance with the requirements of any portion of paragraphs (2) through (6).

'(B) OPPORTUNITY TO CURE DEFECTS—The rules of the Commission under subparagraph (A) shall provide for appropriate procedures for an issuer to have an opportunity to cure any defects that would be the basis for a prohibition under subparagraph (A), before the imposition of such prohibition.

'(2) RESPONSIBILITIES RELATING TO REGISTERED PUBLIC ACCOUNTING FIRMS—The audit committee of each issuer, in its capacity as a committee of the board of directors, shall be directly responsible for the appointment, compensation, and oversight of the work of any registered public accounting firm employed by that issuer (including resolution of disagreements between management and the auditor regarding financial reporting) for the purpose of preparing or issuing an audit report or related work, and each such registered public accounting firm shall report directly to the audit committee.

'(3) INDEPENDENCE—

'(A) IN GENERAL—Each member of the audit committee of the issuer shall be a member of the board of directors of the issuer, and shall otherwise be independent.

'(B) CRITERIA—In order to be considered to be independent for purposes of this paragraph, a member of an audit committee of an issuer may not, other than in his or her capacity as a member of the audit committee, the board of directors, or any other board committee—

'(i) accept any consulting, advisory, or other compensatory fee from the issuer; or

'(ii) be an affiliated person of the issuer or any subsidiary thereof.

'(C) EXEMPTION AUTHORITY—The Commission may exempt from the requirements of subparagraph (B) a particular relationship with respect to audit committee members, as the Commission determines appropriate in light of the circumstances.

'(4) COMPLAINTS—Each audit committee shall establish procedures for—

'(A) the receipt, retention, and treatment of complaints received by the issuer regarding accounting, internal accounting controls, or auditing matters; and

'(B) the confidential, anonymous submission by employees of the issuer of concerns regarding questionable accounting or auditing matters.

'(5) AUTHORITY TO ENGAGE ADVISERS—Each audit committee shall have the authority to engage independent counsel and other advisers, as it determines necessary to carry out its duties.

'(6) FUNDING — Each issuer shall provide for appropriate funding, as determined by the audit committee, in its capacity as a committee of the board of directors, for payment of compensation —

'(A) to the registered public accounting firm employed by the issuer for the purpose of rendering or issuing an audit report; and

'(B) to any advisers employed by the audit committee under paragraph (5).'.

§ 302. Corporate Responsibility for Financial Reports

(a) REGULATIONS REQUIRED — The Commission shall, by rule, require, for each company filing periodic reports under section 13(a) or 15(d) of the Securities Exchange Act of 1934 (15 U.S.C. 78m, 78*o*(d)), that the principal executive officer or officers and the principal financial officer or officers, or persons performing similar functions, certify in each annual or quarterly report filed or submitted under either such section of such Act that —

(1) the signing officer has reviewed the report;

(2) based on the officer's knowledge, the report does not contain any untrue statement of a material fact or omit to state a material fact necessary in order to make the statements made, in light of the circumstances under which such statements were made, not misleading;

(3) based on such officer's knowledge, the financial statements, and other financial information included in the report, fairly present in all material respects the financial condition and results of operations of the issuer as of, and for, the periods presented in the report;

(4) the signing officers —

(A) are responsible for establishing and maintaining internal controls;

(B) have designed such internal controls to ensure that material information relating to the issuer and its consolidated subsidiaries is made known to such officers by others within those entities, particularly during the period in which the periodic reports are being prepared;

(C) have evaluated the effectiveness of the issuer's internal controls as of a date within 90 days prior to the report; and

(D) have presented in the report their conclusions about the effectiveness of their internal controls based on their evaluation as of that date;

(5) the signing officers have disclosed to the issuer's auditors and the audit committee of the board of directors (or persons fulfilling the equivalent function) —

(A) all significant deficiencies in the design or operation of internal controls which could adversely affect the issuer's ability to record, process, summarize, and report financial data and have identified for the issuer's auditors any material weaknesses in internal controls; and

(B) any fraud, whether or not material, that involves management or other employees who have a significant role in the issuer's internal controls; and

(6) the signing officers have indicated in the report whether or not there were significant changes in internal controls or in other factors that could significantly affect internal controls subsequent to the date of their evaluation, including any corrective actions with regard to significant deficiencies and material weaknesses.

(b) FOREIGN REINCORPORATIONS HAVE NO EFFECT—Nothing in this section 302 shall be interpreted or applied in any way to allow any issuer to lessen the legal force of the statement required under this section 302, by an issuer having reincorporated or having engaged in any other transaction that resulted in the transfer of the corporate domicile or offices of the issuer from inside the United States to outside of the United States.

(c) DEADLINE—The rules required by subsection (a) shall be effective not later than 30 days after the date of enactment of this Act.

§ 303. Improper Influence on Conduct of Audits

(a) RULES TO PROHIBIT—It shall be unlawful, in contravention of such rules or regulations as the Commission shall prescribe as necessary and appropriate in the public interest or for the protection of investors, for any officer or director of an issuer, or any other person acting under the direction thereof, to take any action to fraudulently influence, coerce, manipulate, or mislead any independent public or certified accountant engaged in the performance of an audit of the financial statements of that issuer for the purpose of rendering such financial statements materially misleading.

(b) ENFORCEMENT—In any civil proceeding, the Commission shall have exclusive authority to enforce this section and any rule or regulation issued under this section.

(c) NO PREEMPTION OF OTHER LAW—The provisions of subsection (a) shall be in addition to, and shall not supersede or preempt, any other provision of law or any rule or regulation issued thereunder.

(d) DEADLINE FOR RULEMAKING—The Commission shall—

(1) propose the rules or regulations required by this section, not later than 90 days after the date of enactment of this Act; and

(2) issue final rules or regulations required by this section, not later than 270 days after that date of enactment.

§ 304. Forfeiture of Certain Bonuses and Profits

(a) ADDITIONAL COMPENSATION PRIOR TO NONCOMPLIANCE WITH COMMISSION FINANCIAL REPORTING REQUIRE-

MENTS—If an issuer is required to prepare an accounting restatement due to the material noncompliance of the issuer, as a result of misconduct, with any financial reporting requirement under the securities laws, the chief executive officer and chief financial officer of the issuer shall reimburse the issuer for—

(1) any bonus or other incentive-based or equity-based compensation received by that person from the issuer during the 12-month period following the first public issuance or filing with the Commission (whichever first occurs) of the financial document embodying such financial reporting requirement; and

(2) any profits realized from the sale of securities of the issuer during that 12-month period.

(b) COMMISSION EXEMPTION AUTHORITY—The Commission may exempt any person from the application of subsection (a), as it deems necessary and appropriate.

§ 307. Rules of Professional Responsibility for Attorneys

Not later than 180 days after the date of enactment of this Act, the Commission shall issue rules, in the public interest and for the protection of investors, setting forth minimum standards of professional conduct for attorneys appearing and practicing before the Commission in any way in the representation of issuers, including a rule—

(1) requiring an attorney to report evidence of a material violation of securities law or breach of fiduciary duty or similar violation by the company or any agent thereof, to the chief legal counsel or the chief executive officer of the company (or the equivalent thereof); and

(2) if the counsel or officer does not appropriately respond to the evidence (adopting, as necessary, appropriate remedial measures or sanctions with respect to the violation), requiring the attorney to report the evidence to the audit committee of the board of directors of the issuer or to another committee of the board of directors comprised solely of directors not employed directly or indirectly by the issuer, or to the board of directors.

...

Title IV—Enhanced Financial Disclosures

§ 402. Enhanced Conflict of Interest Provisions

(a) PROHIBITION ON PERSONAL LOANS TO EXECUTIVES—Section 13 of the Securities Exchange Act of 1934 (15 U.S.C. 78m), as amended by this Act, is amended by adding at the end the following:

'(k) PROHIBITION ON PERSONAL LOANS TO EXECUTIVES—

'(1) IN GENERAL—It shall be unlawful for any issuer (as defined in section 2 of the Sarbanes-Oxley Act of 2002), directly or indirectly, including through any subsidiary, to extend or maintain credit, to arrange for the extension of credit, or to renew an extension of credit, in the form of a personal loan to or for any director or executive officer (or equivalent thereof) of that issuer. An extension of credit maintained by the issuer on the date of enactment of this subsection shall not be subject to the provisions of this subsection, provided that there is no material modification to any term of any such extension of credit or any renewal of any such extension of credit on or after that date of enactment.

'(2) LIMITATION—Paragraph (1) does not preclude any home improvement and manufactured home loans (as that term is defined in section 5 of the Home Owners' Loan Act (12 U.S.C. 1464)), consumer credit (as defined in section 103 of the Truth in Lending Act (15 U.S.C. 1602)), or any extension of credit under an open end credit plan (as defined in section 103 of the Truth in Lending Act (15 U.S.C. 1602)), or a charge card (as defined in section 127(c)(4)(e) of the Truth in Lending Act (15 U.S.C. 1637(c)(4)(e)), or any extension of credit by a broker or dealer registered under section 15 of this title to an employee of that broker or dealer to buy, trade, or carry securities, that is permitted under rules or regulations of the Board of Governors of the Federal Reserve System pursuant to section 7 of this title (other than an extension of credit that would be used to purchase the stock of that issuer), that is—

'(A) made or provided in the ordinary course of the consumer credit business of such issuer;

'(B) of a type that is generally made available by such issuer to the public; and

'(C) made by such issuer on market terms, or terms that are no more favorable than those offered by the issuer to the general public for such extensions of credit.

'(3) RULE OF CONSTRUCTION FOR CERTAIN LOANS—Paragraph (1) does not apply to any loan made or maintained by an insured depository institution (as defined in section 3 of the Federal Deposit Insurance Act (12 U.S.C. 1813)), if the loan is subject to the insider lending restrictions of section 22(h) of the Federal Reserve Act (12 U.S.C. 375b).'.

...

§ 404. Management Assessment of Internal Controls

(a) RULES REQUIRED—The Commission shall prescribe rules requiring each annual report required by section 13(a) or 15(d) of the Securities Exchange Act of 1934 (15 U.S.C. 78m or 78*o*(d)) to contain an internal control report, which shall—

(1) state the responsibility of management for establishing and maintaining an adequate internal control structure and procedures for financial reporting; and

(2) contain an assessment, as of the end of the most recent fiscal year of the issuer, of the effectiveness of the internal control structure and procedures of the issuer for financial reporting.

(b) INTERNAL CONTROL EVALUATION AND REPORTING—With respect to the internal control assessment required by subsection (a), each registered public accounting firm that prepares or issues the audit report for the issuer shall attest to, and report on, the assessment made by the management of the issuer. An attestation made under this subsection shall be made in accordance with standards for attestation engagements issued or adopted by the Board. Any such attestation shall not be the subject of a separate engagement.

§ 406. Code of Ethics for Senior Financial Officers

(a) CODE OF ETHICS DISCLOSURE—The Commission shall issue rules to require each issuer, together with periodic reports required pursuant to section 13(a) or 15(d) of the Securities Exchange Act of 1934, to disclose whether or not, and if not, the reason therefor, such issuer has adopted a code of ethics for senior financial officers, applicable to its principal financial officer and comptroller or principal accounting officer, or persons performing similar functions.

(b) CHANGES IN CODES OF ETHICS—The Commission shall revise its regulations concerning matters requiring prompt disclosure on Form 8-K (or any successor thereto) to require the immediate disclosure, by means of the filing of such form, dissemination by the Internet or by other electronic means, by any issuer of any change in or waiver of the code of ethics for senior financial officers.

(c) DEFINITION—In this section, the term 'code of ethics' means such standards as are reasonably necessary to promote—

(1) honest and ethical conduct, including the ethical handling of actual or apparent conflicts of interest between personal and professional relationships;

(2) full, fair, accurate, timely, and understandable disclosure in the periodic reports required to be filed by the issuer; and

(3) compliance with applicable governmental rules and regulations.

(d) DEADLINE FOR RULEMAKING—The Commission shall—

(1) propose rules to implement this section, not later than 90 days after the date of enactment of this Act; and

(2) issue final rules to implement this section, not later than 180 days after that date of enactment.

§ 407. Disclosure of Audit Committee Financial Expert

(a) RULES DEFINING 'FINANCIAL EXPERT'—The Commission shall issue rules, as necessary or appropriate in the public interest and consistent with the protection of investors, to require each issuer, together with periodic reports required pursuant to sections 13(a) and 15(d) of the Securities Exchange Act of 1934, to disclose whether or not, and if not, the reasons therefor, the audit committee of that issuer is comprised of at least 1 member who is a financial expert, as such term is defined by the Commission.

(b) CONSIDERATIONS—In defining the term 'financial expert' for purposes of subsection (a), the Commission shall consider whether a person has, through education and experience as a public accountant or auditor or a principal financial officer, comptroller, or principal accounting officer of an issuer, or from a position involving the performance of similar functions—

(1) an understanding of generally accepted accounting principles and financial statements;

(2) experience in—

(A) the preparation or auditing of financial statements of generally comparable issuers; and

(B) the application of such principles in connection with the accounting for estimates, accruals, and reserves;

(3) experience with internal accounting controls; and

(4) an understanding of audit committee functions.

(c) DEADLINE FOR RULEMAKING—The Commission shall—

(1) propose rules to implement this section, not later than 90 days after the date of enactment of this Act; and

(2) issue final rules to implement this section, not later than 180 days after that date of enactment.

NEW YORK STOCK EXCHANGE LISTED COMPANY MANUAL*

Paras. 303A, 312, 313

303A.00. Corporate Governance Standards

303A.01. Independent Directors

Listed companies must have a majority of independent directors.

Commentary: Effective boards of directors exercise independent judgment in carrying out their responsibilities. Requiring a majority of independent directors will increase the quality of board oversight and lessen the possibility of damaging conflicts of interest.

303A.02 Independence Tests

In order to tighten the definition of "independent director" for purposes of these standards:

(a)(i) No director qualifies as "independent" unless the board of directors affirmatively determines that the director has no material relationship with the listed company (either directly or as a partner, shareholder or officer of an organization that has a relationship with the company).

(ii) In addition, in affirmatively determining the independence of any director who will serve on the compensation committee of the listed company's board of directors, the board of directors must consider all factors specifically relevant to determining whether a director has a relationship to the listed company which is material to that director's ability to be independent from management in connection with the duties of a compensation committee member, including, but not limited to:

(A) the source of compensation of such director, including any consulting, advisory or other affiliate of a subsidiary of the listed company.

Commentary: It is not possible to anticipate, or explicitly to provide for, all circumstances that might signal potential conflicts of interest, or that might bear on the materiality of a director's relationship to a listed company (references to "listed company" would include any parent or subsidiary in a consolidated group with the listed company). Accordingly, it is best that boards making "independence" determinations broadly consider all relevant facts and circumstances. In particular, when assessing the materiality of a director's relationship with the listed company, the board should consider the issue not merely from the standpoint of the director, but also from that of persons or organizations with which the director has an affiliation. Material relationships can include commercial, industrial, banking, consulting, legal, accounting, charitable and familial relationships, among others. However, as the concern is independence from management, the Exchange does not view ownership of even a significant amount of stock, by itself, as a bar to an independence finding.

When considering the sources of a director's compensation in determining his independence for purposes of compensation committee service, the board should consider whether the director receives compensation from any person or entity that would impair his ability to make independent judgments about the listed company's executive compensation. Similarly, when considering any affiliate relationship a director has with the company, a subsidiary of the company, or an affiliate of a subsidiary of the company, in determining his independence for purposes of compensation committee service, the board should consider whether the affiliate relationship places the director under the direct or indirect control of the listed company or its senior management, or creates a direct relationship between the director and members of senior management, in each case of a nature that would impair his ability to make independent judgments about the listed company's executive compensation.

Disclosure Requirement: The listed company must comply with the disclosure requirements set forth in Item 407(a) of Regulation S-K.

(b) In addition, a director is not independent if:

(i) The director is, or has been within the last three years, an employee of the listed company, or an immediate family member is, or has been within the last three years, an executive officer, [1] of the listed company.

Commentary: Employment as an interim Chairman or CEO or other executive officer shall not disqualify a director from being considered independent following that employment.

(ii) The director has received, or has an immediate family member who has received, during any twelve-month period within the last three years, more than $120,000 in direct compensation from the listed company, other than director and committee fees and pension or other forms of deferred compensation for prior service (provided such compensation is not contingent in any way on continued service).

Commentary: Compensation received by a director for former service as an interim Chairman or CEO or other executive officer need not be considered in determining independence under this test. Compensation received by an immediate family member for service as an employee of the listed company (other than an executive officer) need not be considered in determining independence under this test.

(iii) (A) The director is a current partner or employee of a firm that is the listed company's internal or external auditor; (B) the director has an immediate family member who is a current partner of such a firm; (C) the director has an immediate family member who is a current employee of such a firm and personally works on the listed company's audit; or (D) the director or an immediate family member was within the last three years a partner or employee of such a firm and personally worked on the listed company's audit within that time.

(iv) The director or an immediate family member is, or has been with the last three years, employed as an executive officer of another company where any of the listed company's present executive officers at the same time serves or served on that company's compensation committee.

(v) The director is a current employee, or an immediate family member is a current executive officer, of a company that has made payments to, or received payments from, the listed company for property or services in an amount which, in any of the last three fiscal years, exceeds the greater of $1 million, or 2% of such other company's consolidated gross revenues.

Commentary: In applying the test in Section 303A.02(b)(v), both the payments and the consolidated gross revenues to be measured shall be those reported in the last completed fiscal year of such other company. The look-back provision for this test applies solely to the financial relationship between the listed company and the director or immediate family member's current employer; a listed company need not consider former employment of the director or immediate family member.

Disclosure Requirement: Contributions to tax exempt organizations shall not be considered payments for purposes of Section 303A.02(b)(v), provided however that a listed company shall disclose either on or through its website or in its annual proxy statement, or if the listed company does not file an annual proxy statement, in the listed company's annual report on Form 10-K filed with the SEC, any such contributions made by the listed company to any tax exempt organization in which any independent director serves as an executive officer if, within the preceding three years, contributions in any single fiscal year from the listed company to the organization exceeded the greater of $1 million, or 2% of such tax exempt organization's consolidated gross revenues. If this disclosure is made on or through the listed company's website, the listed company must disclose that fact in its annual proxy statement or annual report, as applicable, and provide the website address. Listed company boards are reminded of their obligations to consider the materiality of any such relationship in accordance with Section 303A.02(a) above.

General Commentary to Section 303A.02(b): An "immediate family member" includes a person's spouse, parents, children, siblings, mothers and fathers-in-law, sons and daughters-in-law, brothers and sisters-in-law, and anyone (other than domestic employees) who shares such person's home. When applying the look-back provisions in Section 303A.02(b), listed companies need not consider individuals who are no longer immediate family members as a result of legal separation or divorce, or those who have died or become incapacitated.

In addition, references to the "listed company" or "company" include any parent or subsidiary in a consolidated group with the listed company or such other company as is relevant to any determination under the independent standards set forth in this Section 303A.02(b).

For purposes of Section 303A, the term "executive officer" has the same meaning specified for the term "officer" in Rule 16a-1(f) under the Securities Exchange Act of 1934.

303A.03 Executive Sessions

To empower non-management directors to serve as a more effective check on management, the non-management directors of each listed company must meet at regularly scheduled executive sessions without management.

Commentary: To promote open discussion among the non-management directors, companies must schedule regular executive sessions in which those directors meet without management participation. "Non-management" directors are all those who are not executive officers, and includes such directors who are not independent by virtue of a material relationship, former status or family membership, or for any other reason.

Regular scheduling of such meetings is important not only to foster better communication among non-management directors, but also to prevent any negative inference from attaching to the calling of executive sessions. A non-management director must preside over each executive session, although the same director is not required to preside at all executive sessions.

While this Section 303A.03 refers to meetings of non-management directors, listed companies may instead choose to hold regular executive sessions of independent directors only. An independent director must preside over each executive session of the independent directors, although the same director is not required to preside at all executive sessions of the independent directors.

If a listed company chooses to hold regular meetings of all non-management directors, such listed company should hold an executive session including only independent directors at least once a year.

Disclosure Requirements: If one director is chosen to preside at all of these executive sessions, his or her name must be disclosed either on or through the listed company's website or in its annual proxy statement or, if the listed company does not file an annual proxy statement, in its annual report on Form 10-K filed with the SEC. If this disclosure is made on or through the listed company's website, the listed company must disclose that fact in its annual proxy statement or annual report, as applicable, and provide the website address. Alternatively, if the same individual is not the presiding director at every meeting, a listed company must disclose the procedure by which a presiding director is selected for each executive session. For example, a listed company may wish to rotate the presiding position among the chairs of board committees.

In order that all interested parties (not just shareholders) may be able to make their concerns known to the non-management or independent directors, a listed company must also disclose a method for such parties to communicate directly with the presiding director or with those directors as a group either on or through the listed company's website or in its annual proxy statement or, if the listed company does not file an annual proxy statement, in its annual report on Form 10-K filed with the SEC. If this disclosure is made on or through the listed company's website, the listed company must disclose that fact in its annual proxy statement or annual report, as applicable, and provide the website address. Companies may, if they wish, utilize for this purpose the same procedures they have established to comply with the requirement of Rule 10A-3 (b)(3) under the Exchange Act regarding complaints to the audit committee, as applied to listed companies through Section 303A.06.

303A.04 Nominating/Corporate Governance Committee

(a) Listed companies must have a nominating/corporate governance committee composed entirely of independent directors.

(b) The nominating/corporate governance committee must have a written charter that addresses:

(i) the committee's purpose and responsibilities—which, at minimum, must be to: identify individuals qualified to become board members, consistent with criteria approved by the board, and to select, or to recommend that the board select, the director nominees for the next annual meeting of shareholders; develop and recommend to the board a set of corporate governance guidelines applicable to the corporation; and oversee the evaluation of the board and management; and

(ii) an annual performance evaluation of the committee.

Commentary: A nominating/corporate governance committee is central to the effective functioning of the board. New director and board committee nominations are among a board's most important functions. Placing this responsibility in the hands of an independent nominating/corporate governance committee can enhance the independence and quality of nominees. The committee is also responsible for taking a leadership role in shaping the corporate governance of a corporation.

If a listed company is legally required by contract or otherwise to provide third parties with the ability to nominate directors (for example, preferred stock rights to elect directors upon a dividend default, shareholder agreements, and management agreements), the selection and nomination of such directors need not be subject to the nominating committee process.

The nominating/corporate governance committee charter should also address the following items: committee member qualifications; committee member appointment and removal; committee structure and operations (including authority to delegate to subcommittees); and committee reporting to the board. In addition, the charter should give the nominating/corporate governance committee sole authority to retain and terminate any search firm to be used to identify director candidates, including sole authority to approve the search firm's fees and other retention terms.

Boards may allocate the responsibilities of the nominating/corporate governance committee to committees of their own denomination, provided that the committees are composed entirely of independent directors. Any such committee must have a committee charter.

Website Posting Requirement: A listed company must make its nominating/corporate governance committee charter available on or through its website. If any function of the nominating/corporate governance committee has been delegated to another committee, the charter of that committee must also be made available on or through the listed company's website.

Disclosure Requirements: A listed company must disclose in its annual proxy statement or, if it does not file an annual proxy statement, in its annual report on Form 10-K filed with the SEC that its nominating/corporate governance committee charter is available on or through its website and provide the website address.

303A.05 Compensation Committee

(a) Listed companies must have a compensation committee composed entirely of independent directors. Compensation committee members must satisfy the additional independence requirements specific to compensation committee membership set forth in Section 303A.02(a)(ii).

(b) The compensation committee must have a written charter that addresses:

(i) the committee's purpose and responsibilities—which, at minimum, must be to have direct responsibility to:

(A) review and approve corporate goals and objectives relevant to CEO compensation, evaluate the CEO's performance in light of those goals and objectives, and, either as a committee or together with the other independent directors (as directed by the board), determine and approve the CEO's compensation level based on this evaluation;

(B) make recommendations to the board with respect to non-CEO executive officer compensation, and incentive-compensation and equity-based plans that are subject to board approval; and

(C) prepare the disclosure required by Item 407(e)(5) of Regulation S-K;

(ii) an annual performance evaluation of the compensation committee.

(iii) The rights and responsibilities of the compensation committee set forth in Section 303A.05(c).

Commentary: In determining the long-term incentive component of CEO compensation, the committee should consider the listed company's performance and relative shareholder return, the value of similar incentive awards to CEOs at comparable companies, and the awards given to the listed company's CEO in past years. To avoid confusion, note that the compensation committee is not precluded from approving awards (with or without ratification of the board) as may be required to comply with applicable tax laws (i.e., Rule 162(m)). Note also that nothing in Section 303A.05(b)(i)(B) is intended to preclude the board from delegating its authority over such matters to the compensation committee.

The compensation committee charter should also address the following items: committee member qualifications; committee member appointment and removal; committee structure and operations (including authority to delegate to subcommittees); and committee reporting to the board.

Boards may allocate the responsibilities of the compensation committee to committees of their own denomination, provided that the committees are composed entirely of independent directors. Any such committee must have a committee charter.

Nothing in this provision should be construed as precluding discussion of CEO compensation with the board generally, as it is not the intent of this standard to impair communication among members of the board.

Website Posting Requirement: A listed company must make its compensation committee charter available on or through its website. If any function of the compensation committee has been delegated to another committee, the charter of that committee must also be made available on or through the listed company's website.

Disclosure Requirements: A listed company must disclose in its annual proxy statement or, if it does not file an annual proxy statement, in its annual report on Form 10-K filed with the SEC that its compensation committee charter is available on or through its website and provide the website address.

(c)(i) The compensation committee may, in its sole discretion, retain or obtain the advice of a compensation consultant, independent legal counsel or other adviser.

(ii) The compensation committee shall be directly responsible for the appointment, compensation and oversight of the work of any compensation consultant, independent legal counsel or other adviser retained by the compensation committee.

(iii) The listed company must provide for appropriate funding, as determined by the compensation committee, for payment of reasonable compensation to a compensation consultant, independent legal counsel or any other adviser retained by the compensation committee.

(iv) The compensation committee may select a compensation consultant, legal counsel or other adviser to the compensation committee only after taking into consideration, all factors relevant to that person's independence from management, including the following:

(A) The provision of other services to the listed company by the person that employs the compensation consultant, legal counsel or other adviser;

(B) The amount of fees received from the listed company by the person that employs the compensation consultant, legal counsel or other adviser, as a percentage of the total revenue of the person that employs the compensation consultant, legal counsel or other adviser;

(C) The policies and procedures of the person that employs the compensation consultant, legal counsel or other adviser that are designed to prevent conflicts of interest;

(D) Any business or personal relationship of the compensation consultant, legal counsel or other adviser with a member of the compensation committee;

(E) Any stock of the listed company owned by the compensation consultant, legal counsel or other adviser; and

(F) Any business or personal relationship of the compensation consultant, legal counsel, other adviser or the person employing the adviser with an executive officer of the listed company.

Commentary: Nothing in this Section 303A.05(c) shall be construed: (A) to require the compensation committee to implement or act consistently with the advice or recommendations of the compensation consultant, independent legal counsel or other adviser to the compensation committee; or (B) to affect the ability or obligation of the compensation committee to exercise its own judgment in fulfillment of the duties of the compensation committee.

The compensation committee is required to conduct the independence assessment outlined in Section 303A.05(c)(iv) with respect to any compensation consultant, legal counsel or other adviser that provides advice to the compensation committee, other than (i) in-house legal counsel; and (ii) any compensation consultant, legal counsel or other adviser whose role is limited to the following activities for which no disclosure would be required under Item 407(e)(3)(iii) of Regulation S-K: consulting on any broad-based plan that does not discriminate in scope, terms, or operation, in favor of executive officers or directors of the listed company, and that is available generally to all salaried employees; or providing information that either is not customized for a particular company or that is customized based on parameters that are not developed by the compensation consultant, and about which the compensation consultant does not provide advice.

Nothing in this Section 303A.05(c) requires a compensation consultant, legal counsel or other compensation adviser to be independent, only that the compensation committee consider the enumerated independence factors before selecting or receiving advice from a compensation adviser. The compensation committee may select or receive advice from any compensation adviser they prefer including ones that are not independent, after considering the six independence factors outlined in Section 303A.05(c)(iv)(A) — (F).

303A.06 Audit Committee

Listed companies must have an audit committee that satisfies the requirements of Rule 10A-3 under the Exchange Act.

Commentary: The Exchange will apply the requirements of Rule 10A-3 in a manner consistent with the guidance provided by the Securities and Exchange Commission in SEC Release No. 34-47654 (April 1, 2003). Without limiting the generality of the foregoing, the Exchange will provide companies the opportunity to cure defects provided in Rule 10A-3(a)(3) under the Exchange Act.

Disclosure Requirement: Please note that Rule 10A-3(d)(1) and (2) require listed companies to disclose reliance on certain exceptions from Rule 10A-3 and to disclose an assessment of whether, and if so, how, such reliance would materially adversely affect the ability of the audit committee to act independently and to satisfy the other requirements of Rule 10A-3.

303A.07 Audit Committee Additional Requirements

(a) The audit committee must have a minimum of three members. All audit committee members must satisfy the requirements for independence set out in Section 303A.02 and, in the absence of an applicable exemption, Rule 10A-3(b)(1).

Commentary: Each member of the audit committee must be financially literate, as such qualification is interpreted by the listed company's board in its business judgment, or must become financially literate within a reasonable period of time after his or her appointment to the audit committee. In addition, at least one member of the audit committee must have accounting or related financial management expertise, as the listed company's board interprets such qualification in its business judgment. While the Exchange does not require that a listed company's audit committee include a person who satisfies the definition of audit committee financial expert set out in Item 407(d)(5)(ii) of Regulation S-K, a board may presume that such a person has accounting or related financial management expertise.

Because of the audit committee's demanding role and responsibilities, and the time commitment attendant to committee membership, each prospective audit committee member should evaluate carefully the existing demands on his or her time before accepting this important assignment.

Disclosure Requirement: If an audit committee member simultaneously serves on the audit committees of more than three public companies, the board must determine that such simultaneous service would not impair the ability of such member to effectively serve on the listed company's audit committee and must disclose such determination either on or through the listed company's website or in its annual proxy statement or, if the listed company does not file an annual proxy statement, in its annual report on Form 10-K filed with the SEC. If this disclosure is made on or through the listed company's website, the listed company must disclose that fact in its annual proxy statement or annual report, as applicable, and provide the website address.

(b) The audit committee must have a written charter that addresses:

(i) the committee's purpose—which, at minimum, must be to:

(A) assist board oversight of (1) the integrity of the listed company's financial statements, (2) the listed company's compliance with legal and regulatory requirements, (3) the independent auditor's qualifications and independence, and (4) the performance of the listed company's internal audit function and independent auditors (if the listed company does not yet have an internal audit function because it is availing itself of a transition period pursuant to Section 303A.00, the charter must provide that the committee will assist board oversight of the design and implementation of the internal audit function); and

(B) prepare the disclosure required by Item 407(d)(3)(i) of Regulation S-K;

(ii) an annual performance evaluation of the audit committee; and

(iii) the duties and responsibilities of the audit committee—which, at a minimum, must include those set out in Rule 10A-3(b)(2), (3), (4) and (5) of the Exchange Act , as well as to:

(A) at least annually, obtain and review a report by the independent auditor describing: the firm's internal quality-control procedures; any material issues raised by the most recent internal quality-control review, or peer review, of the firm, or by any inquiry or investigation by governmental or professional authorities, within the preceding five years, respecting one or more independent audits carried out by the firm, and any steps taken to deal with any such issues; and (to assess the auditor's independence) all relationships between the independent auditor and the listed company;

Commentary: After reviewing the foregoing report and the independent auditor's work throughout the year, the audit committee will be in a position to evaluate the auditor's qualifications, performance and independence. This evaluation should include the review and evaluation of the lead partner of the independent auditor. In making its evaluation, the audit committee should take into account the opinions of management and the listed company's internal auditors (or other personnel responsible for the internal audit function). In addition to assuring the regular rotation of the lead audit partner as required by law, the audit committee should further consider whether, in order to assure continuing auditor independence, there should be regular rotation of the audit firm itself. The audit committee should present its conclusions with respect to the independent auditor to the full board.

(B) meet to review and discuss the listed company's annual audited financial statements and quarterly financial statements with management and the independent auditor, including reviewing the listed company's specific disclosures under "Management's Discussion and Analysis of Financial Condition and Results of Operations";

Commentary: Meetings may be telephonic if permitted under applicable corporate law; polling of audit committee members, however, is not permitted in lieu of meetings.

With respect to closed-end funds, Section 303A.07(b)(iii)(B) requires that the audit committee meet to review and discuss the fund's annual audited financial statements and semi-annual financial statements. In addition, if a closed-end fund chooses to voluntarily include the section "Management's Discussion of Fund Performance" in its Form N-CSR, then the audit committee is required to meet to review and discuss it.

(C) discuss the listed company's earnings press releases, as well as financial information and earnings guidance provided to analysts and rating agencies;

Commentary: The audit committee's responsibility to discuss earnings releases, as well as financial information and earnings guidance, may be done generally (i.e., discussion of the types of information to be disclosed and the type of presentation to be made). The audit committee need not discuss in advance each earnings release or each instance in which a listed company may provide earnings guidance.

(D) discuss policies with respect to risk assessment and risk management;

Commentary: While it is the job of the CEO and senior management to assess and manage the listed company's exposure to risk, the audit committee must discuss guidelines and policies to govern the process by which this is handled. The audit committee should discuss the listed company's major financial risk exposures and the steps management has taken to monitor and control such exposures. The audit committee is not required to be the sole body responsible for risk assessment and management, but, as stated above, the committee must discuss guidelines and policies to govern the process by which risk assessment and management is undertaken. Many companies, particularly financial companies, manage and assess their risk through mechanisms other than the audit committee. The processes these companies have in place should be reviewed in a general manner by the audit committee, but they need not be replaced by the audit committee.

(E) meet separately, periodically, with management, with internal auditors (or other personnel responsible for the internal audit function) and with independent auditors;

Commentary: To perform its oversight functions most effectively, the audit committee must have the benefit of separate sessions with management, the independent auditors and those responsible for the internal audit function. As noted herein, all listed companies must have an internal audit function. These separate sessions may be more productive than joint sessions in surfacing issues warranting committee attention. If the listed company does not yet have an internal audit function because it is availing itself of a transition period pursuant to Section 303A.00, the committee must meet periodically with the company personnel primarily responsible for the design and implementation of the internal audit function.

(F) review with the independent auditor any audit problems or difficulties and management's response;

Commentary: The audit committee must regularly review with the independent auditor any difficulties the auditor encountered in the course of the audit work, including any restrictions on the scope of the independent auditor's activities or on access to requested information, and any significant disagreements with management. Among the items the audit committee may want to review with the auditor are: any accounting adjustments that were noted or proposed by the auditor but were "passed" (as immaterial or otherwise); any communications between the audit team and the audit firm's national office respecting auditing or accounting issues presented by the engagement; and any "management" or "internal control" letter issued, or proposed to be issued, by the audit firm to the listed company. The review should also include discussion of the responsibilities, budget and staffing of the listed company's internal audit function. If the listed company does not yet have an internal audit function because it is availing itself of a transition period pursuant to Section 303A.00, the review should include discussion of management's plans with respect to the responsibilities, budget and staffing of the internal audit function and its plans for the implementation of the internal audit function.

(G) set clear hiring policies for employees or former employees of the independent auditors; and

Commentary: Employees or former employees of the independent auditor are often valuable additions to corporate management. Such individuals' familiarity with the business, and personal rapport with the employees, may be attractive qualities when filling a key opening. However, the audit committee should set hiring policies taking into account the pressures that may exist for auditors consciously or subconsciously seeking a job with the listed company they audit.

(H) report regularly to the board of directors.

Commentary: The audit committee should review with the full board any issues that arise with respect to the quality or integrity of the listed company's financial statements, the listed company's compliance with legal or regulatory requirements, the performance and independence of the listed company's independent auditors, or the performance of the internal audit function. If the listed company does not yet have an internal audit function because it is availing itself of a transition period pursuant to Section 303A.00, the committee should review with the board management's activities with respect to the design and implementation of the internal audit function.

General Commentary to Section 303A.07(b): While the fundamental responsibility for the listed company's financial statements and disclosures rests with management and the independent auditor, the audit committee must review: (A) major issues regarding accounting principles and financial statement presentations, including any significant changes in the listed company's selection or application of accounting principles, and major issues as to the adequacy of the listed company's internal controls and any special audit steps adopted in light of material control deficiencies; (B) analyses prepared by management and/or the independent auditor setting forth significant financial reporting issues and judgments made in connection with the preparation of the financial statements, including analyses of the effects of alternative GAAP methods on the financial statements; (C) the effect of regulatory and accounting initiatives, as well as off-balance sheet structures, on the financial statements of the listed company; and (D) the type and presentation of information to be included in earnings press releases (paying particular attention to any use of "pro forma," or "adjusted" non-GAAP, information), as well as review any financial information and earnings guidance provided to analysts and rating agencies.

Website Posting Requirement: A listed company must make its audit committee charter available on or through its website. A closed-end fund is not required to comply with this website posting requirement.

Disclosure Requirements: A listed company must disclose in its annual proxy statement or, if it does not file an annual proxy statement, in its annual report on Form 10-K filed with the SEC that its audit committee charter is available on or through its website and provide the website address.

(c) Each listed company must have an internal audit function.

Commentary: Listed companies must maintain an internal audit function to provide management and the audit committee with ongoing assessments of the listed company's risk management processes and system of internal control. A listed company may choose to outsource this function to a third party service provider other than its independent auditor. While Section 303A.00 permits certain categories of newly-listed companies to avail themselves of a transition period to comply with the internal audit function requirement, all listed companies must have an internal audit function in place no later than the first anniversary of the company's listing date.

General Commentary to Section 303A.07: To avoid any confusion, note that the audit committee functions specified in Section 303A.07 are the sole responsibility of the audit committee and may not be allocated to a different committee.

303A.08 Shareholder Approval of Equity Compensation Plans

Shareholders must be given the opportunity to vote on all equity-compensation plans and material revisions thereto, with limited exemptions explained below.

Equity-compensation plans can help align shareholder and management interests, and equity-based awards are often very important components of employee compensation. To provide checks and balances on the potential dilution resulting from the process of earmarking shares to be used for equity-based awards, the Exchange requires that all equity-compensation plans, and any material revisions to the terms of such plans, be subject to shareholder approval, with the limited exemptions explained below.

Definition of Equity-Compensation Plan

An "equity-compensation plan" is a plan or other arrangement that provides for the delivery of equity securities (either newly issued or treasury shares) of the listed company to any employee, director or other service provider as compensation for services. Even a compensatory grant of options or other equity securities that is not made under a plan is, nonetheless, an "equity-compensation plan" for these purposes.

However, the following are not "equity-compensation plans" even if the brokerage and other costs of the plan are paid for by the listed company:

- Plans that are made available to shareholders generally, such as a typical dividend reinvestment plan.
- Plans that merely allow employees, directors or other service providers to elect to buy shares on the open market or from the listed company for their current fair market value, regardless of whether:
  — the shares are delivered immediately or on a deferred basis; or
  — the payments for the shares are made directly or by giving up compensation that is otherwise due (for example, through payroll deductions).

Material Revisions

A "material revision" of an equity-compensation plan includes (but is not limited to), the following:

- A material increase in the number of shares available under the plan (other than an increase solely to reflect a reorganization, stock split, merger, spin-off or similar transaction).
  — If a plan contains a formula for automatic increases in the shares available (sometimes called an "evergreen formula") or for automatic grants pursuant to a formula, each such increase or grant will be considered a revision requiring shareholder approval unless the plan has a term of not more than ten years.

  This type of plan (regardless of its term) is referred to below as a "formula plan." Examples of automatic grants pursuant to a formula are (1) annual grants to directors of restricted stock having a certain dollar value, and (2) "matching contributions," whereby stock is credited to a participant's account based upon the amount of compensation the participant elects to defer.

  — If a plan contains no limit on the number of shares available and is not a formula plan, then each grant under the plan will require separate shareholder approval regardless of whether the plan has a term of not more than ten years.

This type of plan is referred to below as a "discretionary plan." A requirement that grants be made out of treasury shares or repurchased shares will not, in itself, be considered a limit or pre-established formula so as to prevent a plan from being considered a discretionary plan.

- An expansion of the types of awards available under the plan.
- A material expansion of the class of employees, directors or other service providers eligible to participate in the plan.
- A material extension of the term of the plan.
- A material change to the method of determining the strike price of options under the plan.
  —A change in the method of determining "fair market value" from the closing price on the date of grant to the average of the high and low price on the date of grant is an example of a change that the Exchange would not view as material.
- The deletion or limitation of any provision prohibiting repricing of options. See the next section for details.

  Note that an amendment will not be considered a "material revision" if it curtails rather than expands the scope of the plan in question.

Repricings

A plan that does not contain a provision that specifically permits repricing of options will be considered for purposes of this listing standard as prohibiting repricing. Accordingly any actual repricing of options will be considered a material revision of a plan even if the plan itself is not revised. This consideration will not apply to a repricing through an exchange offer that commenced before the date this listing standard became effective.

"Repricing" means any of the following or any other action that has the same effect:

- Lowering the strike price of an option after it is granted.
- Any other action that is treated as a repricing under generally accepted accounting principles.
- Canceling an option at a time when its strike price exceeds the fair market value of the underlying stock, in exchange for another option, restricted stock, or other equity, unless the cancellation and exchange occurs in connection with a merger, acquisition, spin-off or other similar corporate transaction.

Exemptions

This listing standard does not require shareholder approval of employment inducement awards, certain grants, plans and amendments in the context of mergers and acquisitions, and certain specific types of plans, all as described below. However, these exempt grants, plans and amendments may be made only with the approval of the listed company's independent compensation committee or the approval of a majority of the listed company's independent directors. Companies must also notify the Exchange in writing when they use one of these exemptions.

Employment Inducement Awards

An employment inducement award is a grant of options or other equity-based compensation as a material inducement to a person or persons being hired by the listed company or any of its subsidiaries, or being rehired following a bona fide period of interruption of employment. Inducement awards include grants to new employees in connection with a merger or acquisition. Promptly following a grant of any inducement award in reliance on this exemption, the listed company must disclose in a press release the material terms of the award, including the recipient(s) of the award and the number of shares involved.

Mergers and Acquisitions

Two exemptions apply in the context of corporate acquisitions and mergers.

First, shareholder approval will not be required to convert, replace or adjust outstanding options or other equity-compensation awards to reflect the transaction.

Second, shares available under certain plans acquired in corporate acquisitions and mergers may be used for certain post-transaction grants without further shareholder approval. This exemption applies to situations where a party that is not a listed company following the transaction has shares available for grant under pre-existing plans that were previously approved by shareholders. A plan adopted in contemplation of the merger or acquisition transaction would not be considered "pre-existing" for purposes of this exemption.

Shares available under such a pre-existing plan may be used for post-transaction grants of options and other awards with respect to equity of the entity that is the listed company after the transaction, either under the pre-existing plan or another plan, without further shareholder approval, so long as:

- the number of shares available for grants is appropriately adjusted to reflect the transaction;
- the time during which those shares are available is not extended beyond the period when they would have been available under the pre-existing plan, absent the transaction; and
- the options and other awards are not granted to individuals who were employed, immediately before the transaction, by the post-

transaction listed company or entities that were its subsidiaries immediately before the transaction.

Any shares reserved for listing in connection with a transaction pursuant to either of these exemptions would be counted by the Exchange in determining whether the transaction involved the issuance of 20% or more of the listed company's outstanding common stock and thus required shareholder approval under Listed Company Manual Section 312.03(c).

These merger-related exemptions will not result in any increase in the aggregate potential dilution of the combined enterprise. Further, mergers or acquisitions are not routine occurrences, and are not likely to be abused. Therefore, the Exchange considers both of these exemptions to be consistent with the fundamental policy involved in this standard.

Qualified Plans, Parallel Excess Plans and Section 423 Plans

The following types of plans (and material revisions thereto) are exempt from the shareholder approval requirement:

- plans intended to meet the requirements of Section 401(a) of the Internal Revenue Code (e.g., ESOPs);
- plans intended to meet the requirements of Section 423 of the Internal Revenue Code; and
- "parallel excess plans" as defined below.

Section 401(a) plans and Section 423 plans are already regulated under the Internal Revenue Code and Treasury regulations. Section 423 plans, which are stock purchase plans under which an employee can purchase no more than $25,000 worth of stock per year at a plan-specified discount capped at 15%, are also required by the Internal Revenue Code to receive shareholder approval. While Section 401(a) plans and parallel excess plans are not required to be approved by shareholders, U.S. GAAP requires that the shares issued under these plans be "expensed" (i.e., treated as a compensation expense on the income statement) by the company issuing the shares.

An equity-compensation plan that provides non-U.S. employees with substantially the same benefits as a comparable Section 401(a) plan, Section 423 plan or parallel excess plan that the listed company provides to its U.S. employees, but for features necessary to comply with applicable foreign tax law, are also exempt from shareholder approval under this section.

The term "parallel excess plan" means a plan that is a "pension plan" within the meaning of the Employee Retirement Income Security Act ("ERISA") that is designed to work in parallel with a plan intended to be qualified under Internal Revenue Code Section 401(a) to provide benefits that exceed the limits set forth in Internal Revenue Code Section

402(g) (the section that limits an employee's annual pre-tax contributions to a 401(k) plan), Internal Revenue Code Section 401(a)(17) (the section that limits the amount of an employee's compensation that can be taken into account for plan purposes) and/or Internal Revenue Code Section 415 (the section that limits the contributions and benefits under qualified plans) and/or any successor or similar limitations that may hereafter be enacted. A plan will not be considered a parallel excess plan unless (1) it covers all or substantially all employees of an employer who are participants in the related qualified plan whose annual compensation is in excess of the limit of Code Section 401(a)(17) (or any successor or similar limits that may hereafter be enacted); (2) its terms are substantially the same as the qualified plan that it parallels except for the elimination of the limits described in the preceding sentence and the limitation described in clause (3); and (3) no participant receives employer equity contributions under the plan in excess of 25% of the participant's cash compensation.

Transition Rules

Initial Limited Transition Period

Except as provided below, a plan that was adopted before June 30, 2003 will not be subject to shareholder approval under this listing standard unless and until it is materially revised.

In the case of a discretionary plan (as defined in "Material Revisions" above), whether or not previously approved by shareholders, additional grants may not be made without further shareholder approval. In applying this rule, if a plan can be separated into a discretionary plan portion and a portion that is not discretionary, the non-discretionary portion of the plan can continue to be used separately, under the appropriate transition rule. For example, if a shareholder-approved plan permits both grants pursuant to a provision that makes available a specific number of shares, and grants pursuant to a provision authorizing the use of treasury shares without regard to the specific share limit, the former provision (but not the latter) may continue to be used after the transition period, under the general rule above.

Similarly, in the case of a formula plan (as defined in "Material Revisions" above) that either (1) has not previously been approved by shareholders or (2) does not have a term of ten years or less, additional grants may not be made without further shareholder approval.

A shareholder-approved formula plan may continue to be used if it is amended to provide for a term of ten years or less from the date of its original adoption or, if later, the date of its most recent shareholder approval. Such an amendment would not itself be considered a "material revision" requiring shareholder approval.

In addition, a formula plan may continue to be used, without shareholder approval, if the grants after June 30, 2003 are made *only* from the shares available immediately before the effective date, in other words, based on formulaic increases that occurred prior June 30, 2003.

Ongoing Transition Period for a Foreign Private Issuer Whose Status Changes

To the extent that a listed foreign private issuer ceases to qualify as such under SEC rules (so that it is required to file on domestic forms with the SEC) and as a result of such change in status becomes subject to Section 303A.08 for the first time, such listed company will be granted a limited transition period with respect to discretionary plans and formula plans that do not comply with Section 303A.08 that were in place prior to the date that its status changed so that additional grants may be made after the date that its status changed without shareholder approval. This transition period will end upon the later to occur of:

- six months after the date as of which the listed company fails to qualify for foreign private issuer status pursuant to SEC Rule 240.3b-4. Under SEC Rule 240.3b-4, a company tests its status as a foreign private issuer on an annual basis at the end of its most recently completed second fiscal quarter (hereinafter, for purposes of this subsection, the "Determination Date"); and
- the first annual meeting after the Determination Date,

but, in any event no later than one year after the Determination Date.

A shareholder-approved formula plan may continue to be used after the end of this transition period if it is amended to provide for a term of ten years or less from the date of its original adoption or, if later, the date of its most recent shareholder approval. Such an amendment may be made before or after the Determination Date, and would not itself be considered a "material revision" requiring shareholder approval.

In addition, a formula plan may continue to be used, without shareholder approval, if the grants after the date that the listed company's status changed are made only from the shares available immediately before the Determination Date, in other words, based on formulaic increases that occurred prior to the Determination Date.

312.03. Shareholder Approval

Shareholder approval is a prerequisite to issuing securities in the following situations:

(a) Shareholder approval is required for equity compensation plans. See Section 303A.08.

(b) Shareholder approval is required prior to the issuance of common stock, or of securities convertible into or exercisable for common stock, in any transaction or series of related transactions, to:

(1) a director, officer or substantial security holder of the company (each a "Related Party");

(2) a subsidiary, affiliate or other closely-related person of a Related Party; or

(3) any company or entity in which a Related Party has a substantial direct or indirect interest;

if the number of shares of common stock to be issued, or if the number of shares of common stock into which the securities may be convertible or exercisable, exceeds either one percent of the number of shares of common stock or one percent of the voting power outstanding before the issuance.

However, if the Related Party involved in the transaction is classified as such solely because such person is a substantial security holder, and if the issuance relates to a sale of stock for cash at a price at least as great as each of the book and market value of the issuer's common stock, then shareholder approval will not be required unless the number of shares of common stock to be issued, or unless the number of shares of common stock into which the securities may be convertible or exercisable, exceeds either five percent of the number of shares of common stock or five percent of the voting power outstanding before the issuance.

(c) Shareholder approval is required prior to the issuance of common stock, or of securities convertible into or exercisable for common stock, in any transaction or series of related transactions if:

(1) the common stock has, or will have upon issuance, voting power equal to or in excess of 20 percent of the voting power outstanding before the issuance of such stock or of securities convertible into or exercisable for common stock; or

(2) the number of shares of common stock to be issued is, or will be upon issuance, equal to or in excess of 20 percent of the number of shares of common stock outstanding before the issuance of the common stock or of securities convertible into or exercisable for common stock.

However, shareholder approval will not be required for any such issuance involving:

- any public offering for cash;
- any bona fide private financing, if such financing involves a sale of:
- common stock, for cash, at a price at least as great as each of the book and market value of the issuer's common stock; or
- securities convertible into or exercisable for common stock, for cash, if the conversion or exercise price is at least as great as each of the book and market value of the issuer's common stock.

(d) Shareholder approval is required prior to an issuance that will result in a change of control of the issuer.

(e) Sections 312.03 (b), (c) and (d) shall not apply to issuances by limited partnerships.

Limited Transition Period

Prior to December 21, 2006, this rule included an exception from the required calculations for issuances of treasury stock. In light of companies' need for certainty when planning a transaction involving the issuance of shares, if a company has executed a binding contract prior to October 23, 2006 with respect to the issuance of common stock, the existing treasury share exception will continue to be available for the transaction even though the transaction does not close until after the date the SEC approval of this proposed rule change.

313.00. Voting Rights

(A) Voting Rights Policy

On May 5, 1994, the Exchange's Board of Directors voted to modify the Exchange's Voting Rights Policy, which had been based on former SEC Rule 19c-4. The Policy is more flexible than Rule 19c-4. Accordingly, the Exchange will continue to permit corporate actions or issuances by listed companies that would have been permitted under Rule 19c-4, as well as other actions or issuances that are not inconsistent with the new Policy. In evaluating such other actions or issuances, the Exchange will consider, among other things, the economics of such actions or issuances and the voting rights being granted. The Exchange's interpretations under the Policy will be flexible, recognizing that both the capital markets and the circumstances and needs of listed companies change over time. The text of the Exchange's Voting Rights Policy is as follows:

Voting rights of existing shareholders of publicly traded common stock registered under Section 12 of the Exchange Act cannot be disparately reduced or restricted through any corporate action or issuance. Examples of such corporate action or issuance include, but are not limited to, the adoption of time phased voting plans, the adoption of capped voting rights plans, the issuance of super voting stock, or the issuance of stock with voting rights less than the per share voting rights of the existing common stock through an exchange offer.

(B) Non-Voting Common Stock

The Exchange's voting rights policy permits the listing of the voting common stock of a company which also has outstanding a non-voting common stock as well as the listing of non-voting common stock. However, certain safeguards must be provided to holders of a listed non-voting common stock:

(1) Any class of non-voting common stock that is listed on the Exchange must meet all original listing standards.

The rights of the holders of the non-voting common stock should, except for voting rights, be substantially the same as those of the holders of the company's voting common stock.

(2) Although the holders of shares of listed non-voting common stock are not entitled to vote generally on matters submitted for shareholder action, holders of any listed non-voting common stock must receive all communications, including proxy material, sent generally to the holders of the voting securities of the listed company.

(C) Preferred Stock, Minimum Voting Rights Required

Preferred stock, voting as a class, should have the right to elect a minimum of two directors upon default of the equivalent of six quarterly dividends. The right to elect directors should accrue regardless of whether defaulted dividends occurred in consecutive periods.

The right to elect directors should remain in effect until cumulative dividends have been paid in full or until non-cumulative dividends have been paid regularly for at least a year. The preferred stock quorum should be low enough to ensure that the right to elect directors can be exercised as soon as it accrues. In no event should the quorum exceed the percentage required for a quorum of the common stock required for the election of directors. The Exchange prefers that no quorum requirement be fixed in respect of the right of a preferred stock, voting as a class, to elect directors when dividends are in default.

The Exchange recommends that preferred stock should have minimum voting rights even if the preferred stock is not listed.

Increase in Authorized Amount or Creation of a Pari Passu Issue.—

- An increase in the authorized amount of a class of preferred stock or the creation of a pari passu issue should be approved by a majority of the holders of the outstanding shares of the class or classes to be affected. The Board of Directors may increase the authorized amount of a series or create an additional series ranking pari passu without a vote by the existing series if shareholders authorized such action by the Board of Directors at the time the class of preferred stock was created.

Creation of a Senior Issue—

- Creation of a senior equity security should require approval of at least two-thirds of the outstanding preferred shares. The Board of Directors may create a senior series without a vote by the existing series if shareholders authorized such action by the Board of Directors at the time of the existing series of preferred stock was created.
- A vote by an existing class of preferred stock is not required for the creation of a senior issue if the existing class has previously received adequate notice of redemption to occur within 90 days. However, the vote of the existing class should not be denied if all or part of the existing issue is being retired with proceeds from the sale of the new stock.

Alteration of Existing Provisions—

- Approval by the holders of at least two-thirds of the outstanding shares of a preferred stock should be required for adoption of any charter or by-law amendment that would materially affect existing terms of the preferred stock.
- If all series of a class of preferred stock are not equally affected by the proposed changes, there should be a two-thirds approval of the class and a two-thirds approval of the series that will have a diminished status.
- The charter should not hinder the shareholders' right to alter the terms of a preferred stock by limiting modification to specific items, e.g., interest rate, redemption price.

Supplementary Material

.10 Companies with Dual Class Structures—

The restriction against the issuance of super voting stock is primarily intended to apply to the issuance of a new class of stock, and companies with existing dual class capital structures would generally be permitted to issue additional shares of the existing super voting stock without conflict with this Policy.

.20 Consultation with the Exchange—

Violation of the Exchange's Voting Rights Policy could result in the loss of an Issuer's Exchange market or public trading market. The Policy can apply to a variety of corporate actions and securities issuances, not just super voting or so-called "time phase" voting common stock. While the Policy will continue to permit actions previously permitted under Rule 19c-4, it is extremely important that listed companies communicate their intentions to their Exchange representatives as early as possible before taking any action or committing to take any action that may be inconsistent with the Policy. The Exchange urges listed companies not to assume, without first discussing the matter with the Exchange staff, that a particular issuance of common or preferred stock or the taking of some other corporate action will necessarily be consistent with the Policy. It is suggested that copies of preliminary proxy or other material concerning matters subject to the Policy be furnished to the Exchange for review prior to formal filing.

.30 Review of Past Voting Rights Activities—

In reviewing an application for initial listing on the Exchange, the Exchange will review the issuer's past corporate actions to determine whether another self-regulatory organization ("SRO") has found any of the issuer's actions to have been a violation or evasion of the SRO's voting rights policy. Based on such review, the Exchange may take any appropriate action, including the denial of the listing or the placing of restrictions on such listing. The Exchange will also review whether an issuer seeking initial listing on the Exchange has requested a ruling or interpretation from another SRO regarding the application of that SRO's voting rights policy with respect to a proposed transaction. If so, the Exchange will consider that fact in determining its response to any ruling or interpretation that the issuer may request on the same or similar transaction.

.40 Non-U.S. Companies—

The Exchange will accept any action or issuance relating to the voting rights structure of a non-U.S. company that is in compliance with the Exchange's requirements for domestic companies or that is not prohibited by the company's home country law.

EUROPEAN TAKEOVER DIRECTIVE

Article 1. Scope

1. This Directive lays down measures coordinating the laws, regulations, administrative provisions, codes of practice and other arrangements of the Member States, including arrangements established by organisations officially authorised to regulate the markets (hereinafter referred to as 'rules'), relating to takeover bids for the securities of companies governed by the laws of Member States, where all or some of those securities are admitted to trading on a regulated market within the meaning of Directive 93/22/EEC[1] in one or more Member States (hereinafter referred to as a 'regulated market').

2. This Directive shall not apply to takeover bids for securities issued by companies, the object of which is the collective investment of capital provided

1. Council Directive 93/22/EEC of 10 May 1993 on investment services in the securities field (OJ L 141, 11.6.1993, p. 27). Directive as last amended by Directive 2002/87/EC of the European Parliament and of the Council (OJ L 35, 11.2.2003, p. 1).

by the public, which operate on the principle of risk-spreading and the units of which are, at the holders' request, repurchased or redeemed, directly or indirectly, out of the assets of those companies. Action taken by such companies to ensure that the stock exchange value of their units does not vary significantly from their net asset value shall be regarded as equivalent to such repurchase or redemption.

3. This Directive shall not apply to takeover bids for securities issued by the Member States' central banks.

Article 2. Definitions

1. For the purposes of this Directive:

(a) 'takeover bid' or 'bid' shall mean a public offer (other than by the offeree company itself) made to the holders of the securities of a company to acquire all or some of those securities, whether mandatory or voluntary, which follows or has as its objective the acquisition of control of the offeree company in accordance with national law;

(b) 'offeree company' shall mean a company, the securities of which are the subject of a bid;

(c) 'offeror' shall mean any natural or legal person governed by public or private law making a bid;

(d) 'persons acting in concert' shall mean natural or legal persons who cooperate with the offeror or the offeree company on the basis of an agreement, either express or tacit, either oral or written, aimed either at acquiring control of the offeree company or at frustrating the successful outcome of a bid;

(e) 'securities' shall mean transferable securities carrying voting rights in a company;

(f) 'parties to the bid' shall mean the offeror, the members of the offeror's board if the offeror is a company, the offeree company, holders of securities of the offeree company and the members of the board of the offeree company, and persons acting in concert with such parties;

(g) 'multiple-vote securities' shall mean securities included in a distinct and separate class and carrying more than one vote each.

2. For the purposes of paragraph 1(d), persons controlled by another person within the meaning of Article 87 of Directive 2001/34/EC[2] shall be deemed to be persons acting in concert with that other person and with each other.

2. Directive 2001/34/EC of the European Parliament and of the Council of 28 May 2001 on the admission of securities to official stock exchange listing and on information to be published on those securities (OJ L 184, 6.7.2001, p. 1). Directive as last amended by Directive 2003/71/EC (OJ L 345, 31.12.2003, p. 64).

Article 3. General Principles

1. For the purpose of implementing this Directive, Member States shall ensure that the following principles are complied with:

(a) all holders of the securities of an offeree company of the same class must be afforded equivalent treatment; moreover, if a person acquires control of a company, the other holders of securities must be protected;

(b) the holders of the securities of an offeree company must have sufficient time and information to enable them to reach a properly informed decision on the bid; where it advises the holders of securities, the board of the offeree company must give its views on the effects of implementation of the bid on employment, conditions of employment and the locations of the company's places of business;

(c) the board of an offeree company must act in the interests of the company as a whole and must not deny the holders of securities the opportunity to decide on the merits of the bid;

(d) false markets must not be created in the securities of the offeree company, of the offeror company or of any other company concerned by the bid in such a way that the rise or fall of the prices of the securities becomes artificial and the normal functioning of the markets is distorted;

(e) an offeror must announce a bid only after ensuring that he/she can fulfil in full any cash consideration, if such is offered, and after taking all reasonable measures to secure the implementation of any other type of consideration;

(f) an offeree company must not be hindered in the conduct of its affairs for longer than is reasonable by a bid for its securities.

2. With a view to ensuring compliance with the principles laid down in paragraph 1, Member States:

(a) shall ensure that the minimum requirements set out in this Directive are observed;

(b) may lay down additional conditions and provisions more stringent than those of this Directive for the regulation of bids.

Article 5. Protection of Minority Shareholders, the Mandatory Bid and the Equitable Price

1. Where a natural or legal person, as a result of his/her own acquisition or the acquisition by persons acting in concert with him/her, holds securities of a company as referred to in Article 1(1) which, added to any existing holdings of those securities of his/hers and the holdings of those securities of persons acting in concert with him/her, directly or indirectly give him/her a specified percentage of voting rights in that company, giving him/her control of that company, Member States shall ensure that such a person is required to make a bid as a means of protecting the minority shareholders of that company. Such a bid shall be addressed at the earliest opportunity to all the

holders of those securities for all their holdings at the equitable price as defined in paragraph 4.

2. Where control has been acquired following a voluntary bid made in accordance with this Directive to all the holders of securities for all their holdings, the obligation laid down in paragraph 1 to launch a bid shall no longer apply.

3. The percentage of voting rights which confers control for the purposes of paragraph 1 and the method of its calculation shall be determined by the rules of the Member State in which the company has its registered office.

4. The highest price paid for the same securities by the offeror, or by persons acting in concert with him/her, over a period, to be determined by Member States, of not less than six months and not more than 12 before the bid referred to in paragraph 1 shall be regarded as the equitable price. If, after the bid has been made public and before the offer closes for acceptance, the offeror or any person acting in concert with him/her purchases securities at a price higher than the offer price, the offeror shall increase his/her offer so that it is not less than the highest price paid for the securities so acquired.

Provided that the general principles laid down in Article 3(1) are respected, Member States may authorise their supervisory authorities to adjust the price referred to in the first subparagraph in circumstances and in accordance with criteria that are clearly determined. To that end, they may draw up a list of circumstances in which the highest price may be adjusted either upwards or downwards, for example where the highest price was set by agreement between the purchaser and a seller, where the market prices of the securities in question have been manipulated, where market prices in general or certain market prices in particular have been affected by exceptional occurrences, or in order to enable a firm in difficulty to be rescued. They may also determine the criteria to be applied in such cases, for example the average market value over a particular period, the break-up value of the company or other objective valuation criteria generally used in financial analysis. Any decision by a supervisory authority to adjust the equitable price shall be substantiated and made public.

5. By way of consideration the offeror may offer securities, cash or a combination of both.

However, where the consideration offered by the offeror does not consist of liquid securities admitted to trading on a regulated market, it shall include a cash alternative.

In any event, the offeror shall offer a cash consideration at least as an alternative where he/she or persons acting in concert with him/her, over a period beginning at the same time as the period determined by the Member State in accordance with paragraph 4 and ending when the offer closes for acceptance, has purchased for cash securities carrying 5% or more of the voting rights in the offeree company.

Member States may provide that a cash consideration must be offered, at least as an alternative, in all cases.

6. In addition to the protection provided for in paragraph 1, Member States may provide for further instruments intended to protect the interests of the holders of securities in so far as those instruments do not hinder the normal course of a bid.

Article 6. Information Concerning Bids

1. Member States shall ensure that a decision to make a bid is made public without delay and that the supervisory authority is informed of the bid. They may require that the supervisory authority must be informed before such a decision is made public. As soon as the bid has been made public, the boards of the offeree company and of the offeror shall inform the representatives of their respective employees or, where there are no such representatives, the employees themselves.

2. Member States shall ensure that an offeror is required to draw up and make public in good time an offer document containing the information necessary to enable the holders of the offeree company's securities to reach a properly informed decision on the bid. Before the offer document is made public, the offeror shall communicate it to the supervisory authority. When it is made public, the boards of the offeree company and of the offeror shall communicate it to the representatives of their respective employees or, where there are no such representatives, to the employees themselves.

Where the offer document referred to in the first subparagraph is subject to the prior approval of the supervisory authority and has been approved, it shall be recognised, subject to any translation required, in any other Member State on the market of which the offeree company's securities are admitted to trading, without its being necessary to obtain the approval of the supervisory authorities of that Member State. Those authorities may require the inclusion of additional information in the offer document only if such information is specific to the market of a Member State or Member States on which the offeree company's securities are admitted to trading and relates to the formalities to be complied with to accept the bid and to receive the consideration due at the close of the bid as well as to the tax arrangements to which the consideration offered to the holders of the securities will be subject.

3. The offer document referred to in paragraph 2 shall state at least:

(a) the terms of the bid;

(b) the identity of the offeror and, where the offeror is a company, the type, name and registered office of that company;

(c) the securities or, where appropriate, the class or classes of securities for which the bid is made;

(d) the consideration offered for each security or class of securities and, in the case of a mandatory bid, the method employed in determining it, with particulars of the way in which that consideration is to be paid;

(e) the compensation offered for the rights which might be removed as a result of the breakthrough rule laid down in Article 11(4), with particulars of the way in which that compensation is to be paid and the method employed in determining it;

(f) the maximum and minimum percentages or quantities of securities which the offeror undertakes to acquire;

(g) details of any existing holdings of the offeror, and of persons acting in concert with him/her, in the offeree company;

(h) all the conditions to which the bid is subject;

(i) the offeror's intentions with regard to the future business of the offeree company and, in so far as it is affected by the bid, the offeror company and with regard to the safeguarding of the jobs of their employees and management, including any material change in the conditions of employment, and in particular the offeror's strategic plans for the two companies and the likely repercussions on employment and the locations of the companies' places of business;

(j) the time allowed for acceptance of the bid;

(k) where the consideration offered by the offeror includes securities of any kind, information concerning those securities;

(l) information concerning the financing for the bid;

(m) the identity of persons acting in concert with the offeror or with the offeree company and, in the case of companies, their types, names, registered offices and relationships with the offeror and, where possible, with the offeree company;

(n) the national law which will govern contracts concluded between the offeror and the holders of the offeree company's securities as a result of the bid and the competent courts.

4. The Commission shall adopt rules for the application of paragraph 3 in accordance with the procedure referred to in Article 18(2).

5. Member States shall ensure that the parties to a bid are required to provide the supervisory authorities of their Member State at any time on request with all the information in their possession concerning the bid that is necessary for the supervisory authority to discharge its functions.

Article 7. Time Allowed for Acceptance

1. Member States shall provide that the time allowed for the acceptance of a bid may not be less than two weeks nor more than 10 weeks from the date of publication of the offer document. Provided that the general principle laid down in Article 3(1)(f) is respected, Member States may provide that the period of 10 weeks may be extended on condition that the offeror gives at least two weeks' notice of his/her intention of closing the bid.

2. Member States may provide for rules changing the period referred to in paragraph 1 in specific cases. A Member State may authorise a supervisory authority to grant a derogation from the period referred to in paragraph 1 in

order to allow the offeree company to call a general meeting of shareholders to consider the bid.

Article 8. Disclosure

1. Member States shall ensure that a bid is made public in such a way as to ensure market transparency and integrity for the securities of the offeree company, of the offeror or of any other company affected by the bid, in particular in order to prevent the publication or dissemination of false or misleading information.

2. Member States shall provide for the disclosure of all information and documents required by Article 6 in such a manner as to ensure that they are both readily and promptly available to the holders of securities at least in those Member States on the regulated markets of which the offeree company's securities are admitted to trading and to the representatives of the employees of the offeree company and the offeror or, where there are no such representatives, to the employees themselves.

Article 9. Obligations of the Board of the Offeree Company

1. Member States shall ensure that the rules laid down in paragraphs 2 to 5 are complied with.

2. During the period referred to in the second subparagraph, the board of the offeree company shall obtain the prior authorisation of the general meeting of shareholders given for this purpose before taking any action, other than seeking alternative bids, which may result in the frustration of the bid and in particular before issuing any shares which may result in a lasting impediment to the offeror's acquiring control of the offeree company.

Such authorisation shall be mandatory at least from the time the board of the offeree company receives the information referred to in the first sentence of Article 6(1) concerning the bid and until the result of the bid is made public or the bid lapses. Member States may require that such authorisation be obtained at an earlier stage, for example as soon as the board of the offeree company becomes aware that the bid is imminent.

3. As regards decisions taken before the beginning of the period referred to in the second subparagraph of paragraph 2 and not yet partly or fully implemented, the general meeting of shareholders shall approve or confirm any decision which does not form part of the normal course of the company's business and the implementation of which may result in the frustration of the bid.

4. For the purpose of obtaining the prior authorisation, approval or confirmation of the holders of securities referred to in paragraphs 2 and 3, Member States may adopt rules allowing a general meeting of shareholders to be called at short notice, provided that the meeting does not take place within two weeks of notification's being given.

5. The board of the offeree company shall draw up and make public a document setting out its opinion of the bid and the reasons on which it is based, including its views on the effects of implementation of the bid on all the company's interests and specifically employment, and on the offeror's strategic plans for the offeree company and their likely repercussions on employment and the locations of the company's places of business as set out in the offer document in accordance with Article 6(3)(i). The board of the offeree company shall at the same time communicate that opinion to the representatives of its employees or, where there are no such representatives, to the employees themselves. Where the board of the offeree company receives in good time a separate opinion from the representatives of its employees on the effects of the bid on employment, that opinion shall be appended to the document.

6. For the purposes of paragraph 2, where a company has a two-tier board structure 'board' shall mean both the management board and the supervisory board.

Article 10. Information on Companies as Referred to in Article 1(1)

1. Member States shall ensure that companies as referred to in Article 1(1) publish detailed information on the following:

(a) the structure of their capital, including securities which are not admitted to trading on a regulated market in a Member State, where appropriate with an indication of the different classes of shares and, for each class of shares, the rights and obligations attaching to it and the percentage of total share capital that it represents;

(b) any restrictions on the transfer of securities, such as limitations on the holding of securities or the need to obtain the approval of the company or other holders of securities, without prejudice to Article 46 of Directive 2001/34/EC;

(c) significant direct and indirect shareholdings (including indirect shareholdings through pyramid structures and cross-shareholdings) within the meaning of Article 85 of Directive 2001/34/EC;

(d) the holders of any securities with special control rights and a description of those rights;

(e) the system of control of any employee share scheme where the control rights are not exercised directly by the employees;

(f) any restrictions on voting rights, such as limitations of the voting rights of holders of a given percentage or number of votes, deadlines for exercising voting rights, or systems whereby, with the company's cooperation, the financial rights attaching to securities are separated from the holding of securities;

(g) any agreements between shareholders which are known to the company and may result in restrictions on the transfer of securities and/ or voting rights within the meaning of Directive 2001/34/EC;

(h) the rules governing the appointment and replacement of board members and the amendment of the articles of association;

(i) the powers of board members, and in particular the power to issue or buy back shares;

(j) any significant agreements to which the company is a party and which take effect, alter or terminate upon a change of control of the company following a takeover bid, and the effects thereof, except where their nature is such that their disclosure would be seriously prejudicial to the company; this exception shall not apply where the company is specifically obliged to disclose such information on the basis of other legal requirements;

(k) any agreements between the company and its board members or employees providing for compensation if they resign or are made redundant without valid reason or if their employment ceases because of a takeover bid.

2. The information referred to in paragraph 1 shall be published in the company's annual report as provided for in Article 46 of Directive 78/660/EEC[3] and Article 36 of Directive 83/349/EEC.[4]

3. Member States shall ensure, in the case of companies the securities of which are admitted to trading on a regulated market in a Member State, that the board presents an explanatory report to the annual general meeting of shareholders on the matters referred to in paragraph 1.

Article 11. Breakthrough

1. Without prejudice to other rights and obligations provided for in Community law for the companies referred to in Article 1(1), Member States shall ensure that the provisions laid down in paragraphs 2 to 7 apply when a bid has been made public.

2. Any restrictions on the transfer of securities provided for in the articles of association of the offeree company shall not apply vis-à-vis the offeror during the time allowed for acceptance of the bid laid down in Article 7(1).

Any restrictions on the transfer of securities provided for in contractual agreements between the offeree company and holders of its securities, or in contractual agreements between holders of the offeree company's securities entered into after the adoption of this Directive, shall not apply vis-à-vis the offeror during the time allowed for acceptance of the bid laid down in Article 7(1).

3. Restrictions on voting rights provided for in the articles of association of the offeree company shall not have effect at the general meeting of shareholders which decides on any defensive measures in accordance with Article 9.

3. Fourth Council Directive 78/660/EEC of 25 July 1978 on the annual accounts of certain types of companies (OJ L 222, 14.8.1978, p. 11). Directive as last amended by Directive 2003/51/EC of the European Parliament and of the Council (OJ L 178, 17.7.2003, p. 16).

4. Seventh Council Directive 83/349/EEC of 13 June 1983 on consolidated accounts (OJ L 193, 18.7.1983, p. 1). Directive as last amendedby Directive 2003/51/EC.

Restrictions on voting rights provided for in contractual agreements between the offeree company and holders of its securities, or in contractual agreements between holders of the offeree company's securities entered into after the adoption of this Directive, shall not have effect at the general meeting of shareholders which decides on any defensive measures in accordance with Article 9.

Multiple-vote securities shall carry only one vote each at the general meeting of shareholders which decides on any defensive measures in accordance with Article 9.

4. Where, following a bid, the offeror holds 75% or more of the capital carrying voting rights, no restrictions on the transfer of securities or on voting rights referred to in paragraphs 2 and 3 nor any extraordinary rights of shareholders concerning the appointment or removal of board members provided for in the articles of association of the offeree company shall apply; multiple-vote securities shall carry only one vote each at the first general meeting of shareholders following closure of the bid, called by the offeror in order to amend the articles of association or to remove or appoint board members.

To that end, the offeror shall have the right to convene a general meeting of shareholders at short notice, provided that the meeting does not take place within two weeks of notification.

5. Where rights are removed on the basis of paragraphs 2, 3, or 4 and/or Article 12, equitable compensation shall be provided for any loss suffered by the holders of those rights. The terms for determining such compensation and the arrangements for its payment shall be set by Member States.

6. Paragraphs 3 and 4 shall not apply to securities where the restrictions on voting rights are compensated for by specific pecuniary advantages.

7. This Article shall not apply either where Member States hold securities in the offeree company which confer special rights on the Member States which are compatible with the Treaty, or to special rights provided for in national law which are compatible with the Treaty or to cooperatives.

Article 12. Optional Arrangements

1. Member States may reserve the right not to require companies as referred to in Article 1(1) which have their registered offices within their territories to apply Article 9(2) and (3) and/or Article 11.

2. Where Member States make use of the option provided for in paragraph 1, they shall nevertheless grant companies which have their registered offices within their territories the option, which shall be reversible, of applying Article 9(2) and (3) and/or Article 11, without prejudice to Article 11(7).

The decision of the company shall be taken by the general meeting of shareholders, in accordance with the law of the Member State in which the company has its registered office in accordance with the rules applicable to amendment of the articles of association. The decision shall be communicated to the supervisory authority of the Member State in which the company has its registered office and to all the supervisory authorities of Member States in which its securities are admitted to trading on regulated markets or where such admission has been requested.

3. Member States may, under the conditions determined by national law, exempt companies which apply Article 9(2) and (3) and/or Article 11 from applying Article 9(2) and (3) and/or Article 11 if they become the subject of an offer launched by a company which does not apply the same Articles as they do, or by a company controlled, directly or indirectly, by the latter, pursuant to Article 1 of Directive 83/349/EEC.

4. Member States shall ensure that the provisions applicable to the respective companies are disclosed without delay.

5. Any measure applied in accordance with paragraph 3 shall be subject to the authorisation of the general meeting of shareholders of the offeree company, which must be granted no earlier than 18 months before the bid was made public in accordance with Article 6(1).

Article 13. Other Rules Applicable to the Conduct of Bids

Member States shall also lay down rules which govern the conduct of bids, at least as regards the following:

(a) the lapsing of bids;
(b) the revision of bids;
(c) competing bids;
(d) the disclosure of the results of bids;
(e) the irrevocability of bids and the conditions permitted.

Article 15. The Right of Squeeze-Out

1. Member States shall ensure that, following a bid made to all the holders of the offeree company's securities for all of their securities, paragraphs 2 to 5 apply.

2. Member States shall ensure that an offeror is able to require all the holders of the remaining securities to sell him/her those securities at a fair price. Member States shall introduce that right in one of the following situations:

(a) where the offeror holds securities representing not less than 90% of the capital carrying voting rights and 90% of the voting rights in the offeree company, or

(b) where, following acceptance of the bid, he/she has acquired or has firmly contracted to acquire securities representing not less than 90% of the offeree company's capital carrying voting rights and 90% of the voting rights comprised in the bid.

In the case referred to in (a), Member States may set a higher threshold that may not, however, be higher than 95% of the capital carrying voting rights and 95% of the voting rights.

3. Member States shall ensure that rules are in force that make it possible to calculate when the threshold is reached.

Where the offeree company has issued more than one class of securities, Member States may provide that the right of squeeze-out can be exercised only in the class in which the threshold laid down in paragraph 2 has been reached.

4. If the offeror wishes to exercise the right of squeeze-out he/she shall do so within three months of the end of the time allowed for acceptance of the bid referred to in Article 7.

5. Member States shall ensure that a fair price is guaranteed. That price shall take the same form as the consideration offered in the bid or shall be in cash. Member States may provide that cash shall be offered at least as an alternative.

Following a voluntary bid, in both of the cases referred to in paragraph 2(a) and (b), the consideration offered in the bid shall be presumed to be fair where, through acceptance of the bid, the offeror has acquired securities representing not less than 90% of the capital carrying voting rights comprised in the bid.

Following a mandatory bid, the consideration offered in the bid shall be presumed to be fair.

Article 16. The Right of Sell-Out

1. Member States shall ensure that, following a bid made to all the holders of the offeree company's securities for all of their securities, paragraphs 2 and 3 apply.

2. Member States shall ensure that a holder of remaining securities is able to require the offeror to buy his/her securities from him/her at a fair price under the same circumstances as provided for in Article 15(2).

3. Article 15(3) to (5) shall apply *mutatis mutandis*.

Article 17. Sanctions

Member States shall determine the sanctions to be imposed for infringement of the national measures adopted pursuant to this Directive and shall take all necessary steps to ensure that they are put into effect. The sanctions thus provided for shall be effective, proportionate and dissuasive. Member States shall notify the Commission of those measures no later than the date laid down in Article 21(1) and of any subsequent change thereto at the earliest opportunity.

Article 20. Revision

Five years after the date laid down in Article 21(1), the Commission shall examine this Directive in the light of the experience acquired in applying it and, if necessary, propose its revision. That examination shall include a survey of the control structures and barriers to takeover bids that are not covered by this Directive.

To that end, Member States shall provide the Commission annually with information on the takeover bids which have been launched against companies the securities of which are admitted to trading on their regulated markets. That information shall include the nationalities of the companies involved, the results of the offers and any other information relevant to the understanding of how takeover bids operate in practice.

Article 21. Transposition

1. Member States shall bring into force the laws, regulations and administrative provisions necessary to comply with this Directive no later than 20 May 2006. They shall forthwith inform the Commission thereof.

When Member States adopt those provisions, they shall contain a reference to this Directive or shall be accompanied by such reference on the occasion of their official publication. The methods of making such reference shall be laid down by the Member States.

2. Member States shall communicate to the Commission the text of the main provisions of national law that they adopt in the fields covered by this Directive.

Done at Strasbourg, 21 April 2004.

For the European Parliament
The President
P. COX

For the Council
The President
D. ROCHE

HART-SCOTT-RODINO ANTITRUST IMPROVEMENT ACT

§ 801.1 Definitions

(h) Notification threshold. The term "notification threshold" means:

(1) An aggregate total amount of voting securities of the acquired person valued at greater than $50 million (as adjusted) but less than $100 million (as adjusted);

(2) An aggregate total amount of voting securities of the acquired person valued at $100 million (as adjusted) or greater but less than $500 million (as adjusted);

(3) An aggregate total amount of voting securities of the acquired person valued at $500 million (as adjusted) or greater;

(4) Twenty-five percent of the outstanding voting securities of an issuer if valued at greater than $1 billion (as adjusted); or

(5) Fifty percent of the outstanding voting securities of an issuer if valued at greater than $50 million (as adjusted).

(i)(1) Solely for the purpose of investment. Voting securities are held or acquired "solely for the purpose of investment" if the person holding or acquiring such voting securities has no intention of participating in the formulation, determination, or direction of the basic business decisions of the issuer.

§ 801.13 Aggregation of Voting Securities, Assets and Non-Corporate Interests

(a) Voting securities.

(1) Subject to the provisions of § 801.15, and paragraph (a)(3) of this section, all voting securities of the issuer which will be held by the

acquiring person after the consummation of an acquisition shall be deemed voting securities held as a result of the acquisition. The value of such voting securities shall be the sum of the value of the voting securities to be acquired, determined in accordance with § 801.10(a), and the value of the voting securities held by the acquiring person prior to the acquisition, determined in accordance with paragraph (a)(2) of this section...

Example 1. Assume that acquiring person "A" holds in excess of $50 million (as adjusted) of the voting securities of X, and is to acquire another $1 million of the same voting securities. Since under paragraph (a) of this section all voting securities "A" will hold after the acquisition are held "as a result of" the acquisition, "A" will hold in excess of $50 million (as adjusted) of the voting securities of X as a result of the acquisition. "A" must therefore observe the requirements of the act before making the acquisition, unless the present acquisition is exempt under Section 7A(c), § 802.21 or any other rule...

(3) Voting securities held by the acquiring person prior to an acquisition shall not be deemed voting securities held as a result of that subsequent acquisition if:

(i) The acquiring person is, in the subsequent acquisition, acquiring only assets; and

(ii) The acquisition of the previously acquired voting securities was subject to the filing and waiting requirements of the act (and such requirements were observed) or was exempt pursuant to § 802.21....

§ 802.21 Acquisitions of Voting Securities Not Meeting or Exceeding Greater Notification Threshold (as Adjusted)

(a) An acquisition of voting securities shall be exempt from the requirements of the act if:

(1) The acquiring person and all other persons required by the act and these rules to file notification filed notification with respect to an earlier acquisition of voting securities of the same issuer;

(2) The waiting period with respect to the earlier acquisition has expired, or been terminated pursuant to § 803.11, and the acquisition will be consummated within 5 years of such expiration or termination; and

(3) The acquisition will not increase the holdings of the acquiring person to meet or exceed a notification threshold (as adjusted) greater than the greatest notification threshold met or exceeded in the earlier acquisition.

Examples: 1. In 2004, Corporation A acquired $53 million of the voting securities of corporation B and both "A" and "B" filed notification as required, indicating the $50 million threshold. Within five years of the expiration of the original waiting period, "A" acquires additional voting securities of B but not in an amount sufficient to meet or exceed $100 million (as adjusted) or 50 percent of the voting securities of B. No additional notification is required.

2. In 2004, Corporation A acquired $53 million of the voting securities of corporation B and both "A" and "B" filed notification as required, indicating the $50 million threshold. Suppose that in year three following the expiration of the waiting period, the $50 million notification threshold has been adjusted to $56 million pursuant to [Clayton Act] Section 7A(a)(2)(a) of the Act. "A" now intends to acquire an additional $5 million of the voting securities of B. "A" is not required to file another notification even though it now holds voting securities in excess of the $56 million notification threshold (which is greater than the $50 million notification threshold indicated in its filing), because it has not met or exceeded a notification threshold (as adjusted) greater than the notification threshold exceeded in the earlier acquisition (i.e. $100 million (as adjusted) or 50% notification thresholds).

3. Same facts as in Example 2 above except now the five year period has expired. Suppose that, the $50 million notification threshold has been adjusted to $57 million pursuant to [Clayton Act] Section 7A(a)(2)(a) of the Act. "A" now holds $58 million of voting securities of B. Because § 802.21(a)(2) is no longer satisfied, the acquisition of any additional voting securities of B will require a new filing because "A" will hold voting securities valued in excess of the $57 million notification threshold. If, however, the $50 million notification threshold had been adjusted to $60 million at the end of the five-year period, A could acquire up to that threshold without a new filing.

4. This section also allows a person to recross any of the threshold notification levels that were in effect at the time of filing notification any number of times within five years of the expiration of the waiting period following notification. Thus, if in Example 1, "A" had disposed of some voting securities so that it held less than $50 million of the voting securities of B, and thereafter had increased its holdings to more than $50 million but less than $100 million or 50 percent of B, notification would not be required if the increase occurred within 5 years of the expiration of the original waiting period.

5. A files notification at the $50 million notification threshold and acquires $51 million of the voting securities of B in the year following expiration of the waiting period. The next greater notification threshold at the time of filing was $100 million. In year three, the $100 million notification threshold has been adjusted to $106 million. A can now acquire up to, but not meet or exceed, voting securities of B valued at $106 million. As the original $100 million threshold is adjusted upward in years four and five, A can acquire up to those new thresholds as the adjustments are effected.

6. A files notification at the $50 million threshold in January of year one. In February of year one, the $50 million threshold is adjusted to $52 million. A only needs to acquire in excess of $50 million of voting securities of B, not in excess of $52 million, to have exceeded the threshold which was filed for in the year following expiration of the waiting period (see § 803.7). It may then acquire up to the next greater notification threshold (as adjusted) during the five years following expiration of the waiting period.

H.R. 4173 — DODD-FRANK WALL STREET REFORM AND CONSUMER PROTECTION ACT

SUBTITLE E—ACCOUNTABILITY AND EXECUTIVE COMPENSATION

SEC. 951. SHAREHOLDER VOTE ON EXECUTIVE COMPENSATION DISCLOSURES

The Securities Exchange Act of 1934 (15 U.S.C. 78a et seq.) is amended by inserting after section 14 (15 U.S.C. 78n) the following:

"SEC. 14A. SHAREHOLDER APPROVAL OF EXECUTIVE COMPENSATION.

"(a) SEPARATE RESOLUTION REQUIRED. —

"(1) IN GENERAL. — Not less frequently than once every 3 years, a proxy or consent or authorization for an annual or other meeting of the shareholders for which the proxy solicitation rules of the Commission require compensation disclosure shall include a separate resolution subject to shareholder vote to approve the compensation of executives, as disclosed pursuant to section 229.402 of title 17, Code of Federal Regulations, or any successor thereto.

"(2) FREQUENCY OF VOTE.—Not less frequently than once every 6 years, a proxy or consent or authorization for an annual or other meeting of the shareholders for which the proxy solicitation rules of the Commission require compensation disclosure shall include a separate resolution subject to shareholder vote to determine whether votes on the resolutions required under paragraph (1) will occur every 1, 2, or 3 years.

"(3) EFFECTIVE DATE.—The proxy or consent or authorization for the first annual or other meeting of the shareholders occurring after the end of the 6–month period beginning on the date of enactment of this section shall include—

"(A) the resolution described in paragraph (1); and

"(B) a separate resolution subject to shareholder vote to determine whether votes on the resolutions required under paragraph (1) will occur every 1, 2, or 3 years.

"(b) SHAREHOLDER APPROVAL OF GOLDEN PARACHUTE COMPENSATION.—

"(1) DISCLOSURE.—In any proxy or consent solicitation material (the solicitation of which is subject to the rules of the Commission pursuant to subsection (a)) for a meeting of the shareholders occurring after the end of the 6–month period beginning on the date of enactment of this section, at which shareholders are asked to approve an acquisition, merger, consolidation, or proposed sale or other disposition of all or substantially all the assets of an issuer, the person making such solicitation shall disclose in the proxy or consent solicitation material, in a clear and simple form in accordance with regulations to be promulgated by the Commission, any agreements or understandings that such person has with any named executive officers of such issuer (or of the acquiring issuer, if such issuer is not the acquiring issuer) concerning any type of compensation (whether present, deferred, or contingent) that is based on or otherwise relates to the acquisition, merger, consolidation, sale, or other disposition of all or substantially all of the assets of the issuer and the aggregate total of all such compensation that may (and the conditions upon which it may) be paid or become payable to or on behalf of such executive officer.

"(2) SHAREHOLDER APPROVAL.—Any proxy or consent or authorization relating to the proxy or consent solicitation material containing the disclosure required by paragraph (1) shall include a separate resolution subject to shareholder vote to approve such agreements or understandings and compensation as disclosed, unless such agreements or understandings have been subject to a shareholder vote under subsection (a).

"(c) RULE OF CONSTRUCTION.—The shareholder vote referred to in subsections (a) and (b) shall not be binding on the issuer or the board of directors of an issuer, and may not be construed—

"(1) as overruling a decision by such issuer or board of directors;

"(2) to create or imply any change to the fiduciary duties of such issuer or board of directors;

"(3) to create or imply any additional fiduciary duties for such issuer or board of directors; or

"(4) to restrict or limit the ability of shareholders to make proposals for inclusion in proxy materials related to executive compensation.

"(d) DISCLOSURE OF VOTES.—Every institutional investment manager subject to section 13(f) shall report at least annually how it voted on any shareholder vote pursuant to subsections (a) and (b), unless such vote is otherwise required to be reported publicly by rule or regulation of the Commission.

"(e) EXEMPTION.—The Commission may, by rule or order, exempt an issuer or class of issuers from the requirement under subsection (a) or (b). In determining whether to make an exemption under this subsection, the Commission shall take into account, among other considerations, whether the requirements under subsections (a) and (b) disproportionately burdens small issuers.".

SEC. 952. COMPENSATION COMMITTEE INDEPENDENCE.

(a) In General—The Securities Exchange Act of 1934 (15 U.S.C. 78 et seq.) is amended by inserting after section 10B, as added by section 753, the following:

"SEC. 10C. COMPENSATION COMMITTEES.

"(a) INDEPENDENCE OF COMPENSATION COMMITTEES.—

"(1) LISTING STANDARDS.—The Commission shall, by rule, direct the national securities exchanges and national securities associations to prohibit the listing of any equity security of an issuer, other than an issuer that is a controlled company, limited partnership, company in bankruptcy proceedings, open-ended management investment company that is registered under the Investment Company Act of 1940, or a foreign private issuer that provides annual disclosures to shareholders of the reasons that the foreign private issuer does not have an independent compensation committee, that does not comply with the requirements of this subsection.

"(2) INDEPENDENCE OF COMPENSATION COMMITTEES.—The rules of the Commission under paragraph (1) shall require that each member of the compensation committee of the board of directors of an issuer be—

"(A) a member of the board of directors of the issuer; and

"(B) independent.

"(3) INDEPENDENCE.—The rules of the Commission under paragraph (1) shall require that, in determining the definition of the term 'independence' for purposes of paragraph (2), the national securities exchanges and the national securities associations shall consider relevant factors, including—

"(A) the source of compensation of a member of the board of directors of an issuer, including any consulting, advisory, or other compensatory fee paid by the issuer to such member of the board of directors; and

"(B) whether a member of the board of directors of an issuer is affiliated with the issuer, a subsidiary of the issuer, or an affiliate of a subsidiary of the issuer.

"(4) EXEMPTION AUTHORITY.—The rules of the Commission under paragraph (1) shall permit a national securities exchange or a national securities association to exempt a particular relationship from the requirements of paragraph (2), with respect to the members of a compensation committee, as the national securities exchange or national securities association determines is appropriate, taking into consideration the size of an issuer and any other relevant factors.

"(b) INDEPENDENCE OF COMPENSATION CONSULTANTS AND OTHER COMPENSATION COMMITTEE ADVISERS.—

"(1) IN GENERAL.—The compensation committee of an issuer may only select a compensation consultant, legal counsel, or other adviser to the compensation committee after taking into consideration the factors identified by the Commission under paragraph (2).

"(2) RULES.—The Commission shall identify factors that affect the independence of a compensation consultant, legal counsel, or other adviser to a compensation committee of an issuer. Such factors shall be competitively neutral among categories of consultants, legal counsel, or other advisers and preserve the ability of compensation committees to retain the services of members of any such category, and shall include—

"(A) the provision of other services to the issuer by the person that employs the compensation consultant, legal counsel, or other adviser;

"(B) the amount of fees received from the issuer by the person that employs the compensation consultant, legal counsel, or other adviser, as a percentage of the total revenue of the person that employs the compensation consultant, legal counsel, or other adviser;

"(C) the policies and procedures of the person that employs the compensation consultant, legal counsel, or other adviser that are designed to prevent conflicts of interest;

"(D) any business or personal relationship of the compensation consultant, legal counsel, or other adviser with a member of the compensation committee; and

"(E) any stock of the issuer owned by the compensation consultant, legal counsel, or other adviser.

"(c) COMPENSATION COMMITTEE AUTHORITY RELATING TO COMPENSATION CONSULTANTS.—

"(1) AUTHORITY TO RETAIN COMPENSATION CONSULTANT.—

"(A) IN GENERAL.—The compensation committee of an issuer, in its capacity as a committee of the board of directors, may, in its sole discretion, retain or obtain the advice of a compensation consultant.

"(B) DIRECT RESPONSIBILITY OF COMPENSATION COMMITTEE.—The compensation committee of an issuer shall be directly responsible for the appointment, compensation, and oversight of the work of a compensation consultant.

"(C) RULE OF CONSTRUCTION.—This paragraph may not be construed—

"(i) to require the compensation committee to implement or act consistently with the advice or recommendations of the compensation consultant; or

"(ii) to affect the ability or obligation of a compensation committee to exercise its own judgment in fulfillment of the duties of the compensation committee.

"(2) DISCLOSURE.—In any proxy or consent solicitation material for an annual meeting of the shareholders (or a special meeting in lieu of the annual meeting) occurring on or after the date that is 1 year after the date of enactment of this section, each issuer shall disclose in the proxy or consent material, in accordance with regulations of the Commission, whether—

"(A) the compensation committee of the issuer retained or obtained the advice of a compensation consultant; and

"(B) the work of the compensation consultant has raised any conflict of interest and, if so, the nature of the conflict and how the conflict is being addressed.

"(d) AUTHORITY TO ENGAGE INDEPENDENT LEGAL COUNSEL AND OTHER ADVISERS.—

"(1) IN GENERAL.—The compensation committee of an issuer, in its capacity as a committee of the board of directors, may, in its sole discretion, retain and obtain the advice of independent legal counsel and other advisers.

"(2) DIRECT RESPONSIBILITY OF COMPENSATION COMMITTEE.—The compensation committee of an issuer shall be directly responsible for the appointment, compensation, and oversight of the work of independent legal counsel and other advisers.

"(3) RULE OF CONSTRUCTION.—This subsection may not be construed—

"(A) to require a compensation committee to implement or act consistently with the advice or recommendations of independent legal counsel or other advisers under this subsection; or

"(B) to affect the ability or obligation of a compensation committee to exercise its own judgment in fulfillment of the duties of the compensation committee.

"(e) COMPENSATION OF COMPENSATION CONSULTANTS, INDEPENDENT LEGAL COUNSEL, AND OTHER ADVISERS.—Each issuer shall provide for appropriate funding, as determined by the compensation committee in its capacity as a committee of the board of directors, for payment of reasonable compensation—

"(1) to a compensation consultant; and

"(2) to independent legal counsel or any other adviser to the compensation committee.

"(f) COMMISSION RULES.—

"(1) IN GENERAL.—Not later than 360 days after the date of enactment of this section, the Commission shall, by rule, direct the national securities exchanges and national securities associations to prohibit the listing of any security of an issuer that is not in compliance with the requirements of this section.

"(2) OPPORTUNITY TO CURE DEFECTS.—The rules of the Commission under paragraph (1) shall provide for appropriate procedures for an issuer to have a reasonable opportunity to cure any defects that would be the basis for the prohibition under paragraph (1), before the imposition of such prohibition.

"(3) EXEMPTION AUTHORITY.—

"(A) IN GENERAL.—The rules of the Commission under paragraph (1) shall permit a national securities exchange or a national securities association to exempt a category of issuers from the requirements under this section, as the national securities exchange or the national securities association determines is appropriate.

"(B) CONSIDERATIONS.—In determining appropriate exemptions under subparagraph (A), the national securities exchange or the national securities association shall take into account the potential impact of the requirements of this section on smaller reporting issuers.

"(g) CONTROLLED COMPANY EXEMPTION.—

"(1) IN GENERAL.—This section shall not apply to any controlled company.

"(2) DEFINITION.—For purposes of this section, the term 'controlled company' means an issuer—

"(A) that is listed on a national securities exchange or by a national securities association; and

"(B) that holds an election for the board of directors of the issuer in which more than 50 percent of the voting power is held by an individual, a group, or another issuer.".

(b) STUDY AND REPORT.—

(1) STUDY.—The Securities and Exchange Commission shall conduct a study and review of the use of compensation consultants and the effects of such use.

(2) REPORT.—Not later than 2 years after the date of the enactment of this Act, the Commission shall submit a report to Congress on the results of the study and review required by this subsection.

SEC. 953. EXECUTIVE COMPENSATION DISCLOSURES.

(a) DISCLOSURE OF PAY VERSUS PERFORMANCE.—Section 14 of the Securities Exchange Act of 1934 (15 U.S.C. 78n), as amended by this title, is amended by adding at the end the following:

"(i) DISCLOSURE OF PAY VERSUS PERFORMANCE.—The Commission shall, by rule, require each issuer to disclose in any proxy or consent solicitation material for an annual meeting of the shareholders of the issuer a clear description of any compensation required to be disclosed by the issuer under section 229.402 of title 17, Code of Federal Regulations (or any successor thereto), including information that shows the relationship between executive compensation actually paid and the financial performance of the issuer, taking into account any change in the value of the shares of stock and dividends of the issuer and any distributions. The ***1904** disclosure under this subsection may include a graphic representation of the information required to be disclosed.".

(b) ADDITIONAL DISCLOSURE REQUIREMENTS.—

(1) IN GENERAL.—The Commission shall amend section 229.402 of title 17, Code of Federal Regulations, to require each issuer to disclose in any filing of the issuer described in section 229.10(a) of title 17, Code of Federal Regulations (or any successor thereto)—

(A) the median of the annual total compensation of all employees of the issuer, except the chief executive officer (or any equivalent position) of the issuer;

(B) the annual total compensation of the chief executive officer (or any equivalent position) of the issuer; and

(C) the ratio of the amount described in subparagraph (A) to the amount described in subparagraph (B).

(2) TOTAL COMPENSATION.—For purposes of this subsection, the total compensation of an employee of an issuer shall be determined in accordance with section 229.402(c)(2)(x) of title 17, Code of Federal Regulations, as in effect on the day before the date of enactment of this Act.

SEC. 954. RECOVERY OF ERRONEOUSLY AWARDED COMPENSATION.

The Securities Exchange Act of 1934 is amended by inserting after section 10C, as added by section 952, the following:

"SEC. 10D. RECOVERY OF ERRONEOUSLY AWARDED COMPENSATION POLICY.

"(a) LISTING STANDARDS.—The Commission shall, by rule, direct the national securities exchanges and national securities associations to prohibit the listing of any security of an issuer that does not comply with the requirements of this section.

"(b) RECOVERY OF FUNDS.—The rules of the Commission under subsection (a) shall require each issuer to develop and implement a policy providing—

"(1) for disclosure of the policy of the issuer on incentive-based compensation that is based on financial information required to be reported under the securities laws; and

"(2) that, in the event that the issuer is required to prepare an accounting restatement due to the material noncompliance of the issuer with any financial reporting requirement under the securities laws, the issuer will recover from any current or former executive officer of the issuer who received incentive-based compensation (including stock options awarded as compensation) during the 3-year period preceding the date on which the issuer is required to prepare an accounting restatement, based on the erroneous data, in excess of what would have been paid to the executive officer under the accounting restatement.".

SEC. 955. DISCLOSURE REGARDING EMPLOYEE AND DIRECTOR HEDGING.

Section 14 of the Securities Exchange Act of 1934 (15 U.S.C. 78n), as amended by this title, is amended by adding at the end the following:

"(j) DISCLOSURE OF HEDGING BY EMPLOYEES AND DIRECTORS.—The Commission shall, by rule, require each issuer to disclose in any proxy or consent solicitation material for an annual meeting of the shareholders of the issuer whether any employee or member of the board of directors of the issuer, or any designee of such employee or member, is permitted to purchase financial instruments (including prepaid variable forward contracts, equity swaps, collars, and exchange funds) that are designed to hedge or offset any decrease in the market value of equity securities—

"(1) granted to the employee or member of the board of directors by the issuer as part of the compensation of the employee or member of the board of directors; or

"(2) held, directly or indirectly, by the employee or member of the board of directors.".

SEC. 956. ENHANCED COMPENSATION STRUCTURE REPORTING.

(a) ENHANCED DISCLOSURE AND REPORTING OF COMPENSATION ARRANGEMENTS.—

(1) IN GENERAL.—Not later than 9 months after the date of enactment of this title, the appropriate Federal regulators jointly shall prescribe regulations or guidelines to require each covered financial institution to disclose to the appropriate Federal regulator the structures of all incentive-based compensation arrangements offered by such covered financial institutions sufficient to determine whether the compensation structure—

(A) provides an executive officer, employee, director, or principal shareholder of the covered financial institution with excessive compensation, fees, or benefits; or

(B) could lead to material financial loss to the covered financial institution.

(2) RULES OF CONSTRUCTION.—Nothing in this section shall be construed as requiring the reporting of the actual compensation of particular individuals. Nothing in this section shall be construed to require a covered financial institution that does not have an incentive-based payment arrangement to make the disclosures required under this subsection.

(b) PROHIBITION ON CERTAIN COMPENSATION ARRANGEMENTS.—Not later than 9 months after the date of enactment of this title, the appropriate Federal regulators shall jointly prescribe regulations or guidelines that prohibit any types of incentive-based payment arrangement, or any feature of any such arrangement, that the regulators determine encourages inappropriate risks by covered financial institutions—

(1) by providing an executive officer, employee, director, or principal shareholder of the covered financial institution with excessive compensation, fees, or benefits; or

(2) that could lead to material financial loss to the covered financial institution.

(c) STANDARDS.—The appropriate Federal regulators shall—

(1) ensure that any standards for compensation established under subsections (a) or (b) are comparable to the standards established under section of the Federal Deposit Insurance Act (12 U.S.C. 2 1831p–1) for insured depository institutions; and

(2) in establishing such standards under such subsections, take into consideration the compensation standards described in section 39(c) of the Federal Deposit Insurance Act (12 U.S.C. 1831p–9 1(c)).

(d) ENFORCEMENT.—The provisions of this section and the regulations issued under this section shall be enforced under section 505 of the Gramm–Leach–Bliley Act and, for purposes of such section, a violation of this section or such regulations shall be treated as a violation of subtitle A of title V of such Act.

(e) DEFINITIONS.—As used in this section—

(1) the term "appropriate Federal regulator" means the Board of Governors of the Federal Reserve System, the Office of the Comptroller of the Currency, the Board of Directors of the Federal Deposit Insurance Corporation, the Director of the Office of Thrift Supervision, the National Credit Union Administration Board, the Securities and Exchange Commission, the Federal Housing Finance Agency; and

(2) the term "covered financial institution" means—

(A) a depository institution or depository institution holding company, as such terms are defined in section 3 of the Federal Deposit Insurance Act (12 U.S.C. 1813);

(B) a broker-dealer registered under section 15 of the Securities Exchange Act of 1934 (15 U.S.C. 78o);

(C) a credit union, as described in section 19(b)(1)(A)(iv) of the Federal Reserve Act;

(D) an investment advisor, as such term is defined in section 202(a)(11) of the Investment Advisers Act of 1940 (15 U.S.C. 80b–2(a)(11));

(E) the Federal National Mortgage Association;

(F) the Federal Home Loan Mortgage Corporation; and

(G) any other financial institution that the appropriate Federal regulators, jointly, by rule, determine should be treated as a covered financial institution for purposes of this section.

(f) EXEMPTION FOR CERTAIN FINANCIAL INSTITUTIONS.—The requirements of this section shall not apply to covered financial institutions with assets of less than $1,000,000,000.

SEC. 957. VOTING BY BROKERS.

Section 6(b) of the Securities Exchange Act of 1934 (15 U.S.C. 78f(b)) is amended—

(1) in paragraph (9)—

(A) in subparagraph (A), by redesignating clauses (i) through (v) as subclauses (I) through (V), respectively, and adjusting the margins accordingly;

(B) by redesignating subparagraphs (A) through (D) as clauses (i) through (iv), respectively, and adjusting the margins accordingly;

(C) by inserting "(A)" after "(9)"; and

(D) in the matter immediately following clause (iv), as so redesignated, by striking "As used" and inserting the following:

"(B) As used".

(2) by adding at the end the following:

"(10)(A) The rules of the exchange prohibit any member that is not the beneficial owner of a security registered under section 12 from granting a proxy to vote the security in connection with a shareholder vote described in subparagraph (B), unless the beneficial owner of the security has instructed the member to vote the proxy in accordance with the voting instructions of the beneficial owner.

"(B) A shareholder vote described in this subparagraph is a shareholder vote with respect to the election of a member of the board of directors of an issuer, executive compensation, or any other significant matter, as determined by the Commission, by rule, and does not include a vote with respect to the uncontested election of a member of the board of directors of any investment company registered under the Investment Company Act of 1940 (15 U.S.C. 80b–1 et seq.).

"(C) Nothing in this paragraph shall be construed to prohibit a national securities exchange from prohibiting a member that is not the beneficial owner of a security registered under section 12 from granting a proxy to vote the security in connection with a shareholder vote not described in subparagraph (A).".

SUBTITLE G— STRENGTHENING CORPORATE GOVERNANCE

SEC. 971. PROXY ACCESS

(a) PROXY ACCESS.—Section 14(a) of the Securities Exchange Act of 1934 (15 U.S.C. 78n(a)) is amended—

(1) by inserting "(1)" after "(a)"; and

(2) by adding at the end the following:

"(2) The rules and regulations prescribed by the Commission under paragraph (1) may include—

"(A) a requirement that a solicitation of proxy, consent, or authorization by (or on behalf of) an issuer include a nominee submitted by a shareholder to serve on the board of directors of the issuer; and

"(B) a requirement that an issuer follow a certain procedure in relation to a solicitation described in subparagraph (A).".

(b) REGULATIONS.—The Commission may issue rules permitting the use by a shareholder of proxy solicitation materials supplied by an issuer of securities for the purpose of nominating individuals to membership on the board of directors of the issuer, under such terms and conditions as the Commission determines are in the interests of shareholders and for the protection of investors.

(c) EXEMPTIONS.—The Commission may, by rule or order, exempt an issuer or class of issuers from the requirement made by this section or an amendment made by this section. In determining whether to make an exemption under this subsection, the Commission shall take into account, among other considerations, whether the requirement in the amendment made by subsection (a) disproportionately burdens small issuers.

SEC. 972. DISCLOSURES REGARDING CHAIRMAN AND CEO STRUCTURES

The Securities Exchange Act of 1934 (15 U.S.C. 78a et seq.) is amended by inserting after section 14A, as added by this title, the following:

"SEC. 14B. CORPORATE GOVERNANCE.

"Not later than 180 days after the date of enactment of this subsection, the Commission shall issue rules that require an issuer to disclose in the annual proxy sent to investors the reasons why the issuer has chosen—

"(1) the same person to serve as chairman of the board of directors and chief executive officer (or in equivalent positions); or

"(2) different individuals to serve as chairman of the board of directors and chief executive officer (or in equivalent positions of the issuer).".

UNIFORM PARTNERSHIP ACT
(Amended 2013)

Article 1. General Provisions

§ 102. Definitions

(1) "Business" includes every trade, occupation, and profession.

(2) "Contribution", except in the phrase "right of contribution", means property or a benefit described in Section 403 which is provided by a person to a partnership to become a partner or in the person's capacity as a partner.

(3) "Debtor in bankruptcy" means a person that is the subject of:

(A) an order for relief under Title 11 of the United States Code or a comparable order under a successor statute of general application; or

(B) a comparable order under federal, state, or foreign law governing insolvency.

(4) "Distribution" means a transfer of money or other property from a partnership to a person on account of a transferable interest or in a person's capacity as a partner. The term:

(A) includes:

(i) a redemption or other purchase by a partnership of a transferable interest; and

(ii) a transfer to a partner in return for the partner's relinquishment of any right to participate as a partner in the management or conduct of the partnership's business or have access to records or other information concerning the partnership's business; and

(B) does not include amounts constituting reasonable compensation for present or past service or payments made in the ordinary course of business under a bona fide retirement plan or other bona fide benefits program.

(5) "Foreign limited liability partnership" means a foreign partnership whose partners have limited liability for the debts, obligations, or other liabilities of the foreign partnership under a provision similar to Section 306(c).

(6) "Foreign partnership" means an unincorporated entity formed under the law of a jurisdiction other than this state which would be a partnership if formed under the law of this state. The term includes a foreign limited liability partnership.

(7) "Jurisdiction", used to refer to a political entity, means the United States, a state, a foreign country, or a political subdivision of a foreign country.

(8) "Jurisdiction of formation" means the jurisdiction whose law governs the internal affairs of an entity.

(9) "Limited liability partnership", except in the phrase "foreign limited liability partnership" and in [Article] 11, means a partnership that has filed a statement of qualification under Section 901 and does not have a similar statement in effect in any other jurisdiction.

(10) "Partner" means a person that:

(A) has become a partner in a partnership under Section 402 or was a partner in a partnership when the partnership became subject to this [act] under Section 110; and

(B) has not dissociated as a partner under Section 601.

(11) "Partnership", except in [Article] 11, means an association of two or more persons to carry on as co-owners a business for profit formed under this [act] or that becomes subject to this [act] under [Article] 11 or Section 110. The term includes a limited liability partnership.

(12) "Partnership agreement" means the agreement, whether or not referred to as a partnership agreement and whether oral, implied, in a record, or in any combination thereof, of all the partners of a partnership concerning the matters described in Section 105(a). The term includes the agreement as amended or restated.

(13) "Partnership at will" means a partnership in which the partners have not agreed to remain partners until the expiration of a definite term or the completion of a particular undertaking.

(14) "Person" means an individual, business corporation, nonprofit corporation, partnership, limited partnership, limited liability company, [general cooperative association,] limited cooperative association, unincorporated nonprofit association, statutory trust, business trust, common-law business trust, estate, trust, association, joint venture, public corporation, government or governmental subdivision, agency, or instrumentality, or any other legal or commercial entity.

(15) "Principal office" means the principal executive office of a partnership or a foreign limited liability partnership, whether or not the office is located in this state.

(16) "Property" means all property, whether real, personal, or mixed or tangible or intangible, or any right or interest therein.

(17) "Record", used as a noun, means information that is inscribed on a tangible medium or that is stored in an electronic or other medium and is retrievable in perceivable form.

(18) "Registered agent" means an agent of a limited liability partnership or foreign limited liability partnership which is authorized to receive service of any process, notice, or demand required or permitted by law to be served on the partnership.

(19) "Registered foreign limited liability partnership" means a foreign limited liability partnership that is registered to do business in this state pursuant to a statement of registration filed by the [Secretary of State].

(20) "Sign" means, with present intent to authenticate or adopt a record:

(A) to execute or adopt a tangible symbol; or

(B) to attach to or logically associate with the record an electronic symbol, sound, or process.

(21) "State" means a state of the United States, the District of Columbia, Puerto Rico, the United States Virgin Islands, or any territory or insular possession subject to the jurisdiction of the United States.

(22) "Transfer" includes:

(A) an assignment;

(B) a conveyance;

(C) a sale;

(D) a lease;

(E) an encumbrance, including a mortgage or security interest;

(F) a gift; and

(G) a transfer by operation of law.

(23) "Transferable interest" means the right, as initially owned by a person in the person's capacity as a partner, to receive distributions from a partnership, whether or not the person remains a partner or continues to own any part of the right. The term applies to any fraction of the interest, by whomever owned.

(24) "Transferee" means a person to which all or part of a transferable interest has been transferred, whether or not the transferor is a partner.

§ 103. Knowledge and Notice

(a) A person knows a fact if the person:

(1) has actual knowledge of it; or

(2) is deemed to know it under subsection (d)(1) or law other than this [act].

(b) A person has notice of a fact if the person:

(1) has reason to know the fact from all the facts known to the person at the time in question; or

(2) is deemed to have notice of the fact under subsection (d)(2).

(c) Subject to Section 117(f), a person notifies another person of a fact by taking steps reasonably required to inform the other person in ordinary course, whether or not those steps cause the other person to know the fact.

(d) A person not a partner is deemed:

(1) to know of a limitation on authority to transfer real property as provided in Section 303(g); and

(2) to have notice of:

(A) a person's dissociation as a partner 90 days after a statement of dissociation under Section 704 becomes effective; and

(B) a partnership's:

(i) dissolution 90 days after a statement of dissolution under Section 802 becomes effective;

(ii) termination 90 days after a statement of termination under Section 802 becomes effective; and

(iii) participation in a merger, interest exchange, conversion, or domestication, 90 days after articles of merger, interest exchange, conversion, or domestication under [Article] 11 become effective.

(e) A partner's knowledge or notice of a fact relating to the partnership is effective immediately as knowledge of or notice to the partnership, except in the case of a fraud on the partnership committed by or with the consent of that partner.

§ 104. Governing Law

The internal affairs of a partnership and the liability of a partner as a partner for a debt, obligation, or other liability of the partnership are governed by:

(1) in the case of a limited liability partnership, the law of this state; and

(2) in the case of a partnership that is not a limited liability partnership, the law of the jurisdiction in which the partnership has its principal office.

§ 105. Partnership Agreement; Scope, Functions and Limitations

(a) Except as otherwise provided in subsections (c) and (d), the partnership agreement governs:

(1) relations among the partners as partners and between the partners and the partnership;

(2) the business of the partnership and the conduct of that business; and

(3) the means and conditions for amending the partnership agreement.

(b) To the extent the partnership agreement does not provide for a matter described in subsection (a), this [act] governs the matter.

(c) A partnership agreement may not:

(1) vary the law applicable under Section 104(1);

(2) vary the provisions of Section 110;

(3) vary the provisions of Section 307;

(4) unreasonably restrict the duties and rights under Section 408, but the partnership agreement may impose reasonable restrictions on the availability and use of information obtained under that section and may define appropriate remedies, including liquidated damages, for a breach of any reasonable restriction on use;

(5) alter or eliminate the duty of loyalty or the duty of care, except as otherwise provided in subsection (d);

(6) eliminate the contractual obligation of good faith and fair dealing under Section 409(d), but the partnership agreement may prescribe the standards, if not manifestly unreasonable, by which the performance of the obligation is to be measured;

(7) unreasonably restrict the right of a person to maintain an action under Section 410(b);

(8) relieve or exonerate a person from liability for conduct involving bad faith, willful or intentional misconduct, or knowing violation of law;

(9) vary the power of a person to dissociate as a partner under Section 602(a), except to require that the notice under Section 601(1) to be in a record;

(10) vary the grounds for expulsion specified in Section 601(5);

(11) vary the causes of dissolution specified in Section 801(4) or (5);

(12) vary the requirement to wind up the partnership's business as specified in Section 802(a), (b)(1), and (d);

(13) vary the right of a partner under Section 901(f) to vote on or consent to a cancellation of a statement of qualification;

(14) vary the right of a partner to approve a merger, interest exchange, conversion, or domestication under Section 1123(a)(2), 1133(a)(2), 1143(a)(2), or 1153(a)(2);

(15) vary the required contents of a plan of merger under Section 1122(a), plan of interest exchange under Section 1132(a), plan of conversion under Section 1142(a), or plan of domestication under Section 1152(a);

(16) vary any requirement, procedure, or other provision of this [act] pertaining to:

(A) registered agents; or

(B) the [Secretary of State], including provisions pertaining to records authorized or required to be delivered to the [Secretary of State] for filing under this [act]; or

(17) except as otherwise provided in Sections 106 and 107(b), restrict the rights under this [act] of a person other than a partner.

(d) Subject to subsection (c)(8), without limiting other terms that may be included in a partnership agreement, the following rules apply:

(1) The partnership agreement may:

(A) specify the method by which a specific act or transaction that would otherwise violate the duty of loyalty may be authorized or ratified by one or more disinterested and independent persons after full disclosure of all material facts; and

(B) alter the prohibition in Section 406(a)(2) so that the prohibition requires only that the partnership's total assets not be less than the sum of its total liabilities.

(2) To the extent the partnership agreement expressly relieves a partner of a responsibility that the partner would otherwise have under this [act] and imposes the responsibility on one or more other partners, the agreement also may eliminate or limit any fiduciary duty of the partner relieved of the responsibility which would have pertained to the responsibility.

(3) If not manifestly unreasonable, the partnership agreement may:

(A) alter or eliminate the aspects of the duty of loyalty stated in Section 409(b);

(B) identify specific types or categories of activities that do not violate the duty of loyalty;

(C) alter the duty of care, but may not authorize conduct involving bad faith, willful or intentional misconduct, or knowing violation of law; and

(D) alter or eliminate any other fiduciary duty.

(e) The court shall decide as a matter of law whether a term of a partnership agreement is manifestly unreasonable under subsection (c)(6) or (d)(3). The court:

(1) shall make its determination as of the time the challenged term became part of the partnership agreement and by considering only circumstances existing at that time; and

(2) may invalidate the term only if, in light of the purposes and business of the partnership, it is readily apparent that:

(A) the objective of the term is unreasonable; or

(B) the term is an unreasonable means to achieve the term's objective.

Article 2. Nature of Partnership

§ 201. Partnership as Entity

(a) A partnership is an entity distinct from its partners.

(b) A partnership is the same entity regardless of whether the partnership has a statement of qualification in effect under Section 901.

§ 202. Formation of Partnership

(a) Except as otherwise provided in subsection (b), the association of two or more persons to carry on as co-owners a business for profit forms a partnership, whether or not the persons intend to form a partnership.

(b) An association formed under a statute other than this [act], a predecessor statute, or a comparable statute of another jurisdiction is not a partnership under this [act].

(c) In determining whether a partnership is formed, the following rules apply:

(1) Joint tenancy, tenancy in common, tenancy by the entireties, joint property, common property, or part ownership does not by itself establish a partnership, even if the co-owners share profits made by the use of the property.

(2) The sharing of gross returns does not by itself establish a partnership, even if the persons sharing them have a joint or common right or interest in property from which the returns are derived.

(3) A person who receives a share of the profits of a business is presumed to be a partner in the business, unless the profits were received in payment:

(A) of a debt by installments or otherwise;

(B) for services as an independent contractor or of wages or other compensation to an employee;

(C) of rent;

(D) of an annuity or other retirement or health benefit to a deceased or retired partner or a beneficiary, representative, or designee of a deceased or retired partner;

(E) of interest or other charge on a loan, even if the amount of payment varies with the profits of the business, including a direct or indirect present or future ownership of the collateral, or rights to income, proceeds, or increase in value derived from the collateral; or

(F) for the sale of the goodwill of a business or other property by installments or otherwise.

§ 203. Partnership Property

Property acquired by a partnership is property of the partnership and not of the partners individually.

§ 204. When Property Is Partnership Property

(a) Property is partnership property if acquired in the name of:

(1) the partnership; or

(2) one or more partners with an indication in the instrument transferring title to the property of the person's capacity as a partner or of the existence of a partnership but without an indication of the name of the partnership.

(b) Property is acquired in the name of the partnership by a transfer to:

(1) the partnership in its name; or

(2) one or more partners in their capacity as partners in the partnership, if the name of the partnership is indicated in the instrument transferring title to the property.

(c) Property is presumed to be partnership property if purchased with partnership assets, even if not acquired in the name of the partnership or of one or more partners with an indication in the instrument transferring title to the property of the person's capacity as a partner or of the existence of a partnership.

(d) Property acquired in the name of one or more of the partners, without an indication in the instrument transferring title to the property of the person's capacity as a partner or of the existence of a partnership and without use of partnership assets, is presumed to be separate property, even if used for partnership purposes.

Article 3. Relations of Partners to Persons Dealing with Partnership

§ 301. Partner Agent of Partnership

Subject to the effect of a statement of partnership authority under Section 303, the following rules apply:

(1) Each partner is an agent of the partnership for the purpose of its business. An act of a partner, including the signing of an instrument in the partnership name, for apparently carrying on in the ordinary course the partnership business or business of the kind carried on by the partnership binds the partnership, unless the partner did not have authority to act for the partnership in the particular matter and the person with which the partner was dealing knew or had notice that the partner lacked authority.

(2) An act of a partner which is not apparently for carrying on in the ordinary course the partnership's business or business of the kind carried on by the partnership binds the partnership only if the act was actually authorized by all the other partners.

§ 303. Statement of Partnership Authority

(a) A partnership may deliver to the [Secretary of State] for filing a statement of partnership authority. The statement:

(1) must include the name of the partnership and:

(A) if the partnership is not a limited liability partnership, the street and mailing addresses of its principal office; or

(B) if the partnership is a limited liability partnership, the name and street and mailing addresses of its registered agent;

(2) with respect to any position that exists in or with respect to the partnership, may state the authority, or limitations on the authority, of all persons holding the position to:

(A) sign an instrument transferring real property held in the name of the partnership; or

(B) enter into other transactions on behalf of, or otherwise act for or bind, the partnership; and

(3) may state the authority, or limitations on the authority, of a specific person to:

(A) sign an instrument transferring real property held in the name of the partnership; or

(B) enter into other transactions on behalf of, or otherwise act for or bind, the partnership.

(b) To amend or cancel a statement of authority filed by the [Secretary of State], a partnership must deliver to the [Secretary of State] for filing an amendment or cancellation stating:

(1) the name of the partnership;

(2) if the partnership is not a limited liability partnership, the street and mailing addresses of the partnership's principal office;

(3) if the partnership is a limited liability partnership, the name and street and mailing addresses of its registered agent;

(4) the date the statement being affected became effective; and

(5) the contents of the amendment or a declaration that the statement is canceled.

(c) A statement of authority affects only the power of a person to bind a partnership to persons that are not partners.

(d) Subject to subsection (c) and Section 103(d)(1), and except as otherwise provided in subsections (f), (g), and (h), a limitation on the authority of a person or a position contained in an effective statement of authority is not by itself evidence of any person's knowledge or notice of the limitation.

(e) Subject to subsection (c), a grant of authority not pertaining to transfers of real property and contained in an effective statement of authority is conclusive in favor of a person that gives value in reliance on the grant, except to the extent that if the person gives value:

(1) the person has knowledge to the contrary;

(2) the statement has been canceled or restrictively amended under subsection (b); or

(3) a limitation on the grant is contained in another statement of authority that became effective after the statement containing the grant became effective.

(f) Subject to subsection (c), an effective statement of authority that grants authority to transfer real property held in the name of the partnership, a certified copy of which statement is recorded in the office for recording transfers of the real property, is conclusive in favor of a person that gives value in reliance on the grant without knowledge to the contrary, except to the extent that when the person gives value:

(1) the statement has been canceled or restrictively amended under subsection (b), and a certified copy of the cancellation or restrictive amendment has been recorded in the office for recording transfers of the real property; or

(2) a limitation on the grant is contained in another statement of authority that became effective after the statement containing the grant became effective, and a certified copy of the later-effective statement is recorded in the office for recording transfers of the real property.

(g) Subject to subsection (c), if a certified copy of an effective statement containing a limitation on the authority to transfer real property held in the name of a partnership is recorded in the office for recording transfers of that real property, all persons are deemed to know of the limitation.

(h) Subject to subsection (i), an effective statement of dissolution is a cancellation of any filed statement of authority for the purposes of subsection (f) and is a limitation on authority for purposes of subsection (g).

(i) After a statement of dissolution becomes effective, a partnership may deliver to the [Secretary of State] for filing and, if appropriate, may record a statement of authority that is designated as a post-dissolution statement of authority. The statement operates as provided in subsections (f) and (g).

(j) Unless canceled earlier, an effective statement of authority is canceled by operation of law five years after the date on which the statement, or its most recent amendment, becomes effective. The cancellation is effective without recording under subsection (f) or (g).

(k) An effective statement of denial operates as a restrictive amendment under this section and may be recorded by certified copy for purposes of subsection (f)(1).

§ 305. Partnership Liable for Partner's Actionable Conduct

(a) A partnership is liable for loss or injury caused to a person, or for a penalty incurred, as a result of a wrongful act or omission, or other actionable conduct, of a partner acting in the ordinary course of business of the partnership or with the actual or apparent authority of the partnership.

(b) If, in the course of the partnership's business or while acting with actual or apparent authority of the partnership, a partner receives or causes the partnership to receive money or property of a person not a partner, and the money or property is misapplied by a partner, the partnership is liable for the loss.

§ 306. Partner's Liability

(a) Except as otherwise provided in subsections (b) and (c), all partners are liable jointly and severally for all debts, obligations, and other liabilities of the partnership unless otherwise agreed by the claimant or provided by law.

(b) A person that becomes a partner is not personally liable for a debt, obligation, or other liability of the partnership incurred before the person became a partner.

(c) A debt, obligation, or other liability of a partnership incurred while the partnership is a limited liability partnership is solely the debt, obligation, or other liability of the limited liability partnership. A partner is not personally liable, directly or indirectly, by way of contribution or otherwise, for a debt, obligation, or other liability of the limited liability partnership solely by reason of being or acting as a partner. This subsection applies:

(1) despite anything inconsistent in the partnership agreement that existed immediately before the vote or consent required to become a limited liability partnership under Section 901(b); and

(2) regardless of the dissolution of the limited liability partnership.

(d) The failure of a limited liability partnership to observe formalities relating to the exercise of its powers or management of its business is not a ground for imposing liability on a partner for a debt, obligation, or other liability of the partnership.

(e) The cancellation or administrative revocation of a limited liability partnership's statement of qualification does not affect the limitation in this section on the liability of a partner for a debt, obligation, or other liability of the partnership incurred while the statement was in effect.

§ 307. Actions By and Against Partnership and Partners

(a) A partnership may sue and be sued in the name of the partnership.

(b) To the extent not inconsistent with Section 306, a partner may be joined in an action against the partnership or named in a separate action.

(c) A judgment against a partnership is not by itself a judgment against a partner. A judgment against a partnership may not be satisfied from a partner's assets unless there is also a judgment against the partner.

(d) A judgment creditor of a partner may not levy execution against the assets of the partner to satisfy a judgment based on a claim against the partnership unless the partner is personally liable for the claim under Section 306 and:

(1) a judgment based on the same claim has been obtained against the partnership and a writ of execution on the judgment has been returned unsatisfied in whole or in part;

(2) the partnership is a debtor in bankruptcy;

(3) the partner has agreed that the creditor need not exhaust partnership assets;

(4) a court grants permission to the judgment creditor to levy execution against the assets of a partner based on a finding that partnership assets subject to execution are clearly insufficient to satisfy the

judgment, that exhaustion of partnership assets is excessively burdensome, or that the grant of permission is an appropriate exercise of the court's equitable powers; or

(5) liability is imposed on the partner by law or contract independent of the existence of the partnership.

(e) This section applies to any debt, liability, or other obligation of a partnership which results from a representation by a partner or purported partner under Section 308.

§ 308. Liability of Purported Partner

(a) If a person, by words or conduct, purports to be a partner, or consents to being represented by another as a partner, in a partnership or with one or more persons not partners, the purported partner is liable to a person to whom the representation is made, if that person, relying on the representation, enters into a transaction with the actual or purported partnership. If the representation, either by the purported partner or by a person with the purported partner's consent, is made in a public manner, the purported partner is liable to a person who relies upon the purported partnership even if the purported partner is not aware of being held out as a partner to the claimant. If partnership liability results, the purported partner is liable with respect to that liability as if the purported partner were a partner. If no partnership liability results, the purported partner is liable with respect to that liability jointly and severally with any other person consenting to the representation.

(b) If a person is thus represented to be a partner in an existing partnership, or with one or more persons not partners, the purported partner is an agent of persons consenting to the representation to bind them to the same extent and in the same manner as if the purported partner were a partner with respect to persons who enter into transactions in reliance upon the representation. If all the partners of the existing partnership consent to the representation, a partnership act or obligation results. If fewer than all the partners of the existing partnership consent to the representation, the person acting and the partners consenting to the representation are jointly and severally liable.

(c) A person is not liable as a partner merely because the person is named by another as a partner in a statement of partnership authority.

(d) A person does not continue to be liable as a partner merely because of a failure to file a statement of dissociation or to amend a statement of partnership authority to indicate the person's dissociation as a partner.

(e) Except as otherwise provided in subsections (a) and (b), persons who are not partners as to each other are not liable as partners to other persons.

Article 4. Relations of Partners to Each Other and to Partnership

§ 401. Partner's Rights and Duties

(a) Each partner is entitled to an equal share of the partnership distributions and, except in the case of a limited liability partnership, is chargeable with a share of the partnership losses in proportion to the partner's share of the distributions.

(b) A partnership shall reimburse a partner for any payment made by the partner in the course of the partner's activities on behalf of the partnership, if the partner complied with this section and Section 409 in making the payment.

(c) A partnership shall indemnify and hold harmless a person with respect to any claim or demand against the person and any debt, obligation, or other liability incurred by the person by reason of the person's former or present capacity as a partner, if the claim, demand, debt, obligation, or other liability does not arise from the person's breach of this section or Section 407 or 409.

(d) In the ordinary course of its business, a partnership may advance reasonable expenses, including attorney's fees and costs, incurred by a person in connection with a claim or demand against the person by reason of the person's former or present capacity as a partner, if the person promises to repay the partnership if the person ultimately is determined not to be entitled to be indemnified under subsection (c).

(e) A partnership may purchase and maintain insurance on behalf of a partner against liability asserted against or incurred by the partner in that capacity or arising from that status even if, under Section 105(c)(7), the partnership agreement could not eliminate or limit the person's liability to the partnership for the conduct giving rise to the liability.

(f) A partnership shall reimburse a partner for an advance to the partnership beyond the amount of capital the partner agreed to contribute.

(g) A payment or advance made by a partner which gives rise to a partnership obligation under subsection (b) or (f) constitutes a loan to the partnership which accrues interest from the date of the payment or advance.

(h) Each partner has equal rights in the management and conduct of the partnership's business.

(i) A partner may use or possess partnership property only on behalf of the partnership.

(j) A partner is not entitled to remuneration for services performed for the partnership, except for reasonable compensation for services rendered in winding up the business of the partnership.

(k) A difference arising as to a matter in the ordinary course of business of a partnership may be decided by a majority of the partners. An act outside the ordinary course of business of a partnership and an amendment to the partnership agreement may be undertaken only with the affirmative vote or consent of all the partners.

§ 408. Right to Information of Partners and Persons Dissociated as Partners

(a) A partnership shall keep its books and records, if any, at its principal office.

(b) On reasonable notice, a partner may inspect and copy during regular business hours, at a reasonable location specified by the partnership, any record maintained by the partnership regarding the partnership's business, financial condition, and other circumstances, to the extent the information is material to the partner's rights and duties under the partnership agreement or this [act].

(c) The partnership shall furnish to each partner:

(1) without demand, any information concerning the partnership's business, financial condition, and other circumstances which the partnership knows and is material to the proper exercise of the partner's rights and duties under the partnership agreement or this [act], except to the extent the partnership can establish that it reasonably believes the partner already knows the information; and

(2) on demand, any other information concerning the partnership's business, financial condition, and other circumstances, except to the extent the demand or the information demanded is unreasonable or otherwise improper under the circumstances.

(d) The duty to furnish information under subsection (c) also applies to each partner to the extent the partner knows any of the information described in subsection (c).

(e) Subject to subsection (j), on 10 days' demand made in a record received by a partnership, a person dissociated as a partner may have access to information to which the person was entitled while a partner if:

(1) the information pertains to the period during which the person was a partner;

(2) the person seeks the information in good faith; and

(3) the person satisfies the requirements imposed on a partner by subsection (b).

(f) Not later than 10 days after receiving a demand under subsection (e), the partnership in a record shall inform the person that made the demand of:

(1) the information that the partnership will provide in response to the demand and when and where the partnership will provide the information; and

(2) the partnership's reasons for declining, if the partnership declines to provide any demanded information.

(g) A partnership may charge a person that makes a demand under this section the reasonable costs of copying, limited to the costs of labor and material.

(h) A partner or person dissociated as a partner may exercise the rights under this section through an agent or, in the case of an individual under legal disability, a legal representative. Any restriction or condition imposed by the partnership agreement or under subsection (j) applies both to the agent or legal representative and to the partner or person dissociated as a partner.

(i) Subject to Section 505, the rights under this section do not extend to a person as transferee.

(j) In addition to any restriction or condition stated in its partnership agreement, a partnership, as a matter within the ordinary course of its business, may impose reasonable restrictions and conditions on access to and use of information to be furnished under this section, including designating information confidential and imposing nondisclosure and safeguarding obligations on the recipient. In a dispute concerning the reasonableness of a restriction under this subsection, the partnership has the burden of proving reasonableness.

§ 409. Standards of Conduct for Partners

(a) A partner owes to the partnership and the other partners the duties of loyalty and care stated in subsections (b) and (c).

(b) The fiduciary duty of loyalty of a partner includes the duties:

(1) to account to the partnership and hold as trustee for it any property, profit, or benefit derived by the partner:

(A) in the conduct or winding up of the partnership's business;

(B) from a use by the partner of the partnership's property; or

(C) from the appropriation of a partnership opportunity;

(2) to refrain from dealing with the partnership in the conduct or winding up of the partnership business as or on behalf of a person having an interest adverse to the partnership; and

(3) to refrain from competing with the partnership in the conduct of the partnership's business before the dissolution of the partnership.

(c) The duty of care of a partner in the conduct or winding up of the partnership business is to refrain from engaging in grossly negligent or reckless conduct, willful or intentional misconduct, or a knowing violation of law.

(d) A partner shall discharge the duties and obligations under this [act] or under the partnership agreement and exercise any rights consistently with the contractual obligation of good faith and fair dealing.

(e) A partner does not violate a duty or obligation under this [act] or under the partnership agreement solely because the partner's conduct furthers the partner's own interest.

(f) All the partners may authorize or ratify, after full disclosure of all material facts, a specific act or transaction by a partner that otherwise would violate the duty of loyalty.

(g) It is a defense to a claim under subsection (b)(2) and any comparable claim in equity or at common law that the transaction was fair to the partnership.

(h) If, as permitted by subsection (f) or the partnership agreement, a partner enters into a transaction with the partnership which otherwise would be prohibited by subsection (b)(2), the partner's rights and obligations arising from the transaction are the same as those of a person that is not a partner.

Article 5. Transferable Interest and Rights of Transferees and Creditors

§ 501. Partner Not Co-owner of Partnership Property

A partner is not a co-owner of partnership property and has no interest in partnership property which can be transferred, either voluntarily or involuntarily.

§ 502. Nature of Transferable Interest

A transferable interest is personal property.

§ 503. Transfer of Transferable Interest

(a) A transfer, in whole or in part, of a transferable interest:

(1) is permissible;

(2) does not by itself cause a person's dissociation as a partner or a dissolution and winding up of the partnership business; and

(3) subject to Section 505, does not entitle the transferee to:

(A) participate in the management or conduct of the partnership's business; or

(B) except as otherwise provided in subsection (c), have access to records or other information concerning the partnership's business.

(b) A transferee has the right to:

(1) receive, in accordance with the transfer, distributions to which the transferor would otherwise be entitled; and

(2) seek under Section 801(5) a judicial determination that it is equitable to wind up the partnership business.

(c) In a dissolution and winding up of a partnership, a transferee is entitled to an account of the partnership's transactions only from the date of dissolution.

(d) A partnership need not give effect to a transferee's rights under this section until the partnership knows or has notice of the transfer.

(e) A transfer of a transferable interest in violation of a restriction on transfer contained in the partnership agreement is ineffective if the intended transferee has knowledge or notice of the restriction at the time of transfer.

(f) Except as otherwise provided in Section 601(4)(B), if a partner transfers a transferable interest, the transferor retains the rights of a partner other than the transferable interest transferred and retains all the duties and obligations of a partner.

(g) If a partner transfers a transferable interest to a person that becomes a partner with respect to the transferred interest, the transferee is liable for the partner's obligations under Sections 404 and 407 known to the transferee when the transferee becomes a partner.

§ 504. Charging Order

(a) On application by a judgment creditor of a partner or transferee, a court may enter a charging order against the transferable interest of the judgment debtor for the unsatisfied amount of the judgment. A charging order constitutes a lien on a judgment debtor's transferable interest and requires the partnership to pay over to the person to which the charging order was issued any distribution that otherwise would be paid to the judgment debtor.

(b) To the extent necessary to effectuate the collection of distributions pursuant to a charging order in effect under subsection (a), the court may:

(1) appoint a receiver of the distributions subject to the charging order, with the power to make all inquiries the judgment debtor might have made; and

(2) make all other orders necessary to give effect to the charging order.

(c) Upon a showing that distributions under a charging order will not pay the judgment debt within a reasonable time, the court may foreclose the lien and order the sale of the transferable interest. The purchaser at the foreclosure sale obtains only the transferable interest, does not thereby become a partner, and is subject to Section 503.

(d) At any time before foreclosure under subsection (c), the partner or transferee whose transferable interest is subject to a charging order under subsection (a) may extinguish the charging order by satisfying the judgment and filing a certified copy of the satisfaction with the court that issued the charging order.

(e) At any time before foreclosure under subsection (c), a partnership or one or more partners whose transferable interests are not subject to the charging order may pay to the judgment creditor the full amount due under the judgment and thereby succeed to the rights of the judgment creditor, including the charging order.

(f) This [act] does not deprive any partner or transferee of the benefit of any exemption law applicable to the transferable interest of the partner or transferee.

(g) This section provides the exclusive remedy by which a person seeking in the capacity of a judgment creditor to enforce a judgment against a partner or transferee may satisfy the judgment from the judgment debtor's transferable interest.

Article 6. Dissociation

§ 601. Events Causing Dissociation

A person is dissociated as a partner when:

(1) the partnership knows or has notice of the person's express will to withdraw as a partner, but, if the person has specified a withdrawal date later than the date the partnership knew or had notice, on that later date;

(2) an event stated in the partnership agreement as causing the person's dissociation occurs;

(3) the person is expelled as a partner pursuant to the partnership agreement;

(4) the person is expelled as a partner by the affirmative vote or consent of all the other partners if:

(A) it is unlawful to carry on the partnership business with the person as a partner;

(B) there has been a transfer of all of the person's transferable interest in the partnership, other than:

(i) a transfer for security purposes; or

(ii) a charging order in effect under Section 504 which has not been foreclosed;

(C) the person is an entity and:

(i) the partnership notifies the person that it will be expelled as a partner because the person has filed a statement of dissolution or the equivalent, the person has been administratively dissolved, the person's charter or the equivalent has been revoked, or the person's right to conduct business has been suspended by the person's jurisdiction of formation; and

(ii) not later than 90 days after the notification, the statement of dissolution or the equivalent has not been withdrawn, rescinded, or revoked, or the person's charter or the equivalent or right to conduct business has not been reinstated; or

(D) the person is an unincorporated entity that has been dissolved and whose activities and affairs are being wound up;

(5) on application by the partnership or another partner, the person is expelled as a partner by judicial order because the person:

(A) has engaged or is engaging in wrongful conduct that has affected adversely and materially, or will affect adversely and materially, the partnership's business;

(B) has committed willfully or persistently, or is committing willfully or persistently, a material breach of the partnership agreement or a duty or obligation under Section 409; or

(C) has engaged or is engaging in conduct relating to the partnership's business which makes it not reasonably practicable to carry on the business with the person as a partner;

(6) the person:

(A) becomes a debtor in bankruptcy;

(B) signs an assignment for the benefit of creditors; or

(C) seeks, consents to, or acquiesces in the appointment of a trustee, receiver, or liquidator of the person or of all or substantially all the person's property;

(7) in the case of an individual:

(A) the individual dies;

(B) a guardian or general conservator for the individual is appointed; or

(C) a court orders that the individual has otherwise become incapable of performing the individual's duties as a partner under this [act] or the partnership agreement;

(8) in the case of a person that is a testamentary or inter vivos trust or is acting as a partner by virtue of being a trustee of such a trust, the trust's entire transferable interest in the partnership is distributed;

(9) in the case of a person that is an estate or is acting as a partner by virtue of being a personal representative of an estate, the estate's entire transferable interest in the partnership is distributed;

(10) in the case of a person that is not an individual, the existence of the person terminates;

(11) the partnership participates in a merger under [Article] 11 and:

(A) the partnership is not the surviving entity; or

(B) otherwise as a result of the merger, the person ceases to be a partner;

(12) the partnership participates in an interest exchange under [Article] 11 and, as a result of the interest exchange, the person ceases to be a partner;

(13) the partnership participates in a conversion under [Article] 11;

(14) the partnership participates in a domestication under [Article] 11 and, as a result of the domestication, the person ceases to be a partner; or

(15) the partnership dissolves and completes winding up.

§ 602. Power to Dissociate as Partner: Wrongful Dissociation

(a) A person has the power to dissociate as a partner at any time, rightfully or wrongfully, by withdrawing as a partner by express will under Section 601(1).

(b) A person's dissociation as a partner is wrongful only if the dissociation:

(1) is in breach of an express provision of the partnership agreement; or

(2) in the case of a partnership for a definite term or particular undertaking, occurs before the expiration of the term or the completion of the undertaking and:

(A) the person withdraws as a partner by express will, unless the withdrawal follows not later than 90 days after another person's dissociation by death or otherwise under Section 601(6) through (10) or wrongful dissociation under this subsection;

(B) the person is expelled as a partner by judicial order under Section 601(5);

(C) the person is dissociated under Section 601(6); or

(D) in the case of a person that is not a trust other than a business trust, an estate, or an individual, the person is expelled or otherwise dissociated because it willfully dissolved or terminated.

(c) A person that wrongfully dissociates as a partner is liable to the partnership and to the other partners for damages caused by the dissociation. The liability is in addition to any debt, obligation, or other liability of the partner to the partnership or the other partners.

§ 603. Effect of Dissociation

(a) If a person's dissociation results in a dissolution and winding up of the partnership business, [Article] 8 applies; otherwise, [Article] 7 applies.

(b) If a person is dissociated as a partner:

(1) the person's right to participate in the management and conduct of the partnership's business terminates, except as otherwise provided in Section 802(c); and

(2) the person's duties and obligations under Section 409 end with regard to matters arising and events occurring after the person's dissociation, except to the extent the partner participates in winding up the partnership's business pursuant to Section 802.

(c) A person's dissociation does not of itself discharge the person from any debt, obligation, or other liability to the partnership or the other partners which the person incurred while a partner.

Article 7. Person's Dissociation as a Partner When Business not Wound Up

§ 701. Purchase of Interest of Person Dissociated as Partner

(a) If a person is dissociated as a partner without the dissociation resulting in a dissolution and winding up of the partnership business under Section 801, the partnership shall cause the person's interest in the partnership to be purchased for a buyout price determined pursuant to subsection (b).

(b) The buyout price of the interest of a person dissociated as a partner is the amount that would have been distributable to the person under Section 806(b) if, on the date of dissociation, the assets of the partnership were sold and the partnership were wound up, with the sale price equal to the greater of:

(1) the liquidation value; or

(2) the value based on a sale of the entire business as a going concern without the person .

(c) Interest accrues on the buyout price from the date of dissociation to the date of payment, but damages for wrongful dissociation under Section 602(b), and all other amounts owing, whether or not presently due, from the person dissociated as a partner to the partnership, must be offset against the buyout price.

(d) A partnership shall defend, indemnify, and hold harmless a person dissociated as a partner whose interest is being purchased against all partnership liabilities, whether incurred before or after the dissociation, except liabilities incurred by an act of the person under Section 702.

(e) If no agreement for the purchase of the interest of a person dissociated as a partner is reached not later than 120 days after a written demand for payment, the partnership shall pay, or cause to be paid, in money to the person the amount the partnership estimates to be the buyout price and accrued interest, reduced by any offsets and accrued interest under subsection (c).

(f) If a deferred payment is authorized under subsection (h), the partnership may tender a written offer to pay the amount it estimates to be the buyout price and accrued interest, reduced by any offsets under subsection (c), stating the time of payment, the amount and type of security for payment, and the other terms and conditions of the obligation.

(g) The payment or tender required by subsection (e) or (f) must be accompanied by the following:

(1) a statement of partnership assets and liabilities as of the date of dissociation;

(2) the latest available partnership balance sheet and income statement, if any;

(3) an explanation of how the estimated amount of the payment was calculated; and

(4) written notice that the payment is in full satisfaction of the obligation to purchase unless, not later than 120 days after the written notice, the person dissociated as a partner commences an action to determine the buyout price, any offsets under subsection (c), or other terms of the obligation to purchase.

(h) A person that wrongfully dissociates as a partner before the expiration of a definite term or the completion of a particular undertaking is not entitled to payment of any part of the buyout price until the expiration of the term or completion of the undertaking, unless the person establishes to the satisfaction of the court that earlier payment will not cause undue hardship to the business of the partnership. A deferred payment must be adequately secured and bear interest.

(i) A person dissociated as a partner may maintain an action against the partnership, pursuant to Section 410(b)(2), to determine the buyout price of that person's interest, any offsets under subsection (c), or other terms of the obligation to purchase. The action must be commenced not later than 120 days after the partnership has tendered payment or an offer to pay or within one year after written demand for payment if no payment or offer to pay is tendered. The court shall determine the buyout price of the person's interest, any offset due under subsection (c), and accrued interest, and enter judgment for any additional payment or refund. If deferred payment is authorized under subsection (h), the court shall also determine the security for payment and other terms of the obligation to purchase. The court may assess reasonable attorney's fees and the fees and expenses of appraisers or other experts for a party to the action, in amounts the court finds equitable, against a party that the court finds acted arbitrarily, vexatiously, or not in good faith. The finding may be based on the partnership's failure to tender payment or an offer to pay or to comply with subsection (g).

§ 702. Power to Bind and Liability of Person Dissociated as Partner

(a) After a person is dissociated as a partner without the dissociation resulting in a dissolution and winding up of the partnership business and before the partnership is merged out of existence, converted, or domesticated under [Article] 11, or dissolved, the partnership is bound by an act of the person only if:

(1) the act would have bound the partnership under Section 301 before dissociation; and

(2) at the time the other party enters into the transaction:

(A) less than two years has passed since the dissociation; and

(B) the other party does not know or have notice of the dissociation and reasonably believes that the person is a partner.

(b) If a partnership is bound under subsection (a), the person dissociated as a partner which caused the partnership to be bound is liable:

(1) to the partnership for any damage caused to the partnership arising from the obligation incurred under subsection (a); and

(2) if a partner or another person dissociated as a partner is liable for the obligation, to the partner or other person for any damage caused to the partner or other person arising from the liability.

§ 703. Liability to Persons Dissociated as Partner to Other Persons

(a) Except as otherwise provided in subsection (b), a person dissociated as a partner is not liable for a partnership obligation incurred after dissociation.

(b) A person that is dissociated as a partner is liable on a transaction entered into by the partnership after the dissociation only if:

(1) a partner would be liable on the transaction; and

(2) at the time the other party enters into the transaction:

(A) less than two years has passed since the dissociation; and

(B) the other party does not have knowledge or notice of the dissociation and reasonably believes that the person is a partner.

(c) By agreement with a creditor of a partnership and the partnership, a person dissociated as a partner may be released from liability for a debt, obligation, or other liability of the partnership.

(d) A person dissociated as a partner is released from liability for a debt, obligation, or other liability of the partnership if the partnership's creditor, with knowledge or notice of the person's dissociation but without the person's consent, agrees to a material alteration in the nature or time of payment of the debt, obligation, or other liability.

§ 704. Statement of Dissociation

(a) A person dissociated as a partner or the partnership may deliver to the [Secretary of State] for filing a statement of dissociation stating the name of the partnership and that the person has dissociated from the partnership.

(b) A statement of dissociation is a limitation on the authority of a person dissociated as a partner for the purposes of Section 303.

Article 8. Dissolution and Winding Up

§ 801. Events Causing Dissolution

A partnership is dissolved, and its business must be wound up, upon the occurrence of any of the following:

(1) in a partnership at will, the partnership knows or has notice of a person's express will to withdraw as a partner, other than a partner that has dissociated under Section 601(2) through (10), but, if the person has specified a withdrawal date later than the date the partnership knew or had notice, on the later date;

(2) in a partnership for a definite term or particular undertaking:

(A) within 90 days after a person's dissociation by death or otherwise under Section 601(6) through (10) or wrongful dissociation under Section 602(b), the affirmative vote or consent of at least half of the remaining partners to wind up the partnership business, for which purpose a person's rightful dissociation pursuant to Section 602(b)(2)(A) constitutes that partner's consent to wind up the partnership business;

(B) the affirmative vote or consent of all the partners to wind up the partnership business; or

(C) the expiration of the term or the completion of the undertaking;

(3) an event or circumstance that the partnership agreement states causes dissolution;

(4) on application by a partner, the entry by [the appropriate court] of an order dissolving the partnership on the grounds that:

(A) the conduct of all or substantially all the partnership's business is unlawful;

(B) the economic purpose of the partnership is likely to be unreasonably frustrated;

(C) another partner has engaged in conduct relating to the partnership business which makes it not reasonably practicable to carry on the business in partnership with that partner; or

(D) it is otherwise not reasonably practicable to carry on the partnership business in conformity with the partnership agreement;

(5) on application by a transferee, the entry by [the appropriate court] of an order dissolving the partnership on the ground that it is equitable to wind up the partnership business:

(A) after the expiration of the term or completion of the undertaking, if the partnership was for a definite term or particular undertaking at the time of the transfer or entry of the charging order that gave rise to the transfer; or

(B) at any time, if the partnership was a partnership at will at the time of the transfer or entry of the charging order that gave rise to the transfer; or

(6) the passage of 90 consecutive days during which the partnership does not have at least two partners.

§ 802. Winding Up

(a) A dissolved partnership shall wind up its business and, except as otherwise provided in Section 803, the partnership continues after dissolution only for the purpose of winding up.

(b) In winding up its business, the partnership:

(1) shall discharge the partnership's debts, obligations, and other liabilities, settle and close the partnership's business, and marshal and distribute the assets of the partnership; and

(2) may:

(A) deliver to the [Secretary of State] for filing a statement of dissolution stating the name of the partnership and that the partnership is dissolved;

(B) preserve the partnership business and property as a going concern for a reasonable time;

(C) prosecute and defend actions and proceedings, whether civil, criminal, or administrative;

(D) transfer the partnership's property;

(E) settle disputes by mediation or arbitration;

(F) deliver to the [Secretary of State] for filing a statement of termination stating the name of the partnership and that the partnership is terminated; and

(G) perform other acts necessary or appropriate to the winding up.

(c) A person whose dissociation as a partner resulted in dissolution may participate in winding up as if still a partner, unless the dissociation was wrongful.

(d) If a dissolved partnership does not have a partner and no person has the right to participate in winding up under subsection (c), the personal or legal representative of the last person to have been a partner may wind up the partnership's business. If the representative does not exercise that right, a person to wind up the partnership's business may be appointed by the affirmative vote or consent of transferees owning a majority of the rights to receive distributions at the time the consent is to be effective. A person appointed under this subsection has the powers of a partner under Section 804 but is not liable for the debts, obligations, and other liabilities of the partnership solely by reason of having or exercising those powers or otherwise acting to wind up the partnership's business.

(e) On the application of any partner or person entitled under subsection (c) to participate in winding up, the [appropriate court] may order judicial supervision of the winding up of a dissolved partnership, including the appointment of a person to wind up the partnership's business, if:

(1) the partnership does not have a partner and within a reasonable time following the dissolution no person has been appointed under subsection (d); or

(2) the applicant establishes other good cause..

§ 804. Partner's Power to Bind Partnership After Dissolution

(a) A partnership is bound by a partner's act after dissolution which:

(1) is appropriate for winding up the partnership business; or

(2) would have bound the partnership under Section 301 before dissolution if, at the time the other party enters into the transaction, the other party does not know or have notice of the dissolution.

(b) A person dissociated as a partner binds a partnership through an act occurring after dissolution if:

(1) at the time the other party enters into the transaction:

(A) less than two years has passed since the dissociation; and

(B) the other party does not know or have notice of the dissociation and reasonably believes that the person is a partner; and

(2) the act:

(A) is appropriate for winding up the partnership's business; or

(B) would have bound the partnership under Section 301 before dissolution and at the time the other party enters into the transaction the other party does not know or have notice of the dissolution.

§ 805. Liability After Dissolution of Partner and Person Dissociated as Partner

(a) If a partner having knowledge of the dissolution causes a partnership to incur an obligation under Section 804(a) by an act that is not appropriate for winding up the partnership business, the partner is liable:

(1) to the partnership for any damage caused to the partnership arising from the obligation; and

(2) if another partner or person dissociated as a partner is liable for the obligation, to that other partner or person for any damage caused to that other partner or person arising from the liability.

(b) Except as otherwise provided in subsection (c), if a person dissociated as a partner causes a partnership to incur an obligation under Section 804(b), the person is liable:

(1) to the partnership for any damage caused to the partnership arising from the obligation; and

(2) if a partner or another person dissociated as a partner is liable for the obligation, to the partner or other person for any damage caused to the partner or other person arising from the obligation.

(c) A person dissociated as a partner is not liable under subsection (b) if:

(1) Section 802(c) permits the person to participate in winding up; and

(2) the act that causes the partnership to be bound under Section 804(b) is appropriate for winding up the partnership's business.

§ 806. Disposition of Assets in Winding Up; When Contribution Required

(a) In winding up its business, a partnership shall apply its assets, including the contributions required by this section, to discharge the partnership's obligations to creditors, including partners that are creditors.

(b) After a partnership complies with subsection (a), any surplus must be distributed in the following order, subject to any charging order in effect under Section 504:

(1) to each person owning a transferable interest that reflects contributions made and not previously returned, an amount equal to the value of the unreturned contributions; and

(2) among persons owning transferable interests in proportion to their respective rights to share in distributions immediately before the dissolution of the partnership.

(c) If a partnership's assets are insufficient to satisfy all its obligations under subsection (a), with respect to each unsatisfied obligation incurred when the partnership was not a limited liability partnership, the following rules apply:

(1) Each person that was a partner when the obligation was incurred and that has not been released from the obligation under Section 703(c) and (d) shall contribute to the partnership for the purpose of enabling the partnership to satisfy the obligation. The contribution due from each of those persons is in proportion to the right to receive distributions in the capacity of a partner in effect for each of those persons when the obligation was incurred.

(2) If a person does not contribute the full amount required under paragraph (1) with respect to an unsatisfied obligation of the partnership, the other persons required to contribute by paragraph (1) on account of the obligation shall contribute the additional amount necessary to discharge the obligation. The additional contribution due from each of those other persons is in proportion to the right to receive distributions in the capacity of a partner in effect for each of those other persons when the obligation was incurred.

(3) If a person does not make the additional contribution required by paragraph (2), further additional contributions are determined and due in the same manner as provided in that paragraph.

(d) A person that makes an additional contribution under subsection (c)(2) or (3) may recover from any person whose failure to contribute under subsection (c)(1) or (2) necessitated the additional contribution. A person may not recover under this subsection more than the amount additionally contributed. A person's liability under this subsection may not exceed the amount the person failed to contribute.

(e) If a partnership does not have sufficient surplus to comply with subsection (b)(1), any surplus must be distributed among the owners of transferable interests in proportion to the value of the respective unreturned contributions.

(f) All distributions made under subsections (b) and (c) must be paid in money.

Article 9. Limited Liability Partnership

§ 901. Statement of Qualification

(a) A partnership may become a limited liability partnership pursuant to this section.

(b) The terms and conditions on which a partnership becomes a limited liability partnership must be approved by the affirmative vote or consent necessary to amend the partnership agreement except, in the case of a partnership agreement that expressly addresses obligations to contribute to the partnership, the affirmative vote or consent necessary to amend those provisions.

(c) After the approval required by subsection (b), a partnership may become a limited liability partnership by delivering to the [Secretary of State] for filing a statement of qualification. The statement must contain:

(1) the name of the partnership which must comply with Section 902;

(2) the street and mailing addresses of the partnership's principal office and, if different, the street address of an office in this state, if any;

(3) the name and street and mailing addresses in this state of the partnership's registered agent; and

(4) a statement that the partnership elects to become a limited liability partnership.

(d) A partnership's status as a limited liability partnership remains effective, regardless of changes in the partnership, until it is canceled pursuant to subsection (f) or administratively revoked pursuant to Section 903.

(e) The status of a partnership as a limited liability partnership and the protection against liability of its partners for the debts, obligations, or other liabilities of the partnership while it is a limited liability partnership is not affected by errors or later changes in the information required to be contained in the statement of qualification.

(f) A limited liability partnership may amend or cancel its statement of qualification by delivering to the [Secretary of State] for filing a statement of amendment or cancellation. The statement must be approved by the affirmative vote or consent of all the partners and state the name of the limited liability partnership and in the case of:

(1) an amendment, state the text of the amendment; and

(2) a cancellation, state that the statement of qualification is canceled.

§ 902. Permitted Name

(a) The name of a partnership that is not a limited liability partnership may not contain the phrase "Registered Limited Liability Partnership" or

"Limited Liability Partnership" or the abbreviation "R.L.L.P.", "L.L.P.", "RLLP" , or "LLP".

(b) The name of a limited liability partnership must contain the phrase "Registered Limited Liability Partnership" or "Limited Liability Partnership" or the abbreviation "R.L.L.P.", "L.L.P.", "RLLP", or "LLP".

(c) Except as otherwise provided in subsection (f), the name of a limited liability partnership, and the name under which a foreign limited liability partnership may register to do business in this state, must be distinguishable on the records of the [Secretary of State] from any:

(1) name of an existing person whose formation required the filing of a record by the [Secretary of State] and which is not at the time administratively dissolved;

(2) name of a limited liability partnership whose statement of qualification is in effect;

(3) name under which a person that is registered to do business in this state by the filing of a record by the [Secretary of State];

(4) name that is reserved under Section 903 or other law of this state providing for the reservation of a name by a filing of a record by the [Secretary of State];

(5) name that is registered under Section 904 or other law of this state providing for the registration of a name by a filing of a record by the [Secretary of State]; and

(6) a name registered under [this state's assumed or fictitious name statute].

(d) If a person consents in a record to the use of its name and submits an undertaking in a form satisfactory to the [Secretary of State] to change its name to a name that is distinguishable on the records of the [Secretary of State] from any name in any category of names in subsection (c), the name of the consenting person may be used by the person to which the consent was given.

(e) Except as otherwise provided in subsection (f), in determining whether a name is the same as or not distinguishable on the records of the [Secretary of State] from the name of another person, words, phrases, or abbreviations indicating a type of entity, such as "corporation", "corp.", "incorporated", "Inc.", "professional corporation", "PC", "P.C.", "professional association", "PA", "P.A.", "Limited", "Ltd.", "limited partnership", "LP", "L.P.", "limited liability partnership", "LLP", "L.L.P.", "registered limited liability partnership", "RLLP", "R.L.L.P.", "limited liability limited partnership", "LLLP", "L.L.L.P.", "registered limited liability limited partnership", "RLLLP", "R.L.L.L.P.", "limited liability company", "LLC", or "L.L.C.", "limited cooperative association", "limited cooperative", "LCA", or "L.C.A." may not be taken into account.

(f) A person may consent in a record to the use of a name that is not distinguishable on the records of the [Secretary of State] from its name except for the addition of a word, phrase, or abbreviation indicating the type of person as provided in subsection (e). In such a case, the person need not change its name pursuant to subsection (d).

(g) The name of a limited liability partnership or foreign limited liability partnership may not contain the words [insert prohibited words or words that may be used only with approval by an appropriate state agency].

(h) A limited liability partnership or foreign limited liability partnership may use a name that is not distinguishable from a name described in subsection (c)(1) through (6) if the partnership delivers to the [Secretary of State] a certified copy of a final judgment of a court of competent jurisdiction establishing the right of the partnership to use the name in this state.

§ 903. Administrative Revocation of Statement of Qualification

(a) The [Secretary of State] may commence a proceeding under subsection (b) to revoke the statement of qualification of a limited liability partnership administratively if the partnership does not:

(1) pay any fee, tax, interest, or penalty required to be paid to the [Secretary of State] not later than [six months] after it is due;

(2) deliver [an annual] [a biennial] report to the [Secretary of State] not later than [six months] after it is due; or

(3) have a registered agent in this state for [60] consecutive days.

(b) If the [Secretary of State] determines that one or more grounds exist for administratively revoking a statement of qualification, the [Secretary of State] shall serve the partnership with notice in a record of the [Secretary of State's] determination.

(c) If a limited liability partnership, not later than [60] days after service of the notice under subsection (b), does not cure or demonstrate to the satisfaction of the [Secretary of State] the nonexistence of each ground determined by the [Secretary of State], the [Secretary of State] shall administratively revoke the statement of qualification by signing a statement of administrative revocation that recites the grounds for revocation and the effective date of the revocation. The [Secretary of State] shall file the statement and serve a copy on the partnership pursuant to Section 116.

(d) An administrative revocation under subsection (c) affects only a partnership's status as a limited liability partnership and is not an event causing dissolution of the partnership.

(e) The administrative revocation of a statement of qualification of a limited liability partnership does not terminate the authority of its registered agent.

$(x)(.20)$

cost = \$4M

$(.50)(x) = 4M$

$(.50)(.20)(X-4) + (.50)(-2)$

$.1X - .4 - 1 = 0$

$.1X = 1.4$

$X = \frac{1.4}{.1} = 14$